.NET
ARCHITECTURE
and PROGRAMMING
Using VISUAL C++

ISBN 0-13-065207-5

90000

9 780130 652072

The Integrated .NET Series from Object Innovations and Prentice Hall PTR

C#

- Introduction to C# Using .NET
  Oberg

- Application Development Using C# and .NET
  Stiefel/Oberg

VISUAL BASIC

- Introduction to Visual Basic Using .NET
  Wyatt/Oberg

- Application Development Using Visual Basic and .NET
  Oberg/Thorsteinson/Wyatt

VISUAL C++

- .NET Architecture and Programming Using Visual C++
  Thorsteinson/Oberg

WEB APPLICATIONS

- Fundamentals of Web Applications Using .NET and XML
  Bell/Feng/Soong/Zhang/Zhu

PERL

- Programming PERL in the .NET Environment
  Saltzman/Oberg

EXPERT PRACTITIONERS · SEASONED INSTRUCTORS

.NET

.NET

ARCHITECTURE
and PROGRAMMING
Using VISUAL C++

PETER THORSTEINSON · ROBERT J. OBERG

PH
PTR

Prentice Hall PTR, Upper Saddle River, NJ 07458
www.phptr.com

Library of Congress Cataloging-in-Publication Data

A catalog record for this book can be obtained from the Library of Congress

Editorial/Production Supervision: *Nick Radhuber*
Acquisitions Editor: *Jill Harry*
Marketing Manager: *Dan DePasquale*
Manufacturing Buyer: *Maura Zaldivar*
Cover Design: *Anthony Gemmellaro*
Cover Design Direction: *Jerry Votta*
Interior Series Design: *Gail Cocker-Bogusz*

 © 2002 by Peter Thorsteinson and Robert J. Oberg
Published by Prentice Hall PTR
A division of Pearson Education, Inc.
Upper Saddle River, NJ 07458

Prentice Hall books are widely used by corporations and government agencies for training, marketing, and resale.

The publisher offers discounts on this book when ordered in bulk quantities. For more information, contact Corporate Sales Department, phone: 800-382-3419; fax: 201-236-7141; email: corpsales@pren-hall.com
Or write: Corporate Sales Department, Prentice Hall PTR, One Lake Street, Upper Saddle River, NJ 07458.

Product and company names mentioned herein are the trademarks or registered trademarks of their respective owners.

Printed in the United States of America

10 9 8 7 6 5 4 3 2 1

ISBN 0-13-065207-5

Pearson Education LTD.
Pearson Education Australia PTY, Limited
Pearson Education Singapore, Pte. Ltd
Pearson Education North Asia Ltd
Pearson Education Canada, Ltd.
Pearson Educación de Mexico, S.A. de C.V.
Pearson Education—Japan
Pearson Education Malaysia, Pte. Ltd

CONTENTS

v

*F*or several years, Microsoft Visual C++ has been used as the ultimate power tool for Windows software development. Although it requires a substantial investment in acquiring the necessary skills, Visual C++ allows you to do certain things that are just not possible in other programming languages. Now that the .NET world is upon us, it is exciting to know that you can continue to apply Microsoft Visual C++, along with its new managed C++ extensions, to new development efforts to achieve the highest possible power and performance. Managed C++ can be used to develop .NET assemblies and to create amazing new desktop programs, web applications, and web services. Unmanaged C++ can also be used to build ATL Server based Web sites and services.

.NET represents a sea change for Microsoft Windows software development. .NET also represents a significant learning challenge for Microsoft Windows programmers. The new platform includes new C++ language extensions as well as an enormous class library, the .NET Framework.

This book is practical, with many examples and a case study that is used as a realistic demonstration that continues through many of the chapters. The goal is to equip you to begin building significant applications using Visual C++ and the .NET Framework. The book is part of The Integrated .NET Series from Object Innovations and Prentice Hall PTR.

Organization

The book is organized into five major parts and is structured to make it easy for you to navigate to what you need to learn. The first part, chapters 1 and 2, provides an overview that should be read by everyone. It answers the big question, What is Microsoft .NET?, and outlines the programming model of the .NET Framework.

The second part, chapters 3 to 5, covers programming with managed C++. Even if you are familiar with traditional C++, you will want to read these chapters. Chapter 4 introduces the C++ managed extensions. The case study, which is elaborated throughout the entire book, is introduced in Chapter 4. Chapter 5 covers the important topics of interfaces, delegates, and events. This chapter also describes important interactions between managed C++ and the .NET Framework.

The third part, chapters 6 to 9, covers important fundamental topics in the .NET Framework. Chapter 6 covers user interface programming using the Windows Forms classes. Chapter 7 discusses assemblies and deployment, which constitute a major advance in the simplicity and robustness of deploying Windows applications, ending the notorious situation known as "DLL hell." Chapter 8 introduces important .NET Framework classes, including the topics of metadata, serialization, threading, attributes, asynchronous programming, remoting, and memory management. Chapter 9 covers ADO.NET, which provides a consistent set of classes for accessing both relational and XML data.

The fourth part of the book provides an in-depth introduction to Web programming using ASP.NET and SOAP. Chapter 10 introduces the fundamentals of ASP.NET, including the use of Web Forms, for development of Web sites. Chapter 11 covers SOAP and Web Services, which provide an easy-to-use and robust mechanism for heterogeneous systems to interoperate. Chapter 12 shows how to program with the ATL Sever template library to create both Web servers and Web Services.

The final part of the book covers additional important topics in the .NET Framework. Chapter 13 covers the topic of security in detail, including Code Access Security and declarative security. Chapter 14 introduces the debug and trace classes provided by .NET. Chapter 15 covers interoperability of .NET with legacy COM and with Win32 applications.

Sample Programs

The only way to really learn a major framework is to read and write many programs, including some of reasonable size. This book provides many small programs that illustrate pertinent features of .NET in isolation, which makes them easy to understand. The programs are clearly labeled in the text, and they can all be found in the software distribution that accompanies this book.

A major case study, the Acme Travel Agency, is progressively developed in most of the chapters 4 through 12. It illustrates many features of managed C++ and .NET working in combination, as they would in a practical application.

The sample programs are provided in a self-extracting file on the book's Web site. When expanded, a directory structure is created, whose default root is **c:\OI\NetCpp**. The sample programs, which begin with the second chapter, are in directories **Chap02**, **Chap03**, and so on. All the samples for a given chapter are in individual folders within the chapter directories. The names of the folders are clearly identified in the text. An icon in the margin alerts you to a code example. Each chapter that contains a step of the case study has a folder called **CaseStudy**, containing that step. If necessary, there is a **readme.txt** file in each chapter directory to explain any instructions necessary for getting the examples to work.

This book is part of The Integrated .NET Series. The sample programs for other books in the series are located in their own directories underneath **\OI**, so all the .NET examples from all books in the series will be located in a common area as you install them.

These programs are furnished solely for instructional purposes and should not be embedded in any software product. The software (including instructions for use) is provided "as is" without warranty of any kind.

Caveat

The book and the associated code were developed with Beta 2 of the .NET Framework. Microsoft has indicated that this version of .NET is close to what will be the final version. Nonetheless, changes will be made before .NET is released. The code in the examples has been verified to work with Windows 2000. Database code has been verified with SQL Server 2000. Several examples in the database and security chapters have machine names embedded in connection strings or role names. When trying to run these examples, you will have to replace those names with the appropriate name for your machine. To make installation easy, the database examples run with user name "sa" and without a password. Needless to say, in a real system you should *never* have any login ID without a password or have a database application use *sa* to log into a database.

Websites

The web site for the book series is

www.objectinnovations.com/dotnet.htm.

A link is provided at that Web site for downloading the sample programs for this book. Additional information about .NET technology is available at

www.mantasoft.com/dotnet.htm.

The book sample programs are available at this Web site as well.

The Web site for the book will also have a list of .NET learning resources that will be kept up to date.

Acknowledgments

We are indebted to Mike Meehan for helping to get this project off the ground, starting at a meeting at the PDC when Microsoft announced .NET. That conversation put into motion what has become a substantial series of books on .NET technology, in which this volume is the third. We would also like to thank Jill Harry from Prentice Hall for her ongoing support with this ambitious book project. Our editor, Nick Radhuber, has been very helpful, not only with this book but also in coordinating the whole series.

Several people at Microsoft helped in many ways with this book series: Steven Pratschner, Jim Hogg, Michael Pizzo, Michael Day, Krzysztof Cwalina, Keith Ballinger, and Eric Olsen. We thank them for taking time out from their very tight schedules to provide insight and clarification. Connie Sullivan and Stacey Giard coordinated technical sessions and helped assure our access to resources at Microsoft.

Michael Stiefel, an author of another book in our series, was a valuable resource for many of the chapters in this book. Will Provost helped clarify several issues related to XML. We also want to thank all the other authors in the .NET series, because there is much synergy in a group working on parallel books, even if in the heat of writing we did not always collaborate as closely as we might have. These hardworking people include Eric Bell, Howard Feng, Michael Saltzman, Ed Soong, Dana Wyatt, David Zhang, and Sam Zhu.

Robert always has a hard time writing acknowledgments, because there are so many people to thank on such a major project. I (Robert) would like to thank my wife, Marianne, since she has provided enormous support and encouragement for all my writing efforts. This project was especially demanding, and so her support is all the more appreciated. Thank you all, my other colleagues, friends, and students—too numerous to mention individually—who have helped me over the years.

Peter would like to thank his wife Elizabeth and daughter Katherine, for whom his love is a pervasive property of the space-time continuum, throughout the entire universe, for all time, past, present, and future.

> Nú eru Háva mál
> kveðin Háva höllu í,
> allþörf ýta sonum,
> óþörf jötna sonum.
> Heill sá, er kvað,
> heill sá, er kann,
> njóti sá, er nam,
> heilir, þeirs hlýddu.
> —Oðin

November 7, 2001

About this Series
Robert J. Oberg, Series Editor

Introduction

The Integrated .NET Book Series from Object Innovations and Prentice Hall PTR is a unique series of introductory and intermediate books on Microsoft's important .NET technology. These books are based on proven industrial-strength course development experience. The authors are expert practitioners, teachers, and writers who combine subject-matter expertise with years of experience in presenting complex programming technologies such as C++, MFC, OLE, and COM/COM+. These books *teach* in a systematic, step-by-step manner and are not merely summaries of the documentation. All the books come with a rich set of programming examples, and a thematic case study is woven through several of the books.

From the beginning, these books have been conceived as an *integrated whole*, and not as independent efforts by a diverse group of authors.. The initial set of books consists of three introductory books on .NET languages and four intermediate books on the .NET Framework. Each book in the series is targeted at a specific part of the important .NET technology, as illustrated by the diagram below.

		C# Learning Pathway	VB.NET Learning Pathway		
.NET Language Introductions	Programming PERL in the .NET Environment	Introduction to C# Using .NET	Introduction to Programming Visual Basic Using .NET		
Intermediate .NET Framework Titles		Application Development Using C# and .NET	Application Development Using Visual Basic .NET	**.NET Architecture and Programming Using Visual C++**	Fundamentals of Web Applications Using .NET and XML

Introductory .NET Language Books

The first set of books teaches several of the important .NET languages. These books cover their language from the ground up and have no prerequisite other than programming experience in some language. Unlike many .NET language books, which are a mixture of the language and topics in the .NET Framework, these books are focused on the languages, with attention to important interactions between the language and the framework. By concentrating on the languages, these books have much more detail and many more practical examples than similar books.

The languages selected are the new language C#, the greatly changed VB.NET, and Perl.NET, the open source language ported to the .NET environment. Visual C++ .NET is covered in a targeted, intermediate book, and JScript.NET is covered in the intermediate level .NET Web-programming book.

Introduction to C# Using .NET

This book provides thorough coverage of the C# language from the ground up. It is organized with a specific section covering the parts of C# common to other C-like languages. This section can be cleanly skipped by programmers with C experience or the equivalent, making for a good reading path for a diverse group of readers. The book gives thorough attention to the object-oriented aspects of C# and thus serves as an excellent book for programmers migrating to C# from Visual Basic or COBOL. Its gradual pace and many examples make the book an excellent candidate as a college textbook for adventurous professors looking to teach C# early in the language's life-cycle.

Introduction to Programming Visual Basic Using .NET

Learn the VB.NET language from the ground up. Like the companion book on C#, this book gives thorough attention to the object-oriented aspects of VB.NET. Thus the book is excellent for VB programmers migrating to the more sophisticated VB.NET, as well as for programmers experienced in languages such as COBOL. This book would also be suitable as a college textbook.

Programming Perl in the .NET Environment

A very important part of the vision behind Microsoft® .NET is that the platform is designed from the ground up to support multiple programming languages from many sources, and not just Microsoft languages. This book, like other books in the series, is rooted in long experience in industrial teaching. It covers the Perl language from the ground up. Although oriented toward the ActiveState Perl.NET compiler, the book also provides excellent coverage of the Perl language suitable for other versions as well.

Intermediate .NET Framework Books

The second set of books is focused on topics in the .NET Framework, rather than on programming languages. Three parallel books cover the .NET Framework using the important languages C#, VB.NET, and Visual C++. The C# and VB.NET books include self-contained introductions to the languages suitable for experienced programmers, allowing them to rapidly come up to speed on these languages without having to plow through the introductory books. The fourth book covers the important topic of web programming in .NET, with substantial coverage of XML, which is so important in the .NET Framework.

The design of the series makes these intermediate books much more suitable to a wider audience than many similar books. The introductory books focus on languages frees up the intermediate books to cover the important topics of the .NET Framework in greater depth. The series design also makes for flexible reading paths. Less experienced readers can read the introductory language books followed by the intermediate framework books, while more experienced readers can go directly to the intermediate framework books.

Application Development Using C# and .NET

This book does not require prior experience in C#. However, the reader should have experience in some object-oriented language such as C++ or Java™. The book could also be read by seasoned Visual Basic programmers who have experience working with objects and components in VB. Seasoned programmers and also a less experienced reader coming from the introductory C# book can skip the first few chapters on C# and proceed directly to a study of the Framework. The book is practical, with many examples and a major case study. The goal is to equip the reader with the knowledge necessary to begin building significant applications using the .NET Framework.

Application Development Using Visual Basic .NET

This book is for the experienced VB programmer who wishes to learn the new VB.NET version of VB quickly and then move on to learning the .NET Framework. It is also suitable for experienced enterprise programmers in other languages who wish to learn the powerful RAD-oriented Visual Basic language in its .NET incarnation and go on to building applications. Like the companion C# book, this book is very practical, with many examples, and includes the same case study implemented in VB.NET.

.NET Architecture and Programming Using Visual C++

This parallel book is for the experienced Visual C++ programmer who wishes to learn the .NET Framework to build high-performing applications. Unlike the C# and VB.NET book, there is no coverage of the C++ language itself, because C++ is too complex to cover in a brief space. This book is specifically for experienced C++ programmers. Like the companion C# and VB.NET books, this book is very practical, with many examples, and includes the same case study implemented in Visual C++.

Fundamentals of Web Applications Using .NET and XML

The final book in the series provides thorough coverage of building Web applications using .NET. Unlike other books about ASP.NET, this book gives attention to the whole process of Web application development. The book incorporates a review tutorial on classical Web programming, making the book accessible to the experienced programmer new to the Web world. The book contains significant coverage on ASP.NET, Web Forms, Web Services, SOAP, and XML.

What Is Microsoft .NET?

NET is Microsoft's vision of applications in the Internet age. .NET provides enhanced interoperability features based upon open Internet standards. .NET improves the robustness of the classic Windows desktop. .NET offers developers a new programming platform and superb tools with XML playing a fundamental role.

Microsoft .NET is a platform built on top of the operating system. Three years in the making before public announcement, .NET represents a major investment by Microsoft. .NET has been influenced by other technological advances such as XML, Java™ and COM.

Microsoft .NET provides:

- The Common Language Runtime, a robust runtime platform.
- Multiple language development.
- The .NET Framework, an extensible programming model, which provides a very large class library of reusable code available to any .NET language.
- Support for a networking infrastructure built on top of internet standards that allows a high level of communication among applications
- Support for the new industry standard of Web Services. Web Services represent a new mechanism of application delivery that extends the idea of component-based development to the Internet.
- A Security model that is easy for programmers to use in their programs.
- Powerful development tools.

Microsoft and the Web

The World Wide Web has been a big catch-up challenge to Microsoft. Actually the Web coexists quite well with Microsoft's traditional strength, the PC. Through a PC application, the browser, a user gains access to a whole world of information. The Web relies on standards such as HTML, HTTP, and XML, which are essential for communication among diverse users on a wide variety of computer systems and devices.

While complex, the Windows PC is quite standardized. While the Web is based on standard protocols, there is a Tower of Babel of multiple languages, databases, development environments, and devices running on top of those protocols. This exploding complexity of technology exacerbates a growing shortage of knowledge workers who can build the needed systems using the new technologies. .NET provides the infrastructure so that programmers can concentrate on adding value in their applications without having to reinvent solutions to common programming problems.

Applications in the Internet Age

Originally the Web was a vast information repository. Browsers would make requests for pages of existing information, and Web servers would deliver this information as static HTML pages. Even when interactive Web applications were introduced, HTML, which combines information with the details of how it is formatted for viewing, was still used.

XML provides a standard way of transmitting data independently of its formatting. XML can thus provide ways for companies to agree on standards for documents and information flows, such as purchase orders and invoices. E-commerce can then be automated among cooperating companies (B-to-B). XML, however, only describes the data; it does not supply the actions to be performed on that data. For that we need Web Services.

Web Services

One of the most important aspects of .NET is the support for Web Services. Based on the industry standard SOAP protocol, Web Services allow you to expose your applications' functionality across the Internet. From the perspective of a .NET programmer, a Web Service is no different from any other kind of service implemented by a class in a .NET language. The programming model is the same for calling a function within an application, in a separate component on the same machine, or as a Web Service on a different machine.

This inherent simplicity will make it very easy for companies to create and host applications. If desired, a whole application could be completely outsourced, removing issues of development, deployment and maintenance. Or you could use third-party Web Services that did not exist when you designed your application.

ASP.NET

.NET includes a totally redone version of the popular Active Server Pages technology, known as ASP.NET. Whereas ASP relied on interpreted script code in languages with limited capabilities interspersed with page formatting commands, ASP.NET code can be written in any NET language, including C#, VB.NET, JScript and C++ with managed extensions. Since this is compiled code you can separate your interface code from your business logic in a separate "code behind" file. Although C#, VB.NET, and JScript may be left as embedded script within the Web page, managed C++ must be placed in a code behind file.

ASP.NET provides Web Forms that vastly simplify creating Web user interfaces.

Drag and drop in Visual Studio.NET makes it very easy to lay forms out. You can add code to form events such as a button click.

ASP.NET will automatically detect browser capability. For high-end browsers code processing can be performed on the client. For low-end browsers the server does the processing and generates standard HTML. All this is done transparently to the developer by ASP.NET.

The combination of Web Services and compiled full blown languages such as C#, VB.NET, and managed C++ allows Web programming to follow an object-oriented programming model which had not been possible with ASP scripting languages and COM components.

Open Standards and Interoperability

The modern computing environment contains a vast variety of hardware and software systems. Computers range from mainframes and high-end servers, to workstations and PCs, and to small mobile devices such as PDAs and cell phones. Operating systems include traditional mainframe systems, many flavors of UNIX, Linux, several versions of Windows, real-time systems and special systems such as PalmOs for mobile devices. Many different languages, databases, application development tools and middleware products are used.

In the modern environment, few applications are islands unto themselves. Even shrink-wrapped applications deployed on a single PC may use the Internet for registration and updates. The key to interoperability among applications is the use of standards. Since applications typically run over a network, a key standard is the communications protocol used.

Communications Protocols

TCP/IP sockets is highly standard and widely available, but is at too low level for programmers to be productive in writing robust distributed applications. Somewhat higher is the remote procedure call (RPC), but RPC is still very complex, and there are many flavors of RPC. Popular are higher-level protocols, such as CORBA, RMI and DCOM. These are still complex, and require special environments at both ends. These protocols suffer other disadvantages, such as difficulty in going across firewalls.

One communication protocol has become ubiquitous: HTTP. For this reason, Microsoft and other vendors have introduced a new protocol called SOAP (Simple Object Access Protocol). SOAP uses text-based XML to encode object method requests and the accompanying data. The great virtue of SOAP is its simplicity, leading to ease of implementation on multiple devices. While SOAP can run on top of any protocol, its ability to run on top of standard Internet protocols such as HTTP and SMTP, allows it to pass through firewalls without any connectivity problems.

Windows on the Desktop

Microsoft began with the desktop. The modern Windows environment has become ubiquitous. Countless applications are available, and most computer users are at least somewhat at home with Windows. Microsoft has achieved much, but there are also significant problems.

Problems with Windows

Maintaining a Windows PC is a chore, because applications are quite complex. They consist of many files, registry entries, shortcuts, and so on. Different applications can share certain DLLs, and installing a new application can overwrite a DLL that an existing application depends on, possibly breaking the old application ("DLL hell"). Removing an application is complex and is often imperfectly done.

A PC can gradually become less stable, sometimes requiring the drastic cure of reformatting the hard disk and starting from scratch. While there is tremendous economic benefit to using PCs, because standard applications are inexpensive and powerful and the hardware is cheap, the savings are reduced by the cost of maintenance.

Windows was originally developed when personal computers were not connected over a network and security was not an issue. While security was built into Windows NT and Windows2000, the programming model is difficult to use (pop quiz: did you ever pass anything but NULL to a Win32 LPSECURITY_ATTRIBUTES argument?).

The Glass House and Thin Clients

The old "glass house" model of a central computer where all applications are controlled has had an appeal, and there has been a desire to move toward "thin clients" of some sort. But the much heralded "network PC" never really caught on.

There is too much of value in standard PC applications, and users like the idea of their "own" PC, with their data stored conveniently on their local computer. Without very high bandwidth connectivity, a server-based word processor would not perform very well. Security is also a very difficult issue to solve with thin clients. The personal computer is undoubtedly here to stay.

A Robust Windows

With all the hype about .NET and the Internet, it is important to realize that .NET has changed the programming model to allow the creation of much more robust Windows applications. Applications no longer rely on storing extensive configuration data in the fragile Windows registry. .NET applications are self-describing, containing metadata within the program executable files themselves. Different versions of a component can be deployed side-by-side. Applications can share assemblies through the Global Assembly Cache. Versioning is built into the deployment model. A straightforward security model is part of .NET.

A New Programming Platform

Let us now look at what we have just discussed from the point of view of .NET as a new programming platform:

- Type safety and security checking can be done, providing more robust operation.
- It is much easier to program than the Win32 API or COM.
- All or parts of the platform can be implemented on many different kinds of computers (as has been done with Java).
- One class library is used by all .NET languages.
- .NET languages can easily integrate with each other.

There are several important features to the .NET platform:

- .NET Framework
- Common Language Runtime
- Multiple language development
- Development tools

NET Framework

Modern programming relies heavily on reusable code provided in libraries. Object-oriented languages facilitate the creation of class libraries, which are flexible, have a good degree of abstraction, and are extensible by adding new classes and basing new classes on existing ones, "inheriting" existing functionality.

The .NET Framework provides over 2500 classes of reusable code, which can be called by all the .NET languages. The .NET Framework is extensible, and new classes can inherit from existing classes, even those implemented in a different language.

Examples of classes in the .NET Framework include Windows programming, Web programming, database programming, XML, and interoperability with COM and Win32. The .NET Framework is discussed in the next chapter and throughout the rest of the book.

Common Language Runtime

A *runtime* provides services to executing programs. Traditionally there are different runtimes for different programming environments. Examples of runtimes include the standard C library, MFC, the Visual Basic runtime, and the Java Virtual Machine. The runtime environment provided by .NET is called the Common Language Runtime or CLR.

MANAGED CODE AND DATA

The CLR provides a set of services to .NET code (including the .NET Framework which sits on top of the CLR). In order to make use of these services, .NET code has to behave in a predictable fashion, and the CLR has to understand the .NET code. For example, to do runtime checking of array boundaries, all .NET arrays have identical layout. .NET code can also be restricted by type safety restrictions.

The restrictions on .NET code are defined in the Common Type System (CTS) and its implementation in the Microsoft Intermediate Language (MSIL or IL). The Common Type system defines the types and operations that are allowed in code running under the CLR. For example it is the CTS that restricts types to using single implementation inheritance. MSIL code is compiled into the native code of the platform.

.NET applications contain metadata, or descriptions of the code and data in the application. Metadata allows the CLR, for example, to automatically serialize data into storage.

Code that can use the services of the Common Language Runtime is called managed code.

Managed data is allocated and deallocated automatically. This automatic deallocation is called *garbage collection*. Garbage collection reduces memory leaks and similar problems.

Microsoft and ECMA

Microsoft has submitted specifications for the C# programming language and core parts of the .NET Framework to the European Computer Manufacturer's Association (ECMA) for standardization. The ECMA specification, defines the platform independent Common Language Infrastructure (CLI). The CLR can be thought of as the CLI plus the Base Class Libraries (BCL). The BCL has support for the fundamental types of the CTS such as file I/O, strings, and formatting. Since the CLR is platform dependent, it makes use of the process and memory management models of the underlying operating system.

The ECMA specification defines the Common Intermediate Language (CIL). The ECMA specification allows for CIL to be compiled into native code or interpreted.

VERIFIABLE CODE

Managed code can be checked for type safety. Type safe code cannot be easily subverted. For example, a buffer overwrite cannot corrupt other data structures or programs. Security policy can be applied to type safe code. For example, access to certain files or user interface features can be allowed or denied. You can prevent the execution of code from unknown sources.

However, not all programs that make use of the CLR are necessarily type safe. In particular, this is true of C++. Managed C++ code can make use of CLR facilities such as garbage collection, but since C++ can also generate unmanaged code, a C++ program cannot be guaranteed to be type safe. In managed C++ code, you cannot perform pointer arithmetic on a managed pointer, or cast from a managed pointer to an unmanaged pointer. Therefore, managed C++ code is verifiably safe. However, within the same C++ program, you could perform pointer arithmetic and casts on unmanaged pointers, which is inherently unsafe.

Multiple Language Development

As its name suggests, the CLR supports many programming languages. A "managed code" compiler must be implemented for each such language. Microsoft itself has implemented compilers for managed C++, Visual Basic.NET, JScript, and the entirely new language C#.

Well over a dozen other languages are being implemented by third parties, among them COBOL by Fujitsu and Perl by ActiveState. Think of all the billions of lines of COBOL code that, with some porting effort, could become useable within the .NET environment. Programmers do not need to be retrained in a completely new language in order to gain the benefits of .NET.

Development Tools

A practical key to success in software development is a set of effective tools. Microsoft has long provided great tools, including Visual C++ and Visual Basic. With .NET they have combined their development tools into a single integrated environment called Visual Studio.NET.

- VS.NET provides a very high degree of functionality for creating applications in all the languages supported by .NET.
- You can do multi-language programming and debugging.
- VS.NET has many kinds of designers for forms, databases and other software elements.

As with the languages themselves, third parties can provide extension to Visual Studio.NET, creating a seamless development environment for their language that interoperates with the other .NET languages. The tool set includes extensive support for building Web applications and Web Services. There is also great support for database application development.

The Importance of Tools

The importance of tools should not be underestimated. The Ada project provides a good illustration. The project created a very powerful language. Part of the initial vision was to create a standard Ada Programming Support Environment (APSE). But whereas great attention was paid to specifying the language, the APSE received much less attention. Consequently, Ada never did spawn any development environments that compare with Visual Studio, Smalltalk, or many of the Java IDEs.

The advantage of Visual Studio.NET is that it is the standard, so it will be highly tuned for productivity, and there will be much training available, and so on. Microsoft has far more resources to throw at Visual Studio.NET than the many smaller vendors in the highly fragmented tools market. Java is highly standardized in the language and API, but tools, which are required for productivity, are not standard.

The Role of XML

XML is ubiquitous in .NET and is highly important in Microsoft's overall vision. Some uses of XML in .NET include:

- XML is used for encoding requests and responses for Web Services.
- XML can be used to model data within ADO.NET datasets.
- XML is used in configuration files.

- XML documentation can be automatically generated for some .NET languages.
- XML is the lingua franca for the .NET enterprise servers.
- XML is used to describe and transmit data in Web Services.

Success Factors for Web Services

The ultimate success of Microsoft's Internet vision depends on two external factors beyond software: The infrastructure of the Internet and the success of the proposed business model. The widespread use of Web Services depends on higher bandwidth that is now widely available. This capability will probably improve over the next several years. The prospect for the business model remains to be seen!

It is important to understand that the overall .NET technology includes far more than the widely hyped Internet part. The more robust Windows platform and the very powerful .NET Framework and tools will be enduring features.

Summary

Microsoft .NET is a new platform built on top of the operating system. It provides many capabilities for building and deploying both standard applications and new Web-based ones. Web Services allow applications to expose functionality across the Internet, typically using the SOAP protocol. SOAP supports a high degree of interoperability, since it is based on widely adopted standards such as HTTP and XML.

.NET uses managed code running on the Common Language Runtime that uses the Common Type System. The .NET Framework is a very large class library available consistently across many languages. XML plays a fundamental role in .NET. All this functionality can be used to build more robust Windows applications as well as Internet applications.

.NET Fundamentals

*.N*ET solves many problems that have plagued programmers in the past, including deployment, versioning, security, and memory leak issues. .NET allows you to develop powerful, language independent desktop applications and scalable Web-based services built on the powerful new .NET Framework.

Problems of Windows Development

Imagine a symphony orchestra where the violins and the percussion sections had different versions of the score. It would require a heroic effort to play the simplest musical composition. This is the life of the Windows developer. Do I use MFC? Visual Basic or C++? ODBC or OLEDB? COM interface or C style API? Even within COM, do I use IDispatch, dual, or pure vtable interfaces? Where does the Internet fit into all of this? Until .NET, either design had to be contorted by the implementation technologies that the developers understood, or the developer had to learn yet another technological approach that was bound to change in about two years.

Deployment of applications can be a chore. Critical entries have to be made in a registry that is fragile and difficult to back up. There is no good versioning strategy for components. New releases can break existing programs with little clue as to what went wrong. Given the problems with the registry, other technologies have used other configuration stores such as a metabase or SQL Server.

Security in Win32 is another problem. It is difficult to understand and difficult to use. Many developers ignore it. Developers who needed to apply security often do the best they can with a difficult programming model. The rise of Internet-based security threats transforms a bad situation into a potential nightmare.

Even where Microsoft attempted to make development easier, there were still problems. Many system services had to be written from scratch, essentially providing the plumbing code that had nothing to do with your business logic. MTS/COM+ was a giant step in the direction of providing higher level services, but it required yet another development paradigm. COM made real component programming possible. Nonetheless, you either did it simply but inflexibly in Visual Basic, or powerfully but with great difficulty in C++, not to mention the repetitive plumbing code you had to write in C++. If it could disappear, I would not miss IUnknown.

Applications of the Future

Even if .NET fixed all the problems of the past, it would not be enough. One of the unchanging facts of programming life is that the boundaries of customer demand are always being expanded.

The growth of the Internet has made it imperative that applications work seamlessly across network connections. Components have to be able to expose their functionality to other machines. No programmer wants to have to write the underlying plumbing code; they want to solve their customers' problems.

.NET Overview

.NET provides a Common Language Runtime (CLR) that supports managed execution, which has many benefits. The CLR together with the .NET Common Type System (CTS) supports programming language interoperability. .NET also provides a large feature-laden Framework class library.

The Magic of Metadata

To solve all the problems of Windows development, .NET must provide an underlying set of services that is available to all languages at all times. It also has to understand enough about an application to be able to provide these services.

Serialization provides a simple example. Every programmer at some time or another has to save data. Why should every programmer have to reinvent the wheel of how to persist nested objects and complicated data structures? Why should every programmer have to figure out how to do this for a variety of data stores? .NET can do this for the programmer. Programmers can also decide to do it themselves if required.

To see how this is done, look at the **Serialize** sample associated with this chapter. We'll ignore the programming details, which will be covered later, and focus on the concepts.

Code
Example

```
//Serialize.cs

#using <mscorlib.dll>
#using <System.Runtime.Serialization.Formatters.Soap.dll>

using namespace System;
using namespace System::Collections;
using namespace System::IO;
using namespace
   System::Runtime::Serialization::Formatters::Soap;

[Serializable]
__gc class Customer
{
public:
   String *pname;
   long id;
};

__gc class Test
{
public:
   static void Main()
   {
      ArrayList *plist = new ArrayList;

      Customer *pcust = new Customer;
      pcust->pname = "Charles Darwin";
      pcust->id = 10;
      plist->Add(pcust);

      pcust = new Customer;
      pcust->pname = "Isaac Newton";
      pcust->id = 20;
      plist->Add(pcust);

      for (int i=0; i < plist->get_Count(); i++)
      {
         Customer *pcust =
            dynamic_cast<Customer __gc *>
            (plist->get_Item(i));
         Console::WriteLine(
            "{0}: {1}",
            pcust->pname, __box(pcust->id));
```

```
    }

    Console::WriteLine("Saving Customer List");
    FileStream *ps = new FileStream(
        "cust.txt", FileMode::Create);
    SoapFormatter *pf = new SoapFormatter;
    pf->Serialize(ps, plist);
    ps->Close();

    Console::WriteLine("Restoring to New List");
    ps = new FileStream("cust.txt", FileMode::Open);
    pf = new SoapFormatter();
    ArrayList *plist2 =
        dynamic_cast<ArrayList *>
        (pf->Deserialize(ps));
    ps->Close();

    for (int i=0; i < plist->get_Count(); i++)
    {
        Customer *pcust =
            dynamic_cast<Customer __gc *>
            (plist->get_Item(i));
        Console::WriteLine(
            "{0}: {1}",
            pcust->pname, __box(pcust->id));
    }
  }
};

void main(void)
{
    Test::Main();
}
```

We have defined a **Customer** class with two fields: a **pname** and an **id**. The program first creates an instance of a collection class that will be used to hold instances of the **Customer** class. We add two **Customer** objects to the collection and then print out the contents of the collection. The collection is then saved to disk. It is restored to a new collection instance and printed out. The results printed out will be identical to the results printed out before the collection was saved.[1] If you run this program and then open the resulting

---

[1] The sample installation should have already built an instance that you can run. If not, double-click on the Visual Studio.NET solution file that has the .sln suffix. When Visual Studio comes up, hit Ctrl-F5 to build and run the sample.

cust.txt file, you will see that it contains an interesting XML format known as Simple Object Access Protocol (SOAP), specifically designed for storing and transmitting objects.

We wrote no code to indicate how the fields of the customer object are saved or restored. We did have to specify the format (SOAP) and create the medium to which the data was saved. The .NET Framework classes are partitioned so that the choices of where, in what format, and how you load/store an object can be chosen independently. This kind of partitioning exists throughout the .NET Framework.

The **Customer** class was annotated with the **Serializable** attribute in the same way the **public** attribute annotates the name field. If you do not want your objects to be serializable, do not apply the attribute to your class. If an attempt is made to save a nonserializable object, an exception will be thrown and the program will fail.[2]

Attribute-based programming is used extensively throughout .NET to describe how code and data should be treated by the Framework. Security can be set through attributes. You can use attributes to have the framework handle multithreading synchronization. Remoting of objects becomes straightforward using attributes.

The compiler adds this **Serializable** attribute to the *metadata* of the **Customer** class to indicate that the Framework can save and restore the object. Metadata is additional information about the code and data within a .NET application. Metadata, a feature of the CLR, can also provide other information about the code, including

- Version and locale information
- All the types
- Details about each type, including name, visibility, etc.
- Details about the members of each type, such as methods, the signatures of methods, etc.
- Attributes

Since metadata is stored in a programming language-independent fashion with the code, not in a central store such as the Windows registry, it makes .NET applications self-describing. The metadata can be queried at runtime to find out information about the code (such as the presence or absence of the **Serializable** attribute). You can extend the metadata by providing your own custom attributes.

In our example, the Framework can query the metadata to find out the structure of the **Customer** object in order to be able to save and restore it.

---

[2] Comment out the **Serializable** attribute in the program (you can use the C/C++ /* */ comment syntax) and see what happens.

.NET Framework Class Library

The **SoapFormatter** and **FileStream** classes used in the previous **Serialize** example are just two of the over 2,500 classes in the .NET Framework that provide plumbing and system services for .NET applications. Some of the functionality provided by the .NET Framework includes

- Base class library (basic functionality such as strings, arrays, and formatting)
- Networking
- Security
- Remoting
- Diagnostics
- I/O
- Database
- XML
- Web Services that allow us to expose component interfaces over the Internet
- Web programming
- Windows user interface

Interface-Based Programming

Suppose you wanted to encrypt your data and therefore did not want to rely on the Framework's SOAP-based serialization. Your class can inherit from the **ISerializable** interface and provide the appropriate implementation (we will discuss how to do this in a later chapter). The Framework will then use your methods to save and restore the data.

How does the Framework know that you implemented the **ISerializable** interface? It can query the metadata on the class to see if it implements the interface! The Framework can then use either its own algorithm or the class's code to serialize or deserialize the object.

Interface-based programming is used in .NET to allow your objects to provide implementations to standard functionality that can be used by the Framework. Interfaces also allow you to work with objects in terms of a common denominator without having to know the exact type of the object. For example, the formatters (such as the SOAP formatter used in this example) implement the **IFormatter** interface. Programs can be written independently of any particular current (binary, SOAP) or future formatter and still work properly.

Everything Is an Object

If a type has metadata, the runtime can do all kinds of wonderful things. But does everything in .NET have metadata? Yes! Every type, whether it is user-

Types

Types are at the heart of the programming model for the CLR. A type is analogous to a class in most object-oriented programming languages, providing an abstraction of data and behavior, grouped together. A type in the CLR contains

Fields (data members),
Methods,
Properties,
Events.

There are also built-in primitive types, such as integer and floating-point numeric types, strings, and so on.

defined (such as **Customer**) or is part of the Framework (such as **FileStream**) is a .NET object. All .NET objects have the same base class, the system's **Object** class. Hence everything that runs in .NET has a type and therefore has metadata.

In our example, the serialization code can walk through the **ArrayList** of customer objects and save each one as well as the array it belongs to because the metadata allows it to understand the object's type and its layout.

As the next couple of sections will make clear, all .NET objects having the same base class makes several other features possible.

Common Type System

The .NET Framework has to make some assumptions about the nature of the types that will be passed to it. These types are defined by the CTS. The CTS defines the rules for the types and operations that the CLR will support. It is the CTS that limits .NET classes to single implementation inheritance. Since the CTS is defined for a wide range of languages, not all languages need to support all of the data type features of the CTS. In the case of C++, multiple inheritance is still allowed for nonmanaged classes, but disallowed for managed classes.

The Microsoft Intermediate Language (MSIL or IL) defines an instruction set that is used by all .NET compilers. This intermediate language is platform-independent. The MSIL code can later be converted to a platform's native code. We can be sure that the .NET Framework classes will work with all .NET languages. Design no longer dictates language choice; language choice no longer constrains design.

MSIL and the CTS make it possible for multiple languages to use the .NET Framework if their compilers can produce MSIL. This is one of the most visible differences between .NET and Java, which in fact share a great deal in philosophy.

ILDASM

The Microsoft Intermediate Language Disassembler (ILDASM) can display the metadata and MSIL instructions associated with .NET code. It is a very useful tool both for debugging and increasing your understanding of the .NET infrastructure. You can use ILDASM to examine the .NET Framework code itself.[3] Figure 2–1 shows a fragment of the MSIL code from the **Serialize** example where we create two new customer objects and add them to the list.[4]

The **newobj** instruction creates a new object reference using the constructor parameter.[5] The **stloc** instruction stores the value in a local variable.

```
Test::Main : void()                                                    _|□|×|
IL_0000:  ldnull
IL_0001:  stloc.1
IL_0002:  ldnull
IL_0003:  stloc.0
IL_0004:  ldnull
IL_0005:  stloc.s     V_7
IL_0007:  ldnull
IL_0008:  stloc.2
IL_0009:  ldnull
IL_000a:  stloc.s     pf
IL_000c:  ldnull
IL_000d:  stloc.s     plist2
IL_000f:  ldnull
IL_0010:  stloc.s     V_6
IL_0012:  newobj      instance void [mscorlib]System.Collections.ArrayList::.ctor()
IL_0017:  stloc.1
IL_0018:  newobj      instance void Customer::.ctor()
IL_001d:  stloc.0
IL_001e:  ldloc.0
IL_001f:  ldsflda     valuetype $ArrayType$0x5bb2c15a ??_C@_0P@LAAMCGKH@Charles?5Darwin?$AA@
IL_0024:  newobj      instance void [mscorlib]System.String::.ctor(int8*)
IL_0029:  stfld       string Customer::pname
IL_002e:  ldloc.0
IL_002f:  ldc.i4.s    10
IL_0031:  stfld       int32 modopt([Microsoft.VisualC]Microsoft.VisualC.IsLongModifier) Custo
IL_0036:  ldloc.1
IL_0037:  ldloc.0
IL_0038:  callvirt    instance int32 [mscorlib]System.Collections.ArrayList::Add(object)
IL_003d:  pop
IL_003e:  newobj      instance void Customer::.ctor()
IL_0043:  stloc.0
IL_0044:  ldloc.0
IL_0045:  ldsflda     valuetype $ArrayType$0x0de866dc ??_C@_0N@PBPHNJFG@Isaac?5Newton?$AA@
IL_004a:  newobj      instance void [mscorlib]System.String::.ctor(int8*)
IL_004f:  stfld       string Customer::pname
IL_0054:  ldloc.0
IL_0055:  ldc.i4.s    20
IL_0057:  stfld       int32 modopt([Microsoft.VisualC]Microsoft.VisualC.IsLongModifier) Custo
IL_005c:  ldloc.1
IL_005d:  ldloc.0
IL_005e:  callvirt    instance int32 [mscorlib]System.Collections.ArrayList::Add(object)
```

Figure 2–1   *Code fragment from Serialize example.*

---

[3] ILDASM is installed on the Tools menu in Visual Studio.NET. It is also found in the *Microsoft.NET\FrameworkSDK\Bin* subdirectory. You can invoke it by double-clicking on its Explorer entry or from the command line. If you invoke it from the command line (or from VS.NET), you can use the /ADV switch to get some advanced options.

[4] Open Serialize.exe and click on the plus (+) sign next to Test. Double-click on Main to bring up the MSIL for the Main routine.

[5] Technically, it is not a parameter. IL is a stack-based language, and the constructor is a metadata token previously pushed on the stack.

The **ldloc** instruction loads a local variable.[6] It is strongly recommended that you play with ILDASM and learn its features.

Language Interoperability

Having all language compilers use a common intermediate language and common Base Class Library makes it *possible* for languages to interoperate. But since all languages need not implement all parts of the CTS, it is certainly possible for one language to have a feature that another does not.

The *Common Language Specification* (CLS) defines a subset of the CTS that represents the basic functionality that all .NET languages should implement if they are to interoperate with each other. It is this specification that enables a class written in Visual Basic.NET to inherit from a class written in managed C++ or C#. It also makes interlanguage debugging possible. An example of a CLS rule is that method calls need not support a variable number of arguments even though such a construct can be expressed in MSIL.

CLS compliance applies only to publicly visible features. A class, for example, can have a private member that is non-CLS compliant and still be a base class for a class in another .NET language. For example, C++ and C# code should not define public and protected class names that differ only by case sensitivity, since languages such as VB.NET are not case-sensitive. Private fields may have such names.

Microsoft itself is providing several CLS-compliant languages: C#, Visual Basic.NET, and C++ with Managed Extensions. Third parties are providing additional languages (over a dozen so far). ActiveState is implementing Perl and Python. Fujitsu is implementing COBOL.

Managed Code

In the **Serialize** example, a second instance of the **Customer** object was assigned to the same variable as the first instance without freeing it. None of the allocated storage in the example was ever deallocated. .NET uses automatic garbage collection to reclaim memory for objects that are instances of classes declared with the **__gc** keyword. When memory allocated on the managed heap becomes orphaned or passes out of scope, it is placed on a list of memory locations to be freed. Periodically, the system runs a garbage collection thread that returns the memory to the heap.

By having automatic memory management, the system has eliminated memory leaks, which is one of the most common C/C++ programming errors. In most cases, memory allocation is much faster with garbage collection than with classic heap allocation schemes. Note that variables such as **pcust** and

---

[6] You can read all about MSIL in the ECMA documents, specifically, "Partition III: CIL Instruction Set."

plist are managed object pointers, not the objects themselves. This makes garbage collection possible.

Garbage collection is one of several services provided by the CLR to .NET programs.[7]

Data that is under the control of the CLR garbage collection process is called managed data. Managed code is code that is capable of using the services of the CLR. .NET compilers that produce MSIL can produce managed code.

Managed code is not automatically type-safe. C++ provides the classic example. You can use the __**gc** attribute to make a class garbage collected (i.e., managed). The C++ compiler will prevent such classes from using pointer arithmetic. Nonetheless, C++ cannot be reliably verified because of the way C and C++ libraries are used.

Code is typically verified for type safety before compilation. It is optional and can be skipped for trusted code. One of the most significant differences between verified and unverified code is that verified code cannot use pointers. Code that uses pointers could subvert the CTS and produce type-unsafe code.

Type-safe code cannot be easily subverted. For example, a buffer overwrite is not able to corrupt other data structures or programs. Security policy can be applied to type-safe code.[8] For example, access to certain files or user interface features can be allowed or denied. You can prevent the execution of code from unknown sources. You can prevent access to unmanaged code to prevent subversion of .NET security. Type safety also allows paths of execution of .NET code to be isolated from one another.[9]

Assemblies

Another function of the CLR is to load and run .NET programs. .NET programs are deployed as one or more *assemblies*. An assembly is one or more EXEs or DLLs with associated metadata information. The metadata about the entire assembly is stored in the assembly's manifest. The manifest contains, for example, a list of the assemblies on which this assembly is dependent.

In our **Serialize** example there is only one file in the assembly, **Serialize.exe**. That file contains the metadata as well as the code. Since the manifest is stored in the assembly and not in a separate file (like a type library or

---

[7] Technically, metadata, the CTS, the CLS, and the Virtual Execution System (VES) are also part of the CLR. We are using CLR here in the sense that it is commonly used. The VES loads and runs .NET programs and supports late binding. Refer to the Common Language Infrastructure (CLI) "Partition I: Concepts and Architecture" document submitted to ECMA for more details. These documents are loaded with the .NET Framework SDK.

[8] This is discussed in more detail in Chapter 13.

[9] See the discussion of Application Domains in Chapter 8.

registry) the manifest cannot get out of synch with the assembly. Figure 2–2 shows the metadata in the manifest for this example.[10] Note the **assembly extern** statements that indicate the dependencies on the Framework assemblies named **mscorlib** and **System.Runtime.Serialization.Formatters.SOAP**. These statements also indicate the version of those assemblies that Serialize.exe depends on.

Assemblies can be versioned, and the version is part of the name for the assembly. If a unique name is required, you can use a public/private encryption key to generate a unique (strong) name.

Assemblies can be deployed either privately or publicly. For private deployment, all the assemblies that an application needs are copied to the same directory as the application. As we have seen, the version is part of the assembly name. Hence multiple versions can be deployed in the same or different folders without interfering with each other. No more "DLL Hell."

If an assembly is to be publicly shared, an entry is made in the *Global Assembly Cache* (GAC) so that other assemblies can locate it. For assemblies deployed by way of the GAC, a strong name is required.[11] Assembly deployment with language interoperability makes component development almost automatic.

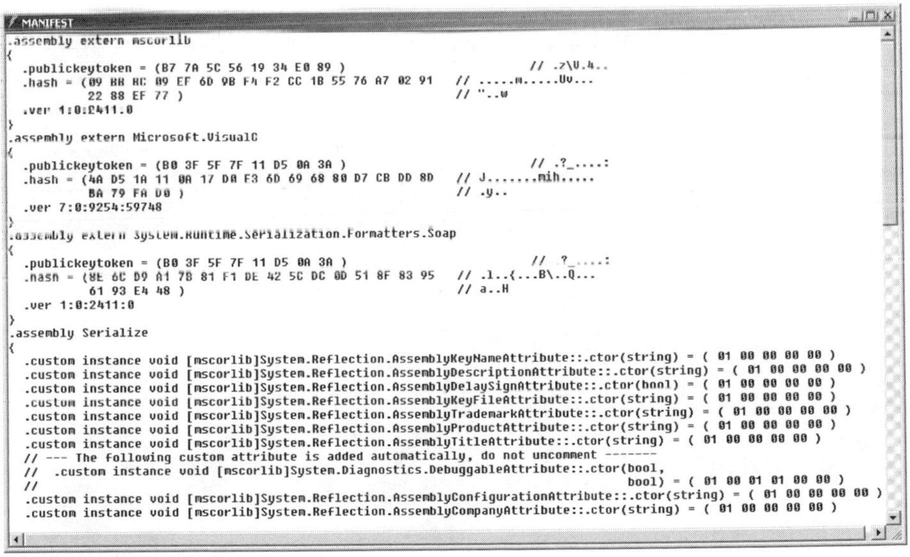

Figure 2–2   *Manifest for the Serialize assembly.*

---

[10]   Open **Serialize.exe** in ILDASM and double-click on the MANIFEST item.

[11]   This is discussed in much more detail in Chapter 7.

JIT Compilation

Before executing on the target machine, MSIL is translated by a just-in-time (JIT) compiler to native code. Some code typically will never be executed during a program run. Hence it may be more efficient to translate MSIL as needed during execution, storing the native code for reuse.

When a type is loaded, the loader attaches a stub to each method of the type. On the first call, the stub passes control to the JIT, which translates to native code and modifies the stub to save the address of the translated native code. On subsequent calls to the method, transfer is then made directly to the native code.

Performance

You may like the safety and ease-of-use features of managed code but be concerned about performance. Early assembly language programmers had similar concerns when high-level languages came out.

The CLR is designed with high performance in mind. With JIT compilation, the first time a method is encountered, the CLR performs verifications and then compiles the method into native code (which will contain safety features, such as array bounds checking). The next time the method is encountered, the native code executes directly. Memory management is designed for high performance. Allocation is almost instantaneous, just taking the next available storage from the managed heap. Deallocation is done by the garbage collector, which has an efficient multiple-generation algorithm.

You do pay a penalty when security checks have to be made that require a stack walk.

Web pages use compiled code, not interpreted code. As a result, ASP.NET is much faster than ASP.

For 95 percent of the code that is written, any small loss in performance is far outweighed by the gains in reliability and ease of development. High-performance server applications might have to use technologies such as ATL Server or unmanaged C++.

Summary

.NET solves many of the problems that have plagued Windows development in the past. There is one development paradigm for all languages. Design and programming language choice are no longer in conflict. Deployment is more rational and includes a sound versioning strategy. Although we will talk more about it later, metadata, attribute-based security, code verification, and type-safe assembly isolation make developing secure applications much easier.

The plumbing code for fundamental system services is there, yet you can extend it or replace it if you must.

The CLR provides a solid base to start developing applications of the future. The CLR is the foundation whose elements are the CTS, metadata, the CLS, and the Virtual Execution System (VES) that executes managed code.[12] As we shall see in future chapters, .NET makes it easier to develop Internet applications for both service providers and customer-based solutions. With the unified development platform .NET provides, it will be much easier than in the past for Microsoft or others to provide extensions.

All this is made possible by old technologies being put together in the CLR creatively: intermediate languages, type-safe verification, and of course metadata. As you will see in many features in .NET, metadata lurks everywhere.

We shall expand on these topics in the course of the book. The next chapter covers the managed C++ language extensions.

---

[12] The Base Class Library (BCL) is also part of the CLR.

THREE

Managed C++ Programming

*M*icrosoft has extended the C++ language in many ways with each new version of Visual C++. Visual C++.NET, being no exception, provides many new features that are supported with new keywords and attributes. In particular, there is substantial new support for developing managed C++ code targeting the .NET platform. This chapter provides several examples that introduce you to a few important .NET Framework classes and help you get started using C++ for writing managed code. Standard input and output is demonstrated using the **Console** class, and the extremely useful **String** and **Array** classes are introduced. The hotel reservation system program is then presented, which is used in subsequent chapters as a recurring example. Important aspects of using managed C++ extensions for writing code for .NET platform are then covered, including the use of managed types, unmanaged types, value types, abstract types, interfaces, boxing and unboxing, delegates, events, properties, and managed exception handling. Finally, C++ attributes are explored in the context of an ATL COM project.

How C++ Fits into the .NET World

One of the great things about the .NET platform is that there is a lot of choice when it comes to deciding what programming languages should be used for developing applications, components, and services. The choices include C++ with managed extensions, C#, and VB.NET, which are provided by Microsoft, as well as many other languages provided by other vendors. Not only can all these languages produce code that can run on the .NET platform, but the code can interact seamlessly across programming languages with respect to object instantiation, method calling, inheritance, event handling, and even exception handling. This is possible because all .NET languages compile into a common Intermediate Language (IL) rather than native code.

Recall from previous chapters that code running under the control of the Common Language Runtime (CLR) is referred to as managed code. Managed code is different from native code in that it is not compiled into the native instruction set of the CPU hardware, but instead is compiled into IL instructions defined by the .NET platform. IL is similar to a traditional CPU instruction set, except that it was designed from the ground up for supporting object-oriented and component-oriented language features, including classes, objects, methods, events, and exceptions. Since all .NET languages target this common IL, they all are fully compatible.

Programs are made up of both data and code, and the CLR provides support for managing data as well as code. As described in previous chapters, managed data is allocated on the managed heap, which provides the convenient feature known as automatic garbage collection. Whereas traditional C++ programmers had to be continually concerned with manual heap management, the CLR eliminates this issue by tracking object references and automatically freeing objects when they are no longer accessible to the program.

C++ with managed extensions can produce managed code and data, however, C++ is unique among .NET programming languages in that it is currently the only one that is capable of producing unmanaged code and data. In fact, managed and unmanaged C++ code and data can be defined within the same C++ source file, and to a certain extent, these two worlds can interoperate directly. Although using managed code and data has many advantages, it can suffer from poorer performance and can lack flexibility. For these reasons, C++ may be the best choice for developing certain types of .NET software. Another reason for choosing C++ over other .NET languages could be that you want to leverage your current investment in C++ programming skills and legacy C++ code.

Enabling C++ Managed Extensions

Managed code development in Visual C++.NET is supported by several newly added keywords as well as extensions made to the C++ compiler for targeting the .NET environment that are enabled with the **/CLR** compiler switch. This compiler switch causes the compiler to generate .NET IL instructions by default rather than native CPU instructions. The new managed extension keywords are specifically intended for developing managed code and are not supported for implementing unmanaged native code. Although the presence or absence of the **/CLR** compiler switch determines whether the compiler generates managed code (IL code) or unmanaged code (native code), you can have finer control over individual portions of code within you source file by using the following pragmas:

```
#pragma managed
//subsequent code is compiled as managed IL code
```

```
#pragma unmanaged
//subsequent code is compiled as unmanaged native code
```

Source code is compiled as managed code by default when the **/CLR** compiler option is used, and the compiler ignores managed or unmanaged pragmas if the **/CLR** option is not used. If the **/CLR** option is not used, all code is compiled as unmanaged.

To use managed extensions you must include a **#using** directive in your source file that accesses required type information contained in the **mscorlib.dll** assembly. An assembly is the unit of deployment on the .NET platform, which is typically in the form of a DLL (or an EXE). You will also typically specify that you intend to use the **System** namespace; however, that is not actually a requirement for using the managed extensions. The C++ concept of namespace is directly mapped to the cross-language .NET concept of namespace that represents a hierarchy of names. These two aspects of developing .NET application code are accomplished by adding the following two lines to the top of your C++ source files:

```
#using <mscorlib.dll>   //required for managed C++ code
using namespace System; //not required, but commonly used
```

The **#using** preprocessor directive serves a purpose similar to that of the **#import** preprocessor directive in previous versions of Visual C++ in that it makes type information available to the current compilation unit. In the case of the **#import** directive, the type information was contained in a type library, which was typically a **TLB**, **DLL**, **OCX**, or **EXE** file. In the case of the **#using** directive, the type information is in the form of metadata contained in a .NET assembly. The **mscorlib.dll** assembly contains type information required by all .NET applications, including the base class for all managed classes, named **System::Object**. Note that **System** refers to a namespace, and **Object** is the name of the root class within the managed type hierarchy.

First Managed C++ .NET Programs

Although you are likely already familiar with C++, we shall start by looking at the very simple but traditional program **HelloWorld**. In this section we explain how to write, build, and run this and other code examples.

The Hello World Program

The following code example shows a very simple managed program that displays one line of text on the console output. You can open the provided solution,[1] or you can create your own project and enter the code yourself. To do this, you will need to create an empty project named HelloWorld, add the source code, and then build and run the project.

How to Create a Managed C++ Console Application

Create an Empty Managed C++ Console Application Project Named HelloWorld:

1. Open Visual Studio.NET. Select the File | New | Project menu sequence to open the New Project dialog.
2. Select Visual C++ Projects as the Project Type.
3. Select Managed C++ Empty Project as the Template.
4. Enter HelloWorld as the Name.
5. Enter a suitable Location.
6. Click OK to close the New Project dialog and create the project.

Add the Source Code:

7. Right-click the Source Files node in the Solution Explorer window.

Select the Add | Add New Item menu sequence to open the Add New Item dialog.

8. Select C++ File as the Template.
9. Enter HelloWorld as the Name.
10. Leave the defaulted Location.
11. Click Open to close the Add New Item dialog and open the Source Editor.
12. Enter the code indicated in the HelloWorld example.

Build and Run the Project:

13. Select the Build | Build menu sequence to build the project.
14. Press Ctrl+F5 to run the program outside of the debugger.

Code Example

The **#using** directive is required by all managed C++ programs, and it makes standard types such as the **Console** and **Object** classes defined within the .NET class library available to the compiler. The **Console** class is contained in the **System** namespace, and its fully qualified name is **System::Console**. The **Console** class exposes a method named **WriteLine** that displays text on the console output with an appended new line character.

```
//HelloWorld.cpp

#using <mscorlib.dll> //required by managed C++ code
```

---

[1] As with all the sample programs in this book, the HelloWorld sample code is provided. The completed example project is located in the *C:\OI\NetCpp\Chap3\HelloWorld* directory. To open it in Visual Studio.NET, double-click *HelloWorld.sln* in Windows Explorer.

```
void main(void)
{
   System::Console::WriteLine("Hello World");
}
```

The program may be built within Visual Studio.NET, or it may be compiled at the command prompt using the **/CLR** (Common Language Runtime compilation) compiler option. If you do this at the command prompt, you will need the proper command-line environment setup. The easiest way to do this is to open a command window using the following sequence: Start | Programs | Microsoft Visual Studio.NET 7.0 | Visual Studio.NET Tools | Visual Studio.NET Command Prompt. In the command line shown below, the source file is compiled and then automatically linked to produce a managed EXE file named **HelloWorld.exe**. Later, you will see how to create a managed DLL.

```
cl /CLR HelloWorld.cpp
```

The resulting managed program can be run from within Visual Studio.NET, or it may be run at the command prompt as a normal executable. The program produces the following output:

```
Hello World
```

The #using Directive and the Using Statement

The **#using** directive makes type information in an assembly available to the compiler. An assembly contains metadata (self-describing type information) and IL code. The **mscorlib.dll** file is an assembly that contains many useful standard classes defined by the .NET Framework, including the **Console** class, which is used in the example above, and **Object**, which is the root class of all managed classes. Note that the **#using** directive is entirely different from the **#include** directive that incorporates other source files into the current compilation unit. As already mentioned, the **#using** directive is more similar in concept to the **#import** directive.

In the previous code example, **System** represents a C++ namespace that maps directly to the .NET namespace of the same name. The fully qualified name of a class is specified by the namespace followed by a double colon followed by the class name, as in **System::Console**. Although the previous example did not make use of a **using namespace** statement, doing so would have allowed us to use the shorter, more convenient name **Console**. Note that the **using namespace** statement (which is ANSI C++) and the **#using** directive (a Microsoft C++ extension) are entirely different from one another. The following code shows how to use the **using namespace** statement, allowing the fully qualified class name **System::Console** to be replaced by the short class name **Console**:

```
//HelloWorld.cpp

#using <mscorlib.dll>
using namespace System; //allows using short class names

void main(void)
{
    Console::WriteLine("Hello World"); //namespace dropped
}
```

Performing Standard Input and Standard Output

The **System::Console** class provides support for standard input and standard output. The **ReadLine** method of **System::Console** reads a line of keyboard input as a text string. The methods **Write** and **WriteLine** of **System::Console** display a text string on the console window, and in the case of the **WriteLine** method, a new line character is appended on the output. An easy way to do console input for various data types is to read the data in as a **String** object and then convert it to the desired data type. The **ToXxx** methods of the **System::Convert** class can be used to perform this data conversion.

The following program uses this technique to read a Fahrenheit value from the console and convert it to a numerical representation. It calculates the corresponding Celsius value and then displays the Fahrenheit and Celsius values on the console output.

```
//ConvertTemp.cpp

#using <mscorlib.dll>
using namespace System;

__gc class InputWrapper
{
public:
    int getInt(String *pprompt)
    {
        Console::Write(pprompt);
        String *pbuf = Console::ReadLine();
        return Convert::ToInt32(pbuf);
    }
    double getDouble(String *pprompt)
    {
        Console::Write(pprompt);
```

```
        String *pbuf = Console::ReadLine();
        return Convert::ToDouble(pbuf);
    }
    Decimal getDecimal(String *pprompt)
    {
        Console::Write(pprompt);
        String *pbuf = Console::ReadLine();
        return Convert::ToDecimal(pbuf);
    }
    String *getString(String *pprompt)
    {
        Console::Write(pprompt);
        String *pbuf = Console::ReadLine();
        return pbuf;
    }
};

void main(void)
{
    InputWrapper *piw = new InputWrapper;
    int numTemp = piw->getInt("How many temp's? ");
    for (int i = 0; i < numTemp; i++)
    {
        int fahr = piw->getInt("Temp. (Fahrenheit): ");
        int celsius = (fahr - 32) * 5 / 9;
        Console::WriteLine(
            "Fahrenheit = {0}", fahr.ToString());
        Console::WriteLine("Celsius = {0}", __box(celsius));
    }
}
```

Notice that the first parameter of the **WriteLine** method is a format string. For example, the first call to **WriteLine** in this example specifies the format string **"Fahrenheit = {0}"**, where {0} is a placeholder that indicates that the second parameter of **WriteLine** is to be inserted into the output string. The zero-based number within the curly braces indicates which subsequent parameter is to be substituted into the format string, which is 0 in this example, since there is only one subsequent parameter. The substitution parameter may be any of several types, including a string or a boxed value, as shown in the example. This program produces the following output for two temperature conversions:

```
How many temp's? 2
Temp. (Fahrenheit): 212
```

```
Fahrenheit = 212
Celsius = 100
Temp. (Fahrenheit): 32
Fahrenheit = 32
Celsius = 0
```

The following program shows how to format several parameters into an output string using the **WriteLine** method. It also shows a bit of the power of formatting codes that can be used to control the text output. For more information on the use of format codes used with **Console::WriteLine** (which are the same as those for **String::Format**), please read the .NET SDK documentation.

```
//FormatString.cpp

#using <mscorlib.dll>
using namespace System;

void main(void)
{
    Console::WriteLine(
        "{0:C}, {1:D}, {2:E}, {3:F}, {4:G}, {5:N}, {6:X}",
        __box(100), //currency
        __box(200), //decimal
        __box(300), //exponent
        __box(400), //fixed point
        __box(500), //general
        __box(600), //number
        __box(700)  //hexadecimal
        );
}
```

This program produces the following output:

```
$100.00, 200, 3.000000E+002, 400.00, 500, 600.00, 2BC
```

The System::String Class

The **System::String** class encapsulates a **Unicode** character string as a managed object. This **String** class is defined in the **System** namespace and is part of the standard .NET Framework. The **String** type is a sealed class, which means that it cannot be used as the base class for any other class. The **String** class inherits directly from the root class **System::Object**. A **String** object is immutable, meaning that once it is initialized, it cannot be modified. The

String class has methods that may appear to change a **String** object, such as **Insert**, **Replace**, and **PadLeft**. However, these methods actually never affect the original object. Instead, they return a new instance of **String** containing the altered text. If you want to be able to modify the original character data, you may want to look at using the **StringBuilder** class rather than the **String** class. The following code proves that the **Replace** method does not affect the original **String** object, but it does modify the original **StringBuilder** object:

Code Example

```
//StringReplace.cpp

#using <mscorlib.dll>
using namespace System; //for Console and String
using namespace System::Text; //for StringBuilder

void main(void)
{
    Console::WriteLine("String is immutable:");
    String *ps1 = S"Hello World";
    String *ps2 = ps1->Replace('H', 'J');
    Console::WriteLine(ps1);
    Console::WriteLine(ps2);
    Console::WriteLine("StringBuilder can be modified.");
    StringBuilder *psb1 = new StringBuilder(S"Hello World");
    StringBuilder *psb2 = psb1->Replace('H', 'J');
    Console::WriteLine(psb1);
    Console::WriteLine(psb2);
}
```

The program's output shows that indeed *ps1* is not changed from its original contents, and therefore, the original **String** object is not modified by the **Replace** method. On the other hand, *psb1* is modified by the **Replace** method.

```
String is immutable:
Hello World
Jello World
StringBuilder can be modified:
Jello World
Jello World
```

In the code example above, you may have noticed string literals being defined with and without the **S** prefix. A string literal defined within unadorned double quotes is simply a pointer to **char**, which is a pointer to a zero-terminated block of **ASCII** data. This is clearly not a pointer to a **String** object. However, a literal string with the **S** prefix defines a pointer to a managed **String** object. The **L** prefix, which is not used in the above example, indicates a Unicode character string, which is also not the same as a **String** object. The following code demonstrates these three types of literal text strings:

```
char     *ps1 = "ASCII string literal";    //unmanaged
__wchar_t *ps2 = L"Unicode string literal"; //unmanaged
String   *ps3 = S"String object literal";  //managed
```

Code Example

There are many useful methods exposed by the **String** class. For example, the **Equals** method can be used to test for equality of objects, as shown in the following example. For details on all the other methods of **String**, please read the .NET SDK documentation.

```
//Strings.cpp

#using <mscorlib.dll>
using namespace System;

void main(void)
{
   String *pstr1 = new String("hello");
   String *pstr2 = new String("hello");
   if (pstr1->Equals(pstr2))
     Console::WriteLine("equal"); //executed
   else
     Console::WriteLine("not equal"); //not executed
   if (pstr1==pstr2)
     Console::WriteLine("equal"); //not executed
   else
     Console::WriteLine("not equal"); //executed
}
```

The code above produces the following output, showing the difference between comparing **String** pointers using the **Equals** method versus the **==** operator. The **Equals** method tests for equality of contents, whereas the **==** operator tests simply for equality of pointers (i.e., equality of memory addresses).

```
equal
not equal
```

The **ToString** method provides a **String** representation for any managed data type. Although **ToString** is not automatically available for any unmanaged types, it is available for boxed value types and boxed primitive types such as **int** or **float**. Boxing and unboxing as well as value types, managed types, and unmanaged types are all described later in this chapter.

ToString is most often used for informational or debugging purposes, and custom managed data types typically override **ToString** to return a customized, human-readable representation of the object. The **Object::ToString** method simply returns the fully qualified class name of the object, which is available as a generic (but not particularly useful) implementation to all managed types via inheritance. The following code example shows several aspects of how **ToString** works:

Code Example

```
//ToString.cpp

#using <mscorlib.dll>
using namespace System;

__gc class ClassWithToString
{
public:
   String *ToString() //override
   {
      return new String("SomeClass - override");
   }
};


__gc class ClassNoToString
{
   //ToString inherited, no override
};

void main(void)
{
   int i = 3;
   Console::WriteLine(i.ToString());     //String* overload
   Console::WriteLine(i);                //int overload
   ClassWithToString *psc = new ClassWithToString;
   Console::WriteLine(psc->ToString());  //String* overload
   Console::WriteLine(psc);              //Object* overload
   ClassNoToString *psoc = new ClassNoToString;
   Console::WriteLine(psoc->ToString()); //String* overload
   Console::WriteLine(psoc);             //Object* overload
```

```
    int array __gc[]= new int __gc[5];
    Console::WriteLine(array->ToString()); //String overload
    Console::WriteLine(array);             //Object* overload
}
```

The result of this program is shown next. Note that the **ToString** method may be called explicitly as a parameter to the **String*** overloaded **WriteLine** method, or you can call on the **Object*** overloaded **WriteLine**, which calls **ToString** internally for you. Also note that even a managed array (which is indeed a managed object) supports the **ToString** method.

```
3
3
SomeClass - override
SomeClass - override
ClassNoToString
ClassNoToString
System.Int32[]
System.Int32[]
```

All identical **String** literals automatically point to the same actual **String** object. This is true for **String** literal objects, but not true for **String** objects that you create directly with the new operator. The following example shows this by comparing the pointers to two identical **String** literals, followed by the comparison between two **String** object pointers created with the new operator. The console output proves that the two identical **String** literal objects are in fact the same actual object (**pstr1==pstr2** is true for the **String** literal objects). On the other hand, the console output proves that the two identical **String** objects created via the **new** operator are not the same actual objects (**pstr1==pstr2** is false for the new **String** objects).

```
//StringLiteral.cpp

#using <mscorlib.dll>
using namespace System;

void main(void)
{
    String *pstr1;
    String *pstr2;
    //comparing literal String objects
    pstr1 = S"hello";
    pstr2 = S"hello";
    if (pstr1->Equals(pstr2))
```

```
      Console::WriteLine("equal"); //executed
   else
      Console::WriteLine("not equal"); //not executed
   if (pstr1==pstr2)
      Console::WriteLine("equal"); // executed
   else
      Console::WriteLine("not equal"); //not executed
   //comparing new String objects (nonliteral)
   pstr1 = new String("hello");
   pstr2 = new String("hello");
   if (pstr1->Equals(pstr2))
      Console::WriteLine("equal"); // executed
   else
      Console::WriteLine("not equal"); //not executed
   if (pstr1==pstr2)
      Console::WriteLine("equal"); //not executed
   else
      Console::WriteLine("not equal"); //executed
}
```

This program produces the following output:

```
equal
equal
equal
not equal
```

Code
Example

Managed **String** literals and even unmanaged **ASCII** or **Unicode** string literals (thanks to automatic boxing) may be used in any expression where a managed **String** object is expected. However, a managed **String** object cannot be used where an unmanaged type is expected. The following code shows this. Note that the two errors have been commented out where necessary to allow successful compilation.

```
//MixingStringTypes.cpp

#using <mscorlib.dll>
using namespace System;
#include <wchar.h> //for wchar_t

void ExpectingManagedString(String *str){}
void ExpectingASCIIString(char *str){}
void ExpectingUnicodeString(wchar_t *str){}
```

```
void main(void)
{
    //expecting a managed type
    ExpectingManagedString(S"hello");    //perfect match
    ExpectingManagedString("hello");     //no error
    ExpectingManagedString(L"hello");    //no error

    //expecting an unmanaged type
    ExpectingASCIIString("hello");        //perfect match
    //ExpectingASCIIString(S"hello");     //error!
    ExpectingUnicodeString(L"hello");     //perfect match
    //ExpectingUnicodeString(S"hello");  //error!
}
```

The System::Array Class

Code
Example

Unlike traditional C++ arrays, which are basically simple pointer types, managed arrays are full-fledged, heap-based managed objects. **System::Array** is the abstract base class for all managed array types. Traditional C++ array syntax can still be used to define unmanaged arrays; however, managed C++ code can define managed arrays either by using the **__gc** keyword or by defining the array's element type as a managed type, as shown in the code below. The **__gc** keyword and managed types are described in more detail later in this chapter. Note the two errors commented out in the following code, where a subscript is being used in the array declaration. A subscript is allowed in an unmanaged array declaration (stack-based), but a subscript is not allowed in a managed array declaration (heap-based). This is because, like all managed objects, a managed array must be heap-based rather than stack-based.

```
//ArraySyntax.cpp

#using <mscorlib.dll>
using namespace System;
#pragma warning(disable : 4101) //kill unrefed var warning

void main(void)
{
    //traditional unmanaged array syntax
    int *pintUnManagedArrayOnHeap = new int [5];
    int intUnManagedArray[5]; //no error for unmanaged array

    //managed array syntax using the __gc keyword
    int intManagedArrayOnHeap __gc[] = new int __gc[5];
```

```
//int intManagedArray __gc[5]; //error for managed array

//managed array syntax using a managed element type
String *strManagedArrayOnHeap[] = new String*[5];
//String *strManagedArray[5]; //error for managed array
}
```

Managed arrays have the following additional features and requirements beyond those of a traditional unmanaged array:

- Managed arrays can only be instantiated on the managed heap. They cannot be declared in-place (i.e., they cannot be stack-based).
- The declaration of a managed array must not specify an array size, since this would imply in-place storage. Instead, the array size must be provided when the new operator is used to create the managed array object on the managed heap.
- All managed arrays inherit from **System::Array**, so the methods of **System::Array**, such as **Copy**, **GetLength**, and **GetType**, as well as the methods of **System::Object**, such as **ToString** and **Equals**, can be used on any managed array object.
- When accessing elements of a managed array, bounds checking is performed to detect a common bug that has plagued many unfortunate C++ programs. If you attempt to access an element outside of the valid index range, an **IndexOutOfRangeException** is thrown.

The following example shows how exception handling can be used with a managed array to gracefully deal with the dreaded index out of range problem. Note that the array has just five elements, but the for loop attempts to go beyond the fifth element. A traditional C++ program would just silently perform the out of bounds assignments and corrupt whatever memory happened to be beyond the last element. What happens after that is unfortunately anybody's guess. Bounds checking does two things: First it prevents the program from corrupting the memory beyond the last element, and second, it lets you know that the attempt was made so that you can recognize it as an error during testing. Traditional C++ code allows the corruption to happen, and the bug's manifestation is often not noticed until completely unrelated pieces of code mysteriously misbehave. Just to be cruel, Murphy's Law often does not kick in until after you have shipped the code to your customers!

```
//IndexOutOfRangeException.cpp

#using <mscorlib.dll>
using namespace System;

void main ()
{
```

```
int intArray __gc[]= new int __gc[5];
for (int i=0; i<6; i++) //over the top!!!
{
   try
   {
      intArray[i] = i;
   }
   catch (IndexOutOfRangeException *piore)
   {
      //should do something more useful to recover here
      Console::WriteLine("Oooops!");
      Console::WriteLine(piore->get_Message());
   }
}
}
```

The output of the above code follows:

```
Oooops!
Exception of type System.IndexOutOfRangeException was thrown.
```

As with unmanaged arrays, managed array indices are zero-based. However, unlike unmanaged arrays, a managed array's elements are automatically initialized to default values according to the type of the array element. Primitive data types, such as **int**, **char**, **double**, and **float**, are automatically initialized to zero. Elements that point to managed objects are also initialized to zero (i.e., zero pointer) by default. Value type elements are initialized using their default constructor (i.e., the no parameter constructor). Value types are described in more detail later in this chapter.

The following code shows some typical examples of working with arrays, and for comparison, it shows a managed 2D array and a traditional unmanaged 2D array. Notice that the unmanaged 2D array uses the old array of arrays syntax **[ ][ ]**, whereas the managed 2D array uses the new **[,]** syntax, which is a true rectangular 2D array. Although the **[ ][ ]** syntax in the following example has each inner array with the same number of elements, it is possible for each of them to be a different length, which is referred to as a jagged-right array. The **[,]** syntax always produces a true rectangular array.

```
//Array1.cpp

#using <mscorlib.dll>
using namespace System;

void main ()
```

```
{
    //managed 1D array of int (using __gc)
    Console::WriteLine("managed 1D array of int");
    int intArray __gc[]= new int __gc[5];
    for (int i=0; i<intArray->Length; i++)
    {
        intArray[i] = i;
        Console::Write(intArray[i]);
        Console::Write("\t");
    }
    Console::WriteLine();

    //managed 2D array of Strings (using managed type)
    Console::WriteLine("managed 2D array of Strings");
    String *str2DArray[,] = new String *[2,3];
    for(int row=0; row<str2DArray->GetLength(0); row++)
    {
        for(int col=0; col<str2DArray->GetLength(1); col++)
        {
            str2DArray[row,col] = (row*10 + col).ToString();
            Console::Write(str2DArray[row,col]);
            Console::Write("\t");
        }
    Console::WriteLine();
    }

    //unmanaged 2D array of int (for comparison)
    Console::WriteLine("unmanaged 2D array of int");
    int int2DArray[2][3];
    for(int row=0; row<2; row++)
    {
        for(int col=0; col<3; col++)
        {
            int2DArray[row][col] = row*10 + col;
            Console::Write(int2DArray[row][col]);
            Console::Write("\t");
        }
    Console::WriteLine();
    }
}
```

This program produces the following output. The managed rectangular 2D array contains elements of type **String***, whereas the unmanaged array of arrays contains elements of type **int**. Although a managed array may contain

managed or unmanaged type elements, an unmanaged array can only contain
elements that are unmanaged types.

```
managed 1D array of int
0         1         2         3         4
managed 2D array of Strings
0         1         2
10        11        12
unmanaged 2D array of int
0         1         2
10        11        12
```

Code
Example

Here is another example that compares an array of arrays declared with
[ ][ ] and a rectangular 2D array declared with [,]. This time an array element
of type **int** is used in both the unmanaged and managed cases for a closer
comparison.

```cpp
//Array2.cpp

#using <mscorlib.dll>
using namespace System;

void main(void)
{
    Console::WriteLine("Rectangular array using [,]");
    int rect2DArray [,] = new int __gc [3,4]; //managed
    for(int row=0; row< rect2DArray ->GetLength(0); row++)
    {
        for(int col=0; col< rect2DArray->GetLength(1); col++)
        {
            rect2DArray [row,col] = row*10 + col;
            Console::Write(rect2DArray[row,col]);
            Console::Write("\t");
        }
        Console::WriteLine();
    }

    Console::WriteLine("Array of arrays using [][]");
    int arrayOfArray[3][4]; //unmanaged
    for(int row=0; row<3 ; row++)
    {
        for(int col=0; col<4; col++)
        {
            arrayOfArray[row][col] = row*10 + col;
```

```
          Console::Write(arrayOfArray[row][col]);
          Console::Write("\t");
      }
    Console::WriteLine();
    }
}
```

This program produces the following output:

```
Rectangular array using [,]
0         1         2         3
10        11        12        13
20        21        22        23
Array of arrays using [][]
0         1         2         3
10        11        12        13
20        21        22        23
```

Figures 3–1 and 3–2 show how the array of arrays declared with **[ ][ ]** and the rectangular 2D array declared with **[,]** in the above example have different memory layouts.

The Hotel Example Program

This section introduces the first version of the hotel reservation system program, which will be used and developed in several subsequent chapters. Note that the **Hotel** class is not packaged as an **EXE**, but rather as a **DLL** assembly.

You can open the provided solution in the **HotelRes\Hotel** directory in the current chapter, or you can create your own project and enter the code yourself. To do this, you will need to create a Managed C++ Class Library

int rect2DArray[,] = new int __gc [3,4];

Figure 3–1   *Memory layout of a rectangular array.*

```
int arrayOfArray[3][4];
```

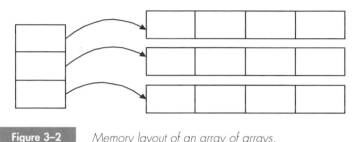

Figure 3–2   *Memory layout of an array of arrays.*

project named Hotel, add the source code, and then build the project. Note that since this is a DLL project, you will not be able to test it until you have created a test client EXE project.

How to Create a Managed C++ Class Library

Create a Managed C++ Class Library Project Named Hotel:
1. Open Visual Studio.NET.
2. Select the File | New | Project menu sequence to open the New Project dialog.
3. Select Visual C++ Projects as the Project Type.
4. Select Managed C++ Class Library Project as the Template.
5. Enter Hotel as the Name.
6. Enter a suitable Location.
7. Click OK to close the New Project dialog and create the project.

Add the Source Code:

8. Double-click the Hotel.cpp source file in the Solution Explorer window.
9. Enter the code indicated in the Hotel example.
   Build and Project:
10. Select the Build | Build menu sequence to build the project.

Although a class definition is usually placed in a header file and used as a data type in CPP files, the following Hotel class definition is placed directly in the **Hotel.cpp** source file for simplicity and demonstration purposes. This also has the effect of making the code look a bit more like C#, which has no **#include** directive. Visual Studio did create a **Hotel.h** file, but it has no effect, since the **#include** directive was removed from **Hotel.cpp**.

```
//Hotel.cpp

#include "stdafx.h" //has a #using <mscorlib.dll>
```

```
using namespace System;

public __gc class Hotel
{
private:
    String *pcity;
    String *pname;
    int number;
    Decimal rate;
public:
    Hotel(String *pcity, String *pname,
    int number, double rate)
    {
        this->pcity = pcity;
        this->pname = pname;
        this->number = number;
        this->rate = rate;
    }
    Hotel()
    {
        this->pcity = 0;
        this->pname = 0;
        this->number = 50; //default to 50
        this->rate = 0;
    }
    String *GetCity()
    {
        return pcity;
    }
    String *GetName()
    {
        return pname;
    }
    int GetNumber()
    {
        return number;
    }
    void SetNumber(int val)
    {
        number = val;
    }
    Decimal GetRate()
    {
        return rate;
```

```
    }
    void SetRate(Decimal val)
    {
        rate = val;
    }
    void RaisePrice(Decimal amount)
    {
        rate = rate+1;
    }
};
```

The above code is then compiled as a .NET assembly named **Hotel.dll**. This can be done within Visual Studio.NET, or it can be done at the command prompt. If you do this at the command prompt, you will need the proper command-line environment setup. The easiest way to do this is to open a command window using the following sequence: Start | Programs | Microsoft Visual Studio.NET 7.0 | Visual Studio.NET Tools | Visual Studio.NET Command Prompt. Here is the command for compiling **Hotel.cpp**.

```
cl /CLR Hotel.cpp /LD
```

The **/LD** option indicates that the linker will produce a DLL rather than an EXE. The **Hotel** class has private instance data (considered to be good design), two constructors that initialize the instance data, and several public methods.

Code Example

To demonstrate the cross-language capabilities of the .NET platform, the following C# program tests the **Hotel** component. This can be created using Visual Studio, or you can open the solution provided in the **Hotel-Res\TestHotel** subdirectory. To create it yourself, you will need to create a C# Console Application project named **TestHotel**, add the source code, add a reference to the **Hotel** assembly, and finally build and then run the program.

```
//TestHotel.cs

using System;

public class TestHotel
{
    public static void Main()
    {
        Hotel generic = new Hotel();
        ShowHotel(generic);
        Hotel ritz = new Hotel("Atlanta", "Ritz", 100, 95);
        ShowHotel(ritz);
```

```
            ritz.RaisePrice(50m);
            ritz.SetNumber(125);
            ShowHotel(ritz);
        }
        private static void ShowHotel(Hotel hotel)
        {
            Console.WriteLine(
                "{0} {1}: number = {2}, rate = {3:C}",
                hotel.GetCity(), hotel.GetName(),
                hotel.GetNumber(), hotel.GetRate());
        }
    }
```

How to Create a C# Console Application

Create a C# Console Application Project Named TestHotel:

1. Open Visual Studio.NET.
2. Select the File | New | Project menu sequence to open the New Project dialog.
3. Select Visual C# Projects as the Project Type.
4. Select Console Application as the Template.
5. Enter TestHotel as the Name.
6. Enter a suitable Location.
7. Click OK to close the New Project dialog and create the project.

To Add the Source Code:

8. Right-click the Class1.cs file in the Solution Explorer window and select Rename.
9. Type the new source filename TestHotel.cs.
10. Double-click the TestHotel.cs file in the Solution Explorer window to open it in the editor
11. Add the provided source code to the TestHotel.cs file.

Add a reference to the Hotel assembly:

12. Select the Project | Add Reference menu sequence.
13. Click Browse.
14. Navigate the directory containing the Hotel.dll assembly.
15. Double-click the Hotel.dll assembly.
16. Click OK.

To Build and Run the Project:

17. Select the Build | Build menu sequence to build the project.
18. Press Ctrl+F5 to run the program outside of the debugger.

Note that Visual Studio automatically copies **Hotel.dll** into the same directory as **TestHotel.exe** client when it is built (i.e., automatic local deployment). This happens because a reference to this assembly has been added to the C# project. This is convenient, because if you try to run the client and the CLR cannot find the assembly, you will get a runtime exception. The output from the above C# program and C++ component is shown next.

```
: number = 50, rate = $0.00
Atlanta Ritz: number = 100, rate = $95.00
Atlanta Ritz: number = 125, rate = $96.00
```

Mapping C++ to the CLS and the .NET Framework

C++ is a powerful language that allows you a great deal of choice in primitive data types, and it allows you to arbitrarily extend the language beyond those primitive data types by defining classes and interfaces. However, one of the main ideas of .NET is that you may want to write code in different languages and then combine the resulting compiled binary code into integrated solutions that can run on the common platform (CLR). To make this possible, the C++ programmer needs to be aware of what subset of C++ data types are compatible with the CLR and the .NET Framework.

C++ Data Types and the CLR

There is a mapping between certain C++ data types and their corresponding data types in the .NET IL defined by the Common Language Specification (CLS). Certain of these types are known as CLS-compliant types, which are guaranteed to be supported by all .NET programming languages. This is defined by the CLS as the Common Type System (CTS). The CLS and its CTS promotes language interoperability, and although C++ supports many non-CLS-compliant data types, those stray data types should only be used internally within a component's implementation, and never exposed across assembly boundaries. This ensures that client code that uses the assembly can be written in any .NET language without running into any data-type mismatch problems. The IL data types listed in Table 3–1 are CLS-compliant. Note that these are IL types, not C++ types, but C++ (and every other .NET language) provides an equivalent type for each of these IL types.

C++ Data Types and the .NET Framework

On the other hand, there is a mapping between certain C++ types and their corresponding .NET Framework classes. For primitive types, such as int and float, the corresponding .NET class is actually a wrapping class, also known as a boxing class. Boxing primitive data types will be discussed in more detail later in this chapter. The following program declares a variety of C++ data

Table 3–1 Intermediate Language Data Types

Intermediate Language Data Type	Contents
bool	True or false
char	Unicode character (16-bit)
System.Object	Object or boxed value type
System.String	Unicode string
float32	IEEE 754 32-bit float
float64	IEEE 754 64-bit float
int8	Signed 8-bit integer
int16	Signed 16-bit integer
int32	Signed 32-bit integer
int64	Signed 64-bit integer
unsigned int8	Unsigned 8-bit integer
unsigned int16	Unsigned 16-bit integer
unsigned int32	Unsigned 32-bit integer
unsigned int64	Unsigned 64-bit integer

Code Example

type variables and then displays the corresponding .NET Framework class for each one, using the **GetType** method of **System::Object**

```
//MappingDataTypes.cpp

#using <mscorlib.dll>
using namespace System;

void main(void)
{
    bool b = false;             //Boolean
    Char ch = '\0';             //Char
    Object *pobj = new Object;  //Object
    String *pstr = S"";         //String
    float f = 1.0F;             //Single
    double d = 1.0;             //Double
    char c = '\0';              //SByte
    unsigned char uc = '\0';    //Byte
```

```
short s = 0;                    //Int16
unsigned short us  = 0;         //UInt16
int i = 0;                      //Int32
unsigned int ui = 0;            //UInt32
long l = 0;                     //Int64
unsigned long ul = 0;           //UInt64
int intManagedArray __gc[] //System.Int32[]
    = new int __gc[5];
Console::WriteLine(__box(b)->GetType());
Console::WriteLine(__box(ch)->GetType());
Console::WriteLine(pobj->GetType());
Console::WriteLine(pstr->GetType());
Console::WriteLine(__box(f)->GetType());
Console::WriteLine(__box(d)->GetType());
Console::WriteLine(__box(c)->GetType());
Console::WriteLine(__box(uc)->GetType());
Console::WriteLine(__box(s)->GetType());
Console::WriteLine(__box(us)->GetType());
Console::WriteLine(__box(i)->GetType());
Console::WriteLine(__box(ui)->GetType());
Console::WriteLine(__box(l)->GetType());
Console::WriteLine(__box(ul)->GetType());
Console::WriteLine(intManagedArray->GetType());
}
```

This program produces the following output:

```
System.Boolean
System.Char
System.Object
System.String
System.Single
System.Double
System.SByte
System.Byte
System.Int16
System.UInt16
System.Int32
System.UInt32
System.Int32
System.UInt32
System.Int32[]
```

To see the unboxed IL data type associated with each of the local variables in the above code, you can run the **Ildasm.exe** tool (IL disassembler) on the **MappingDataTypes.exe** file. **Ildasm.exe** takes any managed binary file (managed EXE or DLL) and disassembles it into its metadata and IL assembly code instructions. The result for the program above is shown in Figure 3–3.

C++ Programming for the .NET Platform

The following subsections describe several key aspects of writing managed C++ code. In particular, each of the managed C++ extension keywords that are provided by Visual C++.NET is described. Note that there are many other keywords in Visual C++ 7.0 that are extensions to ANSI C++ that are not described here, since this chapter is focused primarily on managed C++ extensions. However, a few nonmanaged extensions creep into the discussion

```
Global Functions::main : int32 modopt([mscorlib]System.Runtime...  _ □ ×
.method public static int32 modopt([mscorlib]System.Ru
        main() cil managed
{
  .vtentry 1 : 1
  // Code size       320 (0x140)
  .maxstack  1
  .locals ([0] int32[] V_0,
           [1] int32[] intManagedArray,
           [2] string pstr,
           [3] object pobj,
           [4] unsigned int32 ul,
           [5] int32 l,
           [6] unsigned int32 ui,
           [7] int32 i,
           [8] unsigned int16 us,
           [9] int16 s,
           [10] unsigned int8 uc,
           [11] int8 c,
           [12] float64 d,
           [13] float32 f,
           [14] unsigned int16 ch,
           [15] bool b)
  IL_0000:  ldnull
```

Figure 3–3   *Using Idlasm.exe to reveal the IL data types within managed C++ code.*

here and there. For example, the **__interface** keyword is not limited to use in managed code exclusively, and the last section briefly describes attributes, which are not technically considered to be managed extensions.

VC++.NET and ANSI C++ Compliance

It is good to know that all these Microsoft specific extension keywords and attributes have no impact on ANSI C++ compliance, and in fact VC++.NET is more ANSI C++-compliant than previous VC++ versions.

If you work at the command prompt, you must specify the **/CLR** compiler switch for the compiler to allow the use of the C++ managed extension keywords. If you are using Visual Studio, the correct project settings should already be properly set up if you created the project with the correct template. However, if the need ever arises, the following steps will turn on C++ managed extensions.

1. Right-click on the project node (not the solution node) in the Solution Explorer window.
2. Select the Properties menu to open the Project Property Pages dialog.
3. Select the General node under the C/C++ node, and select Assembly Support (/clr) for the Compile As Managed option.
4. Click OK.

Managed and Unmanaged Types

A managed type is a data type that is instantiated (usually with the new operator) on the managed heap and never created on the unmanaged heap or on the stack. Simply put, a managed type is a type that will be automatically garbage collected by the CLR, and there is no need to use the delete operator to free the object. Instead of explicitly deleting the object, you either let all variables that point to the object go out of scope or explicitly assign them to zero. An unmanaged type is a data type that is ignored by the garbage collector, which means that the programmer becomes responsible for eventually freeing its memory using the delete operator.

An unmanaged type is never created on the managed heap, but is either allocated on the unmanaged heap or declared with in-place storage, such as a stack-based variable or a data member of another unmanaged class. Therefore, an unmanaged type is what C++ programmers have been using all along, whereas managed types are more like the automatically garbage collected reference types in Java.

The **__gc** keyword, which stands for "garbage collect," is used to declare a managed class, or struct, and can also be used on arrays and pointers. The **__gc** keyword is the antonym to the **__nogc** keyword, which stands for "no garbage collect." The **__gc** keyword can be defined only within managed C++ code, meaning that the **/CLR** compiler option must be used and the **#pragma unmanaged** must not be in effect. The **__nogc** keyword may be used in either managed or unmanaged code. The following code shows how **__gc** is typically used to define a managed class:

```
__gc class ManagedClass
{
};
```

The **__nogc** keyword simply indicates that a class, struct, array, or object to which a pointer points is not managed by the .NET garbage collector. The **__nogc** keyword is used to explicitly indicate that the object is never created on the managed heap. It is illegal for a **__gc** type and a **__nogc** type to inherit from one another, and it is illegal to use a **__gc** type anywhere within unmanaged code.

```
__nogc class UnmanagedClass
{
};
```

Note that the automatic garbage collection of managed objects relates only to the freeing of the managed heap memory space, not other resources, such as handles to files and connections to databases.

Managing Garbage Collection

You may have seen the **Finalize** method described in the documentation for other .NET languages for the purpose of cleaning up resources that are not on the managed heap but have been created by a managed object. However, in C++ you must not implement the **Finalize** method. If you do, the compiler will give you an error stating that you must declare a destructor instead of a **Finalize** method in a managed class. The garbage collector will call the destructor automatically on its own thread when it frees the object; however, the timing of the destructor call is not synchronous. This means that you cannot rely on it being called at the time you release your references to the object.

If you do provide a destructor and you explicitly delete the managed object, then the destructor is called synchronously, and the garbage collector then forgets about it. You can also request the garbage collector to make an effort to free objects that are eligible for cleanup by calling the **GC::Collect( )** static method, and you can synchronize with the completion of garbage collection using the **GC::WaitForPendingFinalizers** static method. However, it is generally awkward and inefficient to force collection or synchronize with the call to the destructor method, so it is sometimes recommended that you implement your own method for any synchronous cleanup that may be required, and call it explicitly. For consistency's sake, the recommended name for this synchronous cleanup method is **Dispose**. Consider the following program.

```
//ManagingGC.cpp

#using <mscorlib.dll>
using namespace System;

__gc class ManagedClass
{
public:
   ManagedClass()
   {
      Console::WriteLine("c'tor");
   }
   ~ManagedClass()
   {
         Console::WriteLine("d'tor");
   }
};

void main(void)
{
   Console::WriteLine("start");
   ManagedClass *pmc = new ManagedClass;
   //uncomment the next line to skip d'tor entirely
   //GC::SuppressFinalize(pmc);
   Console::WriteLine("middle");
   //uncomment the next line to get d'tor sooner
   //delete pmc;
   pmc = 0;
   //... or uncomment the next 2 lines to get d'tor sooner
   //GC::Collect();
   //GC::WaitForPendingFinalizers();
   Console::WriteLine("end");
}
```

The above program produces the following output. Note that the destructor is called after **WriteLine** displays **end**.

```
start
c'tor
```

```
middle
end
d'tor
```

However, if you uncomment only the statement that calls **SuppressFinalize**, then the destructor never gets called, as shown in the following:

```
start
c'tor
middle
end
```

Also, if you uncomment only the statement that uses the delete operator on the managed pointer, then the destructor is called before **WriteLine** displays **end**.

```
start
c'tor
middle
d'tor
end
```

Finally, if you uncomment only the two statements that call **Collect** and **WaitForPendingFinalizers**, then again, this causes the destructor to be called before **WriteLine** displays **end**. **Collect** causes the garbage collector to process the pending destructors. **WaitForPendingFinalizers** suspends the current thread until the garbage collector thread completes processing the pending destructors.

```
start
c'tor
middle
d'tor
end
```

Type Safety

C++ programs are not necessarily type-safe. Managed C++ code is type-safe. However, since C++ can also generate unmanaged code, a C++ program cannot be guaranteed to be type safe. You cannot perform pointer arithmetic on a managed pointer. You also cannot cast from a managed pointer to an unmanaged pointer. Therefore, C++ code that deals exclusively with managed code and managed data is verifiably safe.[2] However, any C++ program that performs pointer arithmetic or casts unmanaged pointers is potentially dangerous.

The following program shows an example of unsafe C++ code that casts the unmanaged object pointer **pumc** into an int pointer. In this particular case, it happens to be safe, but in general, this operation may be dangerous. It then performs address arithmetic on the object pointer, which is clearly dangerous in this example, because the result points to rubbish. Further down in this example, you can see that similar antics involving the managed pointer **pmc** are commented out, since these operations on a managed object would generate compiler errors.

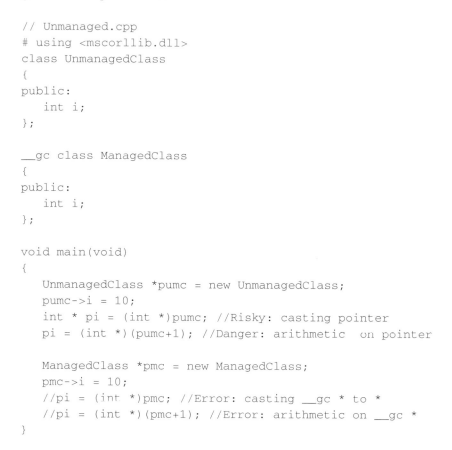

```cpp
// Unmanaged.cpp
# using <mscorllib.dll>
class UnmanagedClass
{
public:
    int i;
};

__gc class ManagedClass
{
public:
    int i;
};

void main(void)
{
    UnmanagedClass *pumc = new UnmanagedClass;
    pumc->i = 10;
    int * pi = (int *)pumc; //Risky: casting pointer
    pi = (int *)(pumc+1); //Danger: arithmetic  on pointer

    ManagedClass *pmc = new ManagedClass;
    pmc->i = 10;
    //pi = (int *)pmc; //Error: casting __gc * to *
    //pi = (int *)(pmc+1); //Error: arithmetic on __gc *
}
```

---

2 Managed C++ can be used to generate verifiably type-safe code if you avoid using certain language features, such as unmanaged pointers and type casts. Peverify.exe can be used to check an assembly's type safety.

Value Types

The __value keyword is similar to the __nogc keyword in that it is used to make a class or struct act as a type that is not garbage collected. This is useful for creating objects on the stack rather than on the managed heap. The main use for this is to be able to create the object without the overhead of garbage collection management. The __value keyword has the side effect of making the class implicitly __sealed and is incompatible with the __abstract keyword.

```
__value struct ValueStruct
{
    int i;
};
```

You may be wondering what syntactic circumstance would allow a __value type but not a __gc type. The following code example shows an example of this (along with several other scenarios for your consideration). Note that you can create **NonManagedClass**, **ValueClass**, and **ManagedClass** as heap-based objects, but only **NonManagedClass** and **ValueClass** can be declared as stack-based variables. The very last statement is commented out, because it would be a compiler error to declare a managed object as a stack based variable.

```
//ValueType.cpp

#using <mscorlib.dll>
using namespace System;

__nogc class NonManagedClass
{
};

__value class ValueClass
{
};

__gc class ManagedClass
{
    NonManagedClass nmc; //strange! but no compiler error
    ValueClass vc; //no error, value type allowed
};

void main(void)
{
```

```
    NonManagedClass *pnmc = new NonManagedClass; //no error
    ValueClass *pvc = __nogc new ValueClass;      //no error
    ManagedClass *pmc = new ManagedClass;         //no error
    NonManagedClass;   //no error on stack
    ValueClass vc;     //no error on stack
    //ManagedClass mc; //error, cannot be stack based
}
```

Abstract Types

The __**abstract** keyword is very similar to the abstract keyword in the Java language. It is also analogous to the tradition that a C++ class that contains at least one pure virtual function is considered to be an abstract class. The __**abstract** keyword simply makes this notion explicit. As with the __**interface** keyword, the __**abstract** keyword is used to define a class as a generalized binding agreement between code that implements the abstract class's methods and client code that calls on those methods. Note that if an abstract class is also to be a managed class, then the __**gc** keyword must be applied to the class as well.

An abstract class is similar to an interface in that it is a vehicle for polymorphism and it cannot be directly instantiated. However, unlike an interface, an abstract class may optionally have implementations for any or all of its methods. An abstract class can be used as a base class for other classes that can be instantiated, and an abstract reference type (i.e., a reference or pointer type, but not a value type) variable may be used to refer to instances of its derived classes.

Note that the __**abstract** keyword is redundant with the __**interface** keyword (which is not a managed extension), since an interface is implicitly abstract. The __**abstract** keyword cannot be used in combination with the __**value** or __**sealed** keywords. The __**value** keyword indicates that an instance directly contains its data, and it does not reference an object stored on the heap. This implies that the class must be capable of being instantiated, and therefore it cannot be abstract. The __**sealed** keyword indicates that a class cannot have any derived classes, which is obviously incompatible with the concept of an abstract class. The following code shows a typical example of using the __**abstract** keyword:

```
//AbstractExample.cpp

#using <mscorlib.dll>
using namespace System;

__abstract class AbstractClass
{
```

```
public:
   virtual void Method1() = 0; //unimplemented here
   virtual void Method2()  //implemented here
   {
      Console::WriteLine("Method2");
   }
};

class DerivedClass : public AbstractClass
{
public:
   void Method1()  //implemented here
   {
      Console::WriteLine("Method1");
   }
};

void main(void)
{
   //AbstractClass *pac = new AbstractClass; //error
   AbstractClass *pac = new DerivedClass; //a pointer
   pac->Method1();
   pac->Method2();
   AbstractClass &ac = *new DerivedClass; //a reference
   ac.Method1();
   ac.Method2();
}
```

The above program produces the following output:

```
Method1
Method2
Method1
Method2
```

Interfaces

The __interface keyword is not technically a managed extension keyword, because it can be effectively used in both managed and unmanaged code. However, it is often used in managed code, so it is worth considering here.

An interface is used as a generalized base type for classes that are required to implement a binding contract. This contract serves to facilitate implementation code and client code by defining a common polymorphic set of functions. You can think of an interface as being an extreme form of an abstract class in that it serves a similar purpose, but it is in a purer form. Conventionally, C++ programmers have used the term "interface" to refer to any class that contains only pure virtual methods. The new **__interface** keyword simply enforces that convention in an explicit manner.

A class declared using the **__interface** keyword must contain only public, pure virtual methods (which is implied in any case). In particular, it must have no implementation of any methods, it must not contain any static or nonstatic data members, and it must not contain any constructors, destructors, static methods, or operator overloading methods. An interface can inherit from any number of base interfaces, but it cannot inherit from any base abstract or nonabstract class. Note that although data members are not allowed, properties (accessed via get/set methods) are allowed in an interface. Properties are described later in this chapter. As with an abstract class, an interface cannot be instantiated directly, but is instead used as a polymorphic base type.

Only the public access specifier is allowed within an interface; however, it is not necessary, since public is the default. Since the only useful purpose for an interface is to provide a base contract for other classes, you may have deduced that it would make no sense for an interface to have the **__sealed** keyword applied to it, and you would be correct.

Code Example

A managed interface (i.e., an interface with **__gc** specified) has an additional requirement. It cannot inherit from any unmanaged interfaces. However, it can inherit from any number of other managed interfaces. The following example code shows how the **__interface** keyword is typically used:

```
//InterfaceExample.cpp

#using <mscorlib.dll>
using namespace System;

__interface SomeInterface
{
public:
   virtual void Method1() = 0; //pure virtual explicit
   void Method2(); //pure virtual implied
};

class DerivedClass : public SomeInterface
{
public:
   void Method1()   //implemented here
   {
      Console::WriteLine("Method1");
   }
```

```
    void Method2()   //implemented here
    {
        Console::WriteLine("Method2");
    }
};

void main(void)
{
    //SomeInterface *psi = new SomeInterface; //error
    SomeInterface *psi = new DerivedClass; //pointer
    psi->Method1();
    psi->Method2();
    SomeInterface &si = *new DerivedClass; //reference
    si.Method1();
    si.Method2();
}
```

The above program produces the following output:

```
Method1
Method2
Method1
Method2
```

Boxing and Unboxing Primitive Data Types

Boxing and unboxing is an important concept in .NET programming regardless of which language you program in. One of the strongest features of .NET is that it has a unified type system. Every type, including the simple boxed built-in types such as **__box(int)**, derive from **System.Object**. A language such as Smalltalk also has this feature in that everything is an object, but pays the price of inefficiency for simple types. Standard C++ treats simple built-in types differently than objects, thus achieving efficiency but at the loss of a unified type system. Managed C++ enjoys the best of both worlds through a scheme known as *boxing*. Boxing converts a value type, such as an **int** or a **double**, to a heap object reference, and this is performed with the **__box** keyword. Unboxing converts a boxed type (stored on heap) back to an unboxed value (stored on stack). Unboxing is done through a type cast. Boxing and unboxing is demonstrated in the following code snippet:

```
int x = 5; //simple built in type int
__box int *po = __box(x); //boxing
x = *po;                   //unboxing
```

The **__box** keyword creates a managed object on the managed heap that encapsulates a copy of a value type expression. The value type expression can be a primitive data type, such as **int**, **float**, **double**, or **char**, or it may be a value type defined as a **class** or **struct** declared with the **__value** keyword. For example, the predefined **__boxed_System_Int32** managed type encapsulates a boxed **int**, and a managed type named **__boxed_ValueStruct** would encapsulate a boxed value type named **ValueStruct**. These strange data type names (**__boxed_System_Int32** and **__boxed_ValueStruct**) do not show up in your source code, but they can be seen using **Ildasm.exe**. Note that **__box int** * is an alias notation for the managed type named **__boxed_System_Int32**, and **__box ValueStruct*** is an alias notation for **__boxed_ValueStruct**.

Once the **__box** keyword is used to create the managed object, the .NET garbage collector will eventually automatically deallocate the resulting managed object. This is similar in concept to using a wrapper class for a primitive data type; however, boxing plays a much more prominent role in the .NET environment than in traditional C++ programming. This is due to the fact that objects in C++ may be treated as value or reference types, whereas managed objects are always treated exclusively as reference types (i.e., a reference or pointer to the object on the managed heap) in the .NET environment.

Code
Example

A value type can be accessed from the boxed version using the same syntax as accessing an unboxed value. This can be seen in the following code, where the assignment ***pIntBox = 50** is performed. In spite of the fact that **pIntBox** points to a managed object, the dereferenced pointer is being used syntactically as if it was simply a pointer to an unboxed **int** type.

```
//BoxExample.cpp

#using <mscorlib.dll>
using namespace System;

__value struct ValueStruct
{
public:
   int i;
};

//function expects to receive a managed object pointer
void ExpectManagedObjectPointer(
   __box ValueStruct* pManagedObject)
{
   pManagedObject->i = 20; //modify the boxed copy
   Console::WriteLine(pManagedObject->i);
}
```

```
//function expects to receive a managed object pointer
void ExpectBoxedPrimitivePointer(__box int* pIntBox)
{
    *pIntBox = 50; //modify boxed copy of primitive type
    Console::WriteLine(*pIntBox);
}

void main(void)
{
    ValueStruct valueStruct; //value type object on stack
    valueStruct.i = 10; //modify the original unboxed copy
    Console::WriteLine(valueStruct.i);
    __box ValueStruct* pManagedObject
        = __box(valueStruct); //__boxed_ValueStruct
    ExpectManagedObjectPointer(pManagedObject);
    pManagedObject->i = 30; //modify the boxed copy
    Console::WriteLine(pManagedObject->i);
    int j; //value type primitive data type
    j = 40; //modify the original unboxed primitive type
    Console::WriteLine(j);
    __box int *pIntBox = __box(j); // boxed_System int32
    ExpectBoxedPrimitivePointer(pIntBox);
}
```

The above program produces the following output:

```
10
20
30
40
50
```

Delegates

The __delegate keyword declares a delegate class based on a method signature. This serves a purpose that is very similar to a traditional C++ pointer to function type definition, except that a delegate may only point to a method of a managed class. The most common use for delegates is in implementing callback functions or handling events within .NET Framework applications. However, they can be used wherever methods need to be called in a dynamically programmatic manner.

There are two types of delegates defined as abstract classes within the .NET Framework, named **System::Delegate** and **System::MulticastDelegate**. These two types of delegates are used as the base classes for single-cast and multicast delegates, respectively. A single-cast delegate binds a function pointer to one managed object method, whereas a multicast delegate binds a function pointer to one or more managed object methods. Invoking a single-cast delegate always results in only a single method being called on a single object, whereas the multicast delegate can result in methods being called on an arbitrary number of methods. Because multicast delegates can be used for one or more method calls, the single-cast form is not actually needed. Generally, only multicast delegates are used in most programs.

The compiler creates a specialized managed class derived from **System::MulticastDelegate** when it sees the **__delegate** keyword. This managed class has a constructor that takes the following two parameters: a pointer to a managed class instance (which may be zero in the case of a static method) and a method that is to be called via the delegate. This managed class also has a method named **Invoke** with a signature that is identical to the method that the delegate invokes. The following code demonstrates how to work with delegates:

Code
Example

```
//DelegateExample.cpp

#using <mscorlib.dll>
using namespace System;

//define managed classes for use as delegates
__delegate int SomeDelegate
    (int i, int j);

__delegate
    void SomeOtherDelegate(int i);

__gc class SomeClass //contains methods called by delegates
{
public:
    int SomeMethod(int i, int j)
    {
        Console::WriteLine(
            "SomeMethod({0}, {1})", __box(i), __box(j));
        return i+j;
    }
    static int SomeStaticMethod(int i, int j)
    {
        Console::WriteLine(
            "SomeStaticMethod({0}, {1})", __box(i), __box(j));
        return i+j;
    }
    void SomeOtherMethod(int i)
```

```
  {
     Console::WriteLine(
        "SomeOtherMethod({0})", __box(i));
  }
};

void main ()
{
   SomeDelegate *pscd;
   int sum;

   //bind delegate to non-static method
   //needs an instance of SomeClass
   SomeClass * psc = new SomeClass();
   pscd = //create instance of sc delegate class
      new SomeDelegate(
         psc, &SomeClass::SomeMethod); //nonstatic
   sum = pscd->Invoke(3, 4); //call method via delegate
   Console::WriteLine(sum);

   //bind delegate to static method - needs no instance
   pscd = //create another instance of sc delegate class
      new SomeDelegate(
         0, &SomeClass::SomeStaticMethod); //static
   sum = pscd->Invoke(3, 4); //call method via delegate
   Console::WriteLine(sum);

   //combine two delegates
   SomeClass * psc1 = new SomeClass();
   SomeClass * psc2 = new SomeClass();
   SomeOtherDelegate *pmcd1 = new SomeOtherDelegate(
      psc1, &SomeClass::SomeOtherMethod);
   SomeOtherDelegate *pmcd2 = new SomeOtherDelegate(
      psc2, &SomeClass::SomeOtherMethod);
   SomeOtherDelegate *pmcd =
   static_cast<SomeOtherDelegate *>(Delegate::Combine(
      pmcd1, pmcd2));
   pmcd->Invoke(1);
}
```

The above program produces the following output:

```
SomeMethod(3, 4)
7
```

```
SomeStaticMethod(3, 4)
7
SomeOtherMethod(1)
SomeOtherMethod(1)
```

Events

An event is a mechanism through which an object can signal the occurrence of something that has happened. An event may represent a user interface action, such as a mouse click, or some programmatic change in state such as a time-out or the completion of a task. The object that generates the event is called the event source or event sender, and the object that responds to the event is called the event sink or event receiver.

Traditional C++ programmers dealt with this design pattern by implementing a callback function and calling back into it via a function pointer. COM programmers dealt with it using the **IConnectionPoint** and **IConnectionPointContainer** interfaces. Now, .NET programmers deal with it using managed events. All these techniques are basically similar in design, so Microsoft has defined the Unified Event Model to consolidate these approaches. To support this new Unified Event Model, the **__event**, **__hook**, and **__unhook** keywords and the **event_source** and **event_receiver** attributes have been added as C++ extensions.

You use the **__event** keyword to establish an event that can be fired from an event source. The **__event** keyword is not limited to use just within managed classes, but is rather quite generalized and can be applied to any of the following:

1. Declaration of a native C++ class method (traditional callback)
2. Declaration of a COM interface (connection point)
3. Declaration of a managed class method (managed event)
4. Declaration of a managed class data member (managed event using delegate)

We will only be concerned here with the third case, where a managed class method is declared as an event source. You use the **__hook** keyword to associate a method of an event receiver class to act as a handler method for a particular event. Once the event has been hooked, the event handler method will then be called whenever the event is fired, until the **__unhook** keyword is used to undo the association. The following code shows a typical example of how the **__event**, **__hook**, and **__unhook** keywords as well as the **event_source** and **event_receiver** attributes are used to establish a callback mechanism:

```
//Event.cpp

#using <mscorlib.dll>
```

```cpp
using namespace System;

[event_source(managed)]
public __gc class ManagedEventSource
{
public:
   __event void ManagedEvent(); //no implementation
   void Fire_ManagedEvent()
   {
      ManagedEvent();
   }
};


[event_receiver(managed)]
__gc class ManagedEventReceiver
{
public:
   void HandleManagedEvent() //called via ManagedEvent
   {
      Console::WriteLine("HandleManagedEvent called");
   }
   void HookEvent(ManagedEventSource *pEventSource)
   {
      __hook(
         &ManagedEventSource::ManagedEvent,
         pEventSource,
         &ManagedEventReceiver::HandleManagedEvent);
   }
   void UnhookEvent(ManagedEventSource* pEventSource)
   {
      __unhook(
         &ManagedEventSource::ManagedEvent,
         pEventSource,
         &ManagedEventReceiver::HandleManagedEvent);
   }
};

void main()
{
   ManagedEventSource* pEventSource =
      new ManagedEventSource;
   ManagedEventReceiver* pReceiver =
      new ManagedEventReceiver;
   pReceiver->HookEvent(pEventSource);
```

```
    pEventSource->Fire_ManagedEvent(); //handler is called
    pReceiver->UnhookEvent(pEventSource);
}
```

The output of the above program is shown next:

```
HandleManagedEvent called
```

Properties

The **__property** keyword is used to indicate that get and/or set methods are used to implement a property of a managed class. Whereas a data member (known also as a field) is quite inflexible, a property may be read/write, read only, or write only, and may be implemented as a simple variable or as a calculated value. For example, a read-only property would be implemented with a **get_** method, but no **set_** method. A property is accessible to client code written in any .NET language using the normal data member access syntax of that language, as if it were a normal data member (i.e., a pseudo data member). You can see this in action in the following code example, where **pmcwp->someProperty** is being used as if there actually was a data member named **someProperty**. In fact, no such data member exists, but rather a **get_someProperty** and **set_someProperty** method pair declared with the **__property** keyword does exist. The example does have a **protected** data member named **m_someProperty**, but this a hidden implementation detail encapsulated within the component. A .NET component property is similar to the notion of an OLE Automation property in a traditional ActiveX component or a bean property in a JavaBean component.

Code Example

Another interesting feature of a managed property that is not supported by a raw exposed data member is that you may choose to test the parameter of the **set_** method for validity and throw an exception if it is not acceptable. This helps in designing components that are responsible for their own sanity.

```
//PropertyExample.cpp

#using <mscorlib.dll>
using namespace System;

__gc class ManagedClassWithProperty
{
public:
    ManagedClassWithProperty() : m_someProperty(0) {}
    __property int get_someProperty() //must be "get_"
    {
        return m_someProperty;
```

```
   }
   __property void set_someProperty(
      int propertyValue) //must be "set_"
   {
      m_someProperty = propertyValue;
   }
protected:
   int m_someProperty; //optionally implement as data member
};

void main()
{
   ManagedClassWithProperty* pmcwp =
      new ManagedClassWithProperty;
   pmcwp->someProperty = 7; //pseudo-data member
   Console::WriteLine(pmcwp->someProperty);
}
```

The above program produces the following output:

7

Pinning Managed Objects

The __**pin** keyword indicates that a pointer to memory in a managed object will remain valid (i.e., the object will not be moved by the CLR) for the lifetime of the pinning pointer. The pinned object remains unmoved for as long as the pinning pointer points to it. If the pinning pointer is assigned to point to a different object, or if it is assigned to zero, then the object becomes eligible for movement by the garbage collector. If the __**pin** keyword is not provided, then the CLR is free to move the object to which it points at any time. Object movement occurs as a natural consequence of the garbage collection and heap compaction activities performed by the CLR. This movement has no detrimental effect on managed code, since the CLR automatically updates managed pointers as part of its routine activities, but object movement is a problem for unmanaged code that uses unmanaged pointers to managed objects.

The __**pin** keyword should be avoided except for situations where it is truly warranted, since pinning an object frustrates the efforts of the garbage collector, thereby reducing its effectiveness. An example of where pinning an object is warranted would be where you pass a parameter pointing to a managed object (or a pointer to a data member within such an object) into an unmanaged function. The problem is that the garbage collector could move the managed object during its normal activities while the unmanaged function continues to use the old invalid pointer. This would cause the unmanaged function to attempt to access invalid memory, often with disastrous results.

An example showing how to use the **__pin** keyword in this situation is shown next. Note that the **pPinnedObject** is pinned in memory so that it is safe to pass a pointer into the pinned object as a parameter into the unmanaged **SetGlobalPointerValue** and **SetGlobalPointerValue** methods. These methods rely on the fact that the global pointer **gx** will remain valid, which can only be guaranteed if the CLR does not move the **ManagedClass** object. Note also that the compiler is aware of this risk, and it generates an error if the **__pin** keyword is removed from this example.

```cpp
//PinExample.cpp

#using <mscorlib.dll>
using namespace System;

__gc class ManagedClass
{
public:
    int x;
};

#pragma unmanaged

int *gx; //global pointer

void SetGlobalPointer(int* pi)
{
    //set global pointer to point into managed object
    gx = pi;
}

void SetGlobalPointerValue(int i)
{
    //set managed object data member via global pointer
    *gx = i;
}

int GetGlobalPointerValue()
{
    //get managed object data member via global pointer
    return *gx;
}
```

```
#pragma managed

void main()
{
    ManagedClass __pin * pPinnedObject = new ManagedClass;
    //note compiler error in the following statement...
    //if the __pin keyword is removed from statement above
    SetGlobalPointer(&pPinnedObject->x); //unmanaged
    SetGlobalPointerValue(1); //unmanaged
    int x = GetGlobalPointerValue();//unmanaged
}
```

Sealed Classes

The __**sealed** keyword indicates that a class or struct cannot be used as a base type. In other words, it is a terminal type in the inheritance hierarchy. The __**scaled** keyword can also be applied to individual methods in a class. A sealed method cannot be overridden in a derived class. Traditional C++ programming had no similar feature; however, the Java keyword *final* provides the same functionality. The following code snippet produces an error, because you cannot derive a class from a sealed class:

```
__sealed class SomeSealedClass
{
};
class SomeDerivedClass : public SomeSealedClass //error
{
};
```

One common reason for using the __**sealed** keyword is to improve the stability of a class hierarchy design by preventing overconfident or underskilled programmers from messing up important or complex behavior in derived classes. Another use of the __**sealed** keyword is to foil attempts on hijacking security-oriented functionality through derived classes that override security-related features. For example, the predefined **String** class is declared to be a sealed class, and this combined with the fact that it is immutable (it has no public methods or data members that allow you to modify its content) makes it ideal for security related purposes, such as passwords. Note that the following code produces a compiler error because the **String** class is sealed:

```
//illegal because System::String is __sealed
class MyString : public String
{
};
```

Managed Type Casting

The **__try_cast** keyword causes a **System::InvalidCastException** to be thrown if a cast is attempted that is not acceptable to the CLR. This is similar to the **bad_cast** exception that can be thrown by the **dynamic_cast** operator in C++ and to the **ClassCastException** exception that is thrown from a bad cast in Java. Although **__try_cast** behaves more like the **dynamic_cast** operator than the **static_cast** operator, the **__try_cast** is really intended as a temporary substitute for the **static_cast** operator during the development phase. Once the testing has thoroughly eradicated all **__try_cast** runtime exceptions, those **__try_cast** exceptions are then typically replaced with the **static_cast**. The following code shows an example where the **__try_cast** is used to detect an invalid cast:

Code
Example

```
//TryCastExample.cpp

#using <mscorlib.dll>
using namespace System;

__gc class Mammal
{
};

__gc class Dog : public Mammal
{
};

__gc struct Cat : public Mammal
{
};

void main()
{
    Mammal *pMammal = new Dog;
    try
    {
        Dog *pDog = __try_cast <Dog *>(pMammal);   //good
        Console::WriteLine("__try_cast <Dog *>"); //good
        Cat *pCat = __try_cast <Cat *>(pMammal);   //bad!
        Console::WriteLine("__try_cast <Cat *>"); //skipped
    }
    catch(InvalidCastException *pe)
    {
        Console::WriteLine("Ooops: {0}", pe->get_Message());
```

```
    }
}
```

The above program produces the following output:

```
__try_cast <Dog *>
Ooops: Exception of type System.InvalidCastException was
thrown.
```

Defining Keyword Identifiers

The **__identifier** keyword allows the use of any name, including any keyword, as an identifier. Use of the **__identifier** keyword for identifiers that are not keywords is permitted, but provides no advantage and is therefore discouraged. It may seem odd that such a feature could ever be useful; however, since the .NET platform is intended for multilanguage development efforts, it makes sense that it may be necessary to refer to a variable or class name (originating in some other language code) that happens to be a keyword in the C++ language. However, it is obvious that using keywords as identifiers can make code very confusing to read, and therefore, it should be avoided except where absolutely necessary. Think of it as a last resort in a desperate situation. The strange-looking code below shows a class named **if** with a data member named **while** (truly bizarre). Then, an instance of **if** is created, and its **while** method is called (OK, now I am feeling queasy). Amazingly, this compiles and runs!

Code Example

```
//IdentifierExample.cpp

#using <mscorlib.dll>
using namespace System;

__gc class __identifier(if)
{
public:
    int __identifier(while);
};

void main(void)
{
    __identifier(if)* pif = new __identifier(if);
    pif->__identifier(while)= 1;
    Console::WriteLine(pif->__identifier(while));
}
```

Exception Handling

You are no doubt already familiar with the standard C++ exception mechanism, which gives a good understanding of how managed exceptions work. It turns out that the .NET platform (i.e., the CLR) supports exceptions that are compatible with managed C++ exceptions, and in fact, managed exceptions thrown by code written in any .NET language can be caught by code written in any other .NET language.

You can make use of the preexisting exceptions, such as **Invalid-CastException** and **OverflowException**, or you may want to define your own **Exception** derived classes that encapsulate application specific exception information. Consider the following example:

```
//Exceptions.cpp

#using <mscorlib.dll>
using namespace System;

__gc class MyException : public Exception
{
};

void TemperamentalFunction(int i) //hates odd numbers
{
   Console::WriteLine(
      "TemperamentalFunction called with {0}",
      i.ToString());
   if (i%2 != 0)
      throw new MyException;
   Console::WriteLine("No exception thrown");
}

void main()
{
   try
   {
      TemperamentalFunction(2); //call with even number
      TemperamentalFunction(3); //call with odd number
   }
   catch (MyException *pe)
   {
      Console::WriteLine("Exception thrown!");
      Console::WriteLine(pe->get_StackTrace());
   }
}
```

The result of the above program is shown next:

```
TemperamentalFunction called with 2
No exception thrown
TemperamentalFunction called with 3
Exception thrown!
   at TemperamentalFunction(Int32 i) in c:\netcpp-
code\chap03\exceptions\exceptio
ns.cpp:line 16
   at main() in c:\netcppcode\chap03\exceptions\excep-
tions.cpp:line 25
```

Note that the **StackTrace** method used in the example returns a text string representing the stack trace at the point where the exception occurred. Although the example does not demonstrate its use, you should remember that Visual C++ also supports the **__finally** keyword, which is a welcome extension to ANSI C++. The **__finally** keyword allows you to place important code that must be executed, regardless of whether or not an exception is thrown from within a try block. It is also nice to know that the **__finally** keyword is completely compatible with the exception mechanism provided by the other .NET languages.

You may want to try breaking the preceding example into two parts. The first part would be a C# component (packaged in a DLL) containing the exception-throwing code. The second part would be a C++ application that calls into **TemperamentalFunction**. This should convince you that indeed exceptions do bridge between different .NET languages.

C++ Attributes

Visual C++.NET supports attributes that allow you to create traditional unmanaged code, such as COM components, more easily than ever before, and also supports new .NET functionality, such as the Unified Event Model. The COM-related attributes were originally used in a separate IDL (Interface Definition Language) file to describe the type information of a COM component. Now, these attributes can be used directly within your C++ source code, eliminating the need for a separately maintained IDL file. The compiler uses these attributes to generate both type information and executable code. One advantage in using C++ attributes for COM programming is that you now have to contend only with C++ source files, not with IDL and RGS (Registry Script) files. This makes a COM component project simpler and more maintainable.

Attributes are used to radically modify or extend the C++ language in a modular manner. Attribute providers, which are made available as independent DLLs, provide a dynamic extension mechanism for the C++ compiler.

Attributes are designed to increase programmer productivity, especially in the area of COM component development. These attributes generate code that is automatically injected into the compiled result. Attributes can generate code for the following purposes:

- COM interfaces and components
- COM events (connection points)
- Unified Event Model events (managed events)
- ATL Server code
- OLE DB consumer code
- Performance counter code
- Module entry points

Although this chapter is titled "Managed C++ Programming," and attributes can be used to build managed code, we will only look briefly at using attributes for unmanaged COM programming in this section. For information on using attributes for managed events, see the section titled "Events" earlier in this chapter. For information on using attributes for all other purposes, please see the .NET SDK documentation. Chapter 8 discusses custom attributes.

The following line of code declaring a function named **AddEmUp** demonstrates the need for C++ attributes. Note that ANSI C++ has no way of describing the **AddEmUp** function completely. For example, it is not possible to stipulate whether each parameter is an in or out parameter. Traditionally, this additional qualifying information, which is important for the generation of COM marshaling code, was defined using IDL attributes in a separate IDL file. IDL attributes are placed within square brackets and can be used to qualify many COM component features, including interfaces, coclasses, and type libraries.

```
//lacks important marshaling information
HRESULT AddEmUp(int i, int j, int* psum);
```

The above C++ function could be described more fully in an IDL file, as shown in the following. Note the **in**, **out**, and **retval** attributes being used.

```
HRESULT AddEmUp(
    [in]int i, [in]int j, [out,retval]int *psum);
```

The Microsoft IDL compiler, **Midl.exe**, is used to parse the **IDL** file and generate a type library and marshaling source files (proxy and stub) for the methods in a COM interface (RPC interfaces are also supported).

You can manually add attributes to your own source code. However, it is instructive to see how attributes are employed within a project generated by the ATL COM Application Wizard, which it is a high productivity tool for building COM components. Figure 3–4 shows how to enable attributes within the ATL COM Application Wizard.

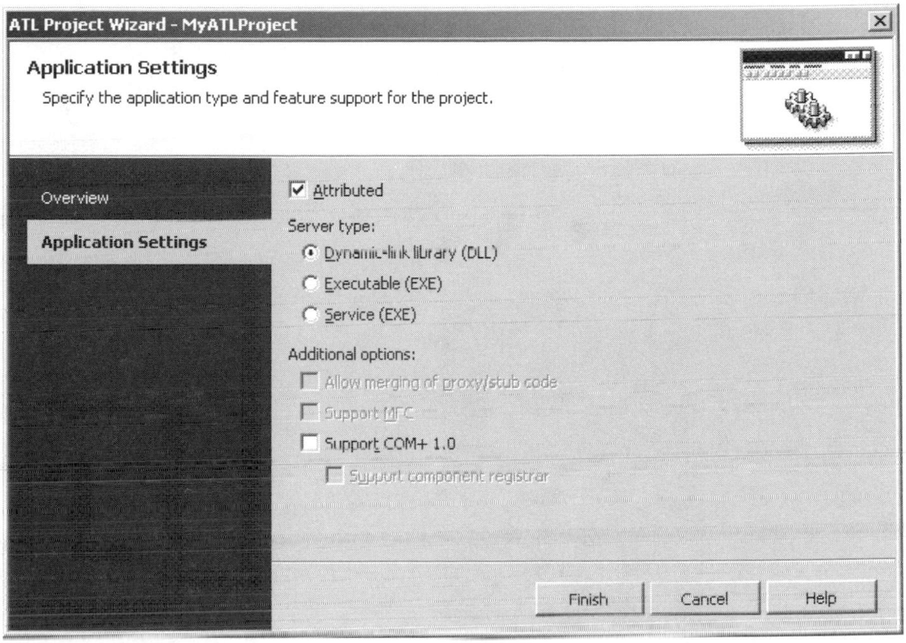

ATL Project Wizard - MyATLProject   ×

Application Settings

Specify the application type and feature support for the project.

Overview

Application Settings

☑ Attributed

Server type:
  ⦿ Dynamic-link library (DLL)
  ○ Executable (EXE)
  ○ Service (EXE)

Additional options:
  ☐ Allow merging of proxy/stub code
  ☐ Support MFC
  ☐ Support COM+ 1.0
      ☐ Support component registrar

  Finish   Cancel   Help

Figure 3–4   *The ATL Project Wizard with the Attributed checkbox checked.*

The following code in **MyATLProject.cpp** was produced using the ATL Project Wizard as a result of checking the Attributed checkbox in the ATL Project Wizard. Note the **module** attribute is applied to the project as a whole, which automatically generates the **DllMain**, **DllRegisterServer**, and **DllUnregisterServer** functions.

```
// MyATLProject.cpp : Implementation of DLL Exports.

#include "stdafx.h"
#include "resource.h"

// The module attribute causes DllMain, DllRegisterServer and
// DllUnregisterServer to be automatically implemented for you
[ module(dll, uuid = "{50434D6D-AAEA-405C-AC49-B9CA769E5D6D}",
     name = "MyATLProject",
     helpstring = "MyATLProject 1.0 Type Library",
     resource_name = "IDR_MYATLPROJECT") ];
```

Figure 3–5 shows the ATL Simple Object Wizard being used to add a simple COM class named **MyATLClass** to the project.

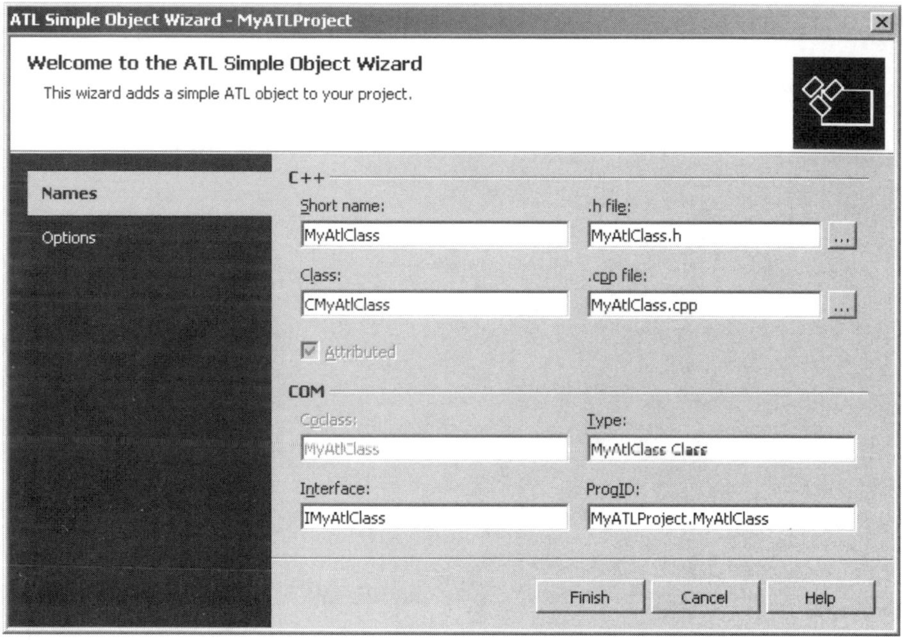

Figure 3–5   *The ATL Simple Object Wizard.*

The ATL Simple Object Wizard then generates the following attributed C++ code in **MyAtlClass.h** (not an IDL file). Note the use of attributes such as **object**, **uuid**, and **dual** to qualify the interface, and **coclass**, **progid**, and **version** to qualify the COM class. These attributes are placed directly into the C++ source code, and therefore no IDL file is required.

```
// IMyAtlClass
[
   object,
   uuid("1F9401D8-58BF-469D-845B-A2069CBAFC84"),
   dual, helpstring("IMyAtlClass Interface"),
   pointer_default(unique)
]
__interface IMyAtlClass : IDispatch
{
};

// CMyAtlClass
[
   coclass,
```

```
    threading("apartment"),
    vi_progid("MyATLProject.MyAtlClass"),
    progid("MyATLProject.MyAtlClass.1"),
    version(1.0),
    uuid("B3321AD5-3ACE-4820-B134-35FD67120A48"),
    helpstring("MyAtlClass Class")
]
class ATL_NO_VTABLE CMyAtlClass :
    public IMyAtlClass
{
public:
    CMyAtlClass()
    {
    }

    DECLARE_PROTECT_FINAL_CONSTRUCT()

    HRESULT FinalConstruct()
    {
        return S_OK;
    }

    void FinalRelease()
    {
    }

public:

};
```

The above code uses the **coclass** attribute but it is missing several features that existed in code generated by previous version of ATL. For example, it has no object map, no interface map, and no registry script. The **coclass** attribute provides all this missing functionality. The missing code is automatically generated by the compiler in response to the **coclass** attribute and injected into the compiled result.

Figure 3–6 shows the Add Method dialog being used to add a method named **AddEmUp**. Note the **in**, **out**, and **retval** attributes being provided.

This makes the following addition to the source code in the project in **MyAtlClass.h**. Note again that the attributes are being applied within the CPP source file rather than a separate IDL file.

```
// IMyAtlClass
[
```

How to Create a Simple ATL Project

Create the ATL Server Project:

1. Select the File | New menu sequence to open the New Project dialog.
2. Select Visual C++ Projects as the Project Type.
3. Select ATL Project as the Template.
4. Enter MyATLProject as the Name.
5. Enter a suitable path as the Location.
6. Click OK to start the ATL Project Wizard.
7. Select the Application Settings tab.
8. Note that the Attributed checkbox is checked.
9. Click Finish.

Create a Simple ATL Object:

10. Select the Project | Add Class Menu sequence to open the Add Class dialog.
11. Select the ATL Simple Object as the Template.
12. Click Open to open the ATL Simple Object Wizard.
13. Enter MyAtlClass as the Short name.
14. Click Finish to generate the project.

Add a Method to the Simple ATL Object:

15. Right-click on the IMyAtlClass interface in the Class View window.
16. Select the Add | Add Method menu sequence to open the Add Method wizard.
17. Enter AddEmUp as the Method name.
18. Select LONG from the Parameter type list.
19. Enter i as the Parameter name.
20. Check the in checkbox.
21. Click Add.
22. Select LONG from the Parameter type list.
23. Enter j as the Parameter name.
24. Check the in checkbox.
25. Click Add.
26. Select LONG* from the Parameter type list.
27. Enter psum as the Parameter name.
28. Check the out and retval checkboxes.
29. Click Add.
30. Click Finish.

```
object,
uuid("1F9401D8-58BF-469D-845B-A2069CBAFC84"),
dual, helpstring("IMyAtlClass Interface"),
pointer_default(unique)
]
__interface IMyAtlClass : IDispatch
```

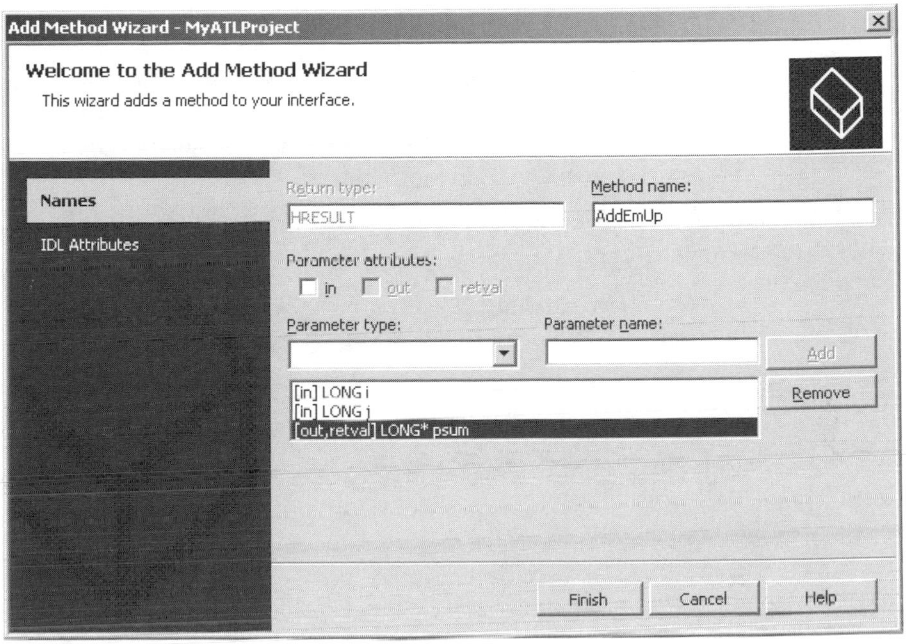

Figure 3-6   *The Add Method dialog specifying parameter attributes.*

```
[
   [id(1), helpstring("method AddEmUp")] HRESULT AddEmUp([in]
LONG i, [in] LONG j, [out,retval] LONG* psum);
};
```

The only thing left to do in this example is to manually provide an implementation for the **AddEmUp** method in **MyAtlClass.cpp** and then build the project. An implementation for the **AddEmUp** method is shown next. Once the project is built, it can be tested with a COM client program. We will not describe the steps involved in doing this, since it is simply conventional COM client programming, using old-fashioned Visual Basic or Visual C++. For more information on how to do this, please refer to the Visual Studio documentation or the many excellent books available on the subject (for example, *Understanding and Programming COM+* by Robert J. Oberg).

```
STDMETHODIMP CMyAtlClass::AddEmUp(LONG i, LONG j, LONG* psum)
{
   // TODO: Add your implementation code here
   *psum = i+j; //added manually
   return S_OK;
}
```

Summary

In this chapter, we have studied how C++ managed extensions can be used to write programs and components for the .NET platform. We first looked at the **HelloWorld**, **ConvertTemp**, and many other programs to get a feel for the basic concepts in writing managed C++ code, including standard input and output. The **String** and **Array** classes were explored, which are used heavily in almost all types of .NET applications. The C++ managed extension keywords were explored in detail, followed by delegates, events, and managed exception handling. Finally, we looked at the topic of using C++ attributes used in COM component development.

Object-Oriented Programming in Managed C++

*I*n the previous chapter we covered the essentials of programming with managed C++. Since we have assumed you are an experienced C++ programmer, we were able to cover quite a lot of ground. This chapter represents a change of pace. Rather than covering a lot of new material, we focus on solidifying our understanding of the object-oriented aspects of managed C++, with an emphasis on abstraction and inheritance. First, we review the fundamentals of object-oriented programming. Next, the Acme Travel Agency case study is introduced. This case study is developed throughout the entire book as we explain more about .NET. We examine what are the suitable abstractions that will enable us to implement a reservation system for a variety of resources that must be reserved, and we provide an implementation of a hotel reservation system. The abstract base classes we define provide reusable code that enables us to easily implement other kinds of reservation systems. The key is finding the right abstractions. We will see how managed C++ language features facilitate object-oriented programming. Certain details of managed C++, such as use of access control (public, private, and protected) and properties, can help express abstractions in a way that is safe and easy to use.

Review of Object-Oriented Concepts

In this preliminary section we review the fundamentals of object-oriented programming. If you are experienced using the object-oriented features of C++, you may skim through this section as a refresher and go on to the following section, where we introduce the case study. On the other hand, if you have been using C++ primarily as a "better C," this section may prove useful background as you learn how to use C++ in a real object-oriented manner, working with inheritance hierarchies that model a real-world system.

Objects

Objects have both a real-world meaning and a software meaning, and an object model describes a relationship between them.

OBJECTS IN THE REAL WORLD

The term *object* has an intuitive real-world meaning. There are concrete, tangible objects, such as a ball, an automobile, and an airplane. There are also more abstract objects that have a definite intellectual meaning, such as a committee, a patent, or an insurance contract.

Objects have both attributes (or characteristics) and operations that can be performed upon them. A ball has a size, a weight, a color, and so on. Operations may be performed on the ball, such as throw, catch, and drop.

There can be various relationships among classes of objects. One relationship is a specialization relationship; for example, an automobile is a special kind of vehicle. Another relationship is a whole–part relationship; an automobile consists of an engine, a chassis, wheels, and other parts.

OBJECT MODELS

Objects can also be used in programs. Objects are useful in programming because you can set up a software model of a real-world system. Software objects abstract the parts of objects in the real world that are relevant to the problem being solved. The model can then be implemented as actual software using a programming language. A software system implemented in this way tends to be more faithful to the real system, and it can be changed more readily when the real system is changed.

There are formal languages for describing object models. The most popular language is UML (Unified Modeling Language), which is a synthesis of several earlier modeling languages. Formal modeling languages are beyond the scope of this book, but we will find that informal models are useful.

REUSABLE SOFTWARE COMPONENTS

Another advantage of objects in software is that they can facilitate reusable software components. Hardware has long enjoyed significant benefits from reusable hardware components. For example, computers can be created from power supplies, printed circuit boards, and other components. Printed circuit boards in turn can be created from chips. The same chip can be reused in many different computers, and new hardware designs do not have to be done from scratch. With appropriate software technology, similar reuse is feasible in software systems. Objects provide the foundation for software reuse.

OBJECTS IN SOFTWARE

An *object* is a software entity containing data *(state)* and related functions *(behavior)* as a self-contained module. For example, a **HotelBroker** may contain a list of hotels (the state) and provide operations to add a hotel and make a reservation (behavior).

ABSTRACTION

An *abstraction* captures the essential features of a real-world object, suppressing unnecessary details. All instances of an abstraction share these common features. Abstraction helps us deal with complexity. For example, consider the problem of booking a reservation. There are many different kinds of things you might want to reserve, such as a hotel, an airplane flight, or a conference room. There are many differences, but every such "reservable" has certain essentials that are always in common, such as a capacity.

ENCAPSULATION

The implementation of an abstraction should be hidden from the rest of the system, or *encapsulated*. For example, the list of hotels may be contained in several different kinds of data structures, such as an array, a collection, or a database. The rest of the system should not need to know the details of the representation.

Classes

A *class* groups all objects with common behavior and common structure. A class allows production of new objects of the same type. An object is an instance of some class. We refer to the process of creating an individual object as *instantiation*. Classes can be related in various ways, such as by *inheritance* and by *containment*.

INHERITANCE

Inheritance is a key feature of the object oriented programming paradigm. You abstract out common features of your classes and put them in a high-level base class. You can add or change features in more specialized derived classes, which "inherit" the standard behavior from the base class. Inheritance facilitates code reuse and extensibility.

Consider **Reservable** as a base class, with derived classes **Hotel** and **Flight**. All reservables share some characteristics, such as a capacity. Different kinds of reservables differ in other respects. For example, a hotel has a city and a name, while a flight has an origin and a destination. Figure 4–1 illustrates the relationship among these different kinds of reservables.

ABSTRACT CLASSES

Sometimes a class is never meant to be instantiated, but only to provide a template for derived classes. The **Reservable** class is an example—it is too abstract to actually instantiate. Only specific kinds of reservable classes, such as **Hotel** and **Flight**, may actually be instantiated. We call a class that cannot

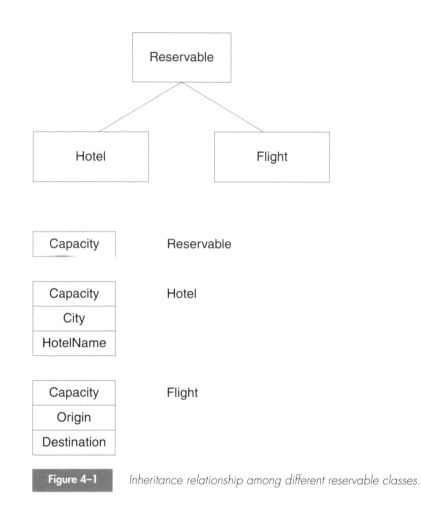

Figure 4–1   *Inheritance relationship among different reservable classes.*

be instantiated, such as **Reservable**, an *abstract* class. A class that can be instantiated, such as **Hotel** or **Flight**, is called a *concrete* class.

RELATIONSHIPS AMONG CLASSES

Classes may be related to each other in various ways.

- The inheritance (IS-A) relationship specifies how one class is a special case of another class. A **Hotel** (subclass or derived class) is a special kind of **Reservable** (superclass or base class).
- The composition (HAS-A) relationship specifies how one class (the whole) is made up of other classes (the parts). A **HotelBroker** (whole) has a list of **Hotel** objects.
- A weaker kind of relationship (USES-A) can be identified when one class merely makes use of some other class when carrying out its responsibilities.

Polymorphism

Consider the problem of generating a payroll for various categories of employees. Different kinds of employees may have pay calculated in a different manner. A salaried employee receives a fixed salary. A wage employee is paid according to the number of hours worked. A sales employee is paid according to the commissions earned on sales that were made.

A traditional approach is to maintain a type field in an employee structure and to perform processing in a switch statement, with cases for each type. Such use of switch statements is error-prone and requires much maintenance when adding a new employee type.

An alternative is to localize the intelligence to calculate pay in each employee class, which will support its own **GetPay** method. Generic payroll code can then be written that will handle different types of employees and will not have to be modified to support an additional employee type. Provide a **GetPay** method in the base class and an override of this method in each derived class. Call **GetPay** through an object reference to a general **Employee** object. Depending on the actual account class referred to, the appropriate **GetPay** method will be called.

The ability for the same method call to result in different behavior depending on the object through which the method is invoked is referred to as *polymorphism*. Polymorphism can greatly simplify complex systems and is an important part of the object-oriented paradigm.

You should not try to coerce your design so that you can take advantage of polymorphism. We will see in our Acme Travel Agency case study that we have three different abstract base classes, but we do not need polymorphism to achieve quite general behavior. On the other hand, the .NET Framework classes use polymorphism heavily, as we shall see beginning in Chapter 5.

Acme Travel Agency Case Study: Design

The Acme Travel Agency provides various services, including the booking of hotel, plane, and car rental reservations. We will use this simple theme of booking reservations to illustrate various features of .NET throughout the book. In this chapter we design the architecture of a general system for booking different kinds of reservations. We illustrate with an implementation of a hotel broker system that supports the following basic features:

- Add a hotel to the list of hotels
- Show all the hotels
- Show all the hotels in a particular city
- Reserve a hotel room for a range of dates
- Show all the reservations
- Show all the reservations for a particular customer

The system also maintains a list of customers. Customers may register by giving their name and email address, and they will be assigned a customer ID. The following features are supported in the basic customer management subsystem:

- Register as a customer
- Change the email address of a customer
- Show a single customer or all the customers

In this chapter various lists, such as hotels, reservations, and customers, will be maintained as arrays. In the next chapter we will use .NET collections in place of arrays, and we will implement more features, such as the ability to delete a hotel and cancel a reservation. In later chapters we will extend the case study in various ways, such as providing a graphical user interface, storing all data in a database, and so on.

The code for our case study is in the **CaseStudy** folder for this chapter.

Designing the Abstractions

Bearing in mind that eventually we want to implement not only a hotel reservation system, but also a system for other kinds of reservations, including plane and car rental, it behooves us at the beginning to look for appropriate abstractions. The more functionality we are able to put in base classes, the less work we will have to do in order to implement a particular kind of reservation system. On the other hand, having more functionality in the base classes can reduce the range of problems to which they are applicable. Good design is a balancing act.

Another attribute of good abstractions is that they will survive major changes in implementation. As we shall see later in this book, our C++ abstractions of the hotel reservation system remain intact as we implement the system on an SQL Server database.

Code Example

These abstractions will be represented in C++ by abstract classes, defined in the file **Broker.cpp** in the **CaseStudy** folder for this chapter.

RESERVABLE

Our first abstraction is the thing we are looking to reserve. We will denote this abstraction as simply **Reservable**. The basic issue in reservations is resource usage. Two users cannot claim the same resource at the same time. Hence the key attribute of a **Reservable** is **capacity**. For example, a hotel may have 100 rooms. A flight may have 250 seats. We will also want a unique identifier for a **Reservable**, which we will denote by **unitid**. (The shorter name **unitid** is used in preference to the longer, more awkward name **reservableid**. Later we will see other use of *unit*. For example, the method to add a reservable is called **AddUnit**.)

For our applications, we are going to introduce an additional attribute, **cost**. There is a room rate for a hotel, a ticket cost for a flight, and so on. Note that this attribute may not be applicable to all things that are being reserved. For example, a conference room within a company may not have a cost assigned to it. However, our applications are for commercial customers, so we choose to include **cost** in our model.

Simplifications

Because our case study is designed to illustrate concepts in managed C++ and .NET, we will choose many simplifications in our design so that we do not become bogged down in overly detailed coding. For example, in real life a hotel has several different kinds of rooms, each with a different rate. Similarly, an airplane flight will have different classes of seats. Here, the situation in real life is even more complicated, because the price of a seat may vary wildly depending on when the reservation was made, travel restrictions, and so on. To make life simple for us, we are assuming that each instance of a particular reservable will have the same cost.

In managed C++, we will represent a **Reservable** by an *abstract class*.

```
public __gc __abstract class Reservable
{
    static private int nextid = 0;
protected:
    int unitid;
public:
    int capacity;
    Decimal cost;
    Reservable(int capacity, Decimal cost)
    {
        this->capacity = capacity;
        this->cost = cost;
        unitid = nextid++;
    }
};
```

A constructor allows us to specify the **capacity** and **cost** when the object is created. The **unitid** is autogenerated by a static variable. This ID starts out at 0, because it is also going to be used in our implementation as an index in a 2D array to track the number of customers having a reservation at a given reservable on a given date.

We will discuss the role of the **private**, **internal**, and **protected** access control specifiers later.

RESERVATION

When a customer books a reservation of a reservable, a record of the reservation will be made. The **Reservation** class holds the information that will be stored.

```
public __gc __abstract class Reservation
{
public:
   int ReservationId;
   int UnitId;
   DateTime Date;
   int NumberDays;
   static private int nextReservationId = 1;
   Reservation()
   {
      ReservationId = nextReservationId++;
   }
};
```

The **ReservationId** is autogenerated. The **UnitId** identifies the reservable at which the reservation was booked. **Date** is the starting date of the reservation, and **NumberDays** specifies the number of days for which the reservation was made.

BROKER

Our third abstraction, **Broker**, models a broker of any kind of reservable, and is also represented by an abstract class. It maintains a list of reservables, represented by the array **units**, and a list of reservations, represented by the array **reservations**. The 2D array **numCust** keeps track of the number of customers having a reservation at a given reservable on a given day.

```
public __gc __abstract class Broker
{
private:
   int MaxDay;
   static const int MAXRESERVATION = 10;
   static int nextReservation = 0;
   static int nextUnit = 0;
   int numCust [,];
protected:
   Reservation *reservations[];
   Reservable *units[];
```

```
public:
    Broker(int MaxDay, int MaxUnit)
    {
        this->MaxDay = MaxDay;
        numCust = new int __gc [MaxDay, MaxUnit];
        units = new Reservable*[MaxUnit];
        reservations = new Reservation*[MAXRESERVATION];
    }
...
```

RESERVATIONRESULT

A simple structure is used for returning the result from making a reservation.

```
public __gc struct ReservationResult
{
public:
    int ReservationId;
    Decimal ReservationCost;
    Decimal Rate;
    String *Comment;
};
```

The **Rate** is the cost for one day, and **ReservationCost** is the total cost, which is equal to the number of days multiplied by the cost for one day. The **ReservationId** is returned as −1 if there was a problem, and an explanation of the problem is provided in the **Comment** field. This structure is created so that result information can be passed in distributed scenarios, such as Web Services, where you cannot throw exceptions.

Base Class Logic

The base class **Broker** not only represents the abstraction of a broker of any kind of reservable, it also contains general logic for booking reservations and maintaining a list of reservations. Our ability to capture this logic abstractly gives the power to this base class, and will make implementing reservations in a derived class relatively simple.

RESERVE

The core method of the **Broker** class is **Reserve**.

```
ReservationResult *Reserve(Reservation *res)
{
    int unitid = res->UnitId;
```

```
DateTime dt = res->Date;
int numDays = res->NumberDays;
ReservationResult *result = new ReservationResult;

// Check if dates are within supported range
int day = dt.DayOfYear - 1;
if (day + numDays > MaxDay)
{
  result->ReservationId = -1;
  result->Comment = "Dates out of range";
  return result;
}

// Check if rooms are available for all dates
for (int i = day; i < day + numDays; i++)
{
    if (numCust[i, unitid] >= units[unitid]->capacity)
    {
        result->ReservationId = -1;
        result->Comment = "Room not available";
        return result;
    }
}

// Reserve a room for requested dates
for (int i = day; i < day + numDays; i++)
    numCust[i, unitid] += 1;

// Add reservation to reservation list, return result
AddReservation(res);
result->ReservationId = res->ReservationId;
result->ReservationCost =
    units[unitid]->cost * numDays;
result->Rate = units[unitid]->cost;
result->Comment = "OK";

return result;
}
```

The **Reserve** method is designed to implement booking several different kinds of reservations. Thus the **Reservation** object, which will be stored
in the list of reservations, is created in a more specialized class derived from
Broker and is passed as a parameter to **Reserve**. For example, a **HotelBroker** will book a **HotelReservation**, and so on. The **UnitId**, **Date**, and

NumberDays fields are extracted from the **Reservation** object, and a **ReservationResult** object is created to be returned.

```
ReservationResult *Reserve(Reservation *res)
{
    int unitid = res->UnitId;
    DateTime dt = res->Date;
    int numDays = res->NumberDays;
    ReservationResult *result = new ReservationResult;
    ...
```

Next, we check that all the dates requested for the reservation are within the supported range (which for simplicity we are taking as a single year). We make use of the **DateTime** structure from the **System** namespace. We return an error if a date lies out of range.

```
// Check if dates are within supported range
int day = dt.DayOfYear - 1;
if (day + numDays > MaxDay)
{
    result->ReservationId = -1;
    result->Comment = "Dates out of range";
    return result;
}
...
```

Now we check that space is available for each date, using the **numCust** array that tracks how many customers currently have reservations for each day and comparing against the capacity. The first dimension of this 2D array indexes on days, and the second dimension indexes on the unit ID. (Note that for simplicity we have named our fields and methods with names suitable for our initial application, a **HotelBroker**.)

```
// Check if rooms are available for all dates
for (int i = day; i < day + numDays; i++)
{
    if (numCust[i, unitid] >= units[unitid]->capacity)
    {
        result->ReservationId = -1;
        result->Comment = "Room not available";
        return result;
    }
}
...
```

Next, we actually reserve the unit for the requested days, which is implemented by incrementing the customer count in **numCust** for each day.

```
// Reserve a room for requested dates
for (int i = day; i < day + numDays; i++)
   numCust[i, unitid] += 1;
...
```

Finally, we add the reservation to the list of reservations and return the result.

```
// Add reservation to reservation list, return result
AddReservation(res);
result->ReservationId = res->ReservationId;
result->ReservationCost =
    units[unitid]->cost * numDays;
result->Rate = units[unitid]->cost;
result->Comment = "OK";

return result;
}
```

LISTS OF RESERVATIONS AND RESERVABLES

The **Broker** class also maintains lists of reservations and reservables. For our simple array implementation, we only implement **Add** methods. In a later version we will provide logic to remove elements from lists.

```
void AddReservation(Reservation *res)
{
   reservations[nextReservation++] = res;
}

void AddUnit(Reservable *unit)
{
   units[nextUnit++] = unit;
}
```

Designing the Encapsulation

In our current implementation of **Broker** all lists are represented by arrays. Since this implementation may not (and in fact will not) be preserved in later versions, we do not want to expose the arrays themselves or the subscripts that are used for manipulating the arrays. We provide public properties **NumberUnits** and

NumberReservations to provide read-only access to the private variables **nextUnit** and **nextReservation**.

```
__property int get_NumberUnits()
{
    return nextUnit;
}

__property int get_NumberReservations()
{
    return nextReservation;
}
```

In our **Reservation** class the simple fields **ReservationId**, **UnitId**, **Date**, and **NumberDays** are not likely to undergo a change in representation, so we do not encapsulate them. Later, if necessary, we could change some of these to properties without breaking client code. For now, and likely forever, we simply use public fields.

```
public __gc __abstract class Reservation
{
public:
    int ReservationId;
    int UnitId;
    DateTime Date;
    int NumberDays;
    static private int nextReservationId = 1;
    Reservation()
    {
        ReservationId = nextReservationId++;
    }
};
```

Inheritance in Managed C++

Managed C++ supports a single inheritance model. Thus a class may derive from a single base class, and not from more than one. This single inheritance model is simple and avoids the complexities and ambiguities associated with multiple inheritance as in unmanaged C++. Although a managed C++ class can only inherit from a single base *class*, it may inherit from several *interfaces*, a topic we will discuss in the next chapter. In this section we review inheritance in connection with a further elaboration of our hotel reservation case study.

Inheritance Fundamentals

With inheritance, factor the abstractions in your object model and put the more reusable abstractions in a high-level base class. You can add or change features in more specialized derived classes, which inherit the standard behavior from the base class. Inheritance facilitates code reuse and extensibility. A derived class can also provide a more appropriate interface to existing members of the base class.

Consider **Reservable** as a base class with derived classes such as **Hotel**. All reservables share some characteristics, such as an ID, a capacity, and a cost. Different kinds of reservables differ in other respects. For example, a hotel has a **City** and a **HotelName**.

MANAGED C++ INHERITANCE SYNTAX

You implement inheritance in managed C++ by specifying the derived class in the **class** statement with a colon followed by the base class. The file **Hotel-Broker.h** in the **CaseStudy** folder illustrates deriving a new class **Hotel** from the class **Reservable**.

```
public __gc class Hotel : public Reservable
{
    ...
};
```

The class **Hotel** automatically has all the members of **Reservable** and also has the fields **City** and **HotelName**.

CHANGING THE INTERFACE TO EXISTING MEMBERS

The base class **Reservable** has members **unitid**, **capacity**, and **cost**, which are designed for internal use and are not intended to be exposed as such to the outside world. In the **Hotel** class we provide public properties **HotelId**, **NumberRooms**, and **Rate** to give clients read-only access to these fields. When we implement a property in this way, we can choose a name that is meaningful, such as **NumberRooms**, in place of a more abstract name, such as **capacity**, used in the base class.

INVOKING BASE CLASS CONSTRUCTORS

If your derived class has a constructor with parameters, you may wish to pass some of these parameters along to the base class constructor. In C++ you can conveniently invoke a base class constructor by using a colon followed by a list of base classes and parameter lists. However, unlike traditional unmanaged C++, a managed C++ class allows only a single base class and parameter list, since only single implementation inheritance is supported.

```
Hotel(
    String *city,
    String *name,
    int number,
    Decimal cost)
    : Reservable(number, cost)
    {
        City = city;
        HotelName = name;
    }
```

Note that the managed C++ allows you to explicitly invoke a constructor only of an immediate base class. You are not allowed to directly invoke a constructor higher up the inheritance hierarchy.

Acme Travel Agency Case Study: Implementation

With the abstractions **Reservable**, **Reservation**, and **Broker** already in place, it now becomes very easy to implement a reservation system for a particular kind of reservable, such as a **Hotel**. Figure 4–2 illustrates our inheritance hierarchy: **Hotel** derives from **Reservable**, **HotelReservation** derives from **Reservation**, and **HotelBroker** derives from **Broker**.

In this section we will examine key pieces of the implementation of the case study, which is in the **CaseStudy** folder for this chapter.

Running the Case Study

Before proceeding with our code walkthrough, it would be a good idea to build and run the case study. The program **TestBroker.exe** is a console

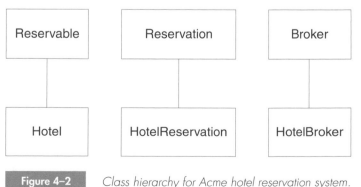

Figure 4–2   *Class hierarchy for Acme hotel reservation system.*

application. By typing "help" at the command prompt, you can obtain a list of commands:

```
Enter command, quit to exit
H> help
The following commands are available:
        hotels    shows all hotels in a city
        all       shows all hotels
        cities    shows all cities
        add       adds a hotel
        book      book a reservation
        bookings  show all bookings
        register  register a customer
        email     change email address
        show      show customers
        quit      exit the program
H>
```

Experiment with this program until you have a clear understanding of its various features.

HotelReservation

HotelReservation is a simple class derived from **Reservation**. The code is in the file **hotelbroker.h**. It adds some additional public fields and provides the property **ArrivalDate** as a more meaningful wrapper around the generic **Date** field of the base class.

```
public __gc class HotelReservation : public Reservation
{
public:
    int CustomerId;
    String *HotelName;
    String *City;
    DateTime DepartureDate;
    __property DateTime get_ArrivalDate()
    {
        return Date;
    }
    __property void set_ArrivalDate(DateTime value)
    {
        Date = value;
    }
};
```

HotelBroker

The heart of the implementation is the **HotelBroker** class, derived from **Broker**. The code is also in the file **hotelbroker.h**.

```
public __gc class HotelBroker : public Broker
{
private:
    static const int MAXDAY = 366;
    static const int MAXUNIT = 10;
    static const int MAXCITY = 5;
    static private int nextCity = 0;
    String *cities[];
public:
    HotelBroker() : Broker(MAXDAY, MAXUNIT)
    {
        cities = new String*[MAXCITY];
        AddHotel("Atlanta", "Dixie", 100, 115.00);
        AddHotel("Atlanta", "Marriott", 500, 70.00);
        AddHotel("Boston", "Sheraton", 250, 95.00);
    }
    ...
};
```

There are constants for various array definitions and a new array to hold the cities. The constructor passes some array definitions to the base class, initializes the **cities** array, and adds some starter hotels as test data.

The next part of the code defines a **NumberCity** property and provides a method to add a hotel.

```
__property int get_NumberCity()
{
    return nextCity;
}

String *AddHotel(
    String *city,
    String *name,
    int number,
    Decimal cost)
    {
        if (FindId(city, name) != -1)
            return "Hotel is already on the list";
        Hotel *hotel =
```

```
            new Hotel(city, name, number, cost);
         AddUnit(hotel);
         AddCity(city);
         return "OK";
      }
...
```

Private helper functions are provided to find the ID of a hotel and to add a city to the list of cities. A city can be added only if it is not already on the list—duplicates are not permitted.

```
int FindId(String *city, String *name)
{
   for (int i = 0; i < NumberUnits; i++)
   {
      Hotel *hotel = dynamic_cast<Hotel *>(units[i]);
      if ((String::Compare(hotel->City, city) == 0)
         && (String::Compare(
            hotel->HotelName, name) == 0))
         return hotel->HotelId;
   }

   return -1;
}

void AddCity(String *city)
{
   // check if city already on list, add if not
   if (!Contains(city))
      cities[nextCity++] = city;
}

bool Contains(String *city)
{
   for (int i = 0; i < NumberCity; i++)
   {
      if (String::Compare(cities[i], city) == 0)
         return true;
   }
   return false;
}
```

Methods are provided to show all the hotels, all the hotels in a given city, and to show the cities. You may wish to examine this code to see how simple text formatting is accomplished.

We finally come to the key method **Reserve**, which is used to book a hotel reservation.

```
ReservationResult *Reserve(
   int customerId, String *city, String *name,
   DateTime dt, int numDays)
{
   int id = FindId(city, name);
   if (id == -1)
   {
      ReservationResult *result =
         new ReservationResult;
      result->ReservationId = -1;
      result->Comment = "Hotel not found";
      return result;
   }
   HotelReservation *res = new HotelReservation;
   res->UnitId = id;
   res->CustomerId = customerId;
   res->HotelName = name;
   res->City = city;
   res->ArrivalDate = dt;
   res->DepartureDate =
      dt.Add(TimeSpan(numDays, 0, 0, 0));
   res->NumberDays = numDays;
   return Broker::Reserve(res);
}
```

The code in this class is very simple, because it relies upon logic in the base class **Broker**. If the hotel cannot be found on the list of hotels, an error is returned. Then a **HotelReservation** object is created, which is passed to the **Reserve** method of the base class. We create the reservation object in the derived class, because we are interested in all the fields of a full **HotelReservation**, not just the fields of a **Reservation**. We have previously used the **DateTime** structure, and we now use the **TimeSpan** structure as part of calculating the departure date by adding the number of days of the stay to the arrival date. This calculation relies on the fact that the **+** operator is overloaded in the **DateTime** structure.

Customers

No reservation system can exist without modeling the customers that use it. The **Customers** class in the file **customer.h** maintains a list of **Customer** objects. Again, we use an array as our representation. This code has very similar structure to code dealing with hotels, and so we show it only in outline form, giving the data structures and the declarations of the public methods and properties.

```
//Customer.h

using namespace System;

namespace OI { namespace NetCpp { namespace Acme {

public __gc class Customer
  {
    public:
      int CustomerId;
      String *FirstName;
      String *LastName;
      String *EmailAddress;
    private:
      static int nextCustId = 1;
    public:
      Customer(String *first, String *last, String *email)
      {
        CustomerId = nextCustId++;
        FirstName = first;
        LastName = last;
        EmailAddress = email;
      }
  };

public __gc class Customers
  {
  private:
    Customer *customers [];
    static int nextCust = 0;
  public:
    Customers(int MaxCust)
    {
      customers = new Customer*[MaxCust];
      RegisterCustomer(
```

```
            "Rocket",
            "Squirrel", "rocky@frosbitefalls.com");
        RegisterCustomer(
            "Bullwinkle", "Moose", "moose@wossamotta.edu");
    }
    __property int get_NumberCustomers()
    ....
    int RegisterCustomer(
        String *firstName,
        String *lastName,
        String *emailAddress)
    ...
    void Add(Customer *cust)
    ...
    void ShowCustomers(int customerId)
    ...
    void ChangeEmailAddress(
        int id, String *emailAddress)
    ...
};
```

Namespace

All case study code is in the namespace **OI::NetCpp::Acme**. All of the files
defining classes begin with a **namespace** directive. There is a corresponding
using directive, which you will see in the file **TestHotel.h**. Here is how the
OI::NetCpp::Acme namespace is defined.

```
namespace OI { namespace NetCpp { namespace Acme {
...
}}}
```

TestHotel

The **TestHotel** class in the file **TestHotel.h** contains an interactive program
to exercise the hotel and customer classes, supporting the commands shown
previously, where we suggested running the case study. There is a command
loop to read in a command and then exercise it. There is a big **try** block
around all the commands, with a **catch** handler afterwards. Note the **using**
statement to gain access to the namespace.

```
//TestHotel.h

using namespace System;
```

```
using namespace OI::NetCpp::Acme;

public __gc class TestHotel
{
public:
   static void Main()
   {
      const int MAXCUST = 10;
      HotelBroker *hotelBroker = new HotelBroker;
      Customers *customers = new Customers(MAXCUST);
      InputWrapper *iw = new InputWrapper;
      String *cmd;
      Console::WriteLine("Enter command, quit to exit");
      cmd = iw->getString("H> ");
      while (! cmd->Equals("quit"))
      {
         try
         {
            if (cmd->Equals("hotels"))
            {
               String *city = iw->getString("city: ");
               hotelBroker->ShowHotels(city);
            }
            else if (cmd->Equals("all"))
               hotelBroker->ShowHotels();
            ...
            else
               hotelhelp();
         }
         catch (Exception *e)
         {
            Console::WriteLine(
               "Exception: {0}", e->Message);
         }
         cmd = iw->getString("H> ");
      }
   }
   ...
};
```

Summary

In this chapter we reviewed the principles of object-oriented programming in managed C++, with an emphasis on inheritance. We introduced the Acme Travel Agency case study, which runs as a strand throughout the remainder of the book. We examined what are the suitable abstractions that enable us to implement a reservation system for a variety of resources that must be reserved, and we provided an implementation of a hotel reservation system. The abstract base classes we defined provide reusable code that can enable us to easily implement other kinds of reservation systems.

FIVE

Managed C++ in the .NET Framework

*T*he C++ language is a powerful tool that has made an enormous impact on the history of computing. Microsoft's managed extensions add a whole new world to the C++ language; that is, the .NET world. To fully use the capabilities of Visual C++ .NET, you need to understand how it works within the .NET Framework. We begin with the primordial root class named **Object** in the **System** namespace. Collections are examined next, including the methods of the **Object** class that should be overridden to leverage the functionality provided by the .NET Framework. We next introduce interfaces, which allow you to rigorously define a contract for classes to implement. In managed C++, a class can implement multiple interfaces even though it can inherit implementation from only one superclass. Interfaces allow for dynamic programming; you can query a class at runtime to see whether it supports a particular interface.

The interfaces supporting collections are examined in detail. Copy semantics are then explored. Instead of using copy constructors as in traditional C++, in managed C++ you can implement the **ICloneable** interface to create object copies. We explore generic interfaces in the .NET Framework programming model and compare the .NET and COM component models. A further illustration of generic interfaces is provided by sorting in different orders, using the **IComparable** interface. These examples offer insight into the workings of an application framework, which supports a program's architecture, rather than just class a library, which provides useful functionality. With a framework, your code calls the framework, and the framework calls back into your code. Your code can be viewed as the middle layer of a sandwich. This key insight can help you grasp what makes .NET programming tick. Callback functions have been used for years in programming. Managed C++ uses this concept in delegates and events. Two simple and intuitive examples are presented: a stock market simulation and an online chat room.

System::Object

As we have already seen, every managed type (declared with **__gc**) in managed C++ ultimately inherits from the root class **System::Object**. Even boxed primitive types such as **System::Int32**, **System::SByte**, and **System::Double** inherit from **System::ValueType**, which in turn inherits from **System::Object**. Added to these are the over 2,500 classes in the .NET Framework, all inheriting from **Object**.[1]

Public Instance Methods of Object

There are four public instance methods of **Object**, three of which are virtual and frequently overridden by managed classes.

EQUALS

```
public: virtual bool Equals(Object*);
```

This method compares an object with the current object and returns **true** if they are equal. **Object** implements this method to test for pointer equality. **ValueType** overrides this method to test for content equality. Many classes override the method to make equality behave appropriately for the particular class. There is also a static version of this method that takes two **Object*** parameters and compares them.

TOSTRING

```
public: virtual String* ToString();
```

This method returns a human-readable string representation of the object. The default implementation inherited from **Object** returns the object's fully qualified type name. Derived classes frequently override this method to return a meaningful string representation of the particular object.

GETHASHCODE

```
public: virtual int GetHashCode();
```

This method returns a hash value for an object that should be suitable for use in hashing algorithms and hash tables. Classes that override **GetHash-Code** should override **Equals** as well to ensure that equal objects produce

---

[1] Since most managed C++ programs have a **using namespace System;** directive, making it possible to refer to **System::Object** as simply **Object**, we will generally refer to it from here on as just **Object**.

equal hash codes. Failing to follow this advice can cause the **Hashtable** class to misbehave.

GETTYPE

```
public: Type* GetType();
```

This method returns type information for the object. This type information can be used to get the associated metadata through *reflection*, a topic we discuss in Chapter 8. This is not a virtual method, and it should not normally be overridden.

Protected Instance Methods

There are two protected instance methods, which can only be used within derived classes.

MEMBERWISECLONE

```
protected: Object* MemberwiseClone();
```

This method creates a shallow copy of the object. This is not a virtual method, and it should not normally be overridden. To perform a deep copy, you should implement the **ICloneable** interface. We will discuss shallow copy and deep copy later in this chapter.

FINALIZE

```
.Object();
```

This method allows an object to free nonmanaged resources and perform other cleanup operations before it is reclaimed by garbage collection. In managed C++ the **Finalize** method is syntactically represented by standard C++ "destructor" notation. But note that the semantics of a managed C++ destructor is totally different from the semantics of a standard C++ destructor. In unmanaged C++ destructors are invoked in a deterministic and synchronous manner, which the programmer can depend upon. In managed C++ the garbage collector performs object finalization on an independent thread.

Generic Interfaces and Standard Behavior

If you are used to a language like Smalltalk, the set of behaviors specified in **Object** may seem quite limited. Smalltalk, which introduced the concept of a class hierarchy rooted in a common base class, has a very rich set of methods defined in its **Object** class. I counted 38 methods![2] These additional methods support features such as comparing objects and copying objects. The .NET Framework class library has similar methods, and many more. But rather than putting them all in a common root class, .NET defines a number of standard interfaces, which classes can optionally implement. This kind of organization, which is also present in Microsoft's Component Object Model (COM) and in Java, is very flexible. We will discuss some of the generic interfaces of the .NET Framework later in this chapter.

Using Object Methods in the Customer Class

As a simple illustration of **Object** methods, let's look at our **Customer** class before and after overriding the **Equals**, **ToString**, and **GetHashCode** methods.

DEFAULT METHODS OF OBJECT

If our class does not provide any overrides of the virtual instance methods of **Object**, our class will inherit the standard behavior. This behavior is demonstrated in **CustomerObject\Step1**.

```
//Customer.cpp

#using <mscorlib.dll>
using namespace System;
#include "Customer.h"


//Customer.h

__gc class Customer
{
public:
   int nCustomerId;
   String *pFirstName;
   String *pLastName;
   String *pEmailAddress;
   Customer(int id, String *pFirst,
      String *pLast, String *eMail)
   {
      nCustomerId = id;
      pFirstName = pFirst;
      pLastName = pLast;
```

---

[2] The methods of Smalltalk's **Object** class are described in Chapters 6 and 14 of *Smalltalk-80: The Language and its Implementation*, by Adele Goldberg and David Robson.

```
        pEmailAddress = eMail;
    }
};


//TestCustomer.cpp

#using <mscorlib.dll>
using namespace System;
#include "Customer.h"
#include "TestCustomer.h"

void main(void)
{
    TestCustomer::Main();
}


//TestCustomer.h

__gc class TestCustomer
{
public:
    static void Main()
    {
        Customer *pCust1, *pCust2;
        pCust1 = new Customer(
            99, "John", "Doe", "john@rocky.com");
        pCust2 = new Customer(
            99, "John", "Doe", "john@rocky.com");
        ShowCustomerObject("pCust1", pCust1);
        ShowCustomerObject("pCust2", pCust2);
        CompareCustomerObjects(pCust1, pCust2);
    }
private:
    static void ShowCustomerObject(
        String *pLabel, Customer *pCust)
    {
        Console::WriteLine("---- {0} ----", pLabel);
        Console::WriteLine(
            "ToString() = {0}", pCust->ToString());
        Console::WriteLine(
            "GetHashCode() = {0}",
            __box(pCust->GetHashCode()));
        Console::WriteLine(
            "GetType() = {0}", pCust->GetType());
```

```
   }
   static void CompareCustomerObjects(
      Customer *pCust1, Customer *pCust2)
   {
      Console::WriteLine(
         "Equals() = {0}",
         __box(pCust1->Equals(
            dynamic_cast<Object __gc *>(pCust2))));
   }
};
```

Run the test program and you will see this output:

```
---- cust1 ----
ToString() = Customer
GetHashCode() = 4
GetType() = Customer
---- cust2 ----
ToString() = Customer
GetHashCode() = 6
GetType() = Customer
Equals() = False
```

The default implementation is not at all what we want for our **Customer** object. The **ToString** method returns the name of the class, not information about a particular customer. The **Equals** method considers only pointer equality rather than content equality. In the example above, we have two pointers to distinct but identical **Customer** objects, and **Equals** returns **false**.

OVERRIDING METHODS OF OBJECT

The version of the project in **CustomerObject\Step2** demonstrates overriding these virtual methods.

```
//Customer.h

__gc class Customer
{
public:
   int nCustomerId;
   String *pFirstName;
   String *pLastName;
   String *pEmailAddress;
   Customer(int id, String *pFirst,
```

```
                String *pLast, String *eMail)
        {
           nCustomerId = id;
           pFirstName = pFirst;
           pLastName = pLast;
           pEmailAddress = eMail;
        }
public:
     bool Equals(Object *pobj)
     {
        Customer *pCust =
            dynamic_cast<Customer *>(pobj);
        return (pCust->nCustomerId == nCustomerId);
     }
     int GetHashCode()
     {
        return nCustomerId;
     }
     String *ToString()
     {
        return String::Format(
            "{0} {1}", pFirstName, pLastName);
     }
};
```

The rest of the program is identical. Here is the new output:

```
---- cust1 ----
ToString() = John Doe
GetHashCode() = 99
GetType() = Customer
---- cust2 ----
ToString() = John Doe
GetHashCode() = 99
GetType() = Customer
Equals() = True
```

Collections

The .NET Framework class library provides an extensive set of classes for working with collections of objects. These classes are all in the **System::Collections** namespace and implement a number of different kinds of collections, including lists, queues, stacks, arrays, and hash tables. The collections contain **Object** instances. Since all managed types derive ultimately from **Object**, any built-in or user-defined managed type may be stored in a collection.

In this section we will look at a representative class in this namespace, **ArrayList**, and see how to use array lists in our programs. Part of our task in using array lists and similar collections is to properly implement our class, whose instances are to be stored in the collection. In particular, our class must override at least the **Equals** method of **Object**, since the implementation of each of the collections classes requires that the **Equals** method be implemented.

ArrayList Example

To get our bearings, let's begin with a simple example of using the **ArrayList** class. An array list, as the name suggests, is a list of items stored like an array. An array list can be dynamically sized and will grow as necessary to accommodate new elements being added.

Collection classes are made up of instances of type **Object**. We will create and manipulate a collection of **Customer** objects. We could also just as easily create a collection of any other built-in or user-defined managed type. If our type were a value type, such as **int**, the instance would need to be boxed before being stored in the collection. When the boxed **int** object is extracted from the collection, it would then be unboxed back to **int**.

Our example program is **CustomerCollection**. It initializes a list of customers and then lets the user show the customers, register a new customer, unregister an existing customer, and change an email address. A simple **help** method displays the commands that are available:

```
Enter command, quit to exit
H> help
The following commands are available:
        register   register a customer
        unregister unregister a customer
        email      change email address
        show       show customers
        quit       exit the program
```

Before examining the code it would be a good idea to run the program to register a new customer, show the customers, change an email address, unregister a customer, and show the customers again. Here is a sample run of the program:

```
H> show
id (-1 for all): -1
    1   Rocket      Squirrel    rocky@frosbitefalls.com
```

```
    2   Bullwinkle   Moose        moose@wossamotta.edu
H> register
first name: Bob
last name: Oberg
email address: oberg@objectinnovations.com
id = 3
H> email
customer id: 1
email address: rocky@objectinnovations.com
H> unregister
id: 2
H> show
id (-1 for all): -1
    1   Rocket       Squirrel     rocky@objectinnovations.com
    3   Bob          Oberg        oberg@objectinnovations.com
```

CUSTOMERS CLASS

All the code for this project is in the folder **CustomerCollection**. The file
customer.h has code for the **Customer** and **Customers** classes. The code
for **Customer** is almost identical to what we looked at previously. The only
addition is a special constructor that instantiates a **Customer** object with a
specified ID. We use this constructor in the **Customers** class when we
remove an element (**UnregisterCustomer**) and when we check if an element
ment is present in the collection (**CheckId**).

```
__gc class Customer
{
public:
...
    Customer(int id)
    {
      nCustomerId = id;
      pFirstName = "";
      pLastName = "";
      pEmailAddress = "";
    }
...
};
```

The **Customers** class contains a list of customers, represented by an
ArrayList.

```
__gc class Customers
{
```

```
private:
   ArrayList *pCustomers;
public:
   Customers()
   {
      pCustomers = new ArrayList;
      RegisterCustomer(
         "Rocket",
         "Squirrel",
         "rocky@frosbitefalls.com");
      RegisterCustomer(
         "Bullwinkle",
         "Moose",
         "moose@wossamotta.edu");
   }
   int RegisterCustomer(
      String *pFirstName,
      String *pLastName,
      String *pEmailAddress)
   {
      Customer *pCust = new Customer(
         pFirstName, pLastName, pEmailAddress);
      pCustomers->Add(pCust);
      return pCust->nCustomerId;
   }
   void UnregisterCustomer(int id)
   {
      Customer *pCust = new Customer(id);
      pCustomers->Remove(pCust);
   }
   void ChangeEmailAddress(int id, String *pEmailAddress)
   {
      IEnumerator *pEnum =
         pCustomers->GetEnumerator();
      while (pEnum->MoveNext())
      {
         Customer *pCust =
            dynamic_cast<Customer *>(pEnum->Current);
         if (pCust->nCustomerId == id)
         {
            pCust->pEmailAddress = pEmailAddress;
            return;
         }
      }
```

```
        String *pStr = String::Format(
            "id {0} {1}", __box(id), S"not found");
        throw new Exception(pStr);
    }
    void ShowCustomers(int id)
    {
        if (!CheckId(id) && id != -1)
            return;
        IEnumerator *pEnum =
            pCustomers->GetEnumerator();
        while (pEnum->MoveNext())
        {
            Customer *pCust =
                dynamic_cast<Customer *>(pEnum->Current);
            if (id == -1 || id == pCust->nCustomerId)
            {
                String *pSid =
                    pCust->nCustomerId.ToString()->PadLeft(4);
                String *pFirst =
                    pCust->pFirstName->PadRight(12);
                String *pLast =
                    pCust->pLastName->PadRight(12);
                String *pEmail =
                    pCust->pEmailAddress->PadRight(20);
                Console::Write("{0}    ", pSid);
                Console::Write("{0}    ", pFirst);
                Console::Write("{0}    ", pLast);
                Console::WriteLine("{0}", pEmail);
            }
        }
    }
    bool CheckId(int id)
    {
        Customer *pCust = new Customer(id);
        return pCustomers->Contains(pCust);
    }
};
```

The bold lines in the listing show the places where we are using collection class features. The **IEnumerator** interface is used to walk through the
collection. The reason that **IEnumerator** can be used is that the **ArrayList**
implements the **IEnumerable** interface. This interface provides support for
the special **foreach** semantics of C#. The **foreach** keyword is not supported

by C++. However, you can see from this example that you can use the **IEnumerable** interface to iterate over an **ArrayList** in a managed C++ while loop. We will discuss **IEnumerable** and the other collection interfaces later in this chapter.

The **Add** and **Remove** methods, as their names suggest, are used for adding and removing elements from a collection. The **Remove** method looks for an object in the collection that **Equals** the object passed as a parameter. Our special constructor creates an object having the ID of the element we want to remove. Since we provided an override of the **Equals** method that bases equality on **CustomerId**, the proper element will be removed.

Similarly, the **Contains** method used in our **CheckId** helper method also relies on the override of the **Equals** method.

Using collections makes it easy to add and remove elements. Using an array instead of a collection would require you to write special code to insert and move array elements and to fill in the space where an element was deleted. Also, collections are not declared to have a specific size, but can grow dynamically as required.

Interfaces

The *interface* concept is a very fundamental idea in modern computer programming. A large system is inevitably decomposed into parts, and it is critical to precisely specify the interfaces between these parts. Interfaces should be quite stable, as changing an interface affects multiple parts of the system. However, an interface may be reimplemented without affecting other interface-dependent code. In Visual C++.NET the **__interface** keyword has a very precise meaning. A managed interface is a reference type, which is similar to an abstract class that *specifies* behavior as a set of methods with defined signatures. An interface is a pure contract. When a class implements an interface, it must adhere to that contract.

Interfaces are a useful way to partition functionality. You should first specify interfaces and then design appropriate classes to implement those interfaces. The methods of a class can be grouped into related interfaces. While a managed C++ class can inherit from only one other class, it can implement multiple interfaces.

Interfaces facilitate very dynamic, flexible, and maintainable programs. The CLR and the BCL (Base Class Library) provides convenient facilities to query a class at runtime to see whether it supports a particular interface. Interfaces in .NET are conceptually very similar to interfaces in Microsoft's COM, but they are *much* easier to work with.

Now we will restructure our case study to take advantage of interfaces and explore their use in detail. After that, we will examine several important generic interfaces in the .NET library, which will help us gain an understanding of how managed C++ and the .NET library support each other to help us develop powerful and useful programs.

Interface Fundamentals

Object-oriented programming is a powerful paradigm for helping to design and implement large systems. Using classes helps us to achieve abstraction and encapsulation. Classes are a natural decomposition of a large system into manageable parts. Inheritance adds another tool for structuring our system, enabling us to factor out common parts into base classes, helping us to accomplish greater code reuse.

The main purpose of an interface is to specify a *contract* independently of implementation. An interface has associated methods, but with no immediate implementation. Each method has a signature, which specifies the parameters with their data types and the data type of the return value.

INTERFACES IN MANAGED C++

In Visual C++ .NET __**interface** is a keyword that you use to define an interface in a manner similar to defining a class. Like classes, interfaces are reference types, and the __**gc** keyword further qualifies it as a managed interface. The big difference between an interface and a class (managed or not) is that there is no implementation code in an interface; it is pure specification. However, just like a class, an interface can have properties and indexers as well as methods.

The **ICustomer** interface shown next specifies the methods to be used by clients in the Acme Travel Agency system.

```
__gc __interface ICustomer
{
public:
    int RegisterCustomer(
        String *pFirstName,
        String *pLastName,
        String *pEmailAddress);
    void UnregisterCustomer(int id);
    ArrayList *GetCustomer(int id);
    void ChangeEmailAddress(int id, String *pEmailAddress);
};
```

The **RegisterCustomer**, **UnregisterCustomer**, and **ChangeEmailAddress** method definitions are exactly the same as the signature of the methods we implemented in the **Customers** class. The **GetCustomer** method is new. Previously, we had a **ShowCustomers** method, which displayed a list of customers to the console. This method was strictly temporary. For general use, we want to return data and let the client decide what to do with it. The **GetCustomer** method returns information about one or all customers in an array list. If –1 is passed for the ID, the list will contain all the registered customers. Otherwise, the list will contain the customer information for the customer with the given ID. If no customer has that ID, the returned list will be empty.

INTERFACE INHERITANCE

Interfaces can inherit from other interfaces (however, they must be compatible with each other with respect to managed versus unmanaged). Unlike classes, for which there is only single inheritance, there can be multiple inheritance of interfaces. For example, the interface **ICustomer** could be declared by inheriting from the two smaller interfaces **IBasicCustomer** and **ICustomerInfo**. Notice that the public access specifier is not present in these three interfaces. That is because public is the default visibility for interfaces.

```
__gc __interface IBasicCustomer
{
    int RegisterCustomer(
        String *pFirstName,
        String *pLastName,
        String *pEmailAddress);
    void UnregisterCustomer(int id);
    void ChangeEmailAddress(int id, String *pEmailAddress);
};


__gc __interface ICustomerInfo
{
    ArrayList *GetCustomer(int id);
};
__gc __interface ICustomer : IBasicCustomer, ICustomerInfo
{
};
```

When declaring a new interface in this way, you can also introduce additional methods, as illustrated for **ICustomer2**.

```
__gc __interface ICustomer2 : IBasicCustomer, ICustomerInfo
{
    void NewMethod();
};
```

Programming with Interfaces

It is easy to program with interfaces in managed C++. You implement interfaces through classes, and you can cast a class pointer to obtain an interface pointer. You can call an interface method through either a class pointer or an interface pointer; however, to leverage the advantages of polymorphism, you will often prefer to use interface pointers where possible.

IMPLEMENTING INTERFACES

In C++ you specify that a class implements one or more interfaces by using the colon notation that is employed for class inheritance. A managed class can inherit both from one managed class and from one or more managed interfaces. In this case the base class should appear first in the derivation list after the colon. Note that unlike managed interfaces, managed classes only support public inheritance.

```
__gc class HotelBroker : public Broker, public IHotelInfo,
public IHotelAdmin, public IHotelReservation
{
...
};
```

In this example the class **HotelBroker** inherits from the class **Broker**, and it implements the interfaces **IHotelInfo**, **IHotelAdmin**, and **IHotelReservation**. **HotelBroker** must implement all the methods of these interfaces, either directly or via implementation inheritance from its base class **Broker**.

We will examine a full-blown example of interfaces with the reservation broker inheritance hierarchy later in the chapter, when we implement Step 2 of the case study.

Code Example

As a small example, consider the program **SmallInterface**. The class **Account** implements the interface **IBasicAccount**. This interface illustrates the syntax for declaring a property in an interface.

```
//Account.h

__gc __interface IBasicAccount
{
    void Deposit(Decimal amount);
    void Withdraw(Decimal amount);
    __property Decimal get_Balance();
};

__gc class Account : public IBasicAccount
{
```

```
private:
   Decimal balance;
public:
   Account(Decimal balance)
   {
      this->balance = balance;
   }
   void Deposit(Decimal amount)
   {
      balance = balance + amount;
   }
   void Withdraw(Decimal amount)
   {
      balance = balance - amount;
   }
   __property Decimal get_Balance()
   {
      return balance;
   }
};
```

USING AN INTERFACE

If you know your class supports an interface, you may simply call its methods through a pointer to the class instance. If you don't know whether your class implements the interface, you may try casting the class pointer to the interface pointer. If the class does not support the interface, you will get an exception thrown. The following code, taken from the **SmallInterface.h** source file, shows how this is done.

```
try
{
   IBasicAccount *pifc2 =
      dynamic_cast<IBasicAccount *>(pacc2);
   pifc2->Deposit(25);
   Console::WriteLine(
      "balance = {0}", __box(pifc2->Balance));
}
catch (NullReferenceException *pe)
{
   Console::WriteLine(
      "IBasicAccount is not supported");
   Console::WriteLine(pe->Message);
}
}
```

In the **SmallInterface** example, we have two almost identical classes. The **Account** class supports the interface **IBasicAccount**, and the other class **NoAccount** does not support that interface. Both classes have exactly the same set of methods and properties. Here is the entire code in **SmallInterface.cpp** and **SmallInterface.h**. Note that the program attempts to cast both an instance of **Account** and an instance of **NoAccount** into an **IBasicAccount** interface.

```cpp
//SmallInterface.cpp

#using <mscorlib.dll>
using namespace System;
#include "Account.h"
#include "NoAccount.h"
#include "SmallInterface.h"

void main()
{
    SmallInterface::Main();
}


//SmallInterface.h

__gc class SmallInterface
{
public:
    static void Main()
    {
        Account *pacc = new Account(100);
        // Use a class reference
        Console::WriteLine(
            "balance = {0}", __box(pacc->Balance));
        pacc->Deposit(25);
        Console::WriteLine(
            "balance = {0}", __box(pacc->Balance));
            // Use an interface reference
        IBasicAccount *pifc =
            dynamic_cast<IBasicAccount *>(pacc);
        pifc->Deposit(25);
        Console::WriteLine(
            "balance = {0}", __box(pifc->Balance));
        // Now try with class not implementing IBasicAccount
        NoAccount *pacc2 = new NoAccount(500);
        // Use a class reference
```

```
    Console::WriteLine(
        "balance = {0}", __box(pacc2->Balance));
    pacc2->Deposit(25);
    Console::WriteLine(
        "balance = {0}", __box(pacc2->Balance));
    // Try an interface pointer
    try
    {
        IBasicAccount *piba=
            dynamic_cast<IBasicAccount *>(pacc2);
        piba->Deposit(25);
        Console::WriteLine(
            "balance = {0}", __box(piba->Balance));
    }
    catch (NullReferenceException *pe)
    {
        Console::WriteLine(
            "IBasicAccount is not supported");
        Console::WriteLine(pe->Message);
    }
    }
};
```

In the above code, we first work with the class **Account**, which does support the interface **IBasicAccount**. We are successful in calling the methods both through a class pointer and through a cast interface pointer. Next, we work with the class **NoAccount**. Although this class has the same methods as **Account**, in its declaration it does not indicate that it is implementing the interface **IBasicAccount**.

```
//NoAccount.h
__gc class NoAccount
{
...
```

When we run the program, we encounter a **NullReferenceException**. This happens when we attempt to use the pointer resulting from the dynamic cast from the **NoAccount** * type to the **IBasicAccount** * interface pointer type. If we had used a traditional C-style cast, we would have produced an **InvalidCastException** instead. However, if you try this, you will see that the compiler generates a warning that C-style casts are deprecated.

```
balance = 100
balance = 125
```

```
balance = 150
balance = 500
balance = 525
IBasicAccount is not supported
Value null was found where an instance of an object was
required.
```

Dynamic Use of Interfaces

A powerful feature of interfaces is their use in dynamic scenarios, allowing us to write generalized code that can test whether an interface is supported by a class. If the interface is supported, our code can take advantage of it; otherwise our program can ignore the interface. We could in fact implement such dynamic behavior through exception handling, as illustrated previously. Although entirely feasible, this approach is very cumbersome and would lead to hard-to-read programs. C++ provides the **dynamic_cast** and **typeid** operators, and the .NET Framework provides the class named **Type**, which facilitates working with interfaces dynamically at runtime.

As an example, consider the interface **ICustomer2** that has a **ShowCustomer** method in addition to the methods of **ICustomer1**.

```
__gc __interface ICustomer2 : ICustomer1
{
public:
    void ShowCustomers(int id);
};
```

Code Example

Assume that a class named **Customer1** supports just **ICustomer1**, while the class **Customers2** implements **ICustomer2**. For a console client program, the original method **ShowCustomers** is actually more efficient than the new method **GetCustomer**, because the new method has to create an array list and copy data into this array list. Thus our client program will prefer to use the **ICustomer2** interface if available. The folder **TestInterfaceBefore-Cast** contains this example program, which is described in the next section.

TESTING FOR AN INTERFACE BEFORE CASTING

We can test for an interface by doing a dynamic cast and catching a possible exception. A neater solution is to test for the interface *before* you do the cast, avoiding the exception altogether. If an object does support the desired interface, we can then perform the cast to obtain the desired interface. C# provides the convenient **is** operator to test if an object supports a specific interface. Unfortunately, in C++ we must use reflection techniques to accomplish this, using the **GetType** and **GetInterface** methods. Since the resulting expression is a bit messy, the following example wraps it up into a **#define** macro named **IS(THIS, THAT_INTERFACE)** that is used in two **if** statements further down.

```cpp
//TestInterfaceBeforeCast.cpp

//MACRO: pObj->GetType()->GetInterface("SomeInterface")!=0
#define IS(THIS, THAT_INTERFACE) (THIS->GetType()->GetInter-
face(THAT_INTERFACE)!=0)

#using <mscorlib.dll>
using namespace System;

__gc __interface ICustomer1 {};

__gc __interface ICustomer2 : ICustomer1
{
public:
    void ShowCustomers(int id);
};

__gc class Customer1 : public ICustomer1 {};

__gc class Customer2 : public ICustomer2
{
public:
    void ShowCustomers(int id)
    {
        Console::WriteLine("Customer2::ShowCustomers:
            succeeded");
    }
};

void main(void)
{
    Customer1 *pCust1 = new Customer1; //no to ICustomer2
    Console::WriteLine(pCust1->GetType());
    // check if type is ICustomer2 before casting
    if (IS(pCust1, "ICustomer2"))
    {
        ICustomer2 *pIcust2 =
            dynamic_cast<ICustomer2 *>(pCust1);
        pIcust2->ShowCustomers(-1);
    }
```

```
   else
      Console::WriteLine
         ("pCust1 does not support ICustomer2 interface");

   Customer2 *pCust2 = new Customer2; //yes to ICustomer2
   Console::WriteLine(pCust2->GetType());
   // check if type is ICustomer2 before casting
   if (IS(pCust2, "ICustomer2"))
   {
      ICustomer2 *pIcust2 =
         dynamic_cast<ICustomer2 *>(pCust2);
      pIcust2->ShowCustomers(-1);
   }
   else
      Console::WriteLine
         ("pCust2 does not support ICustomer2 interface");
}
```

This example is not the most efficient solution, because a check of the type is made *twice*. The first time is when reflection is used to test for the interface with the **IS** macro. But the check is made all over again when the dynamic cast operation is performed, because the runtime will test the type and then throw an exception if the interface is not supported. The output of the program is shown next. As you can see, no exception is thrown.

```
Customer1
pCust1 does not support ICustomer2 interface
Customer2
Customer2::ShowCustomers: succeeded
```

THE DYNAMIC_CAST OPERATOR

Code
Example

When you use the **dynamic_cast** operator, you obtain an interface pointer directly. The interface pointer is set to zero if the class does not support the interface. The type is checked only once in this scenario.[3] The following code is taken from the **CastThenTestForNull** example, which is exactly like the preceding **TestInterfaceBeforeCast** except that the result of the dynamic cast is checked against the value of zero in an **if-else** statement.

```
void main(void)
{
   Customer1 *pCust1 = new Customer1; //no ICustomer2
```

---

[3] The C++ **dynamic_cast** operator is similar to the C# **as** operator.

```
Console::WriteLine(pCust1->GetType());
//Use C++ dynamic_cast operator to check for ICustomer2
ICustomer2 *pIcust2 =
   dynamic_cast<ICustomer2 *>(pCust1);
if (pIcust2 != 0)
   pIcust2->ShowCustomers(-1);
else
   Console::WriteLine
   ("pCust1 does not support ICustomer2 interface");

Customer2 *pCust2 = new Customer2; //yes to ICustomer2
Console::WriteLine(pCust2->GetType());
//Use C++ dynamic_cast operator to check for ICustomer2
pIcust2 =
   dynamic_cast<ICustomer2 *>(pCust2);
if (pIcust2 != 0)
   pIcust2->ShowCustomers(-1);
else
   Console::WriteLine
   ("pCust2 does not support ICustomer2 interface");
}
```

The result of the **CastThenTestForNull** program shows that, again, no exception is thrown, but only one runtime data type check is made on each object.

```
Customer1
pCust1 does not support ICustomer2 interface
Customer2
ICustomer2::ShowCustomers: succeeded
```

If you are experienced with COM, the operation of finding out if an interface is supported should be familiar to you.

Acme Travel Agency Case Study

We will now apply our knowledge of interfaces to do a little restructuring of the Acme case study. One of the big benefits of using interfaces is that they raise the level of abstraction somewhat, helping you to understand the system by way of the interface contacts without worrying about how the system is implemented.

The case study code is in the **CaseStudy** directory for this chapter.

Interfaces in Managed C++ and COM

There are many similarities between .NET and COM. In both, the concept of interface plays a fundamental role. Interfaces are useful for specifying contracts. Interfaces support a very dynamic style of programming.

In COM you must yourself provide a very elaborate infrastructure in order to implement a COM component. You must implement a class factory for the creation of COM objects. You must implement the **QueryInterface** method of **IUnknown** for the dynamic checking of interfaces. You must implement **AddRef** and **Release** for proper memory management.

With .NET languages, the Common Language Runtime does all this for you automatically. You create an object via **new**. You check for and obtain an interface via **dynamic_cast**. The garbage collector takes care of memory management for you.

THE CONTRACT

We have already examined the **ICustomer** interface of the **Customers** class. We will next look at the functionality of the class **HotelBroker**. The methods divide fairly naturally into three groups.

1. Hotel information, such as the cities where hotels are available and the hotels within a city.
2. Hotel administration, such as adding or deleting a hotel or changing the number of rooms and rate of a hotel.
3. Hotel reservations, such as booking or canceling a reservation or obtaining a list of reservations.

Accordingly, we have created three interfaces for the **HotelBroker** class. These interfaces are defined in **AcmeDefinitions.h**.

```
__gc __interface IHotelInfo
{
   ArrayList *GetCities();
   ArrayList *GetHotels();
   ArrayList *GetHotels(String *pCity);
};

__gc __interface IHotelAdmin
{
   String *AddHotel(
      String *pCity,
      String *pName,
      int numberRooms,
      Decimal rate);
```

```
        String *DeleteHotel(String *pCity, String *pName);
        String *ChangeRooms(
            String *pCity,
            String *pName,
            int numberRooms,
            Decimal rate);
    };


    __gc __interface IHotelReservation
    {
        ReservationResult MakeReservation(
            int customerId,
            String *pCity,
            String *pHotel,
            DateTime checkinDate,
            int numberDays);
        void CancelReservation(int id);
        ArrayList *FindReservationsForCustomer(
            int nCustomerId);
    };
```

THE IMPLEMENTATION

We now implement the hotel brokerage system using collections in place of
arrays, and we return displayable information to the client code in the
TestHotel::Main method rather than display information directly in the
HotelBroker class. Earlier in this chapter we examined the new implementation of the **Customers** class. The same principles apply to the implementation of the **HotelBroker** class.

STRUCTURES

One detail concerns the data structures used to pass lists to the client. We use
the **ArrayList** class. But what do we store in each array list? We could use
Customer objects and **Hotel** objects. The problem with this approach is that
these classes have implementation-specific data in them that the client program does not want to see, as well as the information fields that the client
program cares about. To obtain implementation-neutral representations, we
introduce several structures.

In **Customers.h** we define the **CustomerListItem** structure for passing
customer information.

```
    __value struct CustomerListItem
    {
    public:
```

```
    int nCustomerId;
    String *pFirstName;
    String *pLastName;
    String *pEmailAddress;
};
```

In **AcmeDefinitions.h** we define structures for hotels, reservations, and reservation results.

```
__value struct HotelListItem
{
public:
    String *pCity;
    String *pHotelName;
    int nNumberRooms;
    Decimal decRate;
};


__value struct ReservationListItem
{
public:
    int nCustomerId;
    int nReservationId;
    String *pHotelName;
    String *pCity;
    DateTime dtArrivalDate;
    DateTime dtDepartureDate;
    int nNumberDays;
};


__value struct ReservationResult
{
public:
    int nReservationId;
    Decimal decReservationCost;
    Decimal decRate;
    String *pComment;
};
```

The **ReservationResult** returns a **ReservationId** of −1 if there is a problem, along with an explanation of the problem in the **pComment** field. Otherwise "OK" is returned in the **pComment** field.

We invite you to examine the code in the **CaseStudy** folder and to build and run the program.

Explicit Interface Implementation

When working with interfaces, an ambiguity can arise if a class implements two interfaces and each has a method with same name and signature. As an example, consider the following versions of the interfaces **IAccount** and **IStatement**. Each interface contains the method **Show**.

```
__gc __interface IAccount
{
   void Deposit(Decimal amount);
   void Withdraw(Decimal amount);
   __property Decimal get_Balance();
   void Show();
};


__gc __interface IStatement
{
__property int get_Transactions();
   void Show();
};
```

How can the class specify implementations of these methods? The answer is to use the interface name to qualify the method, as illustrated in the program **Ambiguous**. The **IAccount** version **IAccount.Show** will display only the balance, and **IStatement::Show** will display both the number of transactions and the balance.

```
//Account.h
...


__gc class Account : public IAccount, public IStatement
{
private:
   Decimal decBalance;
   int nNumXact;
public:
   Account(Decimal decBalance) : nNumXact(0)
   {
      this->decBalance = decBalance;
   }
   void Deposit(Decimal decAmount)
   {
      decBalance = decBalance + decAmount;
      ++nNumXact;
```

```
}
void Withdraw(Decimal decAmount)
{
   decBalance = decBalance - decAmount;
   ++nNumXact;
}
__property Decimal get_Balance()
{
   return decBalance;
}
void IAccount::Show()
{
   Console::WriteLine(
      "balance = {0}", __box(decBalance));
}
__property int get_Transactions()
{
   return nNumXact;
}
void IStatement::Show()
{
   Console::WriteLine(
      "{0} transactions, balance = {1}",
      __box(nNumXact),
      __box(decBalance));
}
};
```

The methods **IAccount::Show** and **IStatement::Show** *cannot be accessed* through a pointer to a class instance. They can *only* be accessed through an interface pointer of the type explicitly shown in the method definition. The following test program shows that we cannot call the **IAccount::Show** method through an **Account** object pointer but only through an **IAccount** interface pointer. Otherwise, an ambiguous call to function error is flagged by the compiler. By obtaining an **IStatement** interface pointer, we can call **IStatement::Show**. The output is shown next:

```
0 transactions, balance = 100
0 transactions, balance = 100
balance = 115
2 transactions, balance = 115
```

Even when there is no ambiguity, you may wish to use an explicit interface implementation in order to force client programs to use interfaces to call the methods specified in the interfaces. This approach makes it very clear that the client code is programming against specific interfaces and not against a large, amorphous collection of methods of a class. The code will be easily adaptable to using different classes that implement the same interfaces.

Generic Interfaces in .NET

The .NET Framework exposes much standard functionality through generic interfaces, which are implemented in various combinations by classes in the framework itself and which can also be implemented by your own classes in order to tap into standard functionality defined by the framework. In this section we will look at several categories of operations that are supported by these standard, generic interfaces:

- Collections
- Copying objects
- Comparing objects

Our survey of generic interfaces is by no means exhaustive, but our sampling should give you a good understanding of how generic interfaces work in the .NET Framework.

Collection Interfaces

Now that we understand the concept of interfaces, we are equipped to take a closer look at collections, particularly at the **ArrayList** class that we have used so heavily in the case study. If we look at the definition of **ArrayList**, we see that it implements four standard interfaces.

```
__gc class ArrayList : public IList, ICollection,
    IEnumerable, ICloneable
```

The first three interfaces form a simple interface hierarchy, as shown in Figure 5–1. As you go down the hierarchy, additional methods are added until **IList** is a fully featured list.

The fourth interface, **ICloncable**, is independent and is used to support deep copying. As a simple illustration of the collection interfaces, we provide the program **StringList**. Here is the **Main** method in the **StringList** example. We'll look at the individual helper methods as we examine the various collection interfaces.

Code
Example

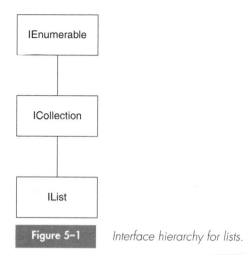

Figure 5–1   *Interface hierarchy for lists.*

```
//StringList.h

__gc class StringList
{
private:
    static ArrayList *pList;
public:
    static void Main()
    {
        // Initialize strings and show starting state
        pList = new ArrayList(4);
        ShowCount();
        AddString("Amy");
        AddString("Bob");
        AddString("Charlie");
        ShowEnum(pList);// enumerator
        ShowCount();
        // Add two more string and show state again
        AddString("David");
        AddString("Ellen");
        ShowList(pList);// simulated foreach
        ShowCount();
        // Remove two strings from list and show state
        RemoveString("David");
        RemoveAt(0);
        ShowArray(pList);// index notation
        ShowCount();
        // Try to remove two strings not in list
```

```cpp
        RemoveString("Amy");
        RemoveAt(3);
    }
private:
    static void ShowEnum(ArrayList *pArray)
    {
        IEnumerator *pIter = pArray->GetEnumerator();
        bool more = pIter->MoveNext();
        while (more)
        {
            String *pStr =
                dynamic_cast<String *>((pIter->Current));
            Console::WriteLine(pStr);
            more = pIter->MoveNext();
        }
    }
    static void ShowList(ArrayList *pArray)
    {
        IEnumerator *pEnum =
            pArray->GetEnumerator();
        while (pEnum->MoveNext())
        {
            String *pStr =
                dynamic_cast<String *>(pEnum->Current);
            Console::WriteLine(pStr);
        }
    }
    static void ShowArray(ArrayList *pArray)
    {
        for (int i = 0; i < pArray->Count; i++)
        {
            Console::WriteLine(
                "pArray->get_Item({0}) = {1}",
                __box(i),
                pArray->get_Item(i));
        }
    }
    static void ShowCount()
    {
        Console::WriteLine(
            "pList->Count = {0}", __box(pList->Count));
        Console::WriteLine(
            "pList->Capacity = {0}", __box(pList->Capacity));
    }
```

```
static void AddString(String *pStr)
{
    if (pList->Contains(pStr))
        throw new Exception(
            String::Format("list contains {0}", pStr));
                pList->Add(pStr);
}
static void RemoveString(String *pStr)
{
    if (pList->Contains(pStr))
        pList->Remove(pStr);
    else
        Console::WriteLine(
            "List does not contain {0}", pStr);
}
static void RemoveAt(int nIndex)
{
    try
    {
        pList->RemoveAt(nIndex);
    }
    catch (ArgumentOutOfRangeException *)
    {
        Console::WriteLine(
            "No element at index {0}", __box(nIndex));
    }
}
};
```

Here is the output:

```
pList->Count = 0
pList->Capacity = 4
Amy
Bob
Charlie
pList->Count = 3
pList->Capacity = 4
Amy
Bob
Charlie
David
Ellen
pList->Count = 5
```

```
pList->Capacity = 8
pArray->get_Item(0) = Bob
pArray->get_Item(1) = Charlie
pArray->get_Item(2) = Ellen
pList->Count = 3
pList->Capacity = 8
List does not contain Amy
No element at index 3
```

IENUMERABLE AND IENUMERATOR

The most basic interface is **IEnumerable**, which has a single method, **GetEnumerator**.

```
__gc __interface IEnumerable
{
    IEnumerator* GetEnumerator();
};
```

GetEnumerator returns an interface pointer to **IEnumerator**, which is the interface used for iterating through a collection. This interface has the property **Current** and the methods **MoveNext** and **Reset**.

```
__gc __interface IEnumerator
{
    __property Object* get_Current();
    bool MoveNext();
    void Reset();
};
```

The enumerator is initially positioned *before* the first element in the collection and it must be advanced before it is used. The **ShowEnum** method illustrates using an enumerator to iterate through a list.

```
static void ShowEnum(ArrayList *pArray)
{
    IEnumerator *pIter =
        pArray->GetEnumerator();
    bool more = pIter->MoveNext();
    while (more)
    {
        String *pStr =
            dynamic_cast<String *>((pIter->Current));
        Console::WriteLine(pStr);
```

```
        more = pIter->MoveNext();
    }
}
```

ICOLLECTION

The **ICollection** interface is derived from **IEnumerable** and adds a **Count** property and a **CopyTo** method.

```
__gc __interface ICollection : public IEnumerable
{
    __property int get_Count();
    __property bool get_IsSynchronized();
    __property Object* get_SyncRoot();
    void CopyTo(Array* array, int index);
};
```

There are also synchronization properties that can help you deal with thread safety issues. "Is it thread safe?" is a question frequently asked about library code. The short answer to this question for the .NET Framework class library is no. This does not mean that the designers of the .NET Framework did not think about thread safety issues. On the contrary, there are many mechanisms to help you write thread-safe code when you need to. The reason that collections are not automatically thread-safe is that your code should not have to pay the performance penalty to enforce synchronization when it is not running in a multi-threading scenario. If you do need thread safety, you may use the thread-safety properties to implement thread safety. We discuss the .NET mechanisms for thread synchronization in Chapter 8.

Our **StringList** program illustrates the use of the **Capacity** property of the **ArrayList** class as well as the **Count** property that **ArrayList** inherits from the **ICollection** interface.

```
    static void ShowCount()
    {
        Console::WriteLine(
            "pList->Count = {0}", __box(pList->Count));
        Console::WriteLine(
            "pList->Capacity = {0}", __box(pList->Capacity));
    }
```

ILIST

The **IList** interface is derived from **ICollection** and provides methods for adding an item to a list, removing an item, and so on.

```
__gc __interface IList : public ICollection
{
    __property bool get_IsFixedSize();
    __property bool get_IsReadOnly();
    __property Object* get_Item(int index);
    __property void set_Item(int index, Object*);
    int Add(Object* value);
    void Clear();
    bool Contains(Object* value);
    int IndexOf(Object* value);
    void Insert(int index, Object* value);
    void Remove(Object* value);
    void RemoveAt(int index);
};
```

Our **StringList** sample code illustrates using the indexer **get_Item** and the **Contains**, **Add**, **Remove**, and **RemoveAt** methods.

```
static void ShowArray(ArrayList *pArray)
{
    for (int i = 0; i < pArray->Count; i++)
    {
        Console::WriteLine(
            "pArray->get_Item({0}) = {1}",
            __box(i),
            pArray->get_Item(i));
    }
}
...
static void AddString(String *pStr)
{
    if (pList->Contains(pStr))
        throw new Exception(
            String::Format("list contains {0}", pStr));
    pList->Add(pStr);
}
static void RemoveString(String *pStr)
{
    if (pList->Contains(pStr))
        pList->Remove(pStr);
    else
        Console::WriteLine(
            "List does not contain {0}", pStr);
```

```
    }
    static void RemoveAt(int nIndex)
    {
        try
        {
            pList->RemoveAt(nIndex);
        }
        catch (ArgumentOutOfRangeException *)
        {
            Console::WriteLine(
                "No element at index {0}", __box(nIndex));
        }
    }
}
```

Copy Semantics and ICloneable

Sometimes you have to make a copy of an object. When you copy objects that contain objects and object pointers, you have to be aware of the copy semantics of **ICloneable**. We will now compare pointer copy, shallow memberwise copy, and deep copy. We will see that by implementing the **ICloneable** interface in your class, you can implement either a shallow or deep copy.

Recall that managed C++ has value types as well as pointer types.[4] A value type contains all its own data, while a pointer type refers to data stored somewhere else. If a pointer variable gets copied to another pointer variable, both will point to the same object. If the object pointed to by the second variable is changed, the first variable will also reflect the new value. Sometimes you want this behavior, but sometimes you do not.

ICLONEABLE

The **ICloneable** interface is a root interface and it has a single method named **Clone**. The **Clone** method may be implemented as either a deep copy or a shallow copy, but the **Object** pointer that is returned must point to an object that is the same type as (or a compatible type) the type that is implementing the **ICloneable** interface. Usually, the **Clone** method is implemented such that it creates a new object on the managed heap. However, there are examples, such as the **String** class, that return a pointer to themselves in their **Clone** method.

```
__gc __interface ICloneable
{
    Object* Clone();
};
```

---

[4] Pointer types and reference types are similar for the purposes of this discussion.

SHALLOW COPY AND DEEP COPY

An unmanaged struct or class in C++ automatically implements a memberwise copy that will be in effect unless you override it with a copy constructor. Memberwise copy is also known as a *shallow copy*. The **Object** root class also has a protected method, **MemberwiseClone**, which will perform a memberwise copy of members of a managed struct or class.

If a member of a struct or class is a pointer type, this memberwise copy may not be what is desired. The result will be that the members point to the same data, not to two independent copies of the data. To actually copy the data itself and not merely the pointers, you will need to perform a *deep copy*. Deep copy can be provided at either the language level or the library level. In unmanaged C++, deep copy is provided at the language level through a *copy constructor*. In managed C++, deep copy is provided by the .NET Framework through a special interface named **ICloneable**, which you can implement in your classes in order to enable them to perform a deep copy.

The following three points describe the possible scenarios for copy semantics involving managed classes and structs, with and without **ICloneable** interface implementations, as well as traditional unmanaged classes and structs.

- Assigning one pointer to another, where the pointers point to a managed or unmanaged class or struct, results in a simple pointer copy. This is neither shallow copy nor deep copy semantics, but rather just *simple pointer assignment*.
- Converting one non-pointer type to another, where each value is an unmanaged class, unmanaged struct, or value type results in a *shallow copy provided automatically by C++*.
- Assigning one pointer to the return of the **Clone** method on another pointer, where the pointer type is a pointer to a managed class or struct with **ICloneable** implemented, results in either a *shallow copy or a deep copy,* depending on how the **Clone** method is implemented.

EXAMPLE PROGRAM

We will illustrate all of these ideas in the program **CopyDemo**. This program makes a copy of a **Course** instance. The **Course** class consists of a title and a collection of students.

```
//Course.h

__gc class Course : public ICloneable
{
public:
    String *pTitle;
```

```
   ArrayList *pRoster;
   Course(String *pTitle)
   {
      this->pTitle = pTitle;
      pRoster = new ArrayList;
   }
   void AddStudent(String *pName)
   {
      pRoster->Add(pName);
   }
   void Show(String *pCaption)
   {
      Console::WriteLine("-----{0}-----", pCaption);
      Console::WriteLine(
         "Course : {0} with {1} students",
         pTitle,
         __box(pRoster->Count));
      IEnumerator *pEnum = pRoster->GetEnumerator();
      while (pEnum->MoveNext())
      {
         String *pName =
            dynamic_cast<String *>(pEnum->Current);
         Console::WriteLine(pName);
      }
   }
   Course *ShallowCopy()
   {
      return dynamic_cast<Course *>(MemberwiseClone());
   }
   Object *Clone()
   {
      Course *pCourse = new Course(pTitle);
      pCourse->pRoster =
         dynamic_cast<ArrayList *>(pRoster->Clone());
      return pCourse;
   }
};
```

The test program constructs a **Course** instance **pC1** and then makes a copy **pC2** by various methods.

```
//CopyDemo.h

__gc class CopyDemo
```

```
{
private:
    static Course *pC1, *pC2;
public:
    static void Main()
    {
        Console::WriteLine("Copy is done via pC2 = pC1");
        InitializeCourse();
        pC1->Show("original");
        pC2 = pC1;
        pC2->Show("copy");
        pC2->pTitle = ".NET Programming";
        pC2->AddStudent("Charlie");
        pC2->Show("copy with changed title and new student");
        pC1->Show("original");

        Console::WriteLine(
            "\nCopy is done via pC2 = pC1->ShallowCopy()");
        InitializeCourse();
        pC2 = pC1->ShallowCopy();
        pC2->pTitle = ".NET Programming";
        pC2->AddStudent("Charlie");
        pC2->Show("copy with changed title and new student");
        pC1->Show("original");

        Console::WriteLine(
            "\nCopy is done via pC2 = pC1->Clone()");
        InitializeCourse();
        pC2 = dynamic_cast<Course *>(pC1->Clone());
        pC2->pTitle = ".NET Programming";
        pC2->AddStudent("Charlie");
        pC2->Show("copy with changed title and new student");
        pC1->Show("original");
    }
private:
    static void InitializeCourse()
    {
        pC1 = new Course("Intro to Managed C++");
        pC1->AddStudent("John");
        pC1->AddStudent("Mary");
    }
};
```

The program output is shown next:

```
Copy is done via pC2 = pC1
-----original-----
Course : Intro to Managed C++ with 2 students
John
Mary
-----copy-----
Course : Intro to Managed C++ with 2 students
John
Mary
-----copy with changed title and new student-----
Course : .NET Programming with 3 students
John
Mary
Charlie
     -original-----
Course : .NET Programming with 3 students
John
Mary
Charlie


Copy is done via pC2 = pC1->ShallowCopy()
-----copy with changed title and new student-----
Course :  .NET Programming with 3 students
John
Mary
Charlie
-----original-----
Course : Intro to Managed C++ with 3 students
John
Mary
Charlie


Copy is done via pC2 = pC1->Clone()
-----copy with changed title and new student-----
Course : .NET Programming with 3 students
John
Mary
Charlie
-----original-----
Course : Intro to Managed C++ with 2 students
John
Mary
```

POINTER COPY BY ASSIGNMENT

The first way the copy is performed is by the straight assignment **pC2 = pC1**. Now we get two pointers to the same object, and if we make any change through the first pointer, we will see the same change through the second pointer. The first part of the test program illustrates such an assignment.

```
__gc class CopyDemo
{
...
public:
   static void Main()
   {
      Console::WriteLine("Copy is done via pC2 = pC1");
      InitializeCourse();
      pC1->Show("original");
      pC2 = pC1;
      pC2->Show("copy");
      pC2->pTitle = ".NET Programming";
      pC2->AddStudent("Charlie");
      pC2->Show("copy with changed title and new student");
      pC1->Show("original");
...
```

We initialize with the title "Intro to Managed C++" and two students in the **InitializeCourse** method. We make the assignment **pC2 = pC1**, and then change the title and add another student for **pC2**. We then show both **pC1** and **pC2**, and we see that both pointers reflect these changes. Here is the output from this first part of the program:

```
Copy is done via pC2 = pC1
-----original-----
Course : Intro to Managed C++ with 2 students
John
Mary
-----copy-----
Course : Intro to Managed C++ with 2 students
John
Mary
-----copy with changed title and new student-----
Course : .NET Programming with 3 students
John
Mary
Charlie
```

```
-----original-----
Course : .NET Programming with 3 students
John
Mary
Charlie
```

MEMBERWISE CLONE

Next, we will illustrate a memberwise copy, which can be accomplished using the **MemberwiseClone** method of **Object**. Since this method is **protected**, we cannot call it directly from outside our **Course** class. Instead, in **Course** we define a method, **ShallowCopy**, which is implemented using **Member-wiseClone**.

```
__gc class Course : public ICloneable
{
   ...
   Course *ShallowCopy()
   {
      return dynamic_cast<Course *>(MemberwiseClone());
   }
   ...
};
```

Here is the second part of the test program, which calls the **Shallow-Copy** method. Again, we change the title and a student in the second copy.

```
__gc class CopyDemo
{
...
public:
   static void Main()
   {
      ...
      Console::WriteLine(
         "\nCopy is done via pC2 = pC1->ShallowCopy()");
      InitializeCourse();
      pC2 = pC1->ShallowCopy();
      pC2->pTitle = ".NET Programming";
      pC2->AddStudent("Charlie");
      pC2->Show("copy with changed title and new student");
      pC1->Show("original");
      ...
```

Here is the output of this second part of the program. Now the **Title** field has its own independent copy, but the **Roster** collection is just copied by pointer, so each copy refers to the same collection of students.

```
Copy is done via pC2 = pC1->ShallowCopy()
-----copy with changed title and new student-----
Course : .NET Programming with 3 students
John
Mary
Charlie
-----original-----
Course : Intro to Managed C++ with 3 students
John
Mary
Charlie
```

USING ICLONEABLE

The final version of copy relies on the fact that our **Course** class supports the **ICloneable** interface and implements the **Clone** method. To clone the **Roster** collection, we use the fact that **ArrayList** implements the **ICloneable** interface, as discussed earlier in this chapter. Note that the **Clone** method returns an **Object** *, so we must cast it to **ArrayList** * before assigning to the **pRoster** field.

```
__gc class Course : public ICloneable
{
   public:
   ...
   Object *Clone()
   {
      Course *pCourse = new Course(pTitle);
      pCourse->pRoster =
         dynamic_cast<ArrayList *>(pRoster->Clone());
      return pCourse;
   }
   ...
};
```

Here is the third part of the test program, which calls the **Clone** method. Again, we change the title and a student in the second copy.

```
__gc class CopyDemo
{
...
```

```
public:
    static void Main()
    {
        ...
        Console::WriteLine(
            "\nCopy is done via pC2 = pC1->Clone()");
        InitializeCourse();
        pC2 = dynamic_cast<Course *>(pC1->Clone());
        pC2->pTitle - ".NET Programming";
        pC2->AddStudent("Charlie");
        pC2->Show("copy with changed title and new student");
        pC1->Show("original");
        ...
```

Here is the output from the third part of the program. Now we have completely independent instances of **Course**. Each has its own title and set of students.

```
Copy is done via pC2 = pC1->Clone()
-----copy with changed title and new student-----
Course : .NET Programming with 3 students
John
Mary
Charlie
-----original-----
Course : Intro to Managed C++ with 2 students
John
Mary
```

This last approach illustrates the generic nature of the .NET interfaces. You can clone an object without knowing or caring exactly what object type it is.

Comparing Objects

We have quite exhaustively studied *copying* objects. We now examine *comparing* objects. To compare objects, the .NET Framework uses the interface **IComparable**. In this section we use the interface **IComparable** to sort an array.

SORTING AN ARRAY

Code Example

The **System::Array** class provides a static method, **Sort**, that can be used for sorting an array. The program **ArrayName** illustrates applying this **Sort** method to an array of **Name** objects, where the **Name** class simply encapsulates a string through a read-only property **Text**. Here is the main program:

```
//ArrayName.cpp
...
__gc class ArrayName
{
public:
   static void Main()
   {
      Name *array[] = new Name*[5];
      array[0] = new Name("Michael");
      array[1] = new Name("Charlie");
      array[2] = new Name("Peter");
      array[3] = new Name("Dana");
      array[4] = new Name("Bob");
      if (dynamic_cast<IComparable *>(array[0]) != 0)
         Array::Sort(array);
      else
         Console::WriteLine(
            "Name does not implement IComparable");
      IEnumerator *pEnum = array->GetEnumerator();
      while (pEnum->MoveNext())
      {
         Name *pName =
            dynamic_cast<Name *>(pEnum->Current);
          if (pName != 0)
             Console::WriteLine(pName);
      }
   }
};
```

IMPLEMENTING ICOMPARABLE

In order for the **Sort** method to function, there must be a way of comparing the objects that are being sorted. This comparison is achieved through the **CompareTo** method of the interface **IComparable**. Thus, to sort an array of a type that you define, you must implement **IComparable** for your type.

```
__gc __interface IComparable
{
int CompareTo(Object* obj);
};
```

Here is the implementation of the **Name** class, with its implementation of **IComparable**:

```
__gc class Name : public IComparable
{
private:
    String *pText;
public:
    Name(String *pText)
    {
        this->pText = pText;
    }
    __property String* get_Item()
    {
        return pText;
    }
    __property void set_Item(String* pText)
    {
        this->pText = pText;
    }
    int CompareTo(Object *pObj)
    {
        String *pS1 = this->pText;
        String *pS2 =
            (dynamic_cast<Name *>(pObj))->pText;
        return String::Compare(pS1, pS2);
    }
    String *ToString()
    {
        return pText;
    }
};
```

The alphabetically ordered output follows:

```
Bob
Charlie
Dana
Michael
Peter
```

Understanding Frameworks

Our example offers some insight into the workings of frameworks. A framework is *more* than a library. In a typical library, you are concerned with your code calling library functions. In a framework, you call into the framework *and the framework might call you*. Your program can be viewed as the middle layer of a sandwich.

- Your code calls the bottom layer.
- The top layer calls your code.

The .NET Framework is an excellent example of such an architecture. There is rich functionality that you can call directly. There are many interfaces, which you can optionally implement to make your program behave appropriately when called by the framework, often on behalf of other objects.

Delegates

Interfaces facilitate writing code so that your program can be *called back into* by some other code. This style of programming has been available for a long time under the guise of callback functions. In this section we examine *delegates* in managed C++, which can be thought of as type-safe and object-oriented callback functions. Delegates are the foundation for a more elaborate callback protocol known as *events*, which we'll look at in the following section.

A *callback function* is one that your program specifies and "registers" in some way, and then gets called by another program. In C and C++ you implement callback functions using function pointers.

In managed C++ you can encapsulate a pointer to a method inside a delegate object. A delegate can point to either a static method or an instance method. When a delegate points to an instance method, it stores both an object instance and an entry point to the instance method. The instance method can then be called through this object instance. When a delegate object points to a static method, it stores just the entry point of this static method.

When the delegate object is passed to other code, it can be used to call back into the target object's method. The code that calls your delegate method is often separately compiled. It does not know which method is actually going to be called at runtime.

A delegate is actually a managed class type derived ultimately from **System::Delegate**. A new delegate instance is created just like any other class instance, using the **new** operator. Delegates are object-oriented and type-safe, and they enjoy the safety of the managed code execution environment.

Declaring a Delegate

You declare a delegate in managed C++ using a special notation with the keyword **__delegate** and the signature of the encapsulated method. A naming convention suggests your name should end with "Callback." Here is an example of a delegate declaration:

```
__delegate void NotifyCallback(Decimal balance);
```

Defining a Method

When you instantiate a delegate, you will need to specify a callback method, which must match the signature in the delegate declaration. The method may be either a static method or an instance method. Here are some examples of callback methods that can be hooked to the **NotifyCallback** delegate declaration shown above:

```
static void NotifyCustomer(Decimal balance)
{
   Console::WriteLine("Dear customer,");
   Console::WriteLine(
      "   Account overdrawn, balance = {0}",
      __box(balance));
}
static void NotifyBank(Decimal balance)
{
   Console::WriteLine("Dear bank,");
   Console::WriteLine(
      "   Account overdrawn, balance = {0}",
      __box(balance));
}
void NotifyInstance(Decimal balance)
{
   Console::WriteLine("Dear instance,");
   Console::WriteLine(
      "   Account overdrawn, balance = {0}",
      __box(balance));
}
```

Creating a Delegate Object

You instantiate a delegate object with the **new** operator, just as you would with any other class. The following code illustrates the creation of two delegate objects. The first one is hooked to a static method, and the second to an instance method. The second delegate object internally stores both a method entry point and an object instance that is used for invoking the method.

```
//create delegate for static method NotifyCustomer
NotifyCallback *pCustDlg = new NotifyCallback(
    0, //zero for static method NotifyCustomer
    NotifyCustomer);
...
//create delegate for instance method NotifyInstance
NotifyCallback *pInstDlg = new NotifyCallback(
    pda, //non-zero for instance method NotifyInstance
    NotifyInstance);
```

Calling a Delegate

You "call" a delegate just as you would a method. The delegate object is not a method, but it has an encapsulated method. The delegate object "delegates" the call to this encapsulated method, hence the name "delegate." In the following code the delegate object **notifyDlg** is called whenever a negative balance occurs on a withdrawal. In this example the **notifyDlg** delegate object is initialized in the method **SetDelegate**.

```
__gc class Account
{
private:
    Decimal balance;
    NotifyCallback *pNotifyDlg;
...
    void SetDelegate(NotifyCallback *pDlg)
    {
        pNotifyDlg = pDlg;
    }
...
    void Withdraw(Decimal amount)
    {
        balance = balance - amount;
        if (balance < 0) //over draft situation
            pNotifyDlg(balance); callback
    }
```

Combining Delegate Objects

Delegates can multicast in that they may have an invocation list of methods. When such a delegate is called, all the methods on the invocation list will be called in turn. A powerful feature of delegates is that you can combine and remove the methods in a delegate's invocation list. The **Delegate::Combine** and **Delegate::Remove** static methods are available for managing these invocation lists. In addition, the += and – = operators are overloaded for the **Delegate** class, providing a shortcut syntax for adding and removing methods.

```
//pseudocode: pCurrDlg = pCustDlg + pBankDlg
pCurrDlg = static_cast<NotityCallback *>(
    Delegate::Combine(pCustDlg, pBankDlg));
...

//alternate code: pCurrDlg -= pBankDlg
pCurrDlg = static_cast<NotifyCallback *>(
    Delegate::Remove(pCurrDlg, pBankDlg));
...

// alternate code: pCurrDlg += pInstDlg
pCurrDlg = static_cast<NotifyCallback *>(
    Delegate::Combine(pCurrDlg, pInstDlg));
```

In this example we construct two static delegate objects and one instance delegate object. It demonstrates several scenarios in which methods are added and removed from the delegate, and each time, the delegate is called back into. This example is provided in the next section, with heavy documentation to clarify the important aspects of how it works.

Complete Example

Code Example

The program **DelegateAccount** illustrates using delegates in our bank account scenario. The file **DelegateAccount.cpp** declares the delegate **NotifyCallback**. The class **DelegateAccount** contains methods matching the signature of the delegate. The **Main** method instantiates delegate objects and combines them in various ways. The delegate objects are passed to the **Account** class, which uses its encapsulated delegate object to invoke suitable notifications when the account is overdrawn.

Observe how dynamic and loosely coupled this structure is. The **Account** class does not know or care which notification methods will be invoked in the case of an overdraft. It simply calls the delegate, which in turn calls all the methods on its invocation list. These methods can be adjusted at runtime.

Here is the code for the **Account** class:

```
//Account.h

__delegate void NotifyCallback(Decimal balance);

__gc class Account
```

```
{
private:
   Decimal balance;
   NotifyCallback *pNotifyDlg;
public:
   Account(Decimal bal, NotifyCallback *pDlg)
   {
      balance = bal;
      pNotifyDlg = pDlg;
   }
   void SetDelegate(NotifyCallback *pDlg)
   {
      pNotifyDlg = pDlg;
   }
   void Deposit(Decimal amount)
   {
      balance = balance + amount;
   }
   void Withdraw(Decimal amount)
   {
      balance = balance - amount;
      if (balance < 0) //overdraft situation
         pNotifyDlg(balance); //callback
   }
   __property Decimal get_Balance()
   {
      return balance;
   }
   __property void set_Balance(Decimal balance)
   {
      this->balance = balance;
   }
};
```

Here is the code declaring and testing the delegate:

```
//DelegateAccount.h

__gc class DelegateAccount
{
public:
   static void Main()
   {
      //create delegate for static method NotifyCustomer
```

```
NotifyCallback *pCustDlg = new NotifyCallback(
    0, //zero for static method NotifyCustomer
    NotifyCustomer);

//create delegate for static method NotifyBank
NotifyCallback *pBankDlg = new NotifyCallback(
    0, //zero for static method NotifyBank
    NotifyBank);

//declare delegate object used by Account object
NotifyCallback *pCurrDlg;

//pseudocode: pCurrDlg = pCustDlg + pBankDlg
pCurrDlg = static_cast<NotifyCallback *>(
    Delegate::Combine(pCustDlg, pBankDlg));

//create Account object and set delegate to be used
Account *pAcc = new Account(100, pCurrDlg);
Console::WriteLine(
    "balance = {0}", __box(pAcc->get_Balance()));

//cause delegate to be called a couple of times
pAcc->Withdraw(125); //calls back via delegate!
Console::WriteLine(
    "balance = {0}", __box(pAcc->get_Balance()));
pAcc->Deposit(200);
pAcc->Withdraw(125); //no overdraft so no call back
Console::WriteLine(
    "balance = {0}", __box(pAcc->get_Balance()));

//alternate: pCurrDlg -= pBankDlg
pCurrDlg = static_cast<NotifyCallback *>(
    Delegate::Remove(pCurrDlg, pBankDlg));

//set new delegate to be used by Account object
pAcc->SetDelegate(pCurrDlg);

//cause delegate to be called
pAcc->Withdraw(125); //calls back via delegate!

//create instance required for instance delegate
DelegateAccount *pda = new DelegateAccount();

//create delegate for instance method NotifyInstance
```

```
        NotifyCallback *pInstDlg = new NotifyCallback(
            pda, //non-zero for instance method NotifyInstance
            NotifyInstance);

        //alternate code: pCurrDlg += pInstDlg
        pCurrDlg = static_cast<NotifyCallback *>(
            Delegate::Combine(pCurrDlg, pInstDlg));

        //set new delegate to be used by Account object
        pAcc->SetDelegate(pCurrDlg);
        pAcc->Withdraw(125); //calls back via delegate!
    }
private:
    static void NotifyCustomer(Decimal balance)
    {
        Console::WriteLine("Dear customer,");
        Console::WriteLine(
            "   Account overdrawn, balance = {0}",
            __box(balance));
    }
    static void NotifyBank(Decimal balance)
    {
        Console::WriteLine("Dear bank,");
        Console::WriteLine(
            "   Account overdrawn, balance = {0}",
            __box(balance));
    }
    void NotifyInstance(Decimal balance)
    {
        Console::WriteLine("Dear instance,");
        Console::WriteLine(
            "   Account overdrawn, balance = {0}",
            __box(balance));
    }
};
```

Here is the output from running the program. Notice which notification methods get invoked, depending upon the operations that have been performed on the current delegate object.

```
balance = 100
Dear customer,
   Account overdrawn, balance = -25
```

```
Dear bank,
    Account overdrawn, balance = -25
balance = -25
balance = 50
Dear customer,
    Account overdrawn, balance = -75
Dear customer,
    Account overdrawn, balance = -200
Dear instance,
    Account overdrawn, balance = -200
```

Stock Market Simulation

As a further illustration of the use of delegates, consider the simple stock market simulation, implemented in the directory **StockMarket**. The simulation consists of two modules:

- The **Admin** module provides a user interface for configuring and running the simulation. It also implements operations called by the simulation engine.
- The **Engine** module is the simulation engine. It maintains an internal clock and invokes randomly generated operations, based on the configuration parameters passed to it.

Figure 5–2 shows the high level architecture of the simulation.

The following operations are available:

- PrintTick: shows each clock tick.
- PrintTrade: shows each trade.

The following configuration parameters can be specified:

- Ticks on/off
- Trades on/off
- Count of how many ticks to run the simulation

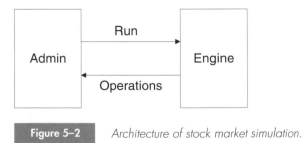

Figure 5–2   *Architecture of stock market simulation.*

RUNNING THE SIMULATION

Build and run the example program in **StockMarket**. Start with the default configuration: Ticks are OFF, Trades are ON, Run count is 100. (Note that the results are random and will be different each time you run the program.)

```
Ticks are OFF
Trades are ON
Run count = 100
Enter command, quit to exit
: run
    2   ACME     23    600
   27   MSFT     63    400
   27   IBM     114    600
   38   MSFT     69    400
   53   MSFT     75    900
   62   INTC     27    800
   64   MSFT     82    200
   68   MSFT     90    300
   81   MSFT     81    600
   83   INTC     30    800
   91   MSFT     73    700
   99   IBM     119    400
:
```

The available commands are listed when you type "help" at the colon prompt. The commands are:

```
count    set run count
ticks    toggle ticks
trades   toggle trades
config   show configuration
run      run the simulation
quit     exit the program
```

The output shows clock tick, stock, price, and volume.

DELEGATE CODE

Two delegates are declared in the **Engine.h** file.

```
__delegate void TickCallback(int ticks);
__delegate void TradeCallback(
   int ticks, String *pStock, int price, int volume);
```

As we saw in the previous section, a delegate is similar to a class, and a delegate object is instantiated using the **new** operator.

```
TickCallback *pTickDlg =
    new TickCallback(0, PrintTick); //0 for static
TradeCallback *pTradeDlg =
    new TradeCallback(0, PrintTrade); //0 for static
```

A method is passed as the parameter to the delegate constructor. The method signature must match that of the delegate.

```
static void PrintTick(int ticks)
{
   Console::Write("{0} ", __box(ticks));
   if (++printcount == LINECOUNT)
   {
      Console::WriteLine();
      printcount = 0;
   }
}
static void PrintTrade(
   int ticks, String *pStock, int price, int volume)
{
   if (printcount != 0)
   {
      Console::WriteLine();
   }
   printcount = 0;
   Console::WriteLine("{0,4}  {1,-4}  {2,4}  {3,4}",
      __box(ticks), pStock,
      __box(price), __box(volume));
}
```

PASSING THE DELEGATES TO THE ENGINE

The **Admin** class passes the delegates to the **Engine** class in the constructor of the **Engine** class.

```
Engine *pEngine = new Engine(pTickDlg, pTradeDlg);
```

RANDOM NUMBER GENERATION

The heart of the simulation is the **Run** method of the **Engine** class. At the core of the **Run** method is assigning simulated data based on random numbers. We use the **System::Random** class, which we discussed in Chapter 3.

```
double r = pRangen->NextDouble();
  if (r < tradeProb[i])
  {
    int delta =
      (int)(price[i] * volatility[i]);
    if (pRangen->NextDouble() < .5)
    {
      delta = -delta;
    }
    price[i] += delta;
    int volume = pRangen->Next(
      minVolume, maxVolume) * 100;
    pTradeOp(
      tick, stocks[i], price[i], volume);
```

USING THE DELEGATES

In the **Engine** class, delegate pointers are declared:

```
TickCallback *pTickOp;
TradeCallback *pTradeOp;
```

The delegate pointers are initialized in the **Engine** constructor:

```
Engine(TickCallback *pTickOp, TradeCallback *pTradeOp)
{
...
  this->pTickOp = pTickOp;
  this->pTradeOp = pTradeOp;
}
```

The method that is wrapped by the delegate object can then be called through the delegate pointer:

```
pTickOp(tick);
...
pTradeOp(
    tick, stocks[i], price[i], volume);
```

Events

Delegates are the foundation for a more elaborate callback protocol known as *events*. Conceptually, servers implement *incoming* interfaces, which are called by clients. In a diagram, such an interface may be shown with a small bubble (a notation used in COM). Sometimes a client may wish to receive notifications from a server when certain "events" occur. In such a case the server will specify an *outgoing* interface. The key concept about events is that the server defines the interface but the client implements it. In a diagram, such an outgoing interface may be shown with an arrow (again, a notation used in COM). Figure 5–3 illustrates a server with one incoming interface and one outgoing interface. In the case of the outgoing interface, the client will implement an incoming interface, which the server will call back into.

Events in Managed C++ and .NET

The .NET Framework provides an easy-to-use implementation of the event paradigm built on delegates. Managed C++ simplifies working with .NET events by providing the keyword **__event** and operators to hook up event handlers to events and to remove them. We will examine this event architecture with the example program **EventDemo**, which simulates a chat room.

Server-Side Event Code

We begin with server-side code, in **ChatServer.h**. The .NET event architecture uses delegates of a specific signature:

```
__delegate void JoinHandler(
   Object *pSender, ChatEventArg *pe);
__delegate void QuitHandler(
   Object *pSender, ChatEventArg *pe);
```

The first parameter specifies the object that sends the event notification. The second parameter is used to pass data along with the notification. Typically, you will derive a class from **EventArg** to hold your event-specific data.

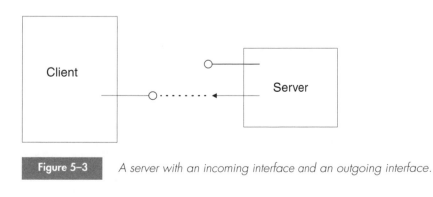

Figure 5–3   *A server with an incoming interface and an outgoing interface.*

```
__gc class ChatEventArg : public EventArgs
{
public:
   String *pName;
   ChatEventArg(String *pName)
   {
      pName = pName;
   }
};
```

A delegate object pointer is declared using the keyword **__event**.

```
__gc class ChatServer
{
...
public:
   __event JoinHandler *pJoin;
   __event QuitHandler *pQuit;
...
```

A helper method is typically provided to facilitate calling the delegate object(s) that have been hooked up to the event. Calling the delegate is often referred to as "firing" the event.

```
__gc class ChatServer
{
...
protected:
   void OnJoin(ChatEventArg *pe)
   {
      if (pJoin != 0)
      {
         pJoin(this, pe); //fire event
      }
   }
   void OnQuit(ChatEventArg *pe)
   {
      if (pQuit != 0)
      {
         pQuit(this, pe); //fire event
      }
   }
...
```

The above helper methods test for **0** in case no delegate objects have been hooked up to the event. Typically, these helper methods are specified as **protected** so that a derived class has access to them.

You can then fire these events by calling the helper methods.

```
__gc class ChatServer
{
...
public:
   void JoinChat(String *pName)
   {
      pMembers->Add(pName);
      OnJoin(new ChatEventArg(pName));
   }
   void QuitChat(String *pName)
   {
      pMembers->Remove(pName);
      OnQuit(new ChatEventArg(pName));
   }
...
```

Client-Side Event Code

The client provides event handler functions.

```
__gc class ChatClient
{
public:
   static void OnJoinChat(Object *pSender, ChatEventArg *pe)
   {
      Console::WriteLine(
         "sender = {0}, {1} has joined the chat",
         pSender,
         pe->pName);
   }
   static void OnQuitChat(Object *pSender, ChatEventArg *pe)
   {
      Console::WriteLine(
         "sender = {0}, {1} has quit the chat",
         pSender,
         pe->pName);
   }
...
```

The client hooks the handler to the event, using the **+=** operator.

```
static void Main()
{
    //create the chat server
    ChatServer *pChat = new ChatServer("OI Chat Room");

    //register to receive event notifications from server
    pChat->pJoin += new JoinHandler(pChat, OnJoinChat);
    pChat->pQuit += new QuitHandler(pChat, OnQuitChat);
    ...
```

The event starts out as **null**, and event handlers get added through **+=**. All of the registered handlers will get invoked when the event delegate is called. You may unregister a handler with the – **=** operator.

Chat Room Example

The chat room example in **EventDemo** illustrates the complete architecture on both the server and client side. The server provides the following methods:

- JoinChat
- QuitChat
- ShowMembers

Whenever a new member joins or quits, the server sends a notification to the client. The event handlers print out an appropriate message. Here is the output from running the program:

```
sender = OI Chat Room, Michael has joined the chat
sender = OI Chat Room, Bob has joined the chat
sender = OI Chat Room, Sam has joined the chat
--- After 3 have joined---
Michael
Bob
Sam
sender = OI Chat Room, Bob has quit the chat
--- After 1 has quit---
Michael
Sam
```

CLIENT CODE

The client program provides event handlers. It instantiates a server object and then hooks up its event handlers to the events. The client then calls methods on the server. These calls will trigger the server firing events back to the client, which get handled by the event handlers.

```
//ChatClient.h

__gc class ChatClient
{
public:
    static void OnJoinChat(Object *pSender, ChatEventArg *pe)
    {
        Console::WriteLine(
            "sender = {0}, {1} has joined the chat",
            pSender,
            pe->pName);
    }
    static void OnQuitChat(Object *pSender, ChatEventArg *pe)
    {
        Console::WriteLine(
            "sender = {0}, {1} has quit the chat",
            pSender,
            pe->pName);
    }
    static void Main()
    {
        //create the chat server
        ChatServer *pChat = new ChatServer("OI Chat Room");

        //register to receive event notifications from server
        pChat->pJoin += new JoinHandler(pChat, OnJoinChat);
        pChat->pQuit += new QuitHandler(pChat, OnQuitChat);

        //call methods on the server
        pChat->JoinChat("Michael");
        pChat->JoinChat("Bob");
        pChat->JoinChat("Sam");
        pChat->ShowMembers("After 3 have joined");
        pChat->QuitChat("Bob");
        pChat->ShowMembers("After 1 has quit");
    }
};
```

SERVER CODE

The server provides code to store in a collection the names of people who have joined the chat. When a person quits the chat, the name is removed from the collection. Joining and quitting the chat triggers firing an event back to the client. The server also contains the plumbing code for setting up the events, including declaration of the delegates, the events, and the event arguments. There are also helper methods for firing the events.

```
//ChatServer.h

__gc class ChatEventArg : public EventArgs
{
public:
   String *pName;
   ChatEventArg(String *pName)
   {
      this->pName = pName;
   }
};

__delegate void JoinHandler(
   Object *pSender, ChatEventArg *pe);
__delegate void QuitHandler(
   Object *pSender, ChatEventArg *pe);

__gc class ChatServer
{
private:
   ArrayList *pMembers;
   String *pChatName;
public:
   __event JoinHandler *pJoin;
   __event QuitHandler *pQuit;
   ChatServer(String *pChatName)
   {
      pMembers = new ArrayList;
      this->pChatName = pChatName;
   }
   String *ToString()
   {
      return pChatName;
   }
protected:
   void OnJoin(ChatEventArg *pe)
   {
      if (pJoin != 0)
      {
```

```
                  pJoin(this, pe);   //fire event
            }
      }
      void OnQuit(ChatEventArg *pe)
      {
            if (pQuit != 0)
            {
                  pQuit(this, pe);   //fire event
            }
      }
public:
      void JoinChat(String *pName)
      {
            pMembers->Add(pName);
            OnJoin(new ChatEventArg(pName));
      }
      void QuitChat(String *pName)
      {
            pMembers->Remove(pName);
            OnQuit(new ChatEventArg(pName));
      }
      void ShowMembers(String *pMsg)
      {
            Console::WriteLine("--- {0} ---", pMsg);
            IEnumerator *pIter = pMembers->GetEnumerator();
            while (pIter->MoveNext())
            {
                  String *pMember =
                        dynamic_cast<String *>((pIter->Current));
                  Console::WriteLine(pMember);
            }
      }
};
```

It may appear that there is a fair amount of plumbing code, but it is *much* simpler than the previous connection point mechanism used by COM events.

Summary

This chapter explored several important interactions between managed C++ and the .NET Framework, beginning with the root class **Object**. We examined collections, including the methods of the **Object** class that should be overridden to tap into the functionality provided by the .NET Framework. We covered in greater depth the concept of interfaces, which allow you to rigorously define a contract for classes to implement. While a class in managed C++ can inherit from only one other class, it can implement multiple interfaces. Another benefit of interfaces is that they facilitate very dynamic programs. Managed C++ provides convenient facilities to query a class at runtime to see whether it supports a particular interface.

The interfaces supporting collections were examined in detail, and copy semantics were explored. While traditional C++ relies on a language feature known as the copy constructor, in managed C++ you provide the same capability by implementing a special interface known as **ICloneable**. This led to an exploration of the role of generic interfaces in the .NET Framework programming model and to a comparison of the .NET and COM component models. Sorting with the **IComparable** interface provided a further illustration of programming with generic interfaces. The examples offered insight into the workings of frameworks, which are more than just class libraries. In a framework, you call the framework, and the framework calls you. Your code can be viewed as the middle layer of a sandwich. This key insight can help you grasp what makes .NET programming tick.

The chapter concluded with a further examination of delegates and events. Two simple and intuitive examples were presented: a stock market simulation and an online chat room.

User Interface Programming

*U*nfortunately, there is no support for working in C++ with the Forms Designer. However, you can use the Forms Designer to work in C#, and then port the resulting C# code to C++. Porting GUI C# code to C++ is an additional effort, and in most cases there is no substantial benefit in doing this. Generally, C++ will not be the most commonly chosen .NET language for developing GUIs, but rather a mixed language approach may be useful, where C# is used for the GUI and C++ is used for various reasons in other aspects of project development. Since you will probably need to implement GUI features in many of your applications, this chapter serves two purposes. First, this chapter shows how you can follow a C#– C++ blended approach. Even if you are primarily a C++ programmer, you should become reasonably familiar with C# and the Forms Designer tool so that you can take advantage of powerful programming tools not supported by C++. Second, for the rare case where porting GUI functionality from C# to C++ is appropriate, this chapter gives several GUI example pairs showing the code before and after the porting task.

A fundamental feature of modern user interaction with a computer is a graphical user interface, or GUI. In this chapter we learn how to implement a GUI using the Windows Forms classes of the .NET Framework. Practical Windows programming involves extensive use of tools and wizards that greatly streamline the process. But all this automation can obscure the fundamentals of what is going on. Hence we begin with the basics, using the .NET Framework SDK to create simple Windows applications from scratch, without use of any fancy tools. We describe the fundamentals of drawing in Windows Forms using a font and a brush. We explain the principles of event handling in Windows Forms and implement handlers for mouse events. We implement menus in Windows Forms and corresponding event handlers. Controls are introduced. At this point we switch over to using Visual Studio.NET, which makes it easy to create a starter GUI C# project, draw controls using the Forms

Designer, create menus, add event handlers, and perform other useful tasks. The resulting C# project can then be ported to C++, if desired. Dialog boxes are covered, and the listbox control is introduced.

Windows Forms Hierarchy

Windows Forms is that part of the .NET Framework that supports building traditional GUI applications on the Windows platform. Windows Forms provides a large set of classes that make it easy to create sophisticated user interfaces. These classes are available to all .NET languages.

Your application will typically have a main window implemented by deriving from the **Form** class. Figure 6–1 illustrates how your class derives from the Windows Forms hierarchy.

Simple Forms Using .NET SDK

To gain insight into the fundamentals of Windows Forms, it will be helpful to build a simple application using only the .NET Framework SDK. See the program **SimpleForm** with several progressive steps. None of these steps has a

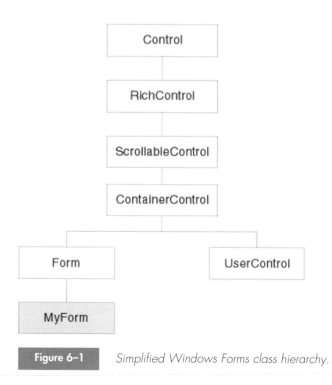

Figure 6–1   *Simplified Windows Forms class hierarchy.*

Visual Studio project. There is a simple batch file **build.bat** that you should run at the command prompt.

Step 0: A Simple Form

Here is a bare bones Windows application. It is Step 0 of the example **SimpleForm**.

```
//SimpleForm.cpp - Step 0
//This version displays a simple form

#using <mscorlib.dll>
#using <System.dll>
#using <System.Drawing.dll>
#using <System.Windows.Forms.dll>

using namespace System;
using namespace System::Windows::Forms;

__gc class Form1 : public Form
{
public:
   Form1()
   {
      Size =
          *__nogc new System::Drawing::Size(300,200);
      Text = "Simple Form - Step 0";
   }
   static void Main()
   {
      Application::Run(new Form1);
   }
};

int __stdcall WinMain(
   long hInstance,        // handle to current instance
   long hPrevInstance,    // handle to previous instance
   long lpCmdLine,        // command line
   int nCmdShow           // show state
)
{
   Form1::Main();
   return 0;
}
```

Our **Form1** class inherits from **System::Windows::Forms::Form**. The class **System::Windows::Forms::Application** has static methods, such as **Run** and **Exit**, to control an application. The **WinMain** method instantiates a new form and runs it as the main window.

Note that in the C++ examples in this chapter, we are using **WinMain** rather than **main** as the program entry point function. Although it is possible to use **main** and create all the same GUI features from within a console style application, doing so would cause a do-nothing console window to be created, which is typically not desirable in a GUI application. Using **WinMain** instead of **main** results in the program simply creating the main window immediately, without creating any console window.

The constructor of the form does initializations: The **Size** field sets the size of the new form in pixels. The **Text** field specifies the caption to be shown in the title bar of the new form.

The key to Windows Forms programming is the **Form** base class. This class contains a great deal of functionality, which is inherited by form classes that we design.

You can build the application at the command line using the batch file **build.bat**. To run the batch file, open up a DOS window and navigate to the **SimpleForm\Step0** directory and type **build**. Remember that you must have the environment variables set up properly, which you can ensure by running the Visual Studio.NET Command Prompt.

```
cl /CLR SimpleForm.cpp
```

The target is, by default, a Windows executable. There are **#using** statements in the source code that provide references to the required .NET libraries, **System.dll**, **System.Drawing.dll**, and **System.Windows.Forms.dll**.

After you have built the application using the batch file, you can run it by typing **SimpleForm** at the command line. You can also double-click on the file **SimpleForm.exe** in Windows Explorer. Figure 6–2 shows this simple application. Although trivial, this application already has a great deal of functionality, which is inherited from the **Form** base class. You can drag the window around, resize it, minimize it, maximize it, open the system menu (click in top left of the window), and so forth.

WINDOWS MESSAGES

Visual Studio.NET supplies a tool called Spy++, which can be used to "spy" on windows, gaining some inkling of things that are taking place under the hood. Spy++ can be started from the Visual Studio Tools menu. With the Step 0 version of **SimpleForm.exe** running, start Spy++. Bring up the Find Window dialog from the menu Spy | Find Window. Click on the Messages radio button. See Figure 6–3.

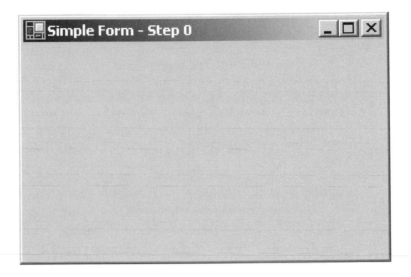

Figure 6–2   *A bare bones Windows Forms application (Step 0).*

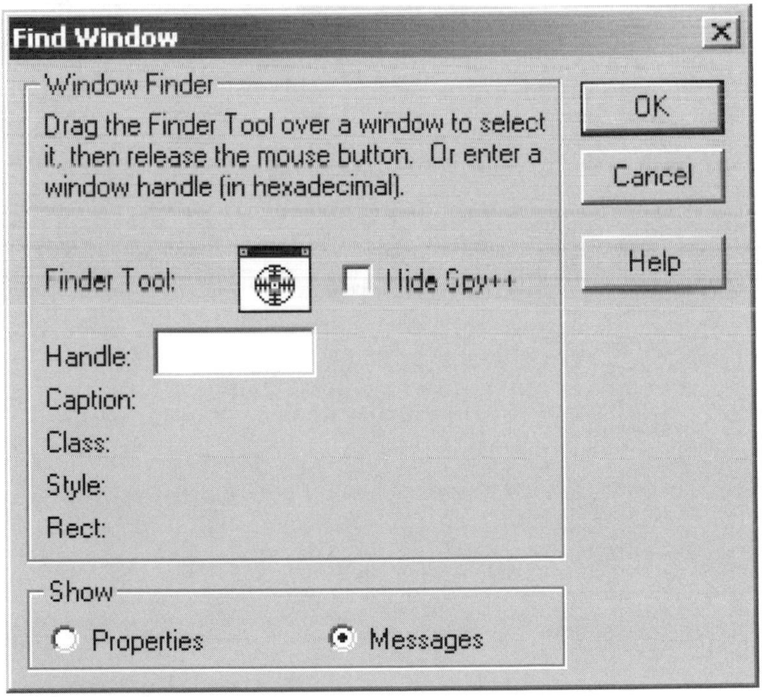

Figure 6–3   *The Finder Tool lets you select a window to spy upon.*

Using the left mouse button, drag the Finder Tool (which appears as a crosshairs icon on the Find Window dialog) over the window of the **Simple-Form** application and release the button, and then click OK. Now as you interact with the **SimpleForm** window, you will see *windows messages* displayed in a window of Spy++, as illustrated in Figure 6–4.

Windows applications are structured to handle events. The Windows operating system sends messages to applications in response to user actions such as clicking a mouse button, selecting a menu, and typing at the keyboard. A Windows application must be structured so that it can respond to such messages.

The nice thing about Windows programming using the .NET Framework classes is that you program at a much higher level of abstraction. We have already seen how simple the Step 0 application is. In the next several sections we will progressively implement some basic features, illustrating the fundamentals of GUI programming using the Windows Forms classes.

Step 1: Drawing Text on a Form

Step 1 illustrates drawing text on a form. Figure 6–5 shows a running instance of the application.

Performing output in Windows programs is very different from doing output in console applications, where we simply use methods such as **Console::WriteLine**. Drawing output in a window is referred to as *painting*. Painting is done in response to a special kind of message, a "paint" message: WM_PAINT. This on-demand style of painting ensures that the output of a

```
Messages (Window 000E020C)                                          _ □ ×
<26897> 000E020C R WM_NCHITTEST nHittest:HTCLIENT
<26898> 000E020C S WM_NCHITTEST xPos:214 yPos:121
<26899> 000E020C R WM_NCHITTEST nHittest:HTCLIENT
<26900> 000E020C S WM_SETCURSOR hwnd:000E020C nHittest:HTCLIENT wMouseMsg:WM_MOUSEMOVE
<26901> 000E020C R WM_SETCURSOR fHaltProcessing:0
<26902> 000E020C P WM_MOUSEMOVE fwKeys:0000 xPos:186 yPos:76
<26903> 000E020C S WM_NCHITTEST xPos:234 yPos:121
<26904> 000E020C R WM_NCHITTEST nHittest:HTCLIENT
<26905> 000E020C S WM_NCHITTEST xPos:234 yPos:121
<26906> 000E020C R WM_NCHITTEST nHittest:HTCLIENT
<26907> 000E020C S WM_SETCURSOR hwnd:000E020C nHittest:HTCLIENT wMouseMsg:WM_MOUSEMOVE
<26908> 000E020C R WM_SETCURSOR fHaltProcessing:0
<26909> 000E020C P WM_MOUSEMOVE fwKeys:0000 xPos:206 yPos:76
<26910> 000E020C S WM_NCHITTEST xPos:256 yPos:121
<26911> 000E020C R WM_NCHITTEST nHittest:HTCLIENT
<26912> 000E020C S WM_NCHITTEST xPos:256 yPos:121
<26913> 000E020C R WM_NCHITTEST nHittest:HTCLIENT
<26914> 000E020C S WM_SETCURSOR hwnd:000E020C nHittest:HTCLIENT wMouseMsg:WM_MOUSEMOVE
<26915> 000E020C R WM_SETCURSOR fHaltProcessing:0
<26916> 000E020C P WM_MOUSEMOVE fwKeys:0000 xPos:228 yPos:76
<26917> 000E020C P WM_MOUSELEAVE
```

Figure 6–4   *The Spy Message Window.*

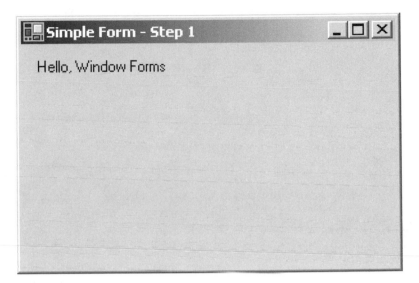

Figure 6–5   *Drawing text on a simple form (Step 1).*

window will still be shown correctly if the window is covered up and uncovered again.

Another difference in output in Windows programs is that you have to specify details, such as the coordinates where it is drawn, a "brush" to draw with, a font for text, and so forth. Here is the code for Step 1.

```cpp
//SimpleForm.cpp - Step 1
//This version displays a greeting

#using <mscorlib.dll>
#using <System.dll>
#using <System.Drawing.dll>
#using <System.Windows.Forms.dll>

using namespace System;
using namespace System::Windows::Forms;
using namespace System::Drawing;

__gc class Form1 : public Form
{
private:
    float x, y;
    Brush *pStdBrush;
public:
```

```
      Form1()
      {
         Size =
            *__nogc new System::Drawing::Size(300,200);
         Text = "Simple Form - Step 1";
         x = y = 10;
         pStdBrush = new SolidBrush(Color::Black);
      }
   protected:
      virtual void OnPaint(PaintEventArgs * ppea)
      {
         ppea->get_Graphics()->Graphics::DrawString
            ("Hello, Window Forms", Font,
            pStdBrush, x, y);
      }
   public:
      static void Main()
      {
         Application::Run(new Form1);
      }
   };

   int __stdcall WinMain(
     long hInstance,        // handle to current instance
     long hPrevInstance,    // handle to previous instance
     long lpCmdLine,        // command line
     int nCmdShow           // show state
   )
   {
      Form1::Main();
      return 0;
   }
```

To draw in Windows Forms, you must override the virtual method **OnPaint**. The class **PaintEventArgs** has a **Graphics** object as a read-only property. The **Graphics** class, part of the **System::Drawing** namespace, has methods for drawing.

The **DrawString** method has parameters for

- The string to be drawn
- The font (**Font** is a property of **Form** that gives the default font for the form)
- The brush to be used
- The pixel coordinates (as **float** numbers)

A black **SolidBrush** is constructed as our standard brush.

Windows Forms Event Handling

GUI applications are event-driven: The application executes code in response to user events, such as clicking the mouse or choosing a menu item. Each form or control has a predefined set of events. For example, every form has a **MouseDown** event.

Windows Forms uses the .NET event model,[1] which uses delegates to bind events to the methods that handle them. The Windows Forms classes use multicast delegates. A multicast delegate maintains a list of the methods it is bound to. When an event occurs in an application, the control raises the event by calling the delegate for that event. The delegate then calls all the methods it is bound to.

The overloaded += C++ operator is provided for adding a delegate to an event. The following code adds the **Form1_MouseDown** method to the **MouseDown** event.

```
MouseDown += new MouseEventHandler
   (this, Form1_MouseDown);
```

We will see this code in context shortly.

Events Documentation

You can find all the events associated with a class in the .NET Framework Reference. The screenshot in Figure 6–6 shows the predefined events associated with the **Form** class.

MouseDown Event

One of the predefined events in the **Control** class, from which the **Form** class derives, is **MouseDown**.

```
public: __event MouseEventHandler* MouseDown;
```

Here is the declaration of **MouseEventHandler**:

```
public __gc __delegate void MouseEventHandler(
   Object* sender,
   MouseEventArgs* e
);
```

---

[1] You may wish to review the discussion of delegates and events in Chapter 5.

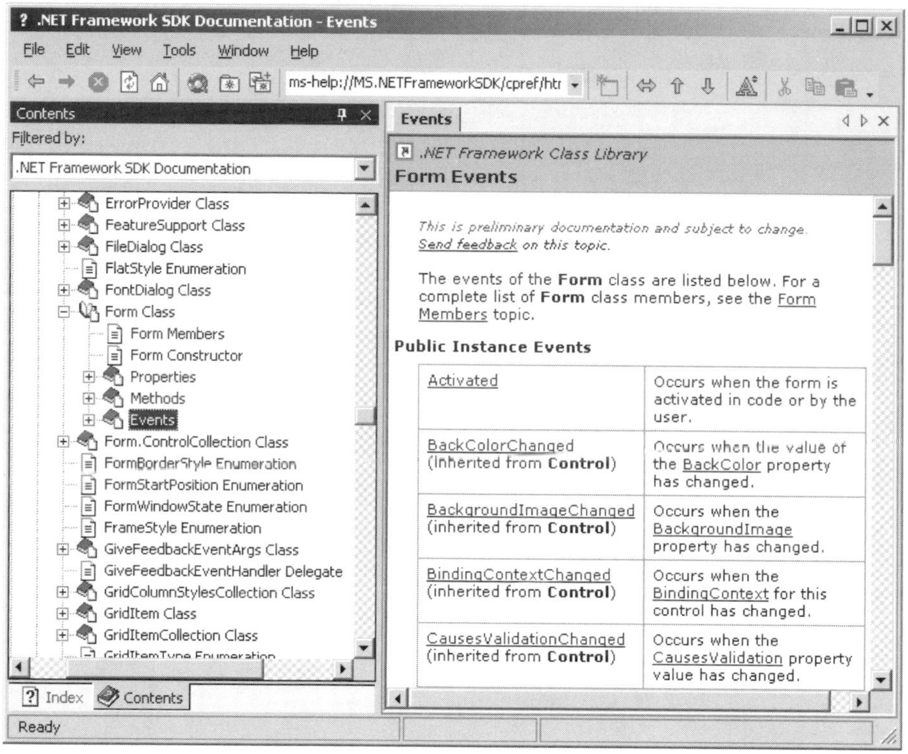

Figure 6–6   *Documentation of events in the **Form** class.*

The event handler receives a **MouseEventArgs** (derived from **EventArgs**), which has read-only properties to provide information specific to this event:

- **Button** specifies which button (left, right, etc.) was pressed.
- **Clicks** indicates how many times the button was pressed and released.
- **Delta** provides a count of rotations of a mouse wheel.
- **X** and **Y** provide the coordinates where the mouse button was pressed.

Step 2: Handling a Mouse Event

In Step 2 a mouse-click (any button) will reposition the location of the greeting string. Figure 6–7 shows the string relocated after we have clicked the mouse.

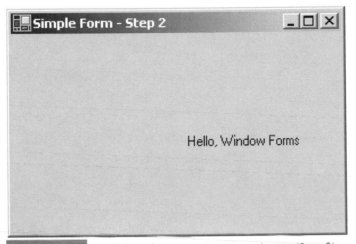

| Figure 6-7 | *Clicking the mouse repositions the text (Step 2).* |

```cpp
//SimpleForm.cpp - Step 2
//This version displays a greeting, which can be relocated
//by clicking a mouse button

#using <mscorlib.dll>
#using <System.dll>
#using <System.Drawing.dll>
#using <System.Windows.Forms.dll>

using namespace System;
using namespace System::Windows::Forms;
using namespace System::Drawing;

__gc class Form1 : public Form
{
private:
   void InitializeComponent()
   {
      MouseDown += new MouseEventHandler
         (this, Form1_MouseDown);
   }
   float x, y;
   Brush *pStdBrush;
public:
   Form1()
   {
      InitializeComponent();
```

```
        Size =
            *__nogc new System::Drawing::Size(300,200);
        Text = "Simple Form - Step 2";
        x = y = 10;
        pStdBrush = new SolidBrush(Color::Black);
    }
protected:
    void Form1_MouseDown
        (Object *pSender, MouseEventArgs *pmea)
    {
        x = pmea->X;
        y = pmea->Y;
        Invalidate();
    }
    ...
```

As part of its initialization, our program registers the **Form1_MouseDown** method with the **MouseDown** event. This method sets the **x** and **y** coordinates of our text to the location where the mouse was clicked. To understand the role of **Invalidate**, comment out the code and build again. Click the mouse to relocate the greeting string. What happens? The string is not relocated. Now cover the **SimpleForm** window with some other window and then uncover it. Now you should see the string relocated.

The **Invalidate** method is defined in the **Control** base class. There are several overloaded versions of this method. They each invalidate some region of the control and cause a paint message to be sent to the control. The method with no parameters causes the entire control to be invalidated. To minimize the amount of redrawing that is done, a more sophisticated application might invalidate just a rectangle.

Step 2M: Multiple Event Handlers

Code Example

Step 2M illustrates tying two different event handlers to the **MouseDown** event. The second handler merely displays a message box.[2]

```
//SimpleForm.cpp - Step 2M
//This version has two MouseDown event handlers
...
__gc class Form1 : public Form
{
private:
    void InitializeComponent()
```

---

[2] A message box is a special kind of dialog box and will be discussed later in this chapter.

```
    {
        MouseDown += new MouseEventHandler
            (this, Form1_MouseDown);
        MouseDown += new MouseEventHandler
            (this, ShowClick);
    }
...
    void Form1_MouseDown
        (Object *pSender, MouseEventArgs *pmea)
    {
        x = pmea->X;
        y = pmea->Y;
        Invalidate();
    }
    void ShowClick
        (Object *pSender, MouseEventArgs *pmea)
    {
        MessageBox::Show("Mouse clicked!!!");
    }
    ...
```

Step 3: MouseDown and KeyPress Events

Step 3 of our demonstration illustrates handling an additional event, **Key-Press**, and also distinguishing between left and right buttons in **Mouse-Down**.

HANDLING LEFT AND RIGHT BUTTONS

We can distinguish between left and right buttons by using the **Button** property of the **MouseEventArgs** parameter. Right button down is used for clearing the message string, which is now stored in a **StringBuilder** data member **str**.

```
    void Form1_MouseDown
        (Object *pSender, MouseEventArgs *pmea)
    {
        if (pmea->Button == MouseButtons::Left)
        {
            x = pmea->X;
            y = pmea->Y;
        }
        else if (pmea->Button == MouseButtons::Right)
        {
            pStr = new StringBuilder();
```

```
    }
    Invalidate();
}
```

KEYPRESS EVENT

Step 3 also illustrates handling a **KeyPress** event. Every time the user presses a key, the corresponding character is appended to the greeting string. Note use of the **StringBuilder** class, which is more efficient to use in this context than **String**. **String** is immutable, and hence **String** objects would be continually created and destroyed while we append characters.

```
StringBuilder *pStr;
...
    void Form1_KeyPress
        (Object *pSender, KeyPressEventArgs *pmea)
    {
        pStr->Append(pmea->KeyChar);
        Invalidate();
    }
```

As with Step 2 we call **Invalidate** to force a repaint after we have made a change in the data to be displayed. Figure 6–8 illustrates our **SimpleForm** window after the starting text has been cleared and some new text typed in.

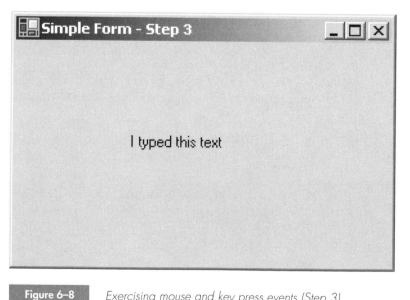

Figure 6–8   *Exercising mouse and key press events (Step 3).*

Menus

As a user of Windows applications, you should be acquainted with menus, which provide a simple mechanism for choosing commands. In .NET menus are implemented in code. There is no separate resource file.

Step 4: A Menu to Exit the Program

Step 4 of our **SimpleForm** program illustrates adding a simple menu. File | Exit is used to exit the program. See Figure 6–9.

| Figure 6–9 | A File | Exit menu is added to our form (Step 4). |

Menu Code

```
//SimpleForm.cpp - Step 4
...
__gc class Form1 : public Form
{
private:
   void InitializeComponent()
   {
      pMainMenu1 = new MainMenu ();
      pMenuFile = new MenuItem ();
      pMenuExit = new MenuItem ();
```

```
      // mainMenu1
      MenuItem* pMainMenu1Items[] = {pMenuFile};
      pMainMenu1->get_MenuItems()
         ->AddRange(pMainMenu1Items);
      // menuFile
      pMenuFile->set_Index(0);
      MenuItem* pMainFileItems[] = {pMenuExit};
      pMenuFile->get_MenuItems()
         ->AddRange(pMainFileItems);
      pMenuFile->set_Text("File");
      // menuExit
      pMenuExit->set_Index(0);
      pMenuExit->set_Text("Exit");
      pMenuExit->Click += new System::EventHandler
         (this, MenuExit Click);

      Menu = pMainMenu1;

      MouseDown += new MouseEventHandler
         (this, Form1_MouseDown);
      KeyPress += new KeyPressEventHandler
         (this, Form1_KeyPress);
   }
   float x, y;
   Brush *pStdBrush;
   StringBuilder *pStr;
   MenuItem *pMenuExit;
   MenuItem *pMenuFile;
   MainMenu *pMainMenu1;
public:
   ...
private:
   void MenuExit_Click(
      Object *pSender, EventArgs *pea)
   {
      Application::Exit();
   }
   ...
```

The code in **InitializeComponent** builds up the hierarchical menu structure, represented by an instance of the **MainMenu** class. A menu is composed of **MenuItem** objects that represent the individual menu commands in the menu structure. Each **MenuItem** can be a command for your application or a parent menu for other submenu items. You bind the **MainMenu** to the

Form that will display it by assigning the **MainMenu** to the **Menu** property of the Form.

When we discuss the Forms Designer later in the chapter, we will see that it is easy to create a menu by dragging a **MainMenu** control from the toolbox to the form. The Forms Designer will take care of generating appropriate boilerplate code.

Menu Event Code

A delegate is hooked to the event, as with other Windows Forms events. Clicking on a menu item causes the corresponding command to be executed.

```
void InitializeComponent()
{
...
    pMenuExit->Click += new System::EventHandler
        (this, MenuExit_Click);
...
}

void MenuExit_Click(
    Object *pSender, EventArgs *pea)
{
    Application::Exit();
}
...
```

Controls

In the program we have just discussed, **pMainMenu1** is an example of a *control*. It is a pointer to an instance of the **MainMenu** class. A control is an object that is contained within a form and is used to add functionality to the form. A control can perform many tasks automatically on behalf of its parent form. It simplifies programming, as you do not have to be concerned with painting, invalidating, working with graphics elements, and so forth. The simple menu that we just illustrated would have required a substantial amount of code if we had to implement it from scratch. Controls provide rich, reusable code, a big benefit from programming with objects.

Step 5: Using a TextBox Control

Code Example

Step 5 of our **SimpleForm** application illustrates using a **TextBox** control to display our greeting text. As with earlier versions of the application, you can reposition the greeting by clicking the left mouse button, and you can clear the greeting by clicking the right mouse button. You can also type in your own greeting text. Now you have full editing capability. You can insert characters wherever you wish in the control, cut and paste (Ctrl+X and Ctrl+V), and so forth. All of this editing capability is provided by the **TextBox** control. Figure 6–10 illustrates the application after the greeting has been repositioned and we have typed in some text of our own.

Here is the new version of our program. Note that it is both simpler and has more functionality. We no longer need member variables for the coordinates or text of the greeting string (this information is now stored in the **TextBox** control **pTxtGreeting)**. We also do not need **OnPaint** any longer, because the text box knows how to paint itself. We can then also get rid of the brush. We don't need to handle **KeyPress** events, because this functionality is handled (in a much more full-blown way) by the **TextBox** control.

Figure 6–10   *The greeting text is now displayed using a control (Step 4).*

```
//SimpleForm.cpp - Step 5
...
__gc class Form1 : public Form
{
private:
    void InitializeComponent()
    {
    ...
        // text greeting
        pTxtGreeting = new TextBox;
```

```
        pTxtGreeting->Location =
            * __nogc new Point(10, 10);
        pTxtGreeting->Size =
            (*__nogc new struct Size(150, 20));
        pTxtGreeting->Text = "Hello, Windows Forms";

        Controls->Add(pTxtGreeting);
    ...
    }
    float x, y;
    Brush *pStdBrush;
    MenuItem *pMenuExit;
    MenuItem *pMenuFile;
    MainMenu *pMainMenu1;
    TextBox *pTxtGreeting;
    ...
protected:
    void Form1_MouseDown
        (Object *pSender, MouseEventArgs *pmea)
    {
        if (pmea->Button == MouseButtons::Left)
        {
            pTxtGreeting->Location =
                * __nogc new Point(pmea->X, pmea->Y);
        }
        else if (pmea->Button == MouseButtons::Right)
        {
            pTxtGreeting->Text = "";
        }
    }
    ...
};
```

Using the **TextBox** control is very easy. As part of the initialization, we instantiate it and assign the **Location**, **Size**, and **Text** properties. We add our new control to the **Controls** collection of our form. In the mouse event handler we reposition the control by assigning the **Location** property. We clear the text by assigning the **Text** property.

Visual Studio.NET and Forms

Although it is perfectly feasible to create Windows Forms applications using only the command-line tools of the .NET Framework SDK, in practice it is much easier to use Visual Studio.NET. Unfortunately, Visual Studio.NET does not provide any tools for generating a Form-based managed C++ starter project, and it does not support a managed C++ Forms Designer tool. You can get started by creating a Windows Application project in C#, which provides starter code and sets up references to the required .NET libraries. You can then use the Forms Designer to drag and drop controls from a toolbox onto your forms. The Forms Designer inserts the needed C# boilerplate code to make your controls work within your forms. There is a Properties window, which makes it easy to set properties of your controls at design time. You can of course also set properties at runtime, which is what we did with our **pTxt-Greeting** text box in the code shown previously. Once you have finished this, you can port it to managed C++, however, this is not usually recommended.

Windows Forms Demonstration

The best way to become acquainted with using Visual Studio.NET to create Windows applications is to build a small C# application from scratch. Our demonstration creates a Windows application to make deposits and withdrawals from a bank account.

1. Create a new C# project **BankGui** of type Windows Application. See Figure 6–11.

Creating a new Windows Application project.

2. Open up the Toolbox by dragging the mouse over the vertical Toolbox tab on the left side of the main Visual Studio window. If the Toolbox tab does not show, you can open it from the menu View | Toolbox. You can make the Toolbox stay open by clicking on the "push-pin" next to the X on the title bar of the Toolbox. (The little yellow box will say "Auto Hide" when you pause the mouse over the push-pin.)

3. From the Toolbox, drag two labels, two textboxes, and two buttons to the form. See Figure 6–12.

4. Click on **label1** in the Forms Designer. This will select that control in the Properties window, just beneath the Solution Explorer. You can use the Properties window to make changes to properties of controls. Change the Text property to **Amount**. After you type the desired value, hit the carriage return. You will then see the new text shown on the form. Figure 6–13 shows the Properties window after you have changed the Text property of the first label.

5. Similarly, change the text of **label2** to **Balance**.

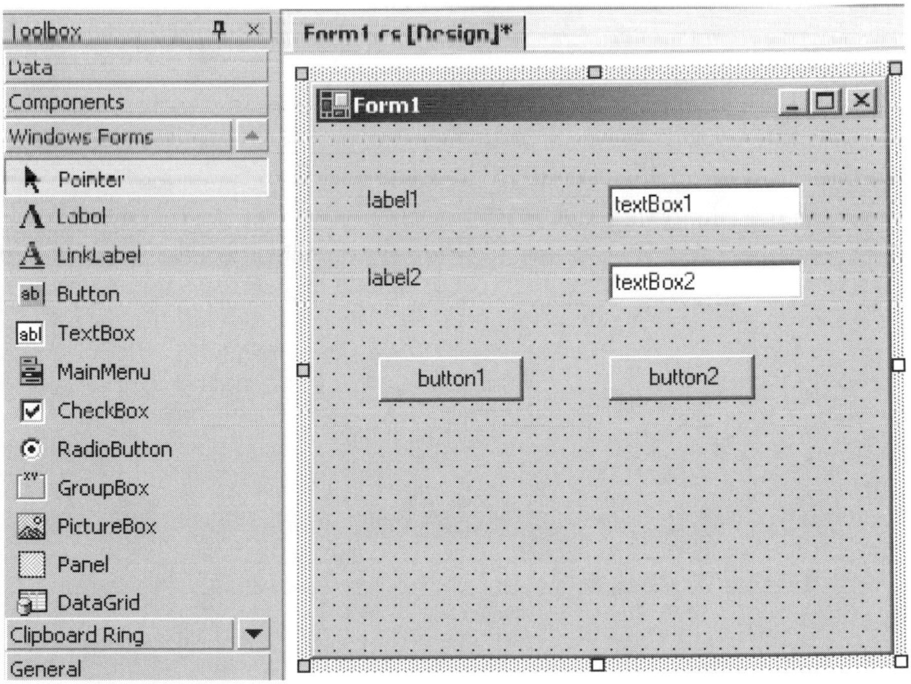

Figure 6–12   *Dragging controls from the Toolbox onto a form.*

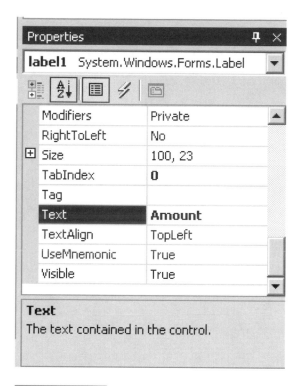

Figure 6–13   *Changing property values in the Properties window.*

6. Enter property values for the textboxes and buttons, as shown in Table 6–1.
7. Resize the form by dragging the sizing handles on the middle of each side. Reposition the controls as desired by dragging with the mouse, and resize the controls with the mouse, if you wish. When you are satisfied with the appearance of your form, save the project. Your form should now look similar to Figure 6–14.

Table 6–1 Property Values for Textboxes and Buttons

Name	Text
txtAmount	(blank)
txtBalance	(blank)
cmdDeposit	Deposit
cmdWithdraw	Withdraw

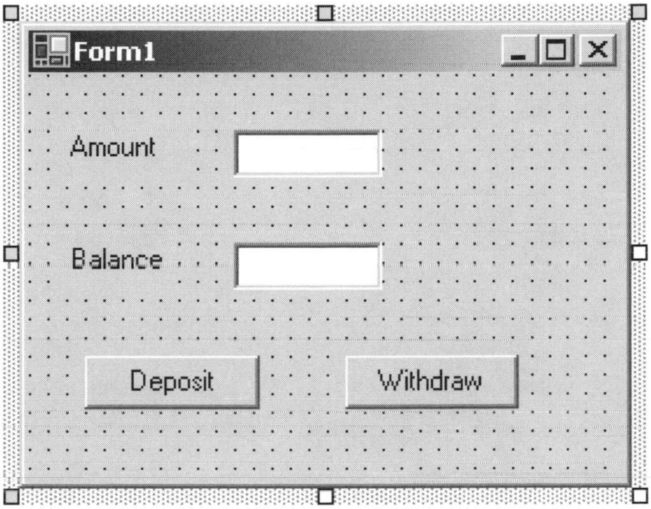

Figure 6–14   *Form for BankGui application.*

8. Add event handlers for the buttons by double-clicking on each button.

9. Add the boldfaced code to the code generated by the wizard:

```
public class Form1 : System.Windows.Forms.Form
{
...
   public Form1()
   {
      //
      // Required for Windows Form Designer support
      //
      InitializeComponent();

      //
      // TODO: Add any constructor code after
      // InitializeComponent call
      //
      txtAmount.Text = "25";
      txtBalance.Text = "100";
   }
   ...
   /// <summary>
   /// The main entry point for the application.
   /// </summary>
```

```csharp
[STAThread]
static void Main()
{
   Application.Run(new Form1());
}

private void cmdDeposit_Click(object sender,
                             System.EventArgs e)
{
   int amount = Convert.ToInt32(txtAmount.Text);
   int balance = Convert.ToInt32(txtBalance.Text);
   balance += amount;
   txtBalance.Text = Convert.ToString(balance);
}

private void cmdWithdraw_Click(object sender,
                              System.EventArgs e)
{
   int amount = Convert.ToInt32(txtAmount.Text);
   int balance = Convert.ToInt32(txtBalance.Text);
   balance -= amount;
   txtBalance.Text = Convert.ToString(balance);
}
```

10. Build and run the application. It should behave like a standard Windows application. You should be able to make deposits and withdrawals. Figure 6–15 illustrates the running application.

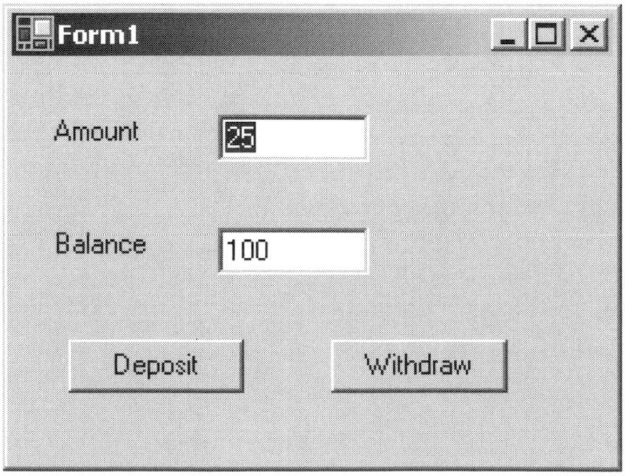

Figure 6–15 *The BankGui Windows application.*

The project is currently implemented in C#. Even though you will usually not choose to do so, we will now port it to C++, just to see how it is done. To proceed with this, create a new C++ project named **BankGuiPort** using the Managed C++ Empty Project template.

Create a source file named Form1.cpp in the **BankGuiPort** project, and copy/paste the C# code from the Form1.cs source file in the **BankGui** project.

Port each line of code from C# to C++ in the Form1.cpp file of the **BankGuiPort** project. There are many issues and situations that you must become familiar with in order to perform such a porting operation, which are not described in detail here. However, you can try opening up the provided solutions for the **BankGui** C# project and the **BankGuiPort** C++ project in two simultaneous instances of Visual Studio .NET, and compare the Form1.cs and Form1.cpp source files visually to get an idea of the many details involved.

Code Example

```
//Form1.cpp

#using <mscorlib.dll>
#using <System.dll>
#using <System.Drawing.dll>
#using <System.Windows.Forms.dll>

using namespace System;

namespace BankGui
{
__gc class Form1 : public System::Windows::Forms::Form
{
private:
    System::Windows::Forms::Label *label1;
    System::Windows::Forms::Label *label2;
    System::Windows::Forms::TextBox *txtAmount;
    System::Windows::Forms::TextBox *txtBalance;
    System::Windows::Forms::Button *cmdDeposit;
    System::Windows::Forms::Button *cmdWithdraw;
    System::ComponentModel::Container *components;
public:
    Form1()
    {
        components = 0;
        InitializeComponent();
        txtAmount->Text = "25";
        txtBalance->Text = "100";
    }
    ...
```

```cpp
private:
    void InitializeComponent()
    {
        cmdWithdraw = new System::Windows::Forms::Button;
        cmdDeposit = new System::Windows::Forms::Button;
        txtBalance = new System::Windows::Forms::TextBox;
        txtAmount = new System::Windows::Forms::TextBox;
        label1 = new System::Windows::Forms::Label;
        label2 = new System::Windows::Forms::Label;
        SuspendLayout();
        //
        // cmdWithdraw
        //
        cmdWithdraw->Location =
            *   nogc new System::Drawing::Point(152, 144);
        cmdWithdraw->Name = "cmdWithdraw";
        cmdWithdraw->TabIndex = 2;
        cmdWithdraw->Text = "Withdraw";
        cmdWithdraw->Click +=
            new System::EventHandler(this, cmdWithdraw_Click);
        ...
        //
        // Form1
        //
        AutoScaleBaseSize =
            * __nogc new System::Drawing::Size(5, 13);
        ClientSize =
            * __nogc new System::Drawing::Size(280, 189);
        System::Windows::Forms::Control* pItems[] = {
            cmdDeposit,
            txtAmount,
            label1,
            label2,
            txtBalance,
            cmdWithdraw};
        Controls->AddRange(pItems);
        Name = "Form1";
        Text = "Form1";
        Load += new System::EventHandler(this, Form1_Load);
        ResumeLayout(false);
    }
    void Form1_Load(
        Object *sender, System::EventArgs *e)
    {
```

```
    }
    ...
    void cmdWithdraw_Click(
        Object *sender, System::EventArgs *e)
    {
        int amount = Convert::ToInt32(txtAmount->Text);
        int balance = Convert::ToInt32(txtBalance->Text);
        balance -= amount;
        txtBalance->Text = Convert::ToString(balance);
    }
    ...
public:
    [STAThread]
    static void Main()
    {
        System::Windows::Forms::Application::Run(new Form1);
    }
};
}
...
```

Design Window and Code Window

The most important thing to understand about navigating Windows Forms projects in Visual Studio is switching between the Design window, where you work with controls on a form, and the Code window, where you work with source code. We can illustrate these two windows from the **VsForm** C# project, where we have provided starter code corresponding to **VsForm\Step1** in the main directory for this chapter. The ported C++ version of this project is provided in **VsFormPort\Step1**. This first version is a starter project that simply displays a fixed greeting string. The state of the project at various points in the demonstration is captured in subsequent numbered steps, and in each case, the Form Designer-friendly C# version is under the **VsForm** directory, and the ported C++ version is in the **VsFormPort** directory.

If you double-click on **Form1.cs** in the Solution Explorer in the **VsForm\Step1** project, you will bring up the Design window, as shown in Figure 6–16.

To bring up the Code window, click on the View Code ▦ toolbar button in the Solution Explorer. This will open up the source code, and you will see horizontal tabs at the top of the principal window area, allowing you to select among the open windows. Now the Design window and the Code window for this one form are open. You may also go back to the Design window by clicking on the View Designer ▦ toolbar button. Figure 6–17 shows the open Code window.

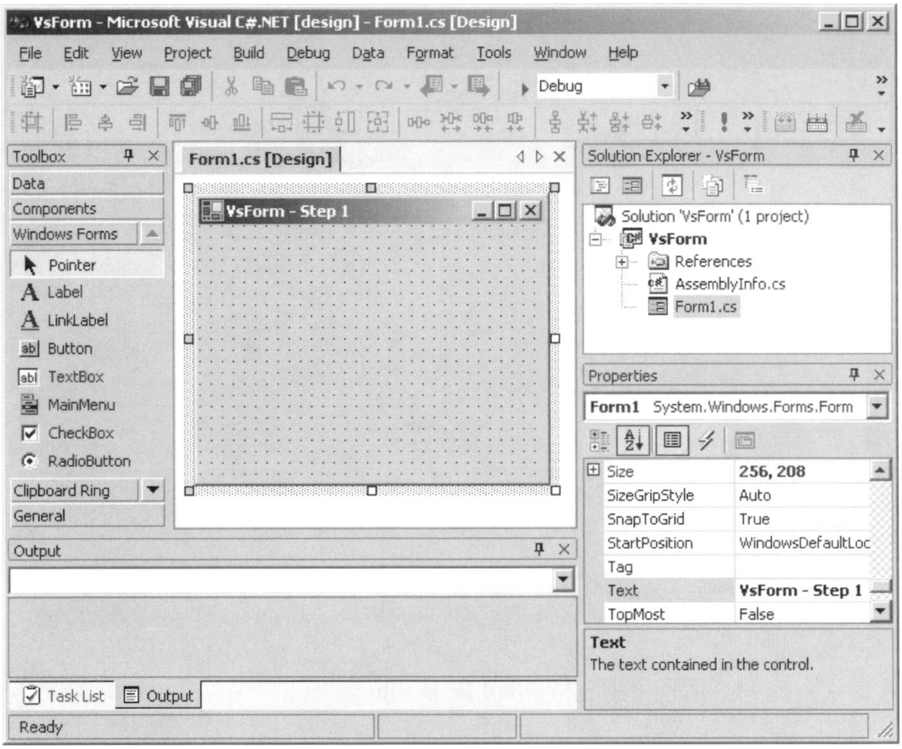

Figure 6–16 *The Design window in a Windows Forms project.*

Adding an Event

1. Build and run both the C# and C++ starter programs in **VsForm\ Step1 and VsFormPort\Step1** and verify that they behave identically. These are completely static applications—they merely display a greeting at a fixed location.

2. Open up the Design window of the form in the C# project in **VsForm\Step1** and click on the Events button ⚡ of the Properties window.

3. Find the **MouseDown** event. See Figure 6–18.

4. Double-click the **MouseDown** event in the Properties window. This will automatically generate code to register a delegate for the event and provide a skeleton for a method tied to the delegate.

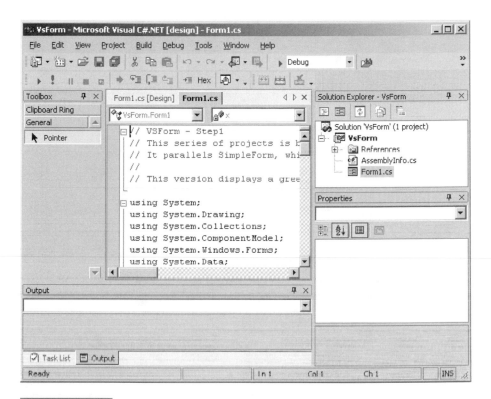

Figure 6-17   *The Code window in a Windows Forms project.*

```
private void InitializeComponent()
{
...
  this.MouseDown +=
    new System.WinForms.MouseEventHandler
        (this.Form1_MouseDown);
}
...

protected void Form1_MouseDown (object sender,
    System.WinForms.MouseEventArgs e)
{

}
...
```

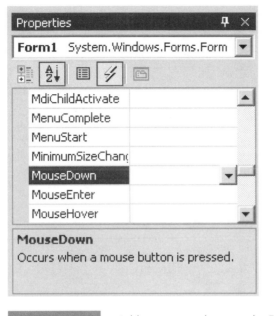

| Figure 6–18 | *Adding an event by using the Events button.* |

Code for Event Handler

1. Add the highlighted code to the mouse-down event handler to set the coordinates of the greeting message. Don't forget to call **Invalidate**!

```
protected void Form1_MouseDown (object sender,
    System.WinForms.MouseEventArgs e)
{
    x = e.X;
    y = e.Y;
    Invalidate();
}
```

2. Build and run. You should now be able to relocate the greeting by clicking the mouse button (either button will work). The project now corresponds to **VsForm\Step2**.

Rather than porting each line of code from C# to C++ in the Form1.cpp file of the **VsForm\Step2** project, just copy the existing project **VsFormPort\Step1** that has already been ported. Then just port the few lines of code that relate to the **MouseDown** event from **VsForm\Step2**.

```
    void InitializeComponent()
    {
```

```
...
MouseDown +=
    new System::Windows::Forms::MouseEventHandler
        (this, Form1_MouseDown);
}

...

void Form1_MouseDown (Object *sender,
    System::Windows::Forms::MouseEventArgs *e)
{
    x = (float)e->X;
    y = (float)e->Y;
    Invalidate();
}
```

Using the Menu Control

3. Open up the Toolbox if not already open (click on the Toolbox vertical tab) and drag the **MainMenu** control 🖳 MainMenu onto the form.

4 Type **File** and **Exit**, creating a popup menu File with a menu item Exit. See Figure 6-19.

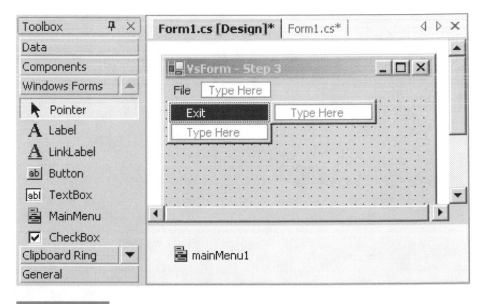

Figure 6–19   *Use the Menu Control to add a menu to a form.*

5. In the Properties window change the names of your two menu items to *menuFile* and *menuExit*.
6. Double-click on Exit to add code for a File | Exit event handler.
7. Add code to the handler to exit the application.

```
protected void menuExit_Click (object sender,
 System.EventArgs e)
{
   Application.Exit();
}
```

8. Build and run. Your menu should now be operational. The project now corresponds to **VsForm\Step3**.

Again, rather than porting each line of code from C# to C++ in the **Form1.cpp** file of the **VsForm\Step3** project, just copy the existing project **VsFormPort\Step2** that has already been ported. Then just port the few lines of code that relate to the new menu functionality from **VsForm\Step3**.

```
// VSForm - Step3
...
__gc class Form1 : public System::Windows::Forms::Form
{
private:
   float x, y;
   Brush *pStdBrush;
   System::Windows::Forms::MainMenu *mainMenu1;
   System::Windows::Forms::MenuItem *menuFile;
   System::Windows::Forms::MenuItem *menuExit;
   ...
private:
   void InitializeComponent()
   {
     menuFile =
       new System::Windows::Forms::MenuItem();
     menuExit =
       new System::Windows::Forms::MenuItem();
     mainMenu1 =
         new System::Windows::Forms::MainMenu();
     //
     // menuFile
     //
     menuFile->Index = 0;
     System::Windows::Forms::MenuItem *pItems[] =
       {menuExit};
```

```
    menuFile->MenuItems->AddRange(pItems);
    menuFile->Text = "File";
    //
    // menuExit
    //
    menuExit->Index = 0;
    menuExit->Text = "Exit";
    menuExit->Click +=
        new System::EventHandler
          (this, menuExit_Click);
    //
    // mainMenu1
    //
    System::Windows::Forms::MenuItem *pMenus[] =
        {menuFile};
    mainMenu1->MenuItems->AddRange(pMenus);
    //
    // Form1
    //
    AutoScaleBaseSize =
        * __nogc new System::Drawing::Size(5, 13);
    ClientSize =
        * __nogc new System::Drawing::Size(248, 181);
    Menu = mainMenu1;

    ...

    }
  ...
private:
  ...
  void menuExit_Click(
    Object *sender, System::EventArgs *pe)
  {
    Application::Exit();
  }
};
...
```

Closing a Form

As an interesting modification to our program, let us arrange it so that whenever the user attempts to close the application, the user will be queried on whether to really close. There are several ways a window can be closed:

- From the "X" at top right of the window
- From the system menu at the top left of the window

- By the keyboard Alt + F4
- In our application, by File | Exit

When a form is about to close, the **Closing** event is raised. You may stop the closing by setting the **Cancel** property in the handler for this event. (First add a handler for the event **Closing** in the usual way.) Just type in the **MessageBox** code as shown.

```
protected void Form1_Closing (object sender,
   System.ComponentModel.CancelEventArgs e)
{
   DialogResult status = MessageBox.Show(
      "Do you want to close",
      "Simple Form (VS)", MessageBoxButtons.YesNo);
   if (status == DialogResult.No)
   {
      e.Cancel = true;
   }
}
```

To tap into this behavior, in your handler for File | Exit you should not exit the application but instead close the main window by calling the **Close** method:

```
protected void menuExit_Click (object sender,
     System.EventArgs e)
{
   //Application.Exit();
   Close();
}
```

The project now corresponds to **VSForm\Step4**. Run your program and try closing in various ways. You should always see the dialog box shown in Figure 6–20.

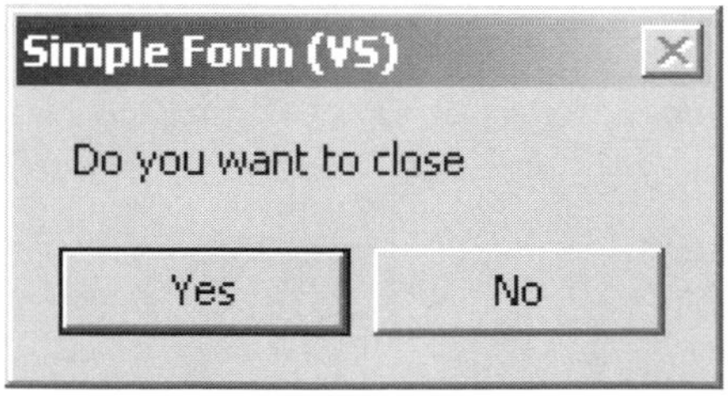

Figure 6–20   *Dialog box that queries the user whether or not to close.*

Finally, port the C# project to C++ in the usual way to **VSFormPort4**. Then build and run the C++ program. You should see that it behaves the same way as the C# program.

```
// VSForm - Step4
...
__gc class Form1 : public System::Windows::Forms::Form
{
...
private:
   void InitializeComponent()
   {
   ...
      Closing +=
         new CancelEventHandler(this, Form1_Closing);
   }
   ...
   void menuExit_Click(
      Object *sender, System::EventArgs *pe)
   {
      //Application::Exit();
      Close();
   }
   void Form1_Closing(
      Object *sender, CancelEventArgs *e)
   {
      int status = MessageBox::Show(
         "Do you want to close",
         "Simple Form (VS)",
         MessageBoxButtons::YesNo);
      if (status == DialogResult::No)
      {
         e->Cancel = true;
      }
   }
};
...
```

All Remaining Examples in this Chapter are C# Only!

For the remainder of this chapter, only C# code is discussed, since even a project that is written primarily in C++ will typical opt for C# code when implementing GUI features. This is due to the lack of Forms Designer support for C++. However, keep in mind that you may develop the GUI in C# initially, and then port that code to C++ if you choose to do so. The code examples in this chapter up to this point have demonstrated how to do this.

Dialog Boxes

Dialog boxes provide a more elaborate way for a user to interact with a Windows application. A dialog box can provide a number of controls to facilitate data input. The code in the previous section illustrated use of a simple message box dialog that allowed the user to answer a yes or no question. This kind of dialog can be created using the **MessageBox** class. You can implement more general dialog boxes by creating forms for them.

We will illustrate a number of dialogs through a GUI to our Acme Travel Agency case study. As usual, the case study code is in the **CaseStudy** folder for this chapter. Let's begin by examining a simple dialog that is used for adding a new hotel to our list of hotels. Build and run the case study. In the main form click the Add... button.[3] The New Hotel dialog is brought up, as illustrated in Figure 6–21.

The user can now enter data. Clicking the OK button will cause the information to be accepted. Clicking the Cancel button will cause the new

| **Figure 6–21** | *Dialog box for adding a new hotel.* |

---

[3] The three dots are a Windows UI style that indicates the action will not be carried out immediately but will prompt the user for additional input, typically through a dialog box.

data to be ignored. This dialog box (like the message box in the previous section) is a *modal* dialog, which means that the user cannot work elsewhere in the application until the dialog is closed. If you try to do something else on the main form while the New Hotel dialog is open—for example, click another button—you will hear a beep. The other kind of dialog is *modeless*, which will allow the user to work elsewhere in the application while the dialog is open.

Dialog boxes normally have special characteristics as forms. For example, they typically do not have a system menu, they have no minimize or maximize buttons, and they have a border that does not permit them to be resized. You can examine these features with the New Hotel dialog.

Continuing the demonstration, enter some data for a new hotel and click OK. You will now be brought back to the main form, and your new hotel will be shown in the list of hotels, as illustrated in Figure 6–22. The main form also illustrates some additional GUI features, such as a listbox for displaying a list of hotels and a multiline text box that can display text that is too long to fit on one line.

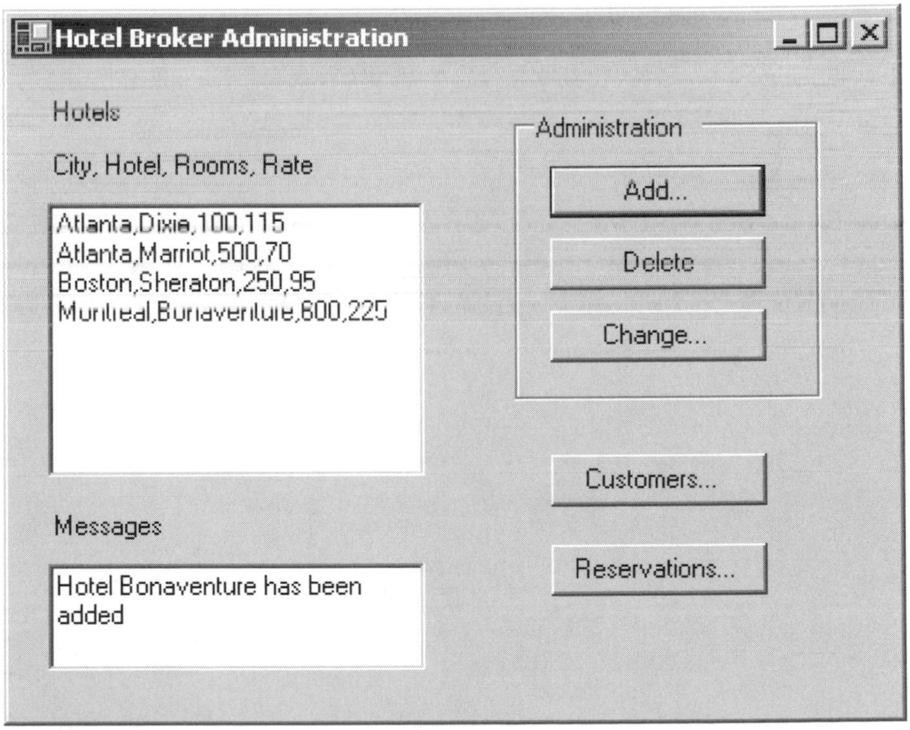

Figure 6–22   *Main form for hotel administration.*

.NET Dialog Documentation

Dialogs are explained clearly in the .NET Framework SDK Documentation. Look in "Dialog Boxes in Windows Forms" under "Introduction to Windows Forms." It is noteworthy that the principles of dialog boxes are the same in all .NET languages. This is in sharp contrast to traditional programming with Visual Basic and Microsoft Foundation Classes, where dialogs are implemented in totally different ways. Figure 6–23 shows the entry point to this documentation.

Dialog Box Demonstration

We will demonstrate the implementation details of a dialog box by creating a dialog to change hotel information in a simplified version of our case study. The starter code is backed up in the folder **HotelAdmin\Step1** in the main folder for this chapter. The completed program is in **HotelAdmin\Step3**. You may run either the case study or the Step 3 solution to see what the completed dialog should look like. In the main form select a hotel by clicking in

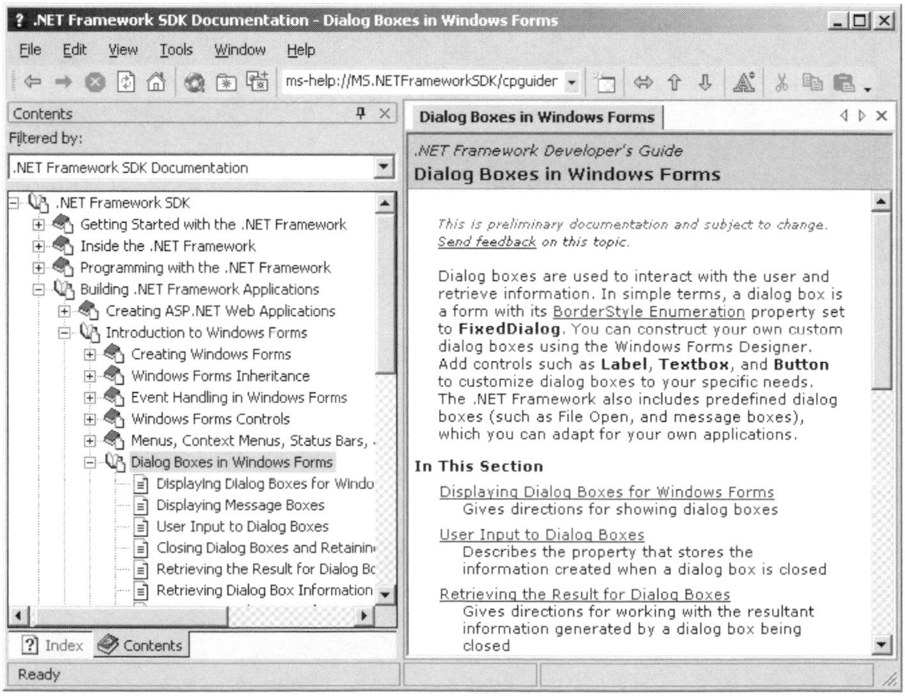

Figure 6–23   *Documentation on dialog boxes using the .NET Framework.*

the listbox of hotels. Then click on the Change... button. This brings up the Change Hotel Information dialog, as illustrated in Figure 6–24. Notice that the City and Hotel Name are grayed out. These items are read-only and cannot be changed. The user can enter new information for the Rooms and Rate.

CREATING A MODAL DIALOG

The first part of our demonstration illustrates how you can create a modal dialog box. We show how to set properties appropriately for the dialog and how to return a dialog result through use of OK and Cancel buttons.

1. Build and run the starter application. The Add... and Delete buttons work, but there is only a stub for Change..., which brings up an empty form. This form is ordinary. It is resizable, it has a system menu, and it has minimize and maximize buttons.
2. Open up **ChangeHotelDialog.cs** in Design mode. In the Properties window, change the **FormBorderStyle** property to **FixedDialog**.
3. Set the **ControlBox**, **MinimizeBox**, and **MaximizeBox** properties to **False**. If you like, you may build and run the application at this point. The dialog now is not resizable, and there is no system menu and no "X" in the top right to close the window.[4]

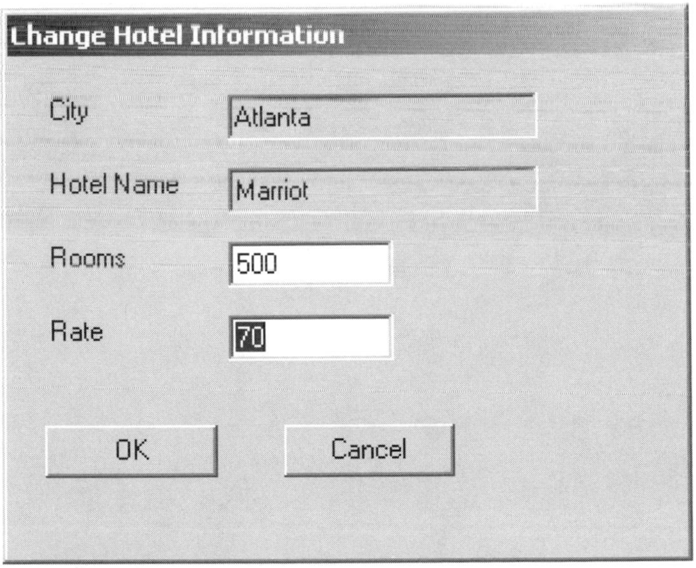

Figure 6–24   *Dialog for changing hotel information.*

---

[4] You may use Alt+F4 to close the window.

4. The next job is to enter labels and text boxes for the hotel information, plus OK and Cancel buttons. You may practice using the Toolbox to add these controls. Alternatively, you may copy and paste from **NewHotelDialog.cs** (open both files in Design mode).

5. If you used copy and paste, the controls will have proper **Name** and **Text** properties. Otherwise, assign values as shown in Table 6–2.

6. Change the **ReadOnly** property of **txtCity** and **txtHotelName** to **true**.

7. Resize the form to better fit the controls we have added.

8. Set the **DialogResult** property of the OK button to OK. Similarly set the property of the Cancel button to Cancel. Save **ChangeHotelDialog.cs**.

9. In **MainAdminForm.cs**, add temporary code to the **cmdChange_Click** handler to display "OK" or "Cancel" in the Messages text box, depending on whether the dialog was closed by clicking OK or Cancel. Notice that a dialog is brought up by the method **ShowDialog** in place of **Show**, which is used for ordinary forms. **ShowDialog** returns a result as an **enum** of type **DialogResult**.

```
private void cmdChange_Click(object sender,
                            System.EventArgs e)
{
   ChangeHotelDialog dlg = new ChangeHotelDialog();
   DialogResult status = dlg.ShowDialog();
   if (status == DialogResult.OK)
   {
      txtMessages.Text = "OK";
   }
   else
   {
      txtMessages.Tcxt = "Cancel";
   }
}
```

Table 6–2 Property Values for Textboxes and Buttons for ChangeHotelDialog.cs

Name	Text
txtCity	(blank)
txtHotelName	(blank)
txtNumberRooms	(blank)
txtRate	(blank)
cmdOK	OK
cmdCancel	Cancel

10. Build and test. You should now be able to bring up the dialog from the menu, and either the OK or Cancel button will close the dialog, and a corresponding message will be displayed. You can verify that the dialog is modal by trying to click elsewhere in the application. The program is now at Step 2.

PASSING INFORMATION BETWEEN PARENT FORM AND A DIALOG

The second part of our demonstration shows how to pass information to a dialog and how to retrieve information from a dialog. The .NET Framework classes do not provide a built-in mechanism for this purpose, but there is a design pattern that you can follow. You create a property in the dialog class for each piece of information you wish to pass between the parent form and the dialog.

In our example we implement write-only[5] properties for **City** and **HotelName** and read-write properties for **Rate** and **NumberRooms**.

1. Add code to the **ChangeHotelDialog** class in **ChangeHotelDialog.cs** to implement these properties.

```
public string City
{
    set
    {
        txtCity.Text = value;
    }
}
public string HotelName
{
    set
    {
        txtHotelName.Text = value;
    }
}
public int NumberRooms
{
    get
    {
        return Convert.ToInt32(txtNumberRooms.Text);
    }
    set
    {
```

---

[5] The properties are write-only from the perspective of the dialog class, because we pass information to a dialog instance. The corresponding controls are read-only, because the user is not allowed to enter new information.

```
      }
   }
   public decimal Rate
   {
      get
      {
         return Convert.ToDecimal(txtRate.Text);
      }
      set
      {
         txtRate.Text = value.ToString();
      }
   }
```

2. Now add code to the main form **MainAdminForm.cs** to set these
   properties prior to bringing up the dialog and to use the properties
   if the dialog box closes via an OK. Comment out or delete your previous test code that displays "OK" or "Cancel" in the Messages box.

```
private void cmdChange_Click(object sender,
                            System.EventArgs e)
{
   ChangeHotelDialog dlg = new ChangeHotelDialog();
   if (currHotel.HotelName != "")
   {
      dlg.City = currHotel.City;
      dlg.HotelName = currHotel.HotelName;
      dlg.NumberRooms = currHotel.NumberRooms;
      dlg.Rate = currHotel.Rate;
   }
   else
   {
      MessageBox.Show("Please select a hotel",
         "Hotel Broker Administration",
         MessageBoxButtons.OK,
         MessageBoxIcon.Exclamation
         );
      return;
   }
   DialogResult status = dlg.ShowDialog();
   if (status == DialogResult.OK)
```

```
    {
        string comment = hotelBroker.ChangeRooms(
            currHotel.City,
            currHotel.HotelName,
            dlg.NumberRooms,
            dlg.Rate);
        if (comment == "OK")
        {
            ShowHotelList(hotelBroker.GetHotels());
            txtMessages.Text = "Hotel " + currHotel.HotelName
                + " has been changed";
        }
        else
            txtMessages.Text = comment;
    }
}
```

The structure **currHotel** holds the fields of the hotel that is currently selected in the listbox. In the next section we will see how to extract information from a listbox and how to populate a listbox.

3.   Build and test. Your dialog should now be fully operational. Your project should now correspond to **HotelAdmin\Step3**.

ListBox Control

The .NET Framework provides a number of controls that you can use to display lists of items to the user. These controls also allow the user to select an item from the list, typically by clicking on the item to be selected. In this section we examine the **ListBox** control.

Code
Example

Our example program is **HotelAdmin\Step3**. The main form in **MainAdminForm.cs** contains the listbox **listHotels**, which maintains a list of hotels. Each hotel is represented by a string with values separated by commas.

Populating a ListBox

When the **HotelAdmin** program starts up, it populates the listbox **listHotels** with a list of hotels as part of the initialization in the **MainAdminForm** constructor.

```
public MainAdminForm()
{
    //
    // Required for Windows Form Designer support
```

```
    //
    InitializeComponent();

    //
    // TODO: Add any constructor code after
    // InitializeComponent call
    //
    hotelBroker = new HotelBroker();
    ShowHotelList(hotelBroker.GetHotels());
}
```

The **ShowHotelList** method displays an array list of hotels in a listbox. This array list is obtained by calling **HotelBroker.GetHotels**. Here is the code for **ShowHotelList**:

```
private void ShowHotelList(ArrayList array)
{
    listHotels.Items.Clear();
    if (array == null)
    {
        return;
    }
    foreach(HotelListItem hotel in array)
    {
        string city = hotel.City.Trim();
        string name = hotel.HotelName.Trim();
        string rooms = hotel.NumberRooms.ToString();
        string rate = hotel.Rate.ToString();
        string str = city + "," + name + ","
                + rooms + "," + rate;
        listHotels.Items.Add(str);
    }
}
```

A **ListBox** has a property **Items** that maintains a collection of object references. We first call **Items.Clear** to clear out the listbox of items currently being displayed. We then loop through the hotels in the array list and build up a string consisting of the fields of the hotel structure, separated by commas. This string is added to the listbox by calling **Items.Add**.

Selecting an Item From a ListBox

An item in a listbox is selected by clicking on the item, generating a **Selected-IndexChanged** event. You can access the selected item through the **Selected-**

Index and **SelectedItem** properties. If no item is selected, **SelectedIndex** is
−1. Here is the code for the event handler for **SelectedIndexChanged**.

```
private void listHotels_SelectedIndexChanged(object sender,
    System.EventArgs e)
{
    if (listHotels.SelectedIndex != -1)
    {
        string selected = (string) listHotels.SelectedItem;
        char[] sep = new char[] {','};
        string[] fields;
        fields = selected.Split(sep);
        currHotel = new HotelListItem();
        currHotel.City = fields[0];
        currHotel.HotelName = fields[1];
        currHotel.NumberRooms = Convert.ToInt32(fields[2]);
        currHotel.Rate = Convert.ToDecimal(fields[3]);
    }
    else
    {
        currHotel.HotelName = "";
    }
}
```

Since the items in a listbox are stored as object references, we cast the
selected item to a **string**. We use **String.Split** to extract the fields that are
separated by commas and store them in the **fields** string array. The values are
then moved from the array and are stored in **currHotel**. In the previous section we saw **currHotel** was used to initialize the New Hotel and Change
Hotel Information dialog boxes.

Acme Travel Agency Case Study — Step 3

The Acme Travel Agency case study was introduced in Chapter 4, where we
used arrays as our data structures for storing lists of hotels, customers, and
reservations. In Chapter 5 we changed the implementation to use collections
in place of arrays. We also specified a number of interfaces and passed lists as
ArrayList object references. In the previous chapters we provided a command-line user interface. In the **CaseStudy** folder of this chapter we provide
a GUI, implemented by using Windows Forms.

We have already looked at the main window (see Figure 6–22), which is the same as in the simplified **HotelAdmin**[6]program we used to illustrate dialog boxes. The Add... button lets us add a new hotel (Figure 6–21), and the Change... button (Figure 6–24) lets us change the number of rooms and the rate of a hotel. The Delete button will delete the currently selected hotel.

The Customers... button brings up a Customer Management form, which shows a list of currently registered customers. You may select a customer by clicking in the listbox. Figure 6–25 shows this form after selecting a customer.

The ID of the selected customer is shown in a textbox. You may unregister this customer by clicking Unregister. You may change the email address of this customer by clicking Change Email, which will bring up a dialog box. You may display the information for just this one customer by clicking One Customer. The All Customers button will again show all the customers in the listbox. The Register button lets you add a new customer.

The third major form of our user interface is Hotel Reservations, which is brought up from the main administration form by clicking Reservations.... To make a reservation, enter the Customer ID, Checkin Date, and Number of Days. You may specify the City and Hotel Name by selecting a hotel from the

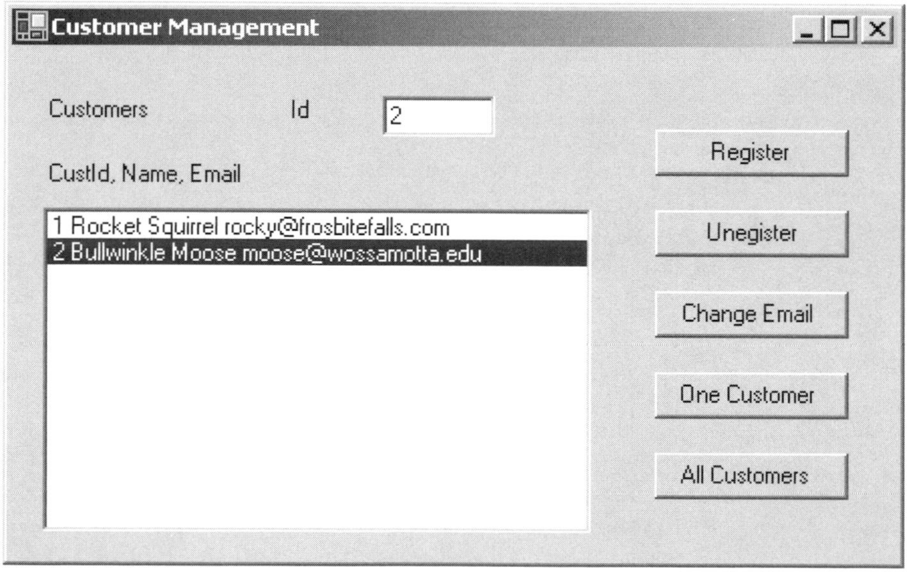

Figure 6–25   *Customer Management form.*

---

[6] The **HotelAdmin** program provides only empty forms as stubs for the Customers... and Reservations... buttons.

listbox. To make the reservation, you then simply click the Make Reservation button. To show all the reservations for a customer with a particular Customer ID,[7] click Show Reservations. Figure 6–26 shows this form after the customer whose ID is 1 has made a reservation, and we have shown the reservations for this customer.

You may clear the reservations listbox by clicking the Clear Reservations button. The Cancel Reservation will cancel the reservation with a particular Reservation ID, which may either be typed in or selected by clicking in the Reservations listbox.

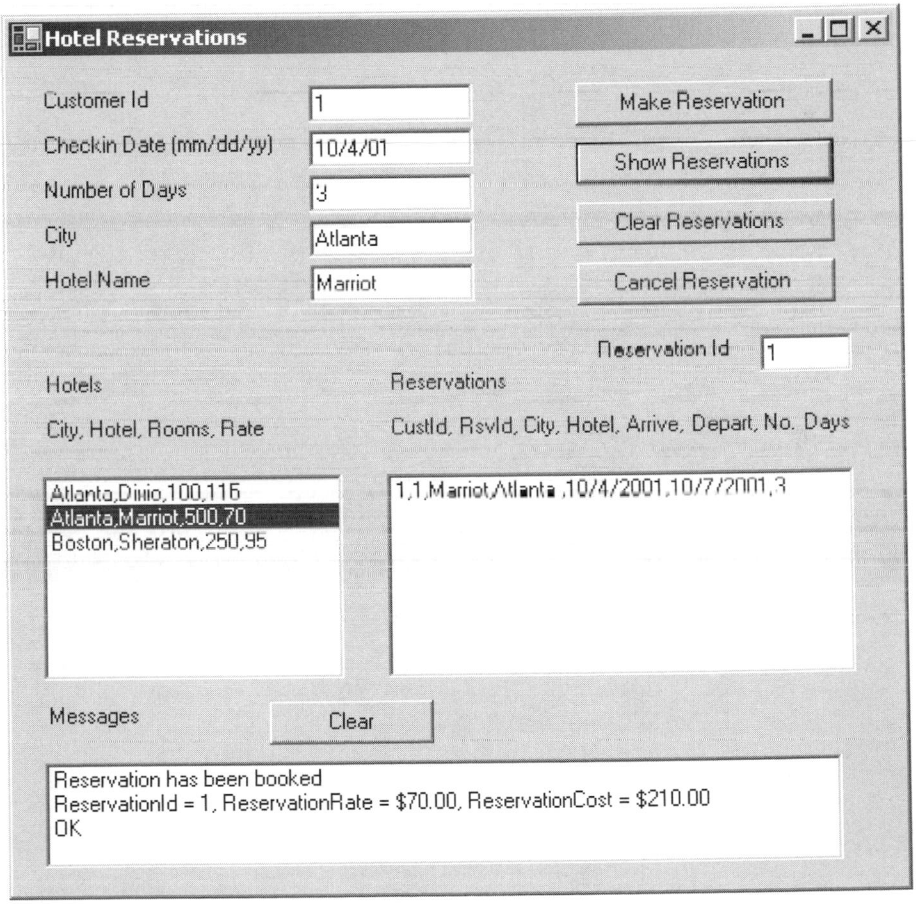

Figure 6–26 *Hotel Reservations form.*

[7] A Customer ID of –1 will show the reservations for all customers.

The Acme Travel Agency case study is used again in subsequent chapters, so you may wish to experiment with it at this point. The GUI makes exercising the case study much easier than our previous command-line interface. On the other hand, the command-line interface and a simple global **try** block around the whole command loop makes it easy to check for all exceptions. Such an approach is not feasible for a GUI program. In an industrial-strength application you should check for exceptions wherever they may occur. Our case study is simplified for instructional purposes, and we have not attempted to be thorough in catching exceptions. Another simplification we made is not checking that a Customer ID used in making a reservation corresponds to a real, registered customer. The database implementation in Chapter 9 does provide such a check.

Summary

In this chapter we learned how to implement a GUI using the Windows Forms classes of the .NET Framework. We began with first principles, using the .NET Framework SDK to create simple Windows applications from scratch without use of any special tools. Drawing is done in an override of **OnPaint**, using a font and a brush. The .NET event mechanism is used to handle user interaction such as mouse events and pressing keys. Controls simplify Windows programming. A menu control makes it easy to add menus to a Windows program. Visual Studio.NET greatly simplifies Windows programming. Unfortunately, the Forms Designer does not support C++ programming efforts. However, the Forms Designer can be used to very quickly create C# projects that can then optionally be ported to C++. The Forms Designer lets you drag controls from the Toolbox onto your forms, and you can set properties of the controls at design time. You can also easily add event handlers. Dialog boxes are a special kind of form, and you can pass information between a parent form and a dialog through use of properties in the dialog. The listbox control makes it easy to display lists of information. We concluded the chapter by presenting a GUI for our Acme Travel Agency case study.

Assemblies and Deployment

*D*eployment makes the programmer's hard work available to the customer. .NET assemblies make deployment much simpler and much more reliable than traditional Windows deployment. Private assembly deployment is as simple as copying the component assembly into the same directory as the client program. Alternatively, shared assembly deployment registers a component with a unique name (known as a strong name) in the global assembly cache, which makes it available for general use.

This chapter begins with a look at assemblies, which are the fundamental unit of deployment in .NET. private assembly deployment and shared assembly deployment are described next. Versioning and digital signing of assemblies are discussed in the context of shared deployment. Then, the Hotel case study is deployed as another example of working with and deploying assemblies. Finally, the Visual Studio.NET deployment and setup wizards are introduced. Throughout our discussion we illustrate a number of useful tools that are part of the .NET Framework SDK.

Assemblies

Assemblies form the basis of .NET component technology. An assembly is the fundamental unit of deployment, security permissions management, versioning, and binary code reuse. An assembly contains binary executable code comprised of managed Intermediate Language (IL) instructions, as well as metadata information that completely describe the assembly contents. Assemblies may also contain resource data and are packaged in the form of either DLL or EXE files. An assembly may be composed of one or more physical disk files, but it is still a single logical unit of deployment. Assemblies are said to be self-describing, since they contain metadata information about themselves, and therefore they do not require any information, to be established externally, such as in the system registry. This makes .NET components much simpler and less error-prone to install and uninstall than traditional COM components, which had extensive registry information requirements. Not only are assemblies conveniently self-describing, but also they contain a hash code representing the binary contents of the assembly. This hash code can be used to authenticate and detect tampering or corruption of digitally signed assemblies.

An assembly that is to be deployed into the global assembly cache must first be digitally signed. Digitally signed assemblies provide cryptographically generated verification information that can be used by the CLR to enforce crucial dependency rules when locating and loading assemblies. Simple version checking ensures that a client program uses shared assemblies correctly with respect to proper versioning determined when the client was originally compiled and tested. This can effectively eliminate the infamous "DLL Hell" problem, where COM clients and COM components could easily get out of synch with one another when an older version was replaced with a newer version, breaking existing clients. A digitally signed assembly can also verify that no unauthorized person has altered the shared assembly contents since the time when it was digitally signed. This assures not only that you cannot accidentally use the wrong version, but also that you will not be tricked into using a maliciously tampered component that could do serious harm.

Although there is often a one-to-one correspondence between namespace and assembly, an assembly may contain multiple namespaces, and one namespace may be distributed among multiple assemblies. Similarly, there is often a one-to-one correspondence between assembly and binary code file (i.e., DLL or EXE). However, one assembly can span multiple binary code files. Remember that the assembly is the unit of deployment, namespaces support a hierarchical naming system, and the DLL or EXE file is the unit of functional packaging within the file system. It is also important to contrast between the assembly, which is the unit of deployment, and the application, which is the unit of configuration.

The identity of an unsigned assembly is defined simply as a human-readable name along with a version number. The identity of a digitally signed assembly also includes its originator, uniquely associated with a cryptographic key pair. Optionally, an assembly's identity may also include a culture code for supporting culturally specific character sets and string formats.

Contents of an Assembly

The **Ildasm.exe** tool can be used to view the assembly contents to better understand how versioning, digital signing, and deployment work. First, we will need an assembly to experiment with. For this purpose, a component named **SimpleComponent** is created with Visual Studio.NET, using the New Project dialog and selecting the managed C++ Class Library template. The name of the project is **SimpleComponent**, and the following source files

Code
Example

show its implementation, which is only slightly modified from the code generated by the wizard. Recall that it is important to declare the method **AddEmUp** as public so that it will be visible to code outside of this assembly.

```
//AssemblyInfo.cpp

#include "stdafx.h" //has a #using <mscorlib.dll>
using namespace System::Reflection;
using namespace System::Runtime::CompilerServices;
[__assembly::AssemblyTitleAttribute("")];
[__assembly::AssemblyDescriptionAttribute("")];
[__assembly::AssemblyConfigurationAttribute("")];
[__assembly::AssemblyCompanyAttribute("")];
[__assembly::AssemblyProductAttribute("")];
[__assembly::AssemblyCopyrightAttribute("")];
[__assembly::AssemblyTrademarkAttribute("")];
[__assembly::AssemblyCultureAttribute("")];
[__assembly::AssemblyVersionAttribute("1.0.*")];
[__assembly::AssemblyDelaySignAttribute(false)];
[__assembly::AssemblyKeyFileAttribute("")];
[__assembly::AssemblyKeyNameAttribute("")];


//SimpleComponent.cpp

#include "stdafx.h" //has a #using <mscorlib.dll>
#include "SimpleComponent.h"


// SimpleComponent.h

using namespace System;
namespace SimpleComponent
{
    public __gc class SomeClass
    {
    public: //must be public to expose from assembly
       int AddEmUp(int i, int j)
       {
           return i+j;
       }
    };
}
```

Once you have created the .NET component assembly containing the above code and have built it, you can view its contents, including its manifest, using **Ildasm.exe**. A manifest provides the following information about an assembly:

- Assembly identity based on name, version, culture, and, optionally, a digital signature.
- Lists files that contribute to the assembly contents.
- Lists other assemblies on which the assembly is dependent.
- Lists permissions required by the assembly to carry out its duties

This can be viewed using the **Ildasm** tool, which is started by executing the following command, and its result is shown in Figure 7–1.

```
Ildasm SimpleComponent.dll
```

To see the manifest for **SimpleComponent**, double click the MANI-FEST node shown in Figure 7–1, and the resulting manifest information is displayed in Figure 7–2.

The manifest contains information about the dependencies and contents of the assembly. You can see that the manifest for **SimpleComponent** contains, among others, the following external dependency:

```
.assembly extern mscorlib
{
  .publickeytoken = (B7 7A 5C 56 19 34 E0 89 )
  .hash = (09 BB BC 09 EF 6D 9B F4 F2 CC 1B 55 76 A7 02 91
          22 88 EF 77 )
  .ver 1:0:2411:0
}
```

The **.assembly extern mscorlib** metadata statement indicates that **SimpleComponent** makes use of, and is therefore dependent on, the standard assembly **mccorlib.dll**, which is required by all managed code. The **mscorlib** assembly is a shared assembly, which can be seen in the **\WINNT\Assembly** directory using Windows Explorer. This dependency appears in the **SimpleComponent.dll** metadata because of the **#using <mscorlib.dll>** statement in the original source code (Stdafx.h). If another **#using** statement was added for another assembly, such as **#using <System.WinForms.dll>**, then the manifest would contain the corresponding **.assembly extern System.WinForms** dependency statement as well.

The **.publickeytoken = (B7 7A 5C 56 19 34 E0 89)** metadata statement provides a public key token, which is a hash of the public key that matches the corresponding private key owned by the **mscorlib** assembly's author. This public key token cannot actually be used directly to authenticate the identity of the author of the **mscorlib**. However, the original public key specified in the **mscorlib** manifest can be used to mathematically verify that

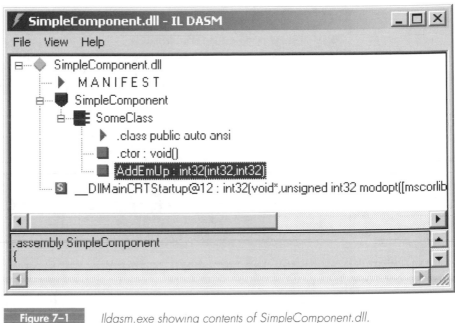

Figure 7–1   Ildasm.exe showing contents of SimpleComponent.dll.

the matching private key was actually used to digitally sign the **mscorlib** assembly. Since Microsoft authored **mscorlib.dll**, the public key token seen above is Microsoft-specific. Of course, the matching private key is a closely guarded corporate secret, and it is believed by most security experts that such a private key is, in practice, very difficult to determine from the public key. However, there is no guarantee that some mathematical genius will not someday find a back door that could make this easier!

As we shall see shortly, the **.publickeytoken** statement is only present in the client assembly's manifest if the referenced assembly has been digitally signed, and all assemblies intended for shared deployment must be digitally signed. Microsoft has digitally signed the standard .NET assemblies, such as **mscorlib.dll** and **System.WinForms.dll**, with private keys belonging to them. This is why the public key token for many of those shared assemblies, seen in the **\WINNT\Assembly** directory using Windows Explorer, have the same value repeated. Assemblies authored and digitally signed by other vendors are signed with their own distinct private keys, and they will therefore result in a different public key token in their client assembly's manifests. Later, we will look at how you can create your own private and public key pair and digitally sign your own assemblies for deployment via the global assembly cache.

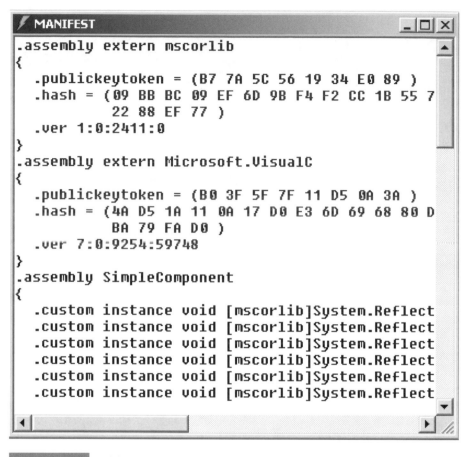

Figure 7–2   *Ildasm.exe showing manifest of SimpleComponent.dll.*

The .publickeytoken Declaration

The **.publickeytoken** declaration provides only the least significant 8 bytes of the SHA1 hash of the producer's public key (which is 128 bytes), which saves some space, but can still be used for fairly reliable verification purposes. Alternatively, the **.publickey** declaration could have been used, which provides the full public key. This would take up more space, but it makes it harder for villains to find a private key that matches the full public key.

It is important to note that, while unique, the digital key by itself cannot identify who the author of a particular module actually is. However, a developer of an assembly can use the **signcode** utility to add a digital certificate that can identify the publisher of the assembly. By registering the digital certificate with a Certificate Authority,[1] such as VeriSign, credence may be established.

The **.hash = (09 BB BC 09 ... 77)** metadata statement provides a fixed sized hash code representation of the binary contents of **mscorlib.dll**. If the contents were to change, this hash code would change as a result. As you may know, a hash code is a highly characteristic yet compact representation that is calculated from the original data to produce a result that can be used for many purposes, including error detection and verification. The hash code for the **mscorlib** assembly shown above is therefore highly characteristic of the binary data within the **mscorlib** assembly. This means that if the contents of **mscorlib.dll** were to be changed accidentally, intentionally, or even maliciously, then, with an astronomically high probability, the new hash code would not match the old one, and the problem would thus be detected. As described later in the section on digitally signing assemblies, a secret private key is used to ensure that only an authorized person can encrypt the hash code, verifying the authenticity of the entire assembly.

The **.ver 1:0:2411:0** metadata statement indicates the version of the **mscorlib** assembly. The format of this version specification is **Major:Minor:Build:Revision**. Over time, as new versions of this assembly are released, existing clients that were built to use this version will continue using this version, at least with respect to major and minor values. Newer client programs will of course be able to access newer versions of this assembly as they become available. The old and new versions can be deployed side–by–side by way of the global assembly cache and can be simultaneously available to old and new client programs. Note that the version **1:0:2411:0** appearing in the client manifest belongs to the current version of the **mscorlib** assembly and is unrelated to the 1.0.* version attribute specified in the **SimpleComponent** source code. We will look more closely at the four fields that make up a version number and how assembly versioning works shortly.

So far, we have been focusing on the dependencies that are defined in the **SimpleComponent** assembly's manifest. Now let's shift our focus to the implemented component information in the manifest. The following manifest information describes the **SimpleComponent** component contained within the assembly. Note that this assembly is not digitally signed, and therefore it does not contain information on its originator (i.e., no public key).

```
.assembly SimpleComponent
{
    .
```

---

[1] A Certificate Authority (CA) is a trusted third-party that verifies a digital signer's credentials, and issues a unique digital certificate of identity. The certificate provides proof that the signer is indeed who he or she claims to be. This is useful in situations where two parties would like to do business with one another, without having to thoroughly know one another beforehand.

.
.
```
.hash algorithm 0x00008004
.ver 1:0:584:39032
}
```

The .assembly Directive

The **.assembly** directive declares the manifest and specifies to which assembly the current module belongs. In this example, the **.assembly** directive specifies the name of the assembly to be **SimpleComponent**. It is this name (combined with the version number and optionally a public key) rather than the name of the DLL or EXE file that is used at runtime to resolve the identity of the assembly. Also note that if the assembly is signed, you will see **.publickey** defined within the **.assembly** directive. The **.assembly** directive also indicates whether any custom attributes have been added to the metadata.

The **.assembly SimpleComponent** metadata statement indicates that the assembly name is **SimpleComponent.** Note that this is not the name of a component class within the assembly, but rather the assembly itself.

The **.hash algorithm 0x00008004** metadata statement indicates that SHA1 is the hash algorithm that is used on the assembly to produce a hash code value. There are many hash code algorithms in existence. However, initially, only MD5 (0x000803) and SHA1 (0x000804) are supported. Since this assembly is not digitally signed with a private key, the hash code will not actually be encrypted. However, the hash code is still calculated to effectively represent the binary content of the assembly.

Hash Algorithms

A hash algorithm is a mathematical function that takes the original data of arbitrary size as input and generates a hash code, also known as a message digest, which is a fixed sized binary output. An effective hash function is a one-way function that is highly collision-free, with a result that is relatively small and fixed in size. Ideally, a hash function is efficient to calculate as well. A one-way function is a function that has no inverse, so you cannot effectively reproduce the original data from the hash code value.[a] The phrase "highly collision-free" means that the probability that two distinct original input data samples generate the same hash code is very small, and it is unlikely to calculate two distinct input data samples that result in the same hash code value. The well-known MD5 and SHA1 hash algorithms are considered to be excellent choices for use in digital signing, and they are both supported by .NET.

---

[a] One way encryption codes are used to store passwords in a passwords database is, when you log in, the password you enter is encrypted and compared with what is stored in the database. If they match, you can log in. The password cannot be reconstructed from the encrypted value stored in the passwords database.

The **.ver 1:0:584:39032** indicates the release version of the **Simple-Component** assembly, which is determined in part by the **AssemblyVersionAttribute** attribute in the component's source code. Versioning is described in more detail in the next subsection.

Versioning an Assembly

As we have just seen, an assembly manifest contains the version of the assembly as well as the version of each of the assemblies that it is dependent on. The detailed set of rules used by the CLR to determine version dependencies is called a version policy. The default version policy is defined by dependencies specified in the assembly manifests, but it can optionally be overridden in an application configuration file or the systemwide configuration file. Automatic version checking is only done by the CLR on assemblies with strong names (i.e., digitally signed assemblies). However, every assembly, regardless of how it is deployed, should be assigned a version number. The version number of an assembly is composed of the following four fields.

- Major version: Major incompatible changes
- Minor version: Minor incompatible changes
- Build number: Backward-compatible changes made during development
- Revision: Backward-compatible Quick Fix Engineering (QFE) changes

The above conventions regarding the purpose of each version number field are not enforced by the CLR. You enforce these conventions, or any other conventions you choose, by testing assemblies for compatibility, and optionally specifying a version policy in a configuration file, which we will discuss later in this chapter.

Conventionally, a change in the value of the major or minor number indicates an explicit incompatibility with the previous version. This is used for substantial changes in a new release of the assembly, and existing clients cannot expect to reliably use the new version. Changes in build number mean that backward compatibility is to be expected, and it is typically changed every time the assembly is rebuilt during development. Backward compatibility between build numbers is clearly intentional; however, this obviously cannot be guaranteed by the CLR, and therefore it must be tested. A change in the revision number supports QFE changes. This is usually used for an emergency fix that is assumed to be backward compatible by the CLR unless instructed otherwise by a configuration file. Again, the CLR cannot guarantee that a QFE is 100 percent backward compatible, but backward compatibility is optimistically expected and should be tested thoroughly.

Version information can be defined in the source code using the assembly attribute **__assembly::AssemblyVersionAttribute**. The **AssemblyVersionAttribute** class is defined in the **System::Runtime::CompilerServices** namespace. If this attribute is not used, a default version number of 0.0.0.0 is listed in the assembly manifest, which is generally not desirable. In a project created with the managed C++ Class Library project wizard, the source file named **AssemblyInfo.cpp** is automatically generated with a version of **1.0.***, producing a major version of 1, a minor version of 0, and automatically generated build and revision values. If you change the **AssemblyVersionAttribute** to, for example, **"1.1.0.0"**, as shown below, the version number displayed in the manifest will be modified accordingly to **1:1:0:0**.

```
//AssemblyInfo.cpp

#using <mscorlib.dll>
.

.

.

[__assembly::AssemblyVersionAttribute("1.1.0.0")];
```

You can use the asterisk (*) character for defaulting the build and revision values. If you specify any version number at all, you must, at a minimum, specify the major number. If you specify only the major number, the remaining values will default to zero. If you also specify the minor value, you can omit the remaining fields, which will then default to zero, or you can specify an asterisk, which will provide automatically generated values. The asterisk will cause the build value to equal the number of days since January 1, 2000, and the revision value will be set to the number of seconds since midnight, divided by 2. If you specify major, minor, and build values, and specify an asterisk for the revision value, then only the revision is defaulted to the number of seconds since midnight, divided by 2. If all four fields are explicitly specified, then all four values will be reflected in the manifest. The following examples show valid version specifications.

```
Specified in source    Result in manifest

None                   0:0:0:0
1                      1:0:0:0
1.1                    1:1:0:0
1.1.*                  1:1:464:27461
1.1.43                 1:1:43:0
1.1.43.*               1:1:43:29832
1.1.43.52              1:1:43:52
```

If you use the asterisk, then the version will automatically change every time you rebuild the component; however, each new version is considered to be backward compatible, since the major and minor numbers are not automatically changed. In order to define a new non-backward-compatible version, you must explicitly change the major and/or minor version number.

Private Assembly Deployment

Private assembly deployment simply means that the end user copies the assembly to the same directory as the client program that uses it. No registration is needed, and no fancy installation program is required. Also, no registry cleanup is required, and no uninstall program is needed to remove the component either. To uninstall the assembly, simply delete it from the hard drive.

Of course, no self-respecting programmer would ever provide a commercial component that required the end user to manually copy or delete any files in this way, even if it is remarkably simple to do. Users have become accustomed to using a formal installation program, so it should be provided even if its work is trivial. However, for testing purposes, manually copying and deleting an assembly is an ideal way to quickly and painlessly manage deployment issues for developing, debugging, or testing purposes. Recall that the deployment of COM components was never this simple, requiring at a minimum a registry script file to provide information about the component to client programs and the COM runtime. Gone are the days where you have to configure the registry on installation, and then later carefully clean out the registry information when you want to discard the component.

Now we shall look at the steps for performing private assembly deployment for a simple .NET component. The next section will show how to deploy such a component as a shared assembly in the global assembly cache.

Once the component assembly has been built, a client program can be created that calls the component's public methods. The following code shows an example of such a client program, which calls into the public method **AddEmUp** shown previously. Of course the path to the **SimpleComponent.dll** assembly in the **#using** statement must be adjusted if necessary to make the compiler happy. Also, it will need to be deployed to allow the CLR to locate and load it at runtime. In this subsection, deployment is accomplished simply by copying it into the directory of the client program.

```
//SimpleComponentClient.cpp

#include "stdafx.h"
#using <mscorlib.dll>
using namespace System;
#using #using <C:\OI\NetCpp\Chap7\SimpleComponent\Debug\
    SimpleComponent.dll>
using namespace SimpleComponent;
void main()
```

```
{
    SomeClass *psc = new SomeClass;
    int sum = psc->AddEmUp(3, 4);
    Console::WriteLine(sum);
}
```

How is SimpleComponent Found?

Note that the **SimpleComponentClient** program has a **#using** statement that tells the compiler where to find the **SimpleComponent** assembly, which the compiler then uses for type checking against the assembly's metadata.

However, if you try to run the client program, you will get an exception **System.IO.FileNotFoundException**. This is because the CLR class loader is unable to find the **SimpleComponent** assembly. To allow the client to run, just copy the **SimpleComponent** assembly into the same directory as the **SimpleComponentClient.exe** program.

Now the assembly manifest of this client program can be viewed, and it can be compared to see how it interacts with the manifest in the **SimpleComponent** assembly shown earlier. To view the client program's manifest, use the following command:

```
Ildasm SimpleComponentClient.exe
```

It can be seen that the client program's manifest contains the following external dependency on the **SimpleComponent** assembly.

```
.assembly extern SimpleComponent
{
  .hash = (2A 1C 2D D7 CA 9E 7E D5 08 5B D0 75 23 D3 50 76
           5E 28 EA 31 )
  .ver 1:0:584:39032 }
```

From this you can see that the client program is expecting to use the **SimpleComponent** assembly version number **1:0:584:39032**. However, since this is a privately deployed assembly, no version number checking is performed by the CLR default version policy when the client loads this assembly. Instead, it is the responsibility of an administrator or an installation program to ensure that the correct version is deployed to this private directory. As we shall see later, it is possible to override this default version policy using a configuration file. Although the client manifest shows the component's hash code, this hash code is also not actually used by the CLR to verify that the binary image is authentic. Again, this is because the assembly is deployed privately. In the next section, we will see that the version number and hash code are used automatically for code content verification on shared assemblies deployed in the global assembly cache.

Shared Assembly Deployment

The assembly cache is a machine-wide, side-by-side component installation facility. The term "side-by-side" means that multiple versions of the same component may reside within the assembly cache along side one another. The global assembly cache contains shared assemblies that are globally accessible to all .NET applications on the machine. There is also a download assembly cache that is accessible to applications such as Internet Explorer that automatically download assemblies over the network. Before an assembly can be deployed into the global assembly cache, a strong name must be created for it.

Strong Names

A strong name is guaranteed to be globally unique for any version of any assembly. Strong names are generated by digitally signing the assembly. This ensures that the strong name is not only unique, but it is a name that can only be generated by an individual that owns a secret private key.

A strong name is made up of a simple text name, a public key, and a hash code that has been encrypted with the matching private key. The hash code is known as a message digest and the encrypted hash code is known as a digital signature. The hash code effectively identifies the binary content of the assembly and the digital signature effectively identifies the assembly's author. Any assemblies that have the same strong name are recognized as being identical assemblies (version numbers are assumed to be identical here as well). Any assemblies that have different strong names are recognized as being distinct. A strong name is considered to be a cryptographically strong name, since, unlike a simple text name, a strong name is guaranteed to uniquely identify the assembly based on its contents and its author's private key. A strong name has the following useful properties:

- A strong name guarantee uniqueness based on encryption technology.
- A strong name establishes a unique namespace based on the use of a private key.
- A strong name prevents unauthorized personnel from modifying the assembly.
- A strong name prevents unauthorized personnel from versioning the assembly.
- A strong name allows the CLR to perform code content verification on shared assemblies.

Digital Signatures

It is required that an assembly be digitally signed if it is to be deployed into the global assembly cache. A digital signature is not required and is not particularly useful for a privately deployed assembly, since a private assembly is custom matched and deployed to work with its specific client program. If a privately deployed assembly is digitally signed, the CLR does not, by default, verify it when it loads the assembly for the client program. It is therefore an entirely administrative responsibility to prevent unauthorized modification or tampering for privately deployed assemblies. On the other hand, publicly deployed (i.e., shared) assemblies benefit greatly from the fact that they must be digitally signed, since many clients typically use them, and multiple versions of an assembly may exist side by side.

Digital signatures are based on public key cryptographic techniques. In the world of cryptography, the two main cryptographic techniques are symmetric ciphers (shared key) and asymmetric ciphers (public key). Symmetric ciphers use one shared secret key for encryption as well as decryption. DES, Triple DES, and RC2 are examples of symmetric cipher algorithms. Symmetric ciphers can be very efficient and powerful for message privacy between two trusted cooperating individuals, but they are not well suited to situations where the sharing of a secret key is problematic. This makes symmetric ciphers generally unsuitable for the purposes of digital signatures. This is because digital signatures are not used for privacy, but are rather used for identification and authentication, which tends to be a more open affair. The problem would be that if you shared your symmetric key with everyone who would potentially want to authenticate you, you could inadvertently share it with people who would want to impersonate you. Asymmetric ciphers are much better suited for use in digital signatures.

Asymmetric ciphers, which are also known as public key ciphers, make use of a public/private key pair. The paired keys are mathematically related and they are generated together; however, it is exceedingly difficult to calculate one key from the other. The public key is typically exposed to everyone who would like to authenticate its owner. On the other hand, the owner keeps the matching private signing key secret so that no one can impersonate him or her. RSA is an example of a public key cipher system.

Public key cryptography is based on a very interesting mathematical scheme that allows plain text to be encrypted with one key and decrypted only with the matching key. For example, if a public key is used to encrypt the original data (known as plain text), then only the matching private key is capable of decrypting it. Not even the encrypting key can decrypt it! This scenario is useful for sending secret messages to only the individual that knows the private key.

The opposite scenario is where only one individual who owns the private key uses that key to encrypt the plain text. The resulting cipher text is by no means a secret, since everyone who is interested can obtain the public to decrypt it. This scenario is useless for secrecy, but very effective for authentication purposes. It is not necessary to encrypt the entire original data, so to improve performance, a compact but highly characteristic hash code is encrypted instead. If you receive a file that contains the encrypted version of its own hash code, and you decrypt it with the matching public key, and you then recalculate the hash code on the original data and find that it matches the hash code that was encrypted, you can be quite certain that the owner of the private key was the digital signer and that the data has not been modified by another party. Assuming that the owner has managed to keep the private key secret, this proves that nobody else could have tampered with it since the time when it was digitally signed. Figure 7–3 shows how a digital signature works.

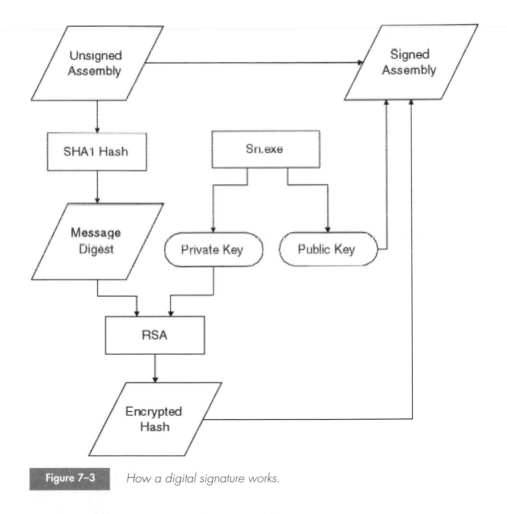

Figure 7–3   *How a digital signature works.*

Digital Signing with SHA1 and RSA

To sign the assembly, the producer calculates a SHA1 hash of the assembly (with the bytes reserved for the signature preset to zero), and then encrypts the hash value with a private key using RSA encryption. The public key and the encrypted hash are then stored in the assembly's metadata.

Digitally Signing and Deploying a Shared Assembly

Before an assembly can be deployed into the global assembly cache, you must digitally sign the assembly. Developers can place the assembly into the global assembly cache by using the Global Assembly Cache utility **Gacutil.exe**, the **Windows Explorer** with the assembly cache viewer Windows shell extension, or the **.NET Admin Tool**. Deploying shared assemblies on an actual end-user machine should be done with a custom installation program.

The process of digitally signing an assembly involves generating a public/private key pair, calculating a hash code on the assembly, encrypting the hash code with the private key, and writing the encrypted hash code along with the public key into the assembly for all to see.

The encrypted hash code and public key together comprise the entire digital signature. Note that the digital signature is written into a reserved area within the assembly that is not included in the hash code calculation. Once this is done, the assembly is deployed into the GAC. All these steps are performed with three simple tools named the Strong Name utility (**Sn.exe),** the Assembly Linker (**Al.exe**), and the Global Assembly Cache utility (**Gacutil.exe)**. To build, digitally sign, and deploy a shared assembly, the following steps are performed:

1. Develop and build the component.
2. Generate a public/private key pair.
3. Calculate a hash code on the contents of the assembly.
4. Encrypt the hash code using the private key.
5. Place the encrypted hash code into the manifest.
6. Place the public key into the manifest.
7. Place the assembly into the global assembly cache.

Step 1 is of course usually performed using Visual Studio.NET. Steps 2 through 6 are known as digital signing. Step 2 is accomplished using the Strong Name utility **Sn.exe**. Steps 3 through 6 are accomplished using either Visual Studio.NET or the Assembly Linking utility **Al.exe** (that's "A-el," not "A-one"). Step 7, placing the assembly into the global assembly cache, is accomplished using the Global Assembly Cache utility **Gacutil.exe,** Windows Explorer, or the .NET Admin Tool.

The first step above, creating the component, is described next. For demonstration purposes, we use an example that is similar to the previous

SimpleComponent assembly example, except this one is called **Shared-Component**, and it will be deployed into the global assembly cache. First, a new project named **SharedComponent** must be created using the managed C++ Class Library template, and the following code must be added:

```
//SharedComponent.cpp

#include "stdafx.h" //has a #using <mscorlib.dll>
#include "SharedComponent.h"

//SharedComponent.h

using namespace System;
namespace SharedComponent
{
    public __gc class SomeClass
    {
        public:
        int AddEmUp(int i, int j)
        {
            return i+j;
        }
    };
}
```

The next step is to generate the key pair using **Sn.exe**, known as the Strong Name utility, but also occasionally referred to as the Shared Name utility (however, this term is now deprecated). This tool generates a cryptographically strong name for the assembly. You generate a public/private key pair and place it into a file named **KeyPair.snk**, as shown in the following command.

```
sn -k KeyPair.snk
```

The resulting **KeyPair.snk** file is a binary file and is not intended to be human readable. If you are curious, you can write these keys into a comma-delimited text file with the following command, and then view it using **Note-pad.exe**; however, this is not a required step.

```
sn -o KeyPair.snk KeyPair.txt
```

The next step is to apply the private key to the assembly. This can be done at compile time, which is generally useful for developing and testing purposes; however, when it comes time to release the assembly, placing the company name on the line, a more formal approach should be taken. For the security concerns of a corporate digital signing authority, the official secret private key may not be made known to the programmer. Instead, the programmer may work on development and testing using an alternate testing key pair that is applied automatically at compile time. Then, when the assembly is about to be released, an authorized individual applies the official corporate digital signature, using a highly secret private key. This is done after compile time, using the **Al.exe** tool. This tool is described later in this subsection. However, to apply the digital signature automatically at compile time, you simply use a certain C++ attribute, as shown in the following code. In particular, note that the **KeyPair.snk** file generated previously with the **Sn.exe** tool is specified in the **AssemblyKeyFileAttribute** attribute.

```
//AssemblyInfo.cpp

#include "stdafx.h" //has a #using <mscorlib.dll>
using namespace System::Reflection;
using namespace System::Runtime::CompilerServices;
[assembly:AssemblyTitleAttribute("")];
[assembly:AssemblyDescriptionAttribute("")];
[assembly:AssemblyConfigurationAttribute("")];
[assembly:AssemblyCompanyAttribute("")];
[assembly:AssemblyProductAttribute("")];
[assembly:AssemblyCopyrightAttribute("")];
[assembly:AssemblyTrademarkAttribute("")];
[assembly:AssemblyCultureAttribute("")];
[assembly:AssemblyVersionAttribute("1.0.*")];
[assembly:AssemblyDelaySignAttribute(false)];
[assembly:AssemblyKeyFileAttribute("KeyPair.snk")];
[assembly:AssemblyKeyNameAttribute("")];
```

Once the **KeyPair.snk** file has been added to the **AssemblyKeyFileAttribute**, it must be recompiled. Then, the following **Ildasm.exe** output shows the resulting information incorporated into the assembly manifest for the **SharedComponent** DLL. Notice the new entry is named **.publickey**, which represents the originator's public key that resides in the **KeyPair.snk** file. It is this public key that can be used to decrypt the message digest to retrieve the original hash code. When the assembly is deployed into the global assembly cache, this decrypted hash code is compared with a fresh recalculation of the hash code from the actual assembly contents. This comparison is made to determine if the assembly is legitimate (i.e., identical to the original) or illegitimate (i.e., corrupt or tampered). Of course, when you use **Sn.exe**, it will produce a different key pair, and the public key shown below will be different in your case accordingly.

```
.assembly SharedComponent
{
   ...
   .publickey = (00 24 00 00 04 80 00 00 94 00 00 00 ...
   ... 56 5A B1 97 D5 FF 39 5F 42 DF 0F 90 7D D4 )
   .hash algorithm 0x00008004
   .ver 1:0:584:42238
}
```

Code
Example

To test the **SharedComponent** assembly developed above, we next have to create a test client program and then, rather than copy the **Shared-Component.dll** to the client directory, we use the **Gacutil.exe** utility, or **Windows Explorer**, or the **.NET Admin Tool** to deploy the assembly into the global assembly cache. The following code represents the test client program.

```
//SharedComponentClient.cpp

#include "stdafx.h"
#using <mscorlib.dll>
using namespace System;
#using <C:\OT\NetCpp\Chap7\SharedComponent\Debug\
    SharedComponent.dll>
using namespace SharedComponent;
using namespace System;
void main()
{
    SomeClass *psc = new SomeClass;
    int sum = psc->AddEmUp(3, 4);
    Console::WriteLine(sum);
}
```

If the above test client program were to be run without first deploying the component assembly, the runtime will throw a **FileNotFoundException** exception because the assembly cannot be found. This time we deploy it into the global assembly cache, using the **Gacutil.exe** utility (one of several techniques). Once you have completed this command, you can go back to the client and you will find that it now works properly.

```
Gacutil -i SharedComponent.dll
```

You should then see the console message Assembly successfully added to the cache. The effect of this command is that a new global assembly cache node named **SharedComponent** is created in the **\WINNT\Assembly** directory. As can be seen in Figure 7–4, the version

Global Assembly Name	Type	Version	Culture	Public Key Token
Microsoft.VisualStudio	PreJit	1.0.2411.0		b03f5f7f11d50a3a
Microsoft.VisualStudio.V...		1.0.0.0		b03f5f7f11d50a3a
Microsoft.Vsa		7.0.0.0		b03f5f7f11d50a3a
Microsoft.Vsa.Vb.Code...		7.0.0.0		b03f5f7f11d50a3a
msatinterop		7.0.0.0		826aaeb3f85826a0
mscorcfg		1.0.2411.0		b03f5f7f11d50a3a
mscorlib	PreJit	1.0.2411.0		b77a5c561934e089
MSDATASRC		1.0.0.0		b03f5f7f11d50a3a
Office		2.2.0.0		b03f5f7f11d50a3a
Regcode		1.0.2411.0		b03f5f7f11d50a3a
SharedComponent		1.0.584.42238		2b02706ec742aab3
SoapSudsCode		1.0.2411.0		b03f5f7f11d50a3a
StdFormat		1.0.0.0		b03f5f7f11d50a3a
stdole		2.0.0.0		b03f5f7f11d50a3a

Figure 7–4   *Windows Explorer showing the global assembly cache.*

number and originator (i.e., public key token) are displayed for the assembly in Windows Explorer.

You can also drag and drop a component into the **Assembly** directory using Windows Explorer to install it in the GAC. Alternatively, you can use the **.NET Admin Tool** to install an assembly into the GAC. The **.NET Admin Tool** is an MMC snap-in located at **\WINNT\Microsoft.NET\Framework\v1.0.2914\mscorcfg.msc.** The directory version number will be different in a later release of the .NET Framework. While it may seem overkill to introduce a third tool, this MMC snap-in is a very useful utility that simplifies many tasks. Figure 7–5 shows the top-level window of this tool. To add an assembly to the GAC using this tool, just select Assembly Cache in the left pane, right mouse-click, and select Add. Using the dialog box that pops up to navigate to the file, select the assembly you want to add, and click the Open button.

Now that the shared assembly is deployed into the global assembly cache, the client program **SharedComponentClient** is able to make use of it. After you have installed the assembly in the GAC, you may then move the client program to another directory. You can then run the client without having to move the assembly installed in the GAC.

But what happens if we change the major or minor version of **SharedComponent** or re-sign it with a different private key without rebuilding the **SharedComponentClient** client program? If we had done this with the privately deployed **SimpleComponent**, we would have found that the CLR made no effort to detect this mismatch (assuming default policies in effect). However, when this is done using a shared assembly, a **FileNotFoundException** is

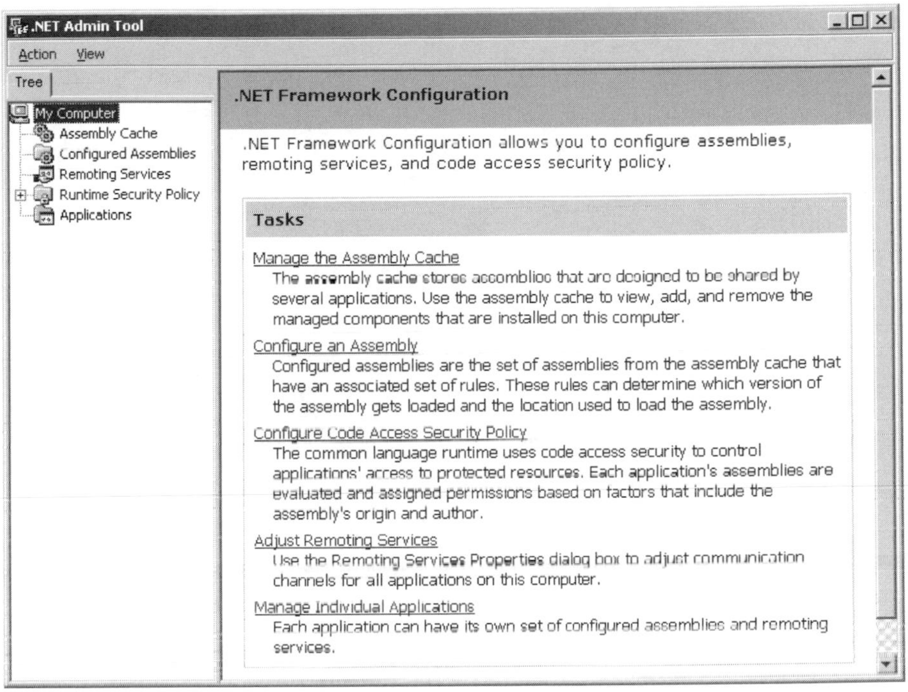

.NET Admin Tool window showing .NET Framework Configuration with a Tree pane (My Computer, Assembly Cache, Configured Assemblies, Remoting Services, Runtime Security Policy, Applications) and a Tasks panel.

.NET Framework Configuration allows you to configure assemblies, remoting services, and code access security policy.

Tasks

Manage the Assembly Cache
The assembly cache stores assemblies that are designed to be shared by several applications. Use the assembly cache to view, add, and remove the managed components that are installed on this computer.

Configure an Assembly
Configured assemblies are the set of assemblies from the assembly cache that have an associated set of rules. These rules can determine which version of the assembly gets loaded and the location used to load the assembly.

Configure Code Access Security Policy
The common language runtime uses code access security to control applications' access to protected resources. Each application's assemblies are evaluated and assigned permissions based on factors that include the assembly's origin and author.

Adjust Remoting Services
Use the Remoting Services Properties dialog box to adjust communication channels for all applications on this computer.

Manage Individual Applications
Each application can have its own set of configured assemblies and remoting services.

Figure 7–5   .NET Admin Tool supports many .NET administrative functions.

thrown by the CLR when it detects a major or minor version or a public key token that is different from that established when the client was built. Note that this exception is not thrown if the implementation is changed but the major and minor version number is not changed, and it is not signed with a different private key.

Versioning Shared Components

As we saw earlier, assemblies are versioned using a version number composed of the four fields: major, minor, build, and revision. Recall that the major and minor fields are used to indicate version changes that are not backward compatible. What happens if you install two incompatible versions of the same assembly? To see the effect of this, try changing the major or minor version numbers of the **SharedComponent** assembly deployed into the global assembly cache in the previous subsection. The previously deployed version was 1.0.584.42238, so if you build a new version with the minor number changed to 1 (i.e., 1:1:*.*), and deploy it to the global assembly cache, you will be able to see both of them side by side with distinct version numbers shown in Windows Explorer. This is shown in Figure 7–6.

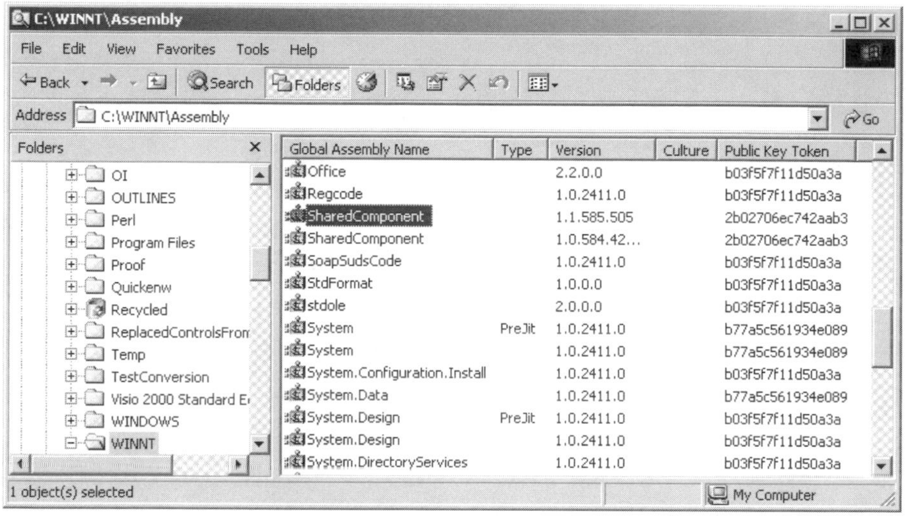

Figure 7–6   *Windows Explorer showing side-by-side components in the global assembly cache.*

Digitally Signing After Compile Time

There is now another issue to deal with regarding the deployment of shared assemblies. The steps described previously accomplished the digital signing of the assembly at compile time using an attribute that specified the key file that contains the public and private keys. It will often be the case that none of the programmers who develop the components to be packaged in an assembly are individuals who are entrusted with the private key that represents the entire organization. This means that those programmers should use a temporary private key for development and testing purposes, but when it comes time to ship the assembly to customers, an assigned individual performs the ultimate digital signing using the organization's official secret private key. This is done with the **Sn.exe** tool, using the **–R** option, where "R" stands for "re-sign." The official key pair will typically have been generated using **Sn.exe** with the **–k** option some time in the past, and the re-signing is performed using **Sn.exe** with the **–R** option on each new assembly. Although you will typically not generate a new key pair every time you re-sign a new assembly, the two commands are shown together. After the second command, you should see the console output `Assembly 'SharedComponent.dll' successfully re-signed`.

```
sn -k TrueKeyPair.snk
sn -R SharedComponent.dll TrueKeyPair.snk
```

Alternatively, you can delay digital signing. When you build the assembly, the public key is supplied to the compiler so that it can be put into the **PublicKey** field in the assembly's manifest. Space is reserved in the file for the signature, but the signature is not generated. When the actual signature is eventually generated, it is placed in the file with the **–R** option to the Strong Name utility (sn.exe).

To indicate to the compiler that you want to use delayed digital signing, you specify **true** for the **AssemblyDelaySignAttribute** in your source code. You also have to include the public key, using the **AssemblyKeyFileAttribute**.

Assuming that you have generated the public/private key pair as described previously, you then use the **–p** option of the Strong Name utility to obtain just the public key without giving out the still secret private key.

```
sn -p TrueKeyPair.snk PublicKey.snk
```

You then add the following two attributes to your code:

```
[assembly:AssemblyDelaySignAttribute(true)];
[assembly:AssemblyKeyFileAttribute("PublicKey.snk")];
```

The assembly still does not have a valid signature. You will not be able to install it into the global assembly cache or load it from an application directory. You can disable signature verification of a particular assembly by using the **–Vr** option on the Strong Name utility.

```
sn -Vr SharedComponent.dll
```

Before you ship the assembly, you must supply the valid signature so that it can be deployed as a shared assembly. You use the **–R** option on the Strong Name utility and supply the public/private key pair.

```
sn -R SharedComponent.dll TrueKeyPair.snk
```

Assembly Configuration

The CLR binds to an assembly when either a static or dynamic reference is made to it at runtime. A static reference is defined permanently in the client assembly manifest when it is compiled. A dynamic reference is produced programmatically at runtime, for example, by calling the method **System.Reflection.Assembly.Load**. In either case, the binding is accomplished in the same manner for any static or dynamic reference to an assembly with a strong name. In addition to its simple name, its version, public key (if present), and culture (if present) also distinguish a shared assembly. For binding purposes, the simple name is the minimum requirement.

The process of binding with a shared assembly is referred to as *probing,* which is nothing more than a set of heuristic rules used by the CLR to locate and load an assembly on demand. These rules only apply to a reference to an assembly with a strong name, and references to non-signed private assemblies are resolved directly, without probing or version checking (assuming that default policies are in effect).

However, you can use a strongly named assembly to force a client to bind to a specific version of an assembly. Suppose you want to allow several backward-compatible assemblies to match (i.e., satisfy CLR assembly loading). You can use an XML configuration file to specify the rules for the CLR to use when it tries to find an assembly that matches. The .NET Admin Tool can be used to create and maintain these files through a GUI.

The name of the configuration file is the client program's name appended with a **.config** extension. The configuration file is then is placed in the same directory as the client executable.

In addition to an application configuration file, there is an administration configuration file called **Machine.config**. It is found in the **Config** subdirectory under the directory where the .NET runtime is installed (**WINNT\\ Microsoft.NET\\Framework\\v1.0.2914**, where the version number reflects the current build of .NET.) An administration version policy is defined with the same XML tags an application configuration file uses. However, the administrator configuration file overrides any corresponding settings in the application configuration file.

Default Version Policy

When binding with publicly deployed assemblies, in the absence of any version policy configuration file, the binding simply uses information in the assembly's manifest to locate and load other assemblies on demand at runtime. By default, only the major and minor version parts of the version number are used, matching the major and minor numbers exactly, and then taking the most advanced build and revision available. This is often the desired effect, since the client assembly specifies dependencies on other assemblies based on major and minor version numbers that were established when client assembly was compiled. Since unchanged major and minor values conventionally indicate backward compatibility, whereas changed build and revision indicate backward-compatible fixes and changes, this default version policy often makes sense. This default version policy is also known as Automatic QFE policy. Where necessary, this behavior can be overridden, for example, to match build and revision numbers exactly, using a version policy configuration file, as described in the next subsection.

Version Policy Configuration Files

The default version policy often does have the desired effect, and this is what happens automatically if no configuration file exists. However, it may be desirable to take more control over the shared assembly binding process. As mentioned earlier, to do this for client executables, a configuration file containing XML is created with same name as the client, but with a **.config** extension, and it is placed in the same directory as the client executable. This can be useful in cases where you want to disable the default automatic QFE policy or you want to use a version of a component assembly other than the one used when the client program was compiled. It is important to note that an application configuration file can only affect the binding behavior of a single client application. It cannot be applied to all client programs that use a particular assembly.

The **<configuration>** is the top-level tag for .NET configuration files. Assembly binding information is found in the **<runtime>** section. An example **configuration** file might look like this:

```
<?xml version="1.0"?>
<configuration>
  <runtime>
    <assemblyBinding xmlns="urn:schemas-microsoft-com:asm.v1">
      <dependentAssembly>
        <assemblyIdentity name="Customer"
          publicKeyToken="8b0e612d60bde0ca" />
        <bindingRedirect oldVersion="1.0.0.0-1.1.0.0"
          newVersion="1.1.0.0" />
      </dependentAssembly>
    </assemblyBinding>
  </runtime>
</configuration>
```

Rules defining version policy are found in the **<assemblyBinding>** section. The XML namespace specification is required. Each assembly whose version policy we want to set is placed in its own **<dependentAssembly>** section. The **assemblyIdentity** element has attributes that define the assembly this section refers to. The **name** attribute is required; the **publicKeyToken** and **culture** attributes are optional.[2] The **bindingRedirect** element's attributes define what versions can map to another version. The **oldVersion**

---

[2] You may ask, why is the publicKeyToken optional. After all, there is no version resolution without it. It turns out that there are other policies that can be defined that do not require a public key.

attribute can be a range; the **newVersion** attribute can only be set to one version. In the above example, any references to versions 1.0.0.0 to 1.1.0.0 can be resolved by using version 1.1.0.0. In other words, 1.1.0.0 is backward compatible with all those versions. You can specify several **bindingRedirect** elements.

You can use the **.NET Admin Tool** to establish the configuration file. To start this tool, double-click on **\WINNT\Microsoft.NET\Framework\ v1.0.2914\mscorcfg.msc** in Windows Explorer. Then add an application to the tool by right-clicking Applications in the left pane, and select Add from the context menu. Navigate to the application you want to configure. Select it and click the Open button. Figure 7–7 shows the Admin Tool after this has been done.

Finding the Assembly's Physical Location

At this point the CLR knows what versions of the assembly will satisfy the reference. The CLR does not yet know where the assembly resides on disk. If the assembly with the right version has been previously loaded because of another reference to that assembly earlier in the program, that assembly is

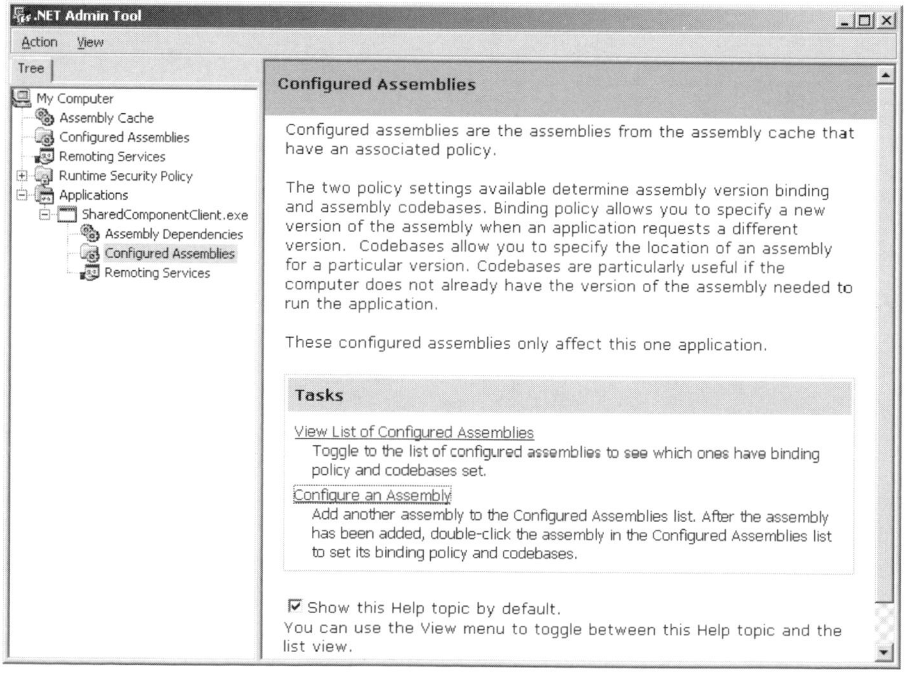

Figure 7–7   *The .NET Admin Tool used to configure a version policy.*

used. If the assembly has a strong name, the assembly cache is checked; if the correct version is found there, that assembly is used.

There are several elements you can specify in the configuration file to tell the CLR where to try and find the assembly.

If the assembly has not yet been found, the runtime checks to see if a codebase has been specified in the configuration file. Under the **<dependentAssembly>** section you can specify a **<codeBase>** element. This element has two attributes, a version and a URI, to check for the assembly. The Codebases tab on the .NET Admin Tool's assembly properties dialog can be used to set them in the configuration file. Examples of this element are:

```
<codeBase version="1.1.1.1" href="http://www.abc.com/
    Customer.dll" />
<codeBase version="1.1.1.2" href="file:///c:\AcmeGui\
    Customer.dll" />
```

To use a Codebase element outside the application's directory or subdirectories, a strong name is required. At this point, whether or not the required assembly is found, the binding process stops. If the assembly is not found, an exception is generated at this point.

If a CodeBase element was not found in the configuration file, the runtime continues to probe for the assembly. At this point all searching is relative to the directory in which the application runs, which is referred to as the *application base*.

The runtime first looks in the application base. It then looks in any subdirectories of the application base that have the same name as the assembly. If a culture is specified in the request, the runtime only looks for the assembly subdirectory under a subdirectory with the name of the culture requested.

Finally, you can specify in the **assemblyBinding** section of the configuration file a privatePath, which is a semicolon-delimited list of subdirectories of the application base to look in.

```
<probing privatePath="\bin;\assemb" />
```

You can also set the privatePath on the properties tab for the application in the .NET Admin Tool.

Multi-Module Assemblies

An assembly can be made up of multiple modules. A module is a DLL (or EXE) that contains managed code plus metadata, but not necessarily a manifest. However, an assembly must have one and only one manifest, so an assembly can contain multiple modules, but only one that contains a manifest that provides information on the contents of all the modules in the assembly. The module with the manifest may have just the manifest, or it can contain other code or resources.

The main advantage of breaking a large assembly into modules is that each module is contained in a separate DLL file. This allows Web downloads to be performed on demand on a per module basis. This can improve performance and memory consumption. Even in a local scenario, the CLR loads classes on the local machine with module granularity, which can improve efficiency. Another reason for constructing an assembly with multiple modules is that you may have written each part of an assembly in a different .NET language. To build an assembly that contains multiple modules, you need to build each module separately and then combine them with the **Al.exe** utility.

There are two ways to go about creating a multi-module assembly. One way is to create all the modules without any manifest, and then create one additional module that contains only a manifest for the entire assembly, but no actual code. The other technique is to have just one module in the assembly that contains both code and a manifest for the entire assembly, and all other modules in the assembly contain only code, with no manifest. We will describe the first of these two alternatives, since it is more symmetric and easier to visualize. The second alternative is not described here; however, it is done in a similar way, with the same tools.

We first create two modules with no manifest, using Visual C++ with managed extensions. Then we create a third module with a manifest that contains information on both of the other two modules, using the Assembly Linker tool **Al.exe**. Together, these three modules form an assembly. Figure 7–8 shows the resulting assembly's structure.

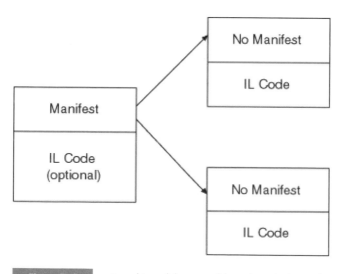

Figure 7–8 *A multi-module assembly with a dedicated manifest module.*

Code
Example

The following source files constitute the first module without a manifest. It contains a public class named **ClassInModuleWithoutManifest1**, which exposes a public method named **SomeMethod**. You can create it using the managed C++ Class Library template.

```
//ModuleWithoutManifest1.h

using namespace System;
namespace ModuleWithoutManifest1
{
    public __gc class ClassInModuleWithoutManifest1
    {
    public:
      void SomeMethod();
    };
}
```

```
//ModuleWithoutManifest1.cpp

#include "stdafx.h" //has a #using <mscorlib.dll>
using namespace System;
#include "ModuleWithoutManifest1.h"
namespace ModuleWithoutManifest1
{
    void ClassInModuleWithoutManifest1::SomeMethod()
    {
      Console::WriteLine(
          "ClassInModuleWithoutManifest1::SomeMethod");
    }
}
```

The **/CLR:noAssembly** compiler option specifies that managed code is generated, but no assembly manifest is to be generated. The **/c** compiler option suppresses automatic linking, since we will do that as a separate command. The **/NOASSEMBLY** link option also prevents manifest information from being generated. Therefore, the following two commands are used at the command prompt to produce the first DLL module with no manifest:

```
cl /CLR:noAssembly /c ModuleWithoutManifest1.cpp
link /NOASSEMBLY /DLL ModuleWithoutManifest1.obj
```

If you prefer to build the module within Visual Studio.NET, you will first need to change these compiler and linker options for the project to prevent manifest information from being added to the module. To set the **/CLR:noAssembly** compiler option in Visual Studio.NET, do the following:

1. Open the project's Property Pages dialog box. To do this, right mouse-click on the ModuleWithoutManifest1 node under the solution node in the ClassView window.
2. Open the Configuration Properties folder.
3. Open the C/C++ folder.
4. Click the General page under the C/C++ folder.
5. Modify the Compile as managed property to be **MetaData Only (/CLR:noAssembly)**.

The result of this compile must now be linked with the **/NOASSEMBLY** linker option in Visual Studio.NET. This linker option requires that you also set the **/NOENTRY** linker option. To make these changes to the project, do the following:

1. Open the project's Property Pages dialog box if it is not still open.
2. Open the Configuration Properties folder if it is not still open.
3. Open the Linker folder.
4. Click the Advanced page under the Linker folder.
5. Modify the Turn Off Assembly Generation property to be **Yes (/NOASSEMBLY)**.
6. Still in the Advanced page, set the Resource Only DLL property to **Yes (/NOENTRY)**.

Then, you can go ahead and build the project in the usual way.

The second DLL module, named **ClassInModuleWithManifest2.dll**, will also be built without a manifest. The following source files, which are very similar to those shown in the first module, constitute the second module with no manifest. It contains a public class named **ClassInModule-WithoutManifest2**, which exposes a public method named **SomeOther-Method**. Again, this project can be created using the managed C++ Class Library template in Visual Studio.NET.

```
//ModuleWithoutManifest2.h

using namespace System;
namespace ModuleWithoutManifest2
{
   public __gc class ClassInModuleWithoutManifest2
   {
   public:
      void SomeOtherMethod();
   };
}
```

```
//ModuleWithoutManifest2.cpp

#include "stdafx.h" //has a #using <mscorlib.dll>
using namespace System;
#include "ModuleWithoutManifest2.h"
namespace ModuleWithoutManifest2
{
    void ClassInModuleWithoutManifest2::SomeOtherMethod()
    {
        Console::WriteLine(
            "ClassInModuleWithoutManifest2::SomeOtherMethod");
    }
}
```

This module will also have no manifest, and it is built with the following commands, which are virtually identical to those shown for the first module:

```
cl /CLR:noAssembly /c ModuleWithoutManifest2.cpp
link /NOASSEMBLY /DLL ModuleWithoutManifest2.obj
```

Again, you can use the same steps as in the previous module if you want to build it within Visual Studio.NET. Just remember to set the Compile as managed property to be **MetaData Only (/CLR:noAssembly)**, set the Turn Off Assembly Generation property to be **Yes (/NOASSEMBLY)**, and set the Resource Only DLL property to **Yes (/NOENTRY)**.

Finally, the two modules must be placed into the same assembly. Note that they are not physically linked together. They remain as distinct DLL files, but they are placed into a combined logical assembly. To do this, the Assembly Linker utility **Al.exe** is used to incorporate the metadata information of both modules into one manifest contained in a third DLL named **Combined-Assembly.dll**. To do this, copy the two existing modules into a common directory named **CombinedAssembly**, and enter the following command:

```
Al ModuleWithoutManifest1.dll, ModuleWithoutManifest2.dll /
    out:CombinedAssembly.dll
```

We have now finished building a multi-module assembly. The assembly's manifest is contained in **CombinedAssembly.dll**. In order to test it, we need to create a test client program. Note that all modules need to be accessible to the client. This could be accomplished by either local or shared deployment. To make this example simple, we will locally deploy the assembly, which means that we will just copy the three DLL modules into the same director as the test client program. The following code implements the test

Code
Example

client program. Note that only the one assembly DLL named **CombinedAssembly.dll** is referenced in the client, since this is the only one that contains a manifest. If you now build this client program and copy the three DLLs, you will see that it successfully calls into methods defined by classes defined in the separate DLL modules. However, only the one **CombinedAssembly.dll** assembly is being referenced. This proves that the three modules are working as a single logical assembly.

```
//MultiModuleAssemblyTestClient.cpp

#include "stdafx.h"
#using <mscorlib.dll>
#using <C:\OI\NetCpp\Chap7\CombinedAssembly\
   CombinedAssembly.dll>
using namespace ModuleWithoutManifest1;
using namespace ModuleWithoutManifest2;
void main()
{
   ClassInModuleWithoutManifest1 *p1 =
      new ClassInModuleWithoutManifest1;
   p1->SomeMethod();
   ClassInModuleWithoutManifest2 *p2 =
      new ClassInModuleWithoutManifest2;
   p2->SomeOtherMethod();
}
```

Deploying the Case Study

As you may recall, the case study in the previous chapter was implemented in C# rather than in managed C++, since it had a great deal of GUI code that is much better suited to C# than C++. For the purposes of this chapter, this would still be fine, since deployment is the same for assemblies written in any .NET language, including C# and managed C++. However, the project has been partially converted from C# to managed C++. For this step of the case study, we have split our Hotel Administrator's program into three assemblies. The **CaseStudy** directory for this chapter has an **AcmeGui** application program (EXE) written in C#, and two component (DLL) assemblies that have been implemented in managed C++: **Customer** and **Hotel**. The C# portion is dedicated to Forms (i.e., GUI functionality). The non-GUI code associated with the **Customer** and **Hotel** classes, as well as related classes, interfaces, and structs in the previous version of the case study, have been moved to the new managed C++ DLL assemblies.

If you look at Figure 7–9, you will see that the Solution Explorer shows that the **AcmeGui** project has references to the **Customer** and **Hotel** DLL assemblies. These references enable the compiler to find the **Hotel** and **Customer** types used by **AcmeGui** and then build the application. They do not dictate where the DLLs have to be when the project is deployed. You will also notice references made to system assemblies such as **System.dll**. Looking at the properties for the reference will show you where the assembly is located.[3]

Creating a managed C++ Class Library as a project within the existing AcmeGui solution is easy. Right-click on the Solution **AcmeGui** node in Solution Explorer, then select Add | New Project. Select the Visual C++ Project type, select the Managed Class Library template, browse to the CaseStudy location, and name the project **Customer**. Select Class Library from the New Project Wizard in Visual Studio.NET, then specify a location and name, and then click OK. The location for the Customer project is under **C:\OI\ NetCpp\Chap7\CaseStudy**. The same is done for the other DLL assembly named **Hotel**. To set up a reference to each DLL assembly from your project, you use the **#using** statement. Of course, the libraries have to be built before they can be referenced.

Figure 7–10 shows the top level that you will see when you open the **Customer.dll** assembly in **ILDASM** and double-click on the **OI.NetCpp. Acme** namespace. You see entries for the MANIFEST, the **Customers** and **Customer** classes, the **ICustomer** interface, and the **CustomerListItem** type. Clicking on the plus (+) button will expand an entry.

To view the manifest, double-click the MANIFEST node, shown in Figure 7–10, and the resulting manifest information is displayed in Figure 7–11. Some of the numbers will vary if you have rebuilt any of the samples or you have a later version of .NET.

The manifest contains information about the dependencies and contents of the assembly. You can see that the manifest for **Customer** contains, among others, the following external dependency:[4]

```
.assembly extern mscorlib
{
  .publickeytoken = (B7 7A 5C 56 19 34 E0 89 )
  .hash = (09 BB BC 09 EF 6D 9B F4 F2 CC 1B 55 ... EF 77 )
  .ver 1:0:2411:0
}
```

The **.assembly extern mscorlib** metadata statement indicates that the **Customer** assembly makes use of, and is therefore dependant on, the standard

---

[3] Select the assembly in the Solution Explorer, right mouse-click, select Properties in the context menu.
[4] If you have rebuilt any of the components, you will of course see different build and revision numbers.

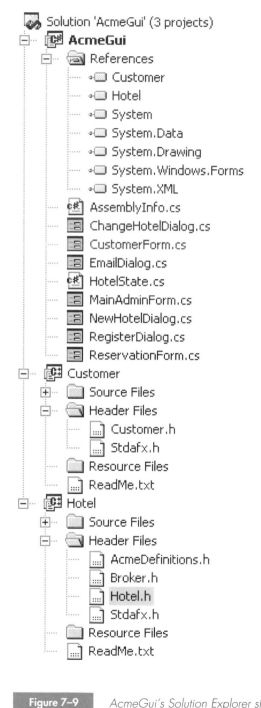

Figure 7–9   *AcmeGui's Solution Explorer showing References.*

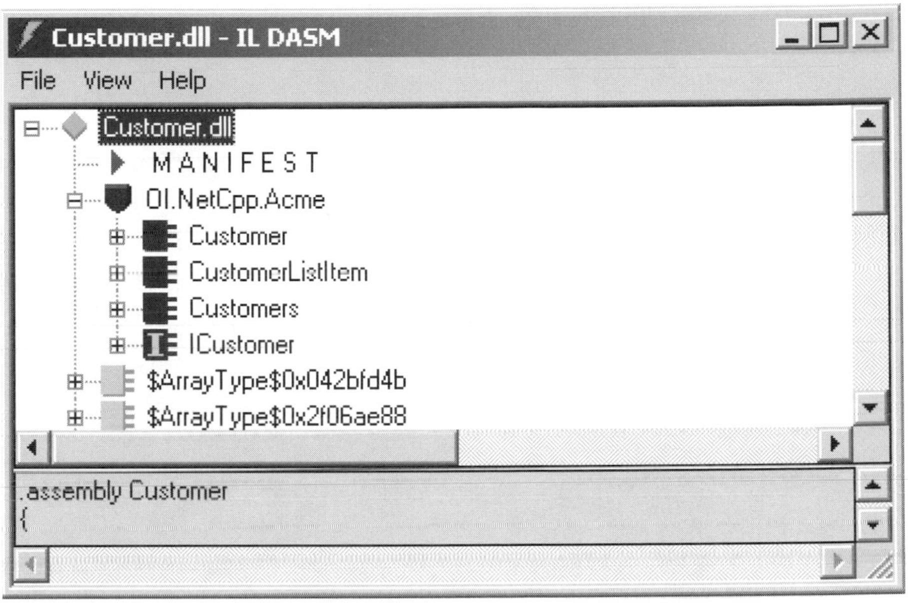

Figure 7–10   *Top Level ILDASM View of Customer Component.*

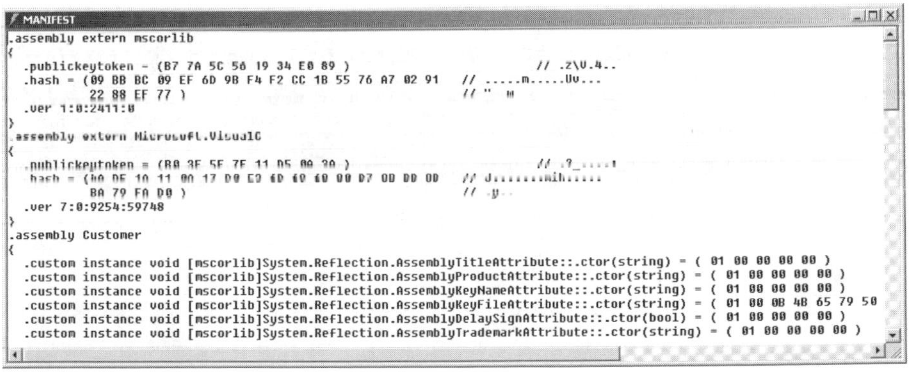

Figure 7–11   *ILDASM showing manifest of Customer.dll.*

assembly **mccorlib.dll**, which is required by all managed code. When an assembly makes a reference to another assembly, you will see an **.assembly extern** metadata statement. If you open **AcmeGui** in ILADASM and look at the manifest, you will see dependencies on several other assemblies, including the **Customer** and **Hotel** assemblies as well as the **System.Drawing** assembly.

```
.assembly extern Customer
{
  .publickeytoken = (8B 0E 61 2D 60 BD E0 CA )
  .ver 1:0:641:33530
}
.assembly extern Hotel
{
  .publickeytoken = (CF 0B C2 2F 8E 2C 15 22 )
  .ver 1:0:641:33536
}
.assembly extern System.Drawing
{
  .publickeytoken = (B0 3F 5F 7F 11 D5 0A 3A )
  .ver 1:0:2411:0
}
```

The **System.Drawing** assembly is a shared assembly, which can be seen in the **\WINNT\Assembly** directory using Windows Explorer. **Mscorlib**, which is a shared assembly, is not deployed in the assembly cache. Microsoft made a single exception here because **mscorlib** is so closely tied with the CLR engine (**mscorwks**[5]) it is installed in the appropriate install directory (**\WINNT\Microsoft.NET\Framework**) for the current .NET version.

In the **System.Drawing** shared assembly, the **.publickeytoken = (B0 3F 5F 7F 11 D5 0A 3A)** metadata statement provides a public key token, which is the lowest 8 bytes of a hash of the public key that matches the corresponding private key owned by the **System.Drawing** assembly's author. This public key token cannot actually be used directly to authenticate the identity of the author of the **System.Drawing**. However, the original public key specified in the **System.Drawing** manifest can be used to mathematically verify that the matching private key was actually used to digitally sign the **System.Drawing** assembly. Since Microsoft authored **System.Drawing.dll**, the public key token seen above is Microsoft-specific.

Setup and Deployment Projects

Assemblies may be deployed as regular standalone binary code files (i.e. DLL or EXE files), or they may be deployed using CAB, MSI, or MSM files. A CAB file is a cabinet file with the **.cab** file name extension. A CAB file is used to compress

---

[5] Or **mscorsvr.dll** for servers.

and combine other files into one convenient manageable file. Although CAB files can be used for general purposes, they have traditionally been used for CD-based and Web-based installation. MSI and MSM files are Microsoft Windows Installer files with the **.msi** and **.msm** file name extensions. MSI files (and, indirectly, MSM files) are used with the **Msiexec.exe** Windows Installer program to deploy standalone applications and reusable components.

MSI files are Microsoft Windows Installer installation packages that have the **.msi** file name extension. MSM files are merge modules that have the **.msm** file name extension. Windows Installer supports software installation, repair, upgrade, and removal. Windows Installer packages are self-contained database files that provide installation information to the Windows Installer service. An MSM file has an internal structure that is similar to an MSI file, but it is somewhat simplified. Unfortunately, an MSM file cannot be used directly by Windows Installer, since it lacks certain important database tables. Instead, the MSM file must be merged into an MSI file to be used in an actual installation session. However, MSM files are useful for separating out shared installation information into an independent package that can then be merged into many other MSI packages.

Installation may be accomplished using the Windows Installer, Internet Explorer, or simply by manually copying assemblies and associated files. To help the programmer develop setup and deployment solutions, Visual Studio.NET provides several templates and wizards for generating starter setup projects. These tools are available by way of the New Project dialog box under the Setup and Deployment Projects node, as shown in Figure 7–12. As you can see, the following templates are provided for generating starter setup and deployment projects:

- Cab Project
- Setup Project
- Setup Wizard
- Merge Module Project
- Web Setup Project

CAB Project

A CAB project creates a cabinet file containing any number of other files that can be used for traditional deployment purposes. CAB files have been used to package legacy COM components deployed over the Internet, and they have also been used in traditional CD-based installation programs. CAB files may now also be used for packaging managed code; however, for .NET deployment, a CAB file can contain only one assembly, and the CAB file be must be assigned the same name as the contained assembly, but with the **.cab** extension. For example, an assembly named **SomeComponent.dll** would have to be contained in a cabinet file named **SomeComponent.cab**.

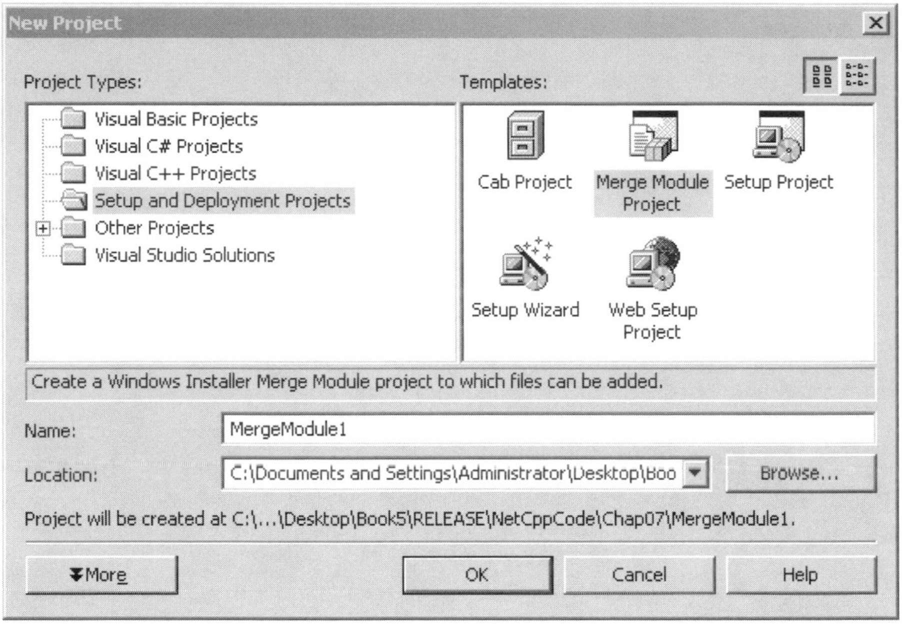

Figure 7–12 *Setup and Deployment Projects templates.*

Setup Project

The Setup Project template creates a Windows Installer **.msi** file for a desktop or distributed application. A setup project is not intended for deployment of Web-based applications, since a specialized Web setup project is used for that purpose. A setup project produces a program that installs an application onto a target machine. You may create setup projects within the same solution that contains the other projects to be deployed. In a multi-tier solution, you can create one setup project for each project that is to be deployed to a particular target computer. For example, in a simple three-tier solution, you would probably have three deployment projects. Two simple deployment projects would setup the client, and server. A third deployment project would then look after the more complex middle-tier business logic. Additional deployment projects may come into play if the solution were highly complex or if merge modules were incorporated into the deployment strategy.

To create a setup project, select File | New, then select Project. In the New Project dialog box, select Setup and Deployment Projects as the Project Type. Finally, select Setup Project as the Template, specify name and location, and then click OK. The result of this is shown in Figure 7–13, showing Solution Explorer and the File System Editor.

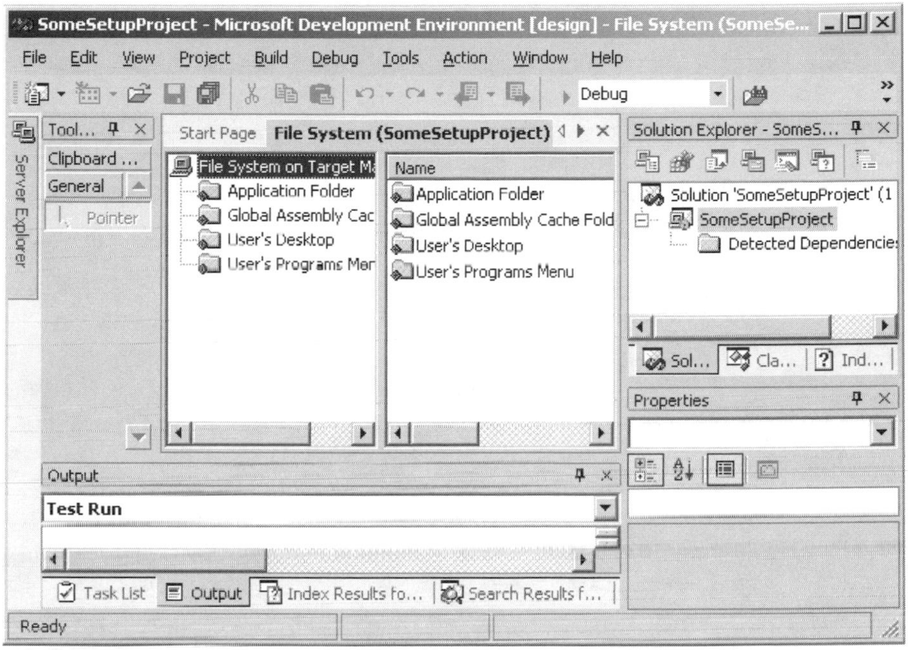

Figure 7-13   *Solution Explorer and the File System Editor in a setup project.*

Once the initial setup project has been created with the Setup Project template, it can be further developed using the File System Editor. The File System Editor allows you to drag and drop or copy and paste files to be deployed by the setup deployment project, and control their destinations on the target machine. Initially, the File System Editor shows an initial list of destination folders that you can deploy into, and you can also add your own folders to this list.

Once you have an MSI file created, you can use Windows Installer, as shown in the following command line:

```
Msiexec /i SomeSetup.msi
```

The Windows Installer program then starts up and displays a series of installation dialogs. After Windows Installer has completed the deployment, you can try running the installed application to verify that the installation was successful. If you run the same command, **Msiexec /i SomeSetup.msi**, it will detect that it already exists, so it gives you the choice to either repair the installation or uninstall the application.

Merge Module Project

A merge module project packages reusable setup information that can be independently maintained and then merged as a shared installation package into other installation packages. A merge module project produces a merge module **.msm** file that can be merged into **.msi** files. This allows you to share common assemblies, associated files, registry values, and setup functionality among multiple applications.

To start the Merge Module Project Wizard, select File | New, then select Project. In the New Project dialog box, select Setup and Deployment Projects as the Project Type. Finally, select Merge Module Project Wizard as the Template, specify name and location, and then click OK.

Typically, an MSI file is intended for use by the end user for installing a complete solution in one simple deployment session. In contrast, an MSM file is typically intended for use by other developers who want to use components that you have developed in their own setup projects. Those other developers can merge your MSM file into their own MSI file for deploying your components into their test and development environments as well as for their ultimate end user. End users should not be provided any MSM files, since they are not directly installable using Windows Installer, and they are not very friendly to work with.

To add an existing merge module project to a setup project, create or open the setup project and Select File | Add Project, and then select Existing Project. In the Add Existing Project dialog box, browse to the location of the desired merge module project, select the associated **.vdp** deployment project file, and then click Open.

We just added the merge module project to the solution. We now have to add it to the setup project itself. Select the setup project and invoke **Add:Project Output**, then select the merge module project in the dialog that appears.

Web-based Deployment

Web-based deployment uses Internet Explorer on the client to automatically download assemblies packaged as EXE, DLL, or CAB files on demand from a .NET Web server. HTML files can dynamically deploy assemblies as well as configuration files to control the binding process. Web-based deployment results in assemblies being downloaded into the client's global assembly download cache on demand.

The **<object>** tag is used to download and install assemblies, using either a relative or absolute URL. The following shows a relative URL example, where the assembly is located relative to the directory of the containing HTML file on the Web server:

```
<object
    id="SomeComponent"
```

```
    classid="./SomeDirectory/MyComponent.dll#SomeClass">
</object>
```

The following shows an absolute URL example, where the assembly is located on a specified Web server:

```
<object
    id="SomeComponent"
    classid="http://www.acme.com/MyComponent.dll#SomeClass">
</object>
```

By default, IE creates a separate application domain for each Web site that it encounters. An application domain is a .NET feature that can be thought of as a scalable lightweight process. An application domain efficiently provides fault isolation without the overhead of running actual multiple processes. Each of these application domains may optionally have its own configuration file to control binding and security. Also, a configuration file may specify an isolated application domain for individual applications on the same Web server. Each HTML file that specifies the same configuration file will be placed into the same application domain.

Summary

Deployment is very important, and it constitutes one of the major phases in software development. If it is not done properly, the entire development effort becomes a waste of time and money. Fortunately, with assemblies, which are the fundamental units of .NET deployment, many of the complexities and problems relating to deployment are conveniently solved. By simply building dynamic-link libraries, you can have reusable components without all the difficulties associated with building and installing COM components.

Private assembly deployment involves no more than simply copying the assembly to the same directory as the client application. Public assembly deployment, involves the creation of a strong name for the assembly, followed by deployment into the global assembly cache. The Strong Name utility (**Sn.exe**) can be used to create the strong name for an assembly. The Global Assembly Cache utility **Gacutil.exe** or the **.NET Admin Tool** can then be used to deploy the shared assembly into the global assembly cache. It is also possible to combine multiple modules into a single logical assembly. To do this, you build separate modules that lack manifest information, and then a manifest module can be generated for the entire set of modules that comprise the assembly. The Visual Studio.NET CAB and setup wizards are very useful for creating starter setup and deployment projects, which can save a great deal of development time.

EIGHT

.NET Framework Classes

*I*t is impossible to cover in one chapter, or even in one book, all of the .NET Framework classes. Although coverage is incomplete, the .NET classes cover a large fraction of the Win32 API, as well as much else. While a lot of attention has been focused on the Internet-related functionality, the development model for Windows applications has changed as well.

This chapter focuses on those classes that illustrate the key concepts and patterns that appear throughout the .NET Framework. You will find this approach more fruitful over the long run than our attempting to explain a little about every class that you might need without giving you much insight. Other chapters will go into more depth about other parts of the framework, such as Windows Forms, ASP.NET, ADO.NET security, and Web Services.

We start out by exploring the concept of reflection and metadata. Meta data appears everywhere in .NET and is critical to understanding how the Common Language Runtime (CLR) can provide services for your applications. Next, we explore file input/output for several reasons. First, it introduces the important topic of serialization. Second, the **Path** class provides an example of how some framework classes provide some or all of their functionality through static methods. Third, the formatter classes are used in several places in .NET.

Understanding serialization will give you a concrete idea of how the framework can handle objects transparently for you. It also appears in a supporting role any place where objects have to be stored or transported. Our discussion of the **ISerializable** interface again demonstrates how much easier it is to implement an interface in .NET than with COM.

To further develop an understanding of the .NET model for applications, we introduce programming with threads under .NET and several .NET synchronization techniques to handle multithreading conflicts. The various synchronization techniques illustrate the tradeoffs of using attributes supplied by the framework versus doing it your self.

To further your understanding of the .NET programming model, we introduce *context* and the use of proxies and stubs to implement system services. We also look at using *application domains*, which are more efficient than Win32 processes in achieving application isolation.

The asynchronous design pattern appears throughout .NET and is discussed in some detail. We give some examples of remoting because it is a key technology and it summarizes many of the concepts developed in this chapter. The chapter uses several attributes provided by the .NET Framework, and we show how to implement and use custom attributes. We discuss finalization so that you can understand how to make sure resources are properly freed in your applications.

Metadata and Reflection

The **Serialization** example in Chapter 2 demonstrates how metadata makes many of the services of the CLR possible. Many of the technologies we cover in the rest of the book rely on metadata, although we will not always stop and point this out.

Metadata is information about the assemblies, modules, and types that constitute .NET programs. If you have ever had to create IDL to generate a type library so that your C++ COM objects could be called by Visual Basic, or to create proxies and stubs, you will appreciate how useful metadata is and will be grateful that it comes "for free."

Compilers emit metadata, and the CLR, the .NET Framework, or your own programs can use it. Since we want to give you an understanding of how metadata works, we will focus our discussion on the use of metadata, not the creation of metadata. Metadata is read using classes in the **System::Reflection** namespace.[1]

When you load an assembly and its associated modules and types, the metadata is loaded along with it. You can then query the assembly to get those associated types. You can also call **GetType** on any CLR type and get its metadata. **GetType** is a method on **System::Object**, which every CLR type inherits from. After you get the **Type** associated with an object, you can use the reflection methods to get the related metadata.

The **Reflection** sample program takes the case study's **Customer** assembly and prints out some of the metadata available. You should examine the output and source code as you read the next sections. You should espe-

---

[1] There is a lower level set of unmanaged COM interfaces for accessing metadata, but we will not discuss them here. See "Metadata in .NET" by Matt Pietrek in the October 2000 *MSDN Magazine*.

cially compare the output of the program with the source code in the file **customer.h**.

The program clearly shows that it is possible to retrieve all of the types in an assembly and reconstruct the structures, interfaces, properties, events, and methods associated with those types.

First we load the assembly into memory and write out its name.

```
Assembly *a = Assembly::Load(assemblyName);
Console::WriteLine(
    "Assembly {0} found.", a->FullName);
```

The output for this statement is appropriate for an unsigned assembly:

```
Assembly Customer, Version=1.0.643.18973, Culture=neutral,
    PublicKeyToken=null found.
```

One of the properties of the **Assembly** class is the **CodeBase**, discussed Chapter 7, "Assemblies and Deployment." The security evidence associated with this assembly is another property.

The following code tries to get the entry point for the assembly:

```
MethodInfo *entryMethodInfo = a->EntryPoint;
```

Since this is a typical C++ component assembly, the entry point is **__DllMainCRTStartup@12**. If this was an executable program, we could use the **Invoke** method on the **MethodInfo** class to run the startup code in the assembly.[2]

The sample uses the assembly's **GetModules** method to find associated modules with this assembly. In this case we have only one, named **customer.dll**. We could then find the types associated with the module. Instead, we use the assembly's **GetTypes** method to return an array of the assembly's types.

Type

The abstract class **Type** in the **System** namespace defines .NET types. Since there are no functions outside of classes or global variables in .NET, getting all the types in an assembly will allow us to get all the metadata about the code in that assembly. **Type** represents all the types present in .NET: classes, structs, interfaces, values, arrays, and enumerations.

The **Type** class is also returned by the **GetType** method on the **System::Object** class and the static **GetType** method on the **Type** class itself. The latter method can be used only with types that can be resolved statically.

---

[2] You can also load and execute the assembly from the AppDomain, as we discuss later in this chapter.

One of **Type**'s properties is the assembly to which it belongs. You can get all the types in the containing assembly once you have the **Type** of one object. **Type** is an abstract class, and at runtime an instance of **System::RuntimeType** is returned.

If you examine the program's output, you will see that each type in the assembly, **CustomerListItem**, **ICustomer**, **Customer**, and **Customers**, is found and its metadata is printed out. We can find out the standard attributes and the type from which the class derives for each type through the **Attributes** and **BaseType** properties.

The methods associated with the **Type** class enable you to get the associated fields, properties, interfaces, events, and methods. For example, the **Customer** type has no interfaces, properties, or events, but it has four fields, three constructors, and the methods inherited from its **BaseType System::Object**:

```
Interfaces:
Fields:
    CustomerId
    FirstName
    LastName
    EmailAddress
Properties:
Events:
Constructors:
    public .ctor(System.String first, System.String last,
        System.String email)
    public .ctor()
    public .ctor(System.Int32 id)
Methods:
    public Int32 GetHashCode()
    public Boolean Equals(System.Object obj)
    public String ToString()
    public Type GetType()
```

The type **Customers** inherits from one interface and has one constructor and four of its own methods in addition to the four it inherited from its **BaseType System::Object**:

```
Interfaces:
    ICustomer
Fields:
Properties:
Events:
Constructors:
```

```
    public .ctor()
Methods:
    public Void ChangeEmailAddress(System.Int32 id,
        System.String emailAddress)
    public ArrayList GetCustomer(System.Int32 id)
    public Void UnregisterCustomer(System.Int32 id)
    public Int32 RegisterCustomer(System.String firstName,
        System.String lastName, System.String emailAddress)
    public Int32 GetHashCode()
    public Boolean Equals(System.Object obj)
    public String ToString()
    public Type GetType()
```

These were obtained with the **GetInterfaces**, **GetFields**, **GetProperties**, **GetEvents**, **GetConstructors**, and **GetMethods** methods on the **Type** class. Since an interface is a type, **GetInterfaces** returns an array of **Types** representing the interfaces inherited or implemented by the **Type** queried. Since fields, properties, events, and methods are not types, their accessor methods do not return **Types**. Each of their accessor methods returns an appropriate class: **FieldInfo**, **PropertyInfo**, **EventInfo**, **ConstructorInfo**, and **MethodInfo**. All these classes, as well as the **Type** class, inherit from the **MemberInfo** class that is the abstract base class for member metadata.

Let us examine some of the metadata associated with a class method. Using the reflection methods, we were able to reconstruct the signatures for all the classes and interfaces in the **Customer** assembly. Here is the output for the methods of the **Customers** class:

```
public Void ChangeEmailAddress(System.Int32 id,
    System.String emailAddress)
public ArrayList GetCustomer(System.Int32 id)
public Void UnregisterCustomer(System.Int32 id)
public Int32 RegisterCustomer(System.String firstName,
    System.String lastName, System.String emailAddress)
public Int32 GetHashCode()
public Boolean Equals(System.Object obj)
public String ToString()
public Type GetType()
```

Here is the code from the example that produced the output:

```
for (int j = 0; j < methodInfo.Length; j++)
{
    if (methodInfo[j]->IsStatic)
        Console::Write("        static ");
```

```
            if (methodInfo[j]->IsPublic)
                Console::Write("          public ");
            if (methodInfo[j]->IsFamily)
                Console::Write("          protected ");
            if (methodInfo[j]->IsAssembly)
                Console::Write("          internal ");
            if (methodInfo[j]->IsPrivate)
                Console::Write("          private ");
            Console::Write(
                "{0} ", methodInfo[j]->ReturnType->Name);
            Console::Write(
                "{0}(", methodInfo[j]->Name);
            ParameterInfo *paramInfo [] =
                methodInfo[j]->GetParameters();
            long last = paramInfo->Length - 1;
            for (int k = 0; k<paramInfo->Length; k++)
            {
                Console::Write(
                    "{0} {1}",
                    paramInfo[k]->ParameterType,
                    paramInfo[k]->Name);
                if (k != last)
                    Console::Write(", ");
            }
            Console::WriteLine(")");
        }
```

Except that a constructor does not have a return type, the exact same code reconstitutes the calling sequences for the class's constructors.

The **MethodInfo** class has properties that help us determine if the method is static, public, protected, internal, or private as well as determine the return type and method name. The method parameters are stored in a property array of type **ParameterInfo** class.

This example should also make it clear that types are assembly relative. The same type name and layout in two different assemblies are treated by the runtime as two separate types. When versioning assemblies, you have to be careful when mixing versioned types or the same types in two different assemblies.

All this metadata allows the CLR and the framework to provide services to your applications, because they can understand the structure of your types.

Late Binding

Reflection can also be used to implement late binding. Late binding is where the method to be called is determined during execution rather than at compilation time. It is one example of how metadata can be used to provide functionality. As the previous example demonstrates, you can extract the signature of a method associated with a type. The **MethodInfo** object has all the needed metadata for a class method. The **Dynamic** sample demonstrates a very simple example of late binding.[3]

We dynamically load an assembly and get the metadata for a method of a particular type:

```
// Load Customer assembly
Assembly *a = Assembly::Load("Customer");

// Get metadata for Customers class and one method
Type *t = a->GetType("OI.NetCpp.Acme.Customers");
MethodInfo *mi = t->GetMethod("GetCustomer");
```

One thing that C++ programmers need to remember when doing reflection programming is that when you deal with strings that contain namespaces or classes, you must use properly formatted strings that are understood by the reflection class methods. So, the fully qualified class name in the code above is OI.NetCpp.Acme.Customers rather than the C++ style format OI::NetCpp::Acme::Customers. Thus, the format used is like that of C#, not C++.

Using the reflection classes, we could have made this completely dynamic by arbitrarily picking types, methods, and constructors from the **Customer** assembly using the techniques of the last example, but we wanted to keep the **Dynamic** example simple. A more ambitious program could do something much more interesting, such as implement an assembly decompiler that generates Managed C++, C#, or VB.NET source code directly from a compiled assembly.

The **System** namespace has an **Activator** class that has overloaded **CreateInstance** methods to create an instance of any .NET type using the appropriate constructor. The **Activator** class is discussed in this chapter's section on remoting. We invoke a constructor with no arguments to create an instance of the **Customers** object.

```
Type *t = a->GetType("OI.NetCpp.Acme.Customers");
...
Object *customerInstance =
    Activator::CreateInstance(t);
```

---

[3] After you build the **Dynamic** project, you must copy **Customer.dll** from the **Dynamic\Customer\Debug** directory to the **Dynamic\Debug** directory before running **Dynamic.exe**.

We then build an argument list and use the **Invoke** method of the **MethodInfo** instance to call the **GetCustomer** method.

```
// invoke the method
Object *arguments [] = new Object*[1];
int customerId = -1;
arguments[0] = __box(customerId);
Object *returnType = mi->Invoke(
   customerInstance, arguments);
```

Using the reflection methods, we get the type information for each field in a return structure. Note that the **GetValue** method of **FieldInfo** returns the data for a particular field in an object.

```
if (returnType->GetType() ==
   Type::GetType("System.Collections.ArrayList"))
{
   ArrayList *arrayList =
      dynamic_cast<ArrayList *>(returnType);
   for (int i = 0; i<arrayList->Count; i++)
   {
      Type *itemType =
         arrayList->get_Item(i)->GetType();
      FieldInfo *fi [] = itemType->GetFields();
      for (int j = 0; j < fi->Length; j++)
      {
         Object *fieldValue =
            fi[j]->GetValue(arrayList->get_Item(i));
         Console::Write(
            "{0, -10} = {1, -15}",
            fi[j]->Name, fieldValue);
      }
      Console::WriteLine();
   }
}
```

Again, note the use of the single periods rather than double colons in the string System.Collections.ArrayList.

This code did not use any specific objects or types from the **Customer** assembly. We did use some knowledge about the assembly to keep the code simple to illustrate the main points. It should be clear, however, how to make this completely general.

You can take this one step further and use the classes that emit metadata (in **System::Reflection::Emit**). You can even dynamically create an assembly in memory, and then load and run it!

Input and Output in .NET

To make a crude generalization, the input/output functions in the .NET Framework can be divided into two broad categories, irrespective of the data storage (disk, memory, etc.) that is being written to or read from.

Data can be treated as a stream of bytes or characters. For example, we could read 500 bytes from a file and write them to a memory buffer. Data can also be treated as a set of objects. Reading and writing the objects is referred to as deserializing and serializing the objects. We can serialize (write) the list of **Customer** objects to disk. We can then deserialize (read) the list of **Customer** objects back into memory.

The **System::IO** namespace has several classes for reading and writing to various types of storage while treating the data as bytes or characters. Serialization functionality can be found in various places in the .NET framework. The **System::Runtime::Serialization** namespace handles serialization of the Common Type System. The **System::Xml::Serialization** namespace handles XML serialization.

Stream Classes

Stream is an abstract class that is the basis for reading from and writing bytes to some storage such as a file. It supports both synchronous and asynchronous reading and writing. Asynchronous methods are discussed later in this chapter. The **Stream** class has the typical methods that you would expect: **Read**, **Write**, **Seek**, **Flush**, and **Close**.

The **FileStream** class is derived from **Stream** to represent the reading and writing of files as a series of bytes. The **FileStream** constructor builds the actual stream instance. The overridden **Stream** methods implement the reading and writing to the file.

Other classes derived from **Stream** include **MemoryStream**, **Buffered-Stream**, and **NetworkStream** (in **System::Net::Sockets**).

The **FileStream** example (in the **FileIO** directory with the IO examples) illustrates how to use the **Stream** classes. If the file does not exist, a new file is created and the numbers from 0 to 9 are written to the file. If the file already exists, the code starts reading 5 bytes from the end of the file and then writes them out. (You should run the example twice. The first time creates and writes the file, and the second time reads and displays the file.)

Code Example

```
unsigned char data __gc[] =
   new unsigned char __gc [10];
FileStream *fs = new FileStream(
   "FileStreamTest.txt", FileMode::OpenOrCreate);
if (fs->Length == 0)
{
   Console::WriteLine("Writing Data...");
```

```
      for (short i = 0; i < 10; i++)
         data[i] = (unsigned char)i;
      fs->Write(data, 0, 10);
   }
   else
   {
      fs->Seek(-5, SeekOrigin::End);
      int count = fs->Read(data, 0, 10);
      for (int i = 0; i < count; i++)
      {
         Console::WriteLine(data[i]);
      }
   }
   fs->Close();
```

Primitive Data Types and Streams

The **Stream**-derived classes work well if you are reading and writing
bytes of data as a block. If you need to read and write the primitive common
types, such as **Boolean**, **String**, and **Int32**, in and out of a stream, you
should use the **BinaryReader** and the **BinaryWriter** classes. The **Binary**
example in the **FileIO** directory shows how to use these classes. You create
the appropriate stream (**FileStream** in the example) and pass it to the **Binary-
Reader** or **BinaryWriter** constructor. You can then use one of the overloaded **Read** or **Write** methods to read or write a data type to or from the
stream. (Again, you should run the example twice. The first time creates and
writes the file, and the second time reads the file.)

```
FileStream *fs = new FileStream(
   "BinaryTest.bin", FileMode::OpenOrCreate);
if (fs->Length == 0)
{
   Console::WriteLine("Writing Data...");
   BinaryWriter *w = new BinaryWriter(fs);
   for (short i = 0; i < 10; i++)
      w->Write(i);
   w->Close();
}
else
{
   BinaryReader *r = new BinaryReader(fs);
   for (int i = 0; i < 10; i++)
      Console::WriteLine(r->ReadInt16());
   r->Close();
```

```
    }
    fs->Close();
```

TextReader and TextWriter

The **TextReader** and **TextWriter** abstract classes treat the data as a sequential stream of characters (i.e., as text). **TextReader** has methods such as **Close**, **Peek**, **Read**, **ReadBlock**, **ReadLine**, and **ReadToEnd**. **TextWriter** has methods such as **Close**, **Flush**, **Write**, and **WriteLine**. The overloaded **Read** methods read characters from the stream. The overloaded **Write** and **WriteLine** methods write various types to the stream. If an object is written to the stream, the object's **ToString** method is used.

StringReader and **StringWriter** are derived from **TextReader** and **TextWriter**, respectively. **StringReader** and **StringWriter** read and write data in a character string, which is stored in an underlying **StringBuilder** object. The **StringWriter** constructor can take a **StringBuilder** object. The **StringBuilder** class was discussed in Chapter 3.

StreamReader and **StreamWriter** are also derived from **TextReader** and **TextWriter**. They read and write text to and from a **Stream** object. As with the **BinaryReader** and **BinaryWriter** class, you can create a **Stream** object and pass it to the **StreamReader** or **StreamWriter** constructor. Hence, these classes can use any **Stream** derived class data storage. The **Text** example in the **FileIO** directory uses the **StreamWriter** and **StreamReader** classes. Run the program twice, first to create the file, and then to read it.

```
FileStream *fs = new FileStream(
    "TextTest.txt", FileMode::OpenOrCreate);
if (fs->Length == 0)
{
    Console::WriteLine("Writing Data...");
    StreamWriter *sw = new StreamWriter(fs);
    sw->Write(100);
    sw->WriteLine(" One Hundred");
    sw->WriteLine("End of File");
    sw->Close();
}
else
{
    String *text;
    StreamReader *sr = new StreamReader(fs);
    text = sr->ReadLine();
    while (text != 0)
    {
        Console::WriteLine(text);
```

```
        text = sr->ReadLine();
    }
    sr->Close();
}
fs->Close();
```

File Manipulation

The framework has two classes named **File** and **FileInfo** that are very useful for working with files. If you need to manipulate the file in addition to reading and writing to it, the **File** class provides the basic functionality. Since the **File** class just has static members, you have to provide the name of the file as an argument. The **FileInfo** class has a constructor that creates an object that represents a file. You then use the methods to manipulate that particular file.

The **File** class methods always perform a security check. If you are going to continually access a particular file, you may want to use the **FileInfo** class because the security check is made only once in the constructor. Security is discussed in more detail in Chapter 13.

FILE CLASS

The **File** class has methods for creating and opening files that return **FileStream**, **StreamWriter**, or **StreamReader** objects that do the actual reading and writing. The overloaded **Create** methods return a **FileStream** object. The **CreateText** method returns a **StreamWriter.** The overloaded **Open** method can either create a new file or open an existing one for reading or writing, depending on the method parameters. The object returned is a **FileStream** object. The **OpenText** method returns a **StreamReader**. The **OpenRead** method returns a **FileStream** object. The **OpenWrite** method returns a **FileStream**.

The **File** class also has methods for copying, deleting, and moving files. You can also test for the existence of a file. File attributes such as the following can be read or modified:

- creation time
- last access time
- last write time
- archive, hidden, normal, system, or temporary
- compressed, encrypted
- read-only
- is the file a directory?

PATH CLASS

Many of the file names needed for input arguments have to be full paths. Or, you might want to manipulate only parts of the path. The **Path** class has static methods that make this easier. The **Path** class has static fields that indicate various platform-specific aspects of pathnames, such as the separator characters for directories, paths, and volumes and the illegal characters for pathnames.

Its static methods let you change the extension of a file or find the directory where temporary files reside. The **GetFullPath** method is particularly useful. You can pass it a relative path, such as \foo.txt, and it will return the full path of the file. This is very useful for the **File** or security classes that require the full file path.

FILEINFO CLASS

The **FileInfo** constructor creates an object that represents a disk file. The constructor takes one argument, a string representing the name of the file. The class has properties that represent file properties such as the creation time, full pathname and the size of the file. It has creation and open methods that are analogous to the **File** class methods, but operate on this file instance and therefore do not need a filename parameter. The **FileInfo** class also has methods to move and copy the file.

FILE EXAMPLE

Code Example

The **File** example in the **FileIO** directory illustrates the use of the **File** and **FileInfo** classes. In this example, the static **Delete** method of the **File** class is used to remove a specified file. The static **CreateText** method then creates a new file and returns a **StreamWriter** instance that is used to write some text to the file. The stream is then closed, and the static **Move** method then renames the file. A **FileInfo** instance is constructed to represent this renamed file. The complete file name, size, and creation date for the file are written to the console. The file is opened as text and a **StreamReader** instance is used to read and write out the contents of the file.

```
File::Delete("file2.txt");

StreamWriter *sw =
    System::IO::File::CreateText("file.txt");
sw->Write("The time has come the Walrus said, ");
sw->WriteLine("to talk of many things.");
sw->Write("Of shoes, and ships, and sealing wax, ");
sw->WriteLine("of cabbages and kings.");
sw->Write("And why the sea is boiling hot, ");
sw->WriteLine("and whether pigs have wings.");
sw->Close();

File::Move("file.txt", "file2.txt");
```

```
FileInfo *fileInfo = new FileInfo("file2.txt");

Console::WriteLine(
    "File {0} is {1} bytes in length, created on {2}",
    fileInfo->FullName,
    __box(fileInfo->Length),
    __box(fileInfo->CreationTime));
Console::WriteLine("");

StreamReader *sr = fileInfo->OpenText();
String *s = sr->ReadLine();
while (s != 0)
{
    Console::WriteLine(s);
    s = sr->ReadLine();
}
sr->Close();
Console::WriteLine("");
```

Serialization

Using the **File** and **Stream** classes can be quite cumbersome if you have to save a complicated data structure with linked objects. You have to save the individual fields to disk, remembering which field belongs to which object, and which object instance was linked to another object instance. When restoring the data structure, you have to reconstitute that arrangement of fields and object references.

The serialization technology provided by the .NET Framework does this for you. Serialization converts objects, such as classes, structs, and arrays, to a byte stream. Deserialization converts the byte stream back into the objects. Serializing and deserializing can be done on different machines as long as they both host the CLR.

Objects can be serialized without writing special code because, as we have seen, the runtime can query the object's metadata to allow it to understand the memory layout of the object. To inform the framework that a class can be serialized, mark the class with the **System::Serializable** attribute. Any field or property that should not be serialized can be marked with the **System::NonSerialized** attribute. For example, fields that represent cached values need not be serialized. All you have to do is mark the class with the serializable attribute, and you then do not have to write any other code to serialize the object's fields.

The **Serialization** example shows how to apply serialization to the case study's **HotelBroker** class in the **Hotel** assembly.[4] The **Serializable** attribute has been applied to the **HotelBroker** class definition. The **Serializable** attribute has also been applied to all the classes that get used by **HotelBroker** or that **HotelBroker** derives from—**Broker**, **Hotel**, **HotelReservation**, **Reservable**, and **Reservation**—because in order for **HotelBroker** to be serializable, those classes must be serializable as well. If any of those classes were not marked, a runtime exception would be thrown when the framework tries to serialize an object of that type.

```
[Serializable]
public __gc class HotelBroker :
    public Broker,
    public IHotelInfo,
    public IHotelAdmin,
    public IHotelReservation
{
private:
    const int MAXDAY;
    const int MAXUNIT;
    [NonSerialized] ArrayList *cities;
    ...
};

[Serializable]
public __gc class Hotel : public Reservable
{
    ...
};

[Serializable]
public __gc class HotelReservation : public Reservation
{
    ...
};

[Serializable]
public __gc __abstract class Reservable
{
    ...
};

[Serializable]
```

---

[4] After you build the **Serialization** project, you must copy **Hotel.dll** from the **Serialization\Hotel\Debug** directory to the **Serialization\Debug** directory before running **Serialization.exe**.

```
public __gc __abstract class Reservation
{
   ...
};

[Serializable]
public __gc __abstract class Broker
{
   ...
};
```

The cities field has been marked as **NonSerialized**, since the hotel's city is saved with the serialized hotels, and therefore can be restored as the modified **AddCity** method demonstrates. The cities field would be null if the **HotelBroker** class had been deserialized, because the cities field was not saved.[5]

```
private:
   void AddCity(String *city)
   {
      if (cities == 0)
      {
         cities = new ArrayList;
         IEnumerator *pEnum = units->GetEnumerator();
         while (pEnum->MoveNext())
         {
            Hotel *h =
               dynamic_cast<Hotel *>(pEnum->Current);
            AddCity(h->City);
         }
      }
      // check if city already on list, add if not
      if (!cities->Contains(city))
         cities->Add(city);
   }
```

Serialization Objects

Although the framework knows how to save an object marked with the **Serializable** attribute, you still have to specify the format in which the object is

---

[5] Of course we could have serialized the cities field and not have to deal with the case where cities could be null, but we wanted to demonstrate the **NonSerialized** attribute.

saved and the storage medium. To specify the format that an object is saved in, you use an instance of an object that supports the **IFormatter** interface.[6]

The Framework ships with two such classes: **System::Runtime::Serialization::Formatters::Binary::BinaryFormatter** and **System::Runtime::Serialization::Formatters::Soap::SoapFormatter**. The **BinaryFormatter** uses a binary, compact format for serializing and deserializing on platforms that support the CLR. The **SoapFormatter** uses the industry standard SOAP protocol that is discussed in Chapter 11, "Web Services." Since it is an XML-based, and therefore text-based, protocol, it can be used to communicate with a non CLR-based platform. The binary format is faster when serializing and deserializing data.

You can, of course, implement your own formatter classes. You might do this if you have to talk to a foreign system with its own persistent object byte format.

The **Serialization** example has code to demonstrate saving and restoring both binary and SOAP formats using a **FileStream**. Of course you could use any **Stream**-based class representing some data medium. Notice the special care taken to ensure that the **Load** method is able to modify the parameter that points to the **HotelBroker**. To enable this, the parameter is declared to be a reference to a pointer to a **HotelBroker**.

```
static void Save(
   HotelBroker *broker, String *formatter)
{
   FileStream *s;
   if (String::Equals(formatter, "b"))
   {
      s = new FileStream(
         "hotels.bin", FileMode::Create);
      BinaryFormatter *b = new BinaryFormatter;
      b->Serialize(s, broker);
   }
   else
   {
      s = new FileStream(
         "hotels.txt", FileMode::Create);
      SoapFormatter *sf = new SoapFormatter;
      sf->Serialize(s, broker);
   }
   s->Close();
}
```

---

[6] How does the runtime know if a class supports the IFormatter interface? It queries the metadata!

```cpp
static void Load(
   HotelBroker *&broker, /*ref to pointer */
   String *formatter)
{

   FileStream *s;
   if (String::Equals(formatter, "b"))
   {
      s = new FileStream("hotels.bin", FileMode::Open);
      BinaryFormatter *b = new BinaryFormatter;
      broker =
         dynamic_cast<HotelBroker *>
            (b->Deserialize(s));
   }
   else
   {
      s = new FileStream("hotels.txt", FileMode::Open);
      SoapFormatter *sf = new SoapFormatter;
      broker =
         dynamic_cast<HotelBroker *>(sf->Deserialize(s));
   }
   s->Close();
   ShowHotelList(broker->GetHotels());
}
```

Here is some sample output from the **Serialization** example: First, we add a hotel and save it with the SOAP formatter. We then exit the program.

```
Enter command: cities
Atlanta
Boston
Commands: quit, cities, list, add, fetch, save

Enter command: list
City            Name                   Rooms     Rate
Atlanta         Dixie                  100       115
Atlanta         Marriott               500       70
Boston          Sheraton               250       95
Commands: quit, cities, list, add, fetch, save

Enter command: add
Hotel City: Philadelphia
Hotel Name: Franklin
Number Rooms: 100
Room Rate: 200
```

```
Commands: quit, cities, list, add, fetch, save

Enter command: save
Formatter: b(inary), s(oap)s
Commands: quit, cities, list, add, fetch, save

Enter command: cities
Atlanta
Boston
Philadelphia
Commands: quit, cities, list, add, fetch, save

Enter command: list
City            Name                    Rooms       Rate
Atlanta         Dixie                   100         115
Atlanta         Marriot                 500         70
Boston          Sheraton                250         95
Philadelphia    Franklin                100         200
Commands: quit, cities, list, add, fetch, save

Enter command: quit
```

We then run the program again and restore what we saved[7] in the first run.

```
Enter command: cities
Atlanta
Boston
Commands: quit, cities, list, add, fetch, save

Enter command: list
City            Name                    Rooms       Rate
Atlanta         Dixie                   100         115
Atlanta         Marriot                 500         70
Boston          Sheraton                250         95
Commands: quit, cities, list, add, fetch, save

Enter command: fetch
Formatter: b(inary), s(oap)s
City            Name                    Rooms       Rate
Atlanta         Dixie                   100         115
Atlanta         Marriot                 500         70
```

---

7 If you look at the **hotels.txt** file, you will see a huge file with a lot of "empty" entries. This stems from the simplistic array data structure we used for reservations, which is very sparse.

```
Boston          Sheraton            250     95
Philadelphia    Franklin            100     200
Commands: quit, cities, list, add, fetch, save

Enter command: cities
Atlanta
Boston
Philadelphia
```

ISerializable

Sometimes the serialization provided by the framework is not satisfactory. You can provide custom serialization for a class by implementing the **ISerializable** interface and adding a constructor to the class, as shown in the **Serialization** project in the **ISerializable** directory. The **ISerializable** interface has one member: **GetObjectData**. This method is used when data is serialized.

The **ISerializable** example[8] demonstrates how this is done. As before, the class has to be marked as **Serializable**.

```
[Serializable]
public __gc class HotelBroker :
   public Broker,
   public IHotelInfo,
   public IHotelAdmin,
   public IHotelReservation,
   public ISerializable
{
   ...
};
```

The **SerializationInfo** class is used to store all the data that needs to be saved in the **ISerializable::GetObjectData** method. The **AddValue** method of **SerializationInfo** is overloaded to handle the saving of various types, including **Object***.[9] When you save the type, you provide a name so that it can be restored later. The **StreamingContext** class gives you information

---

[8] Again, after you build the **Serialization** project, you must copy **Hotel.dll** from the **Serialization\Hotel\Debug** directory to the **Serialization\Debug** directory before running **Serialization.exe**.

[9] Some of the **AddValue** overloads are not CLS-compliant when the types being saved are not CLS-compliant types, such as unsigned integers. Be careful not to use those types where .NET language interoperability is required. You have to watch for this in other places in the framework, such as the **Convert** class or the **Parse** methods of the various CTS types, or any other place where data is formatted, converted, read, or written (such as the **TextWriter** classes).

about the stream being used in the serialization. For example, you can find out if the stream being used is a file or is being remoted to another computer.

```
public:
    void GetObjectData(SerializationInfo *info,
        StreamingContext context)
    {
        long numberHotels = units->Count;
        info->AddValue("NumberHotels", numberHotels);
        info->AddValue("Hotels", units);
    }
```

You also have to implement a special constructor that is used by the framework when the object is deserialized. It has the same arguments as **GetObjectData** has. Here you use the various **GetXXX** methods on **SerializationInfo** to restore the data. Note that since we did not save the cities field, we had to manually restore it. The constructor is private because only the framework uses it. If you forget to add the constructor, you will get a **SerializationException** when you try to restore the object.

```
private:
    HotelBroker(SerializationInfo *info,
        StreamingContext context)
        : Broker(366, 10), MAXDAY(366), MAXUNIT(10)
    {
        long numberHotels =
            info->GetInt32("NumberHotels");
        units = dynamic_cast<ArrayList *>(
            info->GetValue(
                "Hotels", units->GetType()));
        if (numberHotels == units->Count)
            Console::WriteLine("All hotels deserialized.");
        else
            Console::WriteLine("Error in deserialization.");
        cities = new ArrayList;
        IEnumerator *pEnum = units->GetEnumerator();
        while (pEnum->MoveNext())
        {
            Hotel *h =
                dynamic_cast<Hotel *>(pEnum->Current);
            AddCity(h->City);
        }
    }
```

Remember, after you make any changes and build the Hotel project, will need to copy the **Hotel.dll** to the directory of the **Serialization.exe** client program. This does not get done automatically, as in C#, unless you add a custom build step to the project.

In this example we only did custom serialization for the **HotelBroker** object. For all the other objects, we still relied on the framework's serialization. This example works the same way that the **Serialization** example did. The sample output would therefore look the same.

.NET Application Model

Serialization gave you a concrete example of the flexible environment the .NET Framework provides for writing code. Now let us take a look at the model in which .NET applications run. The Win32 environment in which a program runs is called its process. This environment consists of

- An address space in which the code and data of the program resides.
- A set of environment variables that is associated with the program.
- A current drive and directory.
- One or more threads.

Threads

A thread is the actual execution path of a program's code. One or more threads run inside of a process to allow for multiple execution paths inside of a process. For example, with multiple threads a program can update the user interface with partial results on one thread as a calculation proceeds on another thread. All threads in the same process share the process environment so that all the threads can access the process memory.

Threads are scheduled by the operating system. Processes and application domains[10] are not scheduled. Threads are periodically given a limited timeslice in which to run so that they can share the processor with other threads. Higher priority threads will get to run more often than lower priority threads. After some time elapses, a thread will get another chance to run. When a thread is swapped back in, it resumes running from the point it was at when it was swapped out.

Threads maintain a context that is saved and restored when the operating system's scheduler switches from one thread to another. A thread's context includes the CPU registers and stack that contain the state of the executing code.

---

[10] Application domains are discussed later in this chapter.

The **System::Threading::Thread** class models an executing thread. The **Thread** object that represents the current executing thread can be found from the static property **Thread::CurrentThread**.

Unless your code runs on a multiprocessor machine, or you are trying to use time while a uniprocessor waits for some event such as an I/O event, multiple threads do not result in any time saved for your computing tasks. It does, however, make the system seem more responsive to tasks requiring user interaction. Using too many threads can decrease performance, as thread management overhead and contention between competing threads burdens the CPU.

Code Example

To help you understand threads, we have a multiple-step **Threading** example[11] that uses the **Customer** and **Hotel** assemblies from the case study to make reservations. Let us look first at Step 0.

.NET threads run as delegates defined by the **ThreadStart** class. The delegate returns void and takes no parameters.

```
public __gc __delegate void ThreadStart();
```

The **NewReservation** class has a public member function, **MakeReservation**, that will define the thread function. Since the thread function takes no parameters, any data that this function uses is assigned to fields in the **NewReservation** instance.

The thread delegate is created and passed as a parameter to the constructor that creates the **Thread** object. The **Start** method on the **Thread** object is invoked to begin the thread's execution. When we discuss the asynchronous programming model, we will show you how to pass parameters to a thread delegate. The program now has two threads: the original one that executed the code to start the thread and now the thread we just created that attempts to make a hotel reservation.

```
public __gc class NewReservation
{
   ...
public:
   ...
   void MakeReservation()
   {
      Console::WriteLine(
         "Thread {0} starting.",
         Thread::CurrentThread->
            GetHashCode().ToString());
      ...
```

---

[11] In each step, you will need to copy the **Customer** and **Hotel** DLLs into the **Debug** directory of **TestThreading**.

```
        ReservationResult *result =
            hotelBroker->MakeReservation(
            customerId, city, hotel, date, numberDays);
        ...
    }
};
```

Then, in the **Main** method, the following code starts the thread, using a delegate:

```
NewReservation *reserve1 =
    new NewReservation(customers, hotelBroker);

reserve1->customerId = 1;
reserve1->city = "Boston";
reserve1->hotel = "Presidential";
reserve1->sdate = "12/12/2001";
reserve1->numberDays = 3;

// create delegate for threads
ThreadStart *threadStart1 = new ThreadStart(
    reserve1,
    reserve1->MakeReservation);

Thread *thread1 = new Thread(threadStart1);
Console::WriteLine(
    "Thread {0} starting a new thread.",
    Thread::CurrentThread->
        GetHashCode().ToString());
thread1->Start();
```

To cause the original thread to wait until the second thread is done, the **Join** method on the **Thread** object is called. The original thread now blocks (waits) until the reservation thread is complete. The results of the reservation request are written to the console by the reservation thread.

```
// Block this thread until the worker thread is done
thread1->Join();
Console::WriteLine("Done!");
```

THREAD SYNCHRONIZATION

Code Example

An application can create multiple threads. Look at the code in Step 1 of the **Threading** example. Now multiple reservation requests are being made simultaneously.

```
NewReservation *reserve1 =
   new NewReservation(customers, hotelBroker);
...


NewReservation *reserve2 =
   new NewReservation(customers, hotelBroker);
...


// create delegate for threads
ThreadStart *threadStart1 = new ThreadStart(
   reserve1,
   reserve1->MakeReservation);
ThreadStart *threadStart2 = new ThreadStart(
   reserve2,
   reserve2->MakeReservation);

Thread *thread1 = new Thread(threadStart1);
Thread *thread2 = new Thread(threadStart2);

Console::WriteLine(
   "Thread {0} starting a new thread.",
   Thread::CurrentThread->
      GetHashCode().ToString());
thread1->Start();
thread2->Start();

// Block this thread until the worker thread is done
thread1->Join();
thread2->Join();
```

The problem with our reservation system is that there is no guarantee that one thread will not interfere with the work being done by the other thread. Since threads run for only a small period before they give up the processor to another thread, they may not be finished with whatever operation they were working on when their timeslice is up. For example, they might be in the middle of updating a data structure. If another thread tries to use the information in that data structure or to update the data structure, the results of those operations will be inconsistent and incorrect, or a program crash could result (i.e., if references to obsolete structures were not yet updated, an unhandled exception could occur).

Let us look at one of several places in the customer and reservation code where we could have a problem. Examine the code for **Broker::Reserve** in **Broker.h**. First, a check is made of the existing bookings for a given hotel for a given date to see if there are rooms available. Then, if a room is available, it is reserved. Note that we have added a call to **Thread::Sleep** between the code that checks for room availability and the code that reserves a room, which will be explained shortly.

```
. . .
// Check if rooms are available for all dates
for (int i = day; i < day + numDays; i++)
{
    if (numCust[i, unitid] >= unit->capacity)
    {
        result->ReservationId = -1;
        result->Comment = "Room not available";
        return result;
    }
}

Console::WriteLine(
    "Thread {0} finds the room is available in
        Broker::Reserve",
    Thread::CurrentThread->
        GetHashCode().ToString());

Thread::Sleep(0);

// Reserve a room for requested dates
for (int i = day; i < day + numDays; i++)
    numCust[i, unitid] += 1;
. . .
```

This code can produce inconsistent results! One of the threads could be swapped out after it finds that the last room is available, but before it gets a chance to make the booking. The other thread could then run, find the same available room and make the booking. When the first thread runs again, it starts from where it left off, and it will also book the same last room at the hotel.

To simulate this occurrence, this step (Step 1) of the **Threading** example puts a **Thread::Sleep** call between the code that checks for room availability and the code that makes the booking. The **Sleep(0)** call will cause the thread to stop executing and give up the remainder of its timeslice.

To ensure that we see the thread contention problem occur,[12] we have only one room in the entire hotel! We then set up our program so that the two

---

[12] You can see that special care must be taken to make this threading problem manifest itself consistently to make a good example! In real programming, such a problem typically expresses itself inconsistently, which makes it all the more difficult to detect during testing. Of course, it is certain to express itself sooner or later after it has been deployed.

threads try to reserve the only room at the hotel for the same date. Examine the code in the **Main** routine that sets this up:

```
hotelBroker->AddHotel(
    "Boston",
    "Presidential",
    1, //only one room in entire hotel!
    (Decimal) 10000);
...
NewReservation *reserve1 =
    new NewReservation(customers, hotelBroker);
reserve1->customerId = 1;
reserve1->city = "Boston";
reserve1->hotel = "Presidential";
reserve1->sdate = "12/12/2001";
reserve1->numberDays = 3;

NewReservation *reserve2 =
    new NewReservation(customers, hotelBroker);
reserve2->customerId = 2;
reserve2->city = "Boston";
reserve2->hotel = "Presidential";
reserve2->sdate = "12/13/2001";
reserve2->numberDays = 1;
```

Running the program will give results that look something like this:

```
Added Boston Presidential Hotel with one room.
Thread 3 starting a new thread.
Thread 5 starting.
Thread 6 starting.
Reserving for Customer 2 at the Boston Presidential Hotel on
12/13/2001 12:00:00 AM for 1 days
Reserving for Customer 1 at the Boston Presidential Hotel on
12/12/2001 12:00:00 AM for 3 days
Thread 6 entered Broker::Reserve
Thread 6 finds the room is available in Broker::Reserve
Thread 5 entered Broker::Reserve
Thread 5 finds the room is available in Broker::Reserve
Thread 6 left Broker::Reserve
Reservation for Customer 2 has been booked
ReservationId = 1
Thread 5 left Broker::Reserve
Reservation for Customer 1 has been booked
```

```
ReservationId = 2
ReservationRate  = 10000
ReservationCost  = 30000
Comment = OK
ReservationRate  = 10000
ReservationCost  = 10000
Comment = OK
Done!
```

Unfortunately, both customers get to reserve the last (only) room on December 13! Note how one thread enters the **Reserve** method and finds the room is available before it gets swapped out. Then, the other thread enters Reserve and also finds the room is available before it gets swapped out. Both threads then book the same room.

Operating systems provide means for synchronizing the operation of multiple threads or multiple processes accessing shared resources. The .NET Framework provides several mechanisms to prevent threading conflicts.

Every object in the .NET Framework can be used to provide a synchronized section of code (critical section). Only one thread at a time can execute within such a section. If one thread is already executing inside that synchronized code section, any other threads that attempt to access that section will block (wait) until the executing thread leaves that code section.

SYNCHRONIZATION WITH MONITORS

Code Example

The **System::Threading::Monitor** class allows threads to synchronize on an object to avoid the data corruption and indeterminate behavior that can result from race conditions. Step 2 of the **Threading** example demonstrates the use of the **Monitor** class with the **this** pointer of the **HotelBroker** instance.

```
ReservationResult *Reserve(Reservation *res)
{
    Console::WriteLine(
        "Thread {0} trying to enter Broker::Reserve",
        Thread::CurrentThread->
            GetHashCode().ToString());
    Monitor::Enter(this);
    ... (thread contentious code goes here)
    Monitor::Exit(this);
    return result;
}
```

The thread that first calls the **Monitor::Enter(this)** method will be allowed to execute the code of the **Reserve** method because it will acquire the **Monitor** lock based on the **this** pointer. Subsequent threads that try to execute the same code will have to wait until the first thread releases the lock with **Monitor::Exit(this)**. At that point they will be able to call **Monitor::Enter(this)** and acquire the lock.

A thread can call **Monitor::Enter** several times, but each call must be balanced by a call to **Monitor::Exit.** If a thread wants to try to acquire a lock, but does not want to block, it can use the **Monitor::TryEnter** method.

Now that we have provided synchronization, the identical case tried in Step 1 does not result in one reservation too many for the hotel. Notice how the second thread cannot enter the **Reserve** method until the first thread that entered has left. This solves our thread contention problem and enforces the rule that the same room cannot be booked by two customers for the same date.

```
Added Boston Presidential Hotel with one room.
Thread 3 starting a new thread.
Thread 5 starting.
Thread 6 starting.
Reserving for Customer 2 at the Boston Presidential Hotel on
12/13/2001 12:00:00 AM for 1 days
Thread 6 trying to enter Broker::Reserve
Thread 6 entered Broker::Reserve
Thread 6 finds the room is available in Broker::Reserve
Thread 6 left Broker::Reserve
Reservation for Customer 2 has been booked
ReservationId = 1
Reserving for Customer 1 at the Boston Presidential Hotel on
12/12/2001 12:00:00 AM for 3 days
Thread 5 trying to enter Broker::Reserve
Thread 5 entered Broker::Reserve
Reservation for Customer 1 could not be booked
Room not available
ReservationRate = 10000
ReservationCost = 10000
Comment = OK
Done!
```

NOTIFICATION WITH MONITORS

A thread that has acquired a **Monitor** lock can wait for a signal from another thread that is synchronizing on that same object without leaving the synchronization block. The thread invokes the **Monitor::Wait** method and relinquishes the lock. When notified by another thread, it reacquires the synchronization lock.

A thread that has acquired a **Monitor** lock can send notification to another thread waiting on the same object with the **Pulse** or the **PulseAll** methods. It is important that the thread be waiting when the pulse is sent; otherwise, if the pulse is sent before the wait, the other thread will wait forever and will never see the notification. This is unlike the reset events discussed later in this chapter. If multiple threads are waiting, the **Pulse** method will put only one thread on the ready queue to run. The **PulseAll** will put all of them on the ready queue.

The pulsing thread no longer has the **Monitor** lock, but is not blocked from running. Since it is no longer blocked, but does not have the lock, to avoid a deadlock or race condition, this thread should try to reacquire the lock (through a **Monitor::Enter** or **Wait**) before doing any potentially damaging work.

Code Example

The **PulseAll** example illustrates the **Pulse** and **PulseAll** methods. Running the example produces the following output:

```
First thread: 2 started.
Thread: 5 started.
Thread: 5 waiting.
Thread: 6 started.
Thread: 6 waiting.
Thread 5 sleeping.
Done.
Thread 5 awake.
Thread: 5 exited.
Thread 6 sleeping.
Thread 6 awake.
Thread: 6 exited.
```

The class **X** has a field "o" of type **Object** that will be used for a synchronization lock.

The class also has a method **Test** that will be used as a thread delegate. The method acquires the synchronization lock, and then waits for a notification. When it gets the notification, it sleeps for half a second, and then relinquishes the lock.

The main method creates two threads that use the **X::Test** method as their thread delegate and share the same object to use for synchronization. It then sleeps for 2 seconds to allow the threads to issue their wait requests and relinquish their locks. It then calls **PulseAll** to notify both waiting threads and relinquishes its hold on the locks. Eventually, each thread will reacquire the lock, write a message to the console, and relinquish the lock for the last time.

```
__gc class X
{
private:
   Object *o;
```

```
public:
   X(Object *o)
   {
      this->o = o;
   }
   void Test()
   {
      try
      {
         long threadId =
            Thread::CurrentThread->GetHashCode();
         Console::WriteLine(
            "Thread: {0} started.", threadId.ToString());
         Monitor::Enter(o);
         Console::WriteLine(
            "Thread: {0} waiting.", threadId.ToString());
         Monitor::Wait(o);
         Console::WriteLine(
            "Thread {0} sleeping.", threadId.ToString());
         Thread::Sleep(500);
         Console::WriteLine(
            "Thread {0} awake.", threadId.ToString());
         Monitor::Exit(o);
         Console::WriteLine(
            "Thread. {0} exited.", threadId.ToString());
      }
      catch(Exception *e)
      {
         long threadId =
            Thread::CurrentThread->GetHashCode();
         Console::WriteLine(
            "Thread: {0} Exception: {1}",
            threadId.ToString(), e->Message);
         Monitor::Exit(o);
      }
   }
};

__gc class Class1
{
public:
   static Object *o = new Object;
   static void Main()
   {
```

```
        Console::WriteLine(
            "First thread: {0} started.",
            Thread::CurrentThread->GetHashCode().ToString());

        X *a = new X(o);
        X *b = new X(o);

        ThreadStart *ats = new ThreadStart(a, X::Test);
        ThreadStart *bts = new ThreadStart(b, X::Test);

        Thread *at = new Thread(ats);
        Thread *bt = new Thread(bts);

        at->Start();
        bt->Start();

        // Sleep to allow other threads to wait on the
        // object before the Pulse
        Thread::Sleep(2000);
        Monitor::Enter(o);

        Monitor::PulseAll(o);
        //Monitor::Pulse(o);

        Monitor::Exit(o);

        Console::WriteLine("Done.");
    }
};
```

Comment out the **PulseAll** call and uncomment the **Pulse** call, and only one thread completes because the other thread is never put on the ready queue. Remove the **Sleep(2000)** from the main routine, and the other threads block forever because the pulse occurs before the threads get a chance to call the **Wait** method, and hence they will never be notified. These methods can be used to coordinate several threads' use of synchronization locks.

The **Thread::Sleep** method causes the current thread to stop execution (block) for a given time period. Calling **Thread::Suspend** will cause the thread to block until **Thread::Resume** is called by another thread on that same thread. Threads can also block because they are waiting for another thread to finish (**Thread::Join**). This method was used in the **Threading** examples so that the main thread could wait until the reservation requests were completed. Threads can also block because they are waiting on a synchronization lock (critical section).

Calling **Thread::Interrupt** on the blocked thread can awaken it. The thread will receive a **ThreadInterruptedException**. If the thread does not catch this exception, the runtime will catch the exception and kill the thread.

If, as a last resort, you have to kill a thread outright, call the **Thread::Abort** method on the thread. **Thread::Abort** causes the **Thread-AbortException** to be thrown. This exception cannot be caught, but it will cause all the **finally** blocks to be executed. In addition, **Thread::Abort** does not cause the thread to wake up from a wait.

Since **finally** blocks may take a while to execute, or the thread might be waiting, aborted threads may not terminate immediately. If you need to be sure that the thread has finished, you should wait on the thread's termination using **Thread::Join**.

SYNCHRONIZATION CLASSES

The .NET Framework has classes that represent the standard Win32 synchronization objects. These classes all derive from the abstract **WaitHandle** class. This class has static methods, **WaitAll** and **WaitAny**, that allow you to wait on a set or just one of a set of synchronization objects being signaled. It also has an instance method, **WaitOne**, that allows you to wait for this instance to be signaled. How the object gets signaled depends on the particular type of synchronization object that is derived from **WaitHandle**.

A **Mutex** object is used for interprocess synchronization. **Monitors** and synchronized code sections work only within one process. An **AutoResetEvent** and **ManualResetEvent** are used to signal whether an event has occurred. An **AutoResetEvent** remains signaled until a waiting thread is released. A **ManualResetEvent** remains signaled until its state is set to unsignaled with the **Reset** method. Hence, many threads could be signaled by this event. Unlike **Monitors**, code does not have to be waiting for the signal before the pulse is set for the reset events to signal a thread.

The framework has provided classes to solve some standard threading problems. The **Interlocked** class methods allow atomic operations on shared values such as increment, decrement, comparison, and exchange. **Reader-WriterLock** is used to allow single-writer, multiple-reader access to data structures. The **ThreadPool** class can be used to manage a pool of worker threads.

AUTOMATIC SYNCHRONIZATION

You can use attributes to synchronize the access to instance methods and fields of a class. Access to static fields and methods is not synchronized. To do this, you derive the class from the class **System::ContextBoundObject** and apply a **Synchronization** attribute to the class. This attribute cannot be applied to an individual method or field.

Code
Example

The attribute is found in the **System::Runtime::Remoting::Contexts** namespace. It describes the synchronization requirements of an instance of the class to which it is applied. You can pass one of four values, which are static fields of the **SynchronizationAttribute** class, to the **SynchronizationAttribute** constructor: NOT_SUPPORTED, SUPPORTED, REQUIRED, REQUIRES_NEW. The **Threading** example Step 3 illustrates how to do this.

```
...
using namespace System::Runtime::Remoting::Contexts;
...
//SynchronizationAttribute::REQUIRED is 4
[Synchronization(4)]
public __gc __abstract class Broker :
   public ContextBoundObject
{
   ...
};
...
```

In order for the CLR to make sure that the thread in which an object's methods run is synchronized properly, the CLR has to track the threading requirements of the object. This state is referred to as the *context* of the object. If one object needs to be synchronized, and another does not, they are in two separate contexts. The CLR has to acquire a synchronization lock on behalf of the code when a thread that is executing a method on the object that does not need to be synchronized starts executing a method on an object that does. The CLR knows that this has to be done because it can compare the threading requirements of the first object with the threading requirements of the second object by comparing their contexts.

Objects that share the same state are said to live in the same context. For example, two objects that do not need to be synchronized can share the same context. **ContextBoundObject** and contexts are discussed in more detail in the section on contexts.

With this intuitive understanding of contexts, we can now explain the meaning of the various **Synchronization** attributes. NOT_SUPPORTED means that the class cannot support synchronization of its instance methods and fields and therefore must not be created in a synchronized context. REQUIRED means that the class requires synchronization of access to its instance methods and fields. If a thread is already being synchronized, however, it can use the same synchronization lock and live in an existing synchronization context. REQUIRES_NEW means that not only is synchronization required, but access to its instance methods and fields must be with a unique synchronization lock and context. SUPPORTED means that the class does not require synchronization of access to its instance methods and fields, but a new context does not have to be created for it.

You can also pass a bool flag to the constructor to indicate if reentrancy is required. If required, call-outs from methods are synchronized. Otherwise, only calls into methods are synchronized.

With the **Synchronization** attribute, there is no need for **Monitor::Enter** and **Monitor::Exit** in the **Broker::Reserve** method.

Just as in Step 2, this example attempts to make two reservations for the last room in a hotel. Here is the output from running this example:

```
Added Boston Presidential Hotel with one room.
Thread 13 starting a new thread.
Thread 28 starting.
Thread 29 starting.
Reserving for Customer 1 at the Boston Presidential Hotel on
12/12/2001 12:00:00 AM for 3 days
Thread 28 entered Broker::Reserve
Thread 28 finds the room is available in Broker::Reserve
Thread 28 left Broker::Reserve
Reservation for Customer 1 has been booked
ReservationId = 1
ReservationRate = 10000
ReservationCost = 30000
Comment - OK
Reserving for Customer 2 at the Boston Presidential Hotel on
12/13/2001 12:00:00 AM for 1 days
Thread 29 entered Broker::Reserve
Thread 29 left Reserve.
Reservation for Customer 2 could not be booked
Room not available
Done!
```

As in the previous case, the second thread could not enter the **Reserve** method until the thread that entered first finished. Only one reservation is made.

What is different about using this automatic approach is that you get the synchronization in *all* the methods of the class whether you need it or not. Accessing other shared data via other methods in the class is also blocked. You get this behavior whether you want it or not.

Note how only one thread can be in any method of the class at any given time. Assume that you added another method to the class named **CancelReservation**. If one thread called **CancelReservation**, it would block all other threads from calling other methods in the class, including **MakeReservation**.

With a reservation system, this is the behavior you would want, since you do not want the **MakeReservation** attempt to use a data structure that might be in the middle of being modified. In some situations, however, this is not desirable and reduces performance due to unnecessary blocking. The resulting increase in contention can interfere with scalability, since you are not just locking around the specific areas that need synchronizing.

The attribute approach is simpler than using critical sections. You do not have to worry about the details of getting the synchronization implemented correctly. On the other hand, you get behavior that reduces scalability. Different applications or different parts of the same application will benefit from the approach that makes the most sense.

Thread Isolation

Code Example

An exception generated by one thread will not cause another thread to fail. The **ThreadIsolation** example demonstrates this.

```
__gc class tm
{
public:
   void m()
   {
      Console::WriteLine(
         "Thread {0} started",
         Thread::CurrentThread->GetHashCode().ToString());
      Thread::Sleep(1000);
      for(int i = 0; i < 10; i++)
         Console::WriteLine(i);
      Console::WriteLine(
         "Thread {0} done",
         Thread::CurrentThread->GetHashCode().ToString());
   }
};

__gc class te
{
public:
   void tue()
   {
      Console::WriteLine(
         "Thread {0} started",
         Thread::CurrentThread->GetHashCode().ToString());
      Exception *e = new Exception("Thread Exception");
      throw e;
```

```
    }
};

__gc class ThreadIsolation
{
public:
    static void Main()
    {
        tm *tt = new tm;
        te *tex = new te;

        // create delegate for threads
        ThreadStart *ts1 = new ThreadStart(tt, tm::m);
        ThreadStart *ts2 = new ThreadStart(tex, te::tue);

        Thread *thread1 = new Thread(ts1);
        Thread *thread2 = new Thread(ts2);

        Console::WriteLine(
            "Thread {0} starting new threads.",
            Thread::CurrentThread->GetHashCode().ToString());
        thread1->Start();
        thread2->Start();

        Console::WriteLine(
            "Thread {0} done.",
            Thread::CurrentThread->GetHashCode().ToString());
    }
};
```

The following output is generated. Note how the second thread can continue to write out the numbers even though the first thread has aborted from the unhandled exception. Note also how the "main" thread that spawned the other two threads can finish without causing the other threads to terminate.

```
Thread 2 starting new threads.
Thread 2 done.
Thread 5 started
Thread 6 started

Unhandled Exception: System.Exception: Thread Exception
        at te.tue() in c:\oi\netcpp\chap8\threadisolation\
        threadisolation.h:line 32
```

```
0
1
2
3
4
5
6
7
8
9
Thread 5 done
```

The **AppDomain** class (discussed later in the chapter) allows you to set up a handler to catch an **UnhandledException** event.

Synchronization of Collections

Some lists, such as **TraceListeners**, are thread safe. When this collection is modified, a copy is modified and the reference is set to the copy. Most collections, like **ArrayList**, are not thread safe. Making them automatically thread safe would decrease the performance of the collection even when thread safety is not an issue.

An **ArrayList** has a static **Synchronized** method to return a thread-safe version of the **ArrayList**. The **IsSynchronized** property allows you to test if the **ArrayList** you are using is the thread-safe version. The **SyncRoot** property can return an object that can be used to synchronize access to a collection. This allows other threads that might be using the **ArrayList** to be synchronized with the same object.

Context

In order for us to understand how the runtime is able to enforce a threading requirement based on an attribute, we have to introduce the concept of context. Step 4 of the **Threading** example is the same code as Step 3, but with some additional output:

```
Is the customer object a proxy? False
Is the bookings object a proxy? True
Added Boston Presidential Hotel with one room.
Thread 13 ContextId 0 launching threads.
MakeReservation: Thread 28 ContextId 0 starting.
MakeReservation: Thread 29 ContextId 0 starting.
```

```
Reserving for Customer 2 at the Boston Presidential Hotel on
12/13/2001 12:00:00
 AM for 1 days
Thread 29 ContextId 1 entered Reserve.
Thread 29 finds the room is available in Broker::Reserve
Reserving for Customer 1 at the Boston Presidential Hotel on
12/12/2001 12:00:00
 AM for 3 days
Thread 29 ContextId 1 left Reserve.
Thread 28 ContextId 1 entered Reserve.
Thread 28 ContextId 1 left Reserve.
Reservation for Customer 1 could not be booked
Room not available
Reservation for Customer 2 has been booked
ReservationId = 1
ReservationRate = 10000
ReservationCost = 10000
Comment = OK
```

In this last step (Step 4) of the **Threading** example, we see that when a thread enters a method, such as **Reserve** of the **Broker** class, it has a different **ContextId** than when it runs outside of the **Broker** class. It runs in a different context. That is why you see above that thread 28 has the **ContextID** set to 0 before it calls **Reserve**, and then within **Reserve**, its **ContextID** changes to 1. This is due to the **Synchronization** attribute being applied to the **Broker** class.

Broker objects have different runtime requirements than the other objects in the program, since access to **Broker** objects must be synchronized and access to other objects should not be synchronized. The environment that represents the runtime requirements of an object is called a *context*. There are two contexts in the **Threading** Step 3 and Step 4 examples: Context 1 where the **Broker** object lives and Context 0 where all other objects live. Every thread in the program runs in Context 1 when executing inside a **Broker** object, Context 0 everywhere else. Contexts are independent of threads.

A context is a collection of one or more objects that have identical concurrency requirements. The .NET concept of a context is similar to the COM concept of an apartment and the COM+ concept of a context.[13] In general, you cannot say what the runtime must do in a given context because it depends on exactly what the runtime requirements are. A context that has transactional requirements requires different action than one that does not. Or, a context that has to maintain a REQUIRED synchronization requirement

---

[13] At this point in time, COM+ contexts and .NET contexts are different. For a discussion of contexts in COM+, see *Understanding and Programming COM+* by Robert J. Oberg.

is different than one that has to maintain a REQUIRES_NEW synchronization requirement.

You can get the **Context** class instance that represents the current context from the static property **Thread::CurrentContext**. **ContextId** is a property of the **Context** class.

Proxies and Stubs

Code
Example

How does the runtime enforce the different requirements of different contexts? When an object that resides in another context (such as the **HotelBroker** object in the **NewReservation** instance), a pointer to a proxy object is returned instead of a pointer to the object itself. The actual object resides in its original, or home, context. The proxy is an object that represents the original object in a different context. The static method **RemotingServices::IsTransparentProxy** determines if an object reference points to a real object instance or a proxy. Look at the code in the main routine in **Threading.h** of the **TestThreading** project in Step 4:

```
bool bTrans;
bTrans = RemotingServices::IsTransparentProxy(
   customers);
Console::WriteLine(
   "Is the customer object a proxy? {0}",
   bTrans.ToString());

bTrans = RemotingServices::IsTransparentProxy(
   hotelBroker);
Console::WriteLine(
   "Is the bookings object a proxy? {0}",
   bTrans.ToString());
```

This causes the following output:

```
Is the customer object a proxy? False
Is the bookings object a proxy? True
```

When a program starts up, it is given a default context.[14] All objects, like the **Customers** object, that do not have any special requirements are created inside of that context (context 0). An object, such as the **HotelBroker** object, that has a different set of requirements (synchronization) is created in a differ-

---

[14] As will be clear in the next section, the sentence should really read, "When a new application domain starts up, it is given a new default context." Contexts are application domain relative. Two different application domains will have two separate default contexts, each with id 0.

ent context (context 1), and a proxy is returned to the creating context (context 0).

Now when you access the **MakeReservation** method in the **HotelBroker** object, you are actually accessing a method on the proxy. The proxy method can then apply the synchronization lock and then delegate to the actual **HotelBroker** object's method. When the actual object's method returns, it returns to the proxy. The proxy can then remove the synchronization lock and return to the caller. This technique, where the runtime uses a proxy to intercept method calls to the actual object, is called *interception*.

You may also want to look at a similar example named **MarshalByReference** in the example directory; it shows how an object can be created in different ways and the effect on whether or not a proxy object is created.

ContextBoundObject

The **Broker** class has to derive from the class **ContextBoundObject** so that the runtime knows to set up a different context if one is required. If you remove the derivation of **Broker** from **ContextBoundObject**, you will once again get the threading conflict, and both customers will be able to reserve the last room at the hotel, even though the class is still marked with the **Synchronization** attribute. Objects that do not derive from **ContextBoundObject** can run in any context (agile objects).

Since other contexts work with a proxy or a reference to the actual object, the runtime must translate (marshal) the call from one context to another. Hence, **ContextBoundObject** inherits from **MarshalByRefObject**. **MarshalByRefObject** is the base class for objects that need to be able to be marshaled by reference.

One advantage of using synchronization techniques such as a **Monitor** is that a **Monitor** can be called from any context. Another potential disadvantage of using automatic synchronization is the performance hit from marshaling and using proxies rather than the actual object.

As will be clear when we discuss application domains, since the customer object has no dependency on context, it is the actual object that is accessed, not a proxy. It can be copied to any context within the same application domain.

Application Isolation

When writing an application, it is often necessary to isolate parts of the application so that a failure of one part does not cause a failure in another part of the application. In Windows, application isolation has traditionally been at the process level. In other words, if a process is stopped or crashes, other processes will continue running. One process cannot directly address memory in another process's address space; however, several interprocess communication mechanisms may be utilized.

Unfortunately, it is expensive for an application to use separate processes to achieve such isolation. To switch from one process to another, the process state information (context) must be saved and restored. This includes a thread and a process switch. A thread switch requires saving CPU registers, such as the call stack and instruction pointer, and loading the information for a new thread, as well as updating the scheduling information for the threads. A process switch includes IO buffers, accounting information, and processor rights that have to be saved for the old process and restored for the new one.

Application Domain

The .NET application domain (sometimes called the AppDomain) is a more lightweight unit for application isolation, fault tolerance, and security. Multiple application domains can run in one process. Since the .NET code can be checked for type safety and security, the CLR can guarantee that one application domain can run independently of another application domain in the same process. No process switch is required to achieve application isolation.

Application domains can have multiple contexts, but a context exists in only one application domain. Although a thread runs in one context of one application domain at a time, the **Threading** examples Step 3 and Step 4 demonstrate that a thread can execute in more than one context. One or more threads can run in an application domain at the same time. An object lives in only one context.

Each application domain starts with a single thread and one context. Additional threads and contexts are created as needed.

There is no relationship between the number of application domains and threads. A Web server might require an application domain for each hosted application that runs in its process. The number of threads in that process would be far fewer, depending on how much actual concurrency the process can support.

To enforce application isolation, code in one application domain cannot make direct calls into the code (or even reference resources) in another application domain. They must use proxies.

Application Domains and Assemblies

Applications are built from one or more assemblies, but each assembly is loaded into an application domain. Each application domain can be unloaded independently of the others, but you cannot unload an individual assembly from an application domain. The assembly will be unloaded when the application domain is unloaded. Unloading an application domain also frees all resource associated with that application domain.

Each process has a default application domain that is created when the process is started. This default domain can only be unloaded when the process shuts down.

Applications such as ASP.NET or Internet Explorer critically depend on preventing the various applications that run under it from interfering with each other. By never loading application code into the default domain, they can ensure that a crashing program will not bring down a host.

AppDomain Class

The **AppDomain** class abstracts application domains. The **AppDomain** sample illustrates the use of application domains. This class has static methods for creating and unloading application domains:

```
AppDomain *domain = AppDomain::CreateDomain(
    "CreatedDomain2", 0, 0);

. . .

AppDomain::Unload(domain);
```

While the **CreateDomain** method is overloaded, one signature illustrates application domain isolation:

```
static AppDomain CreateDomain(
    String *friendlyName,
    Evidence *securityInfo,
    AppDomainSetup *info);
```

The **Evidence** parameter is a collection of the security constraints on the application domain. While we will discuss this in greater detail in Chapter 13, the domain's creator can modify this collection to control the permissions that the executing application domain can have. The **AppDomainSetup** parameter specifies setup information about the domain. Among the information specified is the location of the application domain's configuration file and where private assemblies are loaded. Hence, application domains can be configured independently of each other. Code isolation, setup isolation, and control over security combine to ensure that application domains are independent of each other.

AppDomain Events

To help in maintaining application isolation, the **AppDomain** class allows you to set up event handlers for

- when a domain unloads.
- when the process exits.

- when an unhandled exception occurs.
- when attempts to resolve assemblies, types, and resources fail.

AppDomain Example

If you run the **AppDomain** example,[15] you will get the following output in Figure 8–1.

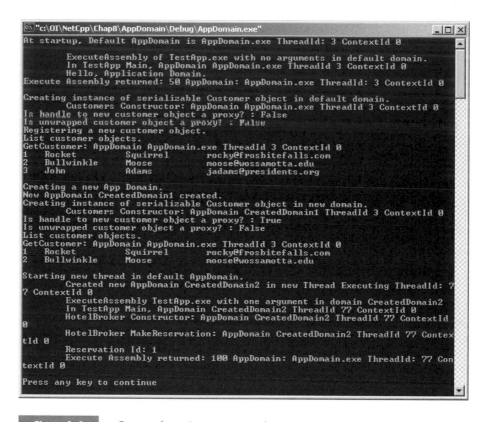

```
"c:\OI\NetCpp\Chap8\AppDomain\Debug\AppDomain.exe"                    _|□|×|
At startup, Default AppDomain is AppDomain.exe ThreadId: 3 ContextId 0

      ExecuteAssembly of TestApp.exe with no arguments in default domain.
      In TestApp Main, AppDomain AppDomain.exe ThreadId 3 ContextId 0
      Hello, Application Domain.
Execute Assembly returned: 50 AppDomain: AppDomain.exe ThreadId: 3 ContextId 0

Creating instance of serializable Customer object in default domain.
      Customers Constructor: AppDomain AppDomain.exe ThreadId 3 ContextId 0
Is handle to new customer object a proxy? : False
Is unwrapped customer object a proxy? : False
Registering a new customer object.
List customer objects.
GetCustomer: AppDomain AppDomain.exe ThreadId 3 ContextId 0
1    Rocket        Squirrel         rocky@frosbitefalls.com
2    Bullwinkle    Moose            moose@wossamotta.edu
3    John          Adams            jadams@presidents.org

Creating a new App Domain.
New AppDomain CreatedDomain1 created.
Creating instance of serializable Customer object in new domain.
      Customers Constructor: AppDomain CreatedDomain1 ThreadId 3 ContextId 0
Is handle to new customer object a proxy? : True
Is unwrapped customer object a proxy? : False
List customer objects.
GetCustomer: AppDomain AppDomain.exe ThreadId 3 ContextId 0
1    Rocket        Squirrel         rocky@frosbitefalls.com
2    Bullwinkle    Moose            moose@wossamotta.edu

Starting new thread in default AppDomain.
      Created new AppDomain CreatedDomain2 in new Thread Executing ThreadId: 7
7 ContextId 0
      ExecuteAssembly TestApp.exe with one argument in domain CreatedDomain2
      In TestApp Main, AppDomain CreatedDomain2 ThreadId 77 ContextId 0
      HotelBroker Constructor: AppDomain CreatedDomain2 ThreadId 77 ContextId
0
      HotelBroker MakeReservation: AppDomain CreatedDomain2 ThreadId 77 Contex
tId 0
      Reservation Id: 1
      Execute Assembly returned: 100 AppDomain: AppDomain.exe ThreadId: 77 Con
textId 0

Press any key to continue
```

Figure 8–1   *Output of AppDomain example.*

---

[15] The TestApp subproject in the AppDomain example is implemented in C# rather than C++. The C++ version is provided in a separate subdirectory that is not part of the AppDomain project. Unfortunately, the C++ version causes a BadImageFormatException to be thrown in the call to ExecuteAssembly, stating that the format of TestApp.exe is invalid. This problem does not occur with the C# version of TestApp.exe. The problem with the C++ version is due to the fact that Managed C++ images can contain unmanaged relocations and unmanaged imports. The initial release of Visual C++.NET cannot load images that contain these unmanaged constructs; however, Microsoft is looking into fixing this in a future version.

First, the name, thread, and context of the default domain is written out.

```
AppDomain *currentDomain = AppDomain::CurrentDomain;
Console::WriteLine(
    "At startup, Default AppDomain is {0} ThreadId: {1}
        ContextId {2}\n",
    currentDomain->FriendlyName,
    Thread::CurrentThread->GetHashCode().ToString(),
    Thread::CurrentContext->ContextID.ToString());
```

We then load and execute an assembly. This code in this assembly just prints out a string and its domain's name, thread, and context. Notice that it executes in the default domain.

```
int val = domain->ExecuteAssembly(
    "TestApp\\bin\\Debug\\TestApp.exe", 0, args);
```

We then create an instance of the **Customers** type from the **Customer** assembly in the default domain. The **CreateInstance** method of the **AppDomain** class returns an **ObjectHandle** instance. You can pass this **ObjectHandle** between application domains without loading the metadata associated with the wrapped type. When you want to use the create object instance, you must unwrap it by calling the **Unwrap** method on the **ObjectHandle** instance.

```
ObjectHandle *oh = currentDomain->CreateInstance(
    "Customer", "OI.NetCpp.Acme.Customers");
...
Customers *custs =
    dynamic_cast<Customers *>(oh->Unwrap());
```

We then add a new customer, and then list all the existing customers. Notice that both the constructor of this type and its methods execute in the same thread and context as the default domain does.

We then create a new domain and create an instance of the same type as before in that new domain.

```
AppDomain *domain = AppDomain::CreateDomain(
    "CreatedDomain1", 0, 0);
...
oh = domain->CreateInstance(
    "Customer", "OI.NetCpp.Acme.Customers");
...
```

```
Customers *custs2 = dynamic_cast
    <Customers *>(oh->Unwrap());
```

Note that the constructor call that results from the **CreateInstance** method executes in the new domain and is therefore in a different context from where the **CreateInstance** call was made, but is executing on the same thread that made the **CreateInstance** call.

When we list the customers in this new object, we get a different list of customers. This is not surprising, since it is a different **Customers** object. Nonetheless, the customer list method executes in the default domain!

Using **RemotingServices::IsTransparentProxy**, we see that the **ObjectHandle** is a proxy to the **Customers** object that lives in the newly created **AppDomain**. However, when you unwrap the object to get an instance handle, you do not get a proxy, but you get an actual object reference. By default, objects are marshaled by value (copied) from one application domain to another.

If the **Customers** object is not serializable, you will get an exception when you try to copy it. This exception would be thrown when you do the **Unwrap**, not the **CreateInstance**. The latter returns a reference. The copy is made only when the **ObjectHandle** is unwrapped. If the object cannot be serialized, it cannot be copied from one application domain to another.

Next, we create a new thread, and that thread creates a new application domain, and then loads and executes an assembly. The assembly starts executing at its entry point, the **Main** routine of the **AppDomainTest** class.

```
AppDomain *domain = AppDomain::CreateDomain(
    "CreatedDomain2", 0, 0);
...
String * args[] = new String *[1];
args[0] = "MakeReservation";
...
int val = domain->ExecuteAssembly(
    "TestApp\\bin\\Debug\\TestApp.exe", 0, args);
...
AppDomain::Unload(domain);
```

The **Main** routine loads the **Hotel** assembly into the newly created application domain. In this example, the **TestApp.exe** application is implemented in C#. It then queries the metadata of the assembly for the **HotelBroker** type information. It then uses that type information to create a **HotelBroker** object. The **HotelBroker** class is marked with a synchronization attribute. As a result, the **HotelBroker** constructor and the **MakeReservation** method run in a different context than the default context.

```
Assembly a = AppDomain.CurrentDomain.Load("Hotel");
Type typeHotelBroker =
```

```
   a.GetType("OI.NetCpp.Acme.HotelBroker");
HotelBroker hotelBroker =
   (HotelBroker)Activator.CreateInstance(typeHotelBroker);
DateTime date = DateTime.Parse("12/2/2001");
ReservationResult rr = hotelBroker.MakeReservation(1,
   "Boston", "Sheraton", date, 3);
Console.WriteLine("\tReservation Id: {0}",
   rr.ReservationId);
```

Marshaling, AppDomains, and Contexts

By default, objects are copied from one application domain to another (marshal by value). The section "Remoting" shows how to marshal by reference between application domains. This ensures that code in one application domain is isolated from another.

Objects are marshaled by reference between contexts. This allows the CLR to enforce the requirements (such as synchronization or transactions) of different objects. This is true whether the client of the object is in the same application domain or not.

Since most objects do not derive from **ContextBoundObject**, they can reside or move from one context to another as required. Threads can cross application domain and context boundaries within the same Win32 process.

Asynchronous Programming

.NET supports a design pattern for asynchronous programming. This pattern is present in many places in .NET (including I/O operations, as noted earlier, and as we will see in Chapter 11). Asynchronous programming provides a way for you to provide a method call without blocking the method caller. From the perspective of the client, the asynchronous model is easier to use than threading. It offers much less control over the synchronization than using synchronization objects, however, and the class designer would probably find threading to be much easier to use.

The Asynchronous Design Pattern

This design pattern is composed of two parts: a set of methods and an interface **IAsyncResult**. The methods of the pattern are

```
IAsyncResult *BeginXXX(
   [InputParams], AsyncCallback *cb, Object *AsyncObject)

[ReturnValue] EndXXX([OutputParams], IAsyncResult *ar);
```

As a design pattern, the XXX represents the actual method being called asynchronously (e.g., **BeginRead/EndRead** for the **System::IO::FileStream** class). The **BeginXXX** should pass all input parameters of the synchronous version (**in**, **in/out**, and **ref**) as well as the **AsyncCallback** and **AsyncObject** parameters. The **EndXXX** should have all the output parameters of the synchronous version (**ref**, **out**, and **in/out**) parameters in its signature. It should return whatever object or value that the synchronous version of the method would return. It should also have an **IAsyncResult** parameter. A **CancelXXX** can also be provided if it makes sense.

The **AsyncCallback** is a delegate that represents a callback function.

```
public __delegate void AsyncCallback(IAsyncResult *ar);
```

The **AsyncObject** is available from **IAsyncResult**. It is provided so that in the callback function you can distinguish which asynchronous read generated the callback.

The framework uses this pattern so that the **FileStream** synchronous **Read** method can be used asynchronously. Here is the synchronous **FileStream::Read** method:

```
int Read(
__in unsigned char* array __gc[],
 int offset, int count);
```

Here is the asynchronous version using the design pattern:

```
IAsyncResult *BeginRead(
    __in unsigned char* array __gc[],
    int offset, int numBytes,
    AsyncCallback *userCallback,
    Object *stateObject);

int EndRead(IAsyncResult *asyncResult);
```

Any exception thrown from **BeginXXX** should be thrown before the asynchronous operation starts. Any exceptions from the asynchronous operation should be thrown from the **EndXXX** method.

IAsyncResult

IAsyncResult is returned by a **BeginXXX** method (such as **BeginRead**). This interface has four elements:

```
public __gc __interface IAsyncResult
{
```

```
public:
    bool get_IsCompleted();
    bool get_CompletedSynchronously();
    WaitHandle* get_AsyncWaitHandle();
    Object* get_AsyncState();
}
```

The **get_IsCompleted** field is set to true after the call has been processed by the server. The client can destroy all resources after **get_IsCompleted** is set to true. If **BeginXXX** completed synchronously, **get_CompletedSynchronously** is set to true. Most of the time this will be ignored and set to the default value of false. In general, a client never knows whether the **BeginXXX** method executed asynchronously or asynchronously. If the asynchronous operation is not finished, the **EndXXX** method will block until the operation is finished.

The **get_AsyncWaitHandle** returns a **WaitHandle** that can be used for synchronization. As we discussed previously, this handle can be signaled so that the client can wait on it. Since you can specify a wait time period, you do not have to block forever if the operation is not yet complete.

The **get_AsyncState** is the object provided as the last argument in the **BeginXXX** call. It allows you to differentiate asynchronous reads in the callback.

Using Delegates for Asynchronous Programming

Any developer of .NET objects who wants to provide an asynchronous interface should follow the pattern just described. Nonetheless, there is no need for most developers to develop a custom asynchronous solution for their objects. Delegates provide a very easy way to support asynchronous operations on any method without any action on the class developer's part. Of course, this has to be done with care because the object may have been written with certain assumptions about which thread it is running on and its synchronization requirements.

Code
Example

The two **Asynch** examples[16] use the **Customers** object from our case study **Customer** assembly. The first example, **AsynchWithoutCallback**, registers new customers asynchronously and does some processing while waiting for each registration to finish. The second example, **AsynchWith Callback**, uses a callback function with the asynchronous processing. In addition to allowing the program to do processing while waiting for the registrations to finish, the callback allows the system to take some asynchronous action for each individual registration.

In the examples, we just print out to the console to show where work could be done. To increase the waiting time to simulate longer processing

---

[16] As usual, you will need to copy the DLL to the **Debug** directory of the test program.

times, we have put calls to **Thread::Sleep()** in **Customers::RegisterCustomer** as well as in the sample programs. Now let us look at the code within the examples.

Suppose the client wants to call the **RegisterCustomer** method asynchronously. The caller simply declares a delegate with the same signature as the method.

```
public __delegate int RegisterCustomerCbk(
    String *FirstName,
    String *LastName,
    String *EmailAddress);
```

You then make the actual method the callback function:

```
RegisterCustomerCbk *rcc = new
    RegisterCustomerCbk(
        customers,
        Customers::RegisterCustomer);
```

BEGIN/END INVOKE

When you declare a delegate, the compiler generates a class with three methods: **BeginInvoke**, **EndInvoke** and **Invoke**. The **BeginInvoke** and **EndInvoke** are type-safe methods that correspond to the **BeginXXX** and **EndXXX** methods and allow you to call the delegate asynchronously. The **Invoke** method is what the compiler uses when you call a delegate.[17] To call **RegisterCustomer** asynchronously, just use the **BeginInvoke** and **EndInvoke** methods.

```
RegisterCustomerCbk *rcc = new
    RegisterCustomerCbk(
        customers,
        Customers::RegisterCustomer);
for(int i = 1; i < 5; i++)
{
    firstName = String::Concat(
        "FirstName", i.ToString());
    lastName = String::Concat(
        "SecondName", (i * 2).ToString());
```

---

[17] If you open the executable from the **DelegateAccount** example in Chapter 5 in ILDASM, you can observe this. The **NotifyCallback** class has the **BeginInvoke**, **EndInvoke**, and **Invoke** methods defined. If you look at the **Withdraw** method for **Account**, you will notice that the line **otifyDlg(balance)** has been transformed to **instance void NotifyCallback::Invoke(valuetype [mscorlib]System.Decimal).**

```
    emailAddress = String::Concat(
        i.ToString(), ".biz");
    IAsyncResult *ar =
        rcc->BeginInvoke(
            firstName,
            lastName,
            emailAddress,
            0,
            0);
    while(!ar->IsCompleted)
    {
        Console::WriteLine(
            "Could do some work here while waiting for customer
                registration to complete.");
        ar->AsyncWaitHandle->WaitOne(1, false);
    }
    customerId = rcc->EndInvoke(ar);
    Console::WriteLine(
        "    Added CustomerId: {0}",
        customerId.ToString());
}
```

The program waits on the **AsyncWaitHandle** periodically to see if the registration has finished. If it has not, some work could be done in the interim. If **EndInvoke** is called before **RegisterCustomer** is complete, **End-Invoke** will block until **RegisterCustomer** is finished.

ASYNCHRONOUS CALLBACK

Instead of waiting on a handle, you could pass a callback function to **Begin-Invoke** (or a **BeginXXX** method). This is done in the **AsynchWithCallback** example.

```
RegisterCustomerCbk *rcc =
    new RegisterCustomerCbk(
        customers,
        Customers::RegisterCustomer);
AsyncCallback *cb =
    new AsyncCallback(this, CustomerCallback);
Object *objectState;
IAsyncResult *ar;
for(int i = 5; i < 10; i++)
{
    firstName = String::Concat(
        "FirstName", i.ToString());
```

```
        lastName = String::Concat(
            "SecondName", (i * 2).ToString());
        emailAddress =
            String::Concat(i.ToString(), ".biz");
        objectState = __box(i);
        ar = rcc->BeginInvoke(
            firstName, lastName,
            emailAddress, cb, objectState);
    }

Console::WriteLine(
    "Finished registrations...could do some work here.");
Thread::Sleep(25);
Console::WriteLine(
    "Finished work..waiting to let registrations complete.");
Thread::Sleep(1000);
```

You then get the results in the callback function:

```
void CustomerCallback(IAsyncResult *ar)
{
    int customerId;
    AsyncResult *asyncResult =
        dynamic_cast<AsyncResult *>(ar);
    RegisterCustomerCbk *rcc =
        dynamic_cast<RegisterCustomerCbk *>
            (asyncResult->AsyncDelegate);

    customerId = rcc->EndInvoke(ar);
    Console::WriteLine(
        "    AsyncState: {0} CustomerId {1} added.",
        ar->AsyncState,
        customerId.ToString());
    Console::WriteLine(
        "        Could do processing here.");
    return;
}
```

You could do some work when each customer registration was finished.

Threading with Parameters

The asynchronous callback runs on a different thread from the one on which **BeginInvoke** was called. If your threading needs are simple and you want to pass parameters to your thread functions, you can use asynchronous delegates to do this. You do not need any reference to the **Threading** namespace. The reference to that namespace in the **AsynchThreading** example is just for the **Thread::Sleep** method needed for demonstration purposes.

PrintNumbers sums the numbers from the starting integer passed to it as an argument to 10 greater than the starting integer. It returns that sum to the caller. **PrintNumbers** can be used for the delegate defined by **Print**.

```
//AsynchThreading.h

using namespace System;
using namespace System::Threading;

public __delegate int Print(int i);

public __gc class Numbers
{
public:
   int PrintNumbers(int start)
   {
      int threadId = Thread::CurrentThread->GetHashCode();
      Console::WriteLine(
         "PrintNumbers Id: {0}",
         threadId.ToString());
      int sum = 0;
      for (int i = start; i < start + 10; i++)
      {
         Console::WriteLine(i.ToString());
         Thread::Sleep(500);
         sum += i;
      }
      return sum;
   }
}
```

The **Main** routine then defines two callbacks and invokes them explicitly with different starting integers. It waits until both of the synchronization handles are signaled. **EndInvoke** is called on both, and the results are written to the console.

```
Numbers *n = new Numbers;
Print *pfn1 = new Print(n, Numbers::PrintNumbers);
Print *pfn2 = new Print(n, Numbers::PrintNumbers);
IAsyncResult *ar1 =
   pfn1->BeginInvoke(0, 0, 0);
```

```
IAsyncResult *ar2 =
    pfn2->BeginInvoke(100, 0, 0);
WaitHandle *wh [] = new WaitHandle*[2];
wh[0] = ar1->AsyncWaitHandle;
wh[1] = ar2->AsyncWaitHandle;
// make sure everything is done before ending
WaitHandle::WaitAll(wh);
int sum1 = pfn1->EndInvoke(ar1);
int sum2 = pfn2->EndInvoke(ar2);
Console::WriteLine(
    "Sum1 = {0} Sum2 = {1}",
    sum1.ToString(), sum2.ToString());
```

The program's output:

```
MainThread Id: 2
PrintNumbers Id: 14
0
1
2
3
4
5
6
7
8
9
PrintNumbers Id: 14
100
101
102
103
104
105
106
107
108
109
Sum1 = 45 Sum2 = 1045
```

Remoting

Remoting technology uses all of the key concepts in the .NET Application Model. While a complete discussion of remoting is beyond the scope of this book, a brief introduction provides a powerful example of how metadata and marshal by reference (MBR) work. Remoting also provides a mechanism that supports executable servers.

Unlike remoting in Microsoft's COM technology, there is a minimal amount of infrastructure programming required. What infrastructure program is required allows programmers either a degree of flexibility or the ability to customize remoting for their particular applications.

The .NET Framework provides two ways to provide connections between two applications on different computers. Web Services, discussed in Chapter 11, enable computers that do not host the CLR to communicate with computers that do. The remoting technology discussed here builds distributed applications between computers that host the CLR.

Remoting Overview

The key parts of Remoting are

- *Interception*, which allows for message generation for communication over the channels.
- *Formatters* to put the messages into a byte stream that is sent over the channel. These are the same formatters that were discussed in the section on serialization.
- Communication *channels* for transport of messages.

INTERCEPTION

Proxies and stubs (referred to in .NET as dispatchers) transform the function calls on the client or server side into messages that are sent over the network. This is called interception, because the proxies and dispatchers intercept a method call to send it to its remote destination. Unlike COM, metadata pro vides the information so the CLR can generate the proxies and stubs for you.

A *proxy* takes the function call off the stackframe of the caller and transforms it into a message. The message is then sent to its destination. A *dispatcher* takes the message and transforms it into a stackframe so that a call can be made to the object.

For example, assume the **UnregisterCustomer** method from the **Customer** assembly runs in one application domain and is called from another. It makes no difference if the application domains are in the same process or on the same machine.

The proxy would take the integer **id** argument on the stackframe of the client making the call and put it in a message that encoded the call and its argument. On the server side, the dispatcher would take that message and create a function call on the server's stack for the call **UnregisterCustomer(int id)** and make that call into the object. The client and server code do not need to know that they are being remoted.

CHANNELS AND FORMATTERS

The formatter converts the message into a byte stream. The .NET Framework comes with two formatters, binary and SOAP (text-based XML, discussed in the Chapter 11). The byte stream is then sent over a communication channel.

The .NET Framework comes with two channels, although you can write your own. The HTTP channel uses the HTTP protocol and is good for communicating over the Internet or through firewalls. The TCP channel uses the TCP (sockets) protocol and is designed for high-speed communication. You have four permutations of formatters and transport: binary over TCP, binary over HTTP, SOAP over HTTP, and SOAP over TCP.

Remote Objects

Clients obtain a proxy by *activating* a remote object. Remote objects must derive from **MarshalByRefObject**, because you work with a proxy to the object reference, not with the object reference itself. This is the same concept discussed in the section on contexts, where marshal by reference is also used to access context bound objects.

Local objects passed as method parameters from one application domain to another can be passed by value (copied) or by reference.

To be passed by value, they must be serializable. The object is serialized, sent across the transport layer, and re-created on the other side. We have already seen an example of this in the **AppDomain** example.

To be passed by reference, the class must derive from **MarshalByRefObject**. The **Remoting** example illustrates pass by reference.

Remote objects can be either server or client activated. Server-activated objects are not created until the first method call on the object. Server-activated objects come in two flavors, **SingleCall** and **Singleton**. **SingleCall** objects are stateless. Each method causes a new object to be created. **Singleton** objects can be used by multiple client activation requests. **Singleton** objects can maintain state. **SingleCall** objects will scale better than **Singleton** objects because they do not retain state and can be load balanced.

Client-activated objects are activated when the client requests them. While they can last for multiple calls and hold state, they cannot store information from different client activations. This is similar to calling **CoCreateInstanceEx** in DCOM.

Activation

Objects are activated on the client side in one of three ways by using the **Activator** class.

- **Activator::GetObject** is used to get a reference to a server-activated object.
- **Activator::CreateInstance** is used to create a client-activated object. You can pass parameters to the object's constructor using

one of the overloaded **CreateInstance** methods that takes an array
of objects to be passed to the constructor.

- The C++ **new** syntax can be used to create a server or a client activated object. A configuration file is used to describe how **new**
  should be used.

Sample Remotable Object

Code
Example

For our remoting example, we remote our **Customers** object from the **Customer** assembly. In the **Remoting** example directory there are two solutions.
One represents the client program, the other the server program. Build the
server solution first, which will also build the dependent **Customer.dll**. Copy
this DLL into the **Debug** directory of both **Server** and **Client**. Start the server
program first. Notice it waits for a client request. You can then run the client program that will run against objects that live inside of the server. We will discuss
the details of the client and server code and output in the next few sections.

Notice that we only had to make two simple changes to our object. The
Customers class in the server project had to be made remotable by inheriting
from **MarshalByRefObject**.

```
public __gc class Customers :
    public MarshalByRefObject, public ICustomer
```

The **CustomerListItem** that was going to be transferred by value had to
be made serializable.

```
[Serializable]
public __value struct CustomerListItem
{
public:
    int CustomerId;
    String *FirstName;
    String *LastName;
    String *EmailAddress;
};
```

SAMPLE REMOTING PROGRAM

In the **Remoting** example the client accesses a server-activated object. The
server is the **TcpServerChannel** class that uses a binary format with the TCP
protocol. The channel will use port 8085. The server registers the type being
remoted, the endpoint name to refer to this object, and the type of activation.
The server then waits for client requests.

```
TcpServerChannel *chan = new TcpServerChannel(8085);
    ChannelServices::RegisterChannel(chan);
```

```
RemotingConfiguration::RegisterWellKnownServiceType(
    __typeof(Customers),
    "AcmeCustomer",
    WellKnownObjectMode::Singleton);
  . . .
```

The server has to be started before the client program can access the object.

The client sets up a **TcpClientChannel** object and then connects to the object. It specifies the type of the object it wants and the endpoint where the server is listening for object requests. If you want to run the client and server on separate machines, substitute the server machine name for localhost in the endpoint. Unlike COM location transparency, the client has to specify a specific endpoint; there is no redirection through an opaque registry entry.

```
TcpClientChannel *chan = new TcpClientChannel;
ChannelServices::RegisterChannel(chan);
Customers *obj = dynamic_cast<Customers *>(
    Activator::GetObject(
        __typeof(Customers),
        "tcp://localhost:8085/AcmeCustomer"));
if (obj == 0)
   Console::WriteLine("Could not locate server");
else
{
    . . .
```

The client then uses the proxy to make calls on the object as if it were a local instance.

```
bool bRet =
    RemotingServices::IsTransparentProxy(obj);
. . .
ArrayList *ar;
ar = obj->GetCustomer(-1);
ShowCustomerArray(ar);
```

To run the program, start the server program in one console window, and then run the client program from another console window.

The output depends on what kind of server-activated object is being activated. If the server activation type is **Singleton**, which supports the maintaining state, you get the behavior you would expect from the non-remoted case. A new customer is added, and you find that new customer in the list when you ask for all the existing customers. As you would expect, the initial activate call results in the **Customers** constructor being called once for each server invocation no matter how many times the client program is run.

```
Object reference a proxy?: True
Client: AppDomain Client.exe Thread 19 Context 0
1    Rocket          Squirrel        rocky@frosbitefalls.com
2    Bullwinkle      Moose           moose@wossamotta.edu

1    Rocket          Squirrel        rocky@frosbitefalls.com
2    Bullwinkle      Moose           moose@wossamotta.edu
3    Boris           Badenough       boris@no-goodnicks.com
```

If the activation type is **SingleCall**, which creates a new object instance for every method call, the results are quite different. Four different objects are created. The first object is created by the initial activate request. The second is created by the initial call to **GetCustomer**. The third object is created by the **RegisterCustomer** call. The fourth object is created by the second call to **GetCustomer**. The last object created never sees the new customer because no state is saved. Note that the static **nextCustId** member of the **Customer** class is treated as static with respect to the new object instances of the **Customer** class, just as you would expect. Same client code, different results! Since the object is already activated, if you run the client program a second time for the same server invocation, the **Customers** constructor will be called only three times.

```
Object reference a proxy?: True
Client: AppDomain Client.exe Thread 19 Context 0
3    Rocket          Squirrel        rocky@frosbitefalls.com
4    Bullwinkle      Moose           moose@wossamotta.edu

8    Rocket          Squirrel        rocky@frosbitefalls.com
9    Bullwinkle      Moose           moose@wossamotta.edu
```

Since the client uses a proxy, the object executes inside the server's application domain, but on a different thread than the main server thread. The object's constructor is not called until the first method call on the object. Notice how in both cases we have remoted an **ArrayList** of types without any special work aside from making the type serializable. The presence of metadata makes the programmer's work much easier.

Metadata and Remoting

In order for the client to request an object of a specific type, metadata about the type has to be available to the client. For the remoting example shown in this chapter, a reference is simply made to the actual assembly where the object is stored. However, for many applications, you do not want to give the client access to your actual assembly, since it can be decompiled into source code via reflection (i.e., reverse engineering). For the metadata that the client needs, a reference need only be made to an object that contains interface information, but no actual implementation details.

One way to do this is to build a version of the object that has methods with no implementation. This interface class can then be built into an assembly that can be given to the client. You can throw the **System::NotSupported-Exception** in the methods if you wish to make sure that they are never used by mistake for the real object.

For Web Services, you use the SOAPSUDS tool to extract the metadata from the service, and then generate an assembly that has the required metadata. You can then build a proxy DLL and have the client program refer to it. This is conceptually equivalent to the first approach. The server, of course, has to reference the real object's assembly.

Unlike the COM model, there is no reference counting, interface negotiation, building and registering separate proxies and stubs, worrying about global identifiers, or use of the registry. Because of metadata, all you have to do is inherit from **MarshalByRefObject** to make an object remotable.

Remoting Configuration Files

You use configuration files to define where the object is activated. The client can then use the **new** operator to create the object. The big advantage in doing this is that as the object location changes (such as a URL or TCP channel), or the formatter you want to use changes, the client does not have to be rebuilt.

Multiple classes can be configured on the client. Configuration files are loaded into the client using the **RemotingConfiguration::Configure** method.

Custom Attributes

Chapter 5 introduced the concept of attributes, which have already appeared in several examples. In this chapter we used the **Serializable** and **Synchronization** attributes, which are provided by .NET Framework classes. The .NET Framework makes the attribute mechanism entirely extensible, allowing you to define custom attributes, which can be added to the class's metadata. This custom metadata is available through reflection and can be used at runtime. To simplify the use of custom attributes, you may declare a base class to do the work of invoking the reflection API to obtain the metadata information.

The example **CustomAttribute** illustrates the custom attribute **Initial-Directory**. **InitialDirectory** controls the initial current directory where the program runs. By default, the current directory is the directory containing the solution, which in this case is **C:\OI\NetCpp\Chap08\CustomAttribute**.

Using a Custom Attribute

Before we discuss implementing the custom attribute, let us look at how the **InitialDirectory** attribute is used. To be able to control the initial directory for a class, we derive the class from the base class **DirectoryContext**. We may then apply to the class the attribute **InitialDirectory**, which takes a **String*** parameter giving a path to what the initial directory should be. The property **DirectoryPath** extracts the path from the metadata. If our class does not have the attribute applied, this path will be the default. Here is the code for our test program.

When you run this sample on your system, you can change the directory in the attribute to one that exists on your machine.

```
//AttributeDemo.h

using namespace System;
using namespace System::IO;

__gc class Normal : public DirectoryContext
{
};

[InitialDirectory("C:\\OI\\NetCpp\\Chap08")]
__gc class Special : public DirectoryContext
{
};

public __gc class AttributeDemo
{
public:
    static void Main()
    {
        Normal *objNormal = new Normal;
        Console::WriteLine(
            "path = {0}", objNormal->DirectoryPath);
        ShowDirectoryContents(objNormal->DirectoryPath);
        Special *objSpecial = new Special;
        Console::WriteLine(
            "path = {0}", objSpecial->DirectoryPath);
```

```
            ShowDirectoryContents(objSpecial->DirectoryPath);
        }
    private:
        static void ShowDirectoryContents(String *path)
        {
            DirectoryInfo *dir = new DirectoryInfo(path);
            FileInfo *files[] = dir->GetFiles();
            Console::WriteLine("Files:");
            IEnumerator *pEnum = files->GetEnumerator();
            while (pEnum->MoveNext())
            {
                FileInfo *f =
                    dynamic_cast<FileInfo *>(pEnum->Current);
                Console::WriteLine("   {0}", f->Name);
            }
            DirectoryInfo *dirs [] = dir->GetDirectories();
            Console::WriteLine("Directories:");
            pEnum = dirs->GetEnumerator();
            while (pEnum->MoveNext())
            {
                DirectoryInfo *d =
                    dynamic_cast<DirectoryInfo *>(pEnum->Current);
                Console::WriteLine("   {0}", d->Name);
            }
        }
    };
```

Here is the output:

```
path = c:\OI\NetCpp\Chap08\CustomAttribute
Files:
    CustomAttribute.vcproj
    CustomAttribute.ncb
    ReadMe.txt
    CustomAttribute.cpp
    AssemblyInfo.cpp
    stdafx.cpp
    stdafx.h
    CustomAttribute.sln
    CustomAttribute.suo
    AttributeDemo.h
    DirectoryContext.h
    DirectoryAttribute.h
Directories:
```

```
      Debug
path = C:\OI\NetCpp\Chap08
Files:
Directories:
   Reflection
   Dynamic
   FileIO
   Serialization
   Hotel
   ISerialization
   Threading
   PulseAll
   ThreadIsolation
   AppDomain
   Asynch
   AsynchThreading
   CustomAttribute
   MarshalByReference
   Remoting
```

Defining an Attribute Class

To create a custom attribute, you must define an attribute class, derived from the base class **Attribute**. By convention, give your class a name ending in "Attribute." The name of your class without the "Attribute" suffix will be the name of the custom attribute. In our example the class name is **InitialDirectoryAttribute**, so the attribute's name is **InitialDirectory**.

You may provide one or more constructors for your attribute class. The constructors define how to pass positional parameters to the attribute (provide a parameter list, separated by commas). It is also possible to provide "named parameters" for a custom attribute, where the parameter information will be passed using the name=value syntax.

You may also provide properties to read the parameter information. In our example, we have a property **Path**, which is initialized in the constructor.

```
//DirectoryAttribute.h

using namespace System;

public __gc class InitialDirectoryAttribute :
   public Attribute
{
private:
   String *path;
```

```
public:
   InitialDirectoryAttribute(String *path)
   {
      this->path = path;
   }
   __property String *get_Path()
   {
      return path;
   }
};
```

Defining a Base Class

The last step in working with custom attributes is to provide a means to extract the custom attribute information from the metadata using the reflection classes. You can obtain the **Type** of any object by calling the method **GetType**, which is provided in the root class **Object**. Using the class's method **GetCustomAttributes** you can read the custom attribute information.

To make the coding of the client program as simple as possible, it is often useful to provide a base class that does the work of reading the custom attribute information.[18] We provide a base class **DirectoryContext**, which is used by a class wishing to take advantage of the **InitialDirectory** attribute. This base class provides the property **DirectoryPath** to return the path information stored in the metadata. Here is the code for the base class:

```
//DirectoryContext.h

using namespace System;
using namespace System::Reflection;
using namespace System::IO;
using namespace System::Collections;

__gc class DirectoryContext
{
public:
   __property String *get_DirectoryPath()
   {
      Type *t = this->GetType();
      IEnumerator *pEnum =
         t->GetCustomAttributes(true)->GetEnumerator();
```

---

[18] With single implementation inheritance, there is a cost to providing a base class. If you need to derive from another class, such as **ContextBoundObject**, the base class has to derive from that class.

```
    while (pEnum->MoveNext())
    {
        Attribute *a =
            dynamic_cast<Attribute *>(pEnum->Current);
        InitialDirectoryAttribute *da =
            dynamic_cast<InitialDirectoryAttribute *>(a);
        if (da != 0)
        {
            return da->Path;
        }
    }
    return Directory::GetCurrentDirectory();
}
};
```

We must import the **System::Reflection** namespace. **GetType** returns the current **Type** object, and we can then use the **GetCustomAttributes** method to obtain a collection of **Attribute** objects from the metadata. Since this collection is heterogeneous, consisting of different types, the dynamic_cast operator is used to test if a given collection element is of the type **InitialDirectoryAttribute**. If we find such an element, we return the **Path** property. Otherwise, we return the default current directory, obtained from **GetCurrentDirectory**.

Garbage Collection

Managed memory allocations are automatically reclaimed through a garbage collection algorithm. The CLR tracks the use of memory that is allocated on the managed heap, and any memory that is no longer referenced is marked as "garbage." When memory is low, the CLR traverses its data structure of tracked memory and reclaims all the memory marked as garbage. Thus the programmer is relieved of this responsibility.

While this prevents memory leaks in the managed heap, it does not help with the reclamation of other types of allocated resources. Examples of these resources include open files or database connections, or server login connections that have to be disconnected. The programmer may need to write explicit code to perform cleanup of these other resources. This can be done in your class destructor[19] or in a specialized cleanup method. The CLR calls your destructor when the memory allocated for an object is reclaimed.

---

[19] The .NET Framework describes a method named **Finalize** in the **Object** base class for this purpose. However, in Managed C++ you do not use the name **Finalize**. Instead, you simply define a destructor for your class.

Another concern with garbage collection is performance. There is some overhead associated with automatic garbage collection. However, the CLR does provide an efficient multi-generational garbage collection algorithm.

Object Destruction

Unless you explicitly use the delete operator on a managed object, destruction time is non-deterministic. The destructor for a particular unreferenced object may run at any time during the garbage collection process, and the order of calling destructors for different objects cannot be predicted. Moreover, under exceptional circumstances, a destructor may not run at all (for example, a thread goes into an infinite loop or a process aborts without giving the run-time a chance to clean up). Also, unless you explicitly use the delete operator, the thread on which the destructor is called is not deterministic.

The fact that the call to the destructor is synchronous, and therefore deterministic, when you explicitly delete a managed pointer is demonstrated in the **ExplicitDelete** example. The following code shows two objects being created. The first one is then passively finalized by assigning it to zero. The garbage collector will call the destructor on its own thread asynchronously. The second object is explicitly destroyed with the delete operator, and the destructor is called synchronously. The program displays details on what is happening to each object, and on what thread, using hash codes. From the output, you can see that with the passively disposed object, the destructor is run on a different thread than the **Main** method thread. In contrast, you can see that with the explicitly deleted object, the destructor is run on the same thread as the **Main** method.

```
//ExplicitDelete.h

using namespace System::Threading;

public __gc class SomeClass
{
public:
   ~SomeClass()
   {
      Console::Write(
         "Destructor running in thread: {0}, ",
         __box(Thread::CurrentThread->GetHashCode()));
      Console::WriteLine(
         "Destroying object: {0}",
         __box(this->GetHashCode()));
   }
};
```

```
public __gc class ExplicitDelete
{
public:
   static void Main()
   {
      Console::WriteLine(
         "Main thread: {0}",
         __box(Thread::CurrentThread->GetHashCode()));

      SomeClass *sc = new SomeClass;
      Console::WriteLine(
         "Main thread creating object: {0}",
         __box(sc->GetHashCode()));
      Console::WriteLine(
         "Nulling pointer to object: {0}",
         __box(sc->GetHashCode()));
      sc = 0;
      GC::Collect();
      GC::WaitForPendingFinalizers();

      sc = new SomeClass;
      Console::WriteLine(
         "Main thread creating object: {0}",
         __box(sc->GetHashCode()));
      Console::WriteLine(
         "Deleting pointer to object: {0}",
          __box(sc->GetHashCode()));
      delete sc;

      Console::WriteLine("All done.");
   }
};
```

Here is the output.

```
Main thread: 2
Main thread creating object: 5
Nulling pointer to object: 5
Destructor running in thread: 6, Destroying object: 5
Main thread creating object: 7
Deleting pointer to object: 7
Destructor running in thread: 2, Destroying object: 7
All done.
```

To avoid unnecessary overhead, you should not implement a destructor for a class unless you have a good reason for doing so. And if you do provide a destructor, you should probably provide an alternate, deterministic mechanism for a class to perform necessary cleanup. The .NET Framework recommends a **Dispose** design pattern for deterministic cleanup, which is described next.

Unmanaged Resources and Dispose

Consider an object that has opened a file, and is then no longer needed and marked for garbage collection. Eventually, the object's destructor will be called, and the file could be closed in that destructor. But, as we discussed, garbage collection is non-deterministic, and the file might remain open for an indefinitely long time. It would be more efficient to have a deterministic mechanism for a client program to clean up the object's resources when it is done with it. The .NET Framework recommends the **IDisposable** interface for this purpose.

```
public __gc __interface IDisposable
{
    void Dispose();
};
```

This design pattern specifies that a client program should call **Dispose** on the object when it is done with it. In the **Dispose** method implementation, the class does the appropriate cleanup. As backup assurance, the class should also implement a destructor in case **Dispose** never gets called, perhaps due to an exception being thrown.[20] Since both **Dispose** and the destructor perform the cleanup, the cleanup code can be placed in **Dispose**, and **the** destructor can be implemented by calling **Dispose**. The **Dispose** method is designed such that a client program can call it when it is done with the object or knows that it is safe to free the resources associated with the object.

One detail is that once **Dispose** has been called, the object's destructor should not be called, because that would involve cleanup being performed twice. The object can be removed from the garbage collection queue by calling **GC::SuppressFinalize**. Also, it is a good idea for the class to maintain a bool flag such as **disposeCalled**, so that if **Dispose** is called twice, cleanup will not be performed a second time.

A **Dispose** method should also call the base class **Dispose** to make sure that all its resources are freed. It should also be written so that if a **Dis-**

---

[20] One of the virtues of the exception handling mechanism is that as the call stack is unwound in handling the exception, local objects go out of scope and so can get marked for finalization. We provide a small demo later in this section.

pose method is called after the resources have been already freed, no exception is thrown.

Since finalization is expensive, any objects that will no longer acquire any more resources should call the static method **GC::SupressFinalize** and pass it the **this** pointer. If you have a **try/finally** block in your code, you can place a call to the object's **Dispose** method in the **finally** block to make sure that resources are freed.

The example program **DisposeDemo** provides an illustration of the dispose pattern. The class **SimpleLog** implements logging to a file, making use of the **StreamWriter** class.

```cpp
//SimpleLog.h

using namespace System;
using namespace System::IO;

public __gc class SimpleLog : public IDisposable
{
private:
   StreamWriter *writer;
   String *name;
   bool disposeCalled;
public:
   SimpleLog(String *fileName) : disposeCalled(false)
   {
      name = fileName;
      writer = new StreamWriter(fileName, false);
      writer->AutoFlush = true;
      Console::WriteLine(
         String::Format("logfile {0} created", name));
   }
   void WriteLine(String *str)
   {
      writer->WriteLine(str);
      Console::WriteLine(str);
   }
   void Dispose()
   {
      if(disposeCalled)
         return;
      writer->Close();
      GC::SupressFinalize(this);
      Console::WriteLine(
         String::Format("logfile {0} disposed", name));
```

```
      disposeCalled = true;
   }
   ~SimpleLog()
   {
      Console::WriteLine(
         String::Format("logfile {0} finalized", name));
      Dispose();
   }
};
```

The class **SimpleLog** supports the **IDisposable** interface and thus implements **Dispose**. The cleanup code simply closes the **StreamWriter** object. To make sure that a disposed object will not also be finalized, **GC::SuppressFinalize** is called. The finalizer simply delegates to **Dispose**. To help monitor object lifetime, a message is written to the console in the constructor, in **Dispose**, and in the finalizer.[21]

Here is the code for the test program:

```
//DisposeDemo.h

using namespace System;
using namespace System::Threading;

public __gc class DisposeDemo
{
public:
   static void Main()
   {
      SimpleLog *log = new SimpleLog("log1.txt");
      log->WriteLine("First line");
      Pause();
      log->Dispose();    // first log disposed
      log->Dispose();    // test Dispose twice
      log = new SimpleLog("log2.txt");
      log->WriteLine("Second line");
      Pause();
      log = new SimpleLog(
         "log3.txt");      // previous (2nd) log released
      log->WriteLine("Third line");
      Pause();
      log = 0;                  // last log released
```

---

[21] The **Console::WriteLine** in the destructor is provided purely for didactic purposes and should not be done in production code, for reasons we shall discuss shortly.

```
      GC::Collect();
      Thread::Sleep(100);
   }
private:
   static void Pause()
   {
      Console::Write("Press enter to continue");
      String *str = Console::ReadLine();
   }
};
```

The **SimpleLog** object pointer **log** is assigned in turn to three different object instances. The first time, it is properly disposed. The second time, **log** is reassigned to refer to a third object, before the second object is disposed, resulting in the second object becoming garbage. The **Pause** method provides an easy way to pause the execution of this console application, allowing us to investigate the condition of the files **log1.txt**, **log2.txt**, and **log3.txt** at various points in the execution of the program.

Running the program results in the following output:

```
logfile log1.txt created
First line
Press enter to continue
logfile log1.txt disposed
logfile log2.txt created
Second line
Press enter to continue
logfile log3.txt created
Third line
Press enter to continue
logfile log3.txt finalized
logfile log3.txt disposed
logfile log2.txt finalized
logfile log2.txt disposed
```

After the first pause, the file **log1.txt** has been created, and you can examine its contents in Notepad. If you try to delete the file, you will get a sharing violation, as illustrated in Figure 8–2.

At the second pause point, **log1.txt** has been disposed, and you will be allowed to delete it. The **log2.txt** file has been created (and is open). At the third pause point, **log3.txt** has been created. But the object reference to **log2.txt** has been reassigned, and so there is now no way for the client program to dispose of the second object.[22] If **Dispose** were the only mechanism to clean up the second object, we would be out of luck. Fortunately, the

Figure 8–2   *Trying to delete an open file results in a sharing violation.*

SimpleObject class has implemented a destructor, so the next time garbage is collected, the second object will be disposed of properly. We can see the effect of finalization by running the program through to completion. The second object is indeed finalized, and thence disposed. In fact, as the application domain shuts down, the destructor is called on all objects not exempt from finalization, even on objects that are still accessible.

In our code we explicitly make the third object inaccessible by the assignment **log = null**, and we then force a garbage collection by a call to **GC::Collect**. Finally, we sleep briefly to give the garbage collector a chance to run through to completion before the application domain shuts down. Coding our test program in this way is a workaround for the fact that the order of garbage collection is non-deterministic. The garbage collector will be called automatically when the program exits and the application domain is shut down. However, at that point, system objects, such as **Console**, are also being closed. Since you cannot rely on the order of finalizations, you may get an exception from the **WriteLine** statement within the finalizer. The explicit call to **GC::Collect** forces a garbage collection while the system objects are still open. If we omitted the last three lines of the **Main** method, we might well get identical output, but we might also get an exception.

ALTERNATE NAME FOR DISPOSE

The standard name for the method that performs cleanup is **Dispose**. The convention is that once an object is disposed, it is finished. In some cases, the same object instance may be reused, as in the case of a file. A file may be

---

[22]   This example illustrates that it is the client's responsibility to help the scalability of the server by cleaning up objects (using **Dispose**) before reassigning them. Once an object has been reassigned, there is no way to call **Dispose**, and the object will hang around for an indeterminate period of time until garbage is collected. Effective memory management involves both the server and client.

opened, closed, and then opened again. In such a case the standard naming convention is that the cleanup method should be called **Close**. In other cases some other natural name may be used.

Our **SimpleLog** class could plausibly have provided an **Open** method, and then it would have made sense to name our cleanup method **Close**. For simplicity, we did not provide an **Open** method, and so we stuck to the name **Dispose**.

GENERATIONS

As an optimization, every object on the managed heap is assigned to a generation. A new object is in generation 0 and is considered a prime candidate for garbage collection. Older objects are in generation 1. Since such an older object has survived for a while, the odds favor its having a longer lifetime than a generation 0 object. Still older objects are assigned to generation 2 and are considered even more likely to survive a garbage collection. The maximum generation number in the current implementation of .NET is 2, as can be confirmed from the **GC::MaxGeneration** property.

In a normal sweep of the garbage collector, only generation 0 will be examined. It is here that the most likely candidates are for memory to be reclaimed. All surviving generation 0 objects are promoted to generation 1. If not enough memory is reclaimed, a sweep will next be performed on generation 1 objects, and the survivors will be promoted. Then, if necessary, a sweep of generation 2 will be performed, and so on up until **MaxGeneration**.

Finalization and Stack Unwinding

Code Example

As mentioned earlier, one of the virtues of the exception handling mechanism is that as the call stack is unwound in handling the exception, local objects go out of scope and so can get marked for finalization. The program **Finalize-StackUnwind** provides a simple illustration. It uses the **SimpleLog** class discussed previously, which implements finalization.

```
//FinalizeStackUnwind.h

using namespace System;
using namespace System::Threading;

public __gc class FinalizeStackUnwind
{
public:
   static void Main()
   {
      try
```

```
        {
            SomeMethod();
        }
        catch(Exception *e)
        {
            Console::WriteLine(e->Message);
        }
        GC::Collect();
        Thread::Sleep(100);
    }
private:
    static void SomeMethod()
    {
        // local variable
        SimpleLog *alpha = new SimpleLog("alpha.txt");
        // force an exception
        throw new Exception("error!!");
    }
};
```

A local pointer variable **alpha** of type **SimpleLog*** is allocated in **SomeMethod**. Before the method exits normally, an exception is thrown. The stack-unwinding mechanism of exception handling detects that **alpha** is no longer accessible, and so is marked for garbage collection. The call to **GC::Collect** forces a garbage collection, and we see from the output of the program that finalization is indeed carried out.

```
logfile alpha.txt created
error!!
logfile alpha.txt finalized
logfile alpha.txt disposed
```

Controlling Garbage Collection with the GC Class

Normally, it is the best practice simply to let the garbage collector perform its work behind the scenes. Sometimes, however, it may be advantageous for the program to intervene. The **System** namespace contains the class **GC**, which enables a program to affect the behavior of the garbage collector. We summarize a few of the important methods of the **GC** class.

SUPPRESSFINALIZE

This method requests the system to not finalize (i.e., not call the destructor) for the specified object. As we saw previously, you should call this method in your implementation of **Dispose** to prevent a disposed object from also being finalized.[23]

COLLECT

You can force a garbage collection by calling the **Collect** method. An optional parameter lets you specify which generations should be collected. Use this method sparingly, since normally the CLR has better information on the current state of memory. A possible use would be a case when your program has just released a number of large objects, and you would like to see all this memory reclaimed right away. Another example was provided in the previous section, where a call to **Collect** forced a collection while system objects were still valid.

MAXGENERATION

This property returns the maximum number of generations that are supported.

GETGENERATION

This method returns the current generation number of an object.

GETTOTALMEMORY

This method returns the number of bytes currently allocated (not the free memory available, and not the total memory size of the heap). A parameter lets you specify whether the system should perform a garbage collection before returning. If no garbage collection is done, the indicated number of bytes is probably larger than the actual number of bytes being used by live objects.

Sample Program

The program **GarbageCollection** illustrates using these methods of the **GC** class. The example is artificial, simply illustrating object lifetime and the effect of the various **GC** methods. The class of objects that are allocated is called **Member**. This class has a **String** property called **Name**. Write statements are provided in the constructor, **Dispose**, and destructor. A **Committee** class maintains an array list of **Member** instances. The **RemoveMember** method

---

[23] You should be careful in the case of an object that might be "closed" (like a file) that is later re-opened again. In such a case it might be better not to suppress finalization. Once finalization is suppressed, it can be made eligible for finalization again by calling **GC::ReRegisterForFinalize**. For a discussion of advanced issues in garbage collection and finalization, refer to the Jeffrey Richter article previously cited.

simply removes the member from the array list. The **DisposeMember** method also calls **Dispose** on the member being expunged from the committee. The **ShowGenerations** method displays the generation number of each **Member** object. **GarbageCollection.h** is a test program to exercise these classes, showing the results of various allocations and deallocations and the use of methods of the **GC** class. The code and output should be quite easy to understand.

All the memory is allocated locally in a method named **Demonstrate-Generations**. After this method returns and its local memory has become inaccessible, we make an explicit call to **GC::Collect**. This forces the destructors to be called before the application domain shuts down, and so we avoid a possible random exception of a stream being closed when a **WriteLine** method is called in a finalizer. This is the same point mentioned previously for the earlier examples.

Summary

This chapter introduced the .NET application model. Through metadata and reflection, the framework can understand enough about your application to provide many services that you do not have to implement. On the other hand, we have seen how the framework is structured so that you can substitute your own objects and implementations where needed.

Type safety enables application domains to provide an effective yet economical form of application isolation. Contexts, proxies, and interception allow the runtime to transparently provide services to parts of applications that require them.

Another aspect of the .NET application model is the pervasive use of attributes, which can be easily added to source code and is stored with the metadata. We saw examples of the use of attributes for serialization and for synchronization, and we demonstrated how to implement and use custom attributes.

.NET simplifies the programming of memory management through an efficient, generational, automatic garbage collection facility. Finalization is non-deterministic, but you can support deterministic cleanup by implementing the dispose pattern or using the delete operator explicitly.

Programming with ADO.NET

*T*he framework database programming classes are referred to as ADO.NET. ADO.NET introduces the **DataSet** class that works with relational data in a relational manner while you are either connected or disconnected from a data source. Disconnected data access has become more important recently in the multitiered and Internet-oriented worlds of data access. You only need to connect with and update or query the database when necessary. You can, of course, also work in the traditional connected manner if you choose.

ADO.NET data providers[1] allow you to execute commands directly against the data source. Functionality is exposed directly, without intermediary objects such as OLEDB, which stands between ADO and the data source. The **DataAdapter** class models a data source as a set of database commands and a connection to that data source. The **DataAdapter** class implements the **IDataAdapter** interface, forming a bridge between a **DataSet** object and the data source. Differences between data sources are hidden by the **IData Adapter** interface. The OLEDB data provider allows for nested transactions; the SqlServer data provider does not.[2]

.NET data providers supply data to a dataset or a data reader. A dataset is a memory-resident, lightweight relational database that is not directly connected to any database. You can also obtain a dataset from an XML document or create an XML document from a dataset. This allows you to work, if it makes sense, with your data as relational data or as hierarchical XML data.[3] Data readers model the traditional method of working with a database.

---

[1] Data providers were called managed providers in the beta literature. You may still see them referred to by that term.

[2] There is a **Begin** method on the **OleDbTransaction** class. The **SqlTransaction** class does not have such a method.

[3] Hierarchies do not automatically map to the many-to-many relations that you can have in a relational database, but this is no different from working with the classic object-relational model clash.

The data access classes that currently ship with the framework are found in the namespaces **System::Data**, **System::Data::SqlClient**, **System:: Data::OleDb**, **System::Data::Common**, and **System::Data::SqlTypes**. The **Sql** and **OleDb** namespaces reflect the SqlServer and OleDb data providers. An ODBC data provider has been written, and additional ones will be written in the future.

This chapter changes the implementation of the **Customer** and **Hotel** assemblies of the case study to use SQL Server. An air travel service that the Acme Travel Agency can use to make air travel reservations is added to illustrate the use of XML.

To make our examples concrete, we use SQL Server 2000 and the SQL Server data provider.[4] Nonetheless, much of the basic functionality discussed in this chapter applies to the OleDb data provider as well.

This chapter assumes you have some understanding of database concepts.

Setting Up the Example Databases

This chapter assumes that SQL Server 2000 has been installed using the Local System account, with authentication mode set to Mixed Mode. The user is assumed to be sa, with a blank password.

Several examples in this chapter make use of the Northwind Traders sample database, which is installed along with SQL Server. In addition, there are other example programs that use the HotelBroker and AirlineBroker databases, which are supplied specifically for use with this book.

Some of the example programs make changes to these databases, and other examples assume a freshly installed database. This means that some of the examples will not always work as expected unless you initialize them again. You can initialize each of these databases by running the SQL scripts that are provided. For details, see the readme.txt file provided for this chapter.

Data Providers

The prefix on the database classes and methods indicates the data provider used to access the data source. For example the OleDb prefix applies to the OleDb data provider. The Sql prefix applies to the SqlServer data provider.

---

[4] If you do not have an SQL Server available, you can go to the Microsoft site and download the Microsoft Data Engine (MSDE), which is a scaled down version of SQL Server. As of this writing, MSDE is available for free. Microsoft suggests using MSDE in the future instead of the Microsoft Jet database engine (Microsoft Access). Since we use vanilla functionality, you should be able to use the OleDb data provider against the Access version of the Northwind Traders by changing the Sql classes to the corresponding OleDb classes. We have not yet tested this scenario, however.

The SQL Server data provider uses the native SQL Server wire protocol. The OleDb data provider goes through the COM interop layer to talk to the various OleDb providers. For example, you could talk to SqlServer through the OleDb data provider to the OLEDB provider for SQL Server. Nonetheless, the performance of going through the SqlServer data provider will be superior. The advantage of the OleDb and the ODBC data providers is that you can work with ADO.NET against most data sources that you work with today.

There are some interfaces that define common functionality and some base classes that can be used to provide common functionality, but there is no requirement for a data provider to fit a specification that does not correspond to the way the underlying data source works.

For example, the **SqlDataAdapter** class and the **OleDbDataAdapter** class both use the abstract base classes **DbDataAdapter** and **DataAdapter** that are found in the **System::Data::Common** namespace. On the other hand, the **SqlTransaction** and the **OleDbTransaction** classes do not inherit any implementation from any database classes.[5] The **OleDbError** class and the **SqlError** classes do not resemble each other at all. Server-side cursors are not in the ADO.NET model because some databases (such as Oracle and DB2) do not have native support for them. Any support for them in the SQL Server data provider would be an extension.

As Table 9-1 shows, the prefixed classes of the Ole and Sql data providers for connection, command, data reader, data adapter, and data parameter do have some parallels that are defined by the **IDbConnection**, **IDbCommand**, **IDataReader**, **IDbDataAdapter**, and **IDataParameter** interfaces. Nothing, of course, prevents an implementation of these classes from having additional methods beyond those specified in the interfaces.

Table 9–1 Comparison of Parallel Classes in the OleDb and SqlServer Data Providers

Interface	OleDb	SQL Server
IDbConnection	OleDbConnection	SqlConnection
IDbCommand	OleDbCommand	SqlCommand
IDataReader	OleDbDataReader	SqlDataReader
IDbDataAdapter	OleDbDataAdapter	SqlDataAdapter
IDataParameter	OleDbDataParameter	SqlDataParameter

---

[5] They both inherit from **MarshalByRef** object, but as was discussed in Chapter 8, this allows the references to the transaction classes to be marshaled across application domain boundaries. This has nothing to do with database functionality. They also both implement the **IDbTransaction** interface, which of course provides no actual implementation.

Classes, such as **DataSet** or **DataTable**, that are independent of any data provider do not have any prefix.

If database scalability is important, it is desirable to suppress finalization on any of your classes that do not require it. You will get improved performance because you will reduce the amount of time the finalizer thread needs to run.

The Visual Studio.NET Server Explorer

Visual Studio.NET Server Explorer is a very useful tool for working with databases. While not as powerful as the SQL Server Enterprise Manager, it can give you the basic functionality you need when writing or debugging database applications.

To access the Server Explorer, use the View | Server Explorer menu item. The Server Explorer window is dockable, and it can be moved around as required. Figure 9–1 illustrates the Server Explorer.

You can find out information about all the fields in a table, or look at and edit the data in the tables. You can create or edit stored procedures and design tables. We will use the Server Explorer in a couple of examples to show a little bit of how it can be used.

Getting Connected

Code
Example

We start by looking at the **JustConnect** example, which is a tiny program that simply connects to a database. This example just proves that SQL Server is properly installed and that the desired database exists, which in this case is the Northwind database that is a standard part of the SQL Server installation.

```
SqlConnection *conn = 0;
String *ConnString =
   "server=localhost;uid=sa;pwd=;database=Northwind";
try
{
   conn = new SqlConnection(ConnString);
   conn->Open();
   Console::WriteLine(
      "Connection to {0} opened successfully.",
      conn->Database);
}
catch(Exception *e)
{
   Console::WriteLine(e->Message);
```

```
   }
   __finally
   {
      if (conn->State == ConnectionState::Open)
         conn->Close();
   }
```

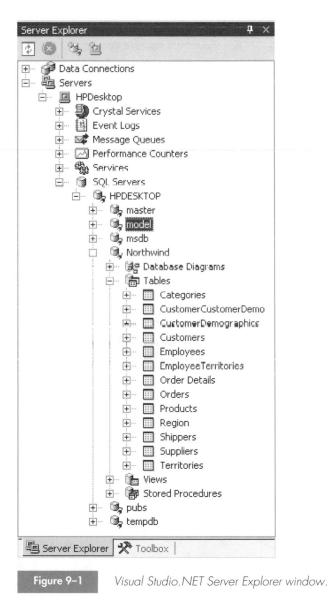

Figure 9-1 *Visual Studio.NET Server Explorer window.*

If SQL Server is properly installed and running, and the Northwind database exists, then the **JustConnect** example program displays the following message:

```
Connection to Northwind opened successfully.
```

If something goes wrong, the **Open** method throws an exception, and you will see a message displayed in the exception handler. For example, if you have stopped SQL Server, then the program displays the following message:

```
General network error.  Check your network documentation.
```

If you change the name of the database in the connection string to a non-existent database, such as Southwind, then the following message is displayed:

```
Cannot open database requested in login 'Southwind'. Login
    fails.
Login failed for user 'sa'.
```

Data Readers

Code Example

As our second example, let us use some of the ADO.NET classes to access data in a database. This example is found in this chapter's **Connected** subdirectory.

We will need a connection to the database, a command to issue against the database, and a reader to retrieve the data, so we declare three variables that point to **SqlConnection**, **SqlCommand**, and **SqlDataReader** classes:[6]

```
SqlConnection *conn = 0;
SqlCommand *command = 0;
SqlDataReader *reader = 0;
```

The connection string that is used to connect to the database is set next. You may replace the server element with the appropriate name for your machine. You will also have to specify the appropriate user and password for

---

[6] The variables are declared outside of the try/catch block so that they can be used in the finally block. They are set to zero because their use in the finally block could theoretically occur before they are initialized inside the try, and it is considered bad programming style to allow uninitialized variables to be used.

the database.[7] You can also set the connect string as an **SqlConnection** property. A simple select statement is the command run against the database in this example.

```
String *ConnString =
    "server=localhost;uid=sa;pwd=;database=Northwind";
String *cmd =
    "select CustomerId, CompanyName from Customers";
```

Figure 9–2 shows the tables and stored procedures for the Northwind database.

Within a try block, we create an **SqlConnection** object. A connection to the database is then opened, since this must be done before any command can be executed. Then we create an **SqlCommand** object that is attached to the connection just created.

```
conn = new SqlConnection(ConnString);
conn->Open();
command = new SqlCommand(cmd, conn);
```

When the command is executed using the **ExecuteReader** method on the **SqlCommand** object, an **SqlDataReader** instance is returned. This reader object can be used to iterate through the result set. The column names can be used to fetch the data elements from the current result set row.

```
reader = command->ExecuteReader();
if (reader != 0)
{
    Console::WriteLine(
        "CustomerId\tCompanyName");
    while (reader->Read())
        Console::WriteLine(
            "{0}\t\t{1}",
            reader->get_Item("CustomerId"),
            reader->get_Item("CompanyName"));
}
```

---

[7] For Northwind, the usual uid=sa;pwd=; will work on many installations.

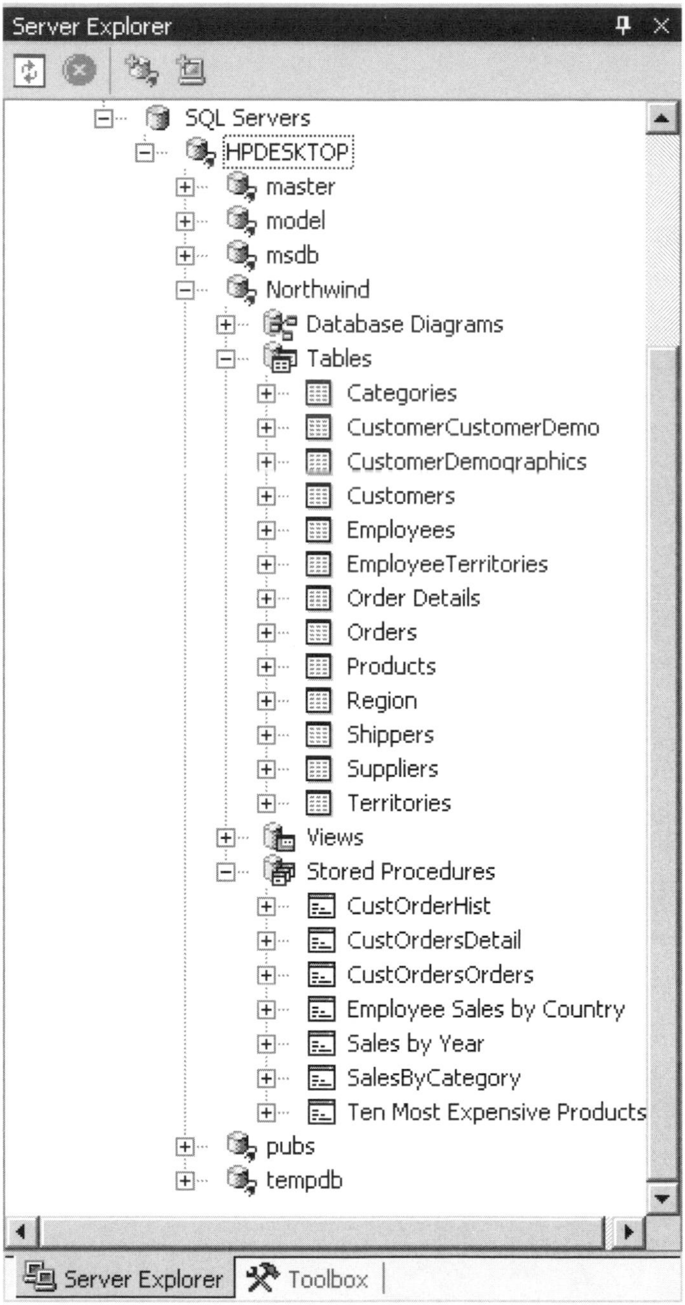

Figure 9–2   *Server Explorer showing Northwind database tables and stored procedures.*

The reader and the connection are closed in the finally block.

```
if (reader != 0)
    reader->Close();
if (conn->State == ConnectionState::Open)
    conn->Close();
```

If the connection is not closed explicitly, the finalizer on the **SqlCon-nection** object will eventually get called and the connection will be closed. Since the garbage collector is not deterministic, there is no way to know when this will happen. Therefore, always close your connections explicitly. If you do not, you will use more connections than you need (even with connection pooling), and this could interfere with your application's scalability. You could also run out of connections.

Here is the output the program produced:

```
CustomerId        CompanyName
ALFKI             Alfreds Futterkiste
ANATR             Ana Trujillo Emparedados y helados
ANTON             Antonio Moreno Taquería
AROUT             Around the Horn
BERGS             Berglunds snabbköp
BLAUS             Blauer See Delikatessen
BLONP             Blondesddsl père et fils
BOLID             Bólido Comidas preparadas
BONAP             Bon app'
BOTTM             Bottom-Dollar Markets
BSBEV             B's Beverages
...
```

You can use the Visual Studio.NET Server Explorer to check the results of the program. Select the Customers table under the Northwind database explorer and right-click to get a context menu. Select Retrieve Data from Table, and you can retrieve the data associated with the table and compare it with the results of the program. You will see that they are the same. Figure 9–3 shows this.

The Connected Database Scenario

This scenario of working with a database is referred to as *connected*. The program connects to the database, does the work it needs to do, and then disconnects. You can run through the returned data only in the forward direction. This corresponds to the classic ADO forward-only cursor/recordset.

	CustomerID	CompanyName	ContactName	ContactTitle
▶	ALFKI	Alfreds Futterkiste	Foo	Sales Represer
	ANATR	Ana Trujillo Empare	Ana Trujillo	Owner
	ANTON	Antonio Moreno Ta	Antonio Moreno	Owner
	AROUT	Around the Horn	Thomas Hardy	Sales Represer
	BERGS	Berglunds snabbköj	Christina Berglund	Order Administ
	BLAUS	Blauer See Delikate	Hanna Moos	Sales Represer
	BLONP	Blondesddsl père el	Frédérique Citeaux	Marketing Mana
	BOLID	Bólido Comidas pre|	Martín Sommer	Owner
	BONAP	Bon app'	Laurence Lebihan	Owner
	BOTTM	Bottom-Dollar Mark	Elizabeth Lincoln	Accounting Mar
	BSBEV	B's Beverages	Victoria Ashworth	Sales Represer
	CACTU	Cactus Comidas pa	Patricio Simpson	Sales Agent
	CENTC	Centro comercial M	Francisco Chang	Marketing Mana
	CHOPS	Chop-suey Chinese	Yang Wang	Owner
	COMMI	Comércio Mineiro	Pedro Afonso	Sales Associate
	CONSH	Consolidated Holdir	Elizabeth Brown	Sales Represer
	DRACD	Drachenblut Delikat	Sven Ottlieb	Order Administ
	DUMON	Du monde entier	Janine Labrune	Owner
	EASTC	Eastern Connection	Ann Devon	Sales Agent
	ERNSH	Ernst Handel	Roland Mendel	Sales Manager
	FAMIA	Familia Arquibaldo	Aria Cruz	Marketing Assis
	FISSA	FISSA Fabrica Inter	Diego Roel	Accounting Mar
	FOLIG	Folies gourmandes	Martine Rancé	Assistant Sales
	FOLKO	Folk och fä HB	Maria Larsson	Owner
	FRANK	Frankenversand	Peter Franken	Marketing Mana
	FRAND	France restauration	Carine Schmitt	Marketing Mana

Figure 9–3 *Server Explorer showing Customers table, fields, and data.*

In the connected mode you must open and close the database connection explicitly.

Keeping a connection continually open is not the best way to work in an environment where you want to minimize the resources consumed (connections are expensive) to allow for scalability. Nonetheless, as will be discussed later, depending on your concurrency assumptions, the **SqlDataReader** might still be the right approach.

As will also be discussed later, the **SqlConnection** is used with **DataSet** as well as with the **SqlDataReader** to establish connections with the database in the same way as illustrated here with the **SqlCommand**. **SqlConnection** also controls database properties such as transactions and isolation levels. A root transaction is issued by invoking the **BeginTransaction** method on the **SqlConnection** class.[8] The equivalent connection string to connect to SQL Server through the **OleDbConnection** class would be

```
"Provider=SQLOLEDB.1;server=localhost;uid=sa;pwd=;
                            database=Northwind";
```

You would have to provide the correct server, user ID, and password.

---

[8] Since OLEDB allows for nested transactions, nested transactions can be started by invoking the **Begin** method on the **OleDbTransaction** class.

While the **SqlCommand** executes a command against a database when you use a **Dataset** as well as **SqlDataReader**, the way it does so is different. This will become clearer when we discuss the **SqlDataAdapter** class.

You specify the type of **SqlCommand** with the **CommandType** property. For the Sql data provider, this can be either Text (the default) or Stored-Procedure. The CommandText can also be specified as a property. We will soon show how parameters can be applied to database commands.

An **SqlDataReader** instance is returned by the **ExecuteReader** method on an **SqlCommand** instance. If you wanted to program in a way that was independent of a data provider, you could use the **IDataReader** interface instead. You can then invoke methods on the interface instead of the class of the actual object.

```
IDataReader *idr = command->ExecuteReader();
```

Similar techniques can be used with the other data provider classes that implement interfaces used by multiple data providers. Until the **SqlDataReader** instance is closed, the **SqlCommand** object cannot be used for any other purpose except executing its Close method.

Executing SQL Statements

The **ExecuteReader** method on the **SqlCommand** returns a **DataReader** instance. Data is returned when the command is a select statement. You could use this method with update, insert, or delete SQL statements. The **SQLCommand::ExecuteReader** method uses the stored procedure **sp_executesql**. Some commands that use SET statements may not work properly. Other providers might have different restrictions when using their **ExecuteReader** method.

Code
Example

In general, for commands that do not return data, use the **SqlCommand::ExecuteNonQuery** method. The **NonQuery** example shows how this works. For illustrative purposes, this example connects to SQL Server through the OleDb data provider.

```
String *cmd = "update Customers set ContactName =
    'Foo' where ContactName = 'Maria Anders'";
try
{
   conn = new OleDbConnection(ConnString);
   conn->Open();
   command = new OleDbCommand(cmd, conn);
   int NumberRows = command->ExecuteNonQuery();
   Console::WriteLine(
      "Number Rows: {0}", NumberRows.ToString());
}
```

The number of rows affected, which should be 1, is displayed in the console window output. If you immediately run this program again, it will fail to find the record because it has just been changed (no more Maria Anders), and it will display 0. To reinitialize the database in its pristine state, you will need to run the SQL script, as described in the readme.txt file for this chapter.[9] Figure 9–4 shows the results of the change to the first row, where Maria Anders has been replaced with Foo in the ContactName field.

For insert, update, and delete statements, the number of rows affected is returned. SQL Server returns –1 for all other statements (native or OLEDB provider). Other providers might return 0 or –1.

To fetch a single value (such as an aggregate computation), use the **ExecuteScalar** method. For data sources that can produce XML output,[10] the **SqlCommand::ExecuteXmlReader** method is more memory-efficient than going to a **DataSet** and using it to generate the XML.

CustomerID	CompanyName	ContactName	ContactTitle	Address	City
ALFKI	Alfreds Futterkiste	Foo	Sales Representati	Obere Str. 57	Berlin
ANATR	Ana Trujillo Empare	Ana Trujillo	Owner	Avda. de la Constit	México D
ANTON	Antonio Moreno Ta	Antonio Moreno	Owner	Mataderos 2312	México D
AROUT	Around the Horn	Thomas Hardy	Sales Representati	120 Hanover Sq.	London
BERGS	Berglunds snabbkö	Christina Berglund	Order Administrato	Berguvsvägen 8	Luleå
BLAUS	Blauer See Delikate	Hanna Moos	Sales Representati	Forsterstr. 57	Mannheir
BLONP	Blondesddsl père el	Frédérique Citeaux	Marketing Manager	24, place Kléber	Strasbou
BOLID	Bólido Comidas pre	Martín Sommer	Owner	C/ Araquil, 67	Madrid
BONAP	Bon app'	Laurence Lebihan	Owner	12, rue des Bouche	Marseille
BOTTM	Bottom-Dollar Mark	Elizabeth Lincoln	Accounting Manage	23 Tsawassen Blvd	Tsawass
BSBEV	B's Beverages	Victoria Ashworth	Sales Representati	Fauntleroy Circus	London
CACTU	Cactus Comidas pa	Patricio Simpson	Sales Agent	Cerrito 333	Buenos A
CENTC	Centro comercial M	Francisco Chang	Marketing Manager	Sierras de Granada	México D
CHOPS	Chop-suey Chinese	Yang Wang	Owner	Hauptstr. 29	Bern
COMMI	Comércio Mineiro	Pedro Afonso	Sales Associate	Av. dos Lusíadas, 2	Sao Paul
CONSH	Consolidated Holdir	Elizabeth Brown	Sales Representati	Berkeley Gardens 1	London
DRACD	Drachenblut Delikat	Sven Ottlieb	Order Administrato	Walserweg 21	Aachen
DUMON	Du monde entier	Janine Labrune	Owner	67, rue des Cinqua	Nantes
EASTC	Eastern Connection	Ann Devon	Sales Agent	35 King George	London

Figure 9–4   *Rows in Customers table in the Server Explorer showing the changed ContactName. Compare with Figure 9–3 to see the original value of the first row.*

---

[9] To avoid potential problems, you are advised to close all connections to the database before running the script.

[10] Such as SqlServer2000 with the FOR XML syntax.

DataReader

When created, the **SqlDataReader** is positioned before the first record returned of the first result set. You must invoke the **Read** method before accessing any data. As the **Connected** example illustrated, the **Item** property can be used to access the individual fields or column values in the current row. All the fields in a row can be accessed with the **GetValues** method.

```
Object *fields [] = new Object *[NumberFields];
...
int NumberFields = reader->GetValues(fields);
```

GetValue returns the column value in its native format. You can also access the column values as particular data types, such as **GetBoolean**, **Get-Decimal**, and **GetString**. The **GetName** method returns the column name of a particular column.

To reinforce what was mentioned earlier, only one record at a time is accessible with a **DataReader**. Make sure you close the **DataReader** when you are done with it.

Multiple Result Sets

Code Example

The **SqlDataReader** class can handle multiple result sets, as the **DataReader** example demonstrates. Two queries separated by a semicolon represent two SQL statements that will cause two result sets to be generated, one for each statement.

```
String *ConnString =
   "server=localhost;uid=sa;pwd=;database=Northwind";
String *cmd =
   "select CustomerId, CompanyName from Customers where
   CustomerId like 'T%';select CustomerId, CompanyName ..."
...
   int ResultSetCounter = -1;
   int NumberFields = 0;
...
   reader = command->ExecuteReader();
   if (reader != 0)
   {
      NumberFields = reader->FieldCount;
      Object *fields[] = new Object*[NumberFields];
      Console::WriteLine(
         "Result Set\tCustomerId\tCompanyName");
```

```
        do
        {
            ResultSetCounter++;
            while(reader->Read() == true)
            {
                NumberFields =
                reader->GetValues(fields);
                Console::Write(
                    "{0}",
                    ResultSetCounter.ToString());
                for (int i = 0; i<NumberFields; i++)
                {
                    Console::Write(
                        "\t\t{0}", fields[i]);
                }
                Console::Write("\n");
            };
        }while(reader->NextResult() == true);
    }
    ...
```

The **FieldCount** method returns the number of columns in the result set. Since the **GetValues** method returns the native format of the data, an array of objects is passed to it. The **NextResult** method navigates to the next result set.

The output of the **DataReader** example appears as follows:

```
Result Set      CustomerId      CompanyName
0               THEBI           The Big Cheese
0               THECR           The Cracker Box
0               TOMSP           Toms Spezialitäten
0               TORTU           Tortuga Restaurante
0               TRADH           Tradiçao Hipermercados
0               TRAIH           Trail's Head Gourmet
                                Provisioners
1               WANDK           Die Wandernde Kuh
1               WARTH           Wartian Herkku
1               WELLI           Wellington Importadora
1               WHITC           White Clover Markets
1               WILMK           Wilman Kala
1               WOLZA           Wolski  Zajazd
```

Parameters Collection

Sometimes you have to parameterize an SQL statement. You also might have to associate the input and output arguments of a stored procedure with variables in your program.

To do this, you build the **Parameters** property of the **SqlCommand** class, which is a collection of **SqlParameter** instances. The installation procedure that accompanies this book has added the **get_customers** stored procedure to the Northwind database. This can be done manually with Server Explorer within Visual Studio.NET, or with SQL Query Analyzer. Or you can run the SQL script provided for this chapter. The **get_customers** stored procedure illustrates how to use a simple stored procedure that takes one input argument that is the company name, and returns the customer ID for that customer.

```
CREATE PROCEDURE get_customers
(@companyname nvarchar(40), @customerid nchar(5) OUTPUT)
AS
select @customerid = CustomerID from Customers where
  CompanyName = @companyname
RETURN

GO
```

The **StoredProcedure** example shows how to do this.

```
command =
    new SqlCommand("get_customers", conn);
command->CommandType =
    CommandType::StoredProcedure;

SqlParameter *p = 0;
p = new SqlParameter(
    "@companyname", SqlDbType::NVarChar, 40);
p->Direction = ParameterDirection::Input;
p->set_Value(S"Ernst Handel");
command->Parameters->Add(p);

p = new SqlParameter(
    "@customerid", SqlDbType::NChar, 5);
p->Direction = ParameterDirection::Output;
command->Parameters->Add(p);
```

```
command->ExecuteNonQuery();
Console::WriteLine(
    "{0} CustomerId = {1}",
    command->get_Parameters()->
        get_Item("@companyname")->Value,
    command->get_Parameters()->
        get_Item("@customerid")->Value);
```

Each individual **SqlParameter** member of the **SqlParameterCollection** represents one parameter of an SQL statement or stored procedure. As this example illustrates, the parameters need not have any relationship to any particular table or column in the database.

At a minimum you have to specify, either through the constructor or by setting properties, the name and database type of the parameter. If the parameter is of variable length, you have to specify the size.

In this example two parameters are added to the parameters collection. The first represents the input argument to the stored procedure. The second represents the return value from the stored procedure.

The name of the parameter corresponds to the name of the argument in the stored procedure get_customers. The other parameters to the **SqlParameter** constructor define the data type of the parameter. The first is a variable Unicode string up to 40 characters in length. The second variable is a 5–character, fixed-length Unicode string. The **SqlDbType::NVarChar** enumeration signifies a fixed-length stream of Unicode characters.

The **Value** property is used to set or get the value of the parameter. It is used to initialize the @companyname parameter for input to the stored procedure. It is also used to obtain the value that the stored procedure set for the @customerid parameter.

Output parameters must be specified as such with the **Direction** property. In this example the @companyname parameter is set as an input parameter with the value **ParameterDirection::Input**. The @customerid parameter is set as an output parameter with the value **ParameterDirection::Output**. Output parameters must be specified, since input parameters are the default. To bind to the return value of a stored procedure, use **ParameterDirection::ReturnValue**. For bidirectional parameters, use **ParameterDirection::InputOutput**.

You can use the parameter names to access individual parameters in the **SqlCommand** parameters collection. Parameterized commands work with both **SqlDataReader** and **DataSet** classes. When the **DataSet** class is discussed, you will see how to specify the **Source** property of the parameter, which indicates which column in the **DataSet** the parameter represents.

SqlDataAdapter and the DataSet Class

The **DataSet** class is a memory-resident, lightweight relational database class. It has properties that reflect the tables (**Tables**) and relationships between tables (**Relations**) within the dataset. You can control whether these constraints are enforced with the **EnforceConstraints** property. You can name the dataset with the **DataSetName** property. You can also set the name of the dataset in the **DataSet** constructor.

The **SqlDataAdapter** class is used to get data from the database into the **DataSet**. The constructor of the **HotelBroker** class shows how to use a data adapter class to populate a dataset. The **CaseStudy** example for this chapter uses the code shown below.[11] This code is found in **HotelBroker.h** in the **CaseStudy\HotelBrokerAdmin\Hotel** directory.

```
conn = new SqlConnection(connString);
citiesAdapter = new SqlDataAdapter();
citiesAdapter->SelectCommand = new SqlCommand(
    "select distinct City from Hotels", conn);
citiesDataset = new DataSet;
citiesAdapter->Fill(citiesDataset, "Cities");
```

The **SqlDataAdapter** class has properties associated with it for selecting, inserting, updating, and deleting data from a data source. Here, the **SqlCommand** instance is associated with the **SelectCommand** property of the **SqlDataAdapter** instead of being executed independently through one of its own execute methods.

The **Fill** method of the **SqlDataAdapter** is then used to execute the select command and fill the **DataSet** with information to be put in a table whose name is supplied as an argument. If the database connection were closed when the **Fill** method was executed, it would be opened. When finished, the **Fill** method will leave the connection in the same state as it was when it was first called.

At this point the connection to the database may be closed. You can then continue to work with the **DataSet** and its contained data independently of the connection to the database.

---

[11] The CaseStudy example for this chapter is in a solution named AcmeGui, which contains three projects named AcmeGui, Customer, and Hotel. While the Customer and Hotel projects are implemented in Managed C++, the AcmeGui project is implemented in C#. This is because the AcmeGui project deals with the GUI aspects of the program, and C# provides better GUI development tools than managed C++. However, since this chapter deals with database access, all code that deals with database functionality is implemented in managed C++.

SqlDataAdapter is implemented with the **SqlDataReader** class, so you can expect better performance with the latter. The **SqlDataReader** might also be more memory-efficient, depending on how your application is structured. If you do not need the features of the **DataSet**, there is no point incurring the overhead.

Disconnected Mode

This scenario of working with a database without a current connection is referred to as *disconnected*. Connected mode represents a tightly coupled, connected environment where state and connections can be maintained. Client-server environments are examples of where this is true. ADO and OLEDB were designed for this approach. In a connected mode environment, data readers can be used. If necessary, ADO can be used through the COM interop facility for this purpose. In fact, ADO was not rewritten for .NET so that absolute backwards compatibility could be maintained, bugs and all.

Connections, however, are expensive to maintain in environments where you want to be able to scale to large number of users, such as multitier and Internet-based solutions. In these environments, there is often no need to hold locks on database tables. This aids scalability because it reduces contention on database tables. The **DataTable** objects in the **DataSet's Tables** collection, with their associated constraints, can mimic the tables and relationships in the original database. For applications that are implemented completely with .NET, **DataSet** instances can be passed around or remoted to the various parts of an application. For applications that can make optimistic assumptions about concurrency, this can produce large gains in scalability and performance. This is true of many types of Internet–based or intranet-based applications.

In the disconnected mode, a connection is made in the same way as with the connected mode of operation. Data is retrieved using the data provider's data adapter class. The **SelectCommand** property specifies the SQL statement used to place data into the dataset. Unlike the data reader, which is related to a particular database connection, the dataset has no relationship to any database, including the one from which the data originally came.

DataSet Collections

When data is placed into a **DataSet**, the related tables and columns are also retrieved. Each dataset has collections that represent all the tables, columns, and data rows associated with it.

The **HotelBroker** class in the case study of this chapter has a method called **ListHotelsToFile** that illustrates how to retrieve this information and write it to a file named **Hotels.txt**. This method is called when you click on a button in the form defined in **MainAdminForm.cs**. The output is written to the file via redirected console output. The **hotelsDataset** is a dataset that has already been filled with the data from the HotelBroker database. The following is taken from **HotelBroker.h**.

```cpp
TextWriter *tw = new StreamWriter("Hotels.txt");
Console::SetOut(tw); //redirect output
try
{
    Console::WriteLine("Hotels");
    DataTable *t =
        hotelsDataset->Tables->get_Item(
            "Hotels");
    if (t == 0)
        return;
    IEnumerator *pEnum = t->Columns->GetEnumerator();
    while (pEnum->MoveNext())
    {
        DataColumn *c =
            dynamic_cast<DataColumn *>(pEnum->Current);
        Console::Write("{0, -20}", c->ColumnName);
    }

    Console::WriteLine("");

    pEnum = t->Rows->GetEnumerator();
    while (pEnum->MoveNext())
    {
        DataRow *r =
            dynamic_cast<DataRow *>(pEnum->Current);
        for (int i=0; i<t->Columns->Count; i++)
        {
            Type *type = r->get_Item(i)->GetType();
            if (type->FullName->Equals("System::Int32"))
                Console::Write("{0, -20}", r->get_Item(i));
            else
            {
                String *s = r->get_Item(i)->ToString();
                s = s->Trim();
                Console::Write("{0, -20}", s);
            }
        }
        Console::WriteLine("");
    }
```

```
      Console::WriteLine("");
   }
   catch(Exception *e)
   {
      throw e;
   }
   __finally
   {
      tw->Close();
   }
```

The **Tables** collection is a collection of all the **DataTable** instances in the **DataSet**. In this particular case there is only one, so there is no need to iterate through that collection. The program then iterates through all the columns in the table and sets them up as headers for the data that will be printed out. After the headers have been set up, all the rows in the table are iterated through. For each column in the row, we ascertain its type and print out the value appropriately. The program only checks for the types that are in the Hotels database table. Checking for types instead of printing out the row values as **Object** enables us to format the data appropriately.

As we will show later, you can populate the dataset through these collections without having to obtain it from the data source. You can just add tables, columns, and rows to the appropriate collections.

Dataset Fundamentals

You can also fetch a subset of the data in the **DataSet**. The **Select** method on a **DataTable** uses the same syntax as an SQL statement where clause. Column names are used to access the data for a particular row. This example comes from the **HotelBroker** class, where it is used to get the hotels for a particular city.

```
ArrayList *GetHotels(String *city)
{
   try
   {
      DataTable *t = hotelsDataset->
         Tables->get_Item("Hotels");
      DataRow *rows [] = t->Select(
         String::Format("City = '{0}'", city));
      ArrayList *hotels = new ArrayList;
      for (int i = 0; i < rows->Length; i++)
      {
```

```
        String *name = rows[i]->get_Item(
            "HotelName")->ToString()->Trim();
        hotels->Add(name);
    }
    return hotels;
}
catch(Exception *e)
{
    throw e;
}
}
```

The **AddHotel** method of the **HotelBroker** class demonstrates how to add a new row to a **DataSet**. A new **DataRow** instance is created, and the column names are used to add the data to the columns in the row.

If you want to propagate your new row back to a database, you use the **Update** method on the **SqlDataAdapter** class to do so. It is the data adapter that mediates between the **DataSet** and the database. We will discuss later how to do transactional editing on the dataset in order to accept or reject changes before propagating them back to the database.

```
String *AddHotel(
    String *city,
    String *name,
    int number,
    Decimal rate)
{
    try
    {
        DataTable *t = hotelsDataset->Tables->get_Item(
            "Hotels");
        DataRow *r = t->NewRow();
        r->set_Item("HotelName", name);
        r->set_Item("City", city);

        r->set_Item("NumberRooms", __box(number));
        r->set_Item("RoomRate", __box(rate));

        t->Rows->Add(r);

        hotelsAdapter->Update(hotelsDataset, "Hotels");
    }
    catch(Exception *e)
    {
```

```
      throw e;
    }
    ...
}
```

To delete rows from the **DataSet**, you first find the particular row or
rows you want to delete and then invoke the **Delete** method on each
DataRow instance. The **Remove** method removes the **DataRow** from the
collection. It is not marked as deleted, since it is no longer in the **DataSet**.
When the **Update** method on the data adapter is called, it will not be deleted
from the database. This example comes from the **DeleteHotel** method in the
HotelBroker class.

```
String *DeleteHotel(String *city, String *name)
{
    ...
    try
    {
        t = hotelsDataset->Tables->get_Item("Hotels");
        r = t->Select(
            String::Format(
                "City = '{0}' and HotelName = '{1}'",
                city, name));
        ...
        for (i=0; i<r->Length; i++)
            r[i]->Delete();
    ...
}
```

To update a row in a dataset, you just find it and modify the appropriate
columns. This example comes from the **ChangeRooms** method in the **Hotel-
Broker** class. When the **Update** method on the data adapter is called, the
modification will be propagated back to the database.

```
String *ChangeRooms(
    String *city,
    String *name,
    int numberRooms,
    Decimal rate)
{
    DataTable *t = 0;
    try
    {
        t = hotelsDataset->Tables->get_Item("Hotels");
```

```
DataRow *r [] = t->Select(
    String::Format(
        "City = '{0}' and HotelName = '{1}'",
        city, name));
...
for (int i = 0; i < r->Length; i++)
{
    r[i] >set_Item("NumberRooms",
        __box(numberRooms));
    r[i]->set_Item("RoomRate", __box(rate));
}
...
}
...
}
```

Updating the Data Source

How does the **SqlDataAdapter::Update** method propagate changes back to the data source? Changes to the **DataSet** are placed back based on the **Insert-Command**, **UpdateCommand**, and the **DeleteCommand** properties of the **SqlDataAdapter** class. Each of these properties takes an **SqlCommand** instance that can be parameterized to relate the variables in the program to the parts of the related SQL statement. The code fragment we use to show this comes from the **HotelBroker** constructor.

An **SqlCommand** instance is created to represent the parameterized SQL statement that will be used when the **SqlDataAdapter::Update** command is invoked to add a new row to the database. At that point, the actual values will be substituted for the parameters.

```
SqlCommand *cmd = new SqlCommand(
    "insert Hotels(City, HotelName, NumberRooms, RoomRate)
    values(@City, @Name, @NumRooms, @RoomRate)",
    conn);
```

The parameters have to be associated with the appropriate columns in a **DataRow**. In the **AddHotel** method code fragment discussed previously, columns were referenced by the column names: HotelName, City, Number-Rooms, and RoomRate. Notice how they are related to the SQL statement parameters @Name, @City, @NumRooms, @RoomRate in the **SqlParameter** constructor. This last argument sets the **Source** property of the **SqlParame-ter**. The **Source** property sets the **DataSet** column to which the parameter corresponds. The **Add** method places the parameter in the **Parameters** collection associated with the **SqlCommand** instance.

```
SqlParameter *param = new SqlParameter(
   "@City", SqlDbType::Char, 20, "City");
cmd->Parameters->Add(param);

cmd->Parameters->Add(new SqlParameter(
   "@Name", SqlDbType::Char, 20, "HotelName"));
cmd->Parameters->Add(new SqlParameter(
   "@NumRooms", SqlDbType::Int, 4, "NumberRooms"));
cmd->Parameters->Add(new SqlParameter(
   "@RoomRate", SqlDbType::Money, 8, "RoomRate"));
```

Finally, the **InsertCommand** property of the **SqlDataAdapter** class is set to the **SqlCommand** instance. Now this command will be used whenever the adapter has to insert a new row in the database.

```
hotelsAdapter->InsertCommand = cmd;
```

Similar code appears in the **HotelBroker** constructor for the **Update-Command** and **DeleteCommand** properties to be used whenever a row has to be updated or deleted.

```
hotelsAdapter->UpdateCommand = new SqlCommand(
   "update Hotels set NumberRooms = @NumRooms, RoomRate =
   @RoomRate where City = @City and HotelName = @Name",
   conn);
hotelsAdapter->UpdateCommand->Parameters->Add(
   new SqlParameter(
      "@City", SqlDbType::Char,20, "City"));
hotelsAdapter->UpdateCommand->Parameters->Add(
   new SqlParameter(
      "@Name", SqlDbType::Char, 20, "HotelName"));
hotelsAdapter->UpdateCommand->Parameters->Add(
   new SqlParameter(
      "@NumRooms", SqlDbType::Int, 4, "NumberRooms"));
hotelsAdapter->UpdateCommand->Parameters->Add(
   new SqlParameter(
      "@RoomRate",SqlDbType::Money, 8, "RoomRate"));

hotelsAdapter->DeleteCommand = new SqlCommand(
   "delete from Hotels where City = @City and HotelName =
   @Name", conn);
hotelsAdapter->DeleteCommand->Parameters->Add(
   new SqlParameter(
      "@City", SqlDbType::Char, 20, "City"));
hotelsAdapter->DeleteCommand->Parameters->Add(
```

```
new SqlParameter(
    "@Name", SqlDbType::Char, 20, "HotelName"));
```

Whatever changes to the rows in the **DataSet** you have made will be propagated to the database when **SqlDataAdapter::Update** is executed. How to accept and reject changes made to the rows before issuing the **SqlData-Adapter::Update** command is discussed in a later section.

Auto-Generated Command Properties

The **SqlCommandBuilder** class can be used to automatically generate any **InsertCommand**, **UpdateCommand**, and the **DeleteCommand** properties that have not been defined. Since the **SqlCommandBuilder** needs to derive the necessary information to build those properties dynamically, it requires an extra round trip to the database and more processing at runtime. Therefore, if you know your database layout in the design phase, you should explicitly set the **InsertCommand**, **UpdateCommand**, and **DeleteCommand** properties to avoid the performance hit. If the database layout is not known in advance, and the user specifies a query, the **SqlCommandBuilder** can be used if the user subsequently wants to update the results.

This technique works for **DataSet** instances that correspond to single tables. If the data in the **DataSet** is generated by a query that uses a join, or if there are relationships between several tables in the dataset, then the automatic generation mechanism cannot generate the logic to update both tables. You must specify the **SelectCommand** property, since the **SqlCommand-Builder** uses it to generate the command properties.

For this to work, a primary or unique column must exist on the table in the **DataSet**. This column must be returned by the SQL statement set in the **SelectCommand** property. The unique columns are used as a where clause for update and delete.

Column names cannot contain special characters such as spaces, commas, periods, quotation marks, or non-alphanumeric characters. This is true even if the name is delimited by brackets. You can specify a fully qualified table name, such as **SchemaName.OwnerName.TableName**.

A simple way to use the **SqlCommandBuilder** class is to pass the **Sql-DataAdapter** instance to its constructor. The **SqlCommandBuilder** then registers itself as a listener for **RowUpdating** events. It can then generate the needed **InsertCommand**, **UpdateCommand**, or **DeleteCommand** properties before the row update occurs.

Database Transactions and Updates

When the data adapter updates the data source, it is *not* done as a single transaction. If you want all the inserts, updates, and deletes done in one transaction, you must manage the transaction programmatically.

The **SqlConnection** object has a **BeginTransaction** method that returns an **SqlTransaction** object. When you invoke the **BeginTransaction** method, you can optionally specify the isolation level. If you know what you are doing and understand the tradeoffs, you can improve the performance and scalability of your application by setting the appropriate isolation level. If you set the isolation level incorrectly or inappropriately, you can have inconsistent or incorrect data results.[12]

The **SqlTransaction** class has **Commit** and **Rollback** methods to commit or abort the transaction. You open the **SqlConnection**, invoke the **BeginTransaction** method, use the **SqlDataAdapter** as normal, and then call **SqlTransaction::Commit** or **SqlTransaction::Rollback** as appropriate. Then close the connection. The **Save** method on **SqlTransaction** can be used to set a save point in the transaction.

In order to minimize the database resources you hold, and therefore increase the scalability of your application, you want to minimize the time between calling **BeginTransaction** and the call to **Commit** or **Rollback**.

Here is the code from the **Transactions** example. It uses the AirlineBroker database introduced later in the chapter. For illustrative purposes, it uses the **SqlCommandBuilder** introduced in the last section.

```
conn = new SqlConnection(ConnString);
conn->Open();
trans = conn->BeginTransaction();

da = new SqlDataAdapter;
ds = new DataSet;
da->SelectCommand =
   new SqlCommand(cmd, conn, trans);

SqlCommandBuilder *sb = new SqlCommandBuilder(da);

da->Fill(ds, "Airlines");
...
DataRow *newRow = ds->Tables->get_Item(
   "Airlines")->NewRow();
newRow->set_Item("Name", S"Midway");
newRow->set_Item("Abbreviation", S"M");
newRow->set_Item("WebSite", S"www.midway.com");
```

---

[12] Discussing isolation levels in detail would remove our focus from .NET to database programming. Any good intermediate to advanced book on database programming would discuss the concept of isolation levels and locking. For specific information about SQL Server locking mechanism, you can read the Microsoft Press *Inside SQL Server* books, among others. Tim Ewald's book *Transactional COM+* has a good chapter on the issue of isolation and its relation to building scalable applications.

```
newRow->set_Item("ReservationNumber", S"555-555-1212");
ds->Tables->get_Item("Airlines")->Rows->Add(newRow);

Console::WriteLine(
    sb->GetInsertCommand()->CommandText);
Console::WriteLine(
    sb->GetDeleteCommand()->CommandText);
Console::WriteLine(
    sb->GetUpdateCommand()->CommandText);
pEnum =
    sb->GetInsertCommand()->
        Parameters->GetEnumerator();
while (pEnum->MoveNext())
{
    SqlParameter *p =
        dynamic_cast<SqlParameter *>(pEnum->Current);
    Console::WriteLine(
        "{0, -10} {1, -10}",
        p->ParameterName,
        p->SourceColumn);
}
da->Update(ds, "Airlines");
trans->Commit();
trans = 0;
conn->Close();
```

To ensure that the SQL Server data provider operates properly, you should use the **Commit** and **Rollback** methods on the **SqlTransaction** object to commit or roll back the transactions started with **SqlConnection::BeginTransaction**. Do not use the SQL Server transaction statements.

If you use stored procedures for your database work, you can certainly issue SQL Server transaction statements inside the stored procedures instead of using the **SqlTransaction** object. Stored procedures can be used to encapsulate transactional changes. The **MakeReservation** stored procedure in the HotelBroker database does just that.

Optimistic Versus Pessimistic Locking and the DataSet

Transactions only help preserve database consistency. When you move money from your savings to your checking account to pay your phone bill, transaction processing ensures that the credit and withdrawal will both happen, or neither will happen. You will not wind up with a situation where the money goes into your checking, but is not withdrawn from the savings (good for you, but bad for the bank) or the reverse (bad for you, but good for the bank). Nothing about that transaction prevents your spouse from using that same money to eat out at a fancy restaurant.[13]

Under an optimistic locking strategy, you assume this will not happen, but you have to be prepared to deal with it when does.[14] A pessimistic locking strategy requires coordination among all the users of a database table so that this never happens. Of course, the fewer locks you hold on database rows to prevent use by more than one user, the more scalable your application will be.

An understanding of how this affects your application applies to both reads and actual updates. For example, if your spouse sees that money is available and makes plans based on that fact, it could be as much of a problem as the actual withdrawal of money from the joint checking account.

While a discussion of how to solve these problems is beyond the scope of this chapter, it is important to realize that the issue arises because no locks are held on the database records held within a **DataSet**. Just using the **DataSet** with **SqlDataAdapter::Update** assumes an optimistic locking strategy.

Why does this matter? It matters because the performance and scalability of your application can depend on it. Why is it so complicated? Because there is no answer that applies to all applications in all situations. If users do not share the same set of data, optimistic concurrency is an excellent assumption. If you have to lock records for a long period of time, this increases the wait to use these resources, thus decreasing performance and scalability.

You have to understand transaction isolation levels, the database's lock manager, the probability of contention for particular rows, and the probability that this contention results in deadlock in your application. You have to understand how much time and resources you can spend reconciling divergent operations, and how much tolerance for inconsistent or incorrect results your application can stand, in order to decide under what circumstances you want to avoid deadlock at all costs, or if you can deal with the consequences of conflicting operations.[15]

You might have to use the **DataSet** with additional logic to test if the records in the **DataSet** have been changed since the last time they were fetched or modified. Or you might just decide to use **SqlDataReader** and refetch the data. It all depends.

For example, when making a reservation in our HotelBroker case study, you cannot make an optimistic assumption about the availability of rooms. It is not acceptable to assume an infinite supply of rooms at a hotel and let the

---

[13] The failure to distinguish between these two leads to the apparently common problem (as related to me by a bank vice president) of people wondering why their checks bounce when their ATM balance said they had enough money to withdraw some cash.

[14] This is the database equivalent of overdraft protection.

[15] Tim Ewald's book is worth reading to understand this topic. Philip Bernstein and Eric Newcomer's *Principles of Transaction Processing* is another good reference.

reservation clerk deal with what happens when too many people show up for the rooms that are available.[16] We use the **MakeReservation** stored procedure to check on the availability of a room before we make the reservation.[17]

Sometimes, even without concurrency issues, the **DataSet** cannot be used to add new rows in isolation from the database. Sometimes, as in our **HotelBroker** example application, an arbitrary primary key cannot be used.[18] Many users will be making reservations at the same time. Reservation IDs cannot be assigned locally. Some central logic on the database has to be employed to issue them.[19] The **MakeReservation** stored procedure does this as well.

The degree of disconnected operation that your application can tolerate has to be understood before you can decide how to use **SqlDataReader** or the **DataSet** in your applications.

Why then bother to use the **DataSet** at all in our HotelBroker application? In fact, the code for the **Customer** object does not use the **DataSet** at all. The **HotelBroker** object does. The **HotelBroker** object uses the **DataSet** for two reasons. The first is pedagogical. We wanted to show you how a complete application might use the features of the **DataSet**, rather than just isolated sample programs. Secondly, in the Web version of the application, which is developed in subsequent chapters, it is convenient to cache certain pieces of information. For example, it is probably reasonable to assume that a user can work with his or her own local copy of reservations. On the other hand, such information about a customer as an email address can be obtained just once when he or she logs in. There is no need for an elaborate mechanism to cache customer information, so the **Customer** object uses methods on the **SqlCommand** object.

---

[16]   Of course, airlines and hotels overbook. This is a conscious strategy to deal with passengers or guests not making explicit cancellations, not a database concurrency strategy.

[17]   In fact, the transaction in **MakeReservation** includes the checking of the availability of the room as well as the actual making of the reservation in order to maintain consistency. It also breaks up what could be one multiple table join into several queries in order to return better error information.

[18]   For instance, a GUID. Well, theoretically, GUIDs could be used in our case, but when was the last time you got a reservation number from a hotel or airline that was composed of 32 hexadecimal digits? Many times, a primary key has meaning to an organization—for example, a part number whose subsections indicate various categories.

[19]   Of course, if performance were critical, instances of the HotelBroker could be preassigned ranges of reservation IDs to give out. But this would have to be done by some central authority as well (the database, some Singleton object?). But then, this raises the issue of state management in the middle tier. This just reinforces our previous point about the dependency of any solution on the specific requirements of your program. It also reinforces the maxim that any programming problem can be solved either by trading memory against time or adding another level of indirection.

Working with Datasets

Figure 9–5 depicts the hierarchy of classes that exist within the **DataSet** class. It will be helpful to glance at this diagram over the next few sections that discuss these classes.

Multiple Tables in a DataSet

Each **DataSet** has a collection of one or more **DataTable** objects. Each **DataTable** object represents one table. With a **SelectCommand** that contains a join, you can place data from multiple database tables into one **DataTable**. If you want to update the multiple tables, you will have to specify the update commands, because any notion of the original tables is lost. In **HotelBook-**

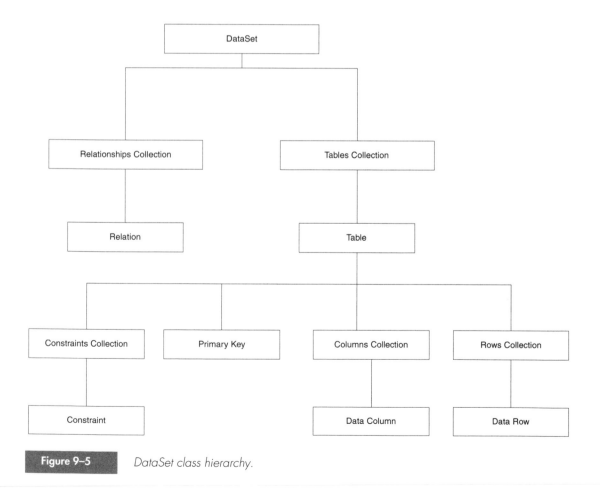

Figure 9–5   *DataSet class hierarchy.*

ings.h of the case study, the **SqlDataAdapter** for the **HotelBroker** object has the following **SelectCommand** property:

```
String *cmd =
   "select CustomerId, HotelName, City, ArrivalDate,
   DepartureDate, ReservationId from Reservations, Hotels
   where Reservations.HotelId = Hotels.HotelId";
adapter->SelectCommand = new SqlCommand(cmd, conn);
dataset = new DataSet;
adapter->Fill(dataset, "Reservations");
```

Code
Example

The **DataSet** will have only one **DataTable**, called Reservations. The fact that some of the data came from the Hotels table is lost.

You can also load more than one table into a dataset. The **DataSchema** example does this with the Northwind database, as shown next.

```
adapter->SelectCommand = new SqlCommand(
   "select * from [Order Details] where ProductId = 1",
   conn);
adapter->FillSchema(
   dataset, SchemaType::Source, "Order Details");
adapter->Fill(dataset, "Order Details");

adapter->SelectCommand =
   new SqlCommand("select * from Shippers", conn);
adapter->FillSchema(
   dataset, SchemaType::Source, "Shippers");
adapter->Fill(dataset, "Shippers");
```

There will be two tables, OrderDetails and Shippers, in the **DataSet**. The method **SqlDataAdapter::FillSchema** fills the **DataSet** with the primary key information associated with the tables. The code can then iterate through the tables and print out both the data and the primary keys of the tables. The **Columns** collection on the **DataTable** enables you to find the **DataColumns** for the **DataTable**.

```
IEnumerator *pEnum = dataset->Tables->GetEnumerator();
while (pEnum->MoveNext())
{
   DataTable *t =
      dynamic_cast<DataTable *>(pEnum->Current);
   Console::WriteLine(t->TableName);
   DataColumn *dc [] = t->PrimaryKey;
   for (int i=0; i<dc->Length; i++)
```

```
      {
         Console::WriteLine(
            "\tPrimary Key Field {0} = {1}",
            __box(i),
            dc[i]->ColumnName);
      }

      Console::Write("\t");
      IEnumerator *pEnum = t->Columns->GetEnumerator();
      while (pEnum->MoveNext())
      {
         DataColumn *c =
            dynamic_cast<DataColumn *>(pEnum->Current);
         Console::Write("{0, -20}", c->ColumnName);
      }
      Console::WriteLine("");
      pEnum = t->Rows->GetEnumerator();
      while (pEnum->MoveNext())
      {
         DataRow *r =
            dynamic_cast<DataRow *>(pEnum->Current);
         Console::Write("\t");
         for (int i=0; i<r->ItemArray.Length; i++)
            Console::Write(
               "{0, -20}",
               r->get_Item(i)->ToString()->Trim());
         Console::WriteLine("");
      }
   }
}
```

The example's output shows the tables, primary keys, columns, and the
data:

```
Order Details
      Primary Key Field 0 = OrderID
      Primary Key Field 1 = ProductID
      OrderID      ProductID  UnitPrice Quantity Discount
      10285        1          14.4      45       0.2
      10294        1          14.4      18       0
...
Shippers
      Primary Key Field 0 = ShipperID
      ShipperID    CompanyName          Phone
      1            Speedy Express       (503) 555-9831
```

```
2          United Package     (503) 555-3199
3          Federal Shipping   (503) 555-9931
```

Table Creation Without a Data Source

Code
Example

You can use a **DataSet** as a memory-resident relational database not based on any database. In fact, we will explore various features of the **DataSet** in the **DataEditing** example by adding the data and relationships directly to the dataset without extracting them from any external database.

First, we create a new **DataSet** and turn on constraint checking. We then add four **DataTables** to the **DataSet**: Books, Categories, Authors, and Book-Categories.

```
DataSet *ds = new DataSet;
ds->EnforceConstraints = true;

// Add tables to Dataset
DataTable *categories =
    ds->Tables->Add("Categories");
DataTable *bookcategories =
    ds->Tables->Add("BookCategories");
DataTable *authors = ds->Tables->Add("Authors");
DataTable *books = ds->Tables->Add("Books");
```

Each **DataTable** object has a collection of **DataColumn** objects. Each object represents one column of the table. We then add columns to the table definition.

```
// define types for column definitions
Type *stringType = Type::GetType("System.String");
Type *intType = Type::GetType("System.Int32");

// Define columns for tables

// Add column to Category table
DataColumn *categoryname =
    categories->Columns->Add(
        "Category",stringType);

// Add columns for BookCategories table
DataColumn *cn = bookcategories->Columns->Add(
    "CategoryName", stringType);
DataColumn *loc = bookcategories->Columns->Add(
    "LibraryofCongressNumber", stringType);
```

```
// Add columns for Authors table
DataColumn *auid = authors->Columns->Add(
    "AuthorId", intType);
authors->Columns->Add(
    "AuthorLastName", stringType);
authors->Columns->Add(
    "AuthorFirstName", stringType);

// Add columns for Books table
DataColumn *ISBN = books->Columns->Add(
    "ISBN", stringType);
DataColumn *booksauid = books->Columns->Add(
    "AuthorId", intType);
books->Columns->Add("Title", stringType);
DataColumn *bloc = books->Columns->Add(
    "LibraryofCongressNumber", stringType);
```

Constraints and Relations

Each **DataTable** object has a collection of **DataRow** objects. Each object represents one row of the table. When you add a **DataRow**, it is subject to the constraints on the **DataColumn** objects (assuming that **EnforceConstraints** property of the **DataSet** has been set to true).

PRIMARY KEYS

There are several possible constraints on a table. The Primary Key constraint is the unique identifier for the table. Other unique constraints force the values in the column (or columns) to which they are applied to be unique. A Foreign Key constraint forces the values in the columns to which it applies to be a primary key in another table in the **DataSet**. The primary key of **DataTable** is a property:

```
// Define PK for BookCategories table
DataColumn *bookcategoriesPK [] =
    new DataColumn*[2];
bookcategoriesPK[0] = cn;
bookcategoriesPK[1] = loc;
bookcategories->PrimaryKey = bookcategoriesPK;

// Define PK for Authors table
DataColumn *authorsPK [] =
    new DataColumn*[1];
authorsPK[0] = auid;
```

```
authors->PrimaryKey = authorsPK;

// Define PK for Books table
DataColumn *booksPK [] =
   new DataColumn*[1];
booksPK[0] = ISBN;
books->PrimaryKey = booksPK;
```

CONSTRAINTS

The other constraints on the table are represented by the abstract base class **Constraint** and its derived classes: **UniqueConstraint** and **ForeignKey-Constraint**. The base class enables the constraints to be placed in the table's constraint collection. Primary Keys also appear in the table's constraint collection as a unique constraint with a system-generated name. The **UniqueConstraint::IsPrimaryKey** property can be used to detect primary keys.

We constrain the Category column in the Categories table to be unique. Since the last argument to the **Add** method is false, this is not a primary key of the table. We do not define a primary key for this table, only a unique constraint. In fact, we do not even have to define any constraint on the table. Although that would violate the rules of relational integrity, you are not forced to use the **DataSet** in a relational manner.

```
// For categories table only define a unique constraint
categories->Constraints->Add(
   "Unique CategoryName Constraint",
   categoryname,
   false);
```

Foreign Keys can specify what action should be taken when the primary key on which it is based is changed. Your choices are the standard database choices: None, Cascade, and SetNull. You can also use SetDefault to set the new value to the **DefaultValue** property of the **DataColumn**. These operations can be specified for both update and delete conditions.

In this example, a foreign key constraint is set so that all author IDs in the Books table have to be found in the Authors table. In other words, when a new book row is inserted, it must have an author. We give this constraint a name, "Authors->Books". If the author ID is changed, the update rule forces the **DataSet** to change all the author IDs in the related rows to the new author ID. If the author ID is deleted, the **DataSet** will set the deleted author IDs in the Book rows to be set to null. If we had set the **DeleteRule** property to Cascade, a cascading delete would be applied to all those rows in the Books table. The **AcceptRejectRule** applies to transactional editing of the **DataSet**, which we will cover in a future section. This rule dictates what happens when the **AcceptChanges** method is invoked on a **DataSet**, **DataRow** or **DataTable**. In this case all changes are cascaded. The alternative rule would be to take no action (i.e., None).

```
// Define FK for Books table
//(AuthorId must be in Authors table)
DataColumn *bookauthorFK [] =
   new DataColumn*[1];
bookauthorFK[0] = booksauid;
ForeignKeyConstraint *fk =
   new ForeignKeyConstraint(
       "Authors->Books", authorsPK, bookauthorFK);
fk->AcceptRejectRule = AcceptRejectRule::Cascade;
fk->DeleteRule = Rule::SetNull;
fk->UpdateRule = Rule::Cascade;
books->Constraints->Add(fk);
```

DATA RELATIONS

Besides constraints, you can add a relation to the **DataRelation** collection in the **DataSet** class. A relation connects two tables so that you can navigate from the parent to the child or the child to the parent. When you add the relation, you also add the equivalent foreign key to the constraint collection.

The Categories table is made the parent of the BookCategories table through the Categories and CategoryName columns. In a relation, both columns have to be of the same type (string). You can use this relation to navigate by finding all the rows in the child table that have the same value in the parent table, or by finding the row in the parent table that is the parent of a row in the child table. Similarly, the Library of Congress number associated with a book has to be found in the Library of Congress field in the BookCategory's Library of Congress field.

```
// Constrain Categories in BookCategories to those
//Categories in Categories table
ds->Relations->Add(
   "Category->BookCategories Relation",
   categoryname,
   cn);

// Constrain Library of Congress Numbers in Books
//to LOC numbers in BookCategories
ds->Relations->Add(
   "Book Category LOC->Book LOC Relation",
   loc,
   bloc);
```

Examining the Schema Information about a DataTable

You can examine the information about a **DataTable**. Here is how to examine the constraint and key information. A previous example has already shown you how to find the **DataColumns** for a **DataTable**. Note the use of the **IsPrimaryKey** property on the **UniqueConstraint** to detect a primary key. The following code continues to show more of the **DataEditing** example.

```
pEnum = ds->Tables->GetEnumerator();
while (pEnum->MoveNext())
{
   DataTable *t =
   dynamic_cast<DataTable *>(pEnum->Current);
   Console::WriteLine("  {0}", t->TableName);
   Console::WriteLine("\tPrimary Key:");
   for (int i = 0; i < t->PrimaryKey.Length; i++)
   {
      DataColumn *c = t->PrimaryKey[i];
      Console::WriteLine("\t\t{0}", c->ColumnName);
   }
   Console::WriteLine("\tConstraints:");
   IEnumerator *pEnum = t->Constraints->GetEnumerator();
   while (pEnum->MoveNext())
   {
      Constraint *c =
         dynamic_cast<Constraint *>(pEnum->Current);
      String *constraintName;
      //if (c is ForeignKeyConstraint)
      if (dynamic_cast<ForeignKeyConstraint *>(c) != 0)
         constraintName =
            String::Concat("Foreign Key:",
               c->ConstraintName);
      else if (dynamic_cast<UniqueConstraint *>(c) != 0)
      {
         UniqueConstraint *u =
            dynamic_cast<UniqueConstraint *>(c);
         if (u->IsPrimaryKey)
            constraintName = "Primary Key";
         else
            constraintName = u->ConstraintName;
      }
      else
         constraintName = "Unknown Name";
```

```
        Console::WriteLine("\t\t{0, -40}", constraintName);
    }
}
```

This produces the following output. Note how the relations defined as a **DataRelation** appear in the table's constraint collection as a **ForeignKey-Constraint** instance. **PrimaryKeys** appear in the constraint collection as a **UniqueConstraint** instance. Constraints defined as unique constraints or foreign keys appear, as you would expect in the collection.

```
Categories
    Primary Key:
    Constraints:
            Unique CategoryName Constraint
BookCategories
    Primary Key:
            CategoryName
            LibraryofCongressNumber
    Constraints:
            Primary Key
            Foreign Key:Category->BookCategories Relation
            Constraint2
Authors
    Primary Key:
            AuthorId
    Constraints:
            Primary Key
Books
    Primary Key:
            ISBN
    Constraints:
            Primary Key
            Foreign Key:Authors->Books
            Foreign Key:Book Category LOC->Book LOC Relation
```

Note the BookCategories constraint with the system-generated name. If you examine the code carefully, you will see we never added this constraint. Where did it come from? If you were to look at the columns in that constraint, you would find the Library of Congress field. The system realized that since the CategoryName is a foreign key in another table, the Library of Congress field should be unique.

You can also examine the **Relations** collection on the **DataSet**. You can examine the parent table and the columns in the parent table involved in the relationship. You can also examine the child table in the relationship and its columns. The following continues showing more code from the **DataEditing** example.

Code
Example

```
pEnum = ds->Relations->GetEnumerator();
while (pEnum->MoveNext())
{
    DataRelation *dr =
        dynamic_cast<DataRelation *>(pEnum->Current);
    DataTable *parentTable = dr->ParentTable;
    DataTable *childTable = dr->ChildTable;
    Console::WriteLine(
        "   Relation: {0} ", dr->RelationName);
    Console::WriteLine(
        "       ParentTable: {0, -10}", parentTable);
    Console::Write("           Columns: ");
    for(int j = 0; j < dr->ParentColumns.Length; j++)
        Console::Write(
            "               {0, -10}",
            dr->ParentColumns[j]->ColumnName);
    Console::WriteLine();
    Console::WriteLine(
        "       ChildTable:  {0, -10}",
        childTable);
    Console::Write("           Columns: ");
    for(int j = 0; j < dr->ChildColumns.Length; j++)
        Console::Write(
            "               {0, -10}",
            dr->ChildColumns[j]->ColumnName);
    Console::WriteLine();
}
```

Here is the resulting output:

```
...
Output Relations between tables in the DataSet...
   Relation: Category->BookCategories Relation
       ParentTable: Categories
           Columns:               Category
       ChildTable:  BookCategories
           Columns:               CategoryName
   Relation: Book Category LOC->Book LOC Relation
       ParentTable: BookCategories
           Columns:               LibraryofCongressNumber
       ChildTable:  Books
           Columns:               LibraryofCongressNumber
...
```

DATABASE EVENTS

Several ADO.NET classes generate events. The **SqlConnection** class generates the **StateChange** and **InfoMessage** events. The **SqlDataAdapter** generates the **RowUpdated** and **RowUpdating** events. The **DataTable** class generates the **ColumnChanging**, **ColumnChanged**, **RowChanged**, **RowChanging**, **RowDeleted**, and **RowDeleting** events.

For example, the **RowChanged** event occurs after an action has been performed on a row. Continuing with our **DataEditing** example, it defines a handler for the **RowChanged** event in the Books table. Every time a row changes in the Books table, the event handler will run.

```
static void Row_Changed(
    Object *sender,
    System::Data::DataRowChangeEventArgs *e)
{
    DataTable *table =
        dynamic_cast<DataTable *>(sender);
    DataColumn *primaryKey [] = table->PrimaryKey;
    String *keyName = primaryKey[0]->ColumnName;

    Console::WriteLine(
        "Rowchanged:Table {0} {1}Row with Primary Key {2}",
        table->TableName,
        __box(e->Action)->ToString(),
        e->Row->get_Item(keyName));
    return;
}
...
books->RowChanged +=
    new DataRowChangeEventHandler(
        books, Row_Changed);
```

The following shows that the code adds some rows, including some to the Books table:

```
DataRow *row;
row = categories->NewRow();
row->set_Item(
    "Category",
    S"UnitedStates:PoliticalHistory");
categories->Rows->Add(row);
...
row = authors->NewRow();
row->set_Item(
```

```
    "AuthorId",
    __box(1));
row->set_Item(
    "AuthorLastName",
    S"Burns");
row->set_Item(
    "AuthorFirstName",
    S"James M.");
authors->Rows->Add(row);
...
row = books->NewRow();
row->set_Item(
    "ISBN",
    S"0-201-62000-3");
row->set_Item(
    "Title",
    S"Freedom and Order");
row->set_Item(
    "AuthorId",
    __box(2));
row->set_Item(
    "LibraryofCongressNumber",
    S"E183.1");
books->Rows->Add(row);
```

We get one output line for each book added, printed by the event handler:

```
Table Books AddRow with Primary Key 0-201-62000-0
Table Books AddRow with Primary Key 0-201-62000-3
```

If we were to change the ISBN numbers of the two books that were added to the same value, a **ConstraintException** would be thrown. If we change the **DataSet::EnforceConstraints** property to false, however, no exception would be thrown.

NAVIGATING RELATIONSHIPS

Using the schema information, we can navigate from parent table to child table and print out the results. This cannot be done with relationships defined as **ForeignKeyConstraint**, only as a **DataRelation** in the **Relations** collection of the **DataSet**.

We previously printed out the schema information associated with the relationships. Now we use this information to print out the parent and child rows in the relationships. By using relationships appropriately, you can walk through the data without using relational queries. This can be quite useful for finding all the books in a certain category or all order items in an order.

Code
Example

Note the use of the **DataRow** methods **GetChildRows** and **GetParentRows** to do the navigation. For a given relation, first we navigate from parent to children, then from the children to its parent. The following code continues with the **DataEditing** example.

```
pEnum = ds->Relations->GetEnumerator();
while (pEnum->MoveNext())
{
   DataRelation *dr =
      dynamic_cast<DataRelation *>(pEnum->Current);
   Console::WriteLine(dr->RelationName);
   DataTable *parentTable = dr->ParentTable;
   DataTable *childTable = dr->ChildTable;

   IEnumerator *pEnum2 =
      parentTable->Rows->GetEnumerator();
   while (pEnum2->MoveNext())
   {
   DataRow *r =
      dynamic_cast<DataRow *>(pEnum2->Current);
   Console::Write("      Parent Row: ");
   for(int m=0; m<parentTable->Columns->Count; m++)
      Console::Write(
         " {0} ",
         r->get_Item(
            parentTable->Columns->get_Item(m)->
               ColumnName->ToString()->Trim()));

   Console::WriteLine();

   DataRow *childRows [] = r->GetChildRows(dr);
   for(int k=0; k<childRows.Length; k++)
   {
      Console::Write("         Child Row: ");

      for(int l=0; l<childTable->Columns->Count; l++)
         Console::Write(
            " {0} ",
            childRows[k]->get_Item(
               childTable->Columns->get_Item(l)->
                  ColumnName->ToString()->Trim()));
```

```
            Console::WriteLine();
        }
    }

Console::WriteLine();

pEnum2 = childTable->Rows->GetEnumerator();
while (pEnum2->MoveNext())
{
    DataRow *r =
        dynamic_cast<DataRow *>(pEnum2->Current);
    Console::Write("        Child Row: ");
    for(int m=0; m<childTable->Columns->Count; m++)
        Console::Write(
            "   {0} ",
            r->get_Item(
                childTable->Columns->get_Item(m) >
                    ColumnName->ToString()->Trim()));
    Console::WriteLine();

    DataRow *parentRows [] =
        r->GetParentRows(dr);
    for(int o=0; o<parentRows->Length; o++)
    {
        Console::Write("          Parent Row: ");
        for(int p=0; p<parentTable->Columns->Count; p++)
            Console::Write(
                "   {0} ",
                parentRows[o] >get_Item(
                    parentTable->Columns->
                        get_Item(p)->ColumnName
                            ->ToString()->Trim()));
        Console::WriteLine();
    }
}

Console::WriteLine();
}
```

This part of the **DataEditing** example program produces the following output. Note how we loop through each relation. For each relation, we first loop through the parent table and output each row of the parent table with its corresponding child rows. We then loop through the child table and output each row of the child table with its corresponding parent rows.

```
...
Category->BookCategories Relation
  Parent Row:UnitedStates:PoliticalHistory
    Child Row:UnitedStates:PoliticalHistory   E183
  Parent Row:UnitedStates:PoliticalHistory:Opinion
    Child Row:UnitedStates:PoliticalHistory:Opinion E183.1
    Child Row:UnitedStates:PoliticalHistory:Opinion E183.2
  Parent Row:UnitedStates:PoliticalHistory:Predictions
    Child Row:UnitedStates:PoliticalHistory:Predictions
                                          E183.3


  Child Row:UnitedStates:PoliticalHistory   E183
    Parent Row:UnitedStates:PoliticalHistory
  Child Row:UnitedStates:PoliticalHistory:Opinion  E183.1
    Parent Row:UnitedStates:PoliticalHistory:Opinion
  Child Row:UnitedStates:PoliticalHistory:Opinion E183.2
    Parent Row:UnitedStates:PoliticalHistory:Opinion
  Child Row:UnitedStates:PoliticalHistory:Predictions
                                          E183.3
    Parent Row:UnitedStates:PoliticalHistory:Predictions


Book Category LOC->Book LOC Relation
  Parent Row:UnitedStates:PoliticalHistory   E183
  Parent Row:UnitedStates:PoliticalHistory:Opinion E183.1
    Child Row:0-201-62000-0   1
                   The Deadlock of Democracy   E183.1
    Child Row:0-201-62000-3   2
                   Freedom and Order   E183.1
  Parent Row:UnitedStates:PoliticalHistory:Opinion  E183.2
  Parent Row:UnitedStates:PoliticalHistory:Predictions
            E183.3


  Child Row:0-201-62000-0   1
                   The Deadlock of Democracy   E183.1
    Parent Row:UnitedStates:PoliticalHistory:Opinion   E183.1
  Child Row:0-201-62000-3   2   Freedom and Order   E183.1
    Parent Row:UnitedStates:PoliticalHistory:Opinion
            E183.1
```

DataRow Editing

If you want to make multiple edits to a **DataSet** and postpone the checking of constraints and events, you can enter a dataset editing mode.

BEGINEDIT, ENDEDIT, CANCELEDIT

You enter this editing mode by invoking the **BeginEdit** method on the row. You leave this mode by invoking the **EndEdit** or **CancelEdit** row methods.

In the **DataEditing** example, we violate the foreign key constraint by adding a row with a nonexistent author ID. The foreign key constraint exception will not be raised until the **EndEdit** method is called. Since we have called **BeginEdit** in the following code fragment taken from **DataEditing.h** in the **DataEditing** example, there is no exception caught.

```
DataRow *rowToEdit = books->Rows->get_Item(0);
rowToEdit->BeginEdit();
try
{
    rowToEdit->set_Item("AuthorId", __box(21));
    ...
}
catch(Exception *e)
{
    Console::WriteLine(
        "\n {0} while editing a row.", e->Message);
    Console..WriteLine();
}
```

However, when we invoke the **EndEdit** method on the row, the exception is raised.

```
try
{
    rowToEdit->EndEdit();
}
    catch(Exception *e)
{
    Console::WriteLine();
    Console::WriteLine(
        "\n{0} on EndEdit", e->Message);
    Console::WriteLine();
}
```

The following message is printed out because the illegal value was still present when the editing session was finished.

```
ForeignKeyConstraint Authors->Books requires the child key
        values (21) to exist in the parent table. on EndEdit
```

DATAROW VERSIONS

Before the row changes have been accepted, both the original and the changed row data are available. The item property[20] of the row can take a **DataRowVersion** to specify which value you want. The version field can be **Original**, **Default**, **Current**, or **Proposed**.

In the **DataEditing** example, the following code appears before **EndEdit** is called:

```
DataRow *rowToEdit = books->Rows->get_Item(0);
rowToEdit->BeginEdit();
try
{
   rowToEdit->set_Item("AuthorId", __box(21));
   Console::WriteLine(
      "Book Author Id Field Current Value {0}",
      rowToEdit->get_Item(
         "AuthorId", DataRowVersion::Current));
   Console::WriteLine(
      "Book Author Id Field Proposed Value {0}",
      rowToEdit->get_Item(
         "AuthorId", DataRowVersion::Proposed));
   Console::WriteLine(
      "Book Author Id Field Default Value {0}",
      rowToEdit->get_Item(
         "AuthorId", DataRowVersion::Default));
}
...
```

This causes the following output to be displayed:

```
Book Author Id Field Current Value 1
Book Author Id Field Proposed Value 21
Book Author Id Field Default Value 21
```

---

[20] The item property of the **DataRow** is the indexer for the class.

During transactional editing, the Current and Proposed item values are available. After **CancelEdit**, the Proposed value is no longer available. After **EndEdit**, the Proposed value becomes the Current value and the Proposed value is no longer available.

DATAROW ROWSTATE PROPERTY

In addition to the Current and Proposed values of a field, the **DataRow** itself has a property that indicates the state of the particular row. The values can be **Added**, **Deleted**, **Detached**, **Modified**, or **Unchanged**.

A row is in the Detached state when it has been created but has been added to any **DataRow** collection, or when it has been removed from a collection.

The **Default DataRowVersion** of a field returns the appropriate row version, depending on the **RowState** property.

ACCEPTING AND REJECTING CHANGES

Calling **EndEdit** on a **DataRow** does not commit the changes made to the row. Calling the **AcceptChanges** or **RejectChanges** methods on the **DataSet**, **DataTable**, or **DataRow** ends transactional editing on all the contained rows of the appropriate scope. If **EndEdit** or **CancelEdit** has not been called, these methods do it implicitly for all rows within their scope.

After the **AcceptChanges** method, the Proposed value becomes the Original value. If the **RowState** was Added, Modified, or Deleted, it becomes Unchanged and the changes take effect (i.e., rows are added, modified or deleted).

After the **RejectChanges** method, the Proposed value is deleted. If the **RowState** was Deleted or Modified, the values revert to their previous values, and the **RowState** becomes Unchanged. If the **RowState** was Added, the row is removed from the **Rows** collection.

Since the **RowState** after **AcceptChanges** is Unchanged, calling the **DataAdapter** object's **Update** method at this point will not cause any changes to be made on the data source. Therefore, you should call the **Update** method on the **DataAdapter** to update changes to the data source before calling **AcceptChanges** on any row, table, or **DataSet**.

Here is the code for the **CancelReservation** method in the **HotelBroker** class defined in the **CaseStudy** example. This code is found in **Hotel-Bookings.h** under the **CaseStudy\HotelBrokerAdmin\Hotel** directory. Note how **AcceptChanges** on the **DataSet** is called if the **SqlDataAdapter::Update** method succeeds. If an exception is thrown or the update fails, **RejectChanges** is called.

```
void CancelReservation(int id)
{
    DataTable *t = 0;
```

```
try
{
   t = dataset->Tables->get_Item("Reservations");
   DataRow *rc [] = t->Select(
      String::Format("ReservationId = {0} ",
      id.ToString()));
   for (int i=0; i<rc->Length; i++)
      rc[i]->Delete();
   int NumberRows = adapter->Update(
      dataset, "Reservations");
   if (NumberRows > 0)
      t->AcceptChanges();
   else
      t->RejectChanges();
}
catch(Exception *e)
{
   t->RejectChanges();
   throw e;
}
return;
}
```

If you do not reject the changes on failure, the rows will still be in the **DataSet**. The next time an update is requested, the update will be rejected again because the rows are still waiting to be updated. Since the **DataSet** is independent of a database, the fact that an update occurs on the database has nothing to do with accepting or rejecting the changed rows in the **DataSet**.

DATAROW ERRORS

If there have been any data editing errors on a row, the **HasErrors** property on the **DataSet**, **DataTable**, or **DataRow** will be set to true. To get the error, use the **DataRow** object's **GetColumnError** or the **GetColunmsInError** methods.

Acme Travel Agency Case Study

At this point we have covered more than enough material for you to understand the database version of the **Customer** and **HotelBroker** classes in the case study. As usual, the code is under the **CaseStudy** directory for this chapter. Remember to run the SQL script provided for reinitializing the HotelBroker database, in case you have made modifications to it.

Since there will never be any reason for the **Customer** object to hold any state, the **Customer** object methods use **SqlDataReader** to access the database and return the results. Any state that a program might need (e.g., a list of customers) could easily be maintained in the client program and not in a middle tier object. The **HotelBroker** and **HotelBookings** objects are a little more complicated. As mentioned earlier, for pedagogical reasons alone, these objects would have been implemented using a **DataSet** to show you how that technology would work in an application. Nonetheless, we will see that with Web applications, there might be a reason to keep some state in the middle tier. In that scenario, the **DataSet** can serve as an intelligent cache.

Now we will turn away from the case study and look at XML/database integration.

XML Data Access

As we will discuss in the Chapter 11, XML has many advantages for describing data that must move between heterogeneous systems and data sources. Since you can validate your XML against an XML Schema description, you can pass it in many situations where passing a **DataSet** makes no sense. Since XML is text, it can pass through firewall ports that are normally open, unlike the Distributed COM (DCOM) protocol, or Java's RMI protocol that require special ports to be open.

The thrust of these next sections is not to discuss XML in any great detail. We just want to demonstrate how you can move back and forth between looking at data in XML and looking at data with a **DataSet**.

XML Schema and Data

XML does not dictate how data is organized or what the meanings of XML documents are. It only describes the rules on how the documents are put together.[21] On the other hand, an XML schema describes the *metadata* of how the data is organized inside an XML document. XML schemas are written in XML.

For example, XML on its own can be used to describe the data in a relational database, but an XML schema can be used to describe data relationships such as primary and foreign keys. Having the XML schema and the data in one document or text stream is vastly simpler than having to download each table into a dataset and then programmatically set up the relations between the tables.

---

[21] Technically, XML documents in the sense that we speak of are defined by the XML Infoset and consist of documents, element, and attributes.

XmlDataDocument

Documents can include database output within them. For example, a sales report has an explanation as well as the sales data that was pulled from a data source. The **XmlDataDocument** class can be used to represent data in the form of an XML document.

The **XmlDataDocument** class inherits from **XmlDocument**, which represents an XML document for the .NET Xml Framework classes. What makes the **XmlDataDocument** particularly interesting is that you can construct an **XmlDataDocument** from a **DataSet** by passing the **DataSet** instance to the **XmlDataDocument** constructor. The **XmlDataDocument** has a read-only **DataSet** property so that you can work with the XML document as relational data, if that makes sense.

DataSet and XML

The **DataSet** has methods, **WriteXml** and **WriteXmlSchema**, that can write out the data and schema associated with the dataset. The XML schema that the **DataSet** writes out is inferred from the data. Unless you explicitly add the constraints to the **DataSet**, such as primary or foreign key relationships, they will not be part of the schema.

The **DataSet** also has methods to read XML: **ReadXml** and **ReadXmlSchema**. **ReadXml** can read both the data and the schema into the dataset. If a schema is not present, it will try to infer one from the data. If it cannot infer a schema, it will throw an exception. **ReadXmlSchema** will read in a schema document.

If there is no schema in an XML document, the **DataSet** extracts elements that would be defined as tables according to a set of rules. The remaining elements are then assigned as columns to the tables.

You can use the **ColumnMapping** property of the **DataColumn** class to control whether you want columns written as XML elements or attributes. Writing columns as elements is better. Elements that are not scalar values become tables. Attributes and scalar values are columns. The exact procedure is described in the .NET documentation.

AirlineBrokers Database

The AirlineBrokers database will be used to study XML data access. This database can be created and initialized using the SqlServer Query Manager and the SQL script provided for this chapter. The AirlineBrokers database represents another service that the Acme reservation system uses. Acme customers can make airline reservations for the places they wish to go to. The database has several tables:

- Airlines: information about the various airlines in the database.
- PlaneType: the various plane types that the airlines use.
- Flights: information about the various airlines' flights.
- Customers: information about customers.
- Reservations: information about the customers' reservations.

Although in real life, the Airline Broker and the Hotel Broker would not have the same Customers table, for simplicity we use the same table structure, and the same component will be used to access it.

DataSet and XML

To illustrate the relationship between the relational model of the **DataSet** and the XML model, we will first fetch some information from the database. The **DataSetXml** example uses the same commands and techniques we have studied in this chapter to extract the data.

First, the connection, dataset, and the data adapters for the various tables are created.

```
SqlConnection *conn =
    new SqlConnection(connectString);
DataSet *d = new DataSet("AirlineBroker");
SqlDataAdapter *airlinesAdapter =
    new SqlDataAdapter;
SqlDataAdapter *flightsAdapter =
    new SqlDataAdapter;
SqlDataAdapter *planetypeAdapter =
    new SqlDataAdapter;
SqlDataAdapter *customersAdapter =
    new SqlDataAdapter;
SqlDataAdapter *reservationsAdapter =
    new SqlDataAdapter;
```

Then the various **select** commands to fetch the data are created, and the dataset is filled with the data from those tables:

```
airlinesAdapter->SelectCommand =
    new SqlCommand("select * from Airlines", conn);
airlinesAdapter->Fill(d, "Airlines");
```

```
flightsAdapter->SelectCommand =
   new SqlCommand("select * from Flights", conn);
flightsAdapter->Fill(d, "Flights");

planetypeAdapter->SelectCommand =
   new SqlCommand("select * from PlaneType", conn);
planetypeAdapter->Fill(d, "PlaneType");

customersAdapter->SelectCommand =
   new SqlCommand("select * from Customers", conn);
customersAdapter->Fill(d, "Customers");

reservationsAdapter->SelectCommand =
   new SqlCommand("select * from Reservations", conn);
reservationsAdapter->Fill(d, "Reservations");
```

We now have the data for the Airlines, Flights, PlaneType, Customers, and Reservations tables in the dataset. Next, we have the **DataSet** write out an XML schema based on the schema that it infers from the data. Then the **DataSet** writes out the actual data as XML.

```
d->WriteXmlSchema("Airlines.xsd");
d->WriteXml("Airlines.xml");
```

The two statements above create two files named **Airlines.xsd** and **Airlines.xml**. Below, you can see some of the data that was written to **Airlines.xml**. The main element is Airline Broker, which was the name of the **DataSet**. Elements at the next lower level correspond to the various tables that were added to the database: Airlines, Flights, PlaneType, and Customers. There were no reservations in the database. There is one set for each row in the table. The elements under each of these tables correspond to the fields for that particular row.

```
<?xml version="1.0" standalone="yes"?>
<AirlineBroker>
  <Airlines>
    <Name>America West</Name>
    <Abbreviation>AW</Abbreviation>
    <WebSite>www.americawest.com</WebSite>
    <ReservationNumber>555-555-1212</ReservationNumber>
  </Airlines>
  <Airlines>
    <Name>Delta</Name>
```

```
      <Abbreviation>DL</Abbreviation>
      <WebSite>www.delta.com</WebSite>
      <ReservationNumber>800-456-7890</ReservationNumber>
    </Airlines>
...
    <Flights>
      <Airline>DL</Airline>
      <FlightNumber>987</FlightNumber>
      <StartCity>Atlanta</StartCity>
      <EndCity>New Orleans</EndCity>
      <Departure>2001-10-05T20:15:00.0000000-04:00
                </Departure>
      <Arrival>2001-10-05T22:30:00.0000000-04:00</Arrival>
      <PlaneType>737</PlaneType>
      <FirstCost>1300</FirstCost>
      <BusinessCost>0</BusinessCost>
      <EconomyCost>450</EconomyCost>
    </Flights>
...
    <PlaneType>
      <PlaneType>737</PlaneType>
      <FirstClass>10</FirstClass>
      <BusinessClass>0</BusinessClass>
      <EconomyClass>200</EconomyClass>
    </PlaneType>
...
    <Customers>
      <LastName>Adams</LastName>
      <FirstName>John</FirstName>
      <EmailAddress>adams@presidents.org</EmailAddress>
      <CustomerId>1</CustomerId>
    </Customers>
</AirlineBroker>
```

From this data, the **DataSet** infers a schema that was written to **Airlines.xsd**. We discuss here an excerpt from that file. There are no relationships or primary keys defined between any of the tables, such as Airlines and Fights, because none were defined in the database. If you look at the actual generated file, you will see that schema information was inferred for **Reservations** even though there was no data in the table.

The schema preamble in the first line reproduced here defines the name of the schema as AirlineBroker, and we are using two namespaces in this schema document. One namespace, abbreviated **xsd**, contains the XML

Schema standard definitions. The other, abbreviated **msdata**, contains Microsoft definitions.

```
...
<xsd:schema id="AirlineBroker" targetNamespace="" xmlns=""
      xmlns:xsd=http://www.w3.org/2001/XMLSchema
      xmlns:msdata="urn:schemas-microsoft-com:xml-msdata">
```

The next line defines an element called AirlineBroker that has an attribute that indicates this schema came from a **DataSet**. That is a Microsoft-defined attribute, not one defined by the W3C Schema namespace. The element AirlineBroker is a complex type, which means it is a structure composed of other types. This structure can have an unlimited number of any (or even none) of the types defined in the rest of the schema.

```
<xsd:element name="AirlineBroker" msdata:IsDataSet="true">
  <xsd:complexType>
  <xsd:choice maxOccurs="unbounded">
```

The type element is defined next. It too is a structure, or complex type, whose elements, if present, appear in the structure in the order in which they were defined. Those elements, which correspond to the columns in the database table, are all defined to be strings that are optional. No primary keys were defined, and these strings are certainly not optional in the database, but that was what the **DataSet** deduced from the set of tables, constraints, and relationships currently defined in the **DataSet**.

```
    <xsd:element name="Airlines">
      <xsd:complexType>
      <xsd:sequence>
        <xsd:element name="Name" type="xsd:string"
                                   minOccurs="0" />
        <xsd:element name="Abbreviation"
               type="xsd:string" minOccurs="0" />
        <xsd:element name="WebSite" type="xsd:string"
                                       minOccurs="0" />
        <xsd:element name="ReservationNumber"
                 type="xsd:string" minOccurs="0" />
      </xsd:sequence>
      </xsd:complexType>
    </xsd:element>
```

The table Flights is defined similarly to Airlines. In addition to there being no primary key here, there is no foreign key defined for Airline or Plane-Type.

```
<xsd:element name="Flights">
  <xsd:complexType>
  <xsd:sequence>
    <xsd:element name="Airline" type="xsd:string"
                              minOccurs-"0" />
    <xsd:element name="FlightNumber" type="xsd:int"
                              minOccurs="0" />
    <xsd:element name="StartCity" type="xsd:string"
                              minOccurs="0" />
    <xsd:element name="EndCity" type="xsd:string"
                              minOccurs="0" />
    <xsd:element name="Departure" type="xsd:dateTime"
                                minOccurs-"0" />
    <xsd:element name="Arrival" type="xsd:dateTime"
                              minOccurs="0" />
    <xsd:element name="PlaneType" type="xsd:string"
                                minOccurs="0" />
    <xsd:element name="FirstCost" type="xsd:decimal"
                                minOccurs="0" />
    <xsd:element name="BusinessCost"
                    type="xsd:decimal" minOccurs="0" />
    <xsd:element name="EconomyCost"
                    type="xsd:decimal" minOccurs="0" />
  </xsd:sequence>
  </xsd:complexType>
</xsd:element>
...
  </xsd:choice>
  </xsd:complexType>
</xsd:element>
</xsd:schema>
```

We will come back to this schema definition, but for the moment, let us continue to work with this example.

Creating an XML Doc from a Dataset

We can create a new XML document from the **DataSet**. Using the Xpath query to get to the top of the document, we can set up an **XmlNodeReader** to read through the document. We can then print out the contents of the document to the console. The **XmlNodeReader** class knows how to navigate through the XML document. Here is more code taken from the **DataSetXML** example:

```
XmlDataDocument *xmlDataDoc = new XmlDataDocument(d);
XmlNodeReader *xmlNodeReader = 0;
try
{
   XmlNode *node = xmlDataDoc->SelectSingleNode("/");
   xmlNodeReader = new XmlNodeReader (node);
   FormatXml (xmlNodeReader);
}
catch (Exception *e)
{
   Console::WriteLine (
      "Exception: {0}", e->ToString());
}
__finally
{
   if (xmlNodeReader != 0)
      xmlNodeReader->Close();
}
...
static void FormatXml (XmlReader *reader)
{
   while (reader->Read())
   {
      switch (reader->NodeType)
      {
         ...
         case XmlNodeType::Element:
            Format (reader, "Element");
            while(reader->MoveToNextAttribute())
               Format (reader, "Attribute");
            break;
         case XmlNodeType::Text:
            Format (reader, "Text");
            break;
...
static String *lastNodeType = "";
static void Format(XmlReader *reader, String *nodeType)
{
   if (nodeType->Equals("Element"))
   {
```

```
            if (lastNodeType->Equals("Element"))
            {
                Console::WriteLine();
            }
            for (int i=0; i < reader->Depth; i++)
            {
                Console::Write("  ");
            }
            Console::Write(reader->Name);
        }
        else if (nodeType->Equals("Text"))
            Console::WriteLine("={0}", reader->Value);
        else
        {
            Console::Write(String::Format(
                "{0}<{1}>{2}", nodeType, reader->Name,
                reader->Value));
            Console::WriteLine();
        }
        lastNodeType = nodeType;
    }
```

The results resemble the XML that the **DataSet** wrote to a file.

```
AirlineBroker
  Airlines
    Name=America West
    Abbreviation=AW
    WebSite=www.americawest.com
    ReservationNumber=555-555-1212
  Airlines
    Name=Delta
    Abbreviation=DL
    WebSite=www.delta.com
    ReservationNumber=800-456-7890
  Airlines
    Name=Northwest
    Abbreviation=NW
    WebSite=www.northwest.com
    ReservationNumber=888-111-2222
  Airlines
    Name=Piedmont
    Abbreviation=P
    WebSite=www.piedmont.com
```

```
    ReservationNumber=888-222-333
Airlines
  Name=Southwest
  Abbreviation=S
  WebSite=www.southwest.com
  ReservationNumber=1-800-111-222
Airlines
  Name=United
  Abbreviation=UAL
  WebSite=www.ual.com
  ReservationNumber=800-123-4568
Flights
  Airline=DL
  FlightNumber=987
  StartCity=Atlanta
  EndCity=New Orleans
  Departure=2001-10-05T20:15:00.0000000-04:00
  Arrival=2001-10-05T22:30:00.0000000-04:00
  PlaneType=737
  FirstCost=1300
  BusinessCost=0
  EconomyCost=450
Flights
  Airline=UAL
  FlightNumber=54
  StartCity=Boston
  EndCity=Los Angeles
  Departure=2001-10-01T10:00:00.0000000-04:00
  Arrival=2001-10-01T13:00:00.0000000-04:00
  PlaneType=767
  FirstCost=1500
  BusinessCost=1000
  EconomyCost=300
PlaneType
  PlaneType=737
  FirstClass=10
  BusinessClass=0
  EconomyClass=200
PlaneType
  PlaneType=767
  FirstClass=10
  BusinessClass=30
  EconomyClass=300
Customers
```

```
LastName=Adams
FirstName=John
EmailAddress=adams@presidents.org
CustomerId=1
```

Summary

ADO.NET provides classes that enable you to design and build a distributed data architecture. You can access databases in a connected or disconnected mode, depending on your concurrency requirements. The **DataSet** enables you to work with data in a relational manner without being connected to any data source. XML can be used to model relational data inside an XML document that contains nonrelational information. A typed **DataSet** gives you the ability to work in a much easier, type-safe fashion with a **DataSet**, provided that you have an XML schema that defines your data.

ASP.NET and Web Forms

*A*n important part of .NET is its use in creating Web applications through a technology known as ASP.NET. Far more than an incremental enhancement to Active Server Pages (ASP), this new technology is a unified Web development platform that greatly simplifies the implementation of sophisticated Web applications. In this chapter we introduce the fundamentals of ASP.NET and cover Web Forms, which make it easy to develop interactive Web pages. In Chapter 11 we cover ASP.NET-based Web Services, which enable the development of collaborative Web applications that span heterogeneous systems. In Chapter 12, we cover ATL Server-based Web page and Web service development.

What Is ASP.NET?

We will begin our exploration of ASP.NET by looking at a very simple Web application. Along the way we will establish a test bed for ASP.NET programming, and we will review some of the fundamentals of Web processing. Our little example will reveal some of the challenges in developing Web applications, and we can then appreciate the features and benefits of ASP.NET, which we will elaborate on in the rest of the chapter.

Web Application Fundamentals

A Web application consists of document and code pages in various formats. The simplest kind of document is a static HTML page, which contains information that will be formatted and displayed by a Web browser. An HTML page may also contain hyperlinks to other HTML pages. A hyperlink (or just link) contains an address, or a Uniform Resource Locator (URL), specifying where the target document is located. The resulting combination of content

Managed C++ Support for ASP.NET

ASP.NET has only limited support for managed C++. Some other .NET languages, such as C# and VB.NET, can be embedded ASP.NET script within the actual Web page that is dynamically compiled at runtime. However, managed C++ cannot be used as embedded ASP.NET script. Instead, managed C++ can only be used in precompiled assemblies that are referenced within an ASP.NET page, which is referred to as "precompiled code-behind" ASP.NET. Also, the Visual Studio.NET tools for developing the GUI aspects of an ASP.NET Web page support C# and VB.NET code generation, but they do not support C++ code generation. You can still do just about anything with C++, but there will be more manual labor involved.

and links is sometimes called hypertext, and provides easy navigation to a vast amount of information on the World Wide Web.

SETTING UP THE WEB EXAMPLES

As usual, all the example programs for this chapter are in the chapter folder. To run the examples, you will need to have Internet Information Services (IIS) installed on your system. IIS is installed by default with Windows 2000 Server. You will have to explicitly install it with Windows 2000 Workstation. Once installed, you can access the documentation on IIS through Internet Explorer via the URL **http://localhost**, which will redirect you to the starting IIS documentation page, as illustrated in Figure 10–1.

The management tool for IIS is a Microsoft Management Console (MMC) snap-in, the Internet Services Manager, which you can find under Administrative Tools in the Control Panel. Figure 10–2 shows the main window of the Internet Services Manager. You can start and stop the Web server and perform other tasks by right-clicking on Default Web Site. Choosing Properties from the context menu will let you perform a number of configurations on the Web server.

The default home directory for publishing Web files is **\Inetpub\wwwroot** on the drive where Windows is installed. You can change this home directory using Internet Services Manager. You can access Web pages stored at any location on your hard drive by creating a *virtual directory*. The easiest way to create a virtual directory is from Windows Explorer. Right-click over the desired directory, choose Sharing, select the Web Sharing tab, click on the Add button, and enter the desired alias, which will be the name of the virtual directory. Figure 10–3 illustrates creating an alias **NetCpp**, or virtual directory, for the folder **\OI\NetCpp\Chap10**. You should perform this operation on your own system now so that subsequent examples in this chapter will work.

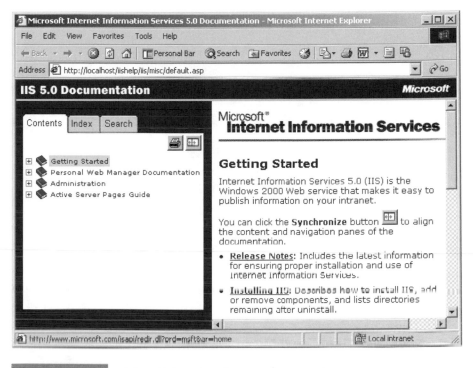

Figure 10–1 Internet Information Services documentation.

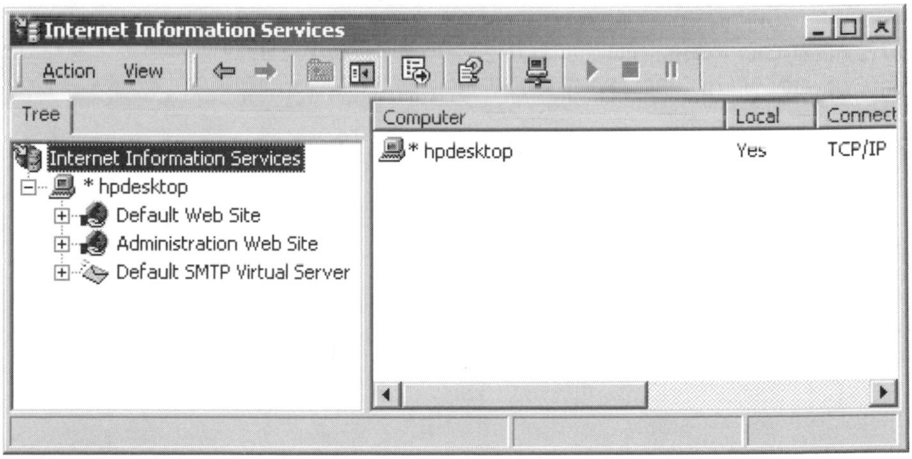

Figure 10–2 Internet Services Manager.

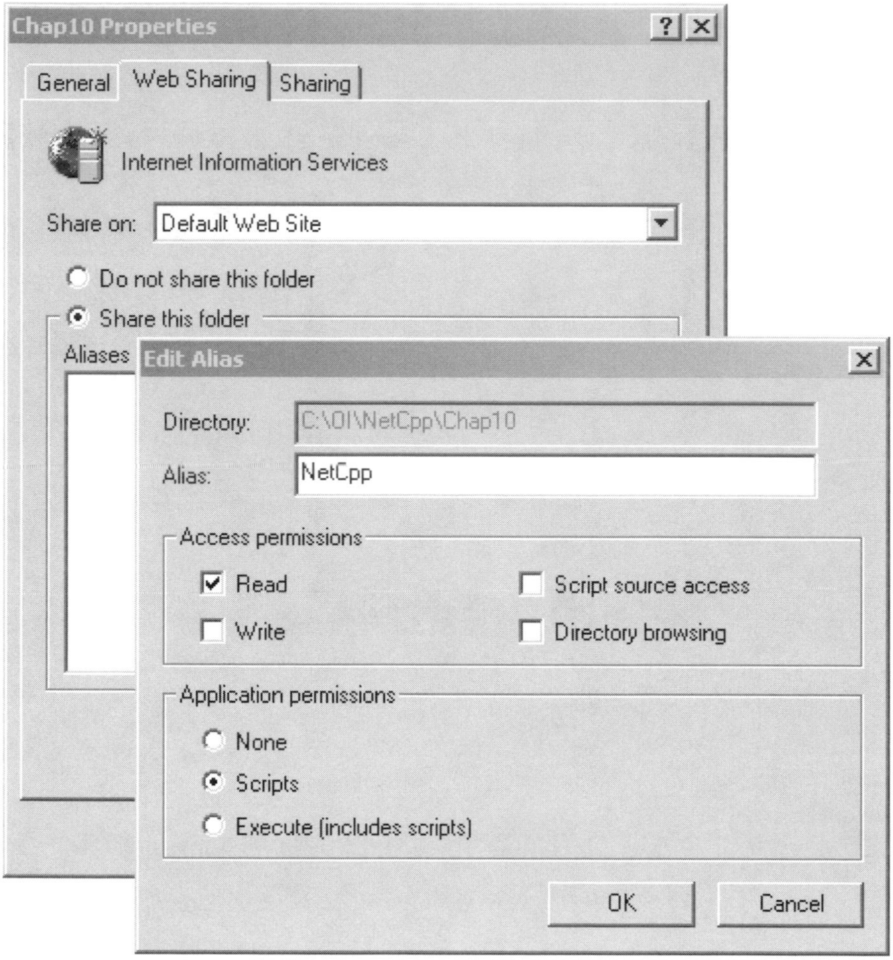

Figure 10–3   *Creating a virtual directory.*

Once a virtual directory has been created, you can access files in this directory by including the virtual directory in the path of the URL. In particular, you can access the file **default.htm** using the URL **http://localhost/ NetCpp/**. The file **default.htm** contains a home page for all the ASP.NET example programs for this chapter. See Figure 10–4.

An Echo Program (in C#)

The first example program for this chapter is **Hello.aspx**, shown as a link on the home page. The example is called "monolithic" because it is complete in

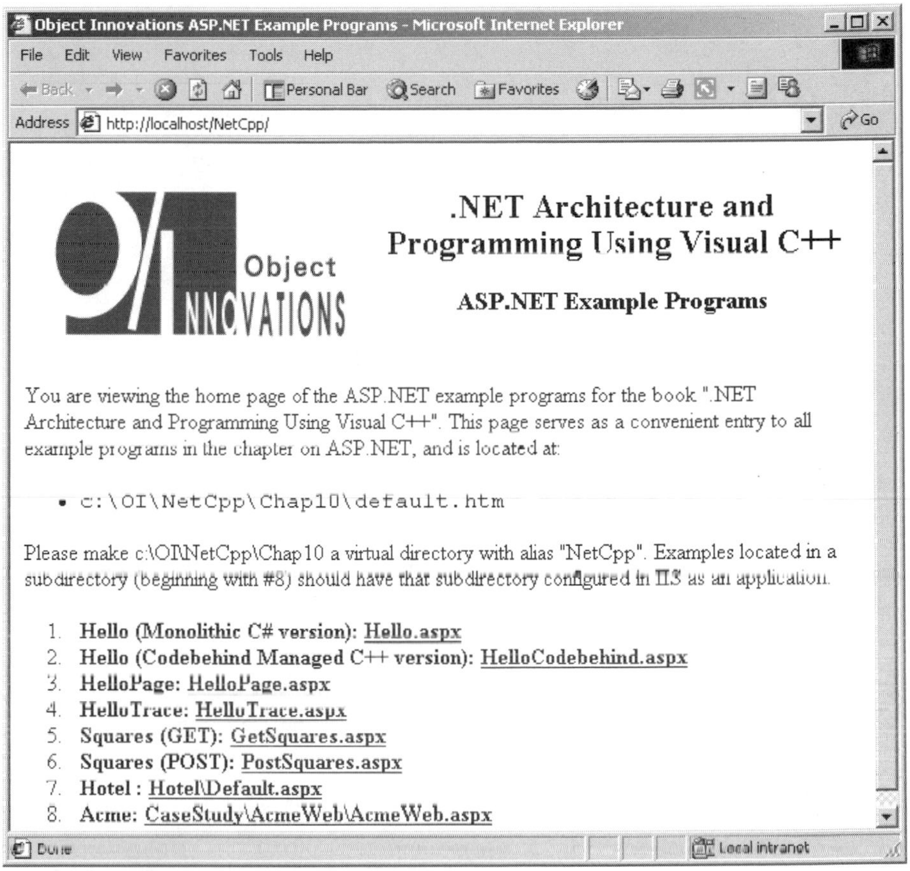

Figure 10-4   Home page for ASP.NET example programs.

one file, with embedded ASP.NET server script code. Since C++ cannot be used as embedded script code, this example is implemented in C#, just to show how this works. We present this C# example for comparison purposes only. Here is the source code, which consists of HTML along with some embedded C# script code. There are also some special tags for *server controls,* recognized by ASP.NET.

```
<!-- Hello.aspx -->
<%@ Page Language="C#" %>
<HTML>
<HEAD>
    <SCRIPT RUNAT="SERVER">
    protected void cmdEcho_Click(object Source, EventArgs e)
```

```
      {
         lblGreeting.Text="Hello, " + txtName.Text;
      }
      </SCRIPT>
</HEAD>
<BODY>
<FORM RUNAT="SERVER">Your name: 
<asp:textbox id=txtName Runat="server"></asp:textbox>
<p><asp:button id=cmdEcho onclick=cmdEcho_Click Text="Echo"
runat="server" tooltip="Click to echo your name">
</asp:button></p>
<asp:label id=lblGreeting runat="server"></asp:label>
<P></P>
</FORM>
</BODY>
</HTML>
```

You can run the program using the URL **http://localhost/NetCpp/ Hello.aspx** or by clicking on the link **Hello.aspx** in the home page of the examples programs. The page shows a text box where you can type in your name, and there is an Echo button. Clicking the button will echo your name back with a "Hello" greeting. The simple form is again displayed, so you could try out other names. If you slide the browser's mouse cursor over the button, you will see the tool tip "Click to echo your name" displayed in a yellow box. Figure 10–5 illustrates a run of this example.

This little program would not be completely trivial to implement with other Web application tools, including ASP. The key user interface feature of such an application is its thoroughly forms-based nature.[1] The user is presented with a form and interacts with the form. The server does some processing, and the user continues to see the same form. This UI model is second nature in desktop applications, but is not so common in Web applications. Typically, the Web server will send back a different page. This kind of application could certainly be implemented using a technology like ASP, but the code would be a little ugly. The server would need to synthesize a new page that looks like the old page, creating the HTML tags for the original page, plus extra information sent back (such as the greeting shown at the bottom in our echo example). A mechanism is needed to remember the current data that is displayed in the controls in the form. Another feature of this Web application is that it does some client-side processing too—the tool tip displayed in the yellow box is performed by the browser. Such rich client-side processing can be performed by Internet Explorer, but not by some other browsers.

---

[1] Forms-based development is wonderful if you have an effective form-editing tool. Visual Studio.NET supports C# and VB.NET form editors, but sadly, C++ is not currently supported by any such tool. That means manual coding is required.

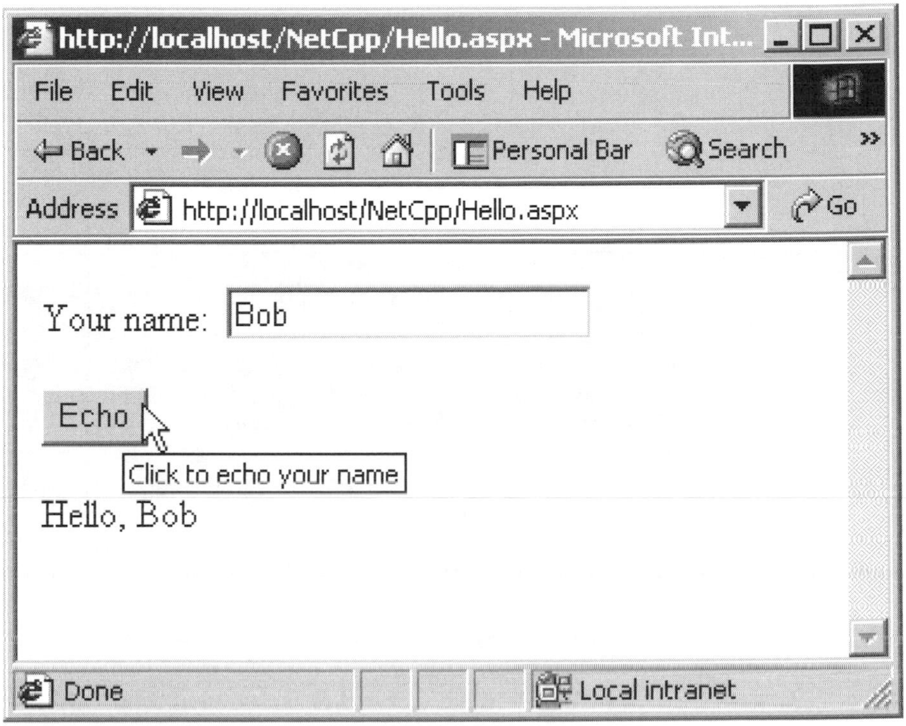

Figure 10–5   *Running the **Hello.aspx** echo program.*

As can be seen by the example code, with ASP.NET it is very easy to implement this kind of Web application (at least it is easy in C# or VB.NET).

ASP.NET Features

ASP.NET provides a programming model and infrastructure that facilitates developing new classes of Web applications. Part of this infrastructure is the .NET runtime and framework. Server-side code is written in .NET languages that are either precompiled or compiled on the fly. There are two main programming models that are supported by ASP.NET.

- Web Forms helps you build form-based Web pages. A WYSIWYG development environment enables you to drag controls onto Web pages. Special server-side controls present the programmer with an event model similar to what is provided by controls in ordinary Windows programming. This chapter discusses Web Forms in detail.
- Web Services make it possible for a Web site to expose functionality via an API that can be called remotely by other applications. Data is exchanged using standard Web protocols and formats such as HTTP

and XML, which will cross firewalls. We will discuss Web Services in the next chapter.

Both Web Forms and Web Services can take advantage of the facilities provided by .NET, such as compiled code and the .NET runtime. In addition, ASP.NET itself provides a number of infrastructure services, including state management, security, configuration, caching, and tracing.

COMPILED CODE

Web Forms (and Web Services) can be written in any .NET language that runs on top of the CLR, including C#, VB.NET, and C++ with managed Extensions. This code is compiled, and thus offers better performance than ASP pages with code written in an interpreted scripting language such as VBScript. All of the benefits, such as a managed execution environment, are available to this code, and of course the entire .NET Framework Class Library is available. Legacy unmanaged code can be called through the .NET interoperability services, which are discussed in Chapter 15.

SERVER CONTROLS

ASP.NET provides a significant innovation known as server controls. These controls have special tags, such as <asp:textbox>. Server-side code interacts with these controls, and the ASP.NET runtime generates straight HTML that is sent to the Web browser. The result is a programming model that is easy to use and yet produces standard HTML that can run in any browser.

BROWSER INDEPENDENCE

Although the World Wide Web is built on standards, the unfortunate fact of life is that browsers are not entirely compatible; they support proprietary features. A Web page designer then has the unattractive options of either writing to a lowest common denominator of browser or else writing special code for different browsers. Server controls help remove some of this pain. ASP.NET takes care of browser compatibility issues when it generates code for a server control. If the requesting browser is upscale, the generated HTML can take advantage of these features, and otherwise the generated code will be plain vanilla HTML. ASP.NET takes care of detecting the type of browser.

SEPARATION OF CODE AND CONTENT

Typical ASP pages have a mixture of scripting code interspersed with HTML elements. In ASP.NET there is a clean separation between code and presentation content. If the server code is written in a language that supports embedded ASP.NET scripting, such as C# (not C++), then it can be isolated within a single <SCRIPT RUNAT="SERVER"> ... </SCRIPT> block. Even better, it can be placed within a "code-behind" page, which is the required mode of operation in the case of C++. We will discuss code-behind in the next major section of this chapter.

STATE MANAGEMENT

HTTP is a stateless protocol. Thus, if a user enters information in various controls on a form and sends this filled-out form to the server, the information will be lost if the form is displayed again, unless the Web application provides special code to preserve this state. ASP.NET makes this kind of state preservation totally transparent. There are also convenient facilities for managing other session state and for managing application state.

Web Forms Architecture

A Web Form consists of two parts:

* The visual content or presentation, typically specified by HTML elements
* Code that contains the logic for interacting with the visual elements.

A Web Form is physically expressed by a file with the extension **.aspx**. Any HTML page could be renamed to have this extension and could be accessed using the new extension with identical results to the original. Thus, Web Forms are upwardly compatible with HTML pages.

The way code can be separated from the form is what makes a Web Form special. This code can be in a separate uncompiled source file (but not a C++ file), or it can be embedded in the **.aspx** file (again, not a C++ file), or it can be in a precompiled DLL assembly (in C#, VB, or C++). When your page is run in the Web server, the user interface code runs and dynamically generates the output for the page.

Code
Example

We can understand the architecture of a C++-based Web Form more clearly by looking at the **HelloCodebehind** example, which again simply echoes user input. You can examine the result of this program at **http://localhost/NetCpp/HelloCodebehind.aspx**. The C++ code is in **Hello-Codebehind.aspx.h**. Note that this project produces a DLL named **Hello-Codebehind.dll**. This DLL is then copied to the **bin** directory under the virtual directory created earlier for the Chapter 10 examples. This is done so that IIS can find the DLL when it needs to load it. Here is the visual content specified by the **HelloCodebehind.aspx** file:

```
<!-- HelloCodebehind.aspx -->

<%@ Assembly Name="HelloCodebehind" %>
<%@ Page Inherits=MyWebPage %>
<HTML>
```

```
  <HEAD>
  </HEAD>
<BODY>
<FORM RUNAT="SERVER">YOUR NAME: 
<asp:textbox id=txtName Runat="server"></asp:textbox>
<p><asp:button id=cmdEcho onclick=cmdEcho_Click Text="Echo"
   runat="server" tooltip="Click to echo your name">
</asp:button></p>
   <asp:label id=lblGreeting runat="server"></asp:label>
<P></P>
</FORM>
</BODY>
</HTML>
```

The user interface code is in the file **HelloCodebehind.h**:

```cpp
//HelloCodebehind.h

#using <System.dll>
#using <System.Web.dll>
using namespace System;
using namespace System::Web;
using namespace System::Web::UI;
using namespace System::Web::UI::WebControls;

public __gc class MyWebPage : public System::Web::UI::Page
{
protected:
   TextBox *txtName;
   Button *cmdEcho;
   Label *lblGreeting;

public:
   void cmdEcho_Click(Object *Source, EventArgs *e)
   {
      lblGreeting->Text =
         String::Format(
         "Hello, {0}. Welcome to Managed C++ ASP.",
         txtName->Text);
   }
};
```

This is manually compiled, and the resulting **HelloCodebehind.dll** assembly is deployed into the **\OI\NetCpp\Chap10\bin** directory, where

IIS can locate it. This is because IIS automatically searches in the **bin** directory under the virtual directory.

Page Class

The key namespace for Web Forms and Web Services is **System::Web**. Support for Web Forms is in the namespace **System::Web::UI**. Support for server controls, such as text boxes and buttons, is in the namespace **System::Web::UI::WebControls**. The classes that dynamically generate the output for an **.aspx** page are the **Page** class (in the **System::Web::UI** namespace) and classes derived from **Page**, as illustrated in the code-behind page in this last example.

INHERITING FROM PAGE CLASS

The elements in the .aspx file, the code in the code-behind file (or script, in the case of C# or VB.NET), and the base **Page** class work together to generate the page output. This cooperation is achieved by ASP.NET, dynamically creating a class for the .aspx file that is derived from the code-behind or script class that is in turn derived from **Page**. Figure 10–6 illustrates the inheritance hierarchy. Here, **MyWebPage** is a class we implement, derived from **Page**.

The most derived **Page** class, shown as My .aspx Page in Figure 10–6, is dynamically created by the ASP.NET runtime. This class extends the **Page**

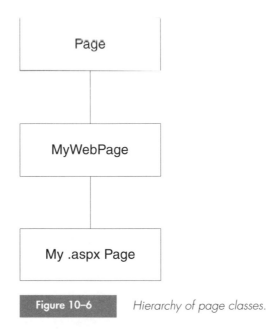

Figure 10–6   *Hierarchy of page classes.*

class, shown as MyWebPage in the figure, to incorporate the controls and HTML text on the Web Form. This class is compiled into an executable, which is run when the page is requested from a browser. The executable code creates the HTML that is sent to the browser.

Web Forms Page Life Cycle

We can get a good, high-level understanding of the Web Forms architecture by following the life cycle of our simple C++-based **HelloCodeBehind** application. This example uses the precompiled code-behind C++ version of **HelloCodebehind.aspx**. With other languages, it is possible to just provide the source code version of the code-behind file. The following steps describe the life cycle of a precompiled code-behind Web Form.

1. The user requests the **HelloCodebehind.aspx** Web page in the browser.
2. The ASP.NET runtime creates a **Page** class that is derived from the class in the precompiled assembly. This class incorporates the visual elements in the .aspx file as well as the code in the precompiled assembly. This class is compiled and executed. This generates HTML, which is then sent to the Web browser. In Internet Explorer you can see this generated HTML with the menu View | Source. If you do this, you will see that the server controls are replaced by regular HTML, as shown in the following:

```
<!-- HelloCodebehind.aspx -->


<HTML>
  <HEAD>
  </HEAD>
<BODY>
<form name="ctrl0" method="post"
action="HelloCodebehind.aspx" id="ctrl0">
<input type="hidden" name="__VIEWSTATE"
value="dDw2MjkzODE3NTs7Pg==" />
YOUR NAME:  <input name="txtName" type="text"
id="txtName" />
<p><input type="submit" name="cmdEcho" value="Echo"
id="cmdEcho" title="Click to echo your name" /></p>
   <span id="lblGreeting"></span>
<P></P>
</form>
</BODY>
</HTML>
```

3. The browser renders the HTML, displaying the simple form shown in Figure 10–7. To distinguish from the first example, we show "YOUR NAME" in all capitals. Since this is the first time the form is displayed, the text box is empty and there is no greeting message displayed.

4. The user types in a name, such as Peter, and clicks the Echo button. The browser recognizes that a Submit button has been clicked. The method for the form is "post," and the action is "HelloCodebehind.aspx." We thus have a "postback" to the original **.aspx** file.

5. The server now performs processing for this page. This time, an event was raised by the user clicking the Echo button, and an event handler in the **MyWebPage** class is invoked.

```
public:
  void cmdEcho_Click(Object *Source, EventArgs *e)
  {
    lblGreeting->Text =
      String::Format(
      "Hello, {0}. Welcome to Managed C++ ASP.NET",
      txtName->Text);
  }
```

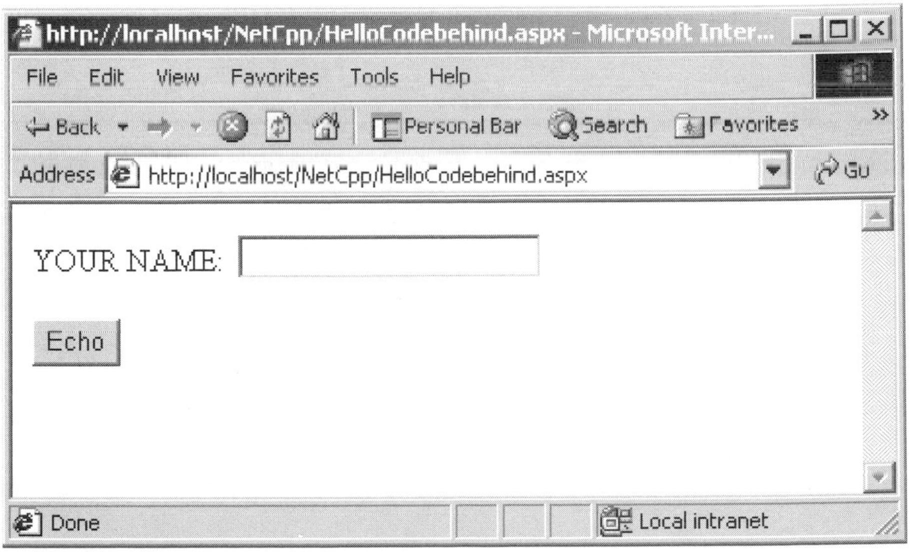

Figure 10–7   *The form for the Echo application is displayed for the first time.*

6. The **Text** property of the **TextBox** server control **txtName** is used to read the name submitted by the user. A greeting string is composed and assigned to the **Label** control **lblGreeting**, again using property notation.

7. The server again generates straight HTML for the server controls, and sends the whole response to the browser. Here is the resulting HTML:

```
...
<form name="ctrl0" method="post"
action="HelloCodebehind.aspx" id="ctrl0">
<input type="hidden" name="__VIEWSTATE"
value="dDw2MjkzODE3NTt0PDtsPGk8Mj47P ... +Oz4+Oz4=" />
YOUR NAME:  <input name="txtName" type="text"
value="Peter" id="txtName" />
<p><input type="submit" name="cmdEcho" value="Echo"
id="cmdEcho" title="Click to echo your name" /></p>
    <span id="lblGreeting">
       Hello, Peter. Welcome to Managed C++ ASP.NET
    </span>
<P></P>
</form>
...
```

8. The browser renders the page, as shown in Figure 10–8. Now a greeting message is displayed.

View State

An important characteristic of Web Forms is that all information on forms is "remembered" by the Web server. Since HTTP is a stateless protocol, this preservation of state does not happen automatically, but must be programmed. A nice feature of ASP.NET is that this state information, referred to as *view state,* is preserved automatically by the Framework, using a "hidden" control. Much of the lengthy value of the view state is omitted for convenience in the following.

```
...
<input type="hidden" name="__VIEWSTATE"
value="dDw2MjkzODE3NTt0PDtsPGk8Mj47P ... +Oz4+Oz4=" />
...
```

Later in the chapter we will examine other facilities provided by ASP.NET for managing session state and application state.

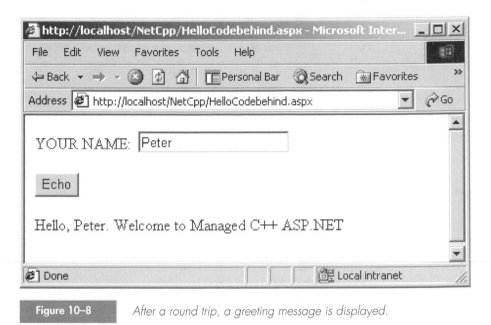

Figure 10–8   *After a round trip, a greeting message is displayed.*

Web Forms Event Model

From the standpoint of the programmer, the event model for Web Forms is very similar to the event model for Windows Forms. Indeed, this similarity is what makes programming with Web Forms so easy. What is actually happening in the case of Web Forms is, however, rather different. The big difference is that events get raised on the client and get processed on the server.[2]

Our simple form with one text box and one button is not rich enough to illustrate event processing very thoroughly. Let's imagine a more elaborate form with several text boxes, list boxes, checkboxes, buttons, and the like. Because round trips to the server are expensive, events do not automatically cause a postback to the server. Server controls have what is known as an *intrinsic event set* of events that automatically cause a postback to the server. The most common such intrinsic event is a button-click. Other events, such as selecting an item in a list box, do not cause an immediate postback to the server. Instead, these events are cached until a button-click causes a post to the server. Then, on the server, the various change events are processed, in no particular order, and the button-click event that caused the post is processed.

---

[2] Some controls, such as the Calendar control, raise some events on the server. Also, the Page itself raises events on the server.

Page Processing

Processing a page is a cooperative endeavor between the Web server, the ASP.NET runtime, and your own code. The **Page** class provides a number of events, which you can handle to hook into page processing. The **Page** class also has properties and methods that you can use. For a complete description, consult the .NET Framework documentation. We cover some of the highlights. The example programs in this chapter will illustrate using features of the **Page** class.

PAGE EVENTS

There are a number of events raised on the server as part of the normal processing of a page. These events are actually defined in the **Control** base class, and so are available to server controls also. The following are the most important events:

- **Init** is the first step in the page's life cycle and occurs when the page is initialized. There is no view-state information for any of the controls at this point.
- **Load** occurs when the controls are loaded into the page. View-state information for the controls is then available.
- **PreRender** occurs just before the controls are rendered to the output stream. Normally, this event is not handled by a page but is important for implementing your own server controls.
- **Unload** occurs when the controls are unloaded from the page. At this point it is too late to write your own data to the output stream.

PAGE PROPERTIES

The **Page** class has a number of important properties. Some of the most useful properties include the following:

- **EnableViewState** indicates whether the page maintains view-state for itself and its controls. You can get or set this property. The default value is true, such that view-state is maintained.
- **ErrorPage** specifies the error page to which the browser should be redirected in case an unhandled exception occurs.
- **IsPostBack** indicates whether the page is being loaded in response to a postback from the client or is being loaded for the first time.
- **IsValid** indicates whether page validation succeeded.
- **Request** gets the HTTP Request object, which allows you to access data from incoming HTTP requests.
- **Response** gets the HTTP Response object, which allows you to send response data to a browser.

- **Session** gets the current Session object, which is provided by ASP.NET for storing session state.
- **Trace** gets a **TraceContext** object for the page, which you can use to write out trace information.

SAMPLE PROGRAM

Code
Example

We can illustrate some of these features of page processing with a simple extension to our Echo program. The page **HelloPage** assembly provides handlers for a number of page events, and we write simple text to the output stream, using the **Response** property. For each event, we show the current text in the **txtName** and **lblGreeting** server controls. In the handler for **Load** we also show the current value of **IsPostBack**, which should be false the first time the page is accessed, and subsequently true.

```
<!-- HelloPage.aspx -->

<%@ Assembly Name="HelloPage" %>
<%@ Page Inherits=MyHelloPage %>
<HTML>
    <HEAD>
    </HEAD>
<BODY>
<FORM RUNAT="SERVER">Your name: 
<asp:textbox id=txtName Runat="server"></asp:textbox>
<p><asp:button id=cmdEcho onclick=cmdEcho_Click Text="Echo"
runat="server"
tooltip="Click to echo your name">
</asp:button></p>
    <asp:label id=lblGreeting runat="server"></asp:label>
<P></P>
</FORM>
</BODY>
</HTML>
```

The .aspx file above refers to the **HelloPage** assembly, which contains the **MyHelloPage** class. It also specifies that the **Page** class inherits from this **MyHelloPage** class. That means that when events are generated for the page, they are handled by methods in the **MyHelloPage** class. The code for the **MyHelloPage** class is shown next.

```
public __gc class MyHelloPage :
   public System::Web::UI::Page
{
```

```
    ...
  public:
    ...
    void Page_Init(Object *sender, EventArgs *e)
    {
       Page *p = dynamic_cast<Page *>(sender);
       HttpResponse *response = p->get_Response();
       response->Write("Page_Init<br>");
       response->Write(String::Concat(
          "txtName = ", txtName->Text, "<br>"));
       response->Write(String::Concat(
          "lblGreeting = ",lblGreeting->Text, "<br>"));
    }
    void Page_Load(Object *sender, EventArgs *e)
    {
       Page *p = dynamic_cast<Page *>(sender);
       HttpResponse *response = p->get_Response();
       response->Write("Page_Load<br>");
       response->Write(String::Format(
          "IsPostBack = {0}<br>", __box(IsPostBack)));
       response->Write(String::Concat(
          "txtName = ", txtName->Text, "<br>"));
       response->Write(String::Concat(
          "lblGreeting = ", lblGreeting->Text, "<br>"));
    }
    void Page_PreRender(Object *sender, EventArgs *e)
    {
       Page *p = dynamic_cast<Page *>(sender);
       HttpResponse *response = p->get_Response();
       response->Write("Page_PreRender<br>");
       response->Write(String::Concat(
          "txtName = ", txtName->Text, "<br>"));
       response->Write(String::Concat(
          "lblGreeting = ", lblGreeting->Text, "<br>"));
    }
    void Page_Unload(Object *sender, EventArgs *e)
    {
       //Response not available in this context
    }
  };
```

When we access the page the first time, both the text box and the labels are empty, since we have entered no information. **IsPostBack** is false. Now

enter the name Robert, and click the Echo button. We obtain the following
output from our handlers for the page events:

```
Page_Init
txtName -
lblGreeting =
Page_Load
IsPostBack = True
txtName = Robert
lblGreeting =
Page_PreRender
txtName = Robert
lblGreeting = Hello, Robert. Welcome again
```

In **Page_Init** there is no information for either control, since view-state
is not available at page initialization. In **Page_Load**, the text box has data, but
the label does not, since the click event handler has not yet been invoked.
IsPostBack is now **true**. In **Page_PreRender** both controls now have data.

Click Echo a second time. Again, the controls have no data in
Page_Init. But this time, in **Page_Load** the view-state provides data for both
controls. Figure 10–9 shows the browser output after Echo has been clicked a
second time.

Page and Assembly Directives

An **.aspx** file may contain an *assembly directive* and a *page directive*. The
assembly directive associates an existing, compiled assembly with the current
page. The page directive defines various attributes that can control how
ASP.NET processes the page. Each directive contains one or more attribute/
value pairs, as shown in the following examples.

```
<@ Assembly Name="HelloCodebehind" @>
<@ Page Inherits=MyWebPage @>
```

Our example **HelloCodebehind.aspx** illustrates an **.aspx** page that
does not contain any script code. If you use other languages, such as C# or
VB.NET, you can embed script directly in the **.aspx** file, and you would not
need to use the assembly directive. These languages also support code-
behind source files, which use the **Src** attribute in the page directive to point
to an uncompiled source file. With C++, neither of these options is available.
Instead, C++ requires the assembly directive to contain a **Name** attribute that
identifies the compiled assembly. The **Inherits** attribute in the Page directive
specifies the **Page**-derived class in the code from which the **.aspx** page class
will inherit.

```
http://localhost/NetCpp/HelloPage.aspx - Microsoft ...

File   Edit   View   Favorites   Tools   Help

Back  ▼  ➡  ▼  ⊗  🔃  🏠  │ 🗂 Personal Bar  🔍 Search  »

Address  🔷 http://localhost/NetCpp/HelloPage.aspx  ▼  ↗ Go

Page_Init
txtName =
lblGreeting =
Page_Load
IsPostBack = True
txtName = Robert
lblGreeting = Hello, Robert. Welcome again.
Page_PreRender
txtName = Robert
lblGreeting = Hello, Robert. Welcome again.


Your name:  Robert


Echo


Hello, Robert. Welcome again.

Done                                      Local intranet
```

Browser output after Echo has been clicked a second time.

Tracing

ASP.NET provides extensive tracing capabilities. Merely setting the **Trace** attribute for a page to true will cause trace output generated by ASP.NET to be sent to the browser. In addition, you can output your own trace information using the **Write** method of the **TraceContext** object, which is obtained from the **Trace** property of the **Page**.

The page **HelloTrace.aspx** illustrates using tracing in place of writing to the **Response** object.

```
<!-- HelloTrace.aspx -->

<%@ Assembly Name="HelloTrace" %>
<%@ Page Inherits=MyHelloTrace Trace = "true" %>
<HTML>
    <HEAD>
    </HEAD>
<BODY>
<FORM RUNAT="SERVER">Your name: 
<asp:textbox id=txtName Runat="server"></asp:textbox>
<p><asp:button id=cmdEcho onclick=cmdEcho_Click Text="Echo"
runat="server" tooltip="Click to echo your name">
</asp:button></p>
    <asp:label id=lblGreeting runat="server"></asp:label>
<P></P>
</FORM>
</BODY>
</HTML>
```

The **MyHelloTrace** class, implemented in the **HelloTrace.dll** assembly, contains the following code that writes trace output:

```
void Page_Init(Object *sender, EventArgs *e)
{
    Page *p = dynamic_cast<Page *>(sender);
    TraceContext *trace = p->get_Trace();
    trace->Write("Page_Init<br>");
    trace->Write(String::Concat(
        "txtName = ", txtName->Text, "<br>"));
    trace->Write(String::Concat(
        "lblGreeting = ",lblGreeting->Text, "<br>"));
}
void Page_Load(Object *sender, EventArgs *e)
{
    Page *p = dynamic_cast<Page *>(sender);
    TraceContext *trace = p->get_Trace();
    trace->Write("Page_Load<br>");
    trace->Write(String::Format(
        "IsPostBack = {0}<br>", __box(IsPostBack)));
    trace->Write(String::Concat(
        "txtName = ", txtName->Text, "<br>"));
```

```
      trace->Write(String::Concat(
         "lblGreeting = ", lblGreeting->Text, "<br>"));
   }
   void Page_PreRender(Object *sender, EventArgs *e)
   {
      Page *p = dynamic_cast<Page *>(sender);
      TraceContext *trace = p->get_Trace();
      trace->Write("Page_PreRender<br>");
      trace->Write(String::Concat(
         "txtName = ", txtName->Text, "<br>"));
      trace->Write(String::Concat(
         "lblGreeting = ", lblGreeting->Text, "<br>"));
   }
```

Figure 10–10 shows the browser output after the initial request for the page. Notice that the trace output is shown *after* the form, along with trace information that is generated by ASP.NET itself.

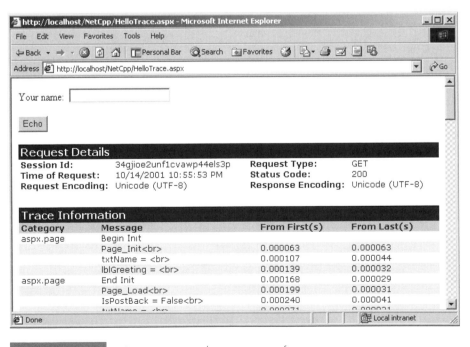

| Figure 10–10 | *Browser output showing trace information.* |

Request/Response Programming

The server control architecture is built on top of a more fundamental processing architecture, which may be called *request/response*. Understanding HTTP request/response is important to solidify our overall grasp of ASP.NET. Also, there are certain programming situations where request/response is the natural approach.

HttpRequest Class

The **System::Web** namespace contains the useful class, **HttpRequest**, that can be used to read the various HTTP values that are sent by a client during a Web request. These HTTP values are what would be used by a classical (CGI) or ISAPI program acting upon a Web request, and are the foundation upon which higher level processing is built. Table 10–1 shows some of the public instance properties of **HttpRequest**. If you are familiar with HTTP, the meaning of these various properties should be largely self-explanatory. Refer to the .NET Framework documentation of the **HttpRequest** class for full details about these and other properties.

The **Request** property of the **Page** class returns an **HttpRequest** object. You may then extract whatever information you need, using the properties of **HttpRequest**. For example, the following code (which is not in any of the code examples) determines the length in bytes of the content sent by the client

Table 10–1 Public Instance Properties of HttpRequest

Property	Meaning
AcceptTypes	String array of client-supported MIME accept types
Browser	Information about client's browser capabilities
ContentLength	Length in bytes of content sent by the client
Cookies	Collection of cookies sent by the client
Form	Collection of form variables
Headers	Collection of HTTP headers
HttpMethod	HTTP transfer method used by client (e.g., GET or POST)
Params	Combined collection of QueryString, Form, ServerVariables, and Cookies items
Path	Virtual request of the current path
QueryString	Collection of HTTP query string variables
ServerVariables	Collection of Web server variables

and writes that information to the **Response** object. This output is then displayed in the browser.

```
Page *p = dynamic_cast<Page *>(sender);
HttpRequest *request = p->get_Request();
int length = request->ContentLength;
HttpResponse *response = p->get_Response();
response->Write(String::Format(
    "ContentLength = {0}<br>", __box(length)));
```

COLLECTIONS

There are a number of useful collections that are exposed as properties of **HttpRequest**. The collections are of type **NamedValueCollection** (in **System::Collections::Specialized** namespace). You can access a value from a string key. For example, the following code extracts values for the QUERY_STRING and HTTP_USER_AGENT server variables using the **ServerVariables** collection.

```
Page *p = dynamic_cast<Page *>(sender);
HttpRequest *request = p->get_Request();
HttpResponse *response = p->get_Response();

String *strQuery =
    request->ServerVariables->get_Item(
        "QUERY_STRING");
response->Write(String::Format(
    "QUERY_STRING = {0}<br>", strQuery));
String *strAgent =
    request->ServerVariables->get_Item(
        "HTTP_USER_AGENT");
response->Write(String::Format(
    "HTTP_USER_AGENT = {0}<br>", strAgent));
```

If you enter the URL for the associated **.aspx** file, followed with the query string **?foo=3,** the above code will display something like the following output in the browser.

```
QUERY_STRING = foo=3
HTTP_USER_AGENT = Mozilla/4.0
```

Server variables such as these are at heart of classical CGI Web server programming. The Web server passes information to a CGI script or program by using environment variables. ASP.NET makes this low-level information available to you, in case you need it.

A common task is to extract information from controls on forms. In HTML, controls are identified by a **name** attribute, which can be used by the server to determine the corresponding value. The way form data is passed to the server depends on whether the form uses the HTTP GET method or the POST method.

With GET, the form data is encoded as part of the query string. The **QueryString** collection can then be used to retrieve the values. With POST, the form data is passed as content after the HTTP header. The **Forms** collection can then be used to extract the control values. You could use the value of the REQUEST_METHOD server variable (GET or POST) to determine which collection to use (the **QueryString** collection in the case of GET and the **Forms** collection in case of POST).

With ASP.NET, you don't have to worry about which HTTP method was used in the request. ASP.NET provides a **Params** collection, which is a combination (union in the mathematical sense) of the **ServerVariables**, **QueryString**, **Forms**, and **Cookies** collections.

EXAMPLE PROGRAM

We illustrate all these ideas with a simple page, **Squares.aspx**, that displays a column of square number values. How many square numbers to display is determined by a number submitted on a form. The page **GetSquares.aspx** submits the request using GET, and **PostSquares.aspx** submits the request using POST. The user interface is identical, and is illustrated in Figure 10–11.

Here is the HTML for **GetSquares.aspx**. Notice that we are using straight HTML. There are no features of ASP.NET, except for the Page directive, which could be used for turning tracing on.

```
<!-- GetSquares.aspx -->

<%@ Page Trace = "false" %>
<html>
<head>
</head>
<body>
<P>This program will print a column of square numbers</P>
<form method="get" action = Squares.aspx>
How many:
<INPUT type=text size_2 value=5 name=txtCount>
<P></P>
<INPUT type=submit value=Squares name=cmdSquares>
</form>
</body>
</html>
```

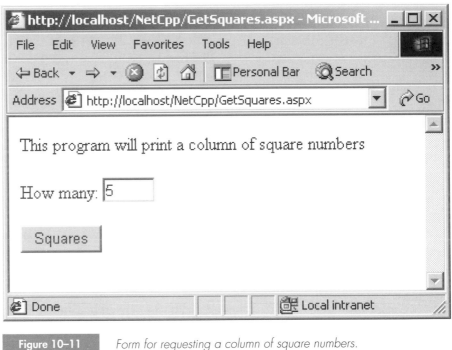

Figure 10–11   *Form for requesting a column of square numbers.*

The **form** tag has attributes specifying the method (GET, rather than POST) and the action (target page **Squares.aspx**). The controls have a **name** attribute, which will be used by server code to retrieve the value.

Run **GetSquares.aspx** and click "Squares." You will then see some HTTP information displayed, followed by the column of squares. Tracing is turned on, so details about the request are displayed by ASP.NET. Figure 10–12 illustrates the output from this GET request.

You can see that form data is encoded in the query string and the content length is 0, since it is a GET rather than a POST. If you scroll down on the trace output, you will see much information. For example, the **QueryString** collection is shown.

Now let's look at **PostSquares.aspx**. Note that the form tag specifies the POST method this time. Everything else is the same as **GetSquares.aspx**.

```
<!-- PostSquares.aspx  -->

<%@ Page Trace = "false" %>
<html>
<head>
</head>
<body>
```

```
<P>This program will print a column of squares</P>
<form method="post" action = Squares.aspx>
How many:
<INPUT type=text size=2 value=5 name=txtCount>
<P></P>
<INPUT type=submit value=Squares name=cmdSquares>
</form>
</body>
</html>
```

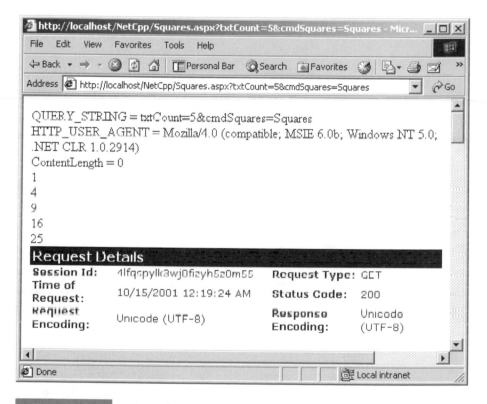

Figure 10–12   *Output from a GET request.*

Run **PostSquares.aspx** and click Squares. Again, you will see some HTTP information displayed, followed by the column of squares. Tracing is turned on, so details about the request are displayed by ASP.NET. Figure 10–13 illustrates the output from this POST request.

You can see that this time, the query string is empty and the content length is 29, since it is a POST rather than a GET. The form data is passed as part of the content following the HTTP header information. If you scroll down on the trace output, you will see that now there is a **Form** collection, which is

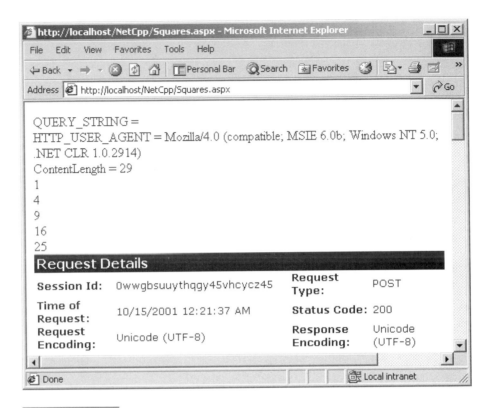

Figure 10–13 *Output from a POST request.*

used by ASP.NET to provide access to the form data in the case of a POST method.

HttpResponse Class

The **HttpResponse** class encapsulates HTTP response information that is built as part of an ASP.NET operation. The Framework uses this class when it is creating a response that includes writing server controls back to the client. Your own server code may also use the **Write** method of the **Response** object to write data to the output stream that will be sent to the client. We have already seen several illustrations of **Response::Write**.

REDIRECT

The **HttpResponse** class has a useful method, **Redirect**, that enables server code to redirect an HTTP request to a different URL. A simple redirection without passing any data is trivial—all you have to do is call the **Redirect** method and pass the URL. An example of such usage would be a reorganization of a Web site, where a certain page is no longer valid and the content has been moved to a new location. You can keep the old page live by simply redirecting traffic to the new location.

It should be noted that redirection always involves an HTTP GET request, like following a simple link to a URL. (POST arises as an option when submitting form data, where the action can be specified as GET or POST.) A more interesting case involves passing data to the new page. One way to pass data is to encode it in the query string. You must preserve standard HTTP conventions for the encoding of the query string. The class **HttpUtility** provides a method **UrlEncode**, which will properly encode an individual item of a query string. You must yourself provide code to separate the URL from the query string with a question mark (?) and to separate items of the query string with an ampersand (&).

The folder **Hotel** provides an example of a simple Web application that illustrates this method of passing data in redirection. The file **default.aspx** provides a form for collecting information to be used in making a hotel reservation. The reservation itself is made on the page **Reservation1.aspx**. You may access the starting **default.aspx** page through the URL

```
http://localhost/NetCpp/Hotel/
```

As usual, we provide a link to this page in our home page of example programs. Figure 10–14 illustrates the starting page of our simple hotel reservation example.

Here is the ASP.NET C++ code that is executed when the Make Reservation button is clicked.

```
void cmdMakeReservation_Click(
    Object *sender, EventArgs *e)
{
    HttpUtility *utility = new HttpUtility;
    String *query = String::Concat(
        "City=", utility->UrlEncode(txtCity->Text));
    query = String::Format(
        "{0}&Hotel={1}",
        query, utility->UrlEncode(txtHotel->Text));
    query = String::Format(
        "{0}&Date={1}",
        query, utility->UrlEncode(txtDate->Text));
    query = String::Format(
        "{0}&NumberDays={1}",
        query, utility->UrlEncode(txtNumberDays->Text));
    Response->Redirect(String::Concat(
        "Reservation1.aspx?", query));
}
```

Starting page for making a hotel reservation.

The **cmdMakeReservation_Click** method builds a query string, which gets appended to the **Reservation1.aspx** URL, separated by a ?. Note the & that is used as a separator of items in the query string. We use the **HttpUtility::UrlEncode** method to encode the individual items. Special encoding is required for the slashes in the date and for the space in names like "San Jose." Clicking the button invokes the method, which then brings up the reservation page. Calling the **Page_Load** method of the **Reservation1** class does this. This method obtains the information on the City, Hotel, Date, and the NumberDays, and displays the results on the returned Web page.

```
void Page_Load(Object *sender, EventArgs *e)
{
    Page *p = dynamic_cast<Page *>(sender);
```

```
HttpRequest *request = p->get_Request();
HttpResponse *response = p->get_Response();
response->Write("Making reservation for ...");
response->Write("<br>");
String *city = request->Params->get_Item("City");
response->Write(String::Concat("City = ", city));
response->Write("<br>");
String *hotel = request->Params->get_Item("Hotel");
response->Write(String::Concat("Hotel = ", hotel));
response->Write("<br>");
String *strDate = request->Params->get_Item("Date");
response->Write(String::Concat("Date = ", strDate));
response->Write("<br>");
String *strDays =
    request->Params->get_Item("NumberDays");
response->Write(String::Concat(
    "NumberDays = ", strDays));
response->Write("<br>");
}
```

You can see the query string in the address window of the browser. Figure 10–15 illustrates the output shown by the browser. (Our program does not actually make the reservation; it simply prints out the parameters passed to it.)

You can turn on tracing, and the trace output should serve to reinforce the ideas we have been discussing about request/response Web programming. In particular, you should examine the **QueryString** collection, as illustrated in Figure 10–16.

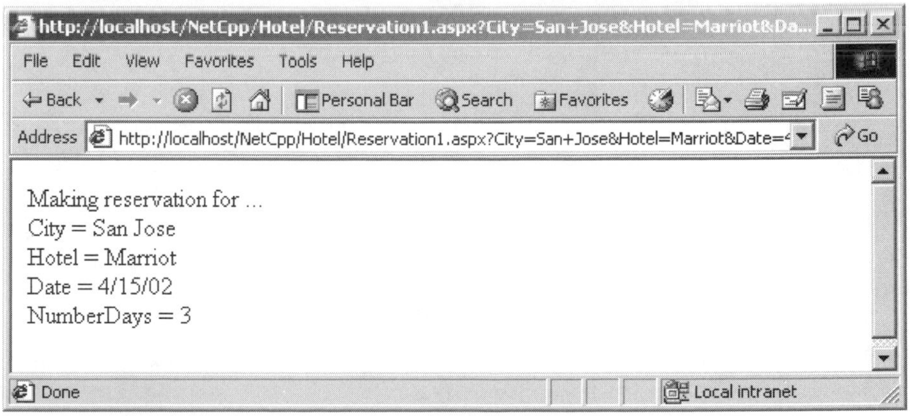

Figure 10–15   *Browser output from making a hotel reservation.*

Querystring Collection	
Name	**Value**
City	San Jose
Hotel	Marriot
Date	4/15/02
NumberDays	3

Figure 10–16   *The query string is used for passing parameters in redirection.*

Case Study

We have examined the fundamentals of ASP.NET, and we have created some simple Web pages simply using the managed C++ Class Library template. We will continue now with the case study for Chapter 10. For C# and VB.NET, there is a special kind of project template, known as an ASP.NET Web Application, that creates boilerplate code. In addition, the Forms Designer makes it very easy to create C# and VB.NET Web forms by dragging controls from a palette. Unfortunately, in C++ we are left to code these forms by hand.

Hotel Information Web Page

We will create a simple C++ ASP.NET Web page that displays information about hotels. Dropdown list boxes are provided to show cities and hotels. Selecting a city from the first dropdown will cause the hotels in that city to be shown in the second dropdown. We obtain the hotel information from the **Hotel.dll** component that is provided in the **CaseStudy\AcmeWeb** directory for this chapter. We use data binding to populate the list boxes. The completed project is in the **CaseStudy\AcmeWeb** directory for this chapter. You can follow the steps and create your own version of this solution in the **Demos** directory provided for this chapter.

To see the result, view *http://localhost/NetCpp/CaseStudy/AcmeWeb/ AcmeWeb.aspx* in your browser. However, before you can view this URL, you will need to set up a virtual directory and configure it as an application in IIS using Internet Server Manager, as described later.

CONFIGURING WEB SERVER CONNECTION

Before getting started, you may wish to check, and possibly change, your Web server connection setting. The two options are File share and FrontPage. If you are doing all your development on a local computer, you might find File share to be faster and more convenient. To access this setting, select the menu Tools | Options. Then choose Web Settings underneath Projects. You can then set the Preferred Access Method by using a radio button, as illustrated in Figure 10–17.

CREATING A C++ ASP.NET WEB APPLICATION

1. In Visual Studio select the menu File | New | Project.
2. In the New Project dialog box choose Visual C++ Projects as the Project Type and Managed C++ Class Library as the Template.
3. Enter *AcmeWeb* as the name of your project.
4. For the location, enter the path **C:\OI\NetCpp\Chap10\Demos**, as illustrated in Figure 10–18.
5. Click OK. The project files, including the **AcmeWeb.sln** solution file, will then be created in **C:\OI\NetCpp\Chap10\Demos**.
6. If you have not already done so, you will need to make **C:\OI\NetCpp\Chap10** a virtual directory with the alias *NetCpp*, as shown earlier in Figure 10–3.

DESIGNING THE FORM

Since there is no C++ form designer in Visual Studio.NET, you can do the design in C# and then port the resulting C# code to C++. To do this, you would first create a dummy C# Form-based project and design your form

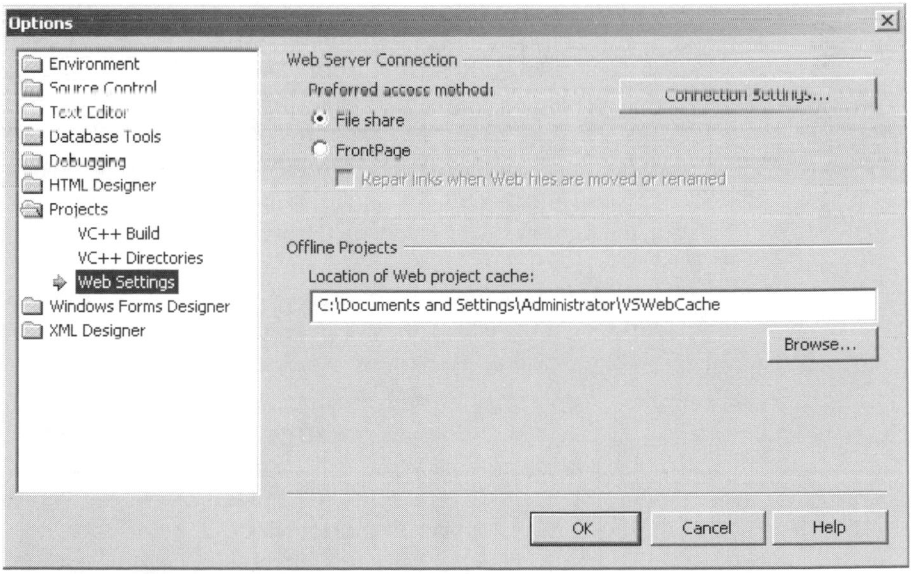

Figure 10–17   *Configuring Web server connection preferred access method.*

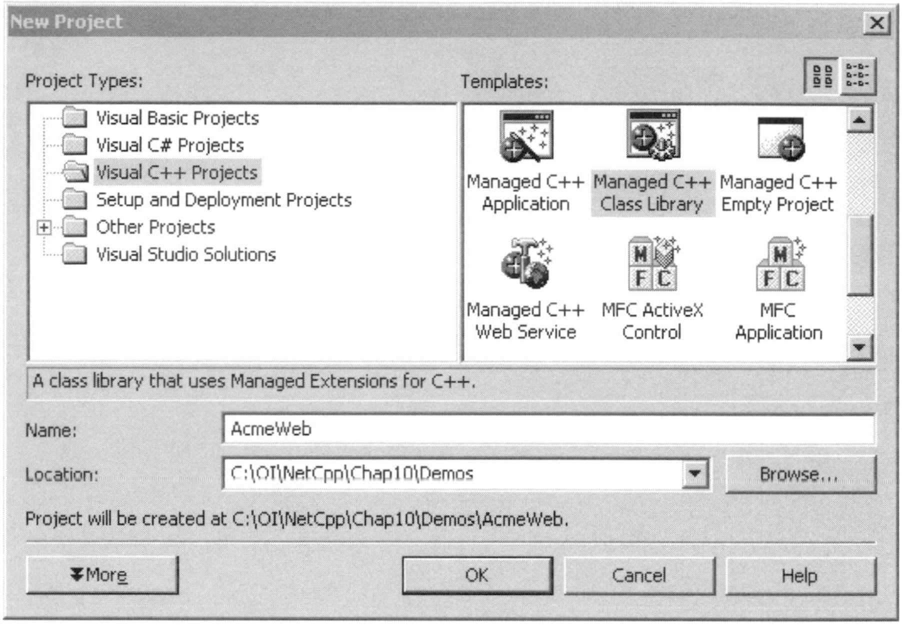

Figure 10–18   *Creating a Visual Studio C++ Class Library project.*

there. This has already been done for you, and you can simply use the ported C++ code provided in **WebForm1.aspx.h** in the **CaseStudy\AcmeWeb** directory to your new project in the **Demos\AcmeWeb** project directory.

Two Label controls, two DropDownList controls, and one Button control were placed onto the form. The Text property of the Labels was set to City and Hotel. The Text property of the Button was set to Make Reservation. The IDs of the DropDownList controls were set to **listCities** and **listHotels**. The ID of the Button was set to **cmdMakeReservation**. The DropDownList controls were resized to look like the image shown in Figure 10–19.

To use the ported C++ code provided in **WebForm1.aspx.h** in the **CaseStudy\AcmeWeb** directory in your new project in the **Demos\AcmeWeb** project directory, do the following:

1. Copy the file **WebForm1.aspx.h** from the **CaseStudy\AcmeWeb** directory into your new **Demos\AcmeWeb** project directory.
2. Open the new project if it is not already open by double-clicking in the **AcmeWeb.sln** file in the **Demos\AcmeWeb** directory.
3. In the Solution Explorer window, right click on the Header Files node under the AcmeWeb project, and select Add | Add Existing Item. Then double click the **WebForm1.aspx.h** file.
4. The project will not need the **AcmeWeb.h** file, so select it in the Solution Explorer window, and hit the Delete key. Since the

Toolbox   ⊉ ✗ | **WebForm1.aspx** ◁ ▷ ✗

Toolbox
Data
Web Forms
▸ Pointer
A Label
ab| TextBox
ab| Button
ab| LinkButton
🖾 ImageButton
A HyperLink
📇 DropDownList
Components ▾
HTML
Clipboard Ring
General

City   [Unbound ▼]

Hotel   [Unbound ▼]

🖫 Design   ⊡ HTML

Figure 10–19   *Using the Form Designer to add controls to the form.*

AcmeWeb.h file is not needed at all, you can also delete it from the disk in **\Demos\AcmeWeb** using Windows Explorer.

5.   Edit the **AcmeWeb.cpp** file to remove the **#include** for **AcmeWeb.h**, and add a **#include** for **WebForm1.aspx.h**. We will soon be adding another header file named **Global.asax.h** to the project, so add a **#include** for it as well.

```
// This is the main DLL file.
#include "stdafx.h"

#include "Global.asax.h"
#include "WebForm1.aspx.h"
```

Here is the **WebForm1.aspx.h** source file. Note that the **Global::hotelBroker** static field is used to retrieve the **HotelBroker** object. We will soon see that this object is created in the **Application_Start** method of the **Global** object defined in the **Global.asax.h** source file.

```
//WebForm1.aspx.h
...
namespace AcmeWeb
{
public __gc class WebForm1 :
     public System::Web::UI::Page
```

```
    {
    protected:
        System::Web::UI::WebControls::Label *Label1;
        System::Web::UI::WebControls::Label *Label2;
        System::Web::UI::WebControls::DropDownList
            *listCities;
        System::Web::UI::WebControls::DropDownList
            *listHotels;
    private:
        static HotelBroker *hotelBroker;
    public:
        WebForm1()
        {
            Page::Init += new System::EventHandler(
                this, Page_Init);
        }
    private:
        void Page_Load(Object *sender, System::EventArgs *e)
        {
            if (!IsPostBack)
            {
                hotelBroker = Global::hotelBroker;
                ArrayList *cities = hotelBroker->GetCities();
                listCities->DataSource = cities;
                ArrayList *hotels = hotelBroker->GetHotels(
                    dynamic_cast<String *>
                        (cities->get_Item(0)));
                BindHotels(hotels);
                DataBind();
            }
        }
    ...
    };
```

DATA BINDING

Next, we populate the first DropDownList with the city data, which can be obtained by the **GetCities** method of **HotelBroker**. We make use of the *data binding* capability of the DropDownList control. You might think data binding is only used with a database. However, in .NET data binding is much more general and can be applied to other data sources besides databases. Binding a control to a database is very useful for two-tier, client/server applications. However, we are implementing a three-tier application in which the presentation logic, whether implemented using Windows Forms or Web Forms, talks to a business logic component and not directly to the database.

The .NET Framework provides a number of data binding options, which can facilitate binding to data obtained through a middle-tier component. A very simple option is binding to an **ArrayList**. This option works perfectly in our example, because we need to populate the DropDownList of cities with strings, and the **GetCities** method returns an array list of strings.

The bottom line is that all we need to do to populate the **listCities** DropDownList is add the following code to the **Page_Load** method of the **WebForm1** class.

```
void Page_Load(Object *sender, System::EventArgs *e)
{
   if (!IsPostBack)
   {
      hotelBroker = new HotelBroker;;
      ArrayList *cities = hotelBroker->GetCities();
      listCities->DataSource = cities;
      ArrayList *hotels = hotelBroker->GetHotels(
         dynamic_cast<String *>
            (cities->get_Item(0)));
      BindHotels(hotels);
      DataBind();
   }
}
```

The call to **DataBind()** binds all the server controls on the form to their data source, which results in the controls being populated with data from the data source. The **DataBind** method can also be invoked on the server controls individually. **DataBind** is a method of the **Control** class and is inherited by the **Page** class and by specific server control classes.

INITIALIZING THE HOTELS

We can populate the second DropDownList with hotel data using a similar procedure. It is a little bit more involved, because **GetHotels** returns an array list of **HotelListItem** structures rather than strings. We want to populate the **listHotels** DropDownList with the names of the hotels. The helper method **BindHotels** loops through the array list of hotels and creates an array list of hotel names, which is bound to **listHotels**. Here is the complete code, which adds the logic for initializing the hotels for the first city (which has index 0).

```
void BindHotels(ArrayList *hotels)
{
   ArrayList *hotelNames =
      new ArrayList(hotels->Count);
   IEnumerator *pEnum = hotels->GetEnumerator();
```

```
      while (pEnum->MoveNext())
      {
         HotelListItem *hotel =
            dynamic_cast<HotelListItem *>
               (pEnum->Current);
         hotelNames->Add(hotel->HotelName->Trim());
      }
      listHotels->DataSource = hotelNames;
   }
```

SELECTING A CITY

Finally, we implement the feature that selecting a city causes the hotels for the selected city to be displayed. We add an event handler for selecting a city. Here is the code for the **SelectedIndexChanged** event.

```
void listCities_SelectedIndexChanged(
   Object *sender, System::EventArgs *e)
{
   String *city = listCities->SelectedItem->Text;
   ArrayList *hotels = hotelBroker->GetHotels(city);
   BindHotels(hotels);
   DataBind();
}
```

ADDING THE GLOBAL CLASS

Add a new file to the project named **Global.asax.h**. Again, you do not need to code this file by hand, since you can copy it from the solution provided in the **CaseStudy\AcmeWeb** directory. To do this, follow these steps:

1. Copy the file **Global.asax.h** from the **CaseStudy\AcmeWeb** directory into your new **Demos\AcmeWeb** project directory.
2. In the Solution Explorer window, right-click on the Header Files node under the AcmeWeb project, and select Add | Add Existing Item. Then double-click the **Global.asax.h** file.

Note that in **Global.asax.h**, the **Application_Start** method creates an instance of the **HotelBroker** class and assigns it to the static field named **hotelBroker**. This is then retrieved in the **WebForm1.aspx.h** source file in the **Page_Load** method shown previously.

```
//Global.asax.h

#using <.\Hotel.dll>
#using <System.dll>
```

```
#using <System.Web.dll>
using namespace System;
using namespace OI::NetCpp::Acme;

namespace AcmeWeb
{
public __gc class Global :
   public System::Web::HttpApplication
   {
   public:
      static HotelBroker *hotelBroker;
   protected:
      void Application_Start(
         Object *sender, EventArgs *e)
      {
         hotelBroker = new HotelBroker;
      }
   ...
   };
}
```

GLOBAL.ASAX AND THE GLOBAL OBJECT

The **Global.asax** file is necessary for the methods of the **Global** class, defined in Global.asax.h, to be called. For example, the **Application_Start** method will not be called by IIS unless the **Global.asax** file is present in the AcmeWeb directory. This is important, since this is the method where the instance of **HotelBroker** is created. This file is provided in the **Case-Study\AcmeWeb** directory, so you can copy it to the **Demos\AcmeWeb** directory. You do not have to add this file to your project. But for convenience, we will. To add this file to the project, do the following.

1. Copy the file **Global.asax** from the **CaseStudy\AcmeWeb** directory into your new **Demos\AcmeWeb** project directory.
2. In the Solution Explorer window, right-click on the AcmeWeb project node, and select Add | Add Existing Item. Set the file type filter to *.*, and then double-click the **Global.asax** file.

The **Global.asax** file contains only the following one line, which specifies that the application object inherit from the **AcmeWeb.Global** class, which is defined in the Global.asax.h source file.

```
<%@ Application Inherits="AcmeWeb.Global" %>
```

ACMEWEB.ASPX

The other ASP.NET file that must exist in the AcmeWeb directory is **AcmeWeb.aspx**. This file specifies the assembly that contains the implementation of the **AcmeWeb::WebForm1** class shown earlier, in the WebForm1. aspx.h source file. The **AcmeWeb.aspx** file also specifies that the page inherits from the **AcmeWeb::WebForm1** class, as well as some HTML to present to the user. This file is provided in the **CaseStudy\AcmeWeb** directory, so you can copy it to the **Demos\AcmeWeb** directory. You do not have to add this file to your project. But for convenience, we will. To add this file to the project, do the following:

1. Copy the file **AcmeWeb.aspx** from the **CaseStudy\AcmeWeb** directory into your new **Demos\AcmeWeb** project directory.
2. In the Solution Explorer window, right-click on the AcmeWeb project node, and select Add | Add Existing Item. Set the file type filter to *.*, and then double-click the **AcmeWeb.aspx** file.

```
<!-- AcmeWeb.aspx -->

<%@ Assembly Name="AcmeWeb" %>
<%@ Page Inherits=AcmeWeb.WebForm1 %>
<HTML>
  <HEAD>
  </HEAD>
<BODY>
<form id="Form1" method="post" runat="server">
<asp:Label id=Label1 style="Z-INDEX: 101; LEFT: 52px;
POSITION: absolute; TOP: 84px" runat="server">City</asp:Label>
<asp:Label id=Label2 style="Z-INDEX: 102; LEFT: 55px;
POSITION: absolute; TOP: 135px" runat="server">Hotel</
asp:Label>
<asp:DropDownList id=listCities style="Z-INDEX: 103; LEFT:
 134px; POSITION: absolute; TOP: 80px" runat="server"
Width="120px" Height="22px" AutoPostBack="True"></asp:Drop-
DownList>
<asp:DropDownList id-listHotels style="Z-INDEX: 104; LEFT:
 134px; POSITION: absolute; TOP: 128px" runat="server"
Width="120px" Height="22px"></asp:DropDownList>
</form>
</BODY>
</HTML>
```

BUILDING ACMEWEB

To build the project, you must copy the **Hotel.dll** to the **Demos\AcmeWeb** directory, since the project has a **#using** directive for this assembly. Once you have copied this file from the **CaseStudy\AcmeWeb** directory, you can perform a build to produce the **AcmeWeb.dll**.

VIEWING ACMEWEB

Before you can view AcmeWeb in your browser, you must first copy the **AcmeWeb.dll** to a subdirectory named *bin* under the **\Demos\AcmeWeb** directory, just as was done in the **CaseStudy\AcmeWeb** directory.

1. Create a directory named *bin* in the **Demos\AcmeWeb** project directory.
2. Copy the **AcmeWeb.dll** file from **Demos\AcmeWeb\Debug** to **Demos\AcmeWeb\bin**.
3. Also, copy the **Hotel.dll** to the **Demos\AcmeWeb\bin** directory.

But, even after copying **AcmeWeb.dll** to the **bin** directory, if you can still not view **http://localhost/NetCpp/Demos/AcmeWeb/AcmeWeb.aspx** in your browser. The virtual directory for this Web page must be configured as an application for IIS. To do this, do the following:

4. Select Start | Programs | Administrative Tools | Internet Server Manager.
5. Open the tree down to **NetCpp\Demos\AcmeWeb** node under Default Web Site.
6. Right-click **NetCpp\Demos\AcmeWeb** and select Properties from the context menu.
7. In the dialog shown in Figure 10–20, click the Create button
8. The result should appear is shown in Figure 10–21
9. Click OK

Once you have done this, you can view **http://localhost/NetCpp/CaseStudy/AcmeWeb/AcmeWeb.aspx**, as shown in Figure 10–22. You can view this directly in your browser or by running it within Visual Studio, which will bring up Internet Explorer to access the application over HTTP. When you drop down the list of cities, you will indeed see the cities returned by the **HotelBroker** component.

DEBUGGING ACMEWEB

In order debug the AcmeWeb project, you will need to provide a configuration file that specifies debug mode, and you will need to enable debugging for the project, as shown in Figure 10–23. To do this, follow these steps:

1. Copy the **Web.config** file provided in the **CaseStudy\AcmeWeb** directory to the **Demos\AcmeWeb** directory. This configuration file

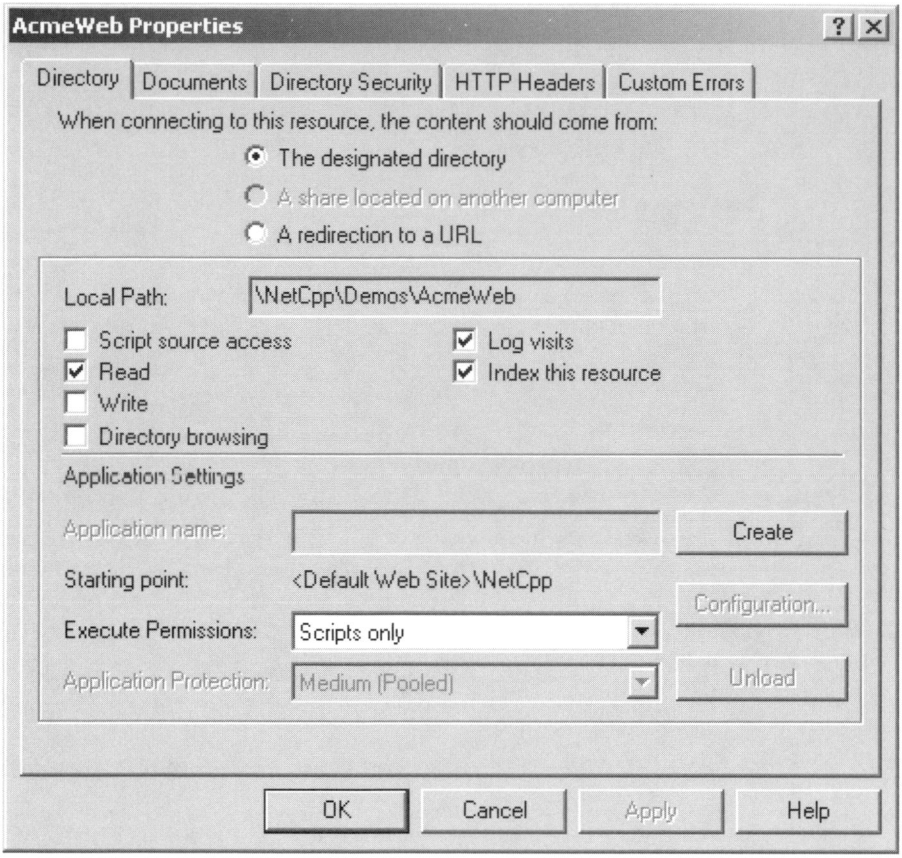

Figure 10–20   *Creating an Application Name for AcmeWeb.*

has several features specified in it, but the significant aspect relating to debugging is the tag that specifies <compilation debug="true"/>.

2. Right-click on the AcmeWeb project in the Solution Explorer window and select Properties.
3. Click on the Debugging node under the Configuration Properties.
4. Set the Command to **aspnet_wp.exe.**
5. Select Yes for Attach.
6. Set HTTP URL to: **http://localhost/NetCpp/Demos/AcmeWeb/ AcmeWeb.aspx**.

You can then run the solution in the debugger by selecting Debug | Start. Figures 10–24 and 10–25 show the debugger stopped at break points in **Global.asax.h** and **WebForm1.aspx.h** respectively.

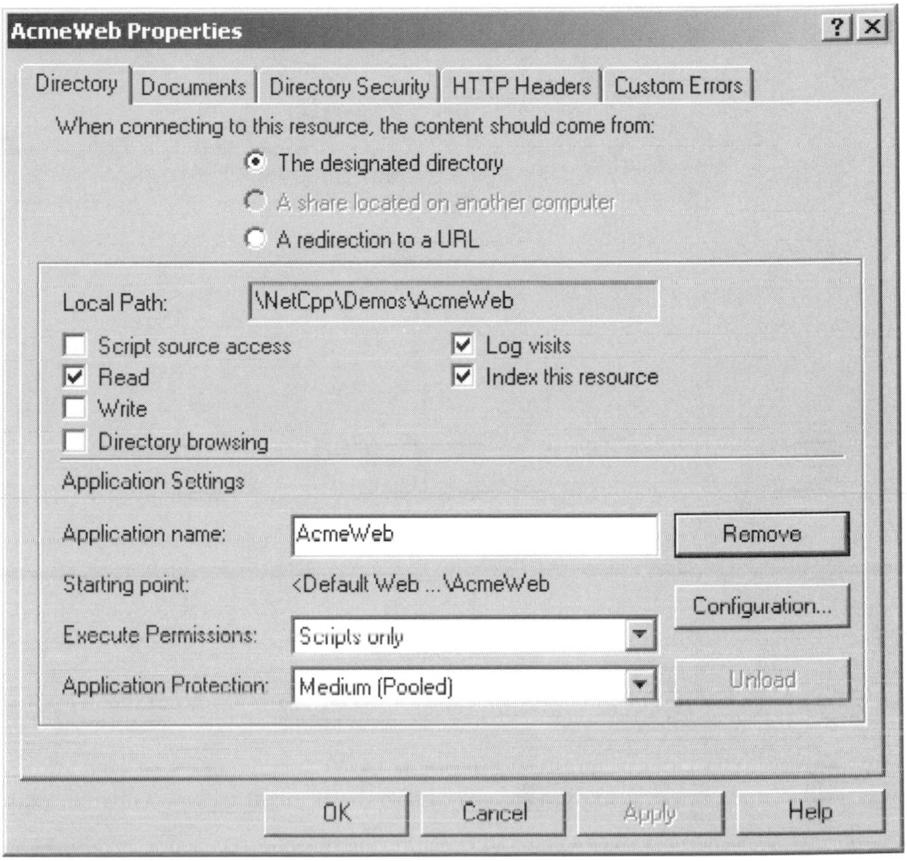

Figure 10–21   *Completed Creation of an Application Name for AcmeWeb.*

ASP.NET Applications

An ASP.NET application consists of all the Web pages and code files that can be invoked from a virtual directory and its subdirectories on a Web server. Besides **.aspx** files and code-behind files such as we have already examined, an application can also have a **global.asax** file and a configuration file **config.web**. In this section we will examine the features of ASP.NET applications. We will then investigate the mechanisms for working with application state and session state and for configuring Web applications.

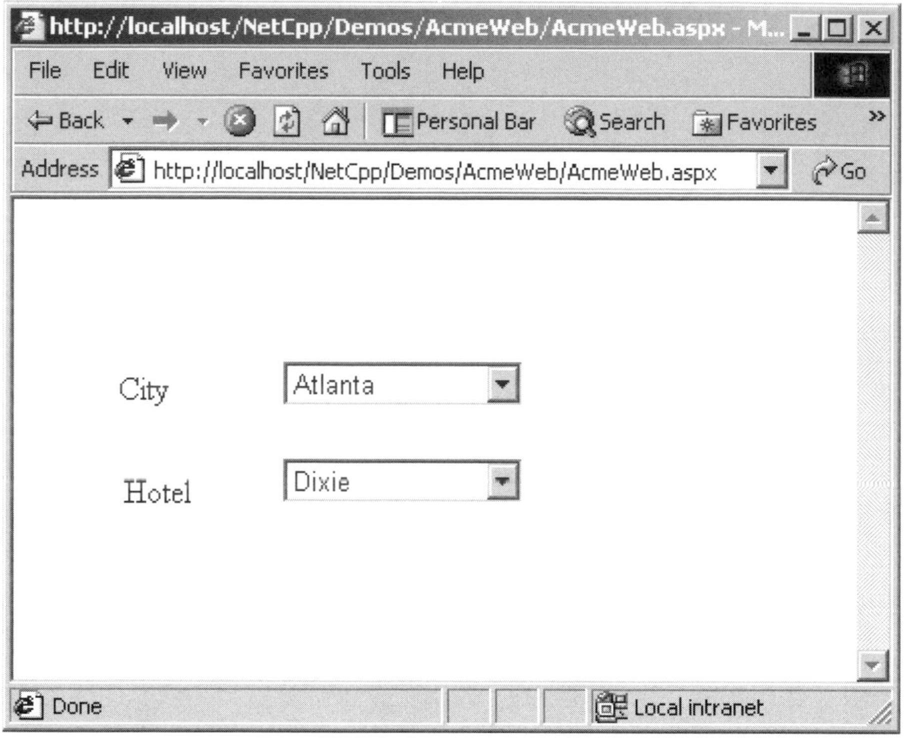

Figure 10–22   *Running the Web page to show information about cities.*

Sessions

To appreciate the Web application support provided by ASP.NET, we need to understand the concept of a Web *session*. HTTP is a stateless protocol. This means that there is no direct way for a Web browser to know whether a sequence of requests is from the same client or from different clients. A Web server such as IIS can provide a mechanism to classify requests coming from a single client into a logical session. ASP.NET makes it very easy to work with sessions.

Global.asax

An ASP.NET application can optionally contain a file **Global.asax**, which contains code for responding to application-level events raised by ASP.NET. This file resides in the root directory of the application. If you do not have a **Global.asax** file in your application, ASP.NET will assume you have not defined any handlers for application-level events.

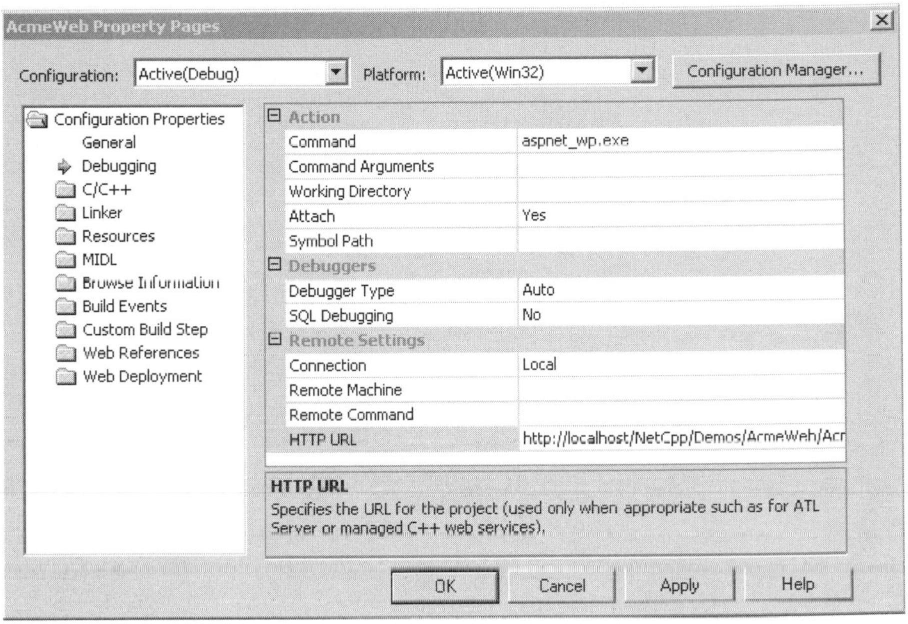

Figure 10–23 *Enabling debugging.*

```
//Global.asax.h

#using <.\Hotel.dll>
#using <System.dll>
#using <System.Web.dll>
using namespace System;
using namespace OI::NetCpp::Acme;

namespace AcmeWeb
{
public __gc class Global : public System::Web::HttpApplication
   {
   public:
      static HotelBroker *hotelBroker;
   protected:
      void Application_Start(
         Object *sender, EventArgs *e)
      {
         hotelBroker = new HotelBroker;
      }
      void Session_Start(
         Object *sender, EventArgs *e)
      {
      }
```

Figure 10–24 | Break point hit in ***Global.asax.h.***

```
namespace AcmeWeb
{
    public __gc class WebForm1 : public System::Web::UI::Page
    {
    protected:
        System::Web::UI::WebControls::Label *Label1;
        System::Web::UI::WebControls::Label *Label2;
        System::Web::UI::WebControls::DropDownList
            *listCities;
        System::Web::UI::WebControls::DropDownList
            *listHotels;
    private:
        static HotelBroker *hotelBroker;
    public:
        WebForm1()
        {
            Page::Init += new System::EventHandler(
                this, Page_Init);
        }
    private:
        void Page_Load(Object *sender, System::EventArgs *e)
        {
            if (!IsPostBack)
            {
                hotelBroker = Global::hotelBroker;
                ArrayList *cities = hotelBroker->GetCities();
                listCities->DataSource = cities;
```

Figure 10–25   *Break point hit in* **WebForm1.aspx.h.**

The most common application-level events are shown in this code. The typical life cycle of a Web application would consist of these events.

- **Application_Start** is raised only once during an application's lifetime, on the first instance of **HttpApplication**. An application starts the first time it is run by IIS for the first user. In your event handler you can initialize state that is shared by the entire application.
- **Session_Start** is raised at the start of each session. Here you can initialize session variables.
- **Application_BeginRequest** is raised at the start of an individual request. Normally, you can do your request processing in the **Page** class.
- **Application_EndRequest** is raised at the end of a request.
- **Session_End** is raised at the end of each session. Normally, you do not need to do cleanup of data initialized in **Session_Start**, because garbage collection will take care of normal cleanup for you. However, if you have opened an expensive resource, such as a database connection, you may wish to call the **Dispose** method here.
- **Application_End** is raised at the very end of an application's lifetime, when the last instance of **HttpApplication** is torn down.

State in ASP.NET Applications

Preserving state across HTTP requests is a major problem in Web programming, and ASP.NET provides several facilities that are convenient to use. There are two main types of state to be preserved.

- **Application state** is global information that is shared across all users of a Web application.
- **Session state** is used to store data for a particular user across multiple requests to a Web application.

Static Data Members

Static data members of a class are shared across all instances of a class. Hence, static data members can be used to hold application state.

Application Object

You can store global application information in the built-in **Application** object, an instance of the class **HttpApplicationState**. You can conveniently access this object through the **Application** property of the **Page** class. The **HttpApplicationState** class provides a key-value dictionary that you can use for storing both objects and scalar values.

Session Object

You can store session information for individual users in the built-in **Session** object, an instance of the class **HttpSessionState**. You can conveniently access this object through the **Session** property of the **Page** class. The **HttpSessionState** class provides a key value dictionary that you can use for storing both objects and scalar values in exactly the same manner employed by **HttpApplicationState**.

There are some interesting issues in the implementation of session variables.

- Typically, cookies are used to identify which requests belong to a particular session. What if the browser does not support cookies, or the user has disabled cookies?
- There is overhead in maintaining session state for many users. Will session state "expire" after a certain time period?
- A common scenario in high performance Web sites is to use a server farm. How can your application access its data if a second request for a page is serviced on a different machine from which the first request was serviced?

SESSION STATE AND COOKIES

Although by default ASP.NET cookies are used to identify which requests belong to a particular session, it is easy to configure ASP.NET to run cookie-less. In this mode the Session ID, normally stored within a cookie, is instead embedded within the URL. We will discuss cookie-less configuration in the next section.

SESSION STATE TIMEOUT

By default, session state times out after 20 minutes. This means if a given user is idle for that period of time, the session is torn down and a request from the client will now be treated as a request from a new user, and a new session will be created. Again, it is easy to configure the timeout period, as we will discuss in the section "ASP.NET Configuration."

SESSION STATE STORE

ASP.NET cleanly solves the Web farm problem, and many other issues, through a session-state model that separates storage from the application's use of the stored information. Thus, different storage scenarios can be implemented without affecting application code. The .NET state server does not maintain "live" objects across requests. Instead, at the end of each Web request, all objects in the session collection are serialized to the session state store. When the same client returns to the page, the session objects are deserialized.

By default, the session-state store is an in-memory cache. It can be configured to be memory on a specific machine or to be stored in an SQL Server database. In these cases the data is not tied to a specific server, and so session data can be safely used with Web farms.

ASP.NET Configuration

In our discussion of session state we have seen a number of cases where it is desirable to be able to configure ASP.NET. There are two types of configurations:

- **Server configuration** specifies default settings that apply to all ASP.NET applications.
- **Application configuration** specifies settings specific to a particular ASP.NET application.

Configuration Files

Configuration is specified in files with an XML format that is easy to read and to modify.

SERVER CONFIGURATION FILE

The configuration file is **machine.config**. This file is located within a version-specific folder under **\WINNT\Microsoft..NET\Framework**. Because there are separate files for each version of .NET, it is perfectly possible to run different versions of ASP.NET side-by-side. Thus, if you have working Web applications running under one version of .NET, you can continue to run them while you develop new applications using a later version.

APPLICATION CONFIGURATION FILES

Optionally, you may provide a file **web.config** at the root of the virtual directory for a Web application. If the file is absent, the default configuration settings in **machine.config** will be used. If the file is present, any settings in **web.config** will override the default settings.

CONFIGURATION FILE FORMAT

Both **machine.config** and **web.config** files have the same XML-based format. There are sections that group related configuration items together and individual items within the sections. The easiest way to get a feel both for the format of **web.config** and for some of the important settings you may wish to adjust, just look at the **web.config** file that is created by Visual Studio when you create a new ASP.NET Web Application project.[3]

```
<?xml version="1.0" encoding="utf-8" ?>
<configuration>

  <system.web>

    <!--  CUSTOM ERROR MESSAGES
          Set mode="on" or "remoteonly" to enable custom
          error messages, "off" to disable. Add
          <error> tags for each of the errors you want to
          handle.
    -->
    <customErrors
    mode="Off"
    />

    <!--  AUTHENTICATION
          This section sets the authentication policies of
          the application. Possible modes are "Windows",
```

---

[3] As discussed, the current Visual Studio can only create ASP.NET Web applications in C# and VB.NET, not in C++.

```
        "Forms", "Passport" and "None"
    -->
    <authentication mode="None" />

    ...

</system.web>
</configuration>
```

More About ASP.NET

Although you can implement ASP.NET Web applications using C++, as we have seen, C++ is not an optimal language for coding the elements of a Web application involving visual interaction. The languages C# and VB.NET are much more suitable for this purpose. To learn more about ASP.NET you can consult the following books in *The Integrated .NET Series* from Object Innovations and Prentice Hall PTR:

- Application Development Using C# and .NET
- Application Development Using Visual Basic and .NET
- Fundamentals of Web Applications Using .NET and XML

Where C++ shines is in creating efficient backend components that can be called from Web pages. Also, there is a technology called ATL Server, which can be used to create high-performance Web applications using C++. Chapter 12 provides an introduction to this interesting technology.

Summary

ASP.NET is a unified Web development platform that greatly simplifies the implementation of sophisticated Web applications. In this chapter we introduced the fundamentals of ASP.NET and covered Web Forms, which can be used to develop interactive Web sites. This high-level programming model rests on a lower level request/response programming model that is common to earlier approaches to Web programming and is still accessible to the ASP.NET programmer.

The Visual Studio.NET development environment includes a Form Designer for C# and VB.NET, but unfortunately, it does not currently support C++. A Form Designer makes it very easy to visually layout Web forms, and with a click you can add event handlers. However, with C++, you must do all this with handwritten code.

In the next chapter we cover Web Services, which enable the development of collaborative Web applications that span heterogeneous systems.

ELEVEN

Web Services

*D*istributing functionality and data beyond the enterprise in which it was developed is the next step in component technology. Developers can integrate into their applications a much more extensive set of services than they could ever hope to develop on their own. Our Acme Reservation System case study is a simple example. The Acme Travel Agency, by using the reservation systems of the airlines and hotels, can provide a wider range of services to their clients.

One vendor will not be able to supply the necessary distributed technology infrastructure. At the very minimum, the worlds of Java, .NET, mobile computers, and legacy systems will continue. Fortunately, TCP/IP and HTTP have established themselves as industry-standard networking protocols and can be the basis for any attempt to interconnect heterogeneous systems. HTTP is a text-based protocol, so using the industry-standard XML to describe the interactions of these systems makes sense. Web Services use XML- and HTTP-based protocols to provide an industry standard to allow diverse systems to interconnect.

Web Services is the second part of the .NET distributed computing story. If all the applications and services that need to interconnect are based on the Common Language Runtime, .NET remoting can be used. The advantage of .NET remoting is that you can remote any .NET data structure through the remoting serialization. Environments that do not run .NET, however, cannot handle the full range of .NET data types. Hence, Web Services transmit a much more limited set of data structures than can be expressed in the XML-based protocols that Web Services use today. The versions of the SOAP protocol used by Web Services and by .NET remoting have different programming models. The latter offers full CLR fidelity. The former is constrained by interoperability standards.

Besides the ability of heterogeneous systems to interconnect, Web Services allow business partners to share information or integrate with legacy systems without having to write specialized interconnection applications. Even within a single enterprise, you will be able to integrate information from internal and external sources. If Web Services are to be more than just distributed application development, however, the necessary financial, reliability, security, and legal infrastructures have to be developed.

Protocols

Behind the Web Services technology are several protocols: XML, XML Namespaces, XML Schema, SOAP, and WSDL. Some of these are formal W3C industry standards. Some, like WSDL, are just gaining widespread use without yet being codified in a standard.

XML

XML is a W3C industry standard[1] that provides a way to structure documents to provide relationships between the basic *elements* of the document. Elements can also have descriptive information called *attributes*. Elements can be composed of other elements so they can have complex structure. Since such documents can be represented as text,[2] XML can provide a platform-neutral way to represent data that is transmitted over a network. In particular, as text it can go safely out through a firewall because HTTP port 80 will invariably be open. Here is an example of an XML document that describes a CustomerList composed of several customers.

```
<CustomerList>
  <Customer>
    <FirstName>John</FirstName>
    <LastName>Smith</LastName>
    <EmailAddress>smith@smith.org</EmailAddress>
  </Customer>
```

---

[1] Technically, W3C final documents are called recommendations. However, we will refer to them as standards or specifications. W3C documents that have not reached recommendation status are referred to by their W3C names: proposed recommendations, candidate recommendations, last-call working drafts, working drafts, and notes.

[2] But does not have to be text. You can build programs using the abstractions defined in the W3C proposed recommendation Information Set. Using these abstractions, such as *document, namespace, element, character,* and *attribute,* to represent the hierarchy of an XML document, you are independent of the particular format in which the XML is stored. For example, mobile solutions will probably use a more efficient binary format for XML encoding rather than text. The XML Schema Recommendation is written based on the Infoset, not the angle bracket syntax. The Information Set assumes the existence of XML namespaces.

```
<Customer>
  <FirstName>Sally</FirstName>
  <LastName>Rutherford</LastName>
  <EmailAddress>srutherford@cando.com</EmailAddress>
</Customer>
</CustomerList>
```

XML Namespaces

A set of elements and attributes in an XML document can be referred to as a vocabulary. This is particularly useful if this vocabulary can model information that might be reused. For example, we could have vocabularies for financial or chemical information. Namespaces not only allow these vocabularies to be uniquely named in order to prevent conflicts, but allow these vocabularies to be reused in many applications.

The following example XML document uses a namespace attribute to uniquely identify the elements <FirstName>, <LastName>, and <EmailAddress> from any other definitions that might use the same tag names with a different meaning or context. The example also shows that abbreviations can be used with namespaces. This is very convenient if multiple namespaces are used in a document.

```
<CustomerList xmlns:cl=
        "urn:uuid 28833F1C-CBE4-4042-9B35-BF641DFB35DC">
  <cl:FirstName>John</cl:FirstName>
  <cl:LastName>Smith</cl:LastName>
  <cl:EmailAddress>smith@smith.org</cl:EmailAddress>
</CustomerList>
```

A Uniform Resource Identifier (URI) is used to identify a particular XML namespace. A URI can either be a Uniform Resource Locator (URL) or a Uniform Resource Name (URN). Both represent a unique name. URLs are the familiar Web site addresses that are unique because URLs are given out by a central naming authority. A URN is just a unique string. For example, you could use a URN defined by a GUID,[3] such as **urn:uuid:28833F1C-CBE4-4042-9B35-BF641DFB35DC.**[4] A URI used for a namespace does not have to resolve to any location on the Web.

---

[3] A GUID, or Globally Unique Identifier, is a 128-bit identifier that is guaranteed to be unique. GUIDs are widely used in COM. You can generate your own GUIDs using the tool **guidgen.exe** (Windows UI) or **uuidgen.exe** (command-line UI). These tools are in the directory ...\Microsoft Visual Studio.NET\Common7\Tools.

[4] GUIDs are used in the examples for simplicity and to reinforce the idea that uniqueness, but not existence, is required for a namespace identifier. In real systems URL-based names are used whether or not the URLs actually exist.

XML Schema

XML with namespaces, however, does not assign any semantics to the data. The XML Schema Definition (XSD) specification defines a basic set of data types and the means to define new data types. In other words, an XML schema can assign meaning to the structure of a document. The schema itself is written in XML. The CustomerList document that was described previously could be described by the following schema:

```
<schema xmlns:xsd="http://www.w3.org/2001/XMLSchema"
        xmlns:cl="http://www.acme.com/CustomerList"
        targetNamespace="http://www.acme.com/CustomerList">
  <xsd:complexType name="Customer">
    <xsd:sequence>
      <xsd:element name="FirstName" type="xsd:string" />
      <xsd:element name="LastName" type="xsd:string" />
      <xsd:element name="EmailAddress" type="xsd:string"/>
    </xsd:sequence>
  </xsd:complexType>
</schema>
```

The **targetNamespace** element defines the name of the schema being defined. This particular string uses the XSD-defined element "string." Using XSD, we can restrict the range of values, specify how often particular instances occur, and provide attributes to the elements. The schema itself is written in XML. Both the document and its associated schema can be validated and managed as XML documents. The same document, interpreted by two different schemas, will have two different meanings.

SOAP

While XML schemas can define the types used by the data, you need a set of conventions to describe how the data and its associated type definitions are transmitted. SOAP, the Simple Object Access Protocol uses XML as a wire protocol to do just this.

While SOAP can use XML schema types to describe the transmitted types, SOAP was designed before the XML Schema specification was finished, so there are some divergences between the two. The reason for this divergence is that XML Schema describes a hierarchy or tree structure. SOAP wants to be able to represent objects, and objects can have far more complicated relationships than a hierarchy. Classes, for example, can have multiple parent classes. As we will discuss later, this has some implications for Web Services. The W3C is currently working on reconciling SOAP with XML Schema.

SOAP 1.1 can be used with several transport protocols, not just HTTP.

The use of SOAP for Web Services on Microsoft platforms is not unique to .NET. Microsoft has released the SOAP Toolkit that has allowed Windows-based platforms to develop Web Services. The support for SOAP, however, is built into .NET. The SOAP Toolkit does contain, however, the SOAP Trace Utility, which is useful for tracking raw and formatted SOAP messages.

WSDL

Objects contain both state and behavior. Schemas define the data. WSDL, the Web Services Description Language, define the methods and the data associated with a Web Service. As a simple example, we shall describe shortly how WSDL is not necessary for writing Web Services. It is important, however, if you want to be able to automatically generate classes that can call Web Services or do anything that requires automatic machine intervention with Web Services.[5] Otherwise, you would have to craft and send the SOAP messages by hand.

As you will see in the following example, the SOAP that is used to describe the Web Service's transport format is defined in the WSDL. WSDL is currently a W3C note.

Web Service Architecture

Besides handling ASP.NET, Microsoft's Internet Information Server (IIS) can handle Web Services, since they come in as HTTP requests. These requests are encoded in the URL or as XML. IIS then creates the required object to fulfill the Web Service request. IIS then calls the object's method that is associated with the request. Any returned values are converted to XML and returned to the client as a response using the HTTP protocol.

The Add Web Service Example

Code Example

To see how this works under Microsoft .NET, we provide a simple Web Service to illustrate this architecture and show how the associated protocols are used. This example is provided in the SimpleWebService directory. Our Web Service will simply add two numbers. To make things clear, we build the Web Service **Add** in the simplest possible way. This example is not created with the Managed C++ Web Service project template, which will be shown later. To keep everything as simple as possible, this first example is created with the

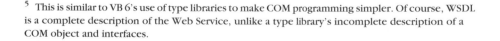

[5] This is similar to VB 6's use of type libraries to make COM programming simpler. Of course, WSDL is a complete description of the Web Service, unlike a type library's incomplete description of a COM object and interfaces.

Managed C++ Class Library project template. If you want to try running the **SimpleWebService** example, follow these steps:

1. Open the project **SimpleWebService\WebService\WebService. sln** in Visual Studio.NET. Build the solution.

2. Copy the resulting WebService.dll into SimpleWebService\WebService\bin. Actually, this has already been done for you, but you would normally have to do this yourself.

3. Right-click on the SimpleWebService\WebService directory in Windows Explorer and select Properties. Select the Web Sharing tab in the Property page, and share the folder using the alias SimpleWebService. Click OK to close the Property page.

4. Either view *http://localhost/SimpleWebService/Add.asmx* in your browser or run the program within Visual Studio.NET in the usual way. This project has been set up to automatically run IE when it is run.

By writing code in a file with the suffix **asmx** and placing it in a subdirectory or virtual subdirectory of the IIS root directory, we can have a simple Web Service.[6] IIS has the concept of virtual directories, so the actual directory does not have to physically be under the IIS root directory. The easiest way to do this is to enable WebSharing on the file folder. To do this, select the folder in the NT Explorer, right-click on the folder, and select Sharing on the context menu. Use the Web Sharing tab to make the directory a virtual directory for IIS.

The file **Add.asmx** defines a reference to the class named **Test**, which implements the service. We put this **.asmx** file in the directory **SimpleWebService**.

    <%@ WebService Class=Test %>

The file **WebService.h** implements the class **Test**, inheriting from the **WebService** class in the namespace **System::Web::Services**. A method of that class can be used as a Web Service method if the attribute **WebMethod** is applied to it, as shown on the **Add** method in **WebService.h**.

```
// WebService.h

#using <mscorlib.dll>
#using <System.dll>
#using <System.Web.dll>
#using <System.EnterpriseServices.dll>
#using <System.Web.Services.dll>
using namespace System;
using namespace System::Web;
```

---

[6] By default, this directory is \inetpub\wwwroot.

```
using namespace System::Web::Services;

public __gc class Test : public WebService
{
public:
    [WebMethod]
    long Add(long x, long y)
    {
        return x + y;
    }
};
```

This file is found in the **WebService** subdirectory of the **SimpleWebService** directory for this chapter. You should make **WebService** a virtual directory with the alias **SimpleWebService**.[7] Then, after building the Add service, create a **bin** directory under the virtual directory **WebService**, and copy the **WebService.dll** assembly into it so that it can be automatically found by IIS.

VIEWING THE ADD WEB SERVICE WITH A BROWSER

IE can be used as a simple client program that uses the HTTP GET protocol's URL encoding of a Web Service request. Figure 11-1 shows the result of viewing **http://localhost/SimpleWebService/Add.asmx** in IE.

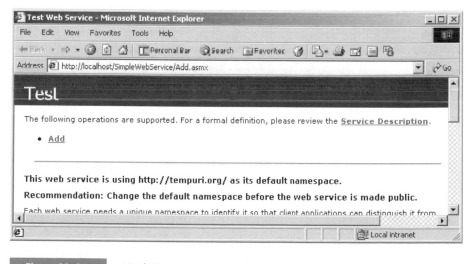

| Figure 11-1 | *Web Service request in Internet Explorer.* |

---

[7] As discussed in Chapter 10, the easiest way to create a virtual directory is through Windows Explorer. Right-click over the directory and choose Properties. From the Web Sharing tab, you can share the folder and add an alias.

Debugging the Add Web Service

Just as you were able to debug the ASP.NET examples in the previous chapter, you can also debug Web Service projects in much the same way. You must first right-click on the project in the Solution Explorer window, and select properties. Then, under Configuration Properties in the Project Property Page, select Debugging and make the following changes:[8]

- Set Command to **aspnet_wp.exe**.
- Set Attach to **Yes**.
- Set HTTP URL to **http://localhost/SimpleWebService/Add.asmx**.

Also, you need to provide a file named **web.config** that enables debugging, and place it in the same directory as the service. The following is an example of such as configuration file.

```
<?xml version="1.0" encoding="utf-8" ?>
<configuration>
  <system.web>
    <compilation debug="true"/>
  </system.web>
</configuration>
```

Once you have done this, you can debug the Web Service project using the Visual Studio.NET debugger in the normal manner. Remember to copy the Web Service DLL from the project directory to the Web service virtual directory each time you change and rebuild the project, or IIS will not be using the same version that you are attempting to debug.

A Client for the Add Web Service

Ultimately, you will want to create client programs that use the Web service in a distributed application. We will do that soon, but we will first look at using IE as a client to study the protocol used to communicate with the Web Service. To start doing this, visit **http://localhost/SimpleWebService/Add.asmx** in IE.

By clicking on the Add link, you will get a form that will enable you submit a request to the Add service. In addition, the form describes the various HTTP protocols that can be used for submitting the request. For our purposes, two of the protocols are worth mentioning: HTTP GET and SOAP.

The HTTP GET protocol is worth exploring because the form that appears in IE uses it. The protocol has boldfaced placeholders for data that has to be entered:

```
GET /SimpleWebService/Add.asmx/Add?x=string&y=string  HTTP/1.1 1
...
```

---

[8] You may select an alternative client program of your own choosing.

The data entered into the form is added to the URL in the standard way any HTTP GET request is made. Data is returned as

```
HTTP/1.1 200 OK
Content-Type: text/xml; charset=utf-8
Content-Length: length

<?xml version="1.0" encoding="utf-8"?>
<int xmlns="http://tempuri.org/">int</int>
```

Figure 11–2 shows values entered into the form. By pressing the Invoke button, you call the Web service.

An IE window will appear with the part of the HTTP response data generated by the Web service that contains the actual returned value:

```
<?xml version="1.0" encoding="utf-8" ?>
<int xmlns="http://tempuri.org/">9</int>
```

This is exactly the format that appeared in the description of the protocol with the answer (9) substituted for the placeholder. HTTP GET, however, can handle only simple types

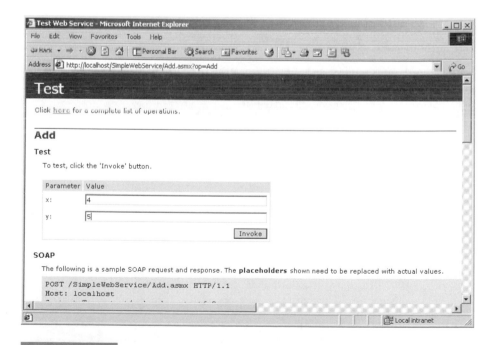

Figure 11–2   *Values entered on the Internet Explorer form.*

The more interesting protocol is SOAP. The SOAP HTTP POST request and response are both described with placeholders for information that has to be provided in the actual call. Those placeholders are in boldface type.

First, let us look at the SOAP HTTP POST request. The first part is a set of HTTP headers. The XML for the SOAP protocol is in the data (entity-body) section of the HTTP request, which is always separated from the headers by a blank line. The content-length header is the length of the data that is dependent on the size of the parameters in the data section.

The method header identifies the file to which the request is directed. It could also name an object that is to handle the request (endpoint). The SOAP-Action header indicates the name of the namespace qualified method to be invoked for the Web Service.[9]

SOAP uses XML to specify the parameters of the method.[10] The SOAP body contains the parameters for the method call. In a real method call, the **int** placeholders would be replaced by the actual parameters to be passed to the Web Service method.

```
POST /SimpleWebService/Add.asmx HTTP/1.1
Host: localhost
Content-Type: text/xml; charset=utf-8
Content-Length: length
SOAPAction: "http://tempuri.org/Add"

<?xml version="1.0" encoding="utf-8"?>
<soap:Envelope xmlns:xsi="http://www.w3.org/2001/XMLSchema-
instance" xmlns:xsd="http://www.w3.org/2001/XMLSchema"
xmlns:soap="http://schemas.xmlsoap.org/soap/envelope/">
  <soap:Body>
    <Add xmlns="http://tempuri.org/">
      <x>int</x>
      <y>int</y>
    </Add>
  </soap:Body>
</soap:Envelope>
```

Next, the SOAP HTTP response is described. The **int** placeholder will be replaced by the actual value returned.

```
HTTP/1.1 200 OK
```

---

[9] For those with a COM background, think of the namespace for the method as equivalent to the GUID that identifies an interface (IID).

[10] The parallel to IDL is WSDL, which we will discuss shortly. SOAP is analogous to NDR, the wire format used for DCOM calls. All these parallels to COM appear in Don Box's March 2000 MSDN article "A Young Person's Guide to the Simple Object Access Protocol."

```
Content-Type: text/xml; charset=utf-8
Content-Length: length

<?xml version="1.0" encoding="utf-8"?>
<soap:Envelope xmlns:xsi="http://www.w3.org/2001/XMLSchema-
instance" xmlns:xsd="http://www.w3.org/2001/XMLSchema"
xmlns:soap="http://schemas.xmlsoap.org/soap/envelope/">
  <soap:Body>
    <AddResponse xmlns="http://tempuri.org/">
      <AddResult>int</AddResult>
    </AddResponse>
  </soap:Body>
</soap:Envelope>
```

WSDL

SOAP does not describe the Web Service interface. While you could encode the SOAP yourself, it would be nice to be able to generate proxy classes for the client to use. Otherwise, you would have to understand all the details of the SOAP specification and how to parse the returned XML.

WSDL provides a description of the Web Service interface. We will now look at the WSDL description for our **SimpleWebService**, which has one method, **Add**. We will ignore the WSDL for invocations of the Web Service that do not use SOAP. You can view the WSDL for the **SimpleWebService** by viewing the following URL in your browser: **http://localhost/SimpleWeb-Service/Add.asmx?WSDL**. The <types> section defines the types:

* **Add** is used when SOAP invokes the Web Service.
* **AddResponse** is used when the SOAP Web Service invocation returns.

Add has two elements; each occurs exactly once. Both are defined with the XSD type long and have the names x and y. The return parameter, whose name is **AddResponse**, has one element, **AddResult**, which occurs once and is defined with the XSD type long. Note how these types were used in the SOAP definitions we looked at previously.

```
...
<types>
...
  <s:element name="Add">
    <s:complexType>
      <s:sequence>
        <s:element minOccurs="1" maxOccurs="1"
          name="x" type="s:int" />
        <s:element minOccurs="1" maxOccurs="1"
```

```
          name="y" type="s:int" />
      </s:sequence>
    </s:complexType>
  </s:element>
  <s:element name="AddResponse">
    <s:complexType>
      <s:sequence>
        <s:element minOccurs="1" maxOccurs="1"
          name="AddResult" type="s:int" />
      </s:sequence>
    </s:complexType>
  </s:element>
  ...
</types>
```

The <message> section relates the types to their use as parameters.

```
<message name="AddSoapIn">
  <part name="parameters" element="s0:Add" />
</message>
<message name="AddSoapOut">
  <part name="parameters" element="s0:AddResponse" />
</message>
...
```

The <portType> section relates the Web service to the individual Web methods defined by the <operation> elements. If there had been more Web methods in the Web Service, there would have been more operation elements associated with the port type.[11] Each method's input and output operations are associated with the appropriate message defined previously.

```
<portType name="TestSoap">
  <operation name="Add">
    <input message="s0:AddSoapIn" />
    <output message="s0:AddSoapOut" />
  </operation>
</portType>
...
```

The <binding> section defines the encodings and protocols to be used for each operation.
```
<binding name="TestSoap" type="s0:TestSoap">
```

---

[11] For those of you keeping score, this is analogous to a COM interface.

```
<soap:binding
        transport="http://schemas.xmlsoap.org/soap/http"
        style="document" />
<operation name="Add">
  <soap:operation soapAction="http://tempuri.org/Add"
      style="document" />
  <input>
    <soap:body use="literal" />
  </input>
  <output>
    <soap:body use="literal" />
  </output>
</operation>
</binding>
...
```

The <service> section relates the Web Service to its port and how it is invoked.

```
<service name="Test">
  <port name="TestSoap" binding-"s0:TestSoap">
    <soap:address location=
        "http://localhost/SimpleWebService/Add.asmx" />
  </port>
...
</service>
...
```

Proxy Classes

The **Wsdl.exe** tool can be used read the WSDL description and generate a proxy class that will make the SOAP calls for you. This tool generates C# as its default language,[12] and C++ is not currently supported. Therefore, this example will proceed using a C#-generated proxy. SOAP is the default protocol for **Wsdl.exe** tool.[13] The following command will generate a C# SOAP proxy class file with the name **addproxy.cs**:

```
wsdl /out:addproxy.cs
        http://localhost/SimpleWebService/Add.asmx?WSDL
```

---

[12] You can choose from CS, VB, JS, or if available, you can specify a class implementing **System::CodeDom::Compiler::CodeDomProvider** for a desired language.
[13] Or you can also choose HttpGet, HttpPost, or custom protocol as specified in a configuration file.

The generated proxy source code in **addproxy.cs** defines a constructor and three methods. The constructor sets the URL that this Web Service uses. One of the methods represents a synchronous, blocking call on the Web Service. The other two methods correspond the asynchronous design pattern discussed in Chapter 8. If you want to call the Web Service asynchronously, you can use the BeginXXX and the EndXXX methods associated with the proxy.[14] The proxy class has the same name as the **WebService** class.

The **Invoke** method of the **SoapHttpClientProtocol** class will make the HTTP request and process the HTTP response associated with the transmitted and received SOAP packets. This example is found in the **SimpleAdd-Client** subdirectory under the **SimpleWebService** directory.

```
...
public class Test :
    System.Web.Services.Protocols.SoapHttpClientProtocol
{
    ...
    public Test()
    {
      this.Url ="http://localhost/SimpleWebService/Add.asmx";
    }


    ...
    public int Add(int x, int y)
    {
       object[] results = this.Invoke("Add",
                                      new object[] {x, y});
       return ((int)(results[0]));
    }
    ...
    public System.IAsyncResult BeginAdd(int x, int y,
       System.AsyncCallback callback, object asyncState)
    {
       return this.BeginInvoke("Add",
       new object[] {x, y}, callback, asyncState);
    }


    ...
    public int EndAdd(System.IAsyncResult asyncResult)
    {
       object[] results = this.EndInvoke(asyncResult);
```

---

[14] Of course, in this particular case, XXX = Add.

```
    return ((int)(results[0]));
    }
}
```

Earlier, we saw how to access the Web Service using a browser. That is useful for testing purposes, but you will generally want to access the service from a client program. You can write a client program to use the generated proxy classes to issue a Web Service request. The following client program, in **Main.cs** under the **SimpleWebService\SimpleAddClient** directory, is written for convenience in C# only because the proxy generated above was C# code. When you run this client program, the Web Service calculates 1 plus 2, and the returned value 3 is displayed in the client console window.

```
public class AddClient
{
    public static void Main(string[] args)
    {
    Test z = new Test();
       long f = z.Add(1, 2);
    Console.WriteLine(f);
       return;
    }
}
```

You cannot mix C++ and C# in the same module. However, if you want to write the equivalent client code in C++, you could compile it into an executable assembly. Then you could compile the generated C# proxy code into a separate DLL assembly. The C++ client code can then use the C# proxy code to access the Web service. We will do this later in the **Arithmetic** example.

Web Service Client with Raw SOAP and HTTP

To show you what the **SoapHttpClientProtocol** class does, the final client program for this set of examples uses sockets to send both the HTTP headers and the SOAP data directly and to receive the response from the Web service. This example is in the **RawAddClient** subdirectory under the **SimpleWebService** directory.

The main routine first reads in a file named **SoapAdd.txt**, which has the SOAP headers for the service to be called. It returns the length of the content, which will have to be placed in one of the HTTP POST headers.

```
    long contentLength = 0;
    StringBuilder *contentData =
    BuildContent(
```

```
      "SoapAdd.txt", &contentLength);
StringBuilder *requestHeader =
   BuildHeader(contentLength);
```

It then connects to the server, sends the data, and receives the response, which it writes out to the console.

```
IPEndPoint *endPoint =
   new IPEndPoint(
      dynamic_cast<IPAddress *>
         (Dns::Resolve(httpServer)->AddressList->
            get_Item(0)),
      httpPort);
Socket *sock =
   new Socket(
      AddressFamily::InterNetwork,
      SocketType::Stream,
      ProtocolType::Tcp);

sock->Connect(endPoint);
...
sock->Send(
   header, header->Length, SocketFlags::None);
sock->Send(
   content, content->Length, SocketFlags::None);
...
bytes = sock->Receive(
   receivedData,
   receivedData->Length,
   SocketFlags::None);
Console::WriteLine(
   ASCII->GetString(receivedData, 0, bytes));

sock->Close();
...
```

The routine **BuildHeader** just builds a standard HTTP POST request with the addition of the SOAPAction header.

```
StringBuilder *sb = new StringBuilder(1024);

sb->Append(
   "POST /SimpleWebService/Add.asmx HTTP/1.1\r\n");
sb->Append("Host: localhost\r\n");
sb->Append(
```

```
   "Content-Type: text/xml; charset=utf-8\r\n");

String *line =
   String::Format("Content-Length: {0}\r\n",
      contentLength.ToString());
sb->Append(line);
sb->Append(
   "SOAPAction: \"http://tempuri.org/Add\"\r\n");

sb->Append("\r\n");;
```
. . .

BuildContent just reads a file to a buffer and calculates the size of the buffer in bytes.

```
*contentLength = 0;

String *line;
while ((line = fileStream->ReadLine()) != 0)
{
   sb->Append(line);
   sb->Append("\r\n");

   *contentLength += line->Length + 2;
}
fileStream->Close();
```

Based on our previous discussion, the SOAP file **SoapAdd.txt** looks like we would expect it to look. The input parameters 9 and 3 appear as the WSDL would dictate.

```
<?xml version="1.0" encoding="utf-8"?>
<soap:Envelope
   xmlns:xsi="http://www.w3.org/2001/XMLSchema-instance"
   xmlns:xsd="http://www.w3.org/2001/XMLSchema"
   xmlns:soap="http://schemas.xmlsoap.org/soap/envelope/">
 <soap:Body>
   <Add xmlns="http://tempuri.org/">
     <x>9</x>
     <y>3</y>
   </Add>
 </soap:Body>
</soap:Envelope>
```

The program first writes out the HTTP POST request with the standard HTTP headers and a special SOAPAction header, then the SOAP encoding of the request. Here is the output:

```
POST /SimpleWebService/Add.asmx HTTP/1.1
Host: localhost
Content-Type: text/xml; charset=utf-8
Content-Length: 355
SOAPAction: "http://tempuri.org/Add"


<?xml version="1.0" encoding="utf-8"?>
<soap:Envelope
   xmlns:xsi="http://www.w3.org/2001/XMLSchema-instance"
   xmlns:xsd="http://www.w3.org/2001/XMLSchema"
   xmlns:soap="http://schemas.xmlsoap.org/soap/envelope/">
  <soap:Body>
    <Add xmlns="http://tempuri.org/">
      <x>9</x>
      <y>3</y>
    </Add>
  </soap:Body>
</soap:Envelope>
```

The program then writes out the response. Again, the HTTP headers come first, then the SOAP encoding of the result, 12.

```
HTTP/1.1 200 OK
Server: Microsoft-IIS/5.0
Date: Tue, 30 Oct 2001 16:49:42 GMT
Cache-Control: private, max-age=0
Content-Type: text/xml; charset=utf-8
Content-Length: 358

<?xml version="1.0" encoding="utf-8"?>
<soap:Envelope
xmlns:soap="http://schemas.xmlsoap.org/soap/envelope/"
xmlns:xsi=
"http://www.w3.org/2001/XMLSchema-instance"
xmlns:xsd="http://www.w3.org/2001/XM
LSchema">
  <soap:Body>
    <AddResponse xmlns="http://tempuri.org/">
      <AddResult>12</AddResult>
```

```
      </AddResponse>
    </soap:Body>
</soap:Envelope>
```

SOAP Formatting Differences

Before we finish our basic examination of SOAP and WSDL, a more detailed look at the relationship of SOAP, WSDL, and the XML Schema specification is in order. As was mentioned earlier, the SOAP encoding used by .NET remoting differs from the SOAP encoding used by Web Services and the XML serializer.

To illustrate the differences between these two types of SOAP encoding, we will serialize the same objects in two different programs. Each program builds a circular list of two customer items, and one uses SOAP serialization encoding while the other uses Web Service SOAP encoding. The two programs are found in the **Formatter** and **WebService** directories under the **SOAP Differences** directory.

The first program, **Formatter**, creates a circular list and then serializes it to disk using the .NET SOAP formatter, creating a file named **cust.xml**. Although it is superfluous to do so, we derive the **Test** class from the **WebService** class to demonstrate that it is the way SOAP is serialized, not the basic idea of Web Services, that makes the difference. The following is taken from **Formatter.h**. Note that the **Serializable** attribute is applied to the **Customer** class.

```
[Serializable]
public __gc class Customer
{
public:
    String *name;
    long id;
    Customer *next;
};


public __gc class Test : public WebService
{
public:
    static void Main()
    {
        Test *test = new Test;
        Customer *list = test->GetList();
        FileStream *s =
            new FileStream("cust.xml", FileMode::Create);
        SoapFormatter *f = new SoapFormatter;
```

```
      f->Serialize(s, list);
      s->Close();
   }

   Customer *GetList()
   {
      Customer *cust1 = new Customer;
      cust1->name = "John Smith";
      cust1->id = 1;

      Customer *cust2 = new Customer;
      cust2->name = "Mary Smith";
      cust2->id = 2;

      cust2->next = cust1;
      cust1->next = cust2;

      return cust1;
   }
};
```

This program produces a file named **cust.xml** that contains the following SOAP encoding. Note the use of the **id** attribute to identify objects and fields, and the **href** attribute that serves as an object reference.

```
...
<SOAP-ENV:Body>
<a1:Customer id="ref-1">
<name id="ref-3">John Smith</name>
<id>1</id>
<next href="#ref-4"/>
</a1:Customer>
<a1:Customer id="ref-4">
<name id="ref-5">Mary Smith</name>
<id>2</id>
<next href-"#ref-1"/>
</a1:Customer>
</SOAP-ENV:Body>
...
```

Code Example

The second version of the program, **WebService**, as its name suggests, is a Web Service. Here is the **CustomerList.asmx** file.

```
<%@ WebService class="Test" %>
```

The source file **WebService.h** contains the following code. Note that this time, the **Serializable** attribute is not applied to the **Customer** class.

```
public __gc class Customer
{
public:
   String *name;
   long id;
   Customer *next;
};

public __gc class Test : public WebService
{
public:
   [WebMethod]
   Customer *GetList()
   {
      Customer *cust1 = new Customer;
      cust1->name = "John Smith";
      cust1->id = 1;

      Customer *cust2 = new Customer;
      cust2->name = "Mary Smith";
      cust2->id = 2;

      cust2->next = cust1;
      cust1->next = cust2;

      return cust1;
   }
};
```

For this to work, you will need to set up the **SOAP Differences\WebService** directory as a virtual directory named **SOAPWebServiceTest**. If you then run this Web Service from IE using the URL **http://localhost/SOAPWebServiceTest/CustomerList.asmx?op=GetList**, IE will indeed recognize it as a Web Service. See Figure 11–3.

However, if you go on to invoke the Web Service, you will get the following error:

```
System.Exception: There was an error generating the XML
    document. ---> System.Exception: A circular reference
    was detected while serializing an object of type
    Customer.
 at System.Xml.Serialization.XmlSerializationWriter.
    WriteStartElement(String name, String ns, Object o,
    Boolean writePrefixed)
...
    at System.Xml.Serialization.XmlSerializer.Serialize
      (XmlWriter xmlWriter, Object o,
       XmlSerializerNamespaces namespaces)
...
```

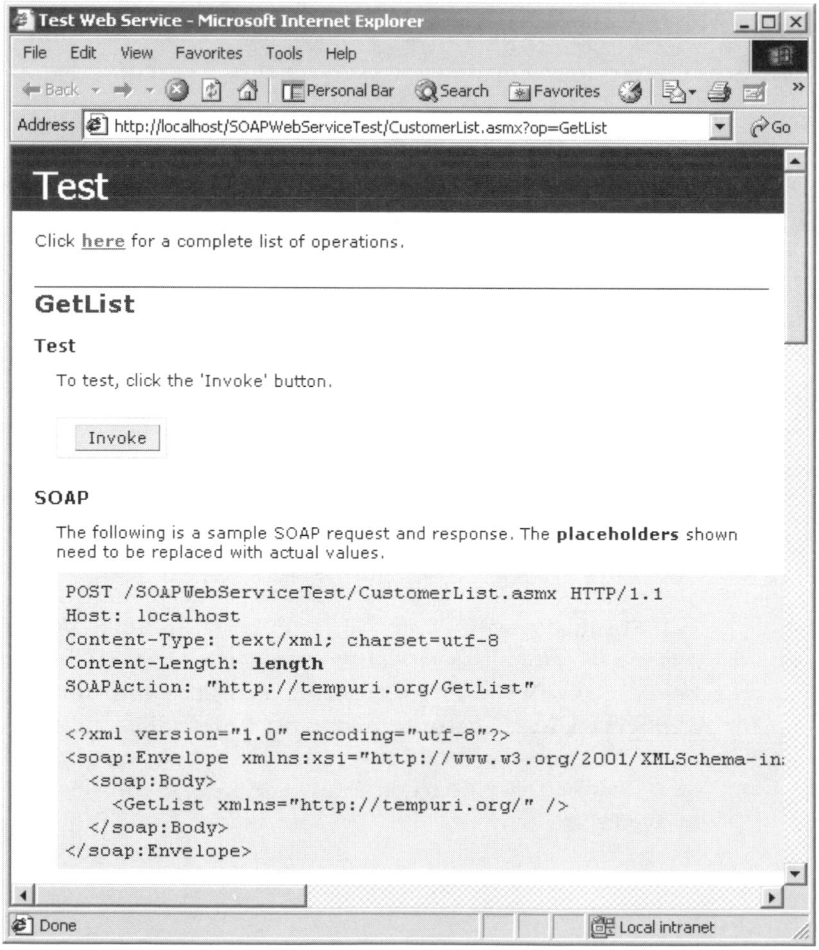

Figure 11–3   *Internet Explorer recognizes **CustomerList.asmx** as a Web Service.*

The XML serializer used to produce the SOAP for Web Services cannot handle the circular reference. If you comment out the line of code **cust2.next = cust1**, rebuild the project, and then copy the **WebService.dll** to the **bin** directory, the Web Service will be able to respond with

```
. . .
  <name>John Smith</name>
  <id>1</id>
  <next>
    <name>Mary Smith</name>
    <id>2</id>
    <next xsi:nil="true" />
  </next>
. . .
```

There is no notion, however, of any real relationship between the items, as was true in the remoting case. Why can the SOAP in .NET remoting handle the relationships and the SOAP in Web Services cannot?

SOAP handles the complicated relationships (multiple parents, graphs, etc.) that exist in an object model. XML Schema still reflects the XML heritage of document processing where you can model a document as a tree with a single root, with each node having one parent. Since SOAP was being developed before XML Schema was finished, SOAP has some extensions to handle those cases. Since these extensions are in Section 5 of the SOAP specification, they are often referred to as the Section 5 encoding rules.

Those parts of the Section 5 encoding rules that are extensions cannot be incorporated in any XML document that has to be validated against a schema. Hence, the .NET XML serialization classes do not use them. On the other hand, the .NET remoting serializer does not care about schema validation. It only cares about the ability to remote full object fidelity and hence uses all the Section 5 rules. In order to maximize interoperability, Web Services implementations tend to use only XML Schema-compliant forms that can be validated against a schema.[15] The counterargument can be made that schema validation is not as important when machines are generating the XML, but the industry has not yet taken that approach.[16]

If you want applications and Web Services that reside on different operating system platforms to interoperate, define your Web Services with XML Schema first, then develop the associated WSDL. You can then create an abstract class that can be the basis for an **.asmx** file by using the **/server** option on the **Wsdl** tool. Starting with an object model and then modeling it

---

[15] For those of you with a COM background, think of the work the proxy has to do to handle pointer aliasing if the pointer_default(unique) attribute is not used.

[16] Although we will not discuss them here, there are attributes you can set on your Web Service class and methods to have them use the Section 5 rules.

with XML schema might result in incompatible systems. Of course, if only simple types and structures are involved, you are not going to have problems. If you have existing object models, you may need a wrapper layer that translates the Web Services layer and moves it into your existing object model. This is the major technological challenge of Web Services, getting the object models on different platforms to work together.[17]

WebService Class

As we have previously demonstrated, a Web Service is nothing but an HTTP request handler. As such, a Web Service can access the intrinsic objects associated with its HTTP request. These are the same intrinsic objects discussed in the section "State in ASP.NET Applications" in Chapter 10. The **WebService** class has properties that access these intrinsic objects.

You need not derive your Web Service class from the framework **WebService** class. This enables you to derive your Web Service class from a different base class if necessary. In this case you can use the current **HttpContext** to access the intrinsic objects. The **WebService** class inherits from **MarshalByRefObject**, however, so if you want your Web Service class to be remotable, and you do inherit from a different base class, make sure that class also inherits from **MarshalByRefObject**. The **HttpContext** enables you to get information about an HTTP request. By using the static **Current** property, you can get access to the current request.

Using the Managed C++ Web Service Template

A managed Web Service can be easily built using C++ with managed extensions. To do this, you generate a starter project with the Managed C++ Web Service template, as described in the following steps. The project described here is provided as a solution in the **ManagedWebService** directory. You can follow these steps to create the same project in the **Demos** directory for this chapter.

1. Select the menu item File | New | Project.
2. Select the Visual C++ Projects node in the Project Types tree.
3. Select the Managed C++ Web Service icon in the Templates window.
4. Enter **ManagedWebService** as the project name.
5. Set **C:\OI\NetCpp\Chap11\Demos** for the project location. You will then see the completed New Project dialog, as shown in Figure 11–4.

---

[17] There is no intent here to slight the security issues associated with Web Services, but if you cannot get the object models to work together in some fashion, security becomes irrelevant because there is nothing to make secure.

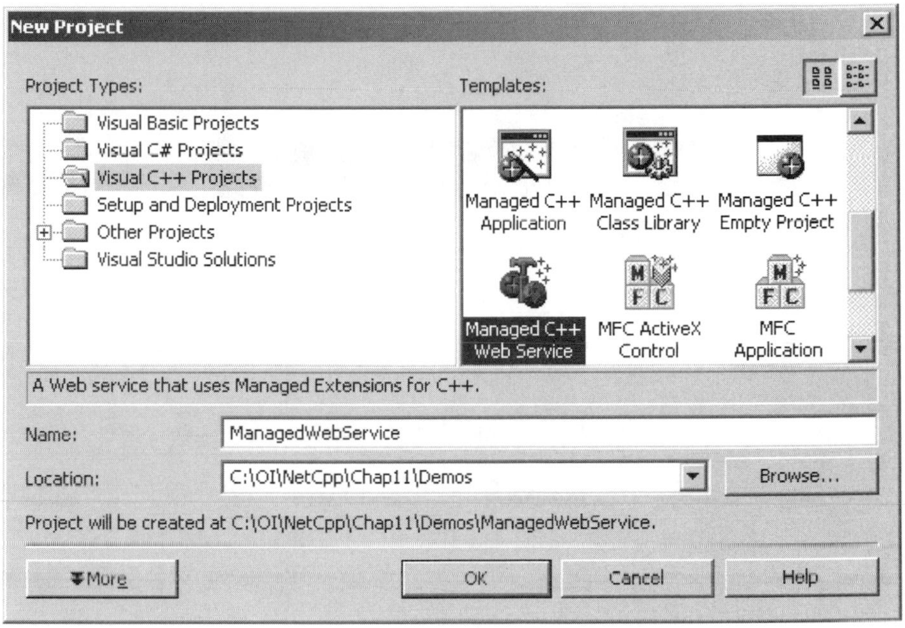

Figure 11-4   *The New Project dialog for a Managed C++ Web Service.*

6.   Click OK.
7.   Later, we will look at the generated code, but for now, build the project with Build | Build or Ctrl+Shift+B, and then run the project without debugging with Debug | Start Without Debugging or Ctrl+F5. Figure 11–5 shows the browser window that should appear.

Managed C++ Web Service Template Generated Code

The Managed C++ Web Service template generates starter code for a Web Service project. Figure 11–6 shows the Solution Explorer window for the **ManagedWebService** project.

The **ManagedWebService.asmx** file just contains the following:

```
<%@ WebService Class= ManagedWebService.Class1 %>
```

There is also a source file named **ManagedWebService.cpp** and an associated header file named **ManagedWebService.h**. Note that the **System.Web.Services.dll** assembly is referenced with a **#using** statement in **ManagedWebService.h**. This assembly contains important type information required by a Web Service. You can also see that a class named **Class1** within the **ManagedWebService** namespace implements the Web Service. This class

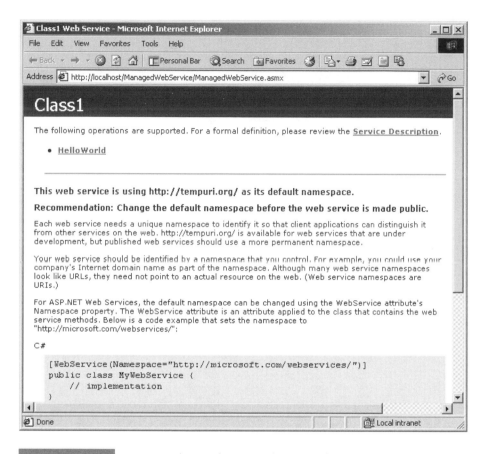

Figure 11–5   *Viewing the initial Managed C++ Web Service.*

has a method named **HelloWorld**, and you can see that it has the **[System::Web::Services::WebMethod]** attribute. This attribute is a requirement for making the method callable from a Web client as a Web Service method. Here is the original **ManagedWebService.cpp** file.

```
#include "stdafx.h"
#include " ManagedWebService.h"
#include "Global.asax.h"


namespace ManagedWebService
{
   // WEB SERVICE EXAMPLE
   // The HelloWorld() example service returns ...
   // To test this web service, ensure that the .asmx ...
```

```
    // set as your Debug HTTP URL, in project properties.
    // and press F5.
    String __gc* Class1::HelloWorld()
    {
        // TODO: Add the implementation of your ...
        return S"Hello World!";
    }
};
```

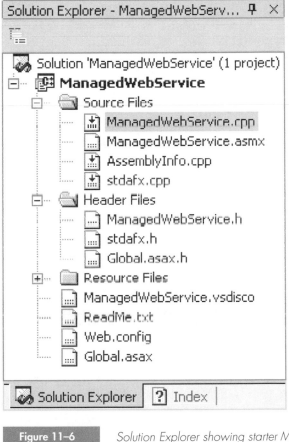

Figure 11-6   *Solution Explorer showing starter Managed C++ Web Service project.*

Here is the original ManagedWebService.h file.

```
// ManagedWebService.h
```

```
#pragma once
#using <System.Web.Services.dll>
using namespace System;
using namespace System::Web;
using namespace System::Web::Services;

namespace ManagedWebService
{
   public __gc
      class Class1 : public WebService
   {
   public:
      // WEB SERVICE EXAMPLE
      // The HelloWorld() example service returns ...
      // To test this web service, ensure that ...
      // set as your Debug HTTP URL, in project ...
      // and press F5.
      [System::Web::Services::WebMethod]
      String __gc* HelloWorld();
      // TODO: Add the methods of your Web Service here
   };
}
```

There are also the following files generated: **Global.asax**, **Managed-WebService.vsdisco**, and **Web.config**. The discovery file is an XML file produced by the wizard. This file is used to make the Web Service known to clients.

You may want to view the service and test its **HelloWorld** method using your browser, just as you did earlier in this chapter. We will not make any modifications of the **ManagedWebService** project. However, in the next section, we will look at a project named **Arithmetic**, which was initially created in the same way that the **ManagedWebService** project was. However, the **Arithmetic** project has been considerably modified after the Managed C++ Web Service template generated the starter code.

The Arithmetic Web Service

In this section we look at a Web Service named **Arithmetic** that was created using the Managed C++ Web Service template. We will see how to work with the intrinsic objects in a Web Service, but before going further, look at what the **Arithmetic** Web service looks like in your browser, as shown in Figure 11–7. From there, you can test each of the Web Service methods to prove that they work correctly.

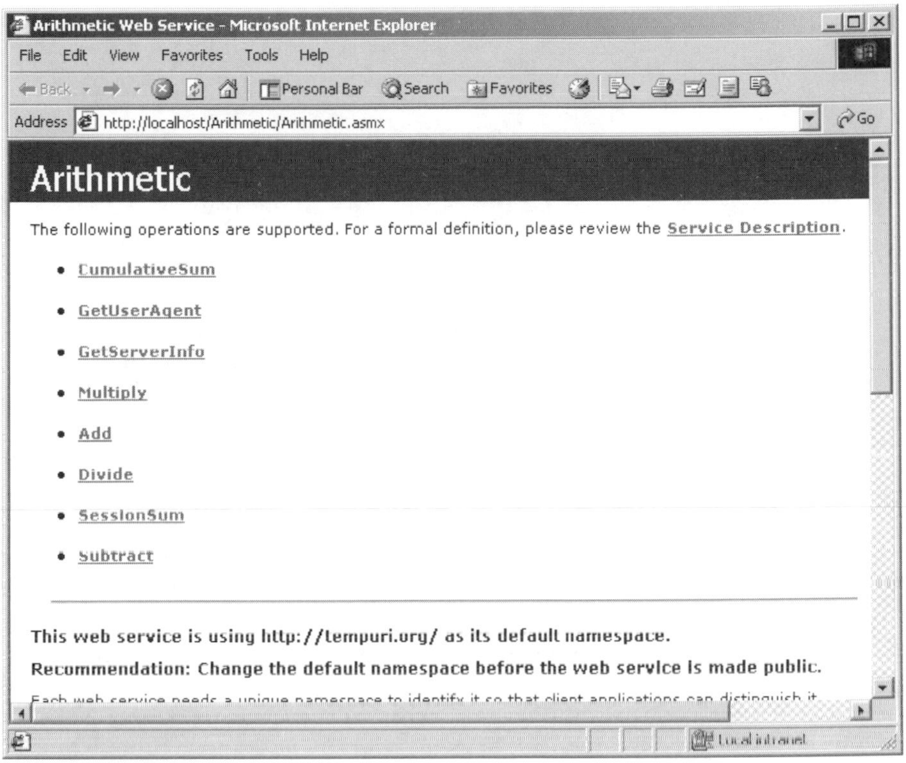

Figure 11-7   *Viewing the completed Managed C++ Web Service.*

Use the Intrinsic Objects

Our Web Service will have several methods that demonstrate how to use the intrinsic objects. As you will see, this is really no different from their use in ASP.NET. Two of the methods will illustrate the use of application and session state by calculating a cumulative sum of numbers.

In the **global.asax.h** file we initialize our sum to zero in the appropriate event handlers. **Global.asax.h** has the same function in Web Services as its analog does in ASP.NET, as discussed in Chapter 10. Since the **Global** class inherits from **System::Web::HttpApplication**, it can access the **Application** and **Session** intrinsic objects.

```
public __gc class Global :
   public System::Web::HttpApplication
{
protected:
   void Application_Start(Object *sender, EventArgs *e)
```

```
      {
         Application->set_Item("TotalSum", __box(0.0));
      }

      void Session_Start(Object *sender, EventArgs *e)
      {
         Session->set_Item("SessionSum", __box(0.0));
      }
   ...
```

Setting the **EnableSession** argument to the **WebMethod** constructor to true, we turn on session state for the **SessionSum** method. Every time a new session is started, the sum is reset to zero. On the other hand, for the **CumulativeSum** Web method, **EnableSession** is set to its default value, or false, so that the sum is reset to zero only when the Web Service application is restarted. The **Application** intrinsic object is used from the **HttpContext** object to show how that class is used.

It should be clear from this code that **HttpApplication**, **WebService**, and **HttpContext** all reference the same intrinsic objects. If you need to save state for the application or session of a Web Service, you can use the collections associated with **HttpApplicationState** and **HttpSessionState** to do so.

```
   ...
   [System::Web::Services::WebMethod(EnableSession = true)]
   double SessionSum(double x)
   {
      double d = *dynamic_cast<Double *>
         (Session->get_Item("SessionSum"));
      Session->set_Item("SessionSum", __box(d + x));
      return *dynamic_cast<Double *>
         (Session->get_Item("SessionSum"));
      }

   [System::Web::Services::WebMethod]
   double CumulativeSum(double x)
   {
      double sum = *dynamic_cast<Double *>
         (Application->get_Item("TotalSum"));
      sum = sum + x;
      Application->set_Item("TotalSum", __box(sum));

      return *dynamic_cast<Double *>
         (Application->get_Item("TotalSum"));
   }
   ...
```

The **GetUserAgent** method shows how to use the **Context** object to access information about the request. We return what kind of application is accessing the Web Service. The **GetServerInfo** method accesses the **Server** intrinsic object.

```
[System::Web::Services::WebMethod]
String *GetUserAgent()
{
   return Context->Request->UserAgent;
}

[System::Web::Services::WebMethod]
String *GetServerInfo()
{
   String *msg = String::Format(
      "Timeout for {0} = {1}; Located at {2}",
      Server->MachineName,
      __box(Server->ScriptTimeout),
         Server->MapPath(""));
   return msg;
}
```

The **ArithmeticClient** console program[18] demonstrates the use of the Web Service. We can create a proxy class from within VisualStudio.NET. On the Project Menu, select Add Web Reference and type in the address of the Web Service in the Address edit box followed by a carriage return. In the example, **http://localhost/Arithmetic/Arithmetic.asmx** was entered. Information about the **Arithmetic** Web Service will appear as in Figure 11-8.

Click on the Add Reference button to add the Web reference. This will add a reference to the proxy in the **WebService.h** file.

```
#using <Arithmetic.dll>
```

We then calculate a sum using the total held by the **Application** intrinsic object. We then calculate a sum for the total held by the **Session** intrinsic object.

---

[18]   You will need to manually copy Arithmetic.dll from Arithmetic\Debug to ArithmeticClient\Debug, or you will get an unhandled Exception (System.IO.FileNotFoundException) when you run ArithmeticClient.exe.

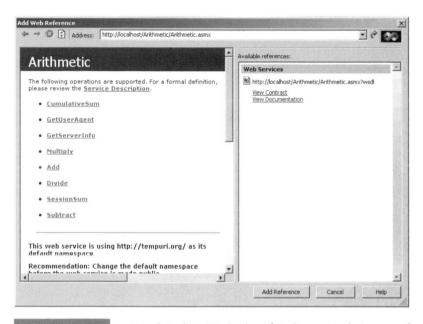

Figure 11-8   *Visual Studio.NET display of Arithmetic Web Service information.*

```
Arithmetic *a = new Arithmetic;

double sum;
for (int i = 0; i < 5; i++)
{
   sum = a->CumulativeSum(i);
   Console::WriteLine(
      "Adding {0}, Application sum is now {1}",
      __box(i), __box(sum));
 }

double sessionSum;
for (int i = 0; i < 5; i++)
{
   sessionSum = a->SessionSum(i);
   Console::WriteLine(
      "Adding {0}, Session sum is now {1}",
      __box(i), __box(sessionSum));
}
```

This will then give us output similar to the following. The exact numbers for the application-based sum will depend on how many times you have run the application.

```
Adding 0, Application sum is now 0
Adding 1, Application sum is now 1
Adding 2, Application sum is now 3
Adding 3, Application sum is now 6
Adding 4, Application sum is now 10
Adding 0, Session sum is now 0
Adding 1, Session sum is now 1
Adding 2, Session sum is now 2
Adding 3, Session sum is now 3
Adding 4, Session sum is now 4
```

We now create another instance of the proxy class, and make the same method calls.

```
Arithmetic *a2 = new Arithmetic;
for (int i = 0; i < 5; i++)
{
    sum = a2->CumulativeSum(i);
    Console::WriteLine(
        "Adding {0}, Application sum is now {1}",
        __box(i), __box(sum));
}
for (int i = 0; i < 5; i++)
    sum = a2->SessionSum(i);
    Console::WriteLine(
        "Adding {0}, Session sum is now {1}",
        __box(i), __box(sum));
}
```

We then get the following output. Notice how the application sum continues to increase, while the session bases sum starts again from zero. A new browser session is not the only way to start a new Web service session.

```
Adding 0, Application sum is now 10
Adding 1, Application sum is now 11
Adding 2, Application sum is now 13
Adding 3, Application sum is now 16
Adding 4, Application sum is now 20
Adding 0, Session sum is now 0
Adding 1, Session sum is now 1
Adding 2, Session sum is now 2
Adding 3, Session sum is now 3
Adding 4, Session sum is now 4
```

Finally, we call the **GetUserAgent** and **GetServerInfo** Web methods.

```
Console::WriteLine(a2->GetUserAgent());
Console::WriteLine(a2->GetServerInfo());
```

This will give you output that will look something like this:

```
Mozilla/4.0 (compatible; MSIE 6.0; MS Web Services Client
Protocol 1.0.2914.16)
Timeout for HPDESKTOP = 90; Located at c:\inetpub\
wwwroot\Arithmetic
```

Hotel Broker Web Service

Code
Example

The next step in the case study is to make the **Customer** and **Hotel** components of the Hotel Broker available as a Web Service. This Web Service is found in the **HotelBrokerWebService** subdirectory of the case study for this chapter. This Web Service will be used by Acme's customers to make reservations as well as for administrative tasks associated with the Hotel Broker. You can see these at the following locations.

- http://localhost/CustomerWebService/CustomerWebService.asmx
- http://localhost/HotelWebService/HotelWebService.asmx

Figures 11–9 and 11–10 show the information on the web services named CustomerWebService and HotelWebService.

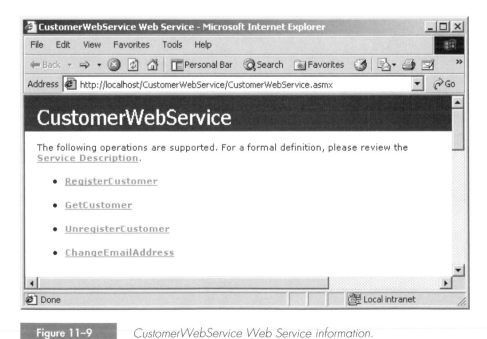

Figure 11–9   *CustomerWebService Web Service information.*

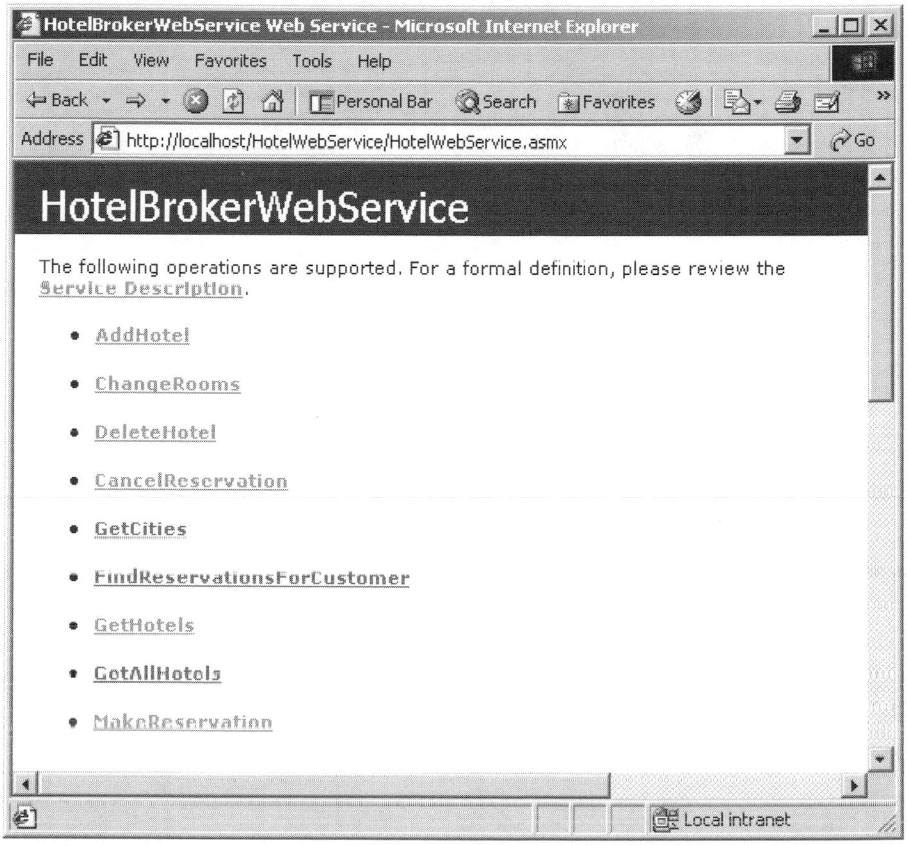

Figure 11–10   *HotelWebService Web Service information.*

The proxy classes themselves are built into an assembly named **proxies.dll**. Two batch files that can be used to create the proxy classes and build this assembly are located in the **WebServiceProxies** subdirectory of the case study.

In the **HotelBrokerAdministration** subdirectory you will find a version of the admin program that uses the proxies assembly instead of the **Customer** and **Hotel** assemblies. Again, this admin program is written in C# rather than C++ because it is GUI intensive, and Visual Studio.NET provides better GUI development support for C# than C++. Figure 11–11 shows **AcmeGui** accessing the Web service.

In the **AcmeWeb2** subdirectory for the Case Study you will find a version of **AcmeLib** that references the **proxies** assembly instead of the **Customer** and **Hotel** assemblies. All references to the **Customer** and **Hotel** components in the Acme reservation Web page and **HotelBrokerAdministration** programs have been removed. Figure 11–12 shows accessing the Web service via IE.

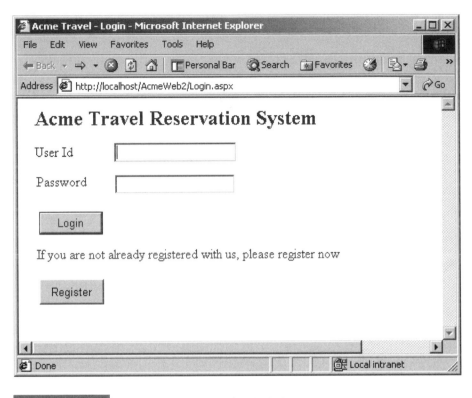

AcmeGui accessing the Web Service.

Customer Web Service

To implement the customer Web Service, we created a Managed C++ Web Service project named **CustomerWebService** that uses the Customer component to implement the details of the Web Service. Here is the **CustomerWebService.asmx** file from this project:

```
<%@ WebService class = "CustomerWebService.CustomerWebService"
%>
```

And here is the implementation code for the **CustomerWebService** class:

```
public __gc class CustomerWebService :
   public WebService
{
private:
   Customers *customers;
```

Figure 11–12   *AcmeWeb2 accessing the Web Service.*

```
public:
   CustomerWebService()
   {
      customers = new Customers("HotelBroker");
   }

   [WebMethod]
   int RegisterCustomer(
      String *firstName,
      String *lastName,
      String *emailAddress)
      {
         int customerId;
         customerId = customers->RegisterCustomer(
            firstName, lastName, emailAddress);
         return customerId;
      }
```

```
[WebMethod]
void UnregisterCustomer(int customerId)
{
   customers->UnregisterCustomer(customerId);
}

[WebMethod]
[XmlInclude(__typeof(CustomerListItem))]
ArrayList *GetCustomer(int customerId)
{
   ArrayList *ar;
   ar = customers->GetCustomer(customerId);
   return ar;
}

[WebMethod]
void ChangeEmailAddress(
int customerId, String *emailAddress)
{
   customers->ChangeEmailAddress(
      customerId, emailAddress);
}
};
```

The only new attribute is **XmlInclude**, which allows the **XmlSerializer** used to create the SOAP protocol to serialize a custom type, in this case **CustomerListItem**. This attribute is found in the **System::Xml::Serialization** namespace. Nonetheless, if you examine the proxy class for this Web Service, which is found in the **WebServiceProxies** directory, you will see that GetCustomer proxy (**customerproxy.cs**) only returns an array of objects.

```
public object[] GetCustomer(int customerId)
```

Although the attribute instructs the serializer to save the custom type, the SOAP protocol only understands how to transmit generic object types, so the AcmeLib code (**Acme.cs**) has to treat the return type as an object and then extract the custom type from it.

```
object[] al = customers.GetCustomer(hotelCustomerId);
foreach(CustomerListItem cust in al)
{
  currentUser.HotelCustomerId = hotelCustomerId;
  currentUser.FirstName = cust.FirstName;
```

```
    currentUser.LastName = cust.LastName;
    currentUser.EmailAddress = cust.EmailAddress;
}
```

All the other **ArrayList** objects in the Customer and Hotel Web Services are treated as arrays of objects where the appropriate type has to be extracted. Those arrays that use types such as strings and integers, however, need no special treatment by the **XmlSerializer**.

Hotel Broker Web Service

For the HotelBroker Web Service, the **Hotel** assembly itself was modified to be a Web Service. The **HotelWebService.asmx file** has to make reference only to the **HotelBroker** class in the Hotel assembly.

```
<%@ WebService class = "OI.NetCpp.Acme.HotelBrokerWebService,
Hotel" %>
```

The code is the same as the previous version of the component except for adding the necessary attributes to convert the code to a Web Service. Since Web Service names have to be unique, we had to use the **Message-Name** property of the **WebMethod** attribute to give one of the overloaded **GetHotels** methods a unique name. The code below is in **Hotel.h** in the **Case-Study\HotelBrokerWebService** directory.

```
[WebMethod(MessageName="GetAllHotels")]
[XmlInclude(__typeof(hotelListitem))]
ArrayList *GetHotels()
{
    . . .
}
```

Design Considerations

Network latency is a major performance consideration. Hence, the number of requests made over the network to a Web Service or a database should be minimized. In the HotelBroker Web Service, the reservations for a customer are kept in the dataset as a cache so that only for database modifications does a database request have to be made. The same is true for tracking the hotels and cities, although there is a tradeoff here, since an administrator might add a new hotel. However, that operation is not likely to happen during the relatively short time a customer is making a reservation. Of course, these types of data could be cached inside the Web form itself, so a call to the Web Service would be unnecessary.

HTTP is stateless protocol, and therefore so is SOAP. Minimizing state will help your applications and Web Services to scale better because objects (such as database connections) can be pooled or reused much more easily; less memory is required so that more resources are available to handle more requests. This means treating your Web Service objects as endpoints of communication, not full-fledged objects. Our case study has not really done this because we wanted to illustrate the use of certain technologies, and the proper way to partition functionality really depends on the details of your actual application and network latencies.

You can also use the **CacheDuration** property on a Web method or the **Cache** property of the **HttpContext** class to cache information to avoid network overhead.

Summary

Web Services provide a means to extend component functionality across the network between platforms and languages from different vendors. Unlike .NET remoting, however, the types that can be used are much more limited.

Nonetheless, if you start your design from the point of view of the XML Schema specification, and then build your WSDL and Web Service classes, you will have a much greater chance of being able to interoperate.

TWELVE

ATL Server Web Sites and Web Services

There are several ways to go about writing Web applications and services. One way, which is supported to varying degrees by most of the .NET-enabled languages, is called ASP.NET. Another approach, which is only supported by Visual C++, is called ATL Server.[1] Other traditional techniques include Common Gateway Interface (CGI) and ISAPI. The advantage of ASP.NET is its simplicity and ease of use. The fact that several languages support it also makes it accessible to more programmers and skill levels. ATL Server's advantage is that it allows for potentially higher performance than ASP.NET.

Although ATL Server is much easier to work with than the traditional C++-based Web development technology known as ISAPI (Internet Services API), it requires a greater degree of experience on the part of the programmer than ASP.NET. The decision to use ASP.NET or ATL Server is not usually a mutually exclusive choice. Often, you will want to take a blended approach. Because ATL is harder to work with, you may want to use ASP.NET for the majority of your Web projects. ATL can then be used for those few areas that really require the greatest performance.

History of Dynamic Web Content Technologies

There have been many techniques for implementing dynamic Web content. The oldest technique, which is supported by most HTTP servers, is CGI. A CGI program uses environment variables to retrieve HTTP request header information sent from the Web browser. It also receives request information through the Web server via redirected standard input and generates dynamic

---

[1] ATL Server is implemented using unmanaged C++, and it therefore falls outside of the main subject area of .NET. However, ATL is an important topic to some Visual C++ programmers.

HTML that is streamed back to the Web server on its way to the client via redirected standard output. Using environment variables, standard input, and standard output is not tremendously efficient, but it is an approach that works uniformly on most Web servers hosted on Unix as well as Windows. Unfortunately, CGI creates a new process for each client request. This is quite expensive in terms of resource usage and performance. Therefore, CGI does not scale well with large numbers of client requests. CGI also suffers from significant interprocess communications overhead because the Web server and CGI process are in separate address spaces.

ISAPI, which is an IIS-specific technology, solved these problems with performance and scaling by replacing the CGI process with an in-process ISAPI DLL. The ISAPI DLL is loaded into the IIS Web server address space on demand, and multiple Web clients can share access to it. ISAPI provides APIs to access the client's requests, including input parameters and HTTP headers. ISAPI provides an input stream to read request information and an output stream that is used to send the dynamically produced HTML content back to the client. This approach is much more efficient that CGI, since no new process is created and no interprocess communications are involved on the server. Visual C++ 6.0 provided the ISAPI Extension Wizard to create an MFC-based ISAPI extension and ISAPI filter projects. MFC provided the **CHttpServer** that wraps the Internet Server API, as well as message map and parse map macros to support working with ISAPI.

ISAPI filters and extensions were excellent for performance-intensive Web application development, but it required considerable programming skill. The programmer not only needed to know C++, but also had to understand and implement thread pooling, synchronization, transaction processing, and security. The programmer also had to be very cautious and had to do extensive testing before deploying the ISAPI DLL, since an in-process DLL takes down the entire process (i.e., the IIS Web server) if it contains a sufficiently nasty bug. Finally, many programmers hated ISAPI because it is more difficult to debug than most other types of C++ programs, since you must attach to the running IIS process.

ASP represents a high-level, convenient approach to developing dynamic Web content. ASP is built on ISAPI technology, but is not as efficient as raw ISAPI. ASP is actually just a prebuilt, generalized ISAPI DLL that implements a scripting engine. This scripting engine then interprets an ASP page, which is like a regular HTML page except that it contains embedded snippets of ASP code written as a script. This ASP code is not compiled, but rather a script engine interprets it. Any scripting language that is installed on the Web server that supports ASP may be used. By default, both VBScript and JScript are supported automatically by IIS. The downside to ASP is that this interpreted code is naturally slower than the equivalent compiled ISAPI code.

Another disadvantage of ASP is that scripting languages are not type-safe, which can result in runtime errors that would be better to catch at compile time. Finally, scripting languages are not object oriented, which makes them unsuitable for highly maintainable, large-scale programming efforts. The big advantage of ASP is that scripting languages are usually very easy to learn, and in particular, VBScript is well known to an enormous number of people. The fact that scripting languages such as VBScript are not object oriented is partially offset by their ability to invoke server-side COM components, which can be implemented in powerful object-oriented languages such as C++. Another advantage of ASP over ISAPI is that ASP is nicely integrated with MTS (Microsoft Transaction Server). This allows threading, synchronization, transaction processing, and security to be managed automatically.

Fortunately, ASP.NET preserves the advantages of traditional ASP and fixes most of its problems, including its poor performance. Instead of relying on a scripting language interpreter, ASP.NET uses compiled .NET languages, such as C#, VB.NET, and even Managed C++.

So now there are several choices that have become available: CGI, ISAPI, ASP, and ASP.NET. Of course, ATL provides yet one more choice. And, just as with ASP.NET, ATL supports both Web site and Web service development. However, ATL servers and services are implemented using a C++ template library based on ISAPI technology.

ATL Server Applications

ATL Server is an unmanaged C++ technology that makes ISAPI development both efficient and convenient.[2] Since ISAPI has been traditionally used in applications where performance is a major requirement, it's not surprising that ATL Server has the same performance advantages.

ATL is provided as a traditional C++ template class library. One of the great things about C++ templates is that they allow you to define new classes based on parameters provided to the compiler. This allows you to efficiently and flexibly extend a class library with new customized classes.

The ATL Server Project template generates starter code for an ISAPI Extension DLL that receives information via IIS from HTTP requests and a companion Web application DLL that implements the actual Web application functionality.

ISAPI Extension and Web application DLLs work in conjunction with SRF files (Service Request File) that contain a combination of HTML and simple script tags or placeholders. Each SRF file provides a template (not a C++ template) for generating a Web page for the client, based on the substitution of placeholders appearing within double curly braces. Each placeholder is given a name that specifies a function implemented in the Web application

---

[2] At least, using ATL is convenient in comparison to traditional ISAPI development. It is not nearly as convenient as ASP.NET development.

DLL. Each of these DLL functions generates a stream of HTML that is substituted in place of the double curly brace tag to produce the response sent back to the client.

Typically, you spend most of your time developing an ATL Server application by adding code to the Web application DLL portion of the solution. However, since you do have the source code, it is possible to modify the ISAPI Extension DLL portion of the solution as well. You would do this only if you wanted to modify the parsing of the SRF file or implement some sort of HTTP stream filtering, which would be a rarely used, advanced technique.

ATL Server Is Based on ISAPI

In order to understand ATL Server, it is important to first have a good understanding of the basic theory behind ISAPI. An ISAPI DLL is used to either filter client HTTP requests as they stream into and out of IIS (an ISAPI filter) or to dynamically generate HTML responses that are returned to the client (an ISAPI extension). Both ISAPI filters and extensions are used to modify or extend the normal behavior of IIS. ISAPI filters are great for things like data encryption, performance monitoring, and custom authentication. ISAPI extensions are great for dynamically generating HTML or transforming non-HTML data, such as database records, into an HTML format on the fly. For example, an ISAPI extension could query a database and place the results into an appropriately formatted HTML page.

ATL Server Application Architecture

Just as with traditional ISAPI extension DLLs, ATL-based ISAPI extension DLLs export functions named **GetExtensionVersion**, **HttpExtensionProc**, and **TerminateExtension**. Also, in the traditional manner, an EXTENSION_CONTROL_BLOCK structure is provided by IIS for each HTTP request. This structure is passed into **HttpExtensionProc** as a parameter. This structure provides access to the HTTP header information as well as access to data streams for communicating with the HTTP client.

The **HttpExtensionProc** function is the main entry point for an ISAPI extension. The **HttpExtensionProc** function is automatically called by IIS when it needs to handle an HTTP request that is intended for the ISAPI Extension. **HttpExtensionProc** uses callback functions provided by the EXTENSION_CONTROL_BLOCK parameter to read client data and respond appropriately. Figure 12–1 shows the overall picture of how ISAPI is used in an ATL Server Web application.

From Figure 12–1, you can see only one ISAPI extension DLL. This is because there can only be one ISAPI extension DLL per IIS virtual directory. The figure shows that there can be multiple Web application DLLs and multi-

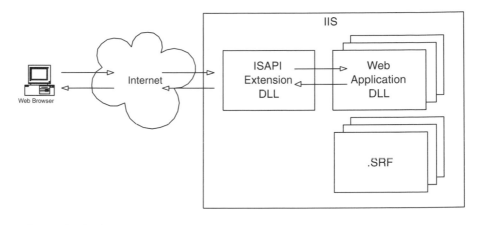

Figure 12–1   *ATL Server application architecture.*

ple **.srf** files within a single virtual directory. Although it is possible to customize the code in the ISAPI extension DLL, typically only the Web application DLLs are customized, since they are the DLLs that implement the request handlers.

Creating an ATL Server Project

The following steps are used to create an initial ATL Server project using the ATL Server Project Wizard. You may follow these steps to create your own project, or you can open the solution **ATLServerApp.sln** provided in the **ATLServerApp** directory.[3]

1. Select the File | New | Project menu item.
2. Open the Visual C++ Projects node in the Project Types tree.
3. Select the ATL Server Project[4] in the Templates window.
4. Enter **ATLServerApp** as the project name.
5. Enter an appropriate directory for the project location. The Demos directory is provided for this purpose.
6. Click OK to start the ATL Server Project Wizard.
7. View the default choices that have been preselected by the Wizard on the Overview tab. Also, look at the Project Settings, Server

---

[3] The solution provided also contains additional code that will be added over the course of the next few pages.

[4] Note that there is also an ATL Server Web Service Project template available. These two choices result in the same ATL Server Project Wizard, but with slightly different preselected choices. They both generate an ISAPI Extension DLL and a Web application DLL, but the ATL Server Project template preselects the stencil support and validation support options. An ATL Server Web Service Project provides a Web Service rather than HTML content.

Options, Application Options, and Developer Support Options tabs
as well. These are shown in Figures 12–2, 12–3, 12–4, 12–5, and 12–6.

8. Without making any changes to these default options, click Finish.

9. Figure 12–2 shows the Project Overview page of the ATL Server
Project Wizard. The information on this tab may be modified using
the other tabs provided. These other tabs are named Project Settings, Server Options, Application Options, and Developer Support
Options.

Figure 12–3 shows the Project Settings page of the ATL Server Project
Wizard. As usual, you can change the name and location of the generated
project. You can also select whether or not the solution generates a Web
application DLL. A Web application DLL implements an HTTP request handler. This page also lets you select whether or not the solution generates an
ISAPI extension DLL. This DLL will contain code that dispatches HTTP
requests to a request handler in a Web application DLL. You can decide
whether or not to combine these two projects into a single DLL. Finally, you
can choose to generate automatic deployment support so that your project is
installed on your Web server as part of the build operation.[5] If you choose

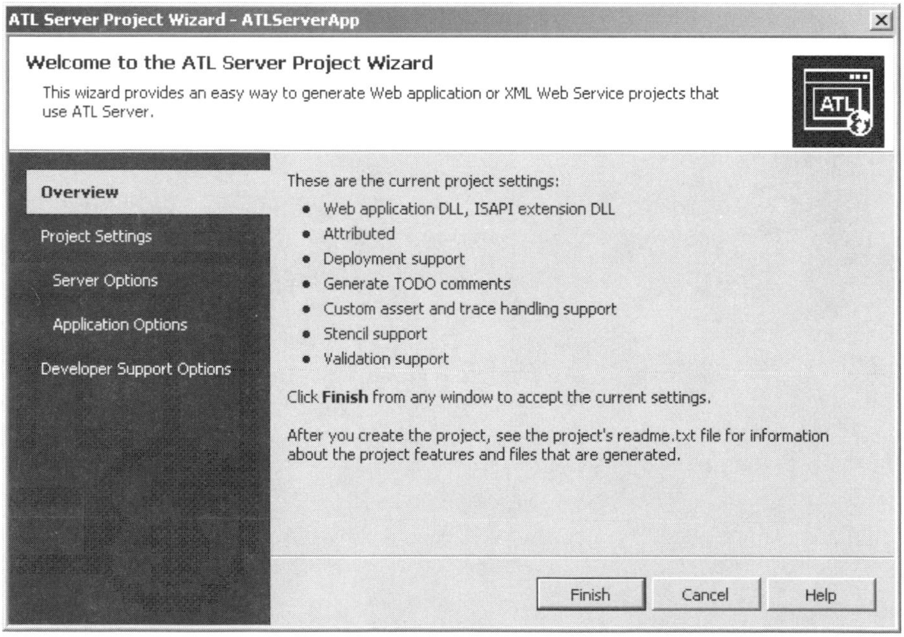

Figure 12–2   *ATL Server Project Wizard Project Overview.*

---

[5] IIS must be installed for automatic build deployment to work.

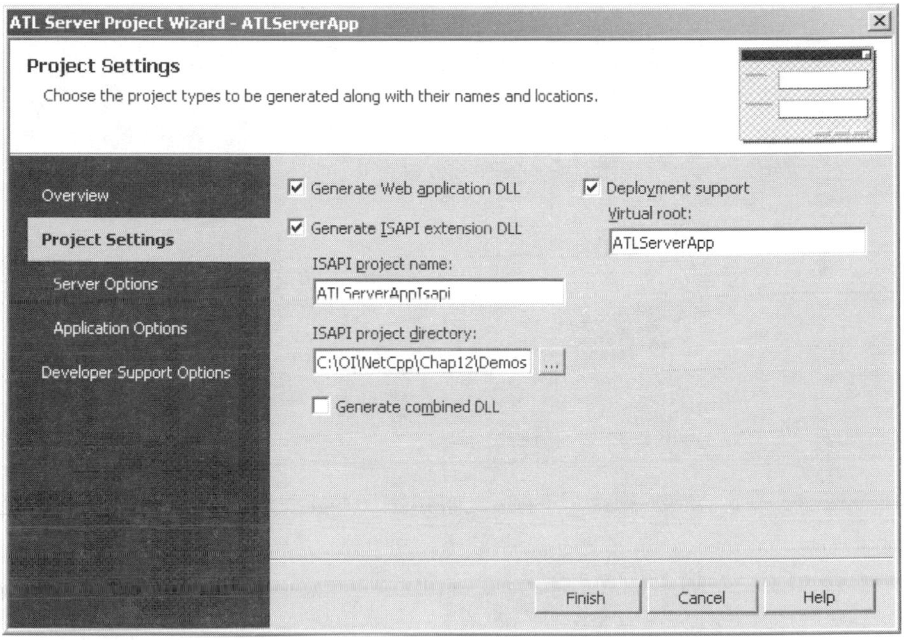

Figure 12–3   *ATL Server Project Wizard Project Settings.*

automatic deployment, you can specify the virtual directory where your project will be installed.

Figure 12–4 shows the Server Options page of the ATL Server Project Wizard. This page allows you to add several features, such as caching support, performance counters, and session state support, to the ISAPI extension DLL.

Figure 12–5 shows the Application Options page of the ATL Server Project Wizard. This page allows you to add several features, such as validation of query parameters and form variables, and stencil tag replacement processing support, to the Web application DLL. It also allows you to specify whether or not you want to create the project as a Web service rather than a Web site.

Figure 12–6 shows the Developer Support Options page of the ATL Server Project Wizard. This page lets you control the insertion of TODO comments, the generation of C++ code that uses attributes,[6] and the use of custom assert and trace handling support.

Now, let's take a look at the code that was just produced by the ATL Server Project Wizard after accepting all the default options. In Solution Explorer, you will see that there are two projects in the solution. There is a

---

[6] Attributes cause the C++ compiler to inject code into the compiled output.

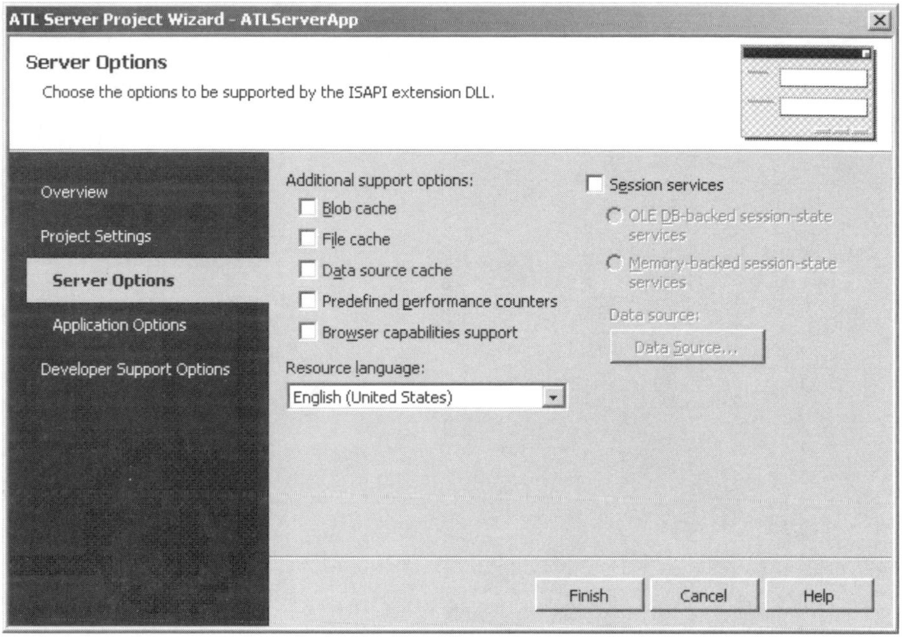

Figure 12–4 *ATL Server Project Wizard Server Options.*

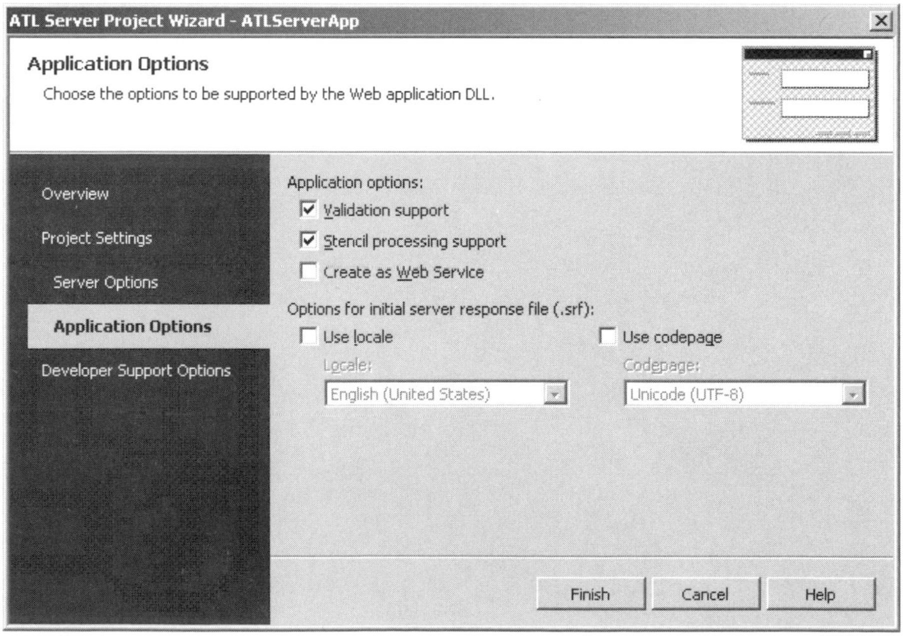

Figure 12–5 *ATL Server Project Wizard Application Options.*

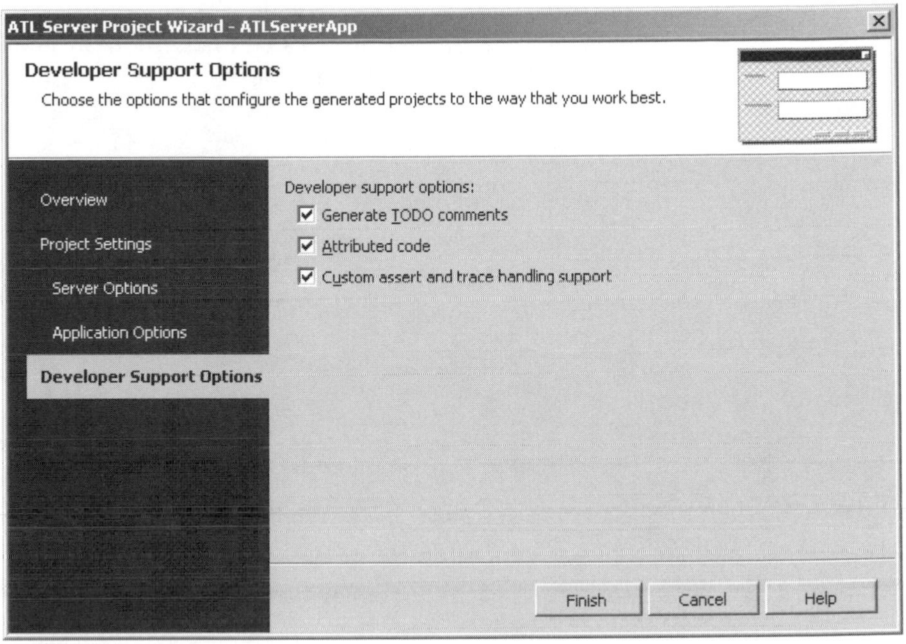

ATL Server Project Wizard Developer Support Options.

Figure 12-6

Web application DLL and an ISAPI extension DLL. There is no deployment project, but if you look at the project settings, you will see that the project does get deployed at build time.

- **ATLServerAppIsapi** is the ISAPI Extension DLL project.
- **ATLServerApp** is the Web application DLL project.

ISAPI Extension DLL

In Solution Explorer open the **ATLServerAppIsapi** project node. Then, open the **ATLServerAppIsapi.def** file and see that this project exports the three standard ISAPI DLL export functions listed below.

- **HttpExtensionProc** is called for each HTTP request to the ISAPI extension.
- **GetExtensionVersion** is called when the ISAPI extension is loaded by IIS.
- **TerminateExtension** is called when the ISAPI extension is unloaded by IIS.

Also, see that **ATLServerAppIsapi.cpp** provides an implementation for each of these exported functions. In each case, it simply uses the **theExtension** object to deal with the details. The **theExtension** object is of type **ExtensionType**, which is defined using the **CIsapiExtension** template. This template looks after all of the tedious and repetitive grunt work associated with implementing a fully featured ISAPI extension, including details such as thread pooling and request dispatching.

```
typedef CIsapiExtension<> ExtensionType;

// The ATL Server ISAPI extension
ExtensionType theExtension;

// Delegate ISAPI exports to theExtension
// extern "C"
DWORD WINAPI HttpExtensionProc(LPEXTENSION_CONTROL_
BLOCK lpECB)
{
    return theExtension.HttpExtensionProc(lpECB);
}

extern "C"
BOOL WINAPI GetExtensionVersion(HSE_VERSION_INFO* pVer)
{
    return theExtension.GetExtensionVersion(pVer);
}

extern "C"
BOOL WINAPI TerminateExtension(DWORD dwFlags)
{
    return theExtension.TerminateExtension(dwFlags);
}
```

The EXTENSION_CONTROL_BLOCK structure that is passed as a parameter into the **HttpExtensionProc** function shown above contains several notable members. The most important members of this structure are shown in the following type definition. Although the **ATLServerAppIsapi** project is often left as is, you can see that you could use this information about the HTPP request to perform customized filtering functionality.

```
typedef struct _EXTENSION_CONTROL_BLOCK
{
    ...
    HCONN ConnID; //in - unique number from HTTP server
    DWORD dwHttpStatusCode; //out - completion status
    ...
    LPSTR lpszMethod;        //in - requested method
```

```
LPSTR lpszQueryString;    //in - query information
...
LPBYTE lpbData;           //in - data sent by the client
LPSTR lpszContentType;    //in - content type of data
...
BOOL ( WINAPI * WriteClient ) //write response to client
  ( HCONN ConnID,
    LPVOID Buffer,
    LPDWORD lpdwBytes,
    DWORD dwReserved );
BOOL ( WINAPI * ReadClient ) //read from HTTP request
  ( HCONN ConnID,
    LPVOID lpvBuffer,
    LPDWORD lpdwSize );
...
} EXTENSION_CONTROL_BLOCK, *LPEXTENSION_CONTROL_BLOCK;
```

Web Application DLL

If you open the **ATLServerApp.h** header file in the Web application DLL
project, you will see the definition of a class named **CATLServerAppHandler**.
The **request handler** attribute specifies that the class will be exposed as an
ATL Server request handler named Default. In this class, an example method
named **OnHello** is provided with the **tag_name** attribute that specifies the
name Hello. We will see how these attributes relate to the actual client request
shortly. Notice how easy it is to send HTML data for a tag replacement back to
the client via the **m_HttpResponse** data member using the stream insertion
operator.

```
[ request_handler("Default") ]
class CATLServerAppHandler
{
private:
   // Put private members here

protected:
   // Put protected members here

public:
   // Put public members here

   HTTP_CODE ValidateAndExchange()
   {
      // TODO: Put all initialization and validation ...
```

```
        // Set the content-type
        m_HttpResponse.SetContentType("text/html");

        return HTTP_SUCCESS;
    }

protected:
    // Here is an example of how to use a replacement ...
    [ tag_name(name="Hello") ]
    HTTP_CODE OnHello(void)
    {
        m_HttpResponse << "Hello World!";
        return HTTP_SUCCESS;
    }
}; // class CATLServerAppHandler
```

The Web application DLL works in conjunction with an .srf. An **.srf** file is really just an HTML file that may contain variable data tags that are placed within double curly braces. These tags are placeholders that will be substituted by the ATL stencil processor when the request is handled. Each placeholder is filled in by a method of a class that you implement in your Web application DLL.

ATL Server provides attributes that are used to associate the double curly brace placeholders in the SRF files with the methods in your Web application DLL. Each such method generates the HTML that is used to substitute for the corresponding placeholder tags in the **.srf** file.

In Solution Explorer open the **ATLServerApp** project node, and then open the **ATLServerApp.srf** file and note that it contains the text and replacement tags shown below. Now compare this **.srf** file with the code in **ATLServerApp.h** shown above. You will notice that the **CATLServerApp-Handler** class is marked with the **request_handler** attribute as "Default," which corresponds with the handler tag below containing the word Default. This tag also specifies the name of the Web application DLL as **ATLServer-App.dll**. This is important because there may be any number of such Web application DLLs in the same virtual directory. The result is that this **.srf** file will use the **CATLServerAppHandler** class to perform tag substitution.

Also, notice that the **tag_name** attribute specifies the name "Hello" in the code above. This corresponds with the tag containing the word Hello in the **.srf** file below. This means that the Hello tag will be replaced by the text written to **m_HttpResponse** in the **OnHello** method above.[7] The starter code provided by the wizard uses "Default" and "Hello" purely as examples

---

[7] It is possible to have more than one Web application DLL specified in a single **.srf** file. See the ATL Server documentation for details.

for us to follow. When we add our own functionality, we provide our own meaningful names for the request handler and tag name attributes.

```
{{handler ATLServerApp.dll/Default}}
This is a test: {{Hello}}
```

Building and Running the ATL Server Project

You build an ATL project in the normal way. During the build, the output window shows the ATLServerApp project being deployed. This copies **ATLServerApp.srf**, **ATLServerApp.dll**, and **ATLServerAppIsapi.dll** to the **\inetpub\wwwroot\ATLServerApp** directory. Figure 12–7 shows the newly deployed ATLServerApp application in IIS.

You can then view the result of the ATL Server project. You can either run the solution within Visual Studio.NET in the usual way or you can just point your Web browser to http://localhost/ATLServerApp/ATLServerApp.srf. Figure 12–8 shows this.

It can be instructive to view what happens within the Web application DLL using the debugger. You will find that the **HttpExtensionProc** function in **ATLServerAppIsapi.dll** is called first, with the EXTENSION_CONTROL_BLOCK parameter containing the structures listed in Table 12–1. The contents of these members originate from the URL specified in the Web browser.

The next function to be called is **ValidateAndExchange**,[8] which just sends the content type text/html to the HTTP response. This function is also useful for adding initialization and validation before the request is handled.

Finally, the **OnHello** method of the **CATLServerAppHandler** class in the Web application DLL is called. It sends the text "Hello World!" to the HTTP response. The resulting data sent to the browser can be seen by viewing the HTML source.

```
<html>
<head>
</head>
<body>
This is a test: Hello World!<br>
</body>
</html>
```

---

[8] Actually, the next function to be called is **DllMain** in **ATLServerApp.dll** for the case DLL_PROCESS_ATTACH. **DllMain** is called several times during the handling of Web requests and will be ignored here. However, note that this first call to **DllMain** is due to the fact that the **ATLServerAppIsapi.dll** ISAPI extension DLL loads the **ATLServerApp.dll** Web application DLL dynamically to handle the Web request.

Figure 12-7   *The newly deployed ATLServerApp.*

Note that the **.srf** file specified the **Default** handler method in **ATLServerApp.dll**, and it also specified the tag **Hello** that will be substituted by the Web application DLL.

```
{{handler ATLServerApp.dll/Default}}
This is a test: {{Hello}}
```

Code
Example

In the specified DLL (**ATLServerApp.dll**) source code, you can see that the **Default** handler attribute is applied to the **CATLServerAppHandler** class, which contains the **OnHello** method with the **tag_name** attribute that matches the tag **Hello**. This means that when IIS gets a request for this particular **.srf** file, it loads the specified DLL, locates the specified class, and calls

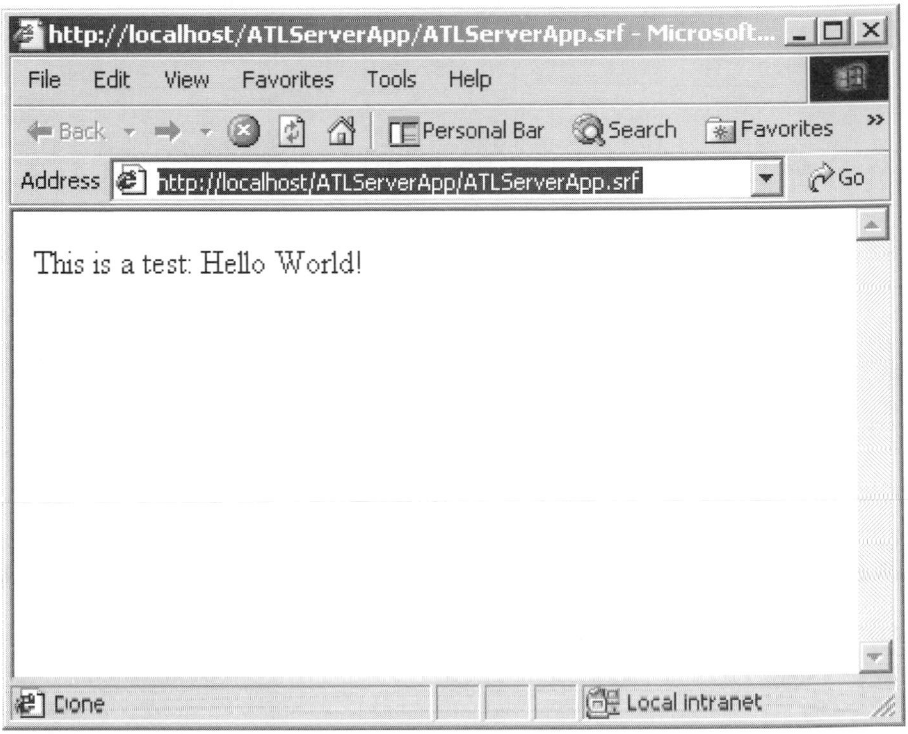

Figure 12–8 *Viewing the default ATLServerApp.srf file.*

Table 12 1 EXTENSION_CONTROL_BLOCK Structure for ATLServerApp.srf

Structure Member	Value
lpszMethod	"GET"
lpszQueryString	""
lpszPathInfo	"/ATLServerApp/ATLServerApp.srf"
pbData	0

on the specified method **OnHello** to provide the text string to be used as the tag replacement that is sent back to the client.

```
[ request_handler("Default") ]
class CATLServerAppHandler
{
```

```
...
[ tag_name(name="Hello") ]
  HTTP_CODE OnHello(void)
  {
      m_HttpResponse << "Hello World!";
      return HTTP_SUCCESS;
  }
```

Adding Another Handler to the Server

Code Example

The request handler generated by the ATL Server Wizard is only meant to provide an example of how to write your own request handlers. As a simple example of adding additional functionality, consider the following code added to **ATLServerApp.h**.[9] This request handler class is marked "Another," and the replacement method is marked with the tag name "Time."

```
//Another handler added to ATLServerApp
[request_handler("Another")]
class CAnotherATLServerAppHandler
{
protected:
  [ tag_name(name="Time") ]
  HTTP_CODE GetTheCurrentTime(void)
  {
     SYSTEMTIME systemTime;
     GetLocalTime(&systemTime);
     m_HttpResponse
        << systemTime.wHour << ":" << systemTime.wMinute;
     return HTTP_SUCCESS;
  }
};
```

The **Another.srf**[10] file shows how you add this additional functionality to the server. If you add this file and rebuild the project, you will automatically deploy this **.srf** file along with the rest of the server. When you view **Another.srf** in your Web browser, you will see it display the current time. Here is the content of the **Another.srf** file.

```
{{handler ATLServerApp.dll/Another}}
{{Time}} is the current time.
```

---

[9] This functionality has also been added to the ATLServerApp example project provided.

[10] Several **.srf** files have been added to the ATLServerApp example project provided. All of the **.srf** files that have been added will be described in the next few pages.

You can see the result at http://localhost/ATLServerApp/Another.srf. Figure 12–9 shows this.

Adding if-else-endif Handling to the Server

The **if_else_endif.srf** file contains an if-else-endif control construct. The associated handler is added to the Web application DLL. Note that for times that have an even number of seconds, the return value is HTTP_SUCCESS, and for an odd number of seconds, the return value is HTTP_S_FALSE. The S in HTTP_S_FALSE indicates that it is a success code rather than an actual error. The probabilities for the two possible outcomes are both 50 percent. This means that if the client is refreshed several times, the two results will be evenly distributed. Note that the **ShouldThisBeDone** method does not actually send any HTML data to the client. Its only purpose is to control the

> **http://localhost/ATLServerApp/Another.srf - Microsoft Interne...**
>
> File   Edit   View   Favorites   Tools   Help
>
> ⇐ Back ▾ ⇒ ▾ ⊗ 🗗 🟐 | ☐ Personal Bar 🔍 Search 🖼 Favorites »
>
> Address 🗐 http://localhost/ATLServerApp/Another.srf ▾ ⌐ Go
>
> 23:18 is the current time.
>
> 🗐 Done   🔌 Local intranet

| **Figure 12–9** | *Viewing Another.srf.* |

expression of text and tags within the if, else, and endif tags in the **.srf** file. Here is the C++ code for this new functionality.

```
//A handler for testing if, else, and endif
[request_handler("if_else_endif")]
class C_if_else_endif_ATLServerAppHandler
{
protected:
   [ tag_name(name="ShouldThisBeDone") ]
   HTTP_CODE ShouldThisBeDone(void)
   {
      SYSTEMTIME systemTime;
      GetLocalTime(&systemTime);
      //return HTTP_SUCCESS 50% of the time
      if (systemTime.wSecond % 2)
         return HTTP_SUCCESS;
      else
         return HTTP_S_FALSE;
   }
};
```

HTTP_SUCCESS and HTTP_S_FALSE effectively represent TRUE and FALSE respectively. If you point your browser to **if_else_endif.srf** and refresh the browser several times, you should see these two outcomes being displayed randomly. Although this example does not show it, you can nest other tags between the if, else, and endif tags.

```
{{handler ATLServerApp.dll/if_else_endif}}
{{if ShouldThisBeDone}}
Here is text that is displayed if ShouldThisBeDone
{{else}}
Here is text that is displayed if *not* ShouldThisBeDone
{{endif}}
```

You can see the result at http://localhost/ATLServerApp/if_else_endif.srf. Figures 12–10 and 12–11 shows the two possible outcomes.

Adding while-endwhile Handling to the Server

The following example supports a while-endwhile loop in the corresponding **while_endwhile.srf** file. A data member of type **int** named count has been added to keep track of the number of times the loop is repeated. This value is initialized to zero in the handler class constructor, and it is incremented in

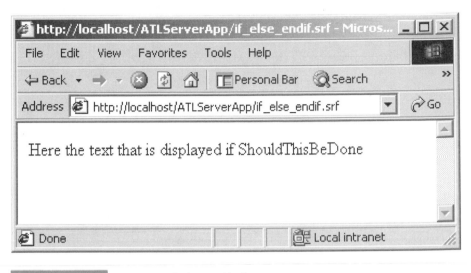

Figure 12–10   *Viewing if_else_endif.srf.*

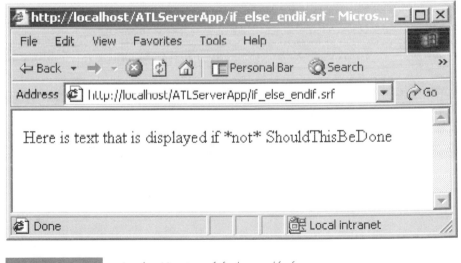

Figure 12–11   *Another Viewing of if_else_endif.srf.*

each call to **ShouldThisBeDoneAgain**. Iteration continues until `count <= 10` is no longer true. Note that there is actually no while loop in the C++ code. Instead, the while loop is located in the corresponding **.srf** file. The handler class also provides two tag replacement methods named **GetNext-**

Number and **GetNextNumberSquared.** These methods correspond to two tags in the **.srf** file that appear in the while loop.

```
//A handler for testing while and endwhile
[request_handler("while_endwhile")]
class C_while_endwhile_ATLServerAppHandler
{
protected:
    int count;
    C_while_endwhile_ATLServerAppHandler() : count(0)
    {
    }
    [ tag_name(name="ShouldThisBeDoneAgain") ]
    HTTP_CODE ShouldThisBeDoneAgain(void)
    {
        count++;
        if (count <= 10)
            return HTTP_SUCCESS;
        else
            return HTTP_S_FALSE;
    }
    [ tag_name(name="GetNextNumber") ]
    HTTP_CODE GetNextNumber(void)
    {
        m_HttpResponse
            << "The square of " << count << " is ";
        return HTTP_SUCCESS;
    }
    [ tag_name(name="GetNextNumberSquared") ]
    HTTP_CODE GetNextNumberSquared(void)
    {
        m_HttpResponse << count*count;
        return HTTP_SUCCESS;
    }
};
```

The corresponding **while_endwhile.srf** file displays a table of numbers and their square values. In this example, you can see that tags may be nested in the expected way. This causes the **GetNextNumber** and **GetNextNumberSquared** tags to be replaced multiple times.

```
<html>
<BODY>
<P>{{handler ATLServerApp.dll/while_endwhile}}</P>
```

```
<P>
<TABLE>
   {{while ShouldThisBeDoneAgain}}
   <TR>
      <TD>{{GetNextNumber}}</TD>
      <TD>{{GetNextNumberSquared}}</TD>
   </TR>
   {{endwhile}}
</TABLE>
</P>
</BODY>
</html>
```

You can see the result at http://localhost/ATLServerApp/while_endwhile.srf. Figure 12–12 shows the outcome.

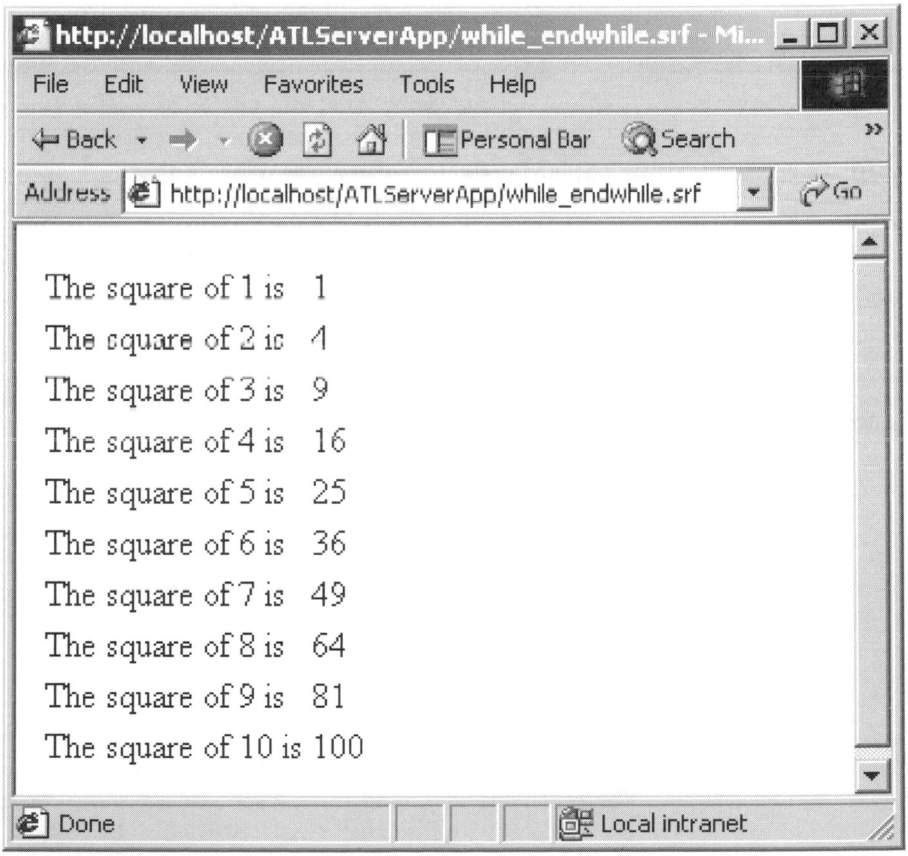

Figure 12-12   *Viewing while_endwhile.srf.*

Passing Parameters to the Server Handler

Code Example

The **pass_parameter.srf** file shows how you can pass parameters into the Web application request handler replacement method. Parse functions are used by the request handler class to convert the original parameter specified in the **.srf** file, which is of type string, into the data type expected by the request handler method. The signature of the parse function in the request handler class must be as follows:

```
HTTP_CODE parseFunction(
    IAtlMemMgr* pMemoryManager,
    LPCSTR szArgumentData,
    parameterType** ppArgument);
```

The memory that is used to store the converted parameter must be allocated using **pMemoryManager->Allocate**. You should not free this memory explicitly, since the ATL Server framework automatically frees it at the appropriate time. The original parameter string data is obtained from **szArgumentData**. The converted parameter to be passed into the request handler method is then stored via the **ppArgument**. The following data types may be used for the parameter, or you may define your own data type using a structure.

- bool
- char
- unsigned char
- short
- unsigned short
- int
- unsigned int
- __int64
- unsigned __int64
- double
- float

The corresponding replacement method in the request handler class then takes an argument as shown in the following signature:

```
HTTP_CODE replacementMethod(
    parameterType* pArgument);
```

The **pArgument** parameter must point to the same data type as that used in the corresponding parse function.

The replacement method and its corresponding parse function can be associated using either of two techniques. In the first technique, if the **parameterType** is one of the supported types for the **tag_name** attribute, the name of the parse function can be omitted and the parse function will be automatically associated with the replacement method based on its type.

In the second technique, the name of the associated parse function can be explicitly specified in the **parse_func** parameter of the **tag_name** attribute. This technique is necessary if you are defining your own parameter type with a structure or if there is more than one method that accepts the same parameter type.

Code Example

The following example supports the passing of a parameter from the corresponding **pass_parameter.srf** file using the first of the two techniques described above. You can see in this example that the passing of a parameter requires both a parse function that converts the parameter from a string to the desired type (**int** in this example) and a replacement method that receives the converted parameter and handles the tag replacement.

```
//A handler for testing parameter passing
[request_handler("pass_parameter")]
class C_parameter_passing_ATLServerAppHandler
{
protected:
    //parse method converts parameter from string to int
    HTTP_CODE parseFunction(
        TAtlMemMgr* pMemoryManager,
        LPCSTR szArgumentData,
        int** ppArgument)
    {
        //allocate memory for the argument to be passed
        int *pparam
            (int *)pMemoryManager->Allocate(sizeof(int));
        //set param value to be passed to replacement method
        *pparam = atoi(szArgumentData);
        //pass parameter back through ppArgument
        ppArgument = &pparam;
        return HTTP_SUCCESS;
    }
    //replacement method accepts int parameter
    [ tag_name(name="SquareOfParameter") ]
    HTTP_CODE SquareOfParameter(int* pArgument)
    {
        m_HttpResponse
            << "Parameter was "
                << *pArgument << "<p>"
            << "Square of parameter is"
                << *pArgument * *pArgument;
```

```
        return HTTP_SUCCESS;
    }
};
```

The corresponding **pass_parameter.srf** file displays the square of the parameter.

```
{{handler ATLServerApp.dll/pass_parameter}}
{{SquareOfParameter(10)}}
```

You can see the result at http://localhost/ATLServerApp/pass_parameter.srf. Figure 12–13 shows the outcome.

You can also pass multiple parameters of differing types from the **.srf** file into the Web application request handler. To do this, you define a structure with members that correspond to the parameters being passed. The following example shows how to pass two parameters from the **.srf** file. The first parameter is a number, and the second parameter is a string. The parsing

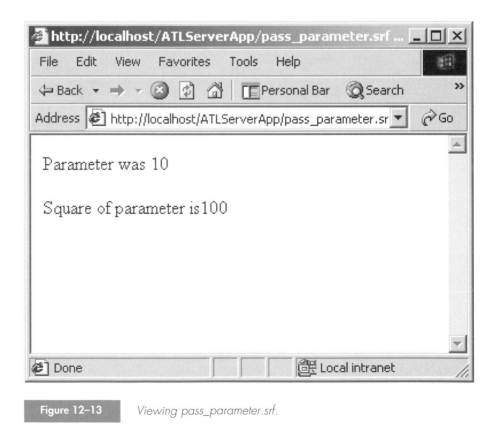

Figure 12–13   *Viewing pass_parameter.srf.*

function separates these two parameters from a single string and packages them up in a custom structure named **PARAMETER_DATA**. The parsing function uses simple string parsing techniques to tokenize the parameter string and convert each parameter into the type expected by the structure member. This structure is then passed into the replacement method as a single composite parameter.

This example also shows how to use the second technique for associating the parsing function with the replacement handler method, mentioned previously. In this technique, the name of the parse method is explicitly specified by **parse_func** in the **tag_name** attribute of the replacement method.

```
//A handler that takes two parameters
[request_handler("pass_two_parameters")]
class C_pass_two_parameters_ATLServerAppHandler
{
protected:
    //custom structure for storing converted parameters
    typedef struct
    {
        short index;
        char string[100];
    } PARAMETER_DATA;
    //parse method converts two parameters from string
    HTTP_CODE parseTwoParametersFunction(
        IAtlMemMgr* pMemoryManager,
        LPCSTR szArgumentData,
        PARAMETER_DATA** ppArgument)
    {
        //allocate memory for the arguments to be passed
        PARAMETER_DATA *pparams =
            (PARAMETER_DATA *)pMemoryManager->Allocate(
                sizeof(PARAMETER_DATA));

        //set params to be passed to replacement method
        char *szToken = strtok(
            (LPSTR)szArgumentData, ", "); //get 1st param
        pparams->index = atoi(szToken); //store 1st param
        szToken = strtok(NULL, "\""); //step over whitespace
        szToken = strtok(NULL, "\""); //get 2nd param
        strcpy(pparams->string, szToken); //store 1st paramr

        //pass parameters back through ppArgument
        ppArgument = &pparams;
        return HTTP_SUCCESS;
    }
}
```

```
//replacement method accepts two parameters in a struct
[ tag_name(name="HandleTwoParameters",
  parse_func="parseTwoParametersFunction") ]
HTTP_CODE HandleTwoParameters(PARAMETER_DATA* pArgument)
{
  m_HttpResponse
     << "First parameter was "
        << pArgument->index << "<p>"
     << "Second parameter was \""
        << pArgument->string << "\"<p>"
     << "The ASCII code for this index is "
        << pArgument->string[pArgument->index];
  return HTTP_SUCCESS;
}
```

The corresponding **pass_two_parameters.srf** file displays the result of passing the two parameters.

```
{{handler ATLServerApp.dll/pass_two_parameters}}
{{HandleTwoParameters(10, "here is a bit of text")}}
```

You can see the result at http://localhost/ATLServerApp/pass_two_parameters.srf. Figure 12–14 shows the outcome.

Maintaining Session State

HTTP is a connectionless protocol; however, ATL Server can maintain session state for the each client from one HTTP request to the next. This can be accomplished using cookies for keeping track of each client session. ATL Server can then retrieve each client session state using the appropriate cookie.

A cookie is initially created by an ISAPI extension. It contains a name and value string pair that is sent in an HTTP response header to the client. Each cookie allows the Web server to store a piece of information in the Web browser that will subsequently be sent back to the server in each HTTP request header that is directed to the specified URL.

ATL Server provides the **CCookie** class to conveniently work with cookies. **CCookie** can be used to encapsulate single-valued and multi-valued cookies.

Code
Example

This example shows how to construct two simple replacement methods named **SendCookieToClient** and **GetCookieFromClient**. This example implements a single-valued cookie that encapsulates the name "nameOfCookie", and a value containing a simple string representation of the current time.

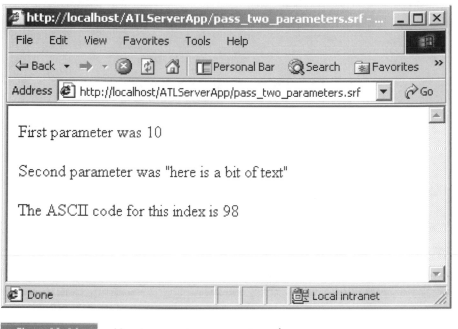

Figure 12–14   *Viewing pass_two_parameters.srf.*

```
//A handler that sends a cookie to the client
[request_handler("send_cookie_to_client")]
class C_send_cookie_to_client_AppHandler
{
protected:
    [ tag_name(name="SendCookieToClient") ]
    HTTP_CODE SendCookieToClient(void)
    {
        CString valueOfCookie;
        SYSTEMTIME systemTime;
        GetLocalTime(&systemTime);
        valueOfCookie.Format(
            "%d:%d", systemTime.wHour, systemTime.wMinute);
        CCookie cookie;
        cookie.SetName("nameOfCookie");
        cookie.SetValue(valueOfCookie);
        cookie.SetPath("/"); //URL where cookie applies
        m_HttpResponse.AppendCookie(&cookie);

        //indicate that we sent the cookie to the client
        m_HttpResponse
            << "SendCookieToClient sent: "
```

```
                << valueOfCookie;
         return HTTP_SUCCESS;
      }
};

//A handler that gets a cookie from the client
[request_handler("get_cookie_from_client")]
class C_get_cookie_from_client_AppHandler
{
protected:
   [ tag_name(name="GetCookieFromClient") ]
   HTTP_CODE GetCookieFromClient(void)
   {
      CString valueOfCookie;
      CCookie cookie =
         m_HttpRequest.Cookies("nameOfCookie");
      BOOL bSuccess = cookie.GetValue(valueOfCookie);
      if (bSuccess)
      {
         //prove that we got the cookie by displaying it
         m_HttpResponse
            << "Proof that GetCookieFromClient worked: "
            << valueOfCookie;
      }
      return HTTP_SUCCESS;
   }
```

Code
Example

The corresponding **send_cookie_to_client.srf** and **get_cookie_from_ client.srf** files interact with the Web browser to exchange information that is stored on the client as a cookie.

First, the **send_cookie_to_client.srf** file is accessed by the Web browser. This .srf file specifies the **SendCookieToClient** replacement method that creates and sends the cookie to the Web browser.

```
{{handler ATLServerApp.dll/send_cookie_to_client}}
{{SendCookieToClient}}
```

Later, the **get_cookie_from_client.srf** file is accessed by the Web browser. This .srf file specifies the **GetCookieFromClient** replacement method that receives the cookie back from the client.

```
{{handler ATLServerApp.dll/get_cookie_from_client}}
{{GetCookieFromClient}}
```

You can see the result of this example by first visiting the URL that sends the cookie to the client, and then visiting the URL that gets the cookie back from the client. If you experiment a bit with it, you will see that the cookie remains unchanged up until the next time you visit the URL that again sends the cookie to the client. The URLs are

- http://localhost/ATLServerApp/send_cookie_to_client.srf.
- http://localhost/ATLServerApp/get_cookie_from_client.srf.

Figure 12–15 shows the first URL, and Figure 12–16 shows the second URL in Internet Explorer.

This example is a bit contrived, but it shows in a very simple and direct way how cookies work. The focus here is on the mechanics of cookies, not realism. In this example, the **send_cookie_to_client.srf** file generates a cookie that contains the current time, which might be a bit unusual in a real application. Then, the **get_cookie_from_client.srf** file sends HTML that displays the contents of the cookie just as a proof that it works, which is even more atypical.

A more realistic application would use cookies to store more meaningful information, such as user preferences and page customization. The first time a user visits a Web page, certain information may be obtained via a form, and the server would then package the information into one or more cookies and send them to the Web client. Then, on subsequent visits to other pages on the same Web site, the server could retrieve these cookies, obtain the information contained in them, and customize the HTML that it generates based on that information.

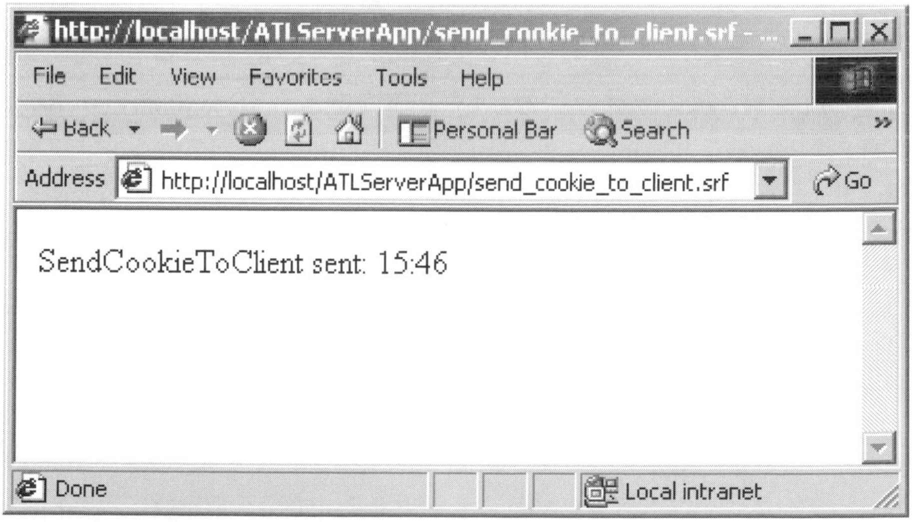

Figure 12–15   *Viewing send_cookie_to_client.srf.*

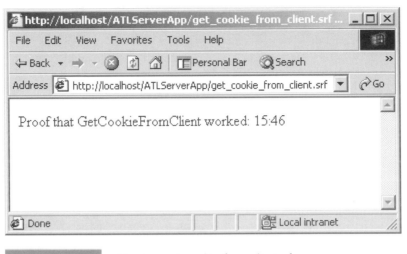

Accessing Server Variables

This example shows how to accesses the HTTP_USER_AGENT server variable. Several other server variables are available that you can make use of as well.

```
//A handler that access a server variable
[request_handler("access_server_variable")]
class C_access_server_variable_AppHandler
{
protected:
   [ tag_name(name="AccessServerVariable") ]
   HTTP_CODE AccessServerVariable(void)
   {
      //use the HTTP_USER_AGENT server variable
      CString strUserAgent;
      m_HttpRequest.GetUserAgent(strUserAgent);
      m_HttpResponse
         << "I see that you are using: "
         << strUserAgent;
      return HTTP_SUCCESS;
   }
};
```

Here is the associated **access_server_variable.srf** file.

```
{{handler ATLServerApp.dll/access_server_variable}}
{{AccessServerVariable}}
```

Figure 12–17 shows the result of viewing **access_server_variable.srf**, which you can access from the URL *http://localhost/ATLServerApp/access_s erver_variable.srf.*

Handling Forms

In this example, a request handler class named **C_process_post_ AppHandler** is added to **ATLServerApp.h**. This class contains a method named **ProcessPost**, which accesses a form variable using the HTTP request object. A **CHttpRequestParams** collection is obtained from the **CHttpRequest::GetFormVars** method. The **CHttpRequestParams::Exchange** method is then used to obtain the named value from the form. In this example, the name of the value is "txtName." Just to prove that it works, we echo the value contained in **szName** back to the client.

```
//A handler that processes a POST
[request_handler("process_post")]
class C_process_post_AppHandler
{
protected:
    [ tag_name(name="ProcessPost") ]
    HTTP_CODE ProcessPost(void)
    {
```

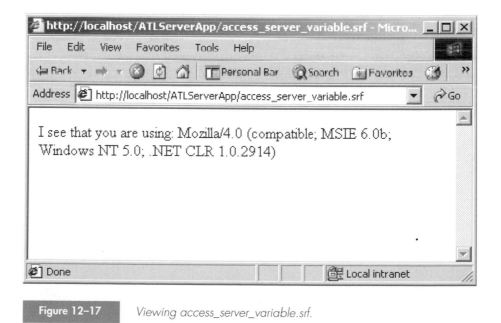

I see that you are using: Mozilla/4.0 (compatible; MSIE 6.0b; Windows NT 5.0; .NET CLR 1.0.2914)

Figure 12–17   *Viewing access_server_variable.srf.*

```
        //use a form variable
        const CHttpRequestParams &request =
            m_HttpRequest.GetFormVars();
        CValidateContext valCtx;
        LPCSTR szName;
        request.Exchange("txtName", &szName, &valCtx);
        m_HttpResponse
            << "Welcome to ATL Server, " << szName << "<p>";
        return HTTP_SUCCESS;
    }
};
```

Here is the **process_post.srf** that provides access to the **ProcessPost** method just described.

```
{{handler ATLServerApp.dll/process_post}}
{{ProcessPost}}
```

This time, rather than access the **process_post.srf** file directly in your browser, you access it via an HTML file that contains a form. This file[11] is named **SimpleForm.htm** and contains the following HTML. Note that it posts a request containing a named value called "txtName."

```
<HTML>
  <HEAD>
  </HEAD>
<BODY>
  <form method="post"
    action=
    "http://localhost/ATLServerApp/process_post.srf">
    Enter your name:
    <input name="txtName" type="text" size="30">
    <input name="cmdEcho" type="submit" value="Echo">
  </form>
</BODY>
</HTML>
```

Again, it can be instructive to view what happens within the ISAPI extension DLL using the debugger. You will find that the **HttpExtensionProc** function in **ATLServerAppIsapi.dll** receives the EXTENSION_CONTROL_BLOCK parameter containing the data listed in Table 12–2. The contents of these

---

[11] The .htm file is copied automatically into the deployment virtual directory along with the .srf files as part of the Visual Studio build process.

members originate from the form specified in **SimpleForm.htm** shown above.

In this example, **SimpleForm.htm** uses a POST method, and the data is carried in the request body. The **FormVars** array is used to access this data in the handler class. If **SimpleForm.htm** were changed to use a GET method, then the data would be contained in the query string.[12] However, the **FormVars** array could still be used in the same way to access the form data. Table12–3 shows the values in the EXTENSION_CONTROL_BLOCK parameter if you were to change the FORM to use a GET method.

Figure 12–18 shows **SimpleForm.htm** being filled in. When you click on the Echo button, the **process_post.srf** is accessed with the form variable containing the value Bob. The result is shown in Figure 12–19.

Session Services

You may recall from Figure 12–4 that the Server Options page of the ATL Server Project Wizard has a checkbox option for Session services. If you select this option, then the resulting project will be automatically configured for

Table 12–2 EXTENSION_CONTROL_BLOCK Structure for POST Method

Structure Member	Value
lpszMethod	"POST"
lpszQueryString	""
lpszPathInfo	"/ATLServerApp/process_post.srf "
pbData	"txtName=Bob&cmdEcho=Echo"

Table 12–3 EXTENSION_CONTROL_BLOCK Structure for GET Method

Structure Member	Value
lpszMethod	"GET"
lpszQueryString	"txtName=Bob&cmdEcho=Echo"
lpszPathInfo	"/ATLServerApp/process_post.srf"
pbData	0

---

[12] The method attribute of the FORM element may specify the GET or POST method of sending the form data to the Web server. The GET method adds a question mark followed by the form data on the end of the URI specified by the action attribute of the FORM. The POST method places the form data into the body of the HTTP request.

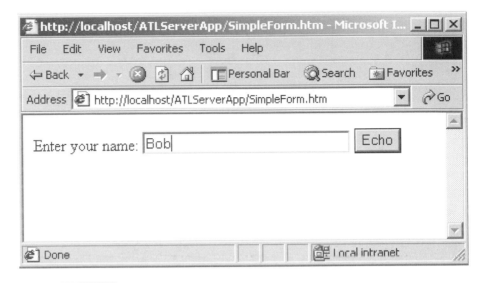

Figure 12–18   *Viewing the form in SimpleForm.htm.*

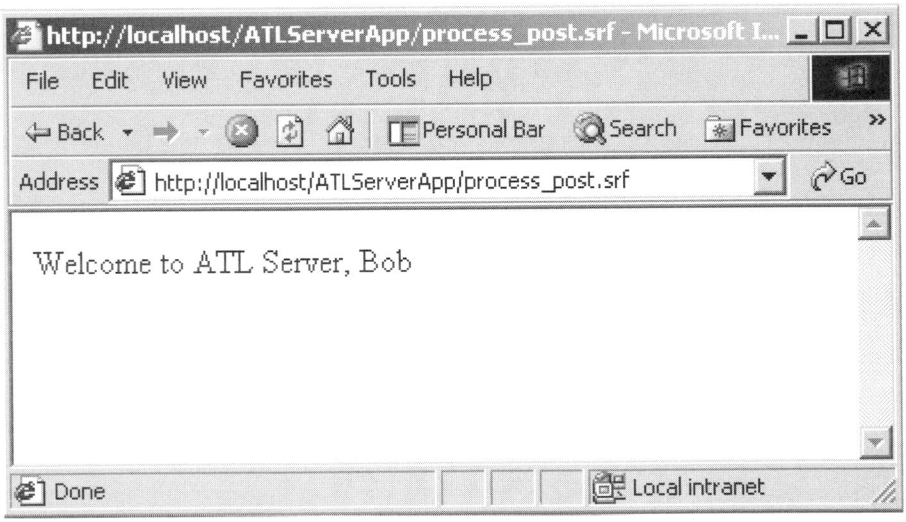

Figure 12–19   *The result of submitting the form in SimpleForm.htm.*

managing session state. The **CSessionStateService** class provides access to session state variables via the **CDBSession** and **CMemSession** classes. The **CDBSession** and **CMemSession** classes implement the **ISession** interface, which specifies methods for storing, modifying, deleting, and enumerating named session variables.[13]

Creating an ATL Server Web Service Project

We saw how Web Services work in Chapter 11, using ASP.NET. We will not repeat the basic theory on how Web Services work here, because the fundamental concepts are the same regardless of whether you use ASP.NET or ATL Server to implement a Web Service. The main difference is that whereas ASP.NET is implemented with managed code and can be written in any .NET language, ATL is implemented as unmanaged code, and it can only be written using Visual C++.

Here are the steps you go through to create a starter ATL Web Service project.[14]

1. Select the File | New | Project menu item.
2. Open the Visual C++ Projects node in the Project Types tree.
3. Select the ATL Server Web Service Project in the Templates window. This results in the ATL Server Project Wizard, but for a Web Service rather than a Web application.
4. Enter **ATLServerWeb** as the project name.
5. Enter an appropriate directory for the project location. The Demos directory is provided for this purpose.
6. Click OK to start the ATL Server Project Wizard.
7. View the default choices that have been preselected by the Wizard on the Overview tab. Also, look at the Project Settings, Server Options, Application Options, and Developer Support Options tabs as well. These are shown in Figures 12–20, 12–21, 12–22, 12–23, and 12–24.
8. Without making any changes to the default options, click Finish.
9. Build the project in the usual way. This builds and deploys the ATL Web service.

As we have just seen, the ATL Server Project Wizard can generate an ATL Server Application Project, or an ATL Server Web Service Project. You can compare Figures 12–2, 12–3, 12–4, 12–5, and 12–6 with the following five figures to see the differences between a newly created ATL Server project and an ATL Web services project. In particular, note that in Figure 12–23, in the Application Options page, the Create as Web Service checkbox is checked.

The following files are created identically in both ATL Server and ATL Web Service projects. These are basic to any ATL-based ISAPI Extension DLL.

- The **.cpp** source that implements **DllMain**.
- The **.cpp** source file that implements the **HttpExtensionProc**, **GetExtensionVersion**, and **TerminateExtension** DLL export functions.
- The **.def** file that exports **HttpExtensionProc**, **GetExtensionVersion**, and **TerminateExtension** functions.

---

[13] For more details on managing session state, please review the ATL Server documentation.

[14] A solution example for this project is provided in the ATLServerWeb directory.

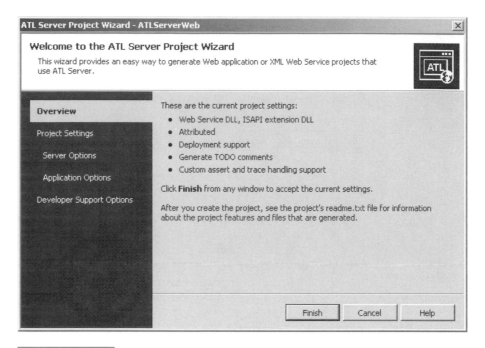

Figure 12–20   *ATL Web Service Project Wizard Overview.*

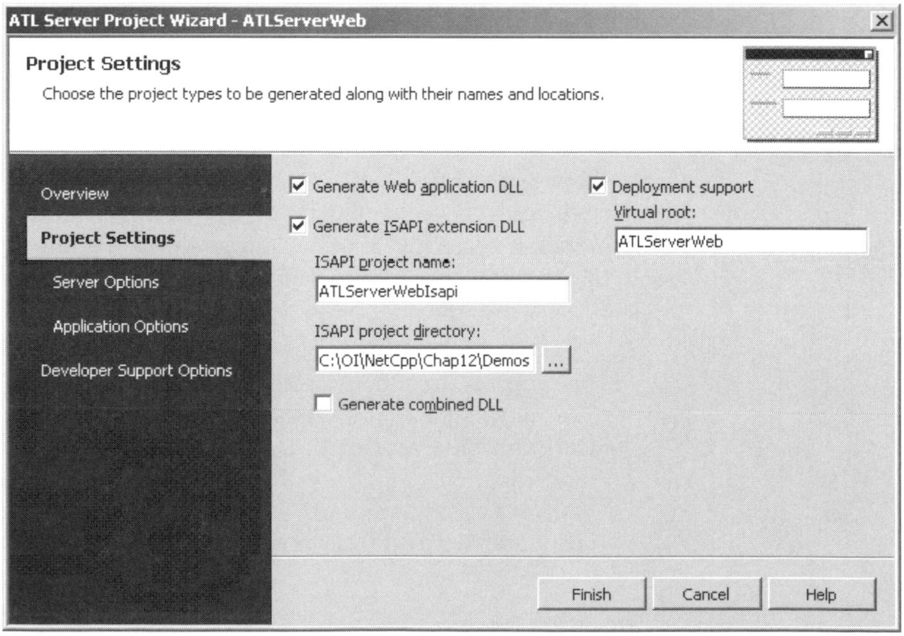

Figure 12–21   *ATL Web Service Project Wizard Project Settings.*

ATL Web Service Project Wizard Server Options.

Web ATL Service Project Wizard Application Options.

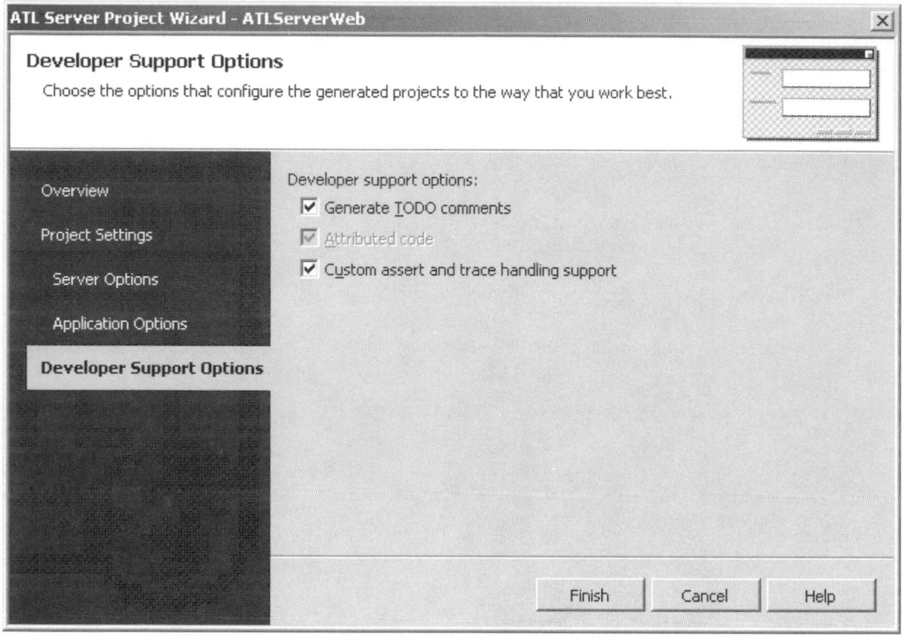

Figure 12–24   *Web ATL Service Project Wizard Developer Support Options.*

The following files are created only in an ATL Web Service project. The discovery file provides XML formatted information to client building tools that need to discover the functional interface exposed by the Web Service. The HTML file provides access to human readable documentation on the Web Service functionality.

- The **.disco** file.
- The **.htm** file.

The **.srf** file is created only in an ATL Server project, not in an ATL Web Service project. Since a Web Service is accessed from a custom client application rather than a Web browser, an .srf file is not of any use.

The only file that exists in both ATL Server and ATL Web Service projects, but is significantly different, is the **.h** file that implements the ATL Server request handler class. In both the ATL Server project and the ATL Web Service project, a namespace is defined. However, only in the ATL Web Service project, the namespace contains an interface for accessing the Web Service methods, as well as a request handler class that has an additional attribute named **soap_handler**. This class also has a starter example method named **HelloWorld**, with the **soap_method** attribute applied to it.

ATL Server Web Service Code: ATLServerWebService.h

The **ATLServerWebService.h** source file is the main difference between what the ATL Wizard generates for a Web application versus a Web Service. It defines the ATL Server request handler class, in both cases, with just a few differences. It also defines a namespace and an interface for accessing the Web Service via the SOAP protocol. Here is the starter code for this file. Note that the **IATLServerWebService** interface is defined. The request handler class in the same source file implements this interface.

```
namespace ATLServerWebService
{
// all struct, enum, and typedefs for your Webservice should go
  inside the namespace

// IATLServerWebService - Web Service interface declaration
//
[
   uuid("53A879FF-9D20-42A8-9978-C0D4B05B10B7"),
   object
]
__interface IATLServerWebService
{
   // HelloWorld is a sample ATL Server Web Service method.
   // It shows how to declare a Web Service method and its
   // in-parameters and out-parameters
   [id(1)] HRESULT HelloWorld(
      [in] BSTR bstrInput, [out, retval] BSTR *bstrOutput);
   // TODO: Add additional Web Service methods here
};

// ATLServerWebService - Web Service implementation
//
[
   request_handler(name="Default",
   sdl="GenATLServerWebWSDL"),
   soap_handler(
      name="ATLServerWebService",
      namespace="urn:ATLServerWebService",
      protocol="soap"
   )
]
class CATLServerWebService :
```

```
    public IATLServerWebService
{
public:
    // This is a sample Web Service method that shows how to
    // use the soap_method attribute to expose a method as a
    // Web method
    [ soap_method ]
    HRESULT HelloWorld(
        /*[in]*/ BSTR bstrInput,
        /*[out, retval]*/ BSTR *bstrOutput)
    {
        CComBSTR bstrOut(L"Hello ");
        bstrOut += bstrInput;
        bstrOut += L"!";
        *bstrOutput = bstrOut.Detach();

        return S_OK;
    }
    // TODO: Add additional Web Service methods here
}; // class CATLServerWebService

} // namespace ATLServerWebService
```

Build the project and then run it in the usual way. The project's default debug properties specify that the URL that you view is at http://localhost/ ATLServerWeb/ATLServerWeb.dll?Handler=GenATLServerWebWSDL. Figure 12–25 shows the result of viewing this URL. This does not actually invoke any functionality in the Web Service. Instead, it just displays an XML representation of the Web Service interface.

Although it is comforting to see this page in your browser, this is not the normal way that a Web Service is accessed or used. Instead, a client typically invokes the Web Service methods within a distributed application. To see this, we will need to create a client program that calls into this Web Service.

Creating a Web Service Client Program

You can make any type of program into a Web Service client program. Here we will build a simple console client program that tests the ATL Web Service just created.[15]

1. Select the File | New | Project menu item.
2. Open the Visual C++ Projects node in the Project Types tree.

---

[15] This client program is provided in the **ATLServerWebClient** directory.

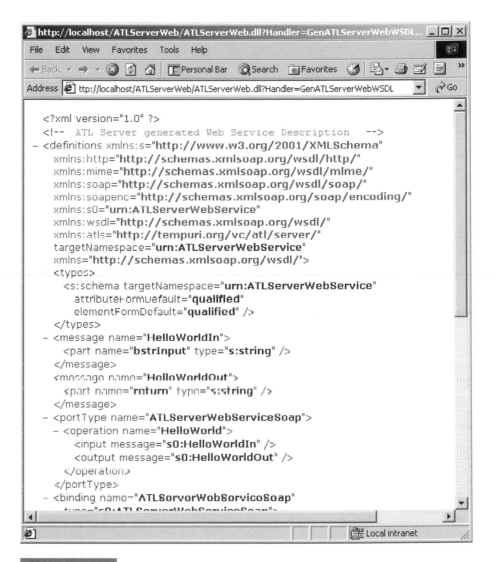

```
http://localhost/ATLServerWeb/ATLServerWeb.dll?Handler=GenATLServerWebWSDL...

File   Edit   View   Favorites   Tools   Help

Back          Personal Bar    Search    Favorites

Address    ttp://localhost/ATLServerWeb/ATLServerWeb.dll?Handler=GenATLServerWebWSDL    Go

<?xml version="1.0" ?>
<!--  ATL Server generated Web Service Description  -->
- <definitions xmlns:s="http://www.w3.org/2001/XMLSchema"
    xmlns:http="http://schemas.xmlsoap.org/wsdl/http/"
    xmlns:mime="http://schemas.xmlsoap.org/wsdl/mime/"
    xmlns:soap="http://schemas.xmlsoap.org/wsdl/soap/"
    xmlns:soapenc="http://schemas.xmlsoap.org/soap/encoding/"
    xmlns:s0="urn:ATLServerWebService"
    xmlns:wsdl="http://schemas.xmlsoap.org/wsdl/"
    xmlns:atls="http://tempuri.org/vc/atl/server/"
    targetNamespace="urn:ATLServerWebService"
    xmlns="http://schemas.xmlsoap.org/wsdl/">
    <types>
      <s:schema targetNamespace="urn:ATLServerWebService"
        attributeFormDefault="qualified"
        elementFormDefault="qualified" />
    </types>
- <message name="HelloWorldIn">
    <part name="bstrInput" type="s:string" />
  </message>
- <message name="HelloWorldOut">
    <part name="return" type="s:string" />
  </message>
- <portType name="ATLServerWebServiceSoap">
  - <operation name="HelloWorld">
      <input message="s0:HelloWorldIn" />
      <output message="s0:HelloWorldOut" />
    </operation>
  </portType>
- <binding name="ATLServerWebServiceSoap"
    type="s0:ATLServerWebServiceSoap">

                                          Local intranet
```

Figure 12–25   *Web ATL Service Project viewed in browser.*

3. Select the Win32 Project in the Templates window. This results in the ATL Server Project Wizard.
4. Enter ATLServerWebClient as the project name.
5. Enter an appropriate directory for the project location.
6. Click OK to start the Win32 Project Wizard.
7. On the Applications Settings tab in the Win32 Application Wizard, select the Console application radio button.
8. Click Finish.

9.   Right-click on the ATLServerWebClient project node in Solution Explorer. Select the Add Web Reference context menu item.

10. In the Add Web Reference dialog, specify the URL of the ATL Web service discovery file ATLServerWeb.disco[16] as shown in Figure 12–26. Then click on Add Reference. This will add the **ATLServerWeb.h** source file to the client project, which implements a proxy object for calling on the Web service methods.[17]

11. Open the **ATLServerWebClient.cpp** source file and add the code indicated in bold text.

```
#include "stdafx.h"
#define _WIN32_WINNT 0x0400 //need _WIN32_WINNT >= 0x0400
#include "ATLServerWeb.h"    //needed to access proxy
```

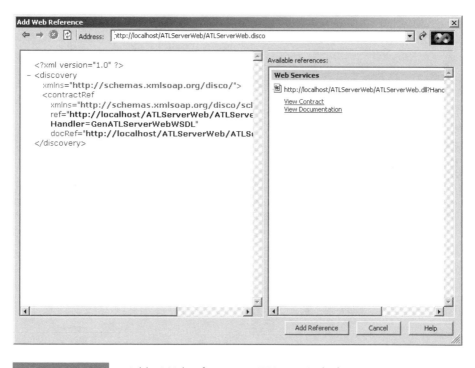

Figure 12–26   *Add a Web reference to ATLServerWeb.disco.*

---

[16] The discovery file was automatically deployed to the appropriate IIS virtual directory when the ATL Web Service project was built.

[17] If the server's interface is ever changed, this step will need to be repeated to generate a new proxy for the client.

```
int _tmain(int argc, _TCHAR* argv[])
{
   CoInitialize(NULL);
   ATLServerWebService::CATLServerWebServiceT<> service;
   CComBSTR bstrInput(L"ATL Web Service");
   CComBSTR bstrOutput;
   service.HelloWorld(bstrInput, &bstrOutput);
   wprintf(
      L"HelloWorld returned bstrOutput: %s\n",
      bstrOutput);
   return 0;
}
```

12. Build and run the ATL Web Service client project in the usual way. Then run the program, and you should then see the following result.

```
HelloWorld returned bstrOutput: Hello ATL Web Service!
```

Adding Functionally to the ATL Server Web Service

You may recall the SimpleWebService example in Chapter 11 that added two numbers. We will now add similar functionality to the ATLServerWeb project that we just created in this chapter. This will provide a method that receives two integer parameters and returns their sum. To do this, just follow these steps.

1. Open the **ATLServerWeb.sln** solution that was just created.
2. In **ATLServerWeb.h**, add the **Add** method definition to the **IATLServerWebService** interface as shown in bold text.[18]

```
__interface IATLServerWebService
{
   ...
   // TODO: Add additional Web Service methods here
   HRESULT Add(
      [in] long x, [in] long y, [out, retval] long *psum);
};
```

3. Also in **ATLServerWeb.h**, add the **Add** method implementation to the **CATLServerWebService** class as shown in bold text.

---

[18] The dispatch ID value is set to 1 in the preexisting HelloWorld method. We will not be using dispatch IDs in this example, but if you did want to assign a dispatch ID to the new Add method, you would use the next available value, which would be 2.

```
class CATLServerWebService :
public IATLServerWebService
{
public:
   ...
   // TODO: Add additional Web Service methods here
   [ soap_method ]
   HRESULT  Add(long x, long y, long *psum)
   {
      *psum = x + y;
      return S_OK;
   }
}; // class CATLServerWebService
```

4.   Build the project.[19]

Now the server is ready to be accessed by any client program that passes two in integer parameters and returns one out integer parameter.

Modifying the Web Service Client Program

Now you will probably want to test the **Add** method with a client program. To do this, follow these steps.

1.   Open the **ATLServerWebClient.sln** project created earlier.
2.   Add http://localhost/ATLServerWeb/ATLServerWeb.disco as a Web reference to the project again. This is done with the Project | Add Web Reference menu item. This was done earlier, but it must be done again now because of the changes just made to the server interface. This will regenerate the proxy used by the client to access the new **Add** method.[20]
3.   Open the **ATLServerWebClient.cpp** file and add the code indicated in bold text.

```
int _tmain(int argc, _TCHAR* argv[])
{
   CoInitialize(NULL);
   ...
   int sum;
   service.Add(3, 4, &sum);
```

---

[19]   If you look at http://localhost/ATLServerWeb/ATLServerWeb.dll?Handler=GenATLServerWeb-WSDL in your browser, you will see the new information on the **Add** method now appears.

[20]   This creates a new header file implementing the client proxy. You will need to either rename the new header file as the old one or modify the #include directive to access the new header file.

```
    wprintf(
        L"The result of calling Add(3, 4) is: %d\n",
        sum);

    return 0;
}
```

4. Build the client project and run it. You should see the following result.

```
The result of calling Add(3, 4) is: 7
```

Passing In and Out Structure Parameters

Here is a simple example of how a Web Service method can take in and out structures as parameters. A structure named **MyStructure**, containing two **int** members, has been added to the **ATLServerWeb.h** source file. The **IATLServerWebService** interface has also been augmented with a new method named **CopyMyStructure**, that takes in and out pointers to **MyStructure** as parameters. This method is then implemented in the **CATLServerWebService** class.

```
namespace ATLServerWebService
{
...
    struct MyStructure
    {
        int x;
        int y;
    };
...
[
    uuid("53A879FF-9D20-42A8-9978-C0D4B05B10B7"),
    object
]
    interface IATLServerWebService
{
    ...
    HRESULT CopyMyStructure(
        [in]MyStructure *pms1, [out]MyStructure *pms2);
};
...
class CATLServerWebService :
```

```
    public IATLServerWebService
{
public:
    ...
    [ soap_method ]
    HRESULT CopyMyStructure(
        MyStructure *pms1, MyStructure *pms2)
    {
        pms2->x = pms1->x;
        pms2->y = pms1->y;
        return S_OK;
    }
};
```

Here is the client code that tests the passing of in and out parameters.[21]

```
//pass in and out pointers to structures
struct ATLServerWebService::MyStructure ms1, ms2;
ms1.x = 10;
ms1.y = 20;
ms2.x = 0;
ms2.y = 0;
wprintf(
    L"ms1.x: %d, ms1.y: %d, ms2.x: %d, ms2.y: %d\n",
    ms1.x, ms1.y, ms2.x, ms2.y);
wprintf(
    L"Calling CopyMyStructure(&ms1, &ms2)\n",
    ms2.x, ms2.y);
service.CopyMyStructure(
    &ms1,
    sizeof(ATLServerWebService::MyStructure),
    &ms2);
wprintf(
    L"ms1.x: %d, ms1.y: %d, ms2.x: %d, ms2.y: %d\n",
    ms1.x, ms1.y, ms2.x, ms2.y);
```

Here is the program output, which proves that the marshaling of the structure works in both directions. The structure named ms2 initially contains zero values for its x and y members. During the call to the **CopyMyStructure** method, the ms2 structure is modified, by copying the members from ms1, and then ms2 is returned to the client.

---

[21] This code is also provided in the solution example.

```
ms1.x: 10, ms1.y: 20, ms2.x: 0, ms2.y: 0
Calling CopyMyStructure(&ms1, &ms2)
ms1.x: 10, ms1.y: 20, ms2.x: 10, ms2.y: 20
```

Now you may be wondering why this is such a big deal. How is this any better than exposing functionality as a DLL, or with RPC or DCOM? The cool thing about a Web Service is that, unlike a DLL, the Web Service can be located anywhere on the Internet. And unlike RPC or DCOM, Web Services are based on XML and SOAP. This will allow some interesting integration possibilities down the road.

Summary

Web Services allow you to build large-scale distributed applications that can take advantage of the widespread nature of the Internet. Because Web Services are built on standard and ubiquitous protocols, such as HTML, XML, and SOAP, it is much more flexible and natural than using traditional distributed computing technologies, such as RPC. ATL provides a means for building Web Services, and because ATL is so efficient, it is ideal for implementing Web Services that need to be optimized for performance.

THIRTEEN

Security

While Security considerations are fundamental to application design and should not be left for last, pedagogically it is easier to talk about security once the .NET application model, ASP.NET, and Web Services have already been introduced. This chapter introduces to you the fundamentals of .NET security.[1]

Security prevents a user or code from doing things it should not be allowed to do. Traditionally, security has focused on restricting user actions. NET allows restrictions to be placed on executing code as well. For example, you can prevent certain sections of code from accessing certain files. This is particularly useful when you have public Web sites or services where it is impractical to create user accounts, lock-down files, or other resources for an unknown number of users. It is critical when you are executing code that was created by third parties.

It is important to realize that .NET security sits on top of the underlying operating system's security system. For the purposes of this chapter, the underlying operating system is assumed to be Windows 2000. While we will discuss some security issues associated with the underlying infrastructure, including Microsoft's Internet Information Server (IIS), we will go into some detail only with those parts of the security story that are relevant to .NET.[2]

To give an example of the interaction of .NET security and the operating system, code always runs under some identity, or in other words, as some user ID. Irrespective of the file creation .NET security permissions, if the file

---

[1] Pedagogical reasons also dictate the form of the sample code. It is easier to demonstrate security by starting with an open environment and then showing you how to restrict operations. Real systems should start with the most restrictive security and then open up only as needed.

[2] For more information about secure Web-based applications, read *Designing Secure Web-Based Applications for Microsoft Windows 2000* by Michael Howard.

Access Control List (ACL) denies you the right to create a file, you will be unable to create a file.

The security story starts with an attempt to answer to two questions. The first is the authentication question: Who are you? The second is the authorization question: Do you have the right to do what you are trying to do? Under .NET this story takes two branches, because the "you" can be either a user identity or an identity associated with an assembly.

We start with a brief telling of the security story by showing how both these types of security exist in .NET. Although it is not needed immediately, a brief excursion into Internet security follows so that we can use that information when we need it. Then we start the detailed narrative with role-based security in .NET.

User-Based Security

From the perspective of traditional user-based security, the authentication question is, Who is the *identity* attempting to do the action? An identity is typically a user or account name. *Credentials* are what you present to prove who you are; they are evidence presented for verification. A credential might be your password, a smart card, or a biometric device. The user's credentials must be verified with some security authority. An example of this is verifying a user's password against his or her login name based on a database of user names and encrypted passwords. Systems that allow unverified access are said to allow anonymous access. In security lingo the identity that can be authenticated is referred to as the *principal*.

The authorization question is, Can the identity perform the action they want? The principal is then compared to some list of rights to determine whether access is allowed. For example, when you access a file, your user name is compared with an ACL for the action you want to do in order to determine whether you can access the file. Of course, access is not always all or nothing. You might have read but not modify rights to a file.

In a multitier architecture, the identity under which the server executes is often very powerful, and you want to restrict the ability of the client that makes a request to some subset of privileges the server has. In other cases, such as anonymous access, the server may not know who the client really is. The server then *impersonates* the client. Server code then temporarily executes under the identity of the client instead of the server. In the case of anonymous access, the server runs under the identity of a special preset user account. For example, the built-in account for anonymous access to IIS is called the Internet Guest Account.

Windows security under .NET and ASP.NET security is based on the concepts of user-based security.

Code Access Security

One of the challenges of the software world of third-party components and downloadable code is that you open your system to damage and compromise from executing code from unknown sources. You might want to restrict Word macros from accessing anything other than the document that contains them. You want to stop potentially malicious Web scripts. You even want to shield your system from bugs of software from known vendors. To handle these situations, .NET security includes *Code Access Security* (CAS).

Security Policy

Code Access Security is based on the idea that you can assign levels of trust to assemblies and restrict the operation of the code within those assemblies to a certain set of operations. Code-based security is also referred to as *evidence-based* security. The name *evidence* stems from the fact that a set of information (or evidence) is used by the CLR to make decisions about what this code is allowed to do. A piece of evidence might be the location from which the code was downloaded or its digital signature (who signed it). *Security policy* is the configurable set of rules that the CLR uses to make those decisions. Administrators set security policy. Security policy can be set at the enterprise, machine, user, or application domain level.

Permissions

Security policy is defined in terms of permissions. Permissions are objects that are used to describe the rights and privileges of assemblies to access other objects or undertake certain actions. Assemblies can request to be granted certain permissions. Security policy dictates what permissions will be granted to an assembly.

Examples of the classes that model permissions include the following:

- **SecurityPermission** controls access to the security system. This includes the right to call unmanaged code, control threads, control principals, application domain, evidence, and the like.
- **FileIOPermission** controls access to the file system.
- **ReflectionPermission** controls access to nonpublic metadata and the dynamic generation of modules, types, and members.

All the permission classes inherit from the **CodeAccessPermission** base class, so they all behave in the same way.

Attributes can be applied to the assembly to represent a request for certain permissions. The CLR will use metadata to determine what permissions are being requested. Based on the code's identity and trust level, the CLR will use security policy to determine whether it can **grant** those permissions.

Code can programmatically demand (i.e., request) that its callers have certain permissions before it will execute certain code paths. If the demand fails, the CLR will throw a **System::Security::SecurityException**. Whenever you demand any permission, you have to be prepared to catch that exception and handle the case where the permission was not granted. Most programmers will not have to demand permissions, because the .NET framework libraries will do that for you on your behalf. You still have to be prepared, though, to handle the exceptions.

Code can also request that permissions it has been granted be restricted or denied. This is important for code that uses third-party components or relies on third-party Web scripts. Since such code may have a lower level of trust than your own code, you might want to restrict the available rights while that code is running. When it is finished running, you can restore the level of permissions.

Determining the identity of the code is equivalent to the authentication question of traditional security. The authorization question is based on the security permissions that are given or taken away from an assembly.

Many of the classes that support permissions are found in the **System::Security::Permissions** namespace. Some are found in the **System::Net** and **System::Data** namespaces.

Internet Security

You can use the Internet Protocol Security (IPSec) to restrict access to your computer to certain IP addresses. This is done using the IP Security Policy Management MMC snap-in. Of course, to do this, you need to know the IP addresses of your clients. The advantage is that you do not have to change your client application, ASP.NET code, or Web Service code to use it. However, this is impractical for public Web sites or services where you do not know who your potential clients are.

Internet Information Server

While the focus of this chapter is .NET security, some knowledge of IIS security is important. Since both Web Services and ASP.NET use IIS, your IIS settings can affect .NET security.

In the previous chapters on ASP.NET and Web Services, we have used the default settings of anonymous access. Anonymous access does not require a user name or password to access an account. You run under a default user account. Anonymous access is useful for public Web sites and services that do their own authentication by asking for a user name and password or by some other means. In such a scenario you could use ASP.NET forms-based authentication. You can build forms to get the user name and password and then validate them against a configuration file or database.

IIS supports the major HTTP authentication schemes. These schemes require you to configure IIS appropriately. The schemes are listed in Table 13–1. In each of these scenarios IIS authenticates the user if the credentials match an existing user account. Secure Sockets Layer (SSL) is used whenever you need to encrypt the HTTP communication channel. SSL does degrade performance. We do not discuss SSL in this chapter.

You will also have to adjust access to the necessary files (graphics, data store files, etc.) and other resources (i.e., databases) to those user accounts (authorization). For public Web sites and Web Services, this approach is not useful because users will not have user accounts.

Microsoft has introduced the *Passport* authentication scheme. While ASP.NET does have support for Passport (**System::Web::Security::Passport-Identity** class) on the server side, as of this writing, developer tools to handle the client side for Passport authentication do not yet exist. Passport avoids the

Table 13–1 IS Authentication Schemes

Scheme	Type of Authentication
Basic	User and password information is effectively sent as plain text. This is standard HTTP authentication and is not secure.
Basic over SSL	Basic authentication, but the communication channel is encoded so that the user name and password are protected.
Digest	Uses secure hashing to transmit user name and password. This is not a completely secure method because the hash codes stored on the server are reversible.[a] It was introduced in HTTP 1.1 to replace basic authentication.
Windows Integrated Security	Traditional Windows security using NTLM or Kerberos protocols. IIS authenticates if credentials match a user account. Cannot be used across proxies and firewalls. NTLM is the legacy Windows security protocol.
Certificates over SSL	Client obtains a certificate that is mapped to a user account.

[a] See the discussion of hash codes in Chapter 7. A message digest is another name for the result of applying a hash code to a message.

problem of requiring specific accounts on specific machines. We will not discuss Passport in this chapter.

The security specification for SOAP is being worked on by the W3C. You could create your own custom authentication using SOAP messages. Since XML is transmitted as text, you want to run using SSL to encrypt the messages (especially if you use tags such as <user> and <password>). In general, secure data has to be encrypted when using SOAP.

Role-Based Security in .NET

Most people have at least an intuitive understanding of users and passwords. MTS and COM+ have provided a well known and easy-to-understand security system based on *roles*. The best place to start a more detailed look at .NET security is with identities and roles. We will look at this from the point of view first of a Windows application and then of ASP.NET.

Principals and Identities

Each thread has associated with it a CLR principal. The principal contains an identity representing the user ID that is running that thread. The static property **Thread::CurrentPrincipal** will return the current principal associated with the calling thread.

Principal objects implement the **IPrincipal** interface. **IPrincipal** has one method and one property. The **Identity** property returns the current identity object, and the method **IsInRole** is used to determine whether a given user is in a specific role. The **RoleBasedSecurity** example illustrates the use of principals, identities, and roles.

Currently, there are two principal classes in the .NET framework: **WindowsPrincipal** and **GenericPrincipal**. The **GenericPrincipal** class is useful if you need to implement your own custom principal. The **WindowsPrincipal** class represents a Windows user and its associated roles.

Code Example

In the **RoleBasedSecurity** example, the program starts out with a demand for a **SecurityPermission** to manipulate the principal object and then proceeds to set the AppDomain principal policy.[3] **SecurityPermission** is the security permission class, which defines a set of security permission flags. The **SecurityPermission** constructor in this example takes **Security-PermissionFlag::ControlPrincipal** as a parameter, specifying the ability to manipulate the principal object. The **Demand** method of **SecurityPermission** is called to determine whether we have the specified permission to manipulate the principal object. If we do, then we proceed to change the

---

[3] The reason for this is to make sure that the example functions properly on your machine. If you get an exception, you will have to set the policy on your local machine to allow you to run the example. This should not happen under normal circumstances.

principal policy. If we do not, then **Demand** will throw a **SecurityException** exception and the program terminates.

```
//determine right to change principal policy
Console::WriteLine(
    "Demanding right to change principal policy");
SecurityPermission *sp = new SecurityPermission(
    SecurityPermissionFlag::ControlPrincipal);

try
{
    //Check if all callers higher in call stack have
    //been granted the permission to manipulate the
    //principal object before operating on it.
    sp->Demand();
}
catch(SecurityException *se)
{
    //cannot manipulate principal object
    Console::WriteLine(se->Message);
    return;
}
```

Next, we change the principal policy from default **Unauthenticated-Principal** to **WindowsPrincipal**. This means that principal and identity objects will be based on the operating system user token of the current thread and that operating system user groups will be mapped into roles.

```
AppDomain *ap = AppDomain::CurrentDomain;
ap->SetPrincipalPolicy(
    PrincipalPolicy::WindowsPrincipal);
Console::WriteLine(
    "AppDomain Principal Policy changed to
    WindowsPrincipal");
```

Next, we get the current thread's principal and verify that it is a **WindowsPrincipal**. Since the **RoleBasedSecurity** example is a Windows (console) application, we should have a **WindowsPrincipal** associated with the **CurrentPrincipal** property.

```
IPrincipal *ip;
ip = Thread::CurrentPrincipal;
WindowsPrincipal *wp =
    dynamic_cast<WindowsPrincipal *>(ip);
```

```
if (wp == 0)
   Console::WriteLine(
      "Thread::CurrentPrincipal is NOT a WindowsPrincipal");
else
   Console::WriteLine(
       "Thread::CurrentPrincipal is a WindowsPrincipal");
```

An identity object implements the **IIdentity** interface. The **IIdentity** interface has three properties:

- **Name** is the string associated with the identity. This is given to the CLR by either the underlying operating system or the authentication provider. ASP.NET is an example of an authentication provider.
- **IsAuthenticated** is a Boolean value indicating whether the user was authenticated or not.
- **AuthenticationType** is a string that indicates which authentication was used by the underlying operating system or authentication provider. Examples of authentication types are Basic, NTLM, Kerberos, Forms, or Passport.

There are several types of identity objects. Since this is a Windows program, we will have a **WindowsIdentity** object associated with the **Windows-Principal**. The example next prints out the property information associated with the identity object. The name of the current thread's user and the type of authentication used is displayed.

```
IIdentity *ii = ip->Identity;
Console::WriteLine(
   "Thread::CurrentPrincipal Name: {0} Type: {1}
   IsAuthenticated: {2}",
ii->Name,
ii->AuthenticationType,
__box(ii->IsAuthenticated));
```

On my machine this is displayed as

```
Thread::CurrentPrincipal Name: HPDESKTOP\Administrator
Type: NTLM IsAuthenticated: Truc
```

Substitute the Name of Your Machine in the Examples

In several of the examples the machine name HPDESKTOP is used. You can substitute the appropriate machine or domain name when you run the samples on your computer.

The operating system on the machine using the NTLM protocol has authenticated the user running this program to be "Administrator." The sample then validates that this is indeed a **WindowsIdentity** object. The **WindowsIdentity** object has additional properties and methods besides those of the **IIdentity** interface. One of them is the Win32 account token ID associated with the currently running thread's user.

```
//get info from Identity from WindowsPrincipal
WindowsIdentity *wi =
    dynamic_cast<WindowsIdentity *>(wp->Identity);
if (wi != 0)
    Console::WriteLine(
        "WindowsPrincipal Identity Name: {0} Type: {1}
         Authenticated: {2} Token: {3}",
        wi->Name,
        wi->AuthenticationType,
        __box(wi->IsAuthenticated),
        __box(wi->Token));
```

You can use the name of the user to programmatically decide (authorize) whether the user has the rights to undertake certain actions by refusing to execute certain code paths. This is shown in the following if-else statement in the **RoleBasedSecurity** example.

```
//use user name to authorize code path
String * name = wp->Identity->Name;
if (name->Equals("HPDESKTOP\\Administrator"))
{
    Console::WriteLine(
        "Name matches HPDESKTOP\\Administrator");
    //authorize code path goes here ...
}
else
{
    Console::WriteLine(
        "Name does not match HPDESKTOP\\Administrator");
    //unauthorize code path goes here ...
}
```

The **RoleBasedSecurity** example then goes on to show how you might undertake certain actions based on membership in a custom role or in built-in roles such as Administrator, Guest, and User.

.NET Windows Roles

Instead of checking each individual user name, you can assign users to **roles**. You can then check to see if a user belongs to a certain role. The standard administrators group is an example of how a role works. You do not have to individually assign a user identity all the privileges that an administrator has and then check to see if individual users have certain privileges. Instead, you just assign the user to the administrators group. Your code can then check to see if the user is in the administrators group before attempting actions such as creating a new user. .NET roles are separate from COM+ roles.

You define roles by defining groups in NT4 or Windows2000. Each group represents one role. Go to the Control Panel and select Administrative Tools. From the Administrative Tools list, select Computer Management. In the Computer Management MMC snap-in expand the Local Users and Groups node. As Figure 13–1 shows, if you select Groups, you will see all the Groups defined on your machine. The CustomerAdmin group has been added.

Some groups, such as Administrators and Guests, are built in because they are predefined for you. CustomerAdmin is a user-defined group that represents administrators who have the right to modify Acme customer information.

To add a new group to the local machine, right-mouse-click on the Groups node and select New Group. A dialog box you can fill in pops up.

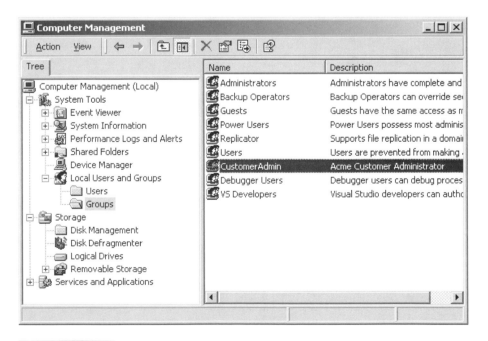

Figure 13–1   *Groups defined on a machine.*

Figure 13–2 shows this dialog box filled for a new group entitled HotelAdmin which is designed to have all users on the machine who can add or modify information about hotels in the HotelBroker system. Clicking the Create button will add the group to the system. You can use the Add and Remove buttons to add or remove users from the group.

To modify an existing group, select that group, right-mouse-click, and select Properties. Clicking the Add button will bring up a dialog of all users on the system. You can then select users and add them to the group. Figure 13–3 shows a user about to be added to the HotelAdmin group. Note that JaneAdmin and PeterT are custom user accounts that have already been created. The Remove button is used to remove users from the group.

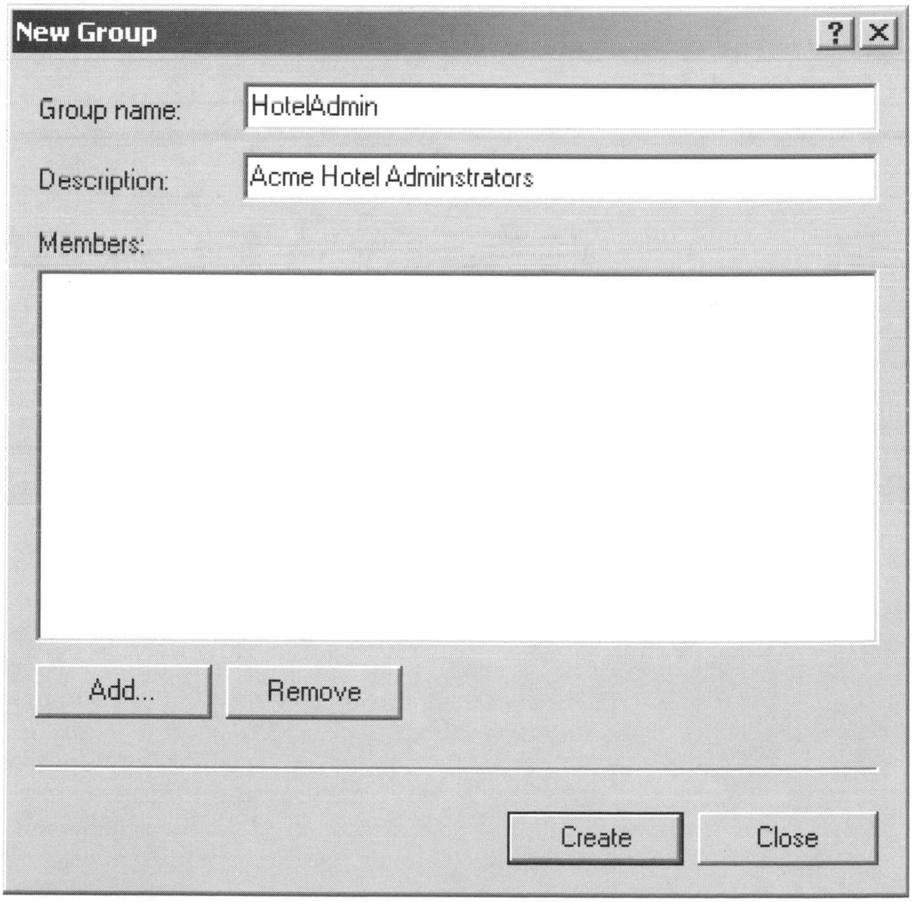

Figure 13–2   *Dialog to create a HotelAdmin group.*

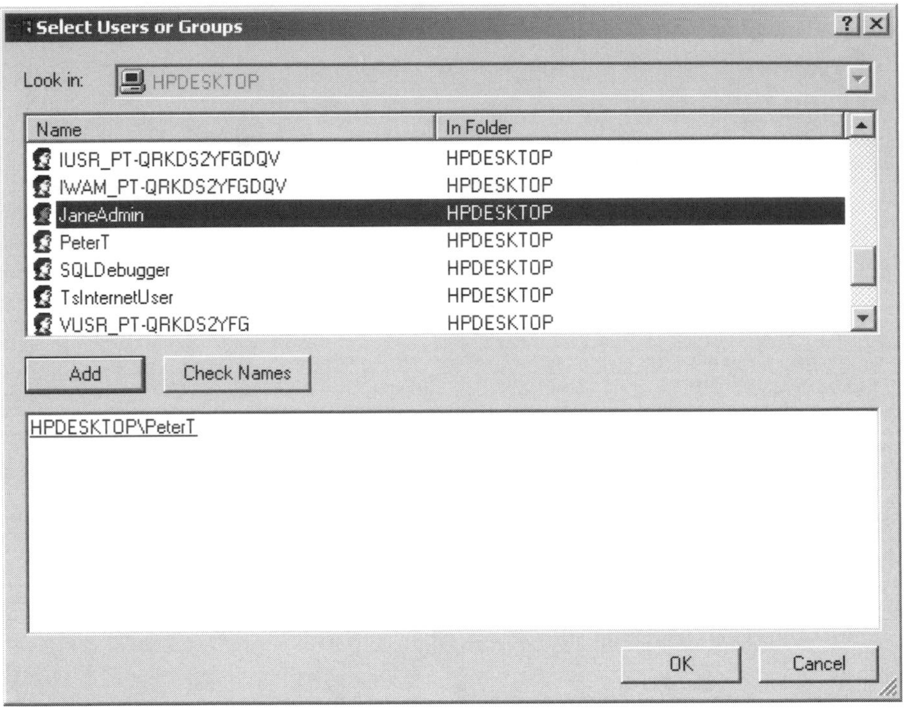

Figure 13–3 *User JaneAdmin about to be added to the HotelAdmin group. User PeterT has already been added.*

Within code, you qualify the name using the domain or machine name. On my machine, the CustomerAdmin role is referred to as "HPDESK-TOP\\CustomerAdmin", and the HotelAdmin role is referred to as "HPDESK-TOP\\HotelAdmin". For groups that are preinstalled, such as the Administrators group, you use the "BUILTIN" prefix—for example, "BUILTIN\\Administrators". To avoid translation and internationalization problems, the **System::Security::Principal::WindowsBuiltInRole** enumeration can be used to refer to built-in roles. Instead of using the "BUILTIN\\Administrators" string, you can refer to the Administrators group as **WindowsBuiltInRole::Administrator**.

The **RoleBasedSecurity** example that we looked at in the previous section checks to see if the current user is in various roles. You can either pass the role as a string or use the **WindowsBuiltInRole** enumeration. Remember that you should modify the program to use the actual name of your machine when you run the example on your computer. The program uses if-else statements to select code paths according to membership in these roles.

```cpp
//use custom role to authorize code path
String *adminRole = "HPDESKTOP\\CustomerAdmin";
if(wp->IsInRole(adminRole))
{
   Console::WriteLine(
      "In Customer Administrator role.");
   //authorize code path for CustomerAdmin ...
}
else
{
   Console::WriteLine(
      "Not in Customer Administrator role.");
   //unauthorize code path for CustomerAdmin ...
}

//using built in roles to authorize code path
if(wp->IsInRole(WindowsBuiltInRole::Administrator))
{
   Console::WriteLine(
      "In Administrator role");
   //authorize code path for Administrator ...
}
else
{
   Console::WriteLine(
      "Not in Administrator role.");
   //unauthorize code path for Administrator ...
}
if(wp->IsInRole(WindowsBuiltInRole::Guest))
{
   Console::WriteLine(
      "In Guest role");
   //authorize code path for Guest...
}
else
{
   Console::WriteLine(
      "Not in Guest role.");
   //unauthorize code path for Guest ...
}
if(wp->IsInRole(WindowsBuiltInRole::User))
{
   Console::WriteLine(
      "In User role");
```

```
      //authorize code path for User ...
}
else
{
   Console::WriteLine(
      "Not in User role");
   //unauthorize code path for User ...
}
```

The **RoleBasedSecurity** example produces the following output if you are logged on as Administrator.

```
Demanding right to change principal policy
AppDomain Principal Policy changed to WindowsPrincipal
Thread::CurrentPrincipal is a WindowsPrincipal
Thread::CurrentPrincipal Name: HPDESKTOP\Administrator
Type: NTLM IsAuthenticated: True
WindowsPrincipal Identity Name: HPDESKTOP\Administrator
Type: NTLM Authenticated: True Token: 260
Name matches HPDESKTOP\Administrator
In Customer Administrator role
In Administrator role
Not in Guest role
In User role
```

The **RoleBasedSecurity** example produces the following output if you are logged on as JaneAdmin.

```
Demanding right to change principal policy
AppDomain Principal Policy changed to WindowsPrincipal
Thread::CurrentPrincipal is a WindowsPrincipal
Thread::CurrentPrincipal Name: HPDESKTOP\JaneAdmin Type:
NTLM IsAuthenticated: T
rue
WindowsPrincipal Identity Name: HPDESKTOP\JaneAdmin Type:
NTLM Authenticated: Tr
ue Token: 260
Name does not match HPDESKTOP\Administrator
Not in Customer Administrator role.
Not in Administrator role.
Not in Guest role.
In User role
```

Other Identity Classes

Now let us look in more detail at the other Identity classes. Currently, there are four in the .NET Framework:

- **FormsIdentity** is used by the **FormsAuthenticationModule** class. We will discuss this class when we discuss ASP.NET forms authentication.
- **GenericIdentity** can represent any user. This class is used with the **GenericPrincipal** for generic or custom identities and principals.
- **PassportIdentity** is used with Passport authentication. Since we do not discuss Passport, we will not discuss this class.
- **WindowsIdentity** represents a Windows user. A **WindowsPrincipal** instance will have a **WindowsIdentity** instance as its **Identity** property. For authenticated users, the type of authentication used (NTLM, Kerberos, etc.) is available.

Note that the properties of the **IIdentity** interface are read-only and therefore cannot be modified.

Even if your users are unauthenticated, you can get the **WindowsIdentity** for any thread using the static method **WindowsIdentity::GetCurrent** to get the **WindowsIdentity** instance of the current user. You can then use the **WindowsPrincipal** constructor to build a **WindowsPrincipal** instance from this **WindowsIdentity**. What this identity represents will be discussed in the next section.

Although this chapter does not provide a version of the **HotelBroker** example program, you could easily modify the previous version yourself so that you cannot run it if you are not in the HotelBrokerAdmin role. See the following code as a guide.

```
AppDomain *ap = AppDomain::CurrentDomain;
ap->SetPrincipalPolicy(
    PrincipalPolicy::WindowsPrincipal);
IPrincipal *ip;
ip = Thread::CurrentPrincipal;
String *hotelAdminRole  = "HPDESKTOP\\HotelAdmin";
if(!ip->IsInRole(hotelAdminRole))
{
    MessageBox::Show(
        "Sorry. You must be a Hotel Administrator.",
        "Acme Customer Management System",
        MessageBoxButtons::OK,
        MessageBoxIcon::Exclamation);
    return 0;
}
```

Operating System Identity and CLR Identity

As we mentioned at the start of the chapter, .NET security sits on top of the underlying operating system security. The identity associated with the thread by the CLR and the identity associated with the thread by the underlying operating system is not the same identity. The identity of the thread from the operating system perspective is reflected by the setting of the **WindowsIdentity** object returned by the static **WindowsIdentity::GetCurrent** method. The CLR identity is reflected by the value of the **Thread::CurrentPrincipal** object.[4] To go back to the example mentioned at the start of the chapter, if you access a file from within .NET, both the managed and unmanaged identities must have rights to the file within their respective environments.

The values of the current **WindowsIdentity** and the **Thread::CurrentPrincipal** are set in two different places: IIS settings and the ASP.NET configuration files.

Code Access Permissions

Code needs permissions in order to access a resource such as a file or to perform some operation. Security Policy (discussed later in the chapter) will give certain permissions to each assembly. Code access permissions can be requested by code. The CLR will decide which permissions to grant based on the security policy for that assembly. We will not discuss how to write a custom permission.

Here are some examples of code access permissions:

- **DNSPermission** controls access to domain name servers on the network.
- **EnvironmentPermission** controls read or write access to environment variables.
- **FileIOPermission** controls access to files and directories.
- **FileDialogPermission** allows files selected in an Open dialog box to be read. This is useful if **FileIOPermission** has not been granted.
- **ReflectionPermission** controls the ability to access nonpublic metadata and emit metadata.
- **RegistryPermission** controls the ability to access and modify the registry.
- **SecurityPermission** controls the use of the security subsystem.

---

[4] The reason why these were identical in the RoleBasedSecurity example is that we set the application domain principal policy in the example to be **PrincipalPolicy::WindowsPrincipal**. With the default ASP.NET settings in **config.web**, the **PrincipalPolicy::UnauthenticatedPrincipal** policy is used. For that policy, **Thread::CurrentPrincipal** returns an unauthenticated **GenericPrincipal** object. We will discuss principal policy later.

- **SocketPermission** controls the ability to make or accept connections on a transport address.
- **UIPPermission** controls the user of various user-interface features, including the clipboard.
- **WebPermission** controls making or accepting connections on a Web address.

The use of these permissions is referred to as *Code Access Security* because this permission is based not on the identity of the user running the code, but on whether the code itself has the right to take some action.

Simple Permission Code Request

Code Example

The **SimplePermissionCodeRequest** example first requests permission to access a file. If the CLR does not grant that request, the CLR will throw a **SecurityException** inside the file constructor. However, this code first tests to see if it has that permission. If it does not, it just returns instead of trying to access the file.[5]

This step is generally superfluous because the CLR will do the demand inside the constructor, but often you want to check permissions before you execute some code to ascertain whether you have the rights you need.

The **FileIOPermission** class models the CLR file permissions. A full path must be supplied to its constructor, and we use the **Path** class we discussed in Chapter 8 to get the full path. We are asking for read, write, and append file access. Other possible access rights are **NoAccess** or **PathDiscovery**. The latter is required to access information about the file path itself. You might want to allow access to the file, but you may want to hide information such as directory structure or user names in the path.

The demand request checks to see if we have the required permission. The **Demand** method checks all the callers on the stack to see if they have this permission. In other words, we want to make sure not only that the assembly this code is running in has this right, but that all the assemblies this code is running on behalf of have this permission. If an exception was generated, we do not have the right we demanded, so we exit the program.

```
static int Main()
{
    String *filename = ".\\read.txt";
    String *fileWithFullPath =
        Path::GetFullPath(filename);
```

---

[5] We have not yet discussed how you set security policy, so you do not yet know how to grant or revoke this permission. By default, however, code running on the same machine that it resides on has this permission. This is another example of how difficult it is to talk about security without knowing the whole picture.

```
try
{
    FileIOPermission *fileIOPerm =
        new FileIOPermission(
            FileIOPermissionAccess::AllAccess,
            fileWithFullPath);
    fileIOPerm->Demand();
}
catch(Exception *e)
{
    Console::WriteLine(e->Message);
    return 1;
}
try
{
    FileInfo *file - new FileInfo(filename);
    StreamReader *sr = file->OpenText();
    String *text;
    text = sr->ReadLine();
    while (text != 0)
    {
        Console::WriteLine(text);
        text = sr->ReadLine();
    }
    sr->Close();
}
catch(Exception *e)
{
    Console::WriteLine(e->Message);
}
return 0;
}
```

Even if the code has the CLR read permission, the user must have read permission from the file system. If the user does not, an **UnauthorizedAccess-Exception** will be thrown when the **OpenText** method is called.

You have to be careful in passing objects that have passed a security check in their constructor to code in other assemblies. Since the check was made in the constructor, no other check is made by the CLR to ascertain access rights. The assembly you pass the object to may not have the same rights as your assembly. If you were to pass this **FileInfo** object to another assembly that did not have the CLR read permission, it would not be prevented from accessing the file by the CLR, because no additional security check would be made. This is a design compromise for performance reasons to avoid making security checks for every operation. This is true for other code access permissions as well.

How a Permission Request Works

To determine whether code is authorized to access a resource or perform an operation, the CLR checks all the callers on the stackframe, making sure that each assembly that has a method on the stack can be granted the requested permission. If any caller in the stack does not have the permission that was demanded, a **SecurityException** is thrown.

Less trusted code is not permitted to use trusted code to perform an unauthorized action. The procedures on the stack could come from different assemblies that have different sets of permissions. For example, an assembly that you build might have all rights, but it might be called by a downloaded component that you would want to have restricted rights (so it doesn't open your email address book).

As discussed in the next sections, you can modify the results of the stack walk by using **Deny** or **Assert** methods on the **CodeAccessPermission** base class.

Strategy for Requesting Permissions

Code should request permissions that it needs before it uses them so that it is easier to recover if the permission request is denied. For example, if you need to access several key files, it is much easier to check to see if you have the permissions when the code starts up rather than when you are halfway through a delicate operation and then have to recover. Users could be told up front that certain functions will not be available to them. Or, as we will discuss later, you could use assembly permission requests, and then fail to load if the required permissions are not present. The problem is that you may not know what permissions request will succeed because you do not know what assemblies will have callers on the stack when the request is made.

You should not request permissions that you do not need. This will minimize the chances that your code will do damaging things from bugs or malicious third-party code and components. In fact you can restrict the permissions you have to the minimum necessary to prevent such damage. For example, if you do not want a program to read and write the files on your disk, you can deny it the right to do so.

Denying Permissions

Code Example

We can apply the **Deny** method to the permission. Then, even though security policy would permit access to the file, any attempt to access the file will fail. The **SimplePermissionCodeDenial** example demonstrates this. Instead of demanding the permission, we invoke the **Deny** method on the **FileIO-Permission** object.

```
...
try
{
    fileIOPerm->Deny();
    Console::WriteLine(
        "File Access Permission Removed");
}
catch(SecurityException *se)
{
    Console::WriteLine(se->Message);
}
...
```

We then try to read the file using the **ReadFile** method. Why we do this inside another method will be explained shortly. Since the permission was denied, the **FileInfo** constructor will throw a **SecurityException**.

```
...
try
{
    FileInfo *file = new FileInfo(filename);
    StreamReader *sr = file->OpenText();
    String *text;
    text = sr->ReadLine();
    while (text != 0)
    {
        Console::WriteLine("    {0}", text);
        text = sr->ReadLine();
    }
    sr->Close();
}
catch(SecurityException *se)
{
    Console::WriteLine(
        "Could not read file: {0}",se->Message);
}
...
```

We then call the static **RevertDeny** method on the **FileIOPermission** class to remove the permission denial, and we attempt to read the file again. This time, the file can be read. The call to **Deny** is good until the containing code returns to its caller or until a subsequent call to **Deny**. **RevertDeny** removes all current **Deny** requests.

```
...
FileIOPermission::RevertDeny();
...
ReadFile();
...
```

We then invoke the **Deny** method to once again remove the permission.

Asserting Permissions

The **Assert** method allows you to demand a permission even though you do not have access rights to do so. You might also want to assert a permission because other calls in the call chain do not have the right, even though your assembly does. You can only assert permissions that your assembly has been granted. If this were otherwise, it would be trivial to circumvent CLR security.[6]

Code Example

The **SimplePermissionCodeDenial** example then asserts the **FileIO Permission** and attempts to read the file.

```
...
fileIOPerm->Deny();

fileIOPerm->Assert();
...
ReadFile();
ReadFileWithAssert(fileIOPerm);
...
ReadFile();
...
```

But the file read fails! The assertion is good only within the method that called. The **ReadFileWithAssert** method can read the file because it asserts the permission within the method and then attempts the read. **Assert** stops the permission stack walk from checking permissions higher in the stackframe and allows the action to proceed, but it does not cause a grant of the permission. Therefore, if code further down the stackframe (like **ReadFile**) tries to demand the denied permission (as the **FileInfo** constructor does), a **SecurityException** will be thrown.[7] Similarly, **Deny** prevents callers higher in the stackframe from an action, but not on the current level.

---

[6] You also need the permission to assert.

[7] This is true as well for code above you on the stackframe.

```
static void ReadFileWithAssert(FileIOPermission *f)
{
   try
   {
      f->Assert();
      Console::WriteLine(
         "File Permission Asserted in same procedure as read.");
      FileInfo *file = new FileInfo(filename);
      StreamReader *sr = file->OpenText();
      String *text;
      text = sr->ReadLine();
      while (text != 0)
      {
         Console::WriteLine("      {0}",  text);
         text = sr->ReadLine();
      }
      sr->Close();
   }
   catch(SecurityException *se)
   {
      Console::WriteLine(
         "Could not read file: {0}", se->Message);
   }
}
```

Remember that the **Assert** applies only to IO operations done in this routine for the specific file that was passed the **FileIOPermission** constructor. The call to **Assert** is good until the containing code returns. Hence, **ReadFile** fails again when it is attempted after **ReadFileWithAssert** returns. **RevertAssert** removes all current **Assert** requests.

Assert opens up security holes, because some caller in the stackframe might be able to use the routine that calls **Assert** to violate security. Any use of **Assert** should be subject to a security review.

Run the **SimplePermissionCodeDenial** example program and observe its output.

Other Permission Methods

PermitOnly specifies the permissions that should succeed. You specify what resources you want to access. The call to **PermitOnly** is good until the containing code returns or until a subsequent call to **PermitOnly**. **RevertPermitOnly** removes all current **PermitOnly** requests. **RevertAll** removes the effect of **Deny**, **PermitOnly**, and **Assert**.

SecurityPermission Class

Code
Example

The **SecurityPermission** class controls "metapermissions" that govern the CLR security subsystem. Let us look again at the **RoleBasedSecurity** example from earlier in the chapter. It used the **AppDomain::SetPrincipalPolicy** method to set the application domain's principal policy:

```
AppDomain *ap = AppDomain::CurrentDomain;
ap->SetPrincipalPolicy(
    PrincipalPolicy::WindowsPrincipal);
```

The type of principal returned by **Thread::CurrentPrincipal** will depend on the application domain's principal policy. An application domain can have one of three authentication policies, as defined by the **System::Security::PrincipalPolicy** enumeration:

- **WindowsPrincipal** uses the current user associated with the thread. **Thread::CurrentPrincipal** returns a **WindowsPrincipal** object.
- **UnauthenticatedPrincipal** uses an unauthenticated user. **Thread::CurrentPrincipal** returns a **GenericPrincipal** object. This is the default.
- **NoPrincipal** returns null for **Thread::CurrentPrincipal**.

You set the policy with the **SetPrincipalPolicy** method on the **AppDomain** instance for the current application domain. The static **method AppDomain::CurrentDomain** will return the current instance. This method should be called before any call to **Thread::CurrentPrincipal**, because the principal object is not created until the first attempt is made to access that property.

In order for the **RoleBasedSecurity** example to set the principal policy, it needs to have the **ControlPrincipal** right. To ascertain if the executing code has that right, you can demand that **SecurityPermission** before you change the policy. A **SecurityException** will be thrown if you do not have that permission.

```
...
    SecurityPermission *sp = new SecurityPermission(
        SecurityPermissionFlag::ControlPrincipal);

    try
    {
        //Check if all callers higher in call stack have
        //been granted the permission to manipulate the
        //principal object before operating on it.
        sp->Demand();
```

```
    }
    catch(SecurityException *se)
    {
        //cannot manipulate principal object
        Console::WriteLine(se->Message);
        return;
    }
```

We first construct a new **SecurityPermission** instance, passing to the constructor the security permission we want to see whether we have the right to use. **SecurityPermissionFlag** is an enumeration of permissions used by the **SecurityPermission** class. The **ControlPolicy** permission represents the right to change policy. Obviously, this should be granted only to trusted code. We then demand (request) the permission.

As mentioned earlier, you can only assert permissions that your assembly actually has so rogue components cannot just assert permissions when running within your code. You can either set security policy or use the **SecurityPermission** class to prevent components from calling **Assert**. Construct an instance of the class with the **SecurityPermissionFlag::Assertion** value and then **Deny** the permission. Other actions you can control with the **SecurityPermission** class include the ability to create and manipulate application domains, specify policy, allow or disallow execution, control whether verification is performed, and access unmanaged code.

Unmanaged Code

Asserts are necessary for controlling access to unmanaged code, since managed should not call unmanaged code directly. In order to call unmanaged code, you need the unmanaged code permission.[8] Since the CLR performs a stack walk to check whether all the callers have unmanaged code permission, you would have to grant all code the unmanaged code permission. Hence, assemblies other than your own trusted ones could perform operations through the Win32 API calls and subvert the framework's security system.[9]

Better would be to make calls through wrapper classes that are contained in an assembly that has the managed-code right. The code in the wrapper class would first ascertain that the caller has the proper CLR rights by demanding the minimal set of permissions necessary to accomplish the task (such as writing to a file). If the demand succeeds, then the wrapper code can assert the right to managed code.[10] No other assembly in the call chain then needs to have the managed-code right.

---

[8] As with all the other security permissions, this is technically a flag on the **SecurityPermission** class, but the common parlance is to call them permissions.

[9] The underlying operating system identity that is running the program must have the rights to perform the operating system function.

[10] By demanding first, then asserting, you ensure that a luring attack is not in progress.

For example, if you ask the .NET file classes to delete a file, they first demand the delete permission on the file. If that permission is granted, then the code asserts the managed code permission and calls the Win32 API to perform the delete.

Attribute-Based Permissions

The **SimplePermissionAttributeRequest** example shows how you can use attributes to make permission requests. This example uses an attribute to put in the metadata for the assembly that you need to have the **ControlPrincipal** permission to run. This enables you to query in advance which components conflict with security policy.

```
[assembly:SecurityPermission(
    SecurityAction::RequestMinimum,
    ControlPrincipal=true)];


public __gc class PermAttrib
{
public:
    static int Main()
    {
...
```

The **SecurityAction** enumeration has several values, some of which can be applied to a class or method and some that can be applied to an assembly, as in this example. For assemblies these are **RequestMinimum**, **RequestOptional**, and **RequestRefuse**. **RequestMinimum** indicates to the metadata those permissions the assembly requires to run. **RequestOptional** indicates to the metadata permissions that the assembly would like to have but can run without. **RequestRefuse** indicates permissions that the assembly would like to be denied.[11]

If you change the attribute in this example to **RequestRefuse** and run it, you will find that the assembly will load, but you will get a **SecurityException** when you attempt to change the policy.

Other values apply to classes and methods. **LinkDemand** is acted upon when a link is made to some type. It requires your immediate caller to have a permission. The other values apply at runtime. **InheritanceDemand** requires a derived class to have a permission. **Assert**, **Deny**, **PermitOnly**, and **Demand** do what you would expect.

---

[11] An assembly would do this to prevent code from another assembly executing on its behalf from having this permission.

Here is an example of a **FileIOPermission** demand being applied to a class through an attribute. **AllAccess** is being demanded for the file. A full file path is required.

```
[FileIOPermission(
   SecurityAction::Demand,
   All = "c:\\foo\\read.txt")]
public class Simple
{
   ...
};
```

Principal Permission

Code Example

Role-based security is controlled by the **PrincipalPermission** class. The **PrincipalPermission** example uses this class to make sure that the user identity under which the program is being run is an administrator. We do that by passing the identity name and a string representing the role to the constructor. Once again, we use the **Demand** method on the permission to check the validity of our permission request.

```
//Demand that executing code be an Administrator
PrincipalPermission *pperm = new PrincipalPermission(
   wi->Name, adminRole);
try
{
   pperm->Demand();
   Console::WriteLine(
      "Code demand for an administrator succeeded.");
}
catch(SecurityException *)
{
   Console::WriteLine(
      "Demand for Administrator failed.");
}
```

If the running user were an administrator, then the demand would succeed; otherwise it would fail with an exception being thrown. The code then checks to see that the user with the name JaneAdmin (not a system administrator, but part of the CustomerAdmin group) and that the designated role is running.

```
String *customerAdminRole =
   "HPDESKTOP\\CustomerAdmin";
PrincipalPermission *pp;
```

```
pp - new PrincipalPermission(
   "HPDESKTOP\\JaneAdmin", customerAdminRole);
try
{
   pp->Demand();
   Console::WriteLine(
      "Demand for Customer Administrator succeeded.");
}
catch(SecurityException *)
{
   Console::WriteLine(
      "Demand for Customer Administrator failed.");
}
```

The **CodeAccessPermission** base class has methods for creating permissions that are the union or the intersection of several permissions. **PrincipalPermission** does not derive from **CodeAccessPermission** because it is based on the identity associated with the code, not on the rights of the code itself. Nonetheless, it shares the same idioms with the **CodeAccessPermission** derived classes.

Next, the example code sees if either of these two administrators is the identity of the running code.

```
String *id1 = "HPDESKTOP\\Administrator";
String *id2 = "HPDESKTOP\\PeterT";

PrincipalPermission *pp1 =
   new PrincipalPermission(id1, adminRole);
PrincipalPermission *pp2 =
   new PrincipalPermission(id2, adminRole);

IPermission *ipermission = pp2->Union(pp1);
try
{
   ipermission >Demand();
   Console::WriteLine(
      "Demand for either administrator succeeded.");
}
catch(SecurityException *)
{
   Console::WriteLine(
      "Demand for either administrator failed.");
}
```

The code then sees whether any administrator is the identity of the running code.[12]

```
PrincipalPermission *pp3 =
    new PrincipalPermission(0, adminRole);
try
{
    pp3->Demand();
    Console::WriteLine(
        "Demand for any administrator succeeded.");
}
catch(SecurityException *)
{
    Console::WriteLine(
        "Demand for any administrator failed.");
}
```

If the users are unauthenticated, even if they do belong to the appropriate roles, the **Demand** will fail.

PermissionSet

You can deal with a set of permissions through the **PermissionSet** class. The **AddPermission** and **RemovePermission** methods allow you to add instances of a **CodeAccessPermission** derived class to the set. You can then **Deny**, **PermitOnly**, or **Assert** sets of permissions instead of individual ones. This makes it easier to restrict what third-party components and scripts might be able to do. The **PermissionSet** example demonstrates how this is done.

We first define an interface **IUserCode** that our "trusted" code will use to access some "third-party" code. While in reality this third-party code would be in a separate assembly, to keep the example simple we put everything in the same assembly.

```
public __gc __interface IUserCode
{
    int PotentialRogueCode();
};

public __gc class ThirdParty : public IUserCode
{
public:
    int PotentialRogueCode()
```

---

[12] A null user and a role as arguments to mean anyone in that role is not an intuitive use of null.

```
    {
        try
        {
            String *filename = ".\\read.txt";
            FileInfo *file = new FileInfo(filename);
            StreamReader *sr = file->OpenText();
            String *text;
            text = sr->ReadLine();
            while (text != 0)
            {
                Console::WriteLine(text);
                text = sr->ReadLine();
            }
            sr->Close();
        }
        catch(Exception *e)
        {
            Console::WriteLine(e->Message);
        }
        return 0;
    }
};
```

Our code will create a new instance of the third party, which would cause the code to be loaded into our assembly. We then invoke the **OurCode** method passing it the third-party code.

```
...
static int Main()
{
    ThirdParty *thirdParty = new ThirdParty;
    OurClass *ourClass = new OurClass;
    ourClass->OurCode(thirdParty);
    return 0;
}
```

Now let us look at the **OurCode** method. It creates a permission set consisting of unrestricted user interface and file access permissions. It then denies the permissions in the permission set.

```
...
void OurCode(IUserCode *code)
{
    UIPermission *uiPerm =
```

```
        new UIPermission(
            PermissionState::Unrestricted);
    FileIOPermission *fileIOPerm =
        new FileIOPermission(
            PermissionState::Unrestricted);
    PermissionSet *ps =
        new PermissionSet(PermissionState::None);
    ps->AddPermission(uiPerm);
    ps->AddPermission(fileIOPerm);
    ps->Deny();
    Console::WriteLine("Permissions denied.");
    ...
    return;
}
...
```

The third-party code is then called. After it returns, the permission denial is revoked and the third-party code is called again.

```
    int v = code->PotentialRogueCode();
    CodeAccessPermission::RevertDeny();
    Console::WriteLine("Permissions allowed.");
    v = code->PotentialRogueCode();
```

The first time **PotentialRogueCode** is called, the code execution fails; the second time, it succeeds. Each stackframe can only have one permission set for denial of permissions. If you call **Deny** on a permission set, it overrides any other calls to **Deny** on a permission set in that stackframe.

Code Identity

The characteristics by which a particular assembly can be identified are its identity permissions. An example would be an assembly's strong name or the Web site that generated the code. Identity permissions are granted by the CLR based on the evidence provided by the loader or trusted host.

Identity Permission Classes

To identify running code, there are several identity permission classes.

- **PublisherIdentityPermission** models the software publisher's digital signature.
- **SiteIdentityPermission** models the Web site where code originated.

- **StrongNameIdentityPermission** models the strong name of an assembly.
- **ZoneIdentityPermission** models the zone where the code originated.
- **URLIdentityPermission** models the URL and the protocol where the code originated.

These permissions represent evidence that can be used to determine security policy. Identity permissions are not code access permissions.

Evidence

Security policy is based on a set of rules that administrators can set. The .NET security system can use those rules to enforce the policy. The evidence, represented by the identity permissions, is used to determine which policy to apply.

The **AppDomain** class has a function **ExecuteAssembly**[13] that causes an assembly to run. One argument to the method is the **Evidence** instance argument. This **Evidence** class is a collection of objects that represent the identity of the assembly. This class is a collection of objects that represent evidence.

The **Evidence** example illustrates this. This example gets the collection of evidence associated with a strongly named assembly and prints out the associated values.

```
Evidence *ev = AppDomain::CurrentDomain->Evidence;
IEnumerator *iEnum = ev->GetEnumerator();
bool bNext;

Console::WriteLine(
    "Evidence Enumerator has {0} members",
    __box(ev->Count));
bNext = iEnum->MoveNext();
while (bNext == true)
{
    Object *x = iEnum->Current;
    Type *t = x->GetType();
    Console::WriteLine(t->ToString());
    if (t == __typeof(Zone))
    {
        Zone *zone = dynamic_cast<Zone *>(x);
        Console::WriteLine(
```

---

[13] At the time of writing, the ExecuteAssembly method had problems dealing with assemblies written in managed C++. It is expected that this function will work in the future.

```
            "    {0}", __box(zone->SecurityZone));
        }
        else if (t == __typeof(Url))
        {
            Url *url = dynamic_cast<Url *>(x);
            Console::WriteLine(
                "    {0}", url->Value);
        }
        else if (t == __typeof(Hash))
        {
            Hash *hash = dynamic_cast<Hash *>(x);
            unsigned char md5Hash __gc [] = hash->MD5;
            unsigned char sha1Hash __gc [] = hash->SHA1;
            Console::WriteLine(
                "    MD5 Hash of Assembly:");
            Console::Write("        ");
            for(int i = 0; i < md5Hash->Length; i++)
                Console::Write(md5Hash[i]);
            Console::WriteLine();
            Console::WriteLine(
                "    SHA1 Hash of Assembly:");
            Console::Write("        ");
            for(int i = 0; i < sha1Hash->Length; i++)
                Console::Write(sha1Hash[i]);
            Console::WriteLine();
        }
        else if (t == __typeof(StrongName))
        {
            StrongName *sn = dynamic_cast<StrongName *>(x);
            Console::WriteLine(
                "    StrongName of Assembly is: {0} version: {1}",
                sn->Name,
                sn->Version);
            Console::WriteLine(
                "    Assembly public key:");
            Console::Write(
                "        ");
            Console::WriteLine(
                sn->PublicKey);
        }
        bNext = iEnum->MoveNext();
    }
```

The example's output should look something like this:

```
Evidence Enumerator has 4 members
System.Security.Policy.Zone
    MyComputer
System.Security.Policy.Url
    file:///C:/OI/NetCpp/Chap13/Evidence/Debug/Evidence.exe
System.Security.Policy.StrongName
    StrongName of Assembly is: Evidence version: 1.0.685.28667
    Assembly public key:
        0024000004800...
    ...EA897BA
System.Security.Policy.Hash
    MD5 Hash of Assembly:
        4160102342262551361424412724852222522668
    SHA1 Hash of Assembly:
        216132245725424821...
```

The evidence associated with the **Zone** for this assembly is MyComputer. The **Url** evidence is the location on disk of the assembly. The **Hash** evidence can give us the MD5 and SHA1 hashes of the assembly. The **StrongName** evidence tells us information about the unique assembly name resulting from the AssemblyKeyFileAttribute("KeyPair.snk") attribute in the AssemblyInfo.cpp source file.

Some of this evidence is convertible to the associated identity permissions. For example, the **Zone** class has a **CreateIdentityPermission** method, which returns an **IPermission** interface represents the **ZoneIdentityPermission** instance associated with this piece of evidence. The **Url** and **StrongName** classes have similar methods.

Another way of looking at the identity permissions is that they answer a series of questions:

- Who published (signed) it?
- What is the name of the assembly?
- What Web site or URL did it come from?
- What zone did the code originate from?

The creator of the application domain (host) can also provide evidence by passing in an **Evidence** collection when the **ExecuteAssembly** method is called. Of course, that code must have the **ControlEvidence** permission. The CLR is also trusted to add evidence, since after all, it enforces the security policy. Evidence is extensible; you can define evidence types and use them in security policy.

Security Policy

Now that we understand evidence and how the evidence about an assembly is gathered, we can discuss security policy. Based on the evidence for an assembly, the assembly is assigned to a code group. Associated with each code group is a set of permissions that represent what code associated with that code group can do.

Security Policy Levels

Security policy is set at several levels. The permissions allowed are defined by the intersection of the policy levels. These levels are enterprise, machine, application domain, and user. If there is a conflict between permissions assigned from a particular level, the more restrictive version overrides. So, enterprise policy can override all the machines in the enterprise, and machine policy can override all policies for an application domain or a particular user.

Code Groups

The enterprise, machine, and user policy levels are a hierarchy of code groups. Associated with each code group is a set of permissions. Code that meets a specified set of conditions belongs to a particular code group.

The root node is referred to as "All_Code." Below this level is a set of child nodes, and each of these children can have children. Each node represents a code group. If code belongs to a code group, it might be a member of one of its children. If it does not belong to a given code group, it cannot belong to any of its children.

By evaluating the evidence, you assign code a group. By assignment to a group, you get an associated set of permissions. This set of conditions corresponds to a named permission set. Since code can belong to more than one group, the set of permissions that can be granted to code is union of all the permission sets from the all groups it belongs to.

Therefore, code policy is determined in two steps. For each level, the union of all the permission sets to which it belongs determines the permissions for an assembly. Each level then effectively has one permission set. Then each of these permission sets is intersected so that the most restrictive of each permission setting is the final value. For example, if the machine level gives all access to an assembly, but the user level restricts the file IO permissions to just read, the assembly will have unlimited permissions for everything but file IO, where it will just have the read permission.

Code groups can have two attributes. The **exclusive** attribute dictates that code will never be allowed more permissions than associated with the exclusive group. Obviously, code can belong to only one group marked exclusive. The **level final** attribute indicates that no policy levels below this one are considered when calculating code group membership. The order of levels is enterprise, machine, user, and application domain.

Named Permission Sets

A named permission set consists of one or more code access permissions that have a name. An administrator can associate a code group with this permission set by means of this name. More than one code group can be associated with a named permission set. Administrators can define their own named permission sets, but several are built in:

- **Nothing**: no permissions (cannot run).
- **Execution**: only permission to run, but no permissions that allow use of protected resources.
- **Internet**: the default policy permission set suitable for content from unknown origin.
- **LocalIntranet**: the default policy permission set for within an enterprise.
- **Everything**: all standard (i.e., built-in) permissions except permission to skip verification.
- **FullTrust:** full access to all resources protected by permissions that can be unrestricted.

Of the built-in named permission sets, only the **Everything** set can be modified. You can define custom permission sets.

Altering Security Policy

Security policy is stored in several XML-based configuration files. Machine security configuration is in the **security.config** file that is stored in the **\WINNT\Microsoft.NET\Framework\vx.x.xxxx\CONFIG** directory. User security configuration is in the **security.config** file that is stored in the **\Documents and Settings\UserName\Application Data\Microsoft\CLR Security Config\vx.x.xxxx** directory.

It is not recommended that you edit these XML files directly. The Code Access Security Policy tool (**caspol.exe**) is a command-line tool that can be used to modify enterprise, machine, and user policy levels.

The .NET Admin Tool introduced in Chapter 7 provides a friendlier interface to changing policy. The .NET Admin Tool is an MMC snap-in that can be started by double clicking **\WINNT\Microsoft.NET\Framework\v1.0.2914\mscorcfg.msc** (you need to change this for newer versions). Figure 13–4 shows the code groups and permission sets defined for the machine and the current user security policy levels as they appear in the left pane in the .NET Admin Tool.

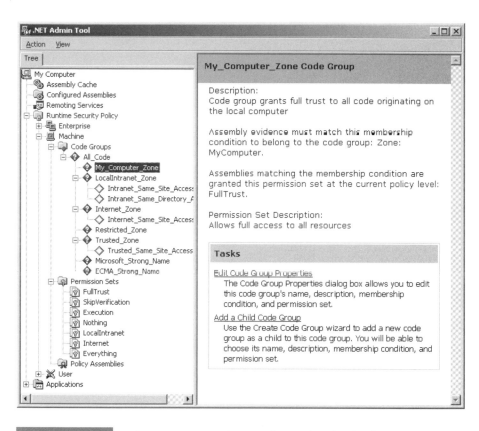

Figure 13–4   *Permission sets and groups for machine level policy.*

Let us use this tool to examine the current policies in the machine level. First, let us look at the named permission sets. As you can see from Figure 13–4, on the machine level no new named permission sets have been created yet; only the default permission sets are present. If you select the Internet permission set and in the right pane select View Permissions, you can then select any permission and look at its settings. Figure 13–5 shows the settings for the UserInterface permission in the Internet named permission set.

Figure 13–6 shows the properties for the Internet zone code group on the machine policy level. You can see that **Zone** condition type is chosen for this group, and the value associated with it is the **Internet** zone. On the Permission Set tab, you can view or select the named permission set associated with the **Internet** zone.

To illustrate how security policy affects running code, we now look at the **Policy** example. The **Policy** example is identical to the **Evidence** exam-

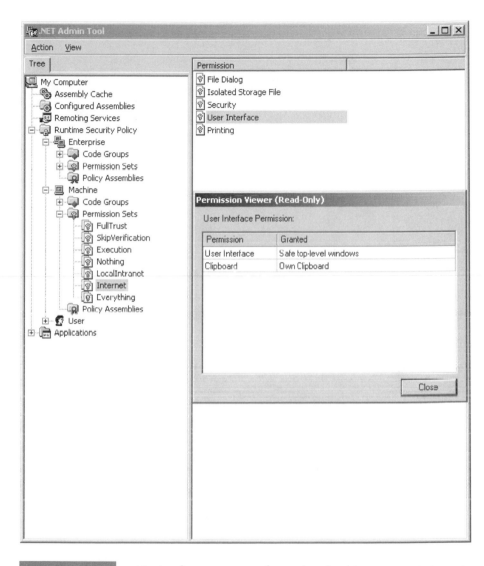

Figure 13-5   *UserInterface permissions for machine level Internet permission set.*

ple shown earlier, except for the additional code shown below. In addition to writing out the associated evidence information, the **Policy** example also displays the contents of a file named read.txt.

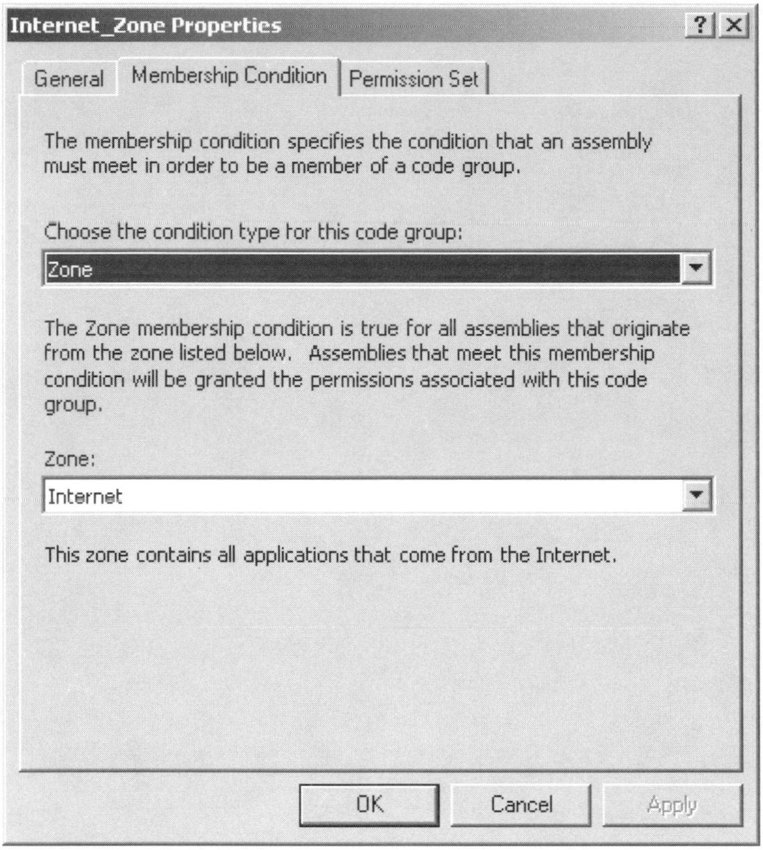

Figure 13-6   *Properties dialog for Internet zone, machine policy level.*

```
String *filename = ".\\read.txt";
try
{
    String *fileWithFullPath =
        Path::GetFullPath(filename);
    FileInfo *file = new FileInfo(filename);
    StreamReader *sr = file->OpenText();
    String *text;
    text = sr->ReadLine();
    while (text != 0)
    {
        Console::WriteLine(text);
        text = sr->ReadLine();
    }
    sr->Close();
```

```
}
catch(Exception *e)
{
    Console::WriteLine(e->Message);
}
```

If you run the Policy example before making any changes to the default user security policy, you will find that it successfully reads the file. If you then make the policy changes described next, you will find that running the Policy example will then fail with a Security Exception when it attempts to read a file.

Figure 13–7 shows the default user policy (we are now working at the user level rather than the machine level).

We will now add a new permission set named TestStrongName, as well as a new code group named TestStrongNameGroup, at the user policy level to control security policy for the **Policy** example assembly.

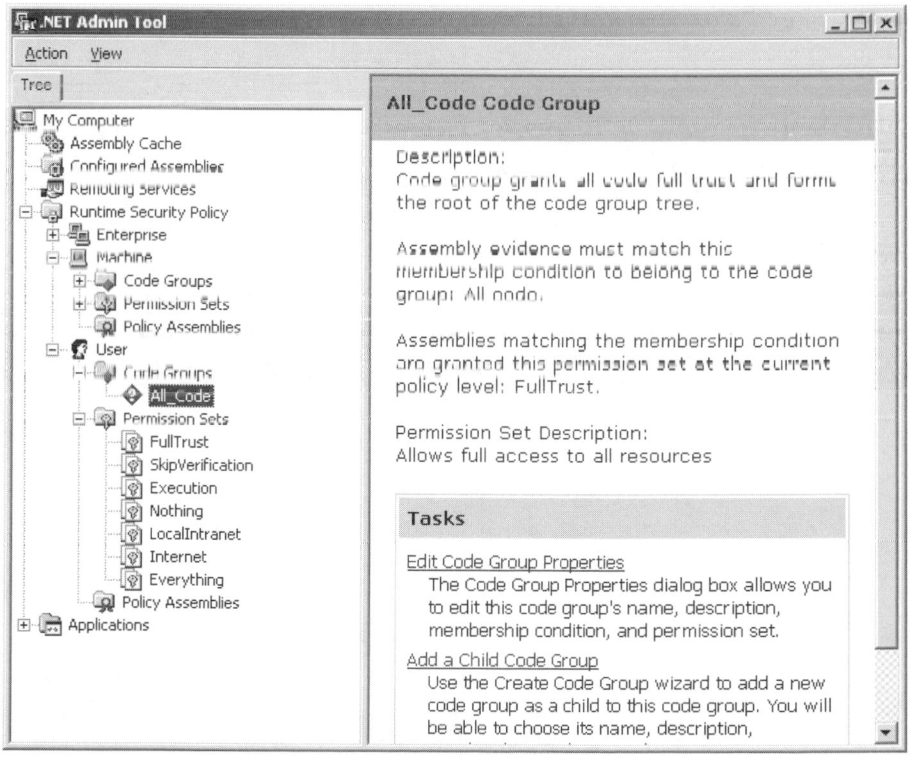

Figure 13–7   *Default user policy.*

We now add a new permission set by right-clicking the PermissionSets node under the desired level (User level in this case). Then select New. The initial Create Permission Set dialog comes up and can be filled in as in Figure 13–8.

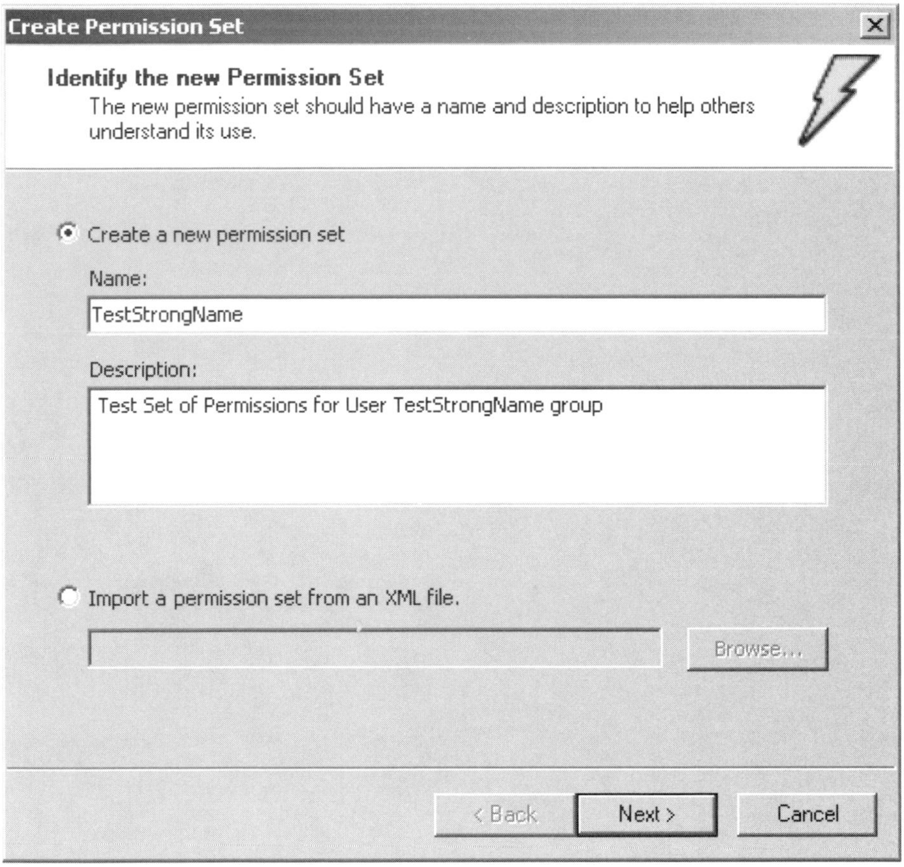

Create Permission Set

Identify the new Permission Set
The new permission set should have a name and description to help others understand its use.

◉ Create a new permission set
Name:
TestStrongName

Description:
Test Set of Permissions for User TestStrongName group

○ Import a permission set from an XML file.

Browse...

< Back   Next >   Cancel

Figure 13–8   *Initial Create Permission Set dialog.*

Continue by clicking on Next. You then see the next step of the Create Permission Set dialog, in Figure 13–9.

Edit the permissions in the permission set, as shown in Figure 13–10, using the Add and Remove buttons. You may control the detailed permission settings for each permission as you add it in the Permission Settings dialog (not shown here). Each Permission Settings dialog provides detailed choices for a particular permission, as well as a radio button to grant assemblies unrestricted access for a particular permission. The result is shown in Figure 13–10.

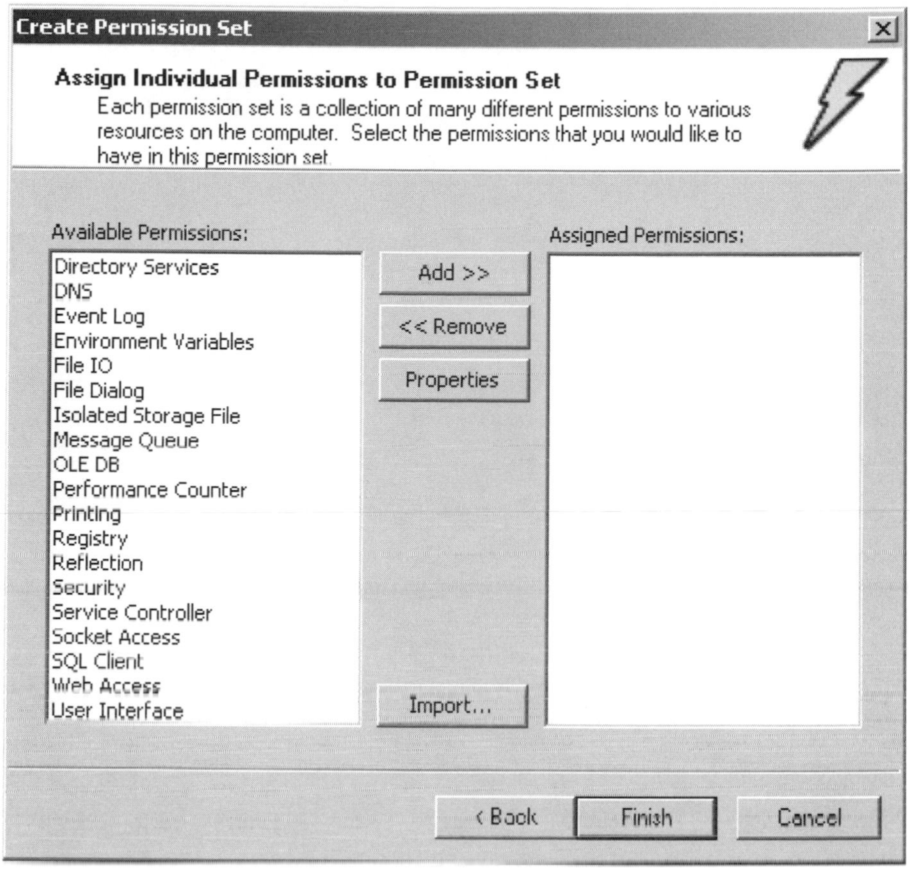

Create Permission Set   [×]

Assign Individual Permissions to Permission Set
Each permission set is a collection of many different permissions to various resources on the computer. Select the permissions that you would like to have in this permission set.

Available Permissions: Assigned Permissions:

Directory Services
DNS
Event Log
Environment Variables
File IO
File Dialog
Isolated Storage File
Message Queue
OLE DB
Performance Counter
Printing
Registry
Reflection
Security
Service Controller
Socket Access
SQL Client
Web Access
User Interface

Add >>
<< Remove
Properties

Import...

< Back   Finish   Cancel

Figure 13–9   *Second step of Create Permission Set dialog.*

Click on Finish to complete the creation of the permission set. The User policy node should now have an asterisk appended, indicating that it has changed but it has not yet been saved. To save the change, right-click on the User policy node and select Save.

To change a permission that you have already added, double-click the permission in the .NET Admin tool, and then make the appropriate changes. Figure 13–11 shows the dialog that appears for changing the UserInterface permission.

If you have changed any policy, you will again have an asterisk appended, indicating that it has not yet been saved. To save the change, right-click on the User policy node and select Save.

Now this permission has to be associated with a code group, and the Policy.exe assembly needs to be assigned to this code group. The name of

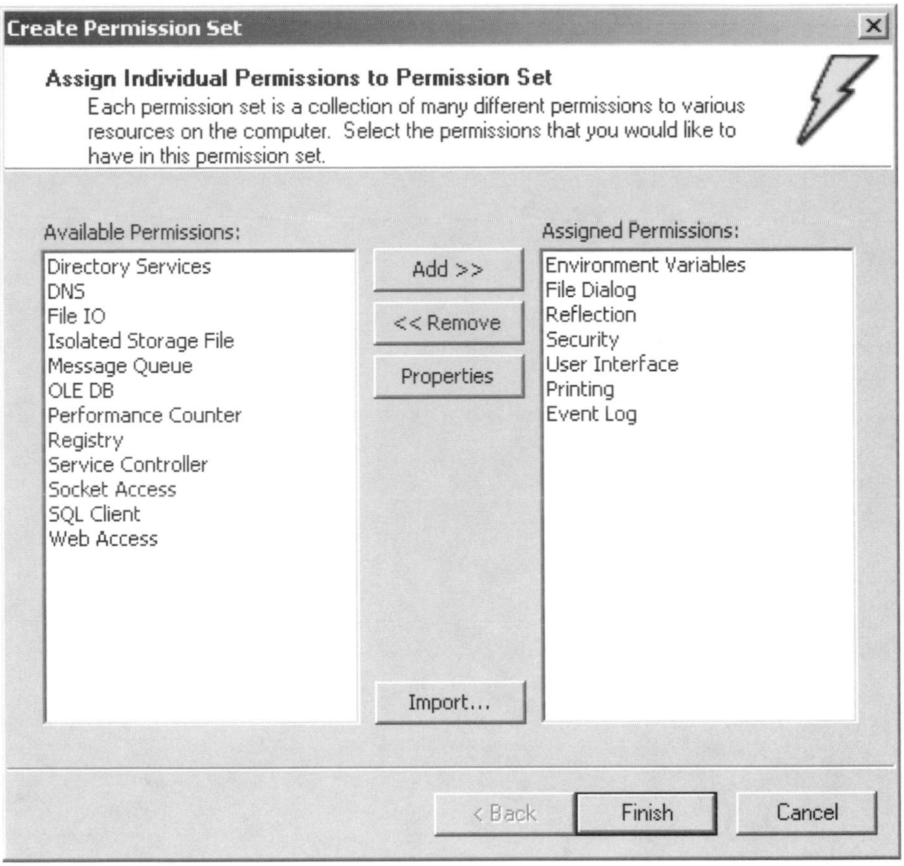

Figure 13-10 *TestStrongName permission set definition.*

this new code group will be TestStrongNameGroup. The TestStrongName-Group code group is created by selecting the parent group (in this case All_Code) and selecting New from its context menu. You then fill in the information requested by the wizard. The Create Code Group dialog will appear, which is filled out as in Figures 13–12.

After entering the information in the Create Code Group dialog, click on Next. This will display the second step of the Create Code Group dialog, which allows you to specify the code membership condition for the code group. Assemblies that meet the specified membership condition will be granted the permissions associated with this code group. In the combo box, select the permission set StrongName, as in Figure 13–13. We also specify the strong name public key of the Policy.exe assembly. This public key is dis-

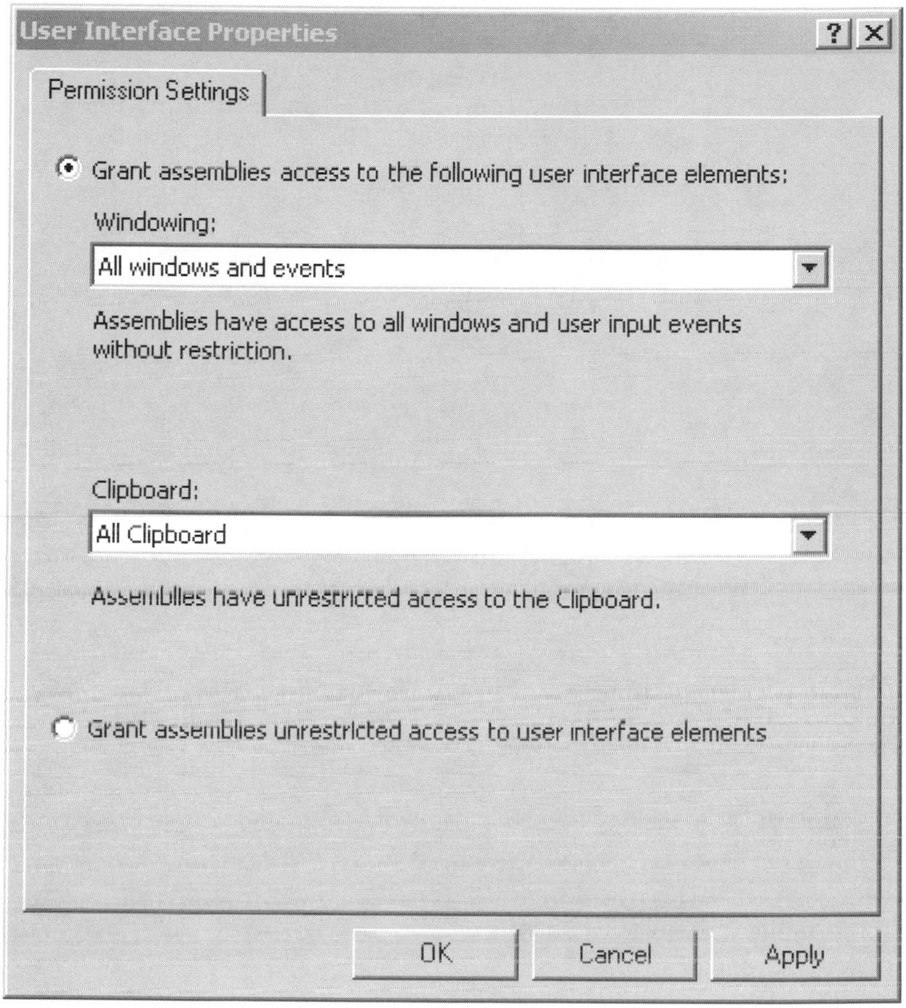

Figure 13-11 *Permission modification.*

played when you run the Policy.exe program, and it can also be obtained from the assembly using Ildasm.exe.

Click on Next, and you will see the third step of the Create Code Group dialog, which allows you to assign a permission set to the code group. Select the TestStrongName permission set that was created earlier, as in Figure 13–14.

Then click on Next, and click on Finish. You will then need to save the User policy node by right-clicking on the User policy node and selecting Save.

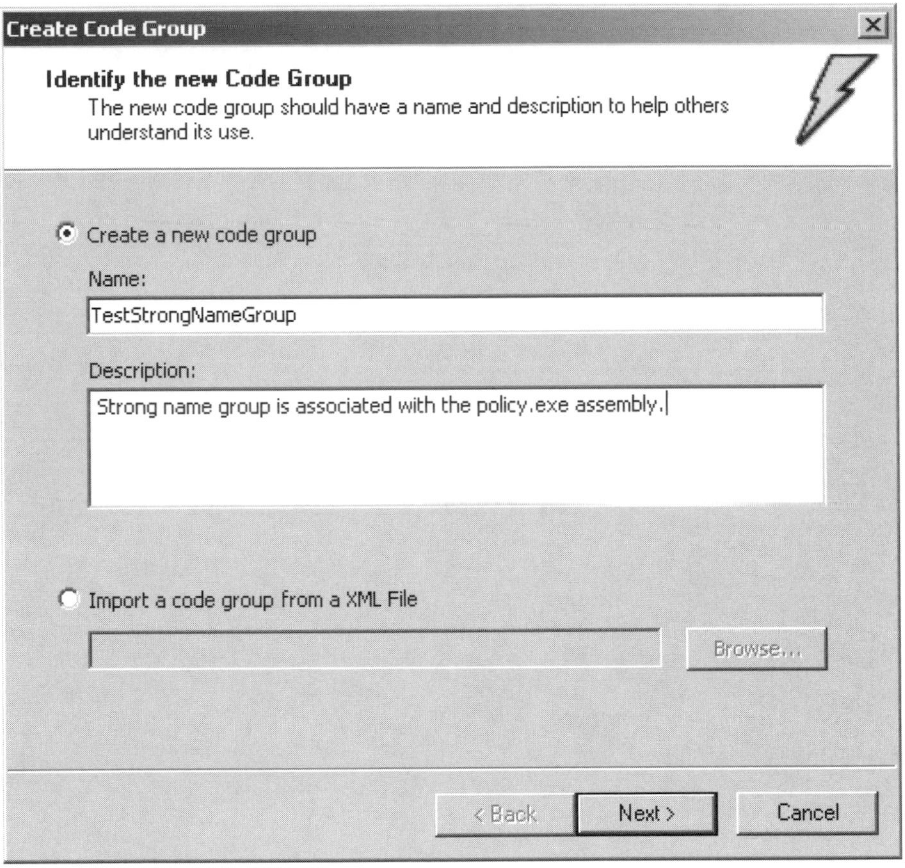

Figure 13–12   *Creating the TestStrongNameGroup code group.*

You can review the changes that you have made by right-clicking on the TestStrongNameGroup in the .NET Admin tool, and selecting Properties. Figure 13–15 shows that the TestStrongNameGroup is associated with the strong name in the policy.exe assembly. Figure 13–16 shows it associated with the TestStrongName permission set.

On the General tab, check the checkbox that states "This policy level will only have the permissions from the permission set associated with this code group," as in Figure 13–17.

Checking this checkbox means that only those permissions that are explicitly specified in the permission set will be used for the assembly. If you do not do this, then you will not see the security exception thrown when the Policy program attempts to write to the file. Click OK. Then right-click on the User node and select Save.

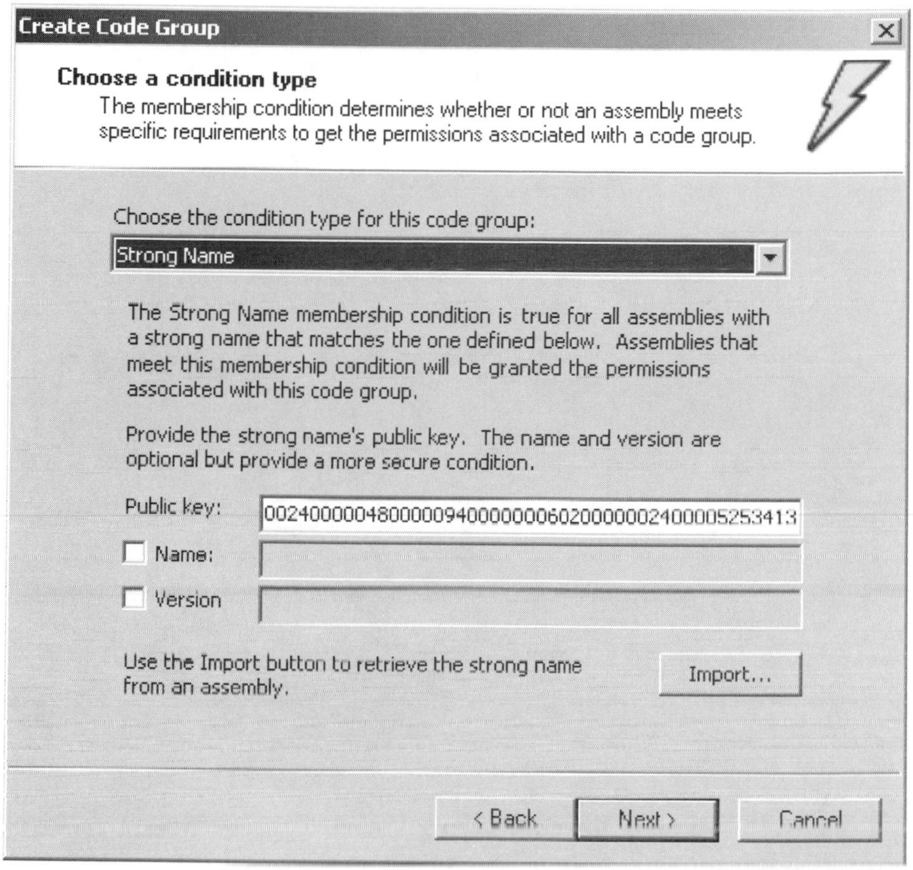

Figure 13-13 *Setting the condition for the TestStrongNameGroup code group*

Recall that there was no FileIOPermission added to the TestStrongName permission set created previously. Also, recall that the Policy.exe program attempts to read a file. To see the effect of this, run the Policy.exe program again, and you will see that it throws a Security exception because of the lack of the FileIOPermission in the associated permission set.

Figure 13–18 shows a new code group named TestStrongNameGroup, as well as the new permission set named TestStrongName, that we have added at the user policy level to control security policy for the **Policy** assembly.

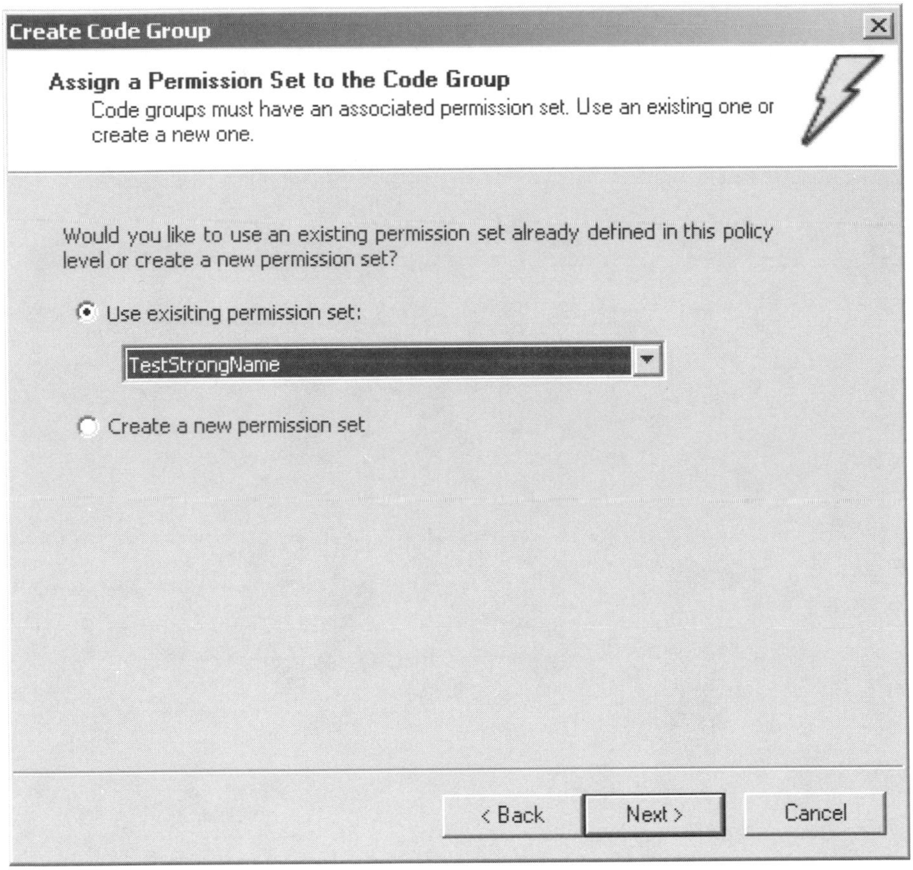

Figure 13–14 *Assign permission set to TestStrongNameGroup code group.*

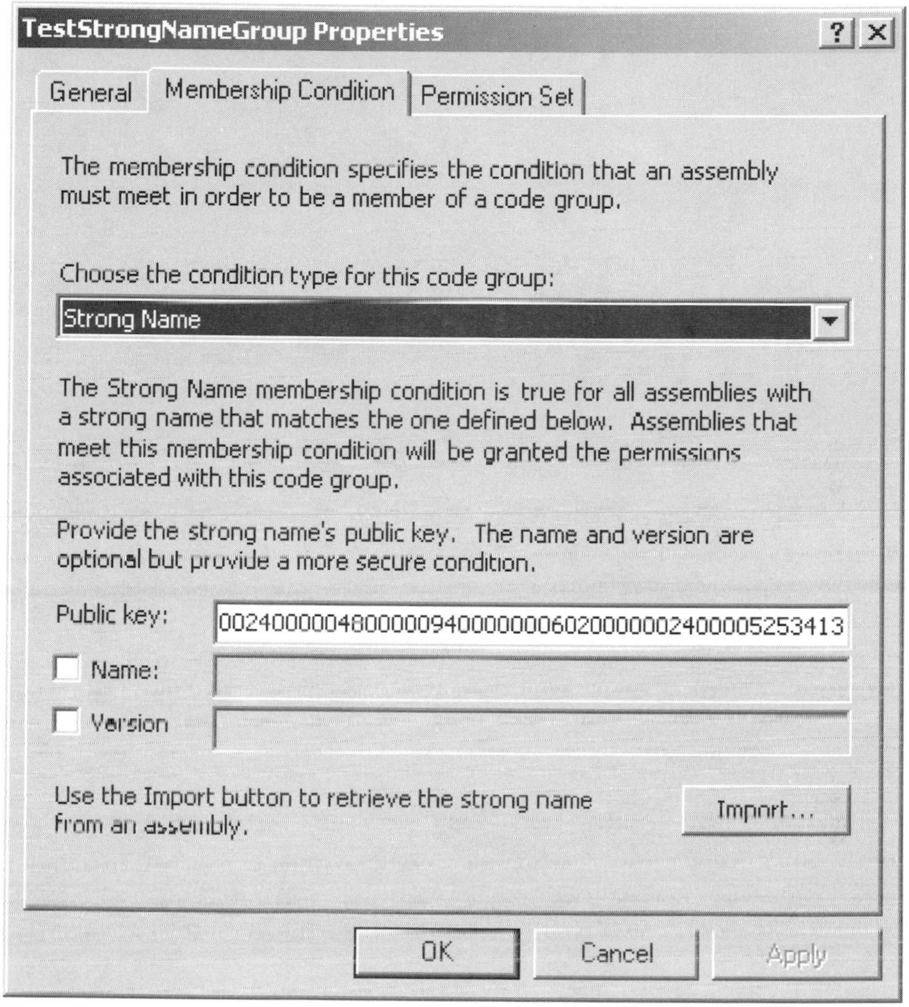

Figure 13–15 *Membership condition for TestStrongNameGroup.*

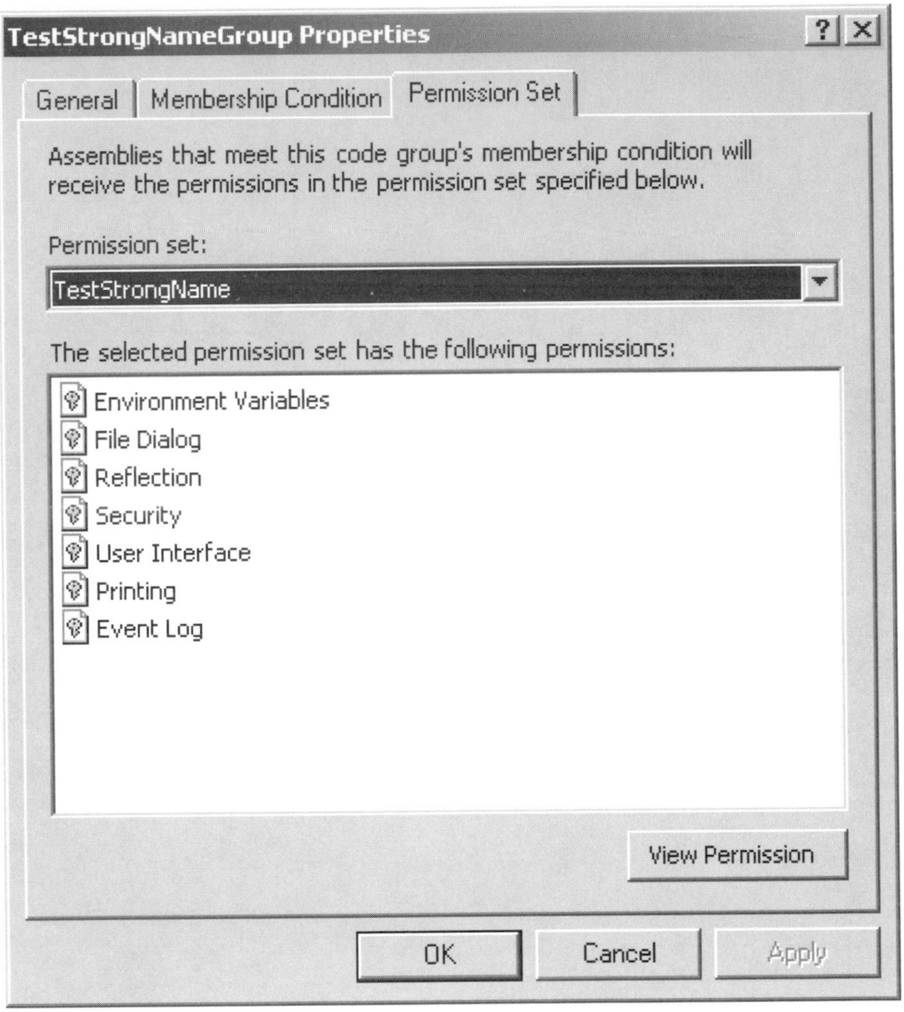

Figure 13–16   *Permissions associated with TestStrongNameGroup from TestStrong-Name permission set.*

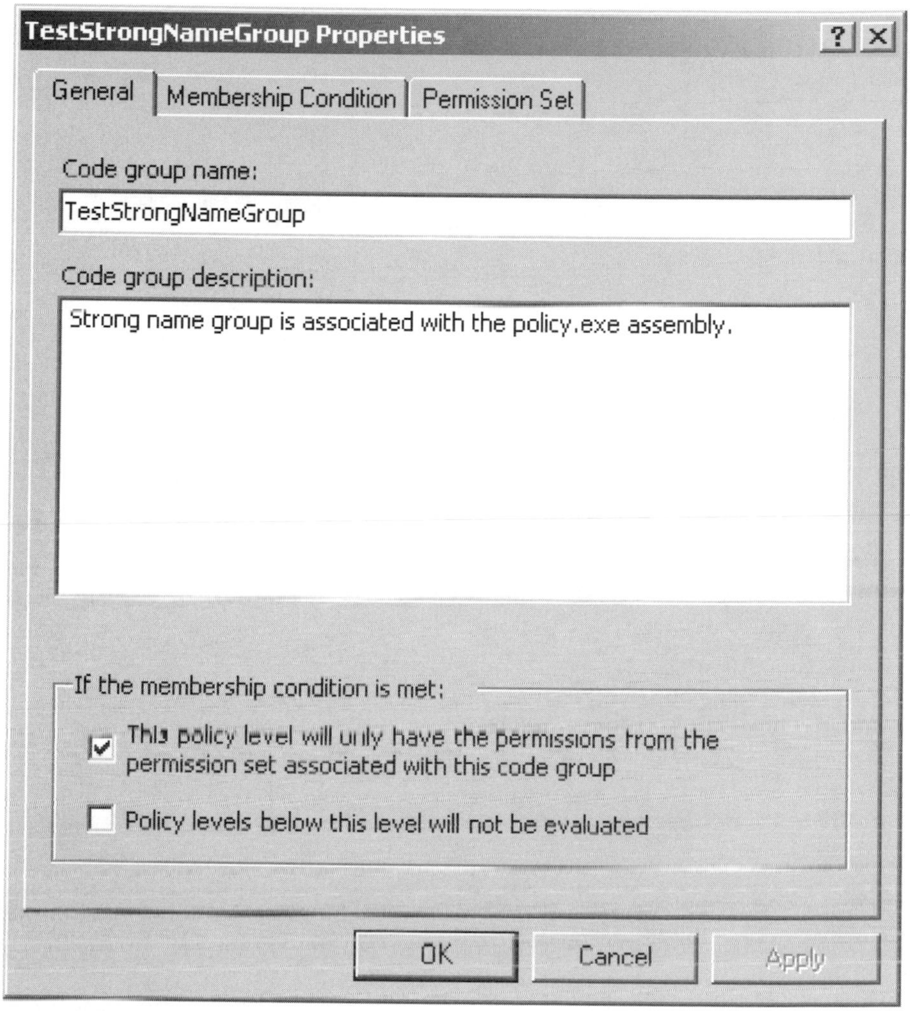

TestStrongNameGroup Properties   ? X

| General | Membership Condition | Permission Set |

Code group name:

TestStrongNameGroup

Code group description:

Strong name group is associated with the policy.exe assembly.

┌─ If the membership condition is met: ─────────────────────

☑ This policy level will only have the permissions from the permission set associated with this code group

☐ Policy levels below this level will not be evaluated

[OK]   [Cancel]   [Apply]

Figure 13-17   *Specifying only permissions from the permission set.*

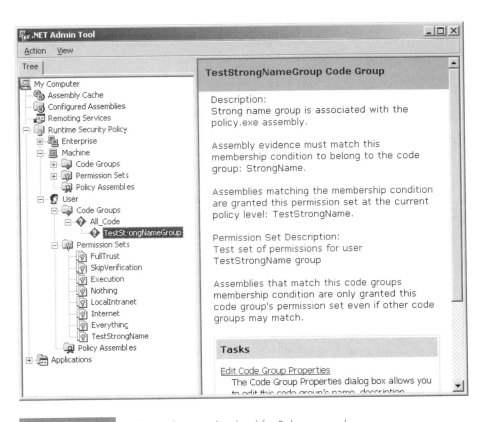

Figure 13–18   *Revised user policy level for Policy example.*

Summary

In this chapter we have attempted to explain the basics of .NET security. .NET security comes in two flavors: user identity security and Code Access Security. The former determines which identity is executing code. The latter determines what rights the executing code has. Between the two, you have the basic tools to provide robust applications.

What is missing from .NET security right now is distributed identity and distributed code access security. Remote code cannot use policy information to make decisions, or identity is not automatically transferred through remote calls.

FOURTEEN

Tracing and Debugging in .NET

Complicated applications cannot always effectively be put under the debugger to find out what went wrong. Duplicating, or even understanding what conditions are needed to replicate, the problem is often difficult. The **System::Diagnostics** namespace has several classes that help you instrument your application.

Instrumenting your application for debugging and tracing will enable you to make your applications more robust. It also illustrates the common pattern of how the framework divides classes into separate tasks (writing the output, controlling the output, and the output destination) so that you can customize parts and still rely on the Framework classes for the rest. The mechanics of instrumenting your application has three aspects.

The **Trace** and **Debug** classes are used to generate the debug or trace output. These classes have identical methods and properties that allow you to write diagnostic output. These classes, however, do not specify the destination of the output.

The **Listeners** classes are used to direct the output to various destinations, although a default destination does exist.

You can use #define DEBUG and #define TRACE along with the appropriate #ifdef and #endif macros for turning on or off the instrumentation. You can use these macro flags to allow different tracing for debug or release builds. You can also have the output of the **Trace** and **Debug** classes depend on the conditional evaluation of expressions. Finally, you can control the verbosity of the output depending on your need for information using the **BooleanSwitch** and **TraceSwitch** classes.

The TraceDemo Example

The **TraceDemo** example illustrates the use of the diagnostic functionality. If you run the example, you will get the following output:

```
Trace Listeners:
        Default

This was compiled with a DEBUG directive!
This was compiled with a TRACE directive!
                Debug Boolean Switch disabled at startup.
                Debug Boolean Switch enabled!
Trace Switch Startup Value = Warning
            TraceError!
            TraceWarning!

Trace Listeners:
        Console::Out Listener
        Output File Listener

File output.txt has been created
```

Refer to this output in the ensuing discussion. You will also find a file called **output.txt** on your computer in the project directory.

Deploying TraceDemo.exe.config

The **TraceDemo** project has a custom-build step (see Figure 14–1) added to copy the **TraceDemo.exe.config** configuration file for the resulting program into the **Debug** directory.[1] This is done so that the program will locate this configuration file at runtime and discover the initial debug and trace options specified there. We will see the contents of this configuration file shortly.

Using the Debug and Trace Classes

All the methods and properties are of **Debug** and **Trace** are static. The over-loaded **WriteLine** and **Write** are used to write debug or trace output. The

---

[1] To see this, right-click on TraceDemo.exe.config in the Solution Explorer window, and view the Custom Build step in the properties dialog. You will see the following command: Copy Trace-Demo.exe.config $(OutDir).

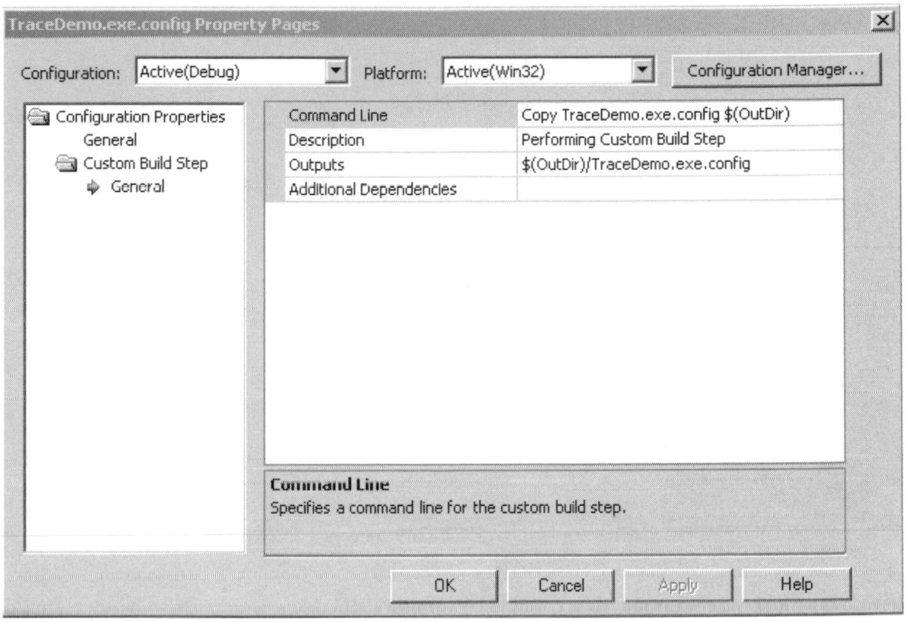

Figure 14-1   *Visual Studio Window for custom-build step.*

overloaded **WriteLineIf** and **WriteIf** write output if the condition in their first argument is true.

```
Debug::WriteLine(
    "This was compiled with a DEBUG directive!");
Trace::WriteLine(
    This was compiled with a TRACE directive!");
...
Debug::WriteLineIf(
    DebugBooleanSwitch->Enabled,
    "Debug Boolean Switch enabled at startup.");
Debug::WriteLineIf(
    !DebugBooleanSwitch->Enabled,
    "Debug Boolean Switch disabled at startup.");
```

Output is indented with the **Indent** and **Unindent** methods in the **Trace** class. The indentation size is controlled with the **IndentSize** property, which can be initially set in the configuration file and changed programmatically at runtime. Here is how you set the indentation size programmatically:

```
...
Trace::IndentSize = 10;
```

Here is how you set the indentation size in the application configuration file.

```
<?xml version="1.0"?>
<configuration>
    <system.diagnostics>
        <trace indentsize="15" />
    </system.diagnostics>
</configuration>
```

The **Assert** method can check an assertion. The **AutoFlush** property and the **Flush** method control the flushing of the output buffer.

Using Switches to Enable Diagnostics

Switches enable you to have fine-grain control over the diagnostic output. You can use the **BooleanSwitch** class to turn output on or off based on the value of its **Enabled** property.

The **TraceSwitch** class gives you five hierarchical levels of control for its **Level** property: **TraceLevel::Error**, **TraceLevel::Warning**, **TraceLevel::Info**, **TraceLevel::Verbose**, and **TraceLevel::Off**. These values are part of the **TraceLevel** enumeration. Setting a lower trace level means the higher ones are set automatically, as well. For example, if the **TraceLevel::Warning** level is set, then both the **TraceLevel::Error** and **TraceLevel::Warning** levels are enabled.

```
DebugBooleanSwitch->Enabled = true;
Debug::WriteLineIf(
    DebugBooleanSwitch->Enabled,
    "Debug Boolean Switch enabled!");
    TraceLevelSwitch->Level = TraceLevel::Warning;
...
Trace::WriteLineIf(
    TraceLevelSwitch->TraceError, "TraceError!");
Trace::WriteLineIf(
    TraceLevelSwitch->TraceWarning, "TraceWarning!");
Trace::WriteLineIf(
    TraceLevelSwitch->TraceInfo, "InfoMessage!");
Trace::WriteLineIf(
    TraceLevelSwitch->TraceVerbose, "VerboseMessage!");
```

The constructors for these switches take two parameters. The first one is the name of the switch, and the second is a text description of the switch. Both **BooleanSwitch** and **TraceSwitch** classes inherit from the abstract class

Switch. You can write your own customized switch classes by inheriting from the **Switch** class. Note that the **Enabled** property of the **BooleanSwitch** and the **Level** property of the **TraceSwitch** are not part of the **Switch** class.

Enabling or Disabling Switches

You can use settings in your application configuration file to enable or disable a switch at startup. This can also be done programmatically.

Config File Switch Settings

You can set the switch's initial setting in the application's configuration file.

```
<configuration>
  <system.diagnostics>
    <switches>
      <add name="DebugSwitch" value = "0" />
      <add name="TraceSwitch" value = "2" />
    </switches>
  </system.diagnostics>
</ configuration>
```

If no values are found, the initial value of the **Enabled** property of **DebugSwitch** is set to false and the **Level** property of **TraceSwitch** is set to off.

Programmatic Switch Settings

The **Enabled** property of **BooleanSwitch** can be set to true or false. The **Level** property of the **TraceSwitch** can be set to one of the **TraceLevel** enumeration values: **TraceLevel::Off**, **TraceLevel::Error**, **TraceLevel::Warning**, **TraceLevel::Info**, **TraceLevel::Verbose**. You can get the level of this **TraceSwitch** setting by examining the **TraceError**, **TraceWarning**, **TraceInfo**, **TraceVerbose** properties.

Using Switches to Control Output

You can test the value of the switch before you write debug or trace output. You can do this with an if statement or as an argument to one of the **Trace** or **Debug** class methods.

```
Trace::WriteLineIf(
  TraceLevelSwitch->TraceError, "TraceError!");
```

```
Trace::WriteLineIf(
    TraceLevelSwitch->TraceWarning, "TraceWarning!");
Trace::WriteLineIf(
    TraceLevelSwitch->TraceInfo, "InfoMessage!");
Trace::WriteLineIf(
    TraceLevelSwitch->TraceVerbose, "VerboseMessage!");
```

Since you can set these values outside of your program's code, you can control under what circumstances you get a particular level of debug or trace output. For example, you can turn on **TraceVerbose** output if you really need a high level of diagnostics, but turn it off after you have found the problem.

TraceListener

Classes derived from the abstract class **TraceListener** represent destinations for the diagnostic output. The **TextWriterTraceListener** is designed to direct output to a **TextWriter**, **Stream**, or **FileStream**. **Console::Out** is an example of a commonly used output stream. The **EventLogTraceListener** class allows you to send output to an **EventLog**. You can create your own event logs with the static method **CreateEventSource** of **EventLog**. The **DefaultTraceListener** sends output to the debugging output window. Default Debug output can be viewed in Visual Studio.NET's Output window or with utilities (such as DBMon, which is included with this project). You can customize where output appears by implementing your own class derived from **TraceListener**.

Listeners Collection

Both the **Debug** and **Trace** classes have a static Listeners collection named **TraceListenerCollection**. This collection represents a list of **TraceListener** objects that want to receive the output from the **Debug** or **Trace** class. Listeners are added or removed from the collection just like any other .NET collection.

```
// create a listener that writes to the console
TextWriterTraceListener *ConsoleOutput =
    new TextWriterTraceListener(
        Console::Out, "Console::Out Listener");
Trace::Listeners->Add(ConsoleOutput);

// create a listener that writes to a text file
Stream *OutputFile = File::Create("output.txt");
```

```
TextWriterTraceListener *OutputFileListener =
    new TextWriterTraceListener(
        OutputFile, "Output File Listener");
Trace::Listeners->Add(OutputFileListener);

// remove the default listener
Trace::Listeners->Remove("Default");
```

In this code extract, the **OutputFileListener** object in the example will send the Trace output to a file called **output.txt**. The **DefaultTraceListener** is added automatically to the **Listener** collections. Any of the listeners, including the default listener, can be removed from the collection by invoking the collection's **Remove** method. To list all listeners in the collection,

```
pEnum =
    Trace::Listeners->GetEnumerator();
while (pEnum->MoveNext())
{
    TraceListener *tr =
        dynamic_cast<TraceListener *>(pEnum->Current);
    Console::WriteLine(
        String::Format("\t{0}", tr->Name));
}
```

Summary

Instrumenting your application for degrees of debugging and diagnostic output is a common program task. The diagnostic classes are an example of how .NET provides classes to handle standard programming tasks so you can concentrate on developing the business logic of your programming, not building debug infrastructure. On the other hand, it is also an example of how the .NET classes are partitioned so that you can customize the infrastructure using as much or as little of the available functionality as you require.

FIFTEEN

Mixing Managed and Unmanaged Code

*T*he .NET architecture supports many choices among programming languages. The primary interest in choosing the C++ language is that there exists a large and valuable investment in Win32 API and in COM (Component Object Model) programming skills and legacy code. Therefore, interoperability between the managed .NET CLR (Common Language Runtime) and existing unmanaged C++-based solutions and components will be of interest to many programmers for the foreseeable future.

Today there are several different forms of interoperability, including the SOAP protocol that allows .NET applications to call Web Services on other platforms, including Unix and mainframes. However, in this chapter we will look at a specific kind of interoperability: that of interfacing managed and unmanaged code running under Windows. The dominant C++ programming models in modern Windows systems are the Win32 API and COM. There exist a great many legacy COM components, and so it is desirable for a .NET program, running as managed code, to be able to call unmanaged COM components. The converse situation, in which a COM client needs to call a .NET server, can also arise. Apart from COM, we may also have need for a .NET program to call any unmanaged code that is exposed as a DLL, including the Win32 API. The .NET Framework supports all these interoperability scenarios through COM Interoperability and the Platform Invocation Services, or PInvoke.

In this chapter we assume that you understand the concepts behind the legacy technologies. Also, to build some of the code examples, you will need Visual Studio 6.0 as well as Visual Studio.NET.

Comparing Managed and Unmanaged Code

Other .NET languages, such as VB.NET and C#, produce managed code that can interoperate with unmanaged Win32 libraries and COM components.

593

However, VC++ .NET is currently the only language that enables you to write both managed and unmanaged code (not to be confused with unsafe code in C#). It even allows mixing of managed and unmanaged code within the same source file. Managed code is simply code that has its dynamically allocated memory managed automatically (i.e., garbage collected) by the CLR. This allows the programmer to allocate objects on the managed heap using the new operator without ever having to explicitly free them with the delete operator. This frees the programmer from having to worry about memory leaks, and it allows the programmer to focus on more interesting and useful tasks, such as accurately implementing a software design. This tends to increase programmer productivity and improve software quality.

Unmanaged C++ .NET code must explicitly manage its own heap memory usage in the traditional C++ manner, using both the **new** and **delete** operators. Since one of the most common software defects in traditional C++ code has always been the dreaded memory leak, using the managed extensions of VC++ .NET can have a dramatically positive effect on many software development efforts. It is also interesting to note that the **delete** operator may be used explicitly on a pointer to a managed object if you want more control over when the object is freed from memory. This can be useful in situations where you would like its destructor to be executed earlier rather than waiting for the garbage collector to do it, to avoid timing issues in a multithreaded program.

Reasons for Mixing Managed and Unmanaged Code

If the C++ managed extensions are so great, then why would you want to write unmanaged code? There are several answers to this question:

1. As with other automatically garbage-collected runtime environments, such as Smalltalk and Java, there is often a noticeable degradation in performance due to the runtime overhead associated with tracking object usage (reference tracking) and also deleting those objects at an appropriate time.

2. Another undesirable side effect that is often associated with automatic garbage collection is an increased amount of physical memory required to store objects that are candidates for deletion but not yet deleted by the garbage collector. More aggressive garbage collection schemes suffer in performance, whereas less aggressive garbage collection schemes suffer from excessive memory consumption. With a traditional C++ program, the programmer is in complete control (for better or for worse) of exactly when each heap object is deleted. This gives the programmer the potential of writing code that achieves both performance and memory efficiency. Unfortunately, this does require greater programmer skill and effort.

3. You may have a legacy C++ Win32 application that you want to convert into a .NET application incrementally over time. This natu-

rally requires that you implement code that contains a mixture of managed and unmanaged code, at least over an interim period.

4. You may have legacy C++ skills and be familiar with traditional unmanaged software development, but you are in need of developing new applications for the .NET platform. In this case, you may want to develop code containing a mixture of managed and unmanaged code as an easier approach to entering the world of .NET programming, rather than suddenly jumping directly into pure C# or VB.NET.

Notice that the preceding arguments for implementing unmanaged code are reasonable in certain circumstances; however, they are not applicable in all situations. For example, consider points 1 and 2 above that focus on performance and memory efficiency issues. In most programs, these issues are most effectively dealt with by focusing on optimizing a relatively small but critical portion of the application's overall code. Therefore, it often makes sense to initially implement all new code using managed extensions (or even C# or VB.NET), and then after careful performance analysis, those portions of code that are found to be critical may be tweaked with an eye for optimization using unmanaged C++. This critical code redesign may or may not be amenable to an unmanaged implementation, in which case you may opt for using managed C++, C#, VB.NET, and so forth. Of course, point 3 is only applicable in situations where legacy code is being upgraded. Point 4 makes total sense to C++ programmers who love their language and would miss it dearly if they could not use it. However, there are C++ programmers who have long been itching to move on to what they perceive as a "better" language, and would not miss C++ for a minute. If none of these four points are applicable to your situation, then you may decide to implement your entire project with C++ managed extensions or select a different .NET language altogether.

Unmanaged Versus Unsafe

Visual C++ .NET is currently the only .NET language that can generate unmanaged code. Other .NET programming languages, such as C# and VB.NET, are capable of generating only managed code. In particular, note that the **unsafe** keyword of C# is entirely unrelated to the issue of managed versus unmanaged code execution. The **unsafe** C# keyword prevents the .NET runtime from providing automatic memory management, permitting the use of pointers to objects.

Although Visual C++ .NET is the only .NET language that can generate unmanaged code, it is quite possible for other .NET languages to be used to create managed code that interoperates with unmanaged code, regardless of whether that managed code is safe or unsafe. For example, a .NET application can call the unmanaged methods on a COM object by way of a simple wrapper facility, and the unmanaged functions exposed by traditional DLLs, including the Win32 API, are accessible via the PInvoke facility. These interoperability features are described later in this chapter.

In Visual C++ .NET, you have the choice of writing managed or unmanaged code; however, you do not have the choice of writing safe or unsafe code. All C++ code is assumed by the CLR to be unsafe. Just as with any C# code using the **unsafe** keyword, all C++ code cannot be verified as safe, and therefore will be executed only when the code is trusted.[1]

Managed and Unmanaged Reference and Value Types

There are fundamental differences between how managed and unmanaged code treats reference and value types. Unmanaged C++ code allows you to declare a local variable, a method parameter, or a class data member to be of a type defined by an unmanaged class or struct. This is known as a value type, because the variable contains the value that actually is the data. C++ also allows you to declare a variable as either a pointer or a reference to a type defined by a class or struct. These are known as reference[2] types, since the variable does not actually contain a value that is the object, but rather, it has the ability to refer to an object of the appropriate type on the unmanaged heap. This can be a bit confusing, since C++ tries to make a conceptual distinction between reference and pointer types. However, in reality, a C++ reference is simply a constant pointer under the covers.

A declaration of a value type represents in situ storage space for the actual value; however, managed code does not allow a managed class or struct to be used to declare a value type (unless of course the **__value** keyword is used). This can be seen in the next code example, **ManagedAndUnmanagedRefAndValTypes**, where the compiler would flag an error on an attempt to declare a variable as a value type using the managed class named **ManagedClass**. To see this, try uncommenting the line of code containing

Code
Example

---

[1] Whether or not code is trusted is determined by security policy and verification. When the CLR JIT compiles the assembly's MSIL code into native code, a verification step may be performed, according to whether or not a security policy requires this verification. If this verification is not skipped, it checks the MSIL code and metadata, and attempts to determine whether or not the code is type-safe. If the code is not recognized to be type-safe, the CLR will throw an exception, and the code will not be allowed to execute.

[2] We are lumping pointer and reference types together as just "reference types" here, which is playing a bit loosely with their definitions. C++ pointers and C++ reference types can be used for very similar purposes (but with different syntax and only slightly different semantics). Technically, it is incorrect to refer to a pointer as a reference type, because when a pointer is passed as a parameter, the pointer value (i.e., variable address) is copied onto the stack. Since this is data that is copied, it is technically not considered to be a reference type, but a value type. However, when you pass a parameter by reference, the compiler actually generates code that treats it as a pointer, but it is still technically considered a reference type rather than a value type.

ManagedClass mcObj;. The resulting error message reminds you that you probably wanted a pointer to be declared rather than a value.

On the other hand, it is not an error to declare a value type variable using the unmanaged class **UnmanagedClass**. Note that it is also not an error to create an instance of either **ManagedClass** on the managed heap or **UnmanagedClass** on the unmanaged heap using the new operator. The only difference between these last two cases is that the managed object does not require a delete operator to prevent a memory leak, whereas the unmanaged object does.

In this particular example, the delete operator is used in the last line to delete the **pmcObj** object, and the comment states that it is "not normally required, but needed here." This **delete** operator was added as the last statement in the program not because explicit clean up is required on a managed object (the garbage collector would have done this for us eventually), but rather, it was added due to a timing issue. This is because the call to **Console::WriteLine** in the managed class's destructor would otherwise be called at the very end of the program execution, after the **Console** output stream has already been closed. In other words, if the destructor were not explicitly invoked using the **delete** operator, the managed object would have attempted to perform output on a nonexistent stream, which would have produced an exception (System.ObjectDisposedException: Cannot access a closed Stream). This illustrates the most common reason for explicitly deleting a managed object, which is that you sometimes need explicit control over when a managed object is destroyed.

Another point to note here is that the compiler treats primitive data types (such as int, float, double, char, and so forth) differently from managed __gc class or __gc struct types in that primitive types are always value types.

```
//ManagedAndUnmanagedRefAndValTypes.cpp

#using <mscorlib.dll>
using namespace System;

__gc class ManagedClass
{
public:
   ManagedClass()
   {
      Console::WriteLine("ManagedClass");
   }
   ~ManagedClass()
   {
      Console::WriteLine("~ManagedClass");
   }
}
```

```
};

__nogc class UnmanagedClass
{
public:
   UnmanagedClass()
   {
      Console::WriteLine("UnmanagedClass");
   }
   ~UnmanagedClass()
   {
      Console::WriteLine("~UnmanagedClass");
   }
};

void main(void)
{
   ManagedClass *pmcObj = new ManagedClass();
   //ManagedClass mcObj; //error, value type not allowed
   UnmanagedClass *pumcObj = new UnmanagedClass();
   delete pumcObj; //required due to no gc
   UnmanagedClass umcObj; //no error, value type allowed
   int i = 3; //no error, value type OK for primitive type
   delete pmcObj; //not normally required, but needed here
}
```

The previous code example produces the following output:

```
ManagedClass
UnmanagedClass
~UnmanagedClass
UnmanagedClass
~ManagedClass
~UnmanagedClass
```

Restrictions on Using Managed Types in C++

There are, unfortunately, many rules that restrict how managed types (class, struct, or interface) may be used, which tend to make them a bit more awkward to work with in comparison to traditional unmanaged C++ types. These rules also have certain effects on how managed and unmanaged code is allowed to interact with one another.

1. A managed type cannot inherit from any unmanaged type. On the other hand, an unmanaged type cannot inherit from any managed type. This means that managed and unmanaged class inheritance hierarchies must always remain completely segregated from one another.

2. Managed types cannot declare friends (i.e., friend functions, classes, structs, or interfaces). This rule is clearly not applicable to traditional unmanaged C++ classes. This may not be such an issue for many programmers, since many consider friendship to be a breach of the important object-oriented concept known as encapsulation. Unmanaged types may declare friends, as in traditional C++ classes; however, an unmanaged type must only declare friends that are themselves unmanaged types.

3. Unlike unmanaged types, managed types do not support multiple implementation inheritance. However, both managed and unmanaged types support multiple interface inheritance. Single implementation inheritance is another limitation that many programmers can probably live with. Although traditional C++ supports multiple implementation inheritance, note that most object-oriented languages, including Java and Smalltalk, do not support it. Even COM, which was, at the binary level, based on a C++-style virtual function table, did not support this feature.

4. A managed type can obviously contain a data member that is a pointer to a managed object. A managed type can also contain a data member that is an unmanaged object or a pointer to an unmanaged object. On the other hand, an unmanaged type cannot have an embedded instance of a managed object or a pointer to a managed type. The points made here regarding pointers apply equally to references.

5. An unmanaged class that specifies no explicit base class is an independent root class. However, a managed class that specifies no explicit base implicitly inherits from the **System::Object** root class.

6. A garbage-collected object (i.e., an instance of a managed class that uses **__gc** keyword rather than the **__value** or **__nogc** keyword) can only be accessed via a pointer (or a reference) to the object on the managed heap. This is different from unmanaged objects, which may be either contained directly within a value type variable or accessed via a pointer on the unmanaged heap.

These rules on using managed types in C++ are summed up in the following code example. The comments should guide you in understanding all of these complicated rules. If you open the **ManagedAndUnmanagedTypes** project provided and try uncommenting each of the statements (one at a time is best) that produce a compiler error, you can learn more about each of these rules. Just click on the error of interest in the Task List window to select it, and then press F1 for the documentation on the error. Of course, double-clicking the error in the Task List window takes you to the offending statement in the source code editor.

```cpp
//ManagedAndUnmanagedTypes.cpp

#using <mscorlib.dll>
using namespace System;
#pragma warning(disable : 4101) //ignore unref local

__gc class MemberManagedClass {}; //used as data member

__nogc class MemberUnmanagedClass {}; //used as data member

__gc class FriendManagedClass {}; //used as friend

__nogc class FriendUnmanagedClass {}; //used as friend

__gc class ManagedClass
{
public:
    MemberUnmanagedClass um;    //OK: embedded unmanaged
    MemberUnmanagedClass *pum; //OK: pointer to unmanaged
    MemberUnmanagedClass &rum; //OK: reference to unmanaged

    //MemberManagedClass m;    //Error: stack-phobic
    MemberManagedClass *pm; //OK: pointer to managed
    MemberManagedClass &rm; //OK: reference to managed

    ManagedClass() : //needed for ref init
        rm(*new MemberManagedClass),    //complier required!
        rum(*new MemberUnmanagedClass), //complier required!
        pm(new MemberManagedClass) //not complier required
    {}

    //Errors: cannot have any friends in a managed class
    //friend FriendManagedClass;
    //friend FriendUnmanagedClass;
};

__nogc class UnmanagedClass
{
public:
```

```
    MemberUnmanagedClass um;    //OK: embedded unmanaged
    MemberUnmanagedClass *pum; //OK: pointer to unmanaged
    MemberUnmanagedClass &rum; //OK: reference to unmanaged

    //MemberManagedClass m;   //Error: stack-phobic
    //MemberManagedClass *pm; //Error: managed* in unmanaged
    MemberManagedClass &rm; //OK: reference to managed (???)

    UnmanagedClass() : //needed for ref init
       rm(*new MemberManagedClass),   //complier required!
       rum(*new MemberUnmanagedClass) //complier required!
    {}

    //Error: cannot declare a managed friend in an unmanaged
    //friend FriendManagedClass;
    friend FriendUnmanagedClass; //OK
};

__gc class SuperManagedClass {};

__nogc class SuperUnmanagedClass {};

//error: managed type cannot derive from an unmanaged type
//__gc class BadSubManagedClass : SuperUnmanagedClass {};

//error: unmanaged type cannot derive from a managed type
//__nogc class BadSubUnmanagedClass : SuperManagedClass {};

//OK: can derive from machine managed/unmanaged super class
__gc class OKSubManagedClass : public SuperManagedClass {};
__nogc class OKSubUnmanagedClass : SuperUnmanagedClass {};

void main(void)
{
    UnmanagedClass *pumc = new UnmanagedClass;   //old C++
    UnmanagedClass umc;                          //old C++
    UnmanagedClass &rumc = *new UnmanagedClass; //old C++

    ManagedClass *pmc = new ManagedClass; //OK: managed heap
    //ManagedClass mc;                    //Error: stack-phobic
    ManagedClass &rmc = *new ManagedClass;//OK: managed heap
}
```

Calling Across the Managed/Unmanaged Boundary

In spite of all the restrictions described in the previous section, it is possible for managed and unmanaged code to cooperate in several ways, even in the same source file. For example, the following code shows that you can call from managed code into unmanaged code. Note that you can pass a pointer to a data member of a managed object as a parameter into an unmanaged object's method. This is made possible by declaring the pointer to the managed object using the **__pin** keyword. The **__pin** keyword prevents the managed object from being moved in memory while the unmanaged code manipulates it. When the **CallingFromManagedToUnmanaged** program is run, you will see the values 0 and 1 being displayed in the console output, proving that the **UnmanagedClassMethod** successfully manipulates the pinned managed object that is passed into it. If you remove the **__pin** keyword in the following code, you will get a compiler error complaining that the parameter being passed into **UnmanagedClassMethod** cannot convert from **int __gc** * to **int** *.

Code
Example

```
//CallingFromManagedToUnmanaged.cpp

#using <mscorlib.dll>
using namespace System;

#pragma managed

__gc class ManagedClass //managed class
{
public:
   int x;
};

#pragma unmanaged

__nogc class UnmanagedClass //unmanaged class
{
public:
   void UnmanagedClassMethod(int *px)
   {
      //px points to the x data member of a managed object
      //but that object is pinned, so this unmanaged code
      //is able to access the data member x safely
      *px = 1; //change value to prove it worked
   }
};
```

```
#pragma managed

void main(void)
{
   ManagedClass __pin *pmcObj = new ManagedClass();
   UnmanagedClass *pumcObj = new UnmanagedClass();
   pmcObj->x = 0;
   Console::WriteLine(pmcObj->x); //show before: 0
   //pass data member of managed object to unmanaged code
   pumcObj->UnmanagedClassMethod(&pmcObj->x);
   Console::WriteLine(pmcObj->x); //show after: 1
}
```

Code Example

The converse of this is shown next in the **CallingFromUnmanagedTo-Managed** program. Notice that the unmanaged code in **main** calls into the managed function named **ManagedFunction**, which creates an instance of the managed class named **ManagedClass** and calls on its method **Managed-ClassMethod**. Unfortunately, the unmanaged code in main is not able to directly instantiate the **ManagedClass**, since unmanaged code cannot refer directly to any managed type. You can prove this by uncommenting the last statement where the **ManagedClass** would be instantiated. Uncommenting this line results in a compiler error (cannot declare a managed object or pointer in an unmanaged function). However, you can see in this example that the managed code in **ManagedFunction** can create an instance of the unmanaged type **UnmanagedClass** and pass it in as a parameter to the managed method **ManagedClassMethod**. This demonstrates one more way that the managed and unmanaged worlds may interact.

```
//CallingFromUnmanagedToManaged.cpp

#using <mscorlib.dll>
using namespace System;

#pragma unmanaged

__nogc class UnmanagedClass //unmanaged class
{
public:
   int x;
};

#pragma managed

__gc class ManagedClass //managed class
```

```
{
public:
   void ManagedClassMethod(UnmanagedClass *pumcObject)
   {
      //pumcObject points to an unmanaged object
      pumcObject->x = 1; //change value to prove it worked
   }
};

void ManagedFunction()
{
   ManagedClass *pmcObj = new ManagedClass();
   UnmanagedClass *pumcObj = new UnmanagedClass();
   pumcObj->x = 0;
   Console::WriteLine(pumcObj->x); //show before: 0
   pmcObj->ManagedClassMethod(pumcObj);
   Console::WriteLine(pumcObj->x); //show before: 1
}

#pragma unmanaged

void main(void)
{
   ManagedFunction(); //call from unmanaged to managed
   //ManagedClass *pmcObj = new ManagedClass(); //error
}
```

Comparing C++ Programming in COM and .NET

A managed interface is used to simply and effectively define a set of methods without any implementation. The idea of programming with interfaces is one of the most important concepts of object-oriented programming. Both Java and C++ support interfaces. Just as with a C++-implemented COM interface, a managed C++-implemented .NET interface contains only methods that are public, pure virtual methods. A managed interface implemented with managed C++ is declared using both the **__gc** and **__interface** keywords together, as shown in the following code example. The compiler enforces the complete implementation of any concrete class that chooses to implement such an interface. This is an important guarantee from the client code's point of view. It allows client code to be written that is interested in using the generic interface, but not interested in any specific details on what concrete class happens to implement that interface.

Code
Example

The following example is provided as a managed C++ Class Library project named **ManagedClassLibrary**, which was created using the New | Project menu sequence in Visual Studio.NET. The resulting .NET DLL component can then be called by .NET clients that are written in any .NET programming languages, such as VC++ .NET, C#, or VB.NET. This time we are introducing a namespace named **ManagedClassLibrary**. This is not strictly required for a .NET assembly, but in larger projects or in situations where you expect to have many other programmers using your component, it is highly recommended that you define a namespace to prevent name collisions.

```cpp
//ManagedClassLibrary.h

#pragma once
using namespace System;

namespace ManagedClassLibrary
{
   public __gc __interface ISomeInterface
   {
      void SomeMethod();
      int SomeOtherMethod();
   };

   public __gc class SomeInterfaceImpl
      : public ISomeInterface
   {
   public:
      void SomeMethod()
      {
         Console::WriteLine("SomeMethod");
      }
      int SomeOtherMethod()
      {
         Console::WriteLine("SomeOtherMethod");
         return 0;
      }
   };
}
```

The example code above shows how easy it is to define and implement a .NET component. Compare that to the considerable complexity of defining and implementing a traditional COM component in C++. For a .NET component, you simply define an interface and then implement that interface with a derived class. Then, all of the great advantages and features traditionally associated with component-oriented programming are realized without all the effort and complexity of COM programming. For example, one of the advantages of COM was its language independence. Notice that without editing the registry and without the need for implementing such things as a class factory, GUIDs, or IUnknown, a client program written in any .NET language can easily use the .NET component above.

Code
Example

For example, the following C# code (note that we have switched temporarily to C#) is able to successfully call into the C++ .NET component shown above. All you have to do is create a new C# console application project named **ManagedClassClient**, add the following code, and add a reference to the project that refers to the **ManagedClassLibrary.dll** assembly created by the code above.[3] You add a reference to another assembly via the Project | Add Reference menu sequence, then click Browse and navigate to the desired assembly. If you forget to add the reference to the assembly, you will get a compiler error stating that the namespace **ManagedClassLibrary** does not exist. If you look at the code above, you will see that it does indeed define a namespace named **ManagedClassLibrary**.

```
//ManagedClassClient.cs

using System;
using ManagedClassLibrary;

namespace ManagedClassClient
{
    public class Test
    {
        public static int Main(string[] args)
        {
            ISomeInterface si =
                new SomeInterfaceImpl();
            si.SomeMethod();
            si.SomeOtherMethod();
            return 0;
        }
    }
}
```

---

[3] If you open the supplied **ManagedClassClient** project, you should first remove the (broken) reference.

The output from the above C# client program is shown in the following:

```
SomeMethod
SomeOtherMethod
```

Accessing COM Components from Managed Code

As shown in the previous section, .NET component programming is very easy using managed C++ code, and it is also easy in the other .NET languages. Probably nobody will miss the annoying complexities of traditional COM component programming now that .NET component programming is such a breeze. However, COM has been a very important technology for Windows programmers for almost a decade. In fact, COM has been the basis of practically every important new technology produced by Microsoft and other major Windows software development companies over the last several years. Clearly, there is a large investment in legacy COM components and COM client applications. This section demonstrates how to call into methods implemented in existing COM components from C++ managed code. Of course, COM components can just as easily be accessed from managed code implemented with other .NET languages using similar techniques.

A managed client application written in Visual C++ .NET (or any .NET language) can use the interoperability facilities provided by the .NET Framework to call into unmanaged legacy COM components. This forms a bridge between the managed execution environment of the .NET client and the native execution environment of the COM component, as shown in Figure 15–1.

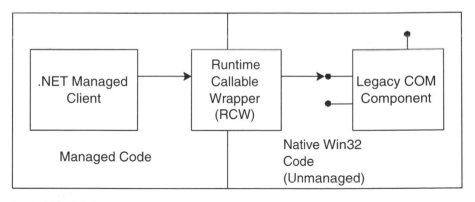

| Figure 15–1 | A Runtime Callable Wrapper between managed and unmanaged code. |

You could implement an RCW assembly yourself, using the PInvoke facility (described in a later section) to call into the necessary APIs, such as **CoCreateInstance** and the **IUnknown** methods directly. But that is not necessary, because the **Tlbimp.exe** tool can read type library information and automatically generate the appropriate RCW for you, as described in the next section.

The Tlbimp.exe Utility

The **Tlbimp.exe** utility (Type Library to .NET Assembly Converter) program is provided in the **\Program Files\Microsoft.NET\FrameworkSDK\Bin** directory. It is used to generate managed classes that wrap unmanaged COM classes. The result is known as a Runtime Callable Wrapper (RCW). The resulting RCW is a .NET component (i.e., a managed DLL assembly) that managed client code can use to access the COM interface methods that are implemented in the COM component. The **Tlbimp.exe** tool is a command-line program[4] that reads COM type library information, generates a managed wrapper class along with the associated metadata, and places the result into the RCW assembly. You can view the resulting contents in this assembly using the **Ildasm.exe** tool. The command-line syntax for **Tlbimp.exe** follows:

```
Tlbimp TypeLibName [options]
Where options may contain the following:
    /out:FileName              Assembly file name
    /namespace:Namespace       Assembly Namespace
    /asmversion:Version        Assembly version number
    /reference:FileName        Reference assembly
    /publickey:FileName        Public key file
    /keyfile:FileName          Key pair file
    /keycontainer:FileName     Key pair key container
    /delaysign                 Delay digital signing
    /unsafe                    Suppress security checks
    /nologo                    Suppress displaying logo
    /silent                    Suppress output except errors
    /verbose                   Display extra information
    /primary                   Make primary interop assembly
    /sysarray                  SAFEARRAY as System.Array
```

---

[4] You will need certain environment settings to be established in order to use .NET SDK tools at the command prompt. The easiest way to do this is via Start | Programs | Microsoft Visual Studio.NET 7.0 | Visual Studio.NET Tools | Visual Studio.NET Command Prompt. If you have not set up the appropriate environment yourself, you cannot use Start | Programs | Accessories | Command Prompt, since this will cause the following error when you try to use Tlbimp.exe: 'Tlbimp' is not recognized as an internal or external command.

```
/strictref                  Only /reference assemblies
/? or /help                 Display help information
```

When the **Tlbimp.exe** tool imports a COM type library, it creates a .NET namespace with the same name as the library defined in the type library (that is, the name of the actual library, not the name of the type library file that contains it). **Tlbimp.exe** converts each COM coclass defined in the type library into a managed .NET wrapper class in the resulting .NET assembly that has one constructor that takes no parameters. **Tlbimp.exe** coverts each COM interface defined in the type library into a .NET interface in the resulting .NET assembly. Consider the typical COM IDL file library statement shown next that would be used to create a type library using **Midl.exe**. The TLB, or DLL file produced by this IDL file, would cause **Tlbimp.exe** to generate the assembly containing metadata, including the namespace **LEGACYCOMSERVERLib**, a managed wrapper class named **LegacyCOMObj**, and a managed interface named **ILegacyCOMObj**.

```
library LEGACYCOMSERVERLib
{
    coclass LegacyCOMObj
    {
        [default] interface ILegacyCOMObj;
    };
};
```

Once you have used **Tlbimp.exe** to generate the wrapper assembly, you can view its contents using the **Ildasm.exe** tool.

```
Tlbimp LegacyCOMServer.tlb
Ildasm LEGACYCOMSERVERLib.dll
```

This command displays the contents of the wrapper assembly, as shown in Figure 15–2. Note that the namespace shown by Ildasm.exe is **LEGACY-COMSERVERLib**, the name of the interface is **ILegacyCOMObj**, and the wrapper class is named **LegacyCOMObj**. In the next subsection, we will look at the source code for this legacy COM component.

A Legacy COM Component

For demonstration purposes, we will need a legacy COM component, which is described in this section. Note that the following IDL file was produced as part of a VC++ 6.0 ATL COM AppWizard DLL project named **LegacyCOM-Server**. This project has an ATL Object Wizard-generated simple object

How to Create and Use a Runtime Callable Wrapper

1. Use Tlbimp.exe on the legacy COM server DLL or TLB file to produce the RCW assembly. This wrapper makes it possible to access the COM component from managed client code.
2. Use Regsvr32.exe on the legacy COM server DLL to register it on your machine if you have not already done so.
3. Optionally, add a using namespace statement to your Managed C++ client code so that you can conveniently refer to the COM class by its short name. This namespace can be found by looking at the library name in the server, using Oleview.exe. Of course, you must also add code to the client that instantiates and calls methods on the COM component. An example of this code will be shown shortly.
4. Deploy the LegacyCOMServer.dll assembly if you have not already done so. The easiest way to do this is to simply copy LegacyCOMServer.dll to your managed client directory. Now the client code can be complied and run to verify that the RCW works properly.

Ildasm.exe showing contents of a COM wrapper assembly.

named **LegacyCOMObj**, containing one dual interface with no aggregation. This dual interface has one method named **AddEmUp**, which takes two **in** parameters of type **int**, named **i** and **j**, and one **out**, **retval** parameter of type **int** * named **psum**.

> If you want to create an ATL COM project yourself, but you do not have Visual Studio 6.0, then you could create a new ATL project with Visual Studio.NET, but you will find that the starter code that is generated looks quite different from the Visual Studio 6.0 example shown here. For example, there is no IDL file, but instead, the **__interface** keyword is used to define the **ILegacyCOMObj** interface directly in the **LegacyCOMObj.h** file. Also, Visual C++ .NET makes considerable use of attributes in its generated code, making it look quite different from traditional Visual C++ code. However, for the purposes of studying how **Tlbimp.exe** is used on a COM component, this will not pose any problems.

```
import "oaidl.idl";
import "ocidl.idl";
   [
      object,
      uuid(7C82D19B-2B04-476B-AEC8-0ABFD7A2E54B),
      dual,
      helpstring("ILegacyCOMObj Interface"),
      pointer_default(unique)
   ]
   interface ILegacyCOMObj : IDispatch
   {
      [id(1), helpstring("method AddEmUp")]
      HRESULT AddEmUp([in] int i, [in] int j,
         [out, retval] int *psum);
   };
[
   uuid(5FBA2BC1-CD8B-4B20-AF94-4CA17714C9C0),
   version(1.0),
   helpstring("LegacyCOMServer 1.0 Type Library")
]
library LEGACYCOMSERVERLib
{
   importlib("stdole32.tlb");
   importlib("stdole2.tlb");
    [
      uuid(EBAC6FD0-D55B-4BA6-B386-8B774255A87C),
      helpstring("LegacyCOMObj Class")
   ]
   coclass LegacyCOMObj
```

```
    {
        [default] interface ILegacyCOMObj;
    };
};
```

The above IDL file is part of the same **LegacyCOMServer** ATL project that contains the following implementation code for the exposed COM interface method **AddEmUp**.

```
STDMETHODIMP CLegacyCOMObj::AddEmUp(int i, int j, int *psum)
{
    // TODO: Add your implementation code here
    *psum = i + j;
    return S_OK;
}
```

When the above COM server project is built, the registry will be automatically updated as one of the build steps; however, if you then deploy it on another machine, you will need to register it there as well. This can be done at the command prompt using the following command:

```
Regsvr32 LegacyCOMServer.dll
```

A release version of the DLL, with no runtime dependency on ATL, is provided. You may register it through the batch file **reg.bat** and unregister it through **unreg.bat**.

A Legacy COM Client

Code Example

For comparison purposes (and of course to test the COM component before we attempt to use **Tlbimp.exe** on it), an unmanaged legacy Win32 console client application is shown next. You may want to look at this example to refresh your memory on how a COM client works (actually, just one of many ways) and to make a comparison with the managed C++ COM client code shown in the next subsection. This unmanaged COM client was created using Visual C++ 6.0 as a Win32 console application. A release version of the EXE is provided.

```
//LegacyCOMClient.cpp

#include <iostream.h>
#include <objbase.h>
#import "..\LegacyCOMServe\LegacyCOMServer.tlb" no_namespace
named_guids
```

```
void main()
{
   { //nested curly braces prevent pointer exception!
     CoInitialize(NULL);
     ILegacyCOMObjPtr pi(CLSID_LegacyCOMObj);
     int i = pi->AddEmUp(3, 4);
     cout << i << endl << flush;
   }
   CoUninitialize();
}
```

The output from the above legacy COM client application is shown below. This is the result of calling the COM interface method **AddEmUp** with the parameters **3** and **4**.

7

A Managed C++ COM Client

Before you can go ahead experimenting with the development of a managed C++ program that can act as a client to the legacy COM component, you will run the **Tlbimp.exe** tool on the **LegacyCOMServer.tlb** to produce the **LEG-ACYCOMSERVERLib.dll** assembly. This was shown previously; however, it is shown again here for convenience. Note that you can run **Tlbimp.exe** on the COM components DLL or the TLB file. The subsequent code example **ManagedCOMClient.cpp** assumes that you have done this in the same directory as the **LEGACYCOMSERVERLib.dll** file (to match the corresponding **#using** statement in the client).

```
Tlbimp LegacyCOMServer.dll
```

Code
Example

Then you will need to make this assembly available to the CLR class loader (i.e., you will need to deploy it). One way to deploy a .NET component is to simply copy it into the same directory as the client program. This is known as "local deployment." But first, we need to create a managed C++ client program, named **ManagedCOMClient** that makes use of this legacy COM component, as shown in the following.

```
//ManagedCOMClient.cpp

#using <mscorlib.dll>
using namespace System;
#using <..\LegacyCOMServer\LEGACYCOMSERVERLib.dll>
```

```
using namespace LEGACYCOMSERVERLib; //library name in IDL
void main()
{
    ILegacyCOMObj *plco; //from name of interface in IDL
    plco = new LegacyCOMObj; //from name of coclass in IDL
    int sum = plco->AddEmUp(3, 4);
    Console::WriteLine(sum);
}
```

Before you run the above program, be sure that you copied the assembly **LEGACYCOMSERVERLib.dll** to the client executable's directory; otherwise, a **System.IO.FileNotFoundException** will be thrown by the CLR when it tries to load the **ILegacyCOMOb** interface from the assembly, which cannot be found. The output from this managed C++ COM client application is exactly the same as that of the legacy COM client application shown previously.

A Managed C# COM Client

Code Example

For comparison purposes, the equivalent C# client program is shown next. Of course, this is a book on managed C++, not C#. However, a few comparisons with C# can provide some insights. The C# code is quite similar to the managed C++ code, but it is just slightly simpler. Note that for this to work, you will need to add a project reference to the **LEGACYCOMSERVERLib.dll** assembly created earlier using the **Tlbimp.exe** utility. Adding a reference to the project is the C# equivalent of the **#using** directive in a managed C++ program. You do not need to manually copy the **LEGACYCOMSERVER-Lib.dll** assembly this time, since this is done automatically when you add the reference to the project in Visual Studio.NET.

```
//ManagedCSharpCOMClient.cs

using System;
using LEGACYCOMSERVERLib;

namespace ManagedCSharpCOMClient
{
    public class Test
    {
        public static void Main(string[] args)
        {
            LegacyCOMObj lco; //interface
            lco = new LegacyCOMObj(); //coclass
            int sum = lco.AddEmUp(3, 4);
```

```
            Console.WriteLine(sum);
        }
    }
}
```

If you run the previous program, you should see the same output produced earlier with the **LegacyCOMClient** and **ManagedCOMClient** client
programs.

A Managed C++ COM Client Without Metadata

An alternative approach for calling from managed C++ code into a legacy
COM component, but without having to generate a wrapper assembly with
Tlbimp.exe is shown next. Rather than using **Tlbimp.exe** to create the **LegacyCOMObj** assembly, the runtime creates the wrapper class dynamically
directly from the COM component's registered type library. Note that this version of the managed C++ client does not need the **#using** directive for accessing the **LEGACYCOMSERVERLib.dll** assembly.

```
//ManagedCOMClientWithoutMetadata.cpp

#using <mscorlib.dll>
using namespace System;
using namespace Reflection;

void main()
{
    Object *args[] = {__box(3), __box(4)};
    __box int *sum;
    Type *type = Type::GetTypeFromProgID(
    "LegacyCOMServer.LegacyCOMObj.1");
    Object *object = Activator::CreateInstance(type);
    sum = static_cast<__box int *>(type->InvokeMember(
       "AddEmUp", //method to be invoked
       BindingFlags::InvokeMethod, //binder flags
       0,       //binder object
       object, //target object
       args    //parameter array
       ));
    Console::WriteLine(sum);
}
```

If you run the above program, you should see the same output produced
earlier with the previous three COM client programs. The only difference is

that in the case of **ManagedCOMClientWithoutMetadata**, the wrapper assembly does not need to be created, and no assembly needs to be deployed to the client (which is cool when you think about it).

A Managed C# COM Client Without Metadata

For comparison purposes, the previous managed C++ program is reimplemented in the C# code shown below, which again produces the same output. As in the previous example, the following code is interesting because it does not need the assembly metadata, so there is no need to add a reference to the project or deploy the assembly. Instead, the type information is discovered at runtime dynamically, using the reflection API.

```
//ManagedCSharpCOMClientWithoutMetadata.cs

using System;
using System.Reflection;

namespace ManagedCSharpCOMClientWithoutMetadata
{
    public class Test
    {
        public static void Main(string[] args)
        {
            Type type;
            Object obj;
            Object[] argArray = new Object[2];
            type = Type.GetTypeFromProgID(
                "LegacyCOMServer.LegacyCOMObj.1");
            obj = Activator.CreateInstance(type);
            argArray[0] = 3;
            argArray[1] = 4;
            Object sum = type.InvokeMember(
                "AddEmUp",
                BindingFlags.InvokeMethod,
                null,
                obj,
                argArray
                );
            Console.WriteLine(sum);
        }
    }
}
```

If you run the previous program, you should see the same output produced as with the previous client programs.

Apartments and Marshaling

In the previous several examples showing how to write managed C++ COM clients that access the legacy COM component named **LegacyCOMObj**, no attention was paid to the issue of apartments and marshaling. That we did not need to concern ourselves with this issue was actually just a fortunate result of the fact that the **ILegacyCOMObj** interface was marked with the **dual** attribute in the **LegacyCOMServer.idl** file. The **dual** attribute causes COM to provide automatic marshaling for the interface, based on type library information.

Dual interfaces are very common, and the default in an ATL wizard-generated COM component has a dual interface. Visual Basic 6.0 also creates COM components with dual interfaces. However, if there is no need for a COM component to be called by a late-binding client, it can be more efficient and flexible to implement only a pure v-table interface.

Therefore, not all legacy COM servers expose only dual interfaces. In such cases, you will find that marshaling becomes an issue, and if you fail to deal with it, your managed client code will throw the **InvalidCastException** exception when you try to call on a method in the interface and no marshaling is available. The problem is that if the .NET client is in a separate apartment, then it needs marshaling. You can use any of the following solutions to deal with this issue. Note that solutions 1 and 2 may not be suitable for legacy code, especially if you do not have the source code, or if it would break other clients, or if it is not feasible to redeploy.

1. Mark the IDL for the interface with **dual** and reimplement the COM server accordingly.
2. Mark the IDL for the interface with **oleautomation** and retrofit the COM server to limit its parameter types to oleautomation-friendly types.
3. Build and register the proxy/stub DLL for the interface to provide marshaling.
4. Mark the **Main** method in the C# client with the **[STAThread]** or **[MTAThread]** attribute (appropriate to the situation) to place it into the same threading model as the COM server. For example, in the scenario above, if the **dual** attribute was not used in the COM server, **[STAThread]** could be used to solve this problem.

Accessing Managed Components from COM Clients

Obviously, it is much more likely that you will want to write new .NET applications that make use of legacy COM components; however, there may be times when you need to go in the opposite direction. For example, you may have an existing application that makes use of one or more COM components, and you would like to rewrite several of those COM components as .NET components to be used in future .NET solutions. However, in the meantime, you may want to make use of those new .NET components in your existing COM client applications as well.

COM client programs may use early binding (v-table interface) or late binding (**IDispatch** interface) to access managed .NET components. Early binding requires that type library information is available at compile time. Late binding does not require any type library information at compile time, since binding takes place at runtime via the **IDispatch** interface methods.

However, regardless of whether the client uses early or late binding, a bridge is required between the unmanaged native execution environment of the COM client and the managed execution environment of the .NET component. This bridge is known as the COM Callable Wrapper (CCW), which acts as a proxy for the managed object, as shown in Figure 15–3. Only one CCW object is created for any given managed object created for a COM client. The CCW manages object lifetime according to the reference counting rules of **IUnknown**, and it also manages marshaling for the method calls made on the object.

Early Binding COM Clients with .NET Components

Early bound COM clients typically make use of type library information to access COM components. This type library information provides a convenient way to create instances of the COM classes defined in those COM components. Type library information can be stored in TLB, DLL, OCX, or EXE files, but the TLB file is the only one that is specifically designed for that purpose alone.

A type library can be generated from the metadata in a .NET assembly using the **Tlbexp.exe** (Assembly to Type Library Converter) tool. This allows COM clients to view .NET components as if they were traditional COM components. The

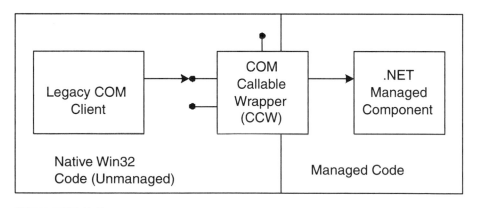

Figure 15–3   *A COM Callable Wrapper between unmanaged and managed code.*

Tlbexp.exe utility is in some ways the complementary tool[5] of **Tlbimp.exe** described in the previous section in this chapter. A traditional COM client can use the resulting type library information to access the .NET component using early binding. The command line syntax for **Tlbexp.exe** is shown next.

```
Tlbexp AssemblyName [options]
Where options may be composed of the following:
/out:FileName          Output typelib file name
/nologo                Prevents displaying logo
/silent                Prevents displaying messages
/verbose               Displays extra information
/? or /help            Display usage help message
```

The **Tlbexp.exe** utility is great for generating the useful type library information for a .NET assembly. However, COM clients also need the necessary registry information to be established so that the COM runtime can locate the appropriate class factory and server path, and so forth. **Regasm.exe** (Assembly Registration Utility) reads the metadata within an assembly and adds these necessary entries to the registry, which allows COM clients to use the .NET assembly's components as if they were just old-fashioned registered COM components (via the CCW proxy).

The syntax for using **Regasm.exe** is shown next. This allows COM client programs to create instances of managed classes defined in the assembly.

```
Regasm AssemblyPath [options]
Where the options may be any of the following.
/unregister            Unregister types
/tlb[:FileName]        Specified typelib
/regfile[:FileName]    Specified output reg file name
/codebase              Sets the code base in the registry
/registered            Only refer to preregistered typelibs
/nologo                Prevents displaying logo
/silent                Prevents displaying of messages
/verbose               Displays extra information
/? or /help            Display usage help message
```

Code
Example

Now let us use the **Tlbexp.exe** and **Regasm.exe** utilities on a real example. Consider the following managed C++ class library code in the directory

---

[5] **Tlbimp.exe** and **Tlbexp.exe** are not truly complementary. **Tlbimp.exe** converts the type information contained in a COM type library into an RCW, which is an assembly containing the equivalent metadata, as well as wrapper methods that provide access to the original COM object's methods. **Tlbexp.exe** only generates a type library containing the type information defined in an assembly. It does not create a CCW. Instead, the CCW is created automatically at runtime for the COM client as a result of registry information established with the **Regasm.exe** tool.

SomeManagedClass. The **Tlbexp.exe** tool exposes only managed public types to COM. This is why the **ManagedClass** class is declared as **public __gc**. Also, without a public default constructor (i.e., parameter-less), COM clients cannot create the type when they call **CoCreateInstance** or **CoCreateInstanceEx**. Therefore, in the following code, the **ManagedClass** class provides a public default constructor.

You may recall from your COM programming experience that a COM client never refers directly to a COM class, but rather refers only to interfaces on the class. However, the code below does not seem to provide any interface. The **AutoDual** value specified in the **ClassInterface(ClassInterfaceType::AutoDual)** attribute automatically generates a dual interface for accessing the **ManagedClass** class. This is convenient, but it is discouraged, because there is no way to version an interface generated with the **AutoDual** value. Later, we will look at an alternative to **AutoDual** that is versionable, but requires an explicit definition for at least one interface.

```
//SomeManagedClass.cpp

#using <mscorlib.dll>
using namespace System;
using namespace System::Runtime::InteropServices;

namespace SomeManagedClass
{
    [ClassInterface(ClassInterfaceType::AutoDual)]
    public __gc class ManagedClass
    {
    public:
        ManagedClass () //public default constructor
        {
        }
        int AddEmUp(int i, int j)
        {
            return i + j;
        }
    };
}
```

Compiling the above code as a managed C++ Class Library project produces an assembly DLL file named **SomeManagedClass.dll**. The following command produces a type library from this assembly named **SomeManagedClass.tlb**.

```
tlbexp SomeManagedClass.dll
```

You can look at the contents of this type library file using the OLE/COM Object viewer tool named **Oleview.exe**, which is located in your .NET SDK tools directory. This is shown in the Figure 15–4.

Early binding COM clients can use this **SomeManagedClass.tlb** file at compile time. For example, the following traditional Win32 console COM client program named **COMClientOfManagedClass** (which was created with VC++ 6.0 to simulate a legacy COM client) uses early binding to call into the .NET component in the **SomeManagedClass.dll** assembly described previously.[6]

```
ITypeLib Viewer                                                          _|□|×|
File  View

SomeManagedClass                  // Generated .IDL file (by the OLE/COM Object Viewer)
  coclass ManagedClass            //
    _ManagedClass                 // typelib filename: SomeManagedClass.tlb
      Methods
        m ToString                [
        m Equals                    uuid(C6C683FF-A753-3078-9EF9-20FCABCA7148),
        m GetHashCode               version(1.0)
        m GetType                 ]
        m AddFml p                library SomeManagedClass
      Inherited Interfaces        {
    _Object                         // TLib :     // TLib : Common Language Runtime Library
  dispinterface _ManagedClass     : {BED7F4EA-1A96-11D2-8F08-00A0C9A6186D}
  interface _ManagedClass            importlib("mscorlib.tlb");
                                     // TLib : OLE Automation : {00020430-0000-0000-C000-
                                  000000000046}
                                     importlib("stdole2.tlb");

                                     // Forward declare all types defined in this typelib
                                     interface _ManagedClass;

                                     [
                                       uuid(C2683887-335E-331D-9B5E-BF79A51F64FA),
                                       version(1.0),
                                         custom({0F21F359-AB84-41E8-9A78-36D11UE6D2F9},
                                  "SomeManagedClass.ManagedClass")
                                     ]
                                     coclass ManagedClass {
                                       [default] interface _ManagedClass;
                                       interface _Object;
                                     };

                                     [
                                       odl,
Ready
```

Figure 15–4   *Oleview.exe showing contents of a COM type library from a .NET assembly generated with Tlbexp.exe.*

---

[6] In the following code, you should replace the .NET version number by the current one. Alternatively, you could copy **mscorlib.tlb** to the local directory, even on a machine without .NET installed.

```
//COMClientOfManagedClass.cpp

#include <iostream.h>
#include <objbase.h>
#import "C:\WINNT\Microsoft.NET\Framework\v1.0.2914\
mscorlib.tlb"
#import "..\SomeManagedClass\Debug\SomeManagedClass.tlb"
no_namespace named_guids

void main()
{
    { //nested curly braces prevent pointer exception!
      CoInitialize(NULL);
      _ManagedClassPtr  psc(CLSID_ManagedClass);
      int i = psc->AddEmUp(3, 4);
      cout << i << endl << flush;
    }
    CoUninitialize();
}
```

However, the .NET component will not be accessible to COM client applications unless the required entries are entered into the registry, and the assembly must be made available to the CLR's class loader (either locally or in the global assembly cache). The tool that is used to do the registration is named **Regasm.exe**. This tool reads the metadata in the .NET component's assembly and writes the required entries to the registry. This allows any COM client to access the .NET component as if it was a legacy COM component.

For example, to register the .NET component above as a COM component, use the following command:

```
Regasm SomeManagedClass.dll
```

You can then use **Regedt32.exe** to verify that the registry information has been properly added to the registry, as shown in Figure 15–5.

Once you have finished registering the **SomeManagedClass.dll** assembly as a COM component, you must deploy that assembly. You can of course do this simply by copying the **SomeManagedClass.dll** assembly into the directory of the **COMClientOfManagedClass** client executable. Once you have done this, you can finally run the **COMClientOfManagedClass** COM client. When you run this client, it should output the number 7 as expected.

Late Binding COM Clients with .NET Components

Legacy COM clients can late bind with managed components, since all managed types implicitly support the standard COM interface **IDispatch**. The way that the .NET CLR does this is somewhat similar to traditional Visual Basic late

Registry Editor - [HKEY_CLASSES_ROOT on Local Machine]

Registry Edit Tree View Security Options Window Help

```
{C20FA58B-B177-11D3-8DE0-00A0C9067A29}      <No Name> : REG_SZ : C:\WINNT\System32\mscoree.dll
{C2349702-EA0B-11CF-9FEC-00AA00A59F69}       Assembly : REG_SZ : SomeManagedClass, Version=1.0.601.24915,
{C237CF82-F9B5-11D2-BEDC-444553540001}       Class : REG_SZ : SomeManagedClass.ManagedClass
{C2530CA6-06D6-11D2-8D70-00A0C98B28E2}       RuntimeVersion : REG_SZ : v1.0.2914
{C2683887-335E-331D-9B5E-BF79A51F64FA}       ThreadingModel : REG_SZ : Both
    Implemented Categories
    InprocServer32
    Progid
{C27CCE32-8596-11D1-B16A-00C0F0283628}
{C27CCE33-8596-11D1-B16A-00C0F0283628}
{C27CCE34-8596-11D1-B16A-00C0F0283628}
{C27CCE35-8596-11D1-B16A-00C0F0283628}
{C27CCE36-8596-11D1-B16A-00C0F0283628}
{C27CCE37-8596-11D1-B16A-00C0F0283628}
{C27CCE38-8596-11D1-B16A-00C0F0283628}
{C27CCE39-8596-11D1-B16A-00C0F0283628}
{C27CCE3A-8596-11D1-B16A-00C0F0283628}
{C27CCE3B-8596-11D1-B16A-00C0F0283628}
```

Figure 15–5   *Regedt32.exe showing the class ID registry contents for a .NET assembly that has been registered for use as a COM component.*

binding. Without any effort on the part of the programmer, the CLR generates an implementation of **IDispatch** on the fly, based on metadata found in the component's assembly. Although a late binding client can be written in Visual C++ 6.0 using an ATL smart pointer or calling on the methods of **IDispatch** directly (yuck!), this can be demonstrated more easily using a client that is implemented with the queen of late binding, Visual Basic.

Just as with any COM client of a .NET component, a VB client requires that **Regasm.exe** be used to establish the necessary registry settings for the .NET component. You only need to do this once to register the component. However, **Regasm.exe** can be used with the **/tlb** flag to generate a type library in addition to registering the types in the assembly. This is something that we want to do for our next VB example, so we will run **Regasm.exe** again, but with the **/tlb** option, as follows:

```
Regasm SomeManagedClass.dll /tlb
```

Then, in Visual Basic, you can add a reference to the **SomeManaged-Class.tlb** file to the project. This makes the class **ManagedClass** available. Also, it is usually necessary to add a reference to the **mscorlib.tlb** type library to access various .NET types. In addition, the **SomeManagedClass.dll** assembly needs to be either copied locally with the client or deployed into the global assembly cache. The following VB code demonstrates late binding with a .NET component:

```
Private Sub Command1_Click()
    Dim obj As Object
    Set obj = CreateObject( _
        "SomeManagedClass.ManagedClass") 'progid
```

```
    i = obj.AddEmUp(3, 4)
    MsgBox (i)
End Sub
```

Once the VB code is entered, you must make an EXE from it and then run it. The result is a message box displaying the expected number 7 result, as shown in Figure 15–6.

Visual Basic client of .NET component.

How to Build and Run a Visual Basic EXE

1. File | Make Project1.exe.
2. Click OK.
3. Double click on Project1.exe in Windows Explorer.

Explicitly Defining an Interface

In a previous section, we defined a public managed class named **Managed-Class** that was automatically exposed by a COM interface generated by the **AutoDual** value specified in the **ClassInterface (ClassInterfaceType::Auto-Dual)** attribute. The resulting dual interface made it possible for the client to able to access the **ManagedClass** class. This is a convenient technique, but it is discouraged because there is no way to version the generated interface, and it produces only a single interface, which can be somewhat restrictive. Now we will look at an alternative to the **AutoDual** value that results in an interface that is versionable but requires an explicit definition for the interface within your code. This time, we specify the **None** value for the **ClassInterface(ClassInterfaceType::None)** attribute. The following code shows the managed component with explicitly defined interface and coclass GUIDs.

```cpp
//SomeManagedClass.cpp

#using <mscorlib.dll>
using namespace System;
using namespace System::Runtime::InteropServices;

namespace SomeManagedClass
{
    //COM interface
    [Guid("C3894DE3-F5D6-46fe-84C7-C6DD0E801C86")]
    public __gc __interface IManagedClass
    {
    //public:
        virtual int AddEmUp(int i, int j) = 0;
    };

    //coclass
    [Guid("8D48DE87-048E-466e-95C3-06F3C21FCEAA"),
        ClassInterface(ClassInterfaceType::None)]
    public __gc class ManagedClass : public IManagedClass
    {
    public:
        ManagedClass () //public default constructor
        {
        }
        int AddEmUp(int i, int j)
        {
            return i + j;
        }
    };
}
```

The following code (which is an unmanaged C++ program created with Visual C++ 6.0) shows the legacy COM client that works with the preceding managed component. Again, the GUIDs are hard coded this time rather than being generated by a type library import statement. Therefore, in this example we do not generate a type library using **Tlbexp.exe**. This makes the example more closely demonstrate the situation where you are working with a true untouched legacy COM client. In other words, you created a managed C++ component that is to be used as a COM component by an existing COM client that is not recompiled.

```cpp
//COMClientOfManagedClass.cpp

#include <unknwn.h>
#include <iostream.h>

// {8D48DE87-048E-466e-95C3-06F3C21FCEAA}
static const GUID CLSID_ManagedClass =
{ 0x8D48DE87, 0x048E, 0x466e, { 0x95, 0xC3, 0x06, 0xF3, 0xC2,
0x1F, 0xCE, 0xAA } };

// {C3894DE3-F5D6-46fe-84C7-C6DD0E801C86}
static const GUID IID_IManagedClass =
{ 0xC3894DE3, 0xF5D6, 0x46fe, { 0x84, 0xC7, 0xC6, 0xDD, 0x0E,
0x80, 0x1C, 0x86 } };

class IManagedClass : public IDispatch
{
public:
virtual HRESULT __stdcall AddEmUp(
   long a,
   long b,
   long* psum) = 0;
};

void main()
{
   HRESULT hResult;
   IManagedClass *pimc;

   hResult = CoInitialize(NULL);
   if (hResult != S_OK)
      return;

   hResult = CoCreateInstance(
      CLSID_ManagedClass,
      NULL,
      CLSCTX_ALL,
      IID_IManagedClass,
```

```
        (void **) &pimc
    );

if (hResult == REGDB_E_CLASSNOTREG)
    cout <<
        "ERROR: CLSID is not properly registered.\n"
        << flush;


if (hResult == S_OK)
{
    cout << "CoCreateInstance succeeded.\n" << flush;
    long sum;
    hResult = pimc->AddEmUp(3, 4, &sum); //should be 6
    if (hResult == S_OK)
        cout << "AddEmUp(3,4) is: "
            << sum << endl << flush;
    pimc->Release();
}

CoUninitialize();
}
```

The resulting program output is shown next.

```
CoCreateInstance succeeded.
AddEmUp(3,4) is: 7
Press any key to continue
```

Platform Invocation Services (PInvoke)

Platform Invocation Services, also known as PInvoke, makes unmanaged exported DLL functions available to managed client code. PInvoke allows this to be done from managed code written in any .NET programming language. Notice that PInvoke is not the name of a class or a method, but is just a nickname for Platform Invocation Services. PInvoke looks after marshaling between CLR data types and native data types, and bridges other differences between the managed and unmanaged runtime environments. Although PInvoke is primarily used to access the Win32 APIs, it can be used to call into your own legacy DLLs that you may find are still useful. Unfortunately, PInvoke is in most circumstances a one-way street. You can use it to call from managed code into unmanaged DLL code and of course return back into managed code. PInvoke is used to access global exported DLL functions, so even though it is possible for DLLs to export class methods, they are currently not accessible via PInvoke.

As a C++ programmer, you can get by without ever thinking about PInvoke. That's because, unlike other .NET languages, Visual C++ .NET allows you to mix managed and unmanaged code directly within your own program. Therefore, to call into a DLL function from managed C++ code, you can simply call into your own unmanaged C++ code, which in turn calls into the unmanaged DLL function in the traditional manner. However, you can use PInvoke to call directly from managed C++ code into unmanaged DLL code, as is shown in the following code example.

```
//PInvoke.cpp

#using <mscorlib.dll>
using namespace System;
using namespace System::Runtime::InteropServices;

typedef void* HWND;

[DllImport("user32")]
extern "C" int MessageBoxA( //WIn32 API
   HWND hWnd,           //owner window handle
   String* pText,      //message box text
   String* pCaption,   //message box title
   unsigned int uType  //message box style
   );

void main(void)
{
   String* pText = L"Hello PInvoke!";
   String* pCaption = L"PInvoke Example";
   MessageBoxA(0, pText, pCaption, 0);
}
```

The resulting message box from program is shown in Figure 15–7.

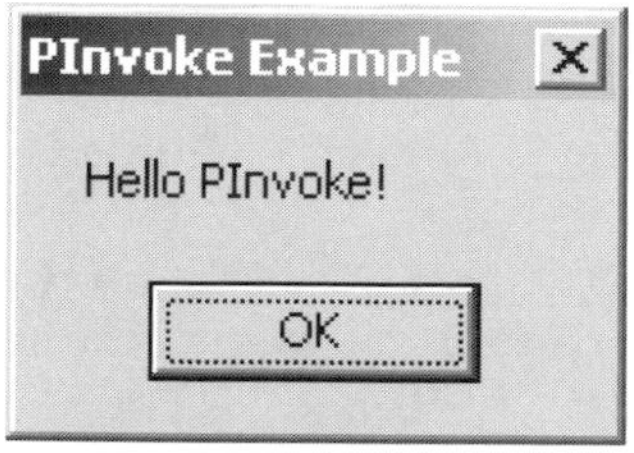

Figure 15–7   *The message box resulting from executing the code in PInvoke.cpp.*

The previous PInvoke example did not demonstrate how PInvoke automatically marshals out parameters for you. This is because the **MessageBox** takes only in parameters. The next example calls the **GetComputerName** and **GetLastError** APIs via PInvoke.

The **GetComputerName** function's first parameter is named **lpBuffer**, which is an out pointer to a buffer that receives a null-terminated string containing the computer name, if successful. The second parameter is named **lpnSize**, which is an in/out parameter. On the way in, it specifies the size of the **lpBuffer** buffer in **TCHAR**s. On the way out, it specifies the actual length of the computer name in **TCHAR**s contained in the **plBuffer**, not including the terminating null character. The return value indicates whether or not the function was successful. A nonzero value return value means success, and a zero value means failure. If the return value is zero, then the **GetLastError** can be used to determine the reason for the failure. For example, if the buffer was not large enough for the actual computer name, **GetLastError** would return **ERROR_BUFFER_OVERFLOW**, which has the value of 111. If you want to try using PInvoke yourself, and you would like an extra little challenge, you could make a call to the **FormatMessage** API to translate this error number into a more meaningful string. If you did this, and you shortened the buffer length sufficiently, you would find that this error produces the string "The file name is too long." The prototypes for **GetComputerName** and **GetLastError** are shown below.

```
BOOL GetComputerName(
  LPTSTR lpBuffer,   // computer name
  LPDWORD lpnSize    // size of name buffer
);


DWORD GetLastError(VOID);
```

Code Example

The following example shows how to call **GetComputerName** and **GetLastError** from managed C++ code using PInvoke. Note that both of these APIs are contained in the **Kernel32.dll**, so the **[DllImport ("Kernel32")]** attribute is used in both cases. Note that the marshaling for each out parameter is done automatically. Although it is not shown in this simple example, it is possible to use attributes to control the details of parameter PInvoke marshaling, which is only useful if the default marshaling provided by PInvoke is not satisfactory.

```
//PInvokeOutParam.cpp

#using <mscorlib.dll>
using namespace System;
using namespace System::Runtime::InteropServices;
```

```
typedef int BOOL;
typedef unsigned long DWORD;
#define MAX_COMPUTERNAME_LENGTH 31

[DllImport("Kernel32")]
extern "C" BOOL GetComputerName(
    signed char *lpBuffer, UInt32* lpnSize);

[DllImport("Kernel32")]
extern "C" DWORD GetLastError();

void main(void)
{
    signed char * lpBuffer =
        new signed char[MAX_COMPUTERNAME_LENGTH + 1];
    UInt32 size = MAX_COMPUTERNAME_LENGTH + 1;
    BOOL bResult = GetComputerName(lpBuffer, &size);
    if (bResult)
    {
        String *pstrComputerName =
            new String((signed char *)lpBuffer);
        Console::WriteLine(
            "Computer Name: {0}", pstrComputerName);
    }
    else
    {
        DWORD dwLastError = GetLastError();
        Console::WriteLine(
            "Last Error: {0}", __box(dwLastError));
    }
}
```

When you run the **PInvokeOutParam** example, you should see something like the following, except that you will see your own machine's name rather than mine.

```
Computer Name: PT-2HBHVPJUGOT9
```

Summary

This chapter has focused on mixing managed and unmanaged code using Visual C++ .NET. We have looked at calling from unmanaged to managed code and calling from managed to unmanaged code within a single source file. Then we looked at calling from the .NET environment to legacy COM components, as well as calling from the COM environment to .NET components, using both early and late binding. Finally, we looked at using Platform Invocation Services (PInvoke), and saw how automatic marshaling is provided for both in and out parameters.

We have come to the end of a long journey, which we hope will be the first of many journeys in the world of .NET. We hope you enjoyed the trip. Good luck on your .NET programming projects!

Visual Studio.NET

*A*lthough it is possible to program .NET using only the command-line compiler, it is much easier and more enjoyable to use Visual Studio.NET. In this appendix we cover the basics of using Visual Studio to edit, compile, run, and debug programs. You will then be equipped to use Visual Studio in the rest of the book. This appendix covers the basics to get you up and running using Visual Studio. We will introduce additional features of Visual Studio in chapters in the book as we encounter a need. This book was developed using beta software, and in the final released product you may encounter some changes to the information presented here. Also, Visual Studio is a very elaborate Windows application that is highly configurable, and you may encounter variations in the exact layout of windows, what is shown by default, and so on. As you work with Visual Studio, a good attitude is to see yourself as an explorer discovering a rich and varied new country.

Overview of Visual Studio.NET

Open up Microsoft Visual Studio.NET 7.0 and you will see a starting window similar to what is shown in Figure A–1.

What you see on default startup is the main window with an HTML page that can help you navigate among various resources, open or create projects, and change your profile information. (If you close the start page, you can get it back anytime from the menu Help | Show Start Page.) Clicking on My Profile will bring up a profile page on which you can change various settings. There is a standard profile for "typical" work in Visual Studio ("Visual Studio Developer" profile), and special ones for various languages. Since Visual Studio.NET is the unification of many development environments, programmers used to one particular previous environment may prefer a particular keyboard

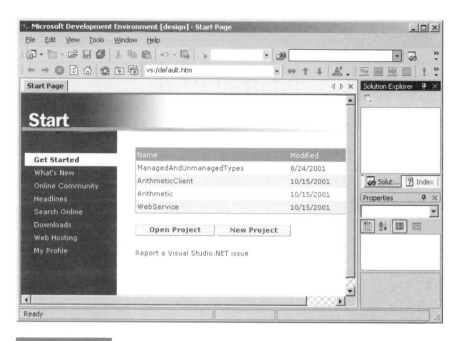

Visual Studio.NET main window.

Visual Studio.NET profile page.

scheme, window layout, and so on. For example, if you choose the profile "Visual Basic Developer," you will get the Visual Basic 6 keyboard scheme. In this book we will use all the defaults, so go back to the profile "Visual Studio Developer" if you made any changes. See Figure A–2.

To gain an appreciation of some of the diverse features in Visual Studio.NET, open up the **Bank** console solution in the **AppA** directory for this appendix (File | Open Solution..., navigate to the **Bank** directory, and open the file **Bank.sln**). You will see quite an elaborate set of windows. See Figure A–3.

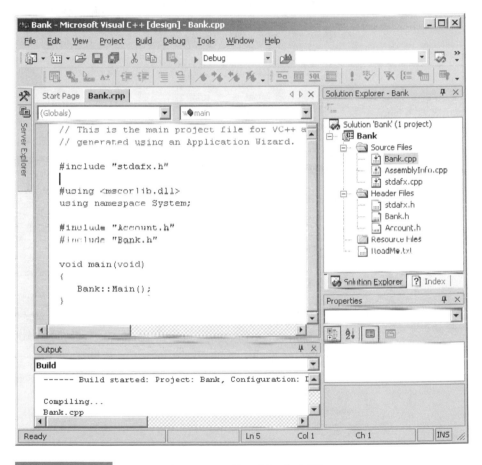

| **Figure A–3** | *A console project in Visual Studio.NET.* |

Starting from the left are icons for the Server Explorer and the Toolbox, followed by the main window area, which currently shows the code in **Bank.cpp**. Underneath the main window is the Output Window, which shows the results of builds and so on. Continuing our tour, on the top right is the Solution Explorer, which enables you to conveniently see all the files in a "solution," which may consist of several "projects." On the bottom right is the Properties window, which lets you conveniently edit properties on forms for Windows applications. The Properties window is very similar to the Properties window in Visual Basic.

From the Solution Explorer you can navigate to files in the projects. In turn, double-click on **Account.h** and **Bank.h**, two of the source files in the **Bank** project. Text editor windows will be brought up in the main window area. Across the top of the main window are horizontal tabs to quickly select any of the open windows. Visual Studio.NET allows you to select the window to show from the Windows menu. Figure A–4 shows the open source files with the horizontal tabs.

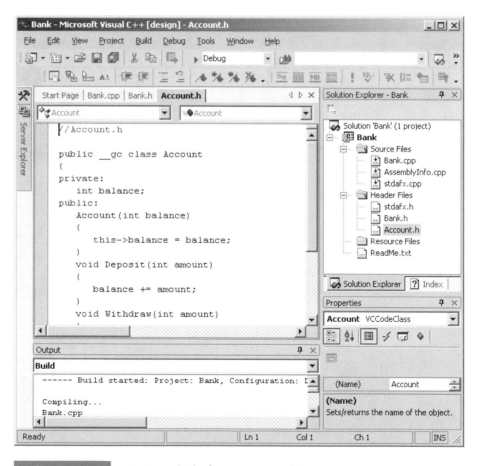

Figure A–4   *Horizontal tabs for open source files.*

Toolbars

Visual Studio comes with many different toolbars. You can configure which toolbars you wish displayed, and you can drag toolbars to position them to where you find them most convenient. You can also customize toolbars by adding or deleting buttons that correspond to different commands.

To specify which toolbars are displayed, bring up the menu View | Toolbars. You can also right-click in any empty area of a toolbar. There will be a check mark next to the toolbars that are currently displayed. By clicking on an item on this menu, you can make the corresponding toolbar button appear or disappear. For your work in this book, add the toolbars

- Build
- Debug

CUSTOMIZING A TOOLBAR

We want to make sure that the "Start Without Debugging" command is available on the Debug toolbar. If it is not already on your Debug toolbar (it is a red exclamation point), you can add it by the following procedure, which can be used to add other commands to toolbars.

1. Select menu Tools | Customize... to bring up the Customize dialog.
2. Select the Commands tab.
3. In Categories, select Debug, and in Commands select Start Without Debugging. See Figure A-5.
4. Drag the selected command onto the Debug toolbar, positioning it where you desire. Place it to the immediate right of the wedge shaped Start ▶ button.
5. Close the Customize dialog.

Creating a Console Application

As our first exercise in using Visual Studio, we will create a simple console application. Our program **Bytes** will attempt to calculate how many bytes there are in a kilobyte, a megabyte, a gigabyte, and a terabyte. If you want to follow along on your PC as you read, you can use the **Demos** directory for this chapter. The first version is in **Bytes\Step1**. A final version can be found in **Bytes\Step3**.

Figure A–5   *Adding a new command to a toolbar.*

Creating a C++ Project

1. From Visual Studio main menu, choose File | New | Project.... This will bring up the New Project dialog.
2. For Project Types choose "Visual C++ Projects" and for Templates choose "Managed C++ Application."
3. Click the Browse button, navigate to **Demos**, and click Open.
4. In the Name field, type **Bytes**. See Figure A–6. Click OK.

Figure A–6   Creating a Managed C++ console project.

Adding a C++ File

At this point you will have a Managed C++ project that contains a main function in **Bytes.cpp**, but no application-specific code. We are now going to add a file **Bytes.h**, which contains a class with a method named Main that will be called from the main function in **Bytes.cpp**.

1. In Solution Explorer, right-click over the project node **Bytcs** and choose Add | Add New Item.... This will bring up the Add New Item dialog.
2. For Categories, choose "Visual C++" and for Templates, choose "Header File (.h)."
3. For Name type **Bytes.h**. See Figure A–7. Click Open.

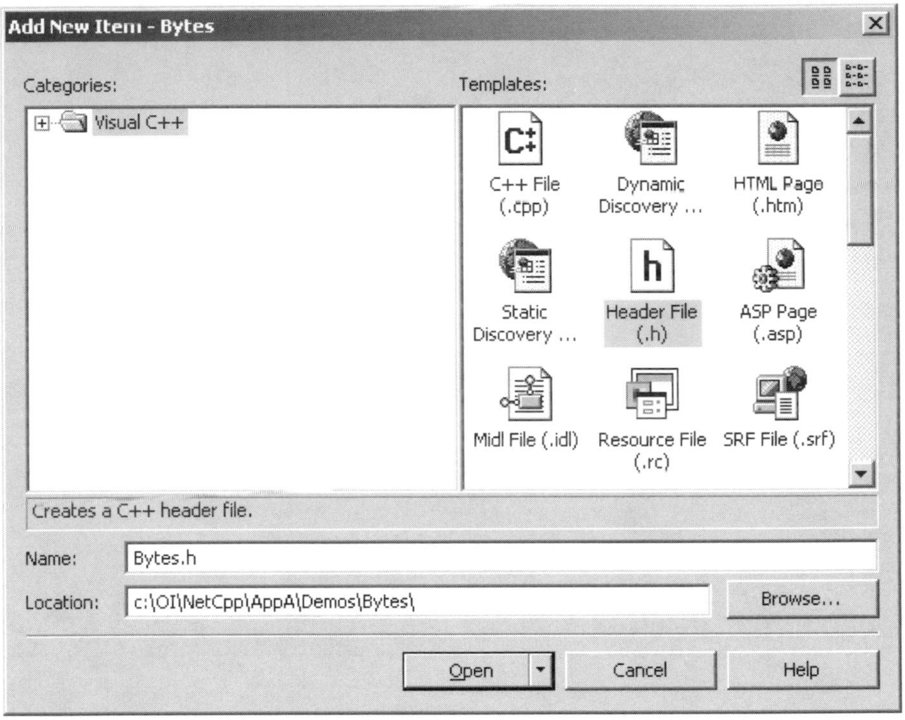

Figure A-7   *Adding an empty C++ header file to a C++ project.*

Using the Visual Studio Text Editor

In the Solution Explorer double-click on **Bytes.h**. This will open up the empty file **Bytes.h** in the Visual Studio text editor. Type in the following program, and notice things like color syntax highlighting to indicate reserved words as you type.

```
//Bytes.h - Step1

public __gc class Bytes
{
public:
   static void Main()
   {
      Int64  bytes = 1024;
      Console::WriteLine("kilo = {0}", __box(bytes));
      bytes = bytes * 1024;
      Console::WriteLine("mega = {0}", __box(bytes));
```

```
    bytes = bytes * 1024;
    Console::WriteLine("giga = {0}", __box(bytes));
    bytes = bytes * 1022;
    Console::WriteLine("tera = {0}", __box(bytes));
    }
};
```

Besides the color syntax highlighting, other features include automatic indenting. All in all, you should find the Visual Studio editor friendly and easy to use.

In the Solution Explorer double-click on **Bytes.cpp**. This will open up the preexisting file **Bytes.cpp** in the Visual Studio text editor. From within the main function of the program, you must call the static **Main** method of the class **Bytes**. To do this, you must first #include the **Bytes.h** header file.

```
#include "stdafx.h"
#using <mscorlib.dll>
using namespace System;
#include "Bytes.h"

#ifdef _UNICODE
int wmain(void)
#else
int main(void)
#endif
{
    Bytes::Main();
    return 0;
}
```

Building the Project

You can build the project by using one of the following:

- Menu Build | Build
- Toolbar 🏛
- Keyboard shortcut Ctrl + Shift + B

Running the Program

You can run the program by using one of the following:

- Menu Debug | Start Without Debugging
- Toolbar ❗
- Keyboard shortcut Ctrl + F5

You will see the following output in a console window that opens up. If you press any key, as indicated, the console window will close.

```
kilo = 1024
mega = 1048576
giga = 1073741824
tera = 1097364144128
Press any key to continue
```

Running the Program in the Debugger

You can run the program in the debugger by using one of the following:

- Menu Debug | Start
- Toolbar ▶
- Keyboard shortcut F5

A console window will briefly open up and then immediately close. If you want the window to stay open, you must explicitly program for it, for example, by asking for input. You can also set a breakpoint to stop execution before the program exits. We will outline features of the debugger later in the appendix.

Project Configurations

A project *configuration* specifies build settings for a project. You can have several different configurations, and each configuration will be built in its own directory, so you can exercise the different configurations independently. Every project in a Visual Studio solution has two default configurations, **Debug** and **Release**. The **Debug** configuration will build a debug version of the project, where you can do source-level debugging by setting breakpoints, and so on. The **Debug** directory will then contain a *program database* file with a **.pdb** extension that holds debugging and project state information.

You can choose the configuration from the main toolbar ▶ Debug ▾ . You can also choose the configuration using the menu Build | Configuration Manager..., which will bring up the Configuration Manager dialog. From the Active Solution Configuration dropdown, choose **Release**. See Figure A–8.

Build the project again. Now a second version of the Managed C++ program **Bytes.exe** is created, this time in the **Release** directory.

Creating a New Configuration

Sometimes it is useful to create additional configurations, which can save alternate build settings. As an example, let's create a configuration that gener-

Figure A–8   *Choosing Release In the Configuration Manager.*

ates the resulting program in an alternate directory. In Visual Studio you set build options through dialog boxes. The following steps will guide you through creating a new configuration called **AlternateDebug**. Subsequently, this new configuration will be modified to generate the resulting program in an alternate directory named **AlternateDebug**.

1. Bring up the Configuration Manager dialog.
2. From the Active Solution Configuration: dropdown, choose <New...>. The New Solution Configuration dialog will come up.
3. Type **AlternateDebug** as the configuration name. Choose Copy Settings from **Debug**. Check "Also create new project configuration(s)." See Figure A–9. Click OK.

Setting Build Settings for a Configuration

Next, we will set the build settings for the new configuration. (You could also set build settings for one of the standard configurations if you wanted to make any changes from the defaults provided.) Check the toolbar to verify that the new **AlternateDebug** is the currently active configuration. After completing

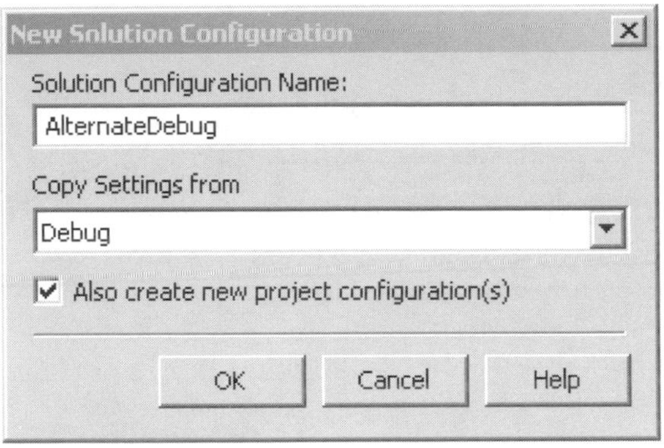

Figure A-9   *Creating a new configuration.*

these steps, you will find that subsequent builds place the **Bytes.exe** program into the **Bytes\AlternateDebug** directory.

1. Right-click over the project node **Bytes** in the Solution Explorer and choose Properties. The "Bytes Property Pages" dialog comes up.
2. In Configuration Properties, select General. Change the setting for "Output Directory" to **AlternateDebug** (see Figure A–10). Click OK.

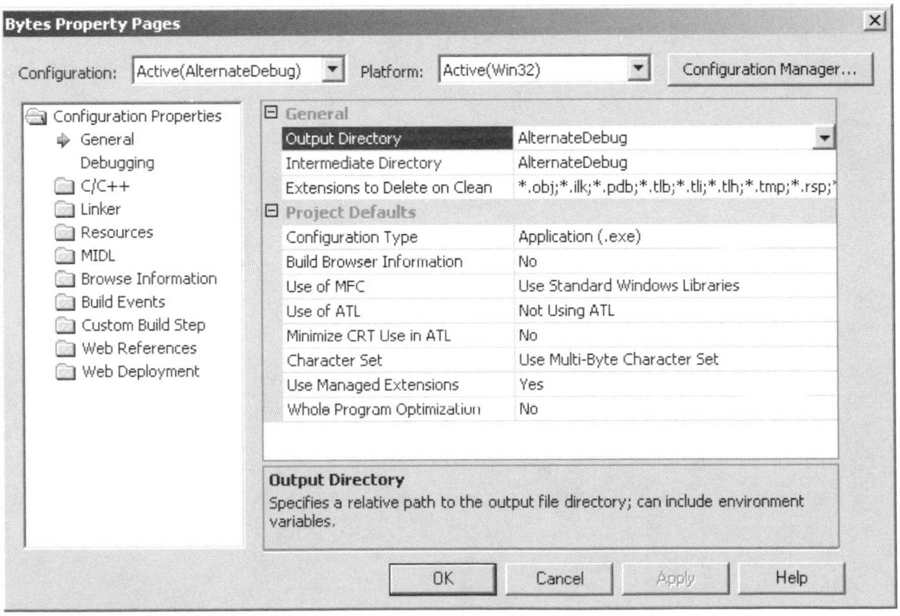

Figure A-10   *Changing the build settings for a configuration.*

Debugging

In this section we will discuss some of the debugging facilities in Visual Studio. To be able to benefit from debugging at the source code level, you should have built your executable using a Debug configuration, as discussed previously. There are two ways to enter the debugger:

- Just-in-Time Debugging. You run normally, and if an exception occurs, you will be allowed to enter the debugger. The program has crashed, so you may not be able to run further, single step, or set breakpoints, and so on. But you will be able to see the value of variables, and you will see the point at which the program failed.
- Standard Debugging. You start the program under the debugger. You may set breakpoints, single step, and so on.

Just-in-Time Debugging

In order to see how just-in-time debugging works, we will artificially add code that causes an unhandled exception to be thrown. This example is in **Bytes\Step2**. The division by zero will cause a **DivideByZeroException** to be thrown.

```
//Bytes.h - Step2

public __gc class Bytes
{
public:
    static void Main()
    {
        Int64  bytes = 1024;
        Console::WriteLine("kilo = {0}", __box(bytes));
        ...
        int zero = 0;
        int i = 3/zero;
    }
};
```

Build and run (without debugging) the **Bytes** program in **Bytes\Step2**, making sure to use the **Debug** configuration. This time, the program will not run through smoothly to completion, but an exception will be thrown. A

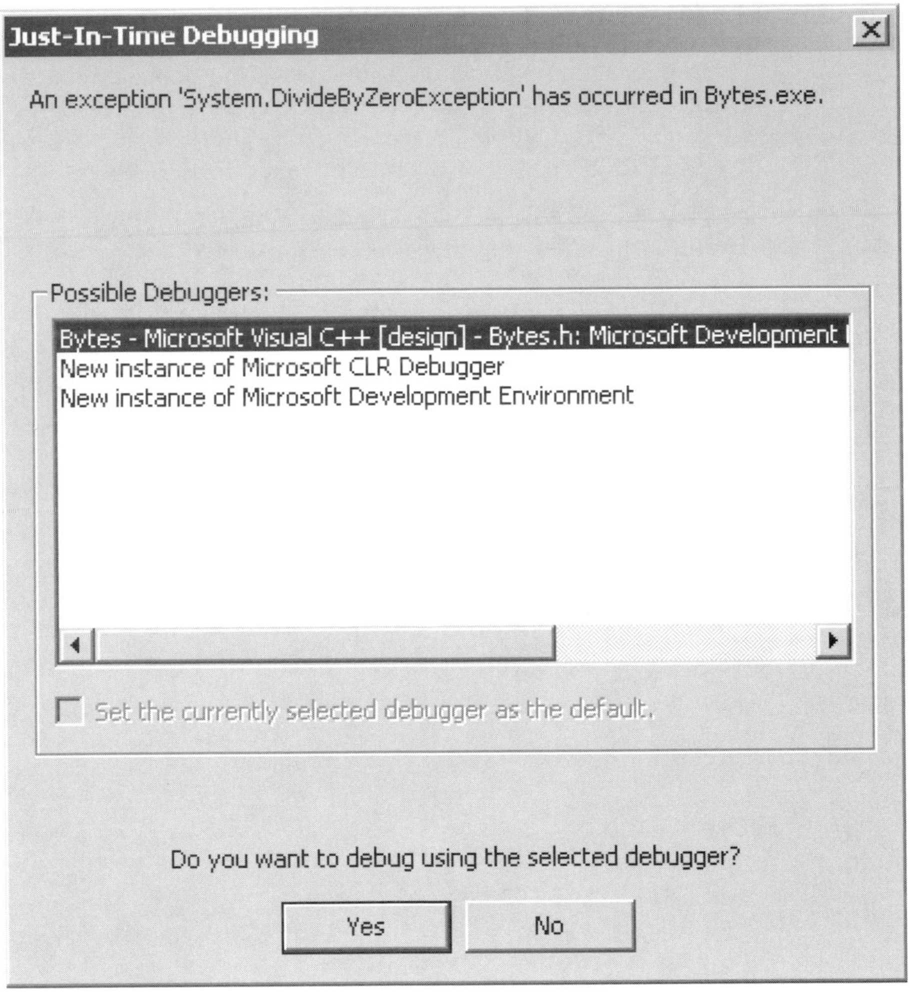

Just-In-Time Debugging ⊠

An exception 'System.DivideByZeroException' has occurred in Bytes.exe.

Possible Debuggers:

```
Bytes - Microsoft Visual C++ [design] - Bytes.h: Microsoft Development
New instance of Microsoft CLR Debugger
New instance of Microsoft Development Environment
```

◄ ▶

☐ Set the currently selected debugger as the default.

Do you want to debug using the selected debugger?

[Yes]   [No]

Figure A-11   *Just-In-Time Debugging dialog is displayed in response to an exception.*

"Just-In-Time Debugging" dialog will be shown (see Figure A–11). Click Yes to debug.

Click OK in the "Attach to Process" dialog and then click Break in the "Microsoft Development Environment" dialog. You will now be brought into a window showing the source code where the problem arose, with an arrow pinpointing the location.

To stop debugging, you can use the ■ toolbar button or the menu Debug | Stop Debugging.

Standard Debugging

BREAKPOINTS

The way you typically do standard debugging is to set a breakpoint and then run using the debugger. As an example, set a breakpoint at the first line:

```
bytes = bytes * 1024;
```

The easiest way to set a breakpoint is by clicking in the gray bar to the left of the source code window. You can also set the cursor on the desired line and click the "hand" toolbar button 🖑 to toggle a breakpoint (set if not set, and remove if a breakpoint is set). Now you can run under the debugger, and the breakpoint should be hit. A yellow arrow over the red dot of the breakpoint shows where the breakpoint has been hit. See Figure A–12.

When you are done with a breakpoint, you can remove it by clicking again in the gray bar or by toggling with the hand toolbar button. If you want

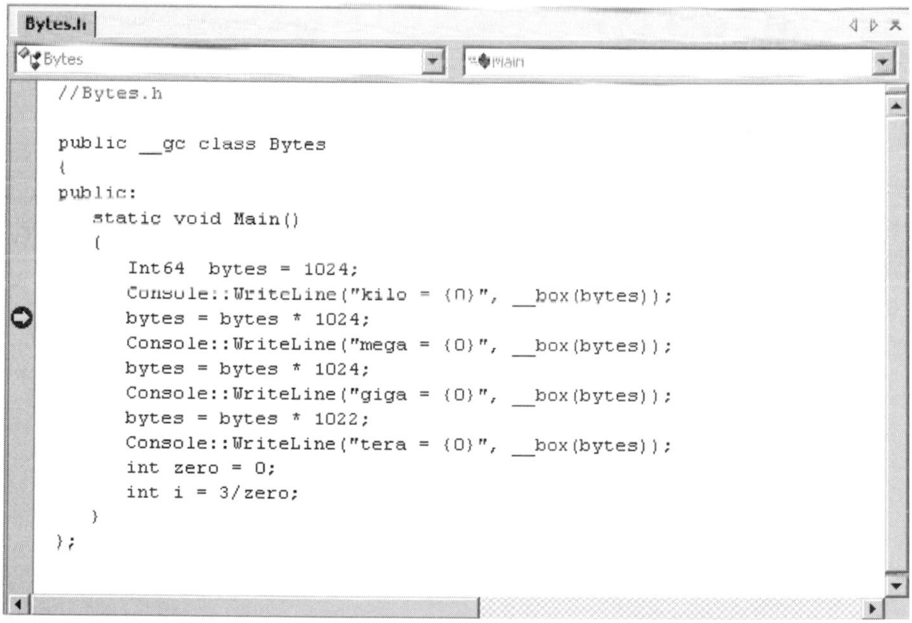

```cpp
//Bytes.h

public __gc class Bytes
{
public:
    static void Main()
    {
        Int64  bytes = 1024;
        Console::WriteLine("kilo = {0}", __box(bytes));
        bytes = bytes * 1024;
        Console::WriteLine("mega = {0}", __box(bytes));
        bytes = bytes * 1024;
        Console::WriteLine("giga = {0}", __box(bytes));
        bytes = bytes * 1022;
        Console::WriteLine("tera = {0}", __box(bytes));
        int zero = 0;
        int i = 3/zero;
    }
};
```

Figure A-12   *A breakpoint has been hit.*

to remove all breakpoints, you can use the menu Debug | Clear All Break-points, or you can use the toolbar button ⚒.

WATCHING VARIABLES

At this point you can inspect variables. The easiest way is to slide the mouse over the variable you are interested in, and the value will be shown as a yellow tool tip. You can also right-click over a variable and choose Quick Watch (or use the eyeglasses toolbar button 👓). Figure A–13 shows a typical Quick Watch window. You can also change the value of a variable from this window.

Figure A–13   *Quick Watch window shows variable, and you can change it.*

When you are stopped in the debugger, you can add a variable to the Watch window by right-clicking over it and choosing Add Watch. The Watch window can show a number of variables, and the Watch window stays open as the program executes. When a variable changes value, the new value is shown in red. Figure A–14 shows the Watch window (note that the display has been changed to hex, as described in the next section).

Figure A–14   *Visual Studio Watch window.*

DEBUGGER OPTIONS

You can change debugger options from the menu Tools | Options, and select Debugging from the list. Figure A–15 illustrates setting a hexadecimal display. If you then go back to a Watch window, you will see a hex value such as **0x400** displayed.

Figure A–15   *Setting hexadecimal display in Debugging Options.*

SINGLE STEPPING

When you are stopped in the debugger, you can *single step*. You can also begin execution by single stepping. There are a number of single-step buttons. The most common are (in the order shown on the toolbar)

- Step Into
- Step Over
- Step Out

There is also a Run to Cursor button.

With Step Into, you will step into a function if the cursor is positioned on a call to a function. With Step Over, you will step to the next line (or statement or instruction, depending on the selection in the dropdown next to the step buttons). To illustrate Step Into, build the **Bytes\Step3** project, where the multiplication by 1,024 has been replaced by a function call to the static method **MultiplyByOneK**. Set a breakpoint at the first function call, and then Step Into. The result is illustrated in Figure A–16. Note the red dot at the breakpoint and the yellow arrow in the function.

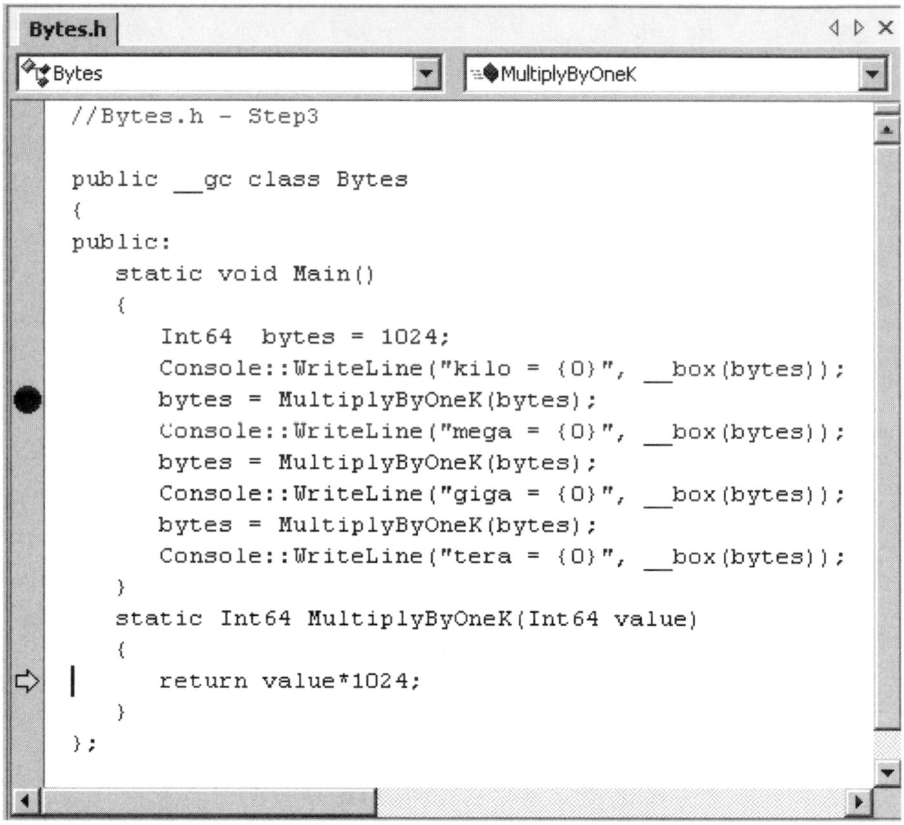
Bytes.h
Bytes
MultiplyByOneK
//Bytes.h - Step3
public __gc class Bytes
{
public:
static void Main()
{
Int64 bytes = 1024;
Console::WriteLine("kilo = {0}", __box(bytes));
bytes = MultiplyByOneK(bytes);
Console::WriteLine("mega = {0}", __box(bytes));
bytes = MultiplyByOneK(bytes);
Console::WriteLine("giga = {0}", __box(bytes));
bytes = MultiplyByOneK(bytes);
Console::WriteLine("tera = {0}", __box(bytes));
}
static Int64 MultiplyByOneK(Int64 value)
{
return value*1024;
}
};

Figure A–16 *Stepping into a function.*

When debugging, Visual Studio maintains a Call Stack. To display the Call Stack, select the Debug | Windows | Call Stack. In our simple example the Call Stack is just four deep. See Figure A–17.

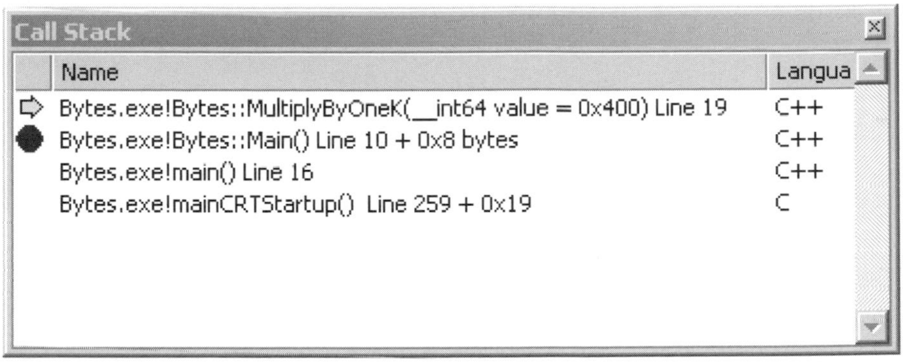

Figure A-17   *The call stack.*

Summary

Visual Studio.NET is a very rich integrated development environment (IDE), with many features to make programming more enjoyable. In this appendix we covered the basics of using Visual Studio to edit, compile, run, and debug programs, so that you will be equipped to use Visual Studio in the rest of the book. Nonetheless, it is worth spending time to become familiar with many more of the Visual Studio features, because understanding how to use them will make your development work much easier. A project can be built in different configurations, such as Debug and Release. Visual Studio.NET has a vast array of features for building database applications, web applications, components, and many other kinds of projects. We discuss some of these additional features in the chapters where they are pertinent.

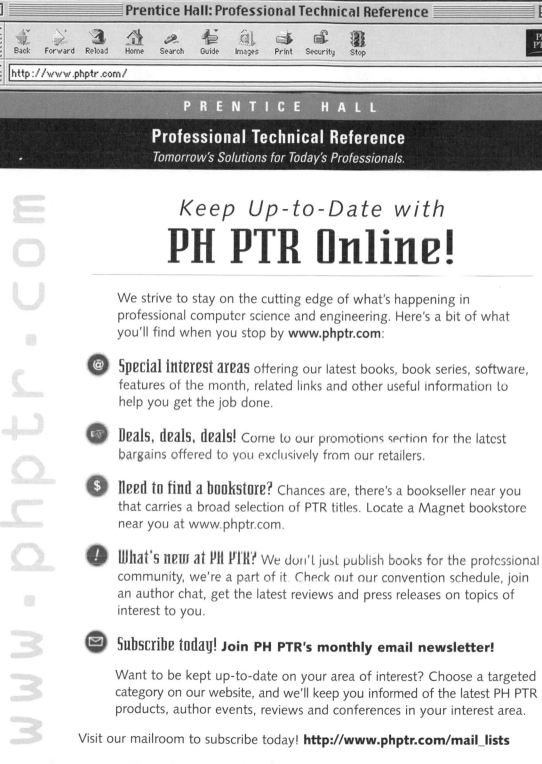

OBJECT INNOVATIONS' .NET TRAINING PARTNERS

For information about .NET training using OBJECT INNOVATIONS courseware,
please check with our .NET Training Partners.

ANEW TECHNOLOGY CORPORATION   www.Anew.net

Specialized in IT consulting, training, mentoring, and development, Anew Technology has been serving many satisfied clients. Our business mission is threefold: to stay at the forefront of IT technologies, to satisfy client needs by applying these technologies, and to provide the best service in our industry. Anew Technology is a business partner with Object Innovations in operations and courseware development.

COMPUTER HORIZONS EDUCATION DIVISION   www.ComputerHorizons.com/Training

For over seventeen years Computer Horizons Education Division (CHED) has been providing on-site, instructor led IT training and customized workshops for organizations nationwide. We have developed extensive curriculum offerings in Web Technologies, Relational Databases, Reporting Tools, Process Improvement, UNIX™ and LINUX™, Client/Server, Mainframe & Legacy Systems, Windows® 2000, and much more. CHED will design, develop and deliver a training solution tailored to each client's training requirements.

COMPUWORKS SYSTEMS, INC.   www.CompuWorks.com

CompuWorks Systems, Inc. is an IT solutions company whose aim is to provide our clients with customized training, support and development services. We are committed to building long term partnerships with our clients in an effort to meet their individual needs. Cutting-edge solutions are our specialty.

CUSTOM TRAINING INSTITUTE   www.4CustomTraining.com

Custom Training Institute is a provider of high quality IT training since 1989. Along with our full line of "off-the-shelf" classes, we excel at providing customized solutions - from technical needs assessment through course development and delivery. We specialize in Legacy Skills Transformation (i.e., COBOL to Java), Oracle (DBA, Developer, Discoverer and Applications), UNIX, C++ and Java for computer professionals.

DB BASICS   www.DBBasics.com

DBBasics, founded in 1988 as a Microsoft® solution development company, has developed and delivered Microsoft technology training since its inception. DBBasics specializes in delivering database and developer technology training to corporate customers. Our vast development experience, coupled with the requirement for instructors to consistently provide hands-on consulting to our customers, enables DBBasics to provide best of breed instruction in the classroom as well as customized eLearning solutions and database technology consulting.

DEVCOM   www.dev-cominc.com

Devcom Corporation offers a full line of courses and seminars for software developers and engineers. Currently Devcom provides technical courses and seminars around the country for Hewlett® Packard, Compaq® Computer, Informix® Software, Silicon Graphics®, Quantum/Maxtor® and Gateway® Inc. Our senior .NET/C# instructor is currently working in conjunction with Microsoft to provide .NET training to their internal technical staff.

FOCAL POINT   www.FocalPoint-Inc.com

Focal Point specializes in providing optimum instructor-led Information Technology technical training for our corporate clients on either an onsite basis, or in regional public course events. All of our course curricula is either developed by our staff of "World Class Instructors" or upon careful evaluation and scrutiny is adopted and acquired from our training partners who are similarly focussed. Our course offerings pay special attention to Real World issues. Our classes are targeted toward topical areas that will ensure immediate productivity upon course completion.

I/SRG   www.isrg.com

The I/S RESOURCE GROUP helps organizations to understand, plan for and implement emerging I/S technologies and methodologies. By combining education, training, briefings and consulting, we assist our clients to effectively apply I/S technologies to achieve business benefits. Our eBusiness Application Bootcamp is an integrated set of courses that prepares learners to utilize XML, OOAD, Java™, JSP, EJB, ASP, CORBA and .NET to build eBusiness applications. Our eBusiness Briefings pinpoint emerging technologies and methodologies.

OBJECT INNOVATIONS' .NET TRAINING PARTNERS

*For information about .NET training using OBJECT INNOVATIONS courseware,
please check with our .NET Training Partners.*

RELIABLE SOFTWARE   www.ReliableSoftware.com

Reliable Software, Inc. uses Microsoft technology to quickly develop cost-effective software solutions for the small to mid-size business or business unit. We use state-of-the-art techniques to allow business rules, database models and the user interface to evolve as your business needs evolve. We can provide design and implementation consulting, or training.

SKILLBRIDGE TRAINING   www.SkillBridgeTraining.com

SkillBridge is a leading provider of blended technical training solutions. The company's service offerings are designed to meet a wide variety of client requirements. Offering an integration of instructor-led training, e-learning and mentoring programs, SkillBridge delivers high value solutions in a cost-effective manner. SkillBridge's technology focus includes, among others, programming languages, operating systems, databases, and internet and web technologies.

/TRAINING/ETC INC.   www.trainingetc.com

A training company dedicated to delivering quality technical training, courseware development, and consulting in a variety of subject matter areas, including Programming Languages and Design (including C, C++, OOAD/UML, Perl, and Java), a complete UNIX curriculum (from UNIX Fundamentals to System Administration), the Internet (including HTML/CGI, XML and JavaScript Programming) and RDBMS (including Oracle and Sybase).

WATERMARK LEARNING   www.WatermarkLearning.com

Watermark Learning provides a wide range of IT skill development training and mentoring services to a variety of industries, software / consulting firms and government. We provide flexible options for delivery: onsite, consortium and public classes in three major areas: project management, requirements analysis and software development, including e-Commerce. Our instructors are seasoned, knowledgeable practitioners, who use their industry experience along with our highly rated courseware to effectively build technical skills relevant to your business need.

Object
INNOVATIONS

DEVELOPER TRAINING

OBJECT INNOVATIONS offers training course materials in fundamental software technologies used in developing applications in modern computing environments. We emphasize object-oriented techniques, with a focus on Microsoft® technologies, XML, Java™, and Linux™. Our courses have been used by businesses, training companies, and universities throughout North America. End clients include IBM®, HP®, Dell®, Compaq®, FedEx®, UPS®, AOL®, U.S. Bank®, Mellon Bank®, and NASA. Our courses are frequently updated to reflect feedback from classroom use. We aggressively track new technologies and endeavor to keep our courseware up-to-date.

Founded in 1993, Object Innovations has a long record of firsts in courseware. Our Visual C++ course was released before Microsoft's, we introduced one of the first courses in JavaServer Pages, and our Linux Internals 2.4 kernel course came out several months before Red Hat's course. Now we are leading the development of comprehensive developer training in Microsoft's .NET technology.

.NET DEVELOPER TRAINING

Object Innovations is writing the premier book series on .NET for Prentice Hall PTR. These authoritative books are the foundation of our curriculum. Each book matches a corresponding course, and the student materials come bundled with the book, so students have comprehensive reference materials after the course. Each core course is five days in length and is very rich in content, containing well over five days worth of material. The courses are modularized, so background information or special topics not needed for a particular class can be cleanly omitted. On the other hand, the courses can be lengthened as required. Thus each course can be easily customized to meet the particular needs and interests of the students. We also have shorter courses.

The first group consists of shorter, overview courses:

  401   Introduction to .NET for Developers   (1 day)
  412   .NET Framework Essentials Using C#   (3 days)
  422   .NET Framework Essentials Using VB.NET   (3 days)
  452   Introduction to ASP.NET   (3 days)

The second group constitutes the full-length courses that correspond to the books in The Integrated .NET Series form Object Innovations and Prentice Hall PTR:

  410   Introduction to C# Using .NET   (5 days)
  414   Application Development Using C# and .NET   (5 days)
  420   Introduction to Visual Basic Using .NET   (5 days)
  424   Application Development Using Visual Basic.NET   (5 days)
  434   .NET Architecture and Programming Using Visual C++   (5 days)
  440   Programming Perl in the .NET Environment   (5 days)
  454   Fundamentals of Web Applications Using .NET and XML   (5 days)

See our .NET website for complete course listings: www.objectinnovations.com/dotnet.htm

MICROSOFT DEVELOPER TRAINING

Our Microsoft curriculum is very extensive, with introductory and advanced courses on C++, Visual C++, MFC, COM/DCOM, OLE, COM+, and advanced topics in Visual Basic™. Selected courses include:

123 Programming COM and DCOM Using ATL (5 days)
127 Programming COM and OLE Using MFC (5 days)
149 Distributed COM+ Programming (5 days)
133 Distributed COM+ Programming Using Visual Basic (5 days)
142 Visual C++ Windows Programming for C Programmers (5 days)
145 MFC Windows Programming for C++ Programmers (5 days)
146 Advanced Windows Programming Using Visual C++ (5 days)
157 Advanced C++ Programming (5 days)

XML DEVELOPER TRAINING

Our XML curriculum covers the broad range of XML technology. We offer courses in "pure" XML – all discussion and exercises based entirely in W3C-recommended standards – as well as training in use of XML through today's dominant enterprise platforms, Java and .NET. Selected courses include:

501 XML for the Enterprise (5 days)
504 Powering Websites with XML (4 days)
506 XML Transformations (3 days)
173 XML and Java (5 days)
454 Fundamentals of Web Applications Using .NET and XML

JAVA DEVELOPER TRAINING

Java training courses span the spectrum from beginning to advanced and provide extensive coverage of both client-side and server-side technologies. Selected courses include:

103 Java Programming (5 days)
105 Using and Developing JavaBeans (4 days)
106 Advanced Java Programming (5 days)
107 CORBA Architecture and Programming Using Java (4 days)
109 Java Server Pages (2 days)
110 Java Servlet Programming (2 days)
111 Introduction to Java RMI (1 day)
163 Enterprise JavaBeans (5 days)
172 Java Foundation Classes (5 days)

LINUX COURSES

Linux courses range from fundamentals and system administration to advanced courses in internals, device drivers and networking. Selected courses include:

135 Fundamentals of Linux (4 days)
310 Linux Internals (5 days)
314 Linux Network Drivers Development (3 days)
320 Linux Network Administration (5 days)

See our .NET website for complete course listings: www.objectinnovations.com/dotnet.htm